THINK
MARKETING

THINK
MARKETING
Second Edition

Keith J. Tuckwell
St. Lawrence College

Marina Jaffey
Camosun College

PEARSON

Toronto

Editor-in-Chief: Claudine O'Donnell
Acquisitions Editor: Carolin Sweig
Marketing Manager: Jessica Saso
Program Manager: Karen Townsend
Project Manager: Jessica Hellen
Developmental Editor: Patti Sayle
Media Editor: Nicole Mellow
Media Producer: Daniel Szabo
Production Services: Aptara®, Inc.
Permissions Project Manager: Joanne Tang
Photo and Text Permissions Research: Natalie Barrington
Cover Designer: Anthony Leung
Interior Designer: Aptara®, Inc.
Cover Image: © Rawpixel-Fotolia.com

Credits and acknowledgments for material borrowed from other sources and reproduced, with permission, in this textbook appear on the appropriate page within the text.

If you purchased this book outside the United States or Canada, you should be aware that it has been imported without the approval of the publisher or the author.

7 17

Library and Archives Canada Cataloguing in Publication
Tuckwell, Keith J. (Keith John), 1950–, author
    Think marketing / Keith J. Tuckwell, St. Lawrence College, Marina Jaffey, Camosun College. — 2nd ed.

Includes bibliographical references and index.
ISBN 978-0-13-381572-6 (pbk.)
    1. Marketing—Textbooks.   I. Jaffey, Marina   II. Title.

HF5415.T755 2015   658.8   C2014-905061-5

PEARSON

ISBN 978-0-13-381572-6

Brief Contents

Contents

About the Authors

Keith J. Tuckwell

Keith Tuckwell is a graduate of Ryerson University in Business Administration Marketing. Following graduation he held various marketing and advertising management positions with leading consumer goods companies, including Reckitt & Coleman, Maple Leaf Mills, and Quaker Oats Company of Canada. Having a desire to teach young marketers, Keith joined St. Lawrence College in 1980 and has taught courses in Introductory Marketing, Advertising, Advertising Management, Media Planning, Integrated Marketing Communications, Public Relations, Business Marketing, Marketing Research, and Personal Selling. He was Coordinator of the Marketing and Advertising programs for many years, and Chair, Marketing and Management, for a three-year term. Keith was also an Adjunct Instructor at Queen's University teaching Introduction to Marketing, Marketing Communications, and Marketing Strategy in the Bachelor of Commerce program and the former two-year MBA program.

Keith has authored several uniquely Canadian textbooks, the first of their kind in the Canadian marketplace. Among his titles are *Canadian Advertising in Action* (now in its tenth edition), *Canadian Marketing in Action* (eight editions), and *Integrated Marketing Communications: Strategic Planning Perspectives* (now in its fourth edition).

Marina Jaffey

Marina Jaffey holds a Master's degree in education from the University of Victoria and a Bachelor of Commerce degree from Carleton University. She has an extensive background in business planning, trade marketing, and sales management with Unilever, a global consumer goods firm. In her role as district sales manager with Unilever, Marina was a three-time recipient of the Sales Excellence Award. Marina has also worked as a consultant for organizations including the National Gallery of Canada and the B.C. government. She has served as board member for Sales and Marketing Executives Victoria and as program co-chair for the Canadian Public Relations Society national conference. Her current position as Program Leader and Instructor at Camosun College in Victoria, B.C., enables her to share her passion for marketing with students. Marina develops and delivers a variety of courses in the Bachelor of Business Administration—Marketing program, including Introduction to Marketing, Marketing Communications, Communication Tools and Media, Business-to-Business Marketing, and Sales Management.

Preface

The Second Edition of *Think Marketing*: Creating More Value for You!

The second edition of *Think Marketing* makes learning and teaching marketing more effective, easier, and more enjoyable than ever. Its streamlined approach strikes a careful balance between depth of coverage and ease of learning. The second edition's brand-new design enhances student understanding. And when combined with our online homework and personalized study tool, *Think Marketing* ensures that you will come to class well prepared and leave class with a richer understanding of basic marketing concepts, strategies, and practices.

The chapters are presented in a logical sequence that reflects the development of a marketing plan. The initial chapters focus on inputs for marketing planning and cover topics such as the external environment, marketing research, and consumer and business buying behaviour. The focus then shifts to the strategic planning process and the marketing plan. Then, the strategic components of the marketing plan—the marketing mix—are presented in detail.

The authors' objectives in preparing this edition were to

1. Present content in a clear and engaging manner
2. Offer examples and illustrations that students would be familiar with so that students can link theoretical concepts with marketing applications
3. Retain a sound balance between theory and practice and introduce students to the process of strategic marketing planning
4. Be as current as possible, recognizing that new technologies are rapidly changing the ways that marketing is practised.

Marketing: Creating Customer Value and Relationships

Top marketers all share a common goal: putting the consumer at the heart of marketing. Today's marketing is all about creating customer value and building profitable customer relationships. It starts with understanding consumer needs and wants, deciding which target markets the organization can serve best, and developing a compelling value proposition by which the organization can attract, keep, and grow the number of targeted consumers. If the organization does these things well, and does so in a socially responsible manner, it will reap the rewards in terms of market share, profits, and customer equity. In the second edition of *Think Marketing*, you'll see how *customer value*—creating it and capturing it—drives every good marketing strategy.

The second edition of *Think Marketing* is truly a Canadian textbook that includes examples and illustrations with which students will readily identify. Illustrations and photographs are presented in a colourful format, with each illustration demonstrating how an important marketing concept is applied. As well, each chapter offers two **Think Marketing** boxes that contain a unique story outlining how an organization or brand has successfully applied the marketing fundamentals students will learn about. Finally, an **Experience Marketing** exercise is included at the end of each chapter. The purpose of these exercises is to have students assume the role of marketer and outline a plan of action to resolve a marketing problem or pursue an opportunity.

Think Marketing is the most up-to-date book on the subject. It includes discussion on all the latest trends and practices, and clearly demonstrates the important role that marketing plays in achieving an organization's business objectives.

New in the Second Edition

The second edition of *Think Marketing* has been thoroughly revised to reflect the major trends and forces that affect marketing in this era of customer value and relationships. Here are just some of the major changes you'll find in this edition.

- **Chapter 1 (Contemporary Marketing)** presents a simplified marketing process model that allows students to quickly grasp the essentials of marketing planning and decision-making. The model focuses on five essential steps:
  - Assessing customer needs
  - Identifying and selecting target markets
  - Devising marketing strategies to attract target markets
  - Devising customer relationship management programs to build customer loyalty and establish long-term relationships
  - Evaluating and controlling programs.
- A new section titled **Ethical Considerations for Marketing** examines the need for organizations to conduct marketing practices in a socially and environmentally productive manner. New content in many other chapters and in several Think Marketing boxes examine the importance of ethical practice and socially responsible marketing by organizations.
- Marketing success today relies heavily on effective customer relationship management programs. Since more companies are establishing longer-term financial and sustainability objectives there is a need for expanded discussion on customer relationship management. Customer relationship management is introduced in **Chapter 1 (Contemporary Marketing)** and expanded upon in **Chapter 3 (Marketing Intelligence), Chapter 5 (Business-to-Business Marketing and Organizational Buying Behaviour)** and **Chapter 13 (Retailing)**.
- In **Chapter 2 (The External Marketing Environment)**, updates and new illustrations of all external influences affecting the development of marketing strategies are provided. Recent trends in mobile marketing and the influence of smart devices on marketing organizations are explored here. New information about external influences that have an impact on marketing planning was also added to **Chapter 6 (Market Segmentation and Target Marketing)**. The rapid pace of change dictates that marketers react to change more quickly than before.
- The introductory discussion of social media marketing has increased in **Chapter 1 (Contemporary Marketing)**. Concepts such as brand democratization, consumer-generated content, and content marketing are introduced to reflect how marketing has become more of a two-way interaction between marketer and customer. Expanded discussion of social media communications has also increased in **Chapter 4 (Consumer Buying Behaviour)** and **Chapter 14 (Integrated Marketing Communications and Emerging Media Platforms)**. Building relationships through effective two-way communications and communication sharing are fast becoming essential components of the communications mix.
- In **Chapter 3 (Marketing Intelligence)** there is enhanced coverage of information collection and analysis of data. Several new stories are included to demonstrate how organizations use information to make astute marketing decisions and develop more impactful marketing strategies. Information plays a key role in attracting and retaining satisfied customers.
- Canadian consumers are changing their shopping habits. **Chapter 4 (Consumer Buying Behaviour)** explores how and why these habits have changed. The impact of social media, the Internet, and the increasingly multicultural nature of the Canadian marketplace are examined in detail.

- In **Chapter 5 (Business-to-Business Marketing and Organizational Buying Behaviour)** ethics and sustainable business practices are given greater emphasis. New examples of marketing organizations that have successfully adopted a triple bottom line philosophy are included.
- In **Chapter 6 (Market Segmentation and Target Marketing)** discussion of ethnic marketing has been expanded. New stories embedded in the chapter and a new Think Marketing box show how various companies are successfully attracting ethnic customers with unique marketing programs.
- A strong focus on strategic planning remains a foundation of this textbook. **Chapter 7 (Strategic Marketing Planning)** draws the links between corporate (executive level) planning and marketing (functional) planning. New illustrations and examples portray the marketing planning process. The content of a typical marketing plan is presented in this chapter.
- In **Chapter 12 (Distribution and Supply Chain Management)** greater emphasis is placed on multi-channelling and electronic distribution systems. The expanding role of e-commerce and its impact on distribution strategy is explored. The changing nature of Canada's retail landscape and the impact of e-commerce on retailer marketing strategies are presented in **Chapter 13 (Retailing)**.
- **Chapter 14 (Integrated Marketing Communications and Emerging Media Platforms)** presents a balanced discussion of all media alternatives. Given the emerging dominance of online communications and social media communications, both topics are presented in greater detail in this edition.
- **Chapter 16 (Services and Not-for-Profit Marketing)** explores recent innovations in services marketing that are driven by digitally empowered consumers and intense global competition.

Effective marketing involves developing strategies that are in tune with rapidly changing market conditions. Therefore, key topics such as ethics, corporate social responsibility, multiculturalism, shifting demographics, customer relationship management, social media communications, and advancing technologies are themes woven throughout the book. An effort has been made to include brand and corporate examples of small and medium enterprises from across the country, in addition to examples of successful Canadian-owned global companies.

Success Stories Dramatize Marketing Practice

Think Marketing features in-depth, real-world examples and stories that show concepts in action and reveal the drama of modern marketing. In the second Canadian edition, every chapter contains an **opening vignette** and **Think Marketing stories** that provide fresh and relevant insights into real marketing practices. By way of example, students will learn how

- IÖGO, a brand with a unique personality, was developed and launched with an effective marketing strategy that made it a leader in the market.
- Google is capitalizing on opportunities created by smart devices and our increasingly connected world.
- West-coast based Monk Office, a leader in corporate social responsibility, is helping its suppliers develop sustainable business practices.
- McDonald's effectively employed marketing research to identify and develop meatless entrees for the Canadian market.
- Walmart and Scotiabank are tailoring their marketing strategies to meet the unique needs of ethnic customers.
- Marketing grad Alex MacLean has successfully launched East Coast Lifestyle, a line of casual clothing and accessories.

- Tim Hortons effectively uses a cup size strategy to improve its profit margins.
- Nike successfully marketed itself during the Olympic Games, even though it was not an official sponsor, an interesting and controversial practice referred to as *ambush marketing*.
- Charities such as Missing Children's Society of Canada are using mobile marketing and social media in creative ways to connect with donors.
- Oreo cookies had to adapt its marketing strategy in China (product, package, and marketing communications) in order to meet the needs and tastes of Chinese consumers.

Beyond these features, each chapter is packed with countless real, relevant, and timely examples that reinforce key concepts. No other text brings marketing to life like the second edition of *Think Marketing*.

Students Will Experience Marketing Decisions

For students to fully appreciate the nature and impact of marketing, it is important that exercises be offered to immerse them in the role of a marketing decision maker. Each chapter includes a section titled **Experience Marketing.** Each Experience Marketing exercise presents a situation that must be analyzed. Based on the analysis, students are asked to present suitable recommendations and marketing strategies to resolve a problem or pursue an opportunity. Among the exercises, students are asked to

- Develop and launch a new flavour of 7Up that will attract a new, younger target market to the brand.
- Develop a profile of Ontario's Aboriginal post-secondary students to help Colleges Ontario develop a relevant advertising campaign for this segment of the market.
- Assess Red Bull's current market position in Canada and devise a new marketing strategy that will continue to build the brand.
- Conduct an audit of the coffee roasting market, and assess the viability of an environmentally friendly storage bag.
- Evaluate the external influences that could impact the distribution strategies of Chapters bookstores.
- Assess competitive market conditions to determine the need for a value menu at Harvey's restaurants.
- Develop a marketing strategy that enables Rumble, a new "nourishing" drink, to grow and expand its market share.
- Devise a marketing strategy for Second Cup, a languishing participant in the retail coffee market, to rejuvenate consumer interest in the brand and encourage more store visits.

Valuable Learning Aids

A wealth of chapter-opening, within-chapter, and end-of-chapter learning devices help students to learn, link, and apply major concepts:

Chapter-Opening Content. The new, more active and integrative opening spread in each chapter features Learning Objectives and an opening vignette—an engaging, deeply developed, illustrated, and annotated marketing story that introduces the chapter material and sparks student interest.

Learning Objectives. Each learning objective (LO) is tied to chapter content, helping students make connections between examples and key concepts easily.

Think Marketing Boxes. Each chapter contains two highlight features that provide an in-depth look at the real marketing practices of large and small companies.

Experience Marketing. To experience marketing, students must assess situations and make recommendations to change marketing strategies when necessary. The **Experience**

Marketing section in the end of chapter content challenges students to consider the details of a given situation, and asks what they would do to resolve it.

Reviewing the Concepts. A summary at the end of each chapter reviews major chapter concepts and links them to chapter objectives.

Key Terms. Key terms are defined in the margins.

Review Questions. These questions ask students to recall the content that was developed throughout the chapter. Chapter questions are linked to learning objectives.

MyMarketingLab Resources

MyMarketingLab delivers **proven results** in helping individual students succeed. It provides **engaging experiences** that personalize, stimulate, and measure learning for each student. For the second Canadian edition, MyMarketingLab includes powerful new learning resources, including a new set of online lesson presentations to help students work through and master key business topics, a completely re-structured Study Plan for student self-study, and a wealth of engaging assessment and teaching aids to help students and instructors explore unique learning pathways. MyMarketingLab online resources include:

- **NEW Interactive Lesson Presentations.** Students can now study key chapter topics and work through interactive assessments to test their knowledge and mastery of marketing concepts. Each presentation allows students to explore through expertly designed steps of reading, practising, and testing to ensure that students not only experience the content, but truly engage with each topic. Instructors also have the ability to assign quizzes, projects, and follow-up discussion questions relating to the online lessons to further develop the valuable learning experiences from the presentations.
- **NEW Study Plan.** MyMarketingLab offers students an engaging and focused self-study experience that is driven by a powerful new Study Plan. Students work through assessments in each chapter to gauge their understanding and target the topics that require additional practice. Along the way, they are recognized for their mastery of each topic and guided toward resources in areas that they might be struggling to understand.
- **NEW Dynamic Study Modules.** These new study modules allow students to work through groups of questions and check their understanding of foundational marketing topics. As students work through questions, the Dynamic Study Modules assess their knowledge and only show questions that still require practice. Dynamic Study Modules can be completed online using a computer, tablet, or mobile device.
- **Decision-Making Simulations.** Decision Making Mini-Simulations walk students through key business decision-making scenarios to help them understand how marketing decisions are made. Students are asked to make important decisions relating to core marketing concepts. At each point, students receive feedback to help them understand the implications of their choices in the marketing environment. These simulations can now be assigned by instructors and graded directly through MyMarketingLab.
- **NEW Business Today Video Database.** Business Today is a dynamic and expanding database of videos that covers the disciplines of business, marketing, management, and more. In addition to the videos that are specifically correlated to this text, you will find new videos posted regularly. Check back often to see up-to-date video examples that are perfect for classroom use.
- **Writing Assignments.** Each assisted-graded writing assignment is based on a question from the text and provides the perfect framework for instructors to efficiently assign, review, and grade students' written work. Questions are accompanied by a clickable rubric that allows instructors to review written work, provide immediate feedback, and assign a grade quickly and consistently.
- **NEW Learning Catalytics.** Learning Catalytics is a "bring your own device" student engagement, assessment, and classroom intelligence system. It allows instructors to

engage students in class with a variety of questions types designed to gauge student understanding.

- **Glossary Flashcards.** These provide a targeted review of the Key Terms in each chapter. The Glossary Flashcards allow learners to select the specific terms and chapters that they would like to study. The cards can also be sorted by Key Term or by definition to give students greater flexibility when studying.
- **NEW Canadian Sketch Animation Series.** Explore a NEW animation series that presents key marketing and business concepts from a uniquely Canadian perspective. This interesting and lively series of videos will help your students to grasp course concepts they find difficult.

The second edition of *Think Marketing* provides an effective and enjoyable total package for moving students down the road to learning marketing!

Teaching and Learning Support

A successful marketing course requires more than a well-written book. Today's classroom requires a dedicated teacher and a fully integrated teaching package. A total package of teaching and learning supplements extends this edition's emphasis on effective teaching and learning. The aids that follow support *Think Marketing*.

Instructor's Resource Manual. This invaluable resource not only includes chapter-by-chapter teaching strategies, it also features notes about the PowerPoint slides. This supplement is available through the Pearson Education Canada's online catalogue at http://vig.pearsoned.ca.

TestGen. This powerful and user-friendly computerized test bank has been thoroughly revised to include more accurate coverage. The test bank includes about 100 questions per chapter, with true/false, multiple choice, and essay questions.

PowerPoint® Presentations. PowerPoint slides are available with this edition, with a minimum of 25 slides per chapter. The PPTs can be accessed on the Instructor's Resource section of the catalogue. The slides are also available to instructors through Pearson Education Canada's online catalogue at http://vig.pearsoned.ca.

Pearson eText. Pearson eText gives students access to the text whenever and wherever they have access to the Internet. The eText pages look exactly like the printed text, offering powerful new functionality for students and instructors. Users can create notes, highlight text in different colours, create bookmarks, zoom, click hyperlinked words and phrases to see definitions, and view in single-page or two-page format. Pearson eText allows for quick navigation to key parts of the eText using a table of contents and provides full-text search. The eText may also offer links to associated media files, enabling users to access videos, animations, or other activities as they read the text.

Learning Solutions Managers. Pearson's Learning Solutions Consultants work with faculty and campus course designers to ensure that Pearson technology products, assessment tools, and online course materials are tailored to meet your specific needs. This highly qualified team is dedicated to helping schools take full advantage of a wide range of educational resources by assisting in the integration of a variety of instructional materials and media formats. Your local Pearson Education sales representative can provide you with more details on this service program.

Pearson Custom Library

For enrollments of at least 25 students, you can create your own textbook by choosing the chapters that best suit your own course needs. To begin building your custom text, visit www.pearsoncustomlibrary.com. You may also work with a dedicated Pearson Custom editor to create your ideal text—publishing your own original content or mixing and matching Pearson content. Contact your local Pearson Representative to get started.

Acknowledgements

I would sincerely like to acknowledge the contribution of Marina Jaffey in the development of the second edition. Marina introduced many new ideas and insights that have improved the overall quality, content, and presentation of material. As always, I would like to thank my family for their support over the years. Another book is complete. To Marnie, Graham, and Gord . . . thank you! As always, a very special thank you to my wife, Esther.

KJT

First, I would like to acknowledge and thank Keith Tuckwell, who has brought a wealth of experience to this project. I am deeply grateful to my students, who are a constant source of inspiration. Finally, I would like to thank my family for the love and support that has enabled me to do this work.

MJ

Both authors would like to thank various people at Pearson Canada and their external suppliers who have helped in so many ways to make this book a success. In particular, we would like to thank Claudine O'Donnell, Managing Editor; Carolin Sweig, Acquisitions Editor; Karen Townsend, Program Manager; Patti Sayle, Developmental Editor; Jessica Hellen, Project Manager; Joanne Tang, Project Manager Permissions; Jeremy Hobbs, Sales & Editorial Representative; Natalie Barrington, Freelance Permissions Researcher; Judy Sturrup, copyeditor; and Jogender Taneja at Aptara.

Keith J. Tuckwell
Marina Jaffey

Scott Olson/Getty Images

LEARNING OBJECTIVES

LO1 Define the term *marketing*. (p. 3)

LO2 Describe the importance of marketing in organizations today. (pp. 3–5)

LO3 Describe how marketing has evolved to become the driving force of business growth. (pp. 5–11)

LO4 Explain the fundamental process of marketing practised by organizations today. (pp. 11–15)

LO5 Explain the concept of the *marketing mix*. (pp. 15–21)

LO6 Explain how an organization maximizes the value of its customers. (pp. 22–23)

LO7 Identify fundamental methods for measuring the effectiveness of marketing activities. (pp. 23–24)

LO8 Explain how ethical considerations impact marketing strategies. (pp. 24–26)

IN JUST A SHORT PERIOD...

the nature of marketing has changed considerably. There was a time when the goal of marketing was to develop and market goods and services that satisfied consumer needs. But modern-day marketing has gone beyond that. We are living in an era of connected consumers who have placed higher expectations on marketers. Today's consumers demand honesty and transparency, and want assurance that organizations are conducting business in a way that helps society and the environment.

Marketing today is awash in social responsibility programs—some good, some not so good. McDonald's has been slammed by consumer advocacy groups for its food and marketing practices, but there is no denying that it has been a good corporate citizen. McDonald's supports community events and worthwhile social causes everywhere! Demonstrating its openness and honesty, McDonald's recently took a very bold step—actually opening itself up to much risk and criticism with its Our Food. Your Questions communications campaign.

The initial video showed how a Quarter Pounder was perfectly styled for an ad—it certainly didn't look like the ones served in their restaurants. McDonald's simply explained why the product in the ad looks different. The video generated more than 10 million views. So what's the rationale behind this campaign? Well, it allowed consumers an opportunity to ask questions about the food and how it is made, in a transparent way.

A multimedia campaign directed consumers to McDonalds.ca/YourQuestions. In a short period, over 15 000 questions were personally answered by a social media team. The website generated 2.9 million interactions. McDonald's encouraged consumers to share the responses with their social network friends, extending the reach of the conversation.

This effort shows McDonald's is in tune with today's consumer. Joel Yanshinky, vice-president, U.S. marketing at McDonald's, says, "We had to engage our consumers in a way that was transparent, and that's unusual, I think, but it's going to become more of the norm in marketing. It's a meaningful step that we needed to make to have dialogue with our customers."

Adapted from Alicia Androich, "Secret sauce," *Marketing*, October 8, 2012, p. 8; and Kristin Laird, "2012 Marketers of the Year: McDonald's Canada," *Marketing*, November 19, 2012, p. 43.

MARKETING TODAY: KEEPING PACE WITH CHANGE

One of the toughest challenges facing a business today is how to anticipate where the business is going and how it will get there. No company can accurately foresee what the future will bring. What any company does know for sure is that change is occurring rapidly, and if it clings to traditional practices it will be heading for failure.

Change is occurring everywhere. There is a heightened interest among consumers about the role of business in society and the need for business to operate in an ethical manner. It is no longer good enough to simply produce and market a good product. Consumers today will consider a company's social responsibility initiatives and examine its business practices. Consumers choose to support those companies that display a social conscience.

Technology today is faster, cheaper, and better, and it has changed the way people live and work. Instruments such as smartphones and tablets (such as Apple's iPad) play key roles in day-to-day business practices and the daily lives of consumers. Further, the manner in which people use these instruments is forcing marketing decision makers to rethink their strategies. There is a shift in control—away from marketers and toward consumers. The prevalence of these electronic devices also allows for direct consumer contact using individualized marketing messages—a situation unheard of only a few years ago.

Populations are getting older, so marketing organizations now face the prospect of attracting new, younger customers while retaining older ones. As well, the ethnic mix of Canada's population is shifting. Finding ways to satisfy the needs of such a diverse population poses a significant challenge to marketers. Marketers must be flexible and adapt their marketing efforts accordingly.

MARKETING DEFINED

LO1 Define the term *marketing*.

In the age of a rapidly changing business environment, it is becoming more difficult to define marketing. There was a time when marketing operated independently of other company functions and was easy to define. It was a process that identified a need and then offered a means (a good or service) to satisfy it. Marketing focused on a transaction or exchange between the organization and the customer, and in the process both parties benefited.

In an attempt to convey the complexity of modern marketing activity, the American Marketing Association (AMA) periodically reviews and changes its definition of marketing. Like the process of marketing itself, the definition must be up to date. The AMA currently defines marketing as follows:

> **Marketing** is the activity, set of institutions, and processes for creating, communicating, delivering, and exchanging offerings that have value for customers, clients, partners, and society at large.[1]

marketing The process of planning the conception, pricing, promotion, and distribution of ideas, goods, and services to create exchanges that satisfy individual and organization objectives.

The essential elements of marketing practice can be divided into several crucial areas. First, marketers assess customers' needs and then find ways to satisfy those needs. Second, marketing programs are designed to attract customers to a good or service and get them to buy for the first time. Third, programs are designed to encourage customer satisfaction and loyalty, the goal of which is to develop a long and profitable relationship with the customer. Finally, marketers must conduct their marketing practices in a manner that benefits numerous stakeholders. These stakeholders include customers, shareholders, partners, and society at large.

Many experts believe marketing must be at the forefront of an organization and positioned as the "philosophy" of an organization, a philosophy that starts at the top executive level and spreads throughout the entire organization. Over time, a marketing-driven business will outperform businesses that have a financial or production focus. When companies stop marketing and focus on other things, the base ultimately falls out from under the business.[2]

Successful global companies and brands such as Apple, Coca-Cola, Starbucks, and McDonald's demonstrate the importance of marketing. It is no coincidence that each of these brands is dominant in its market. Each company or brand has a strong marketing platform, is well known to the public at large, and delivers products and services that are in high demand, all of which demonstrate a strong marketing philosophy and financial commitment to marketing. They listen to their customers and continuously strive to provide customers with better value than expected based on the price tag. These companies have something in common: their leaders think like marketers all the time, they stay a step ahead of their competitors, and they offer goods and services that provide their customers with value.

THE IMPORTANCE OF MARKETING

LO2 Describe the importance of marketing in organizations today.

Marketing is an agent of change, and must lead an organization into the future and set the agenda for how the organization deals with change. It provides a means for companies to constantly assess changing conditions, and then provides the expertise to develop appropriate strategies so that an organization is able to take advantage of the changes. Marketing ensures that an organization creates the right products and services for unique customer groups so that a profitable future for the organization can be sustained.

Marketing is a vital cog in the corporate wheel. Without effective marketing, companies would not grow and prosper. Shoppers Drug Mart serves as a good example. An independent survey conducted by *Marketing* magazine and Leger Marketing placed Shoppers Drug Mart among the top five brands with the best reputations in Canada. Other Canadian brands in this elite group include Tim Hortons and Canadian Tire.

Shoppers Drug Mart offers some insight into its success. Says Sandra Sanderson, then vice-president, marketing at Shoppers Drug Mart: "We've always been true to our value proposition, which is around health, beauty and convenience . . . and we have not deviated."[3] There is a basic marketing lesson here: stick to what you do and do it as best you can.

As you will see from **Figure 1.1**, many well-known brands rank high on the reputation list. The reasons they are there are marketing related. These brands offer

- Popular products
- Strong customer service
- Substantial community involvement
- A large number of locations (if retail)
- An efficient business system to deliver products
- Consistent delivery of brand promise

Marketing is important because it is the means by which an organization connects with customers, and an airtight connection yields profit in the long term. An innovative company such as Apple provides a good example. Apple offers products that are in tune with what people want. Apple is known for being first, being innovative, and being sexy—quite a brand image to have![4] Apple has had a string of product successes—the iPhone, iPod, and iPad are among them. The iPad changed the way people interact with the Internet and serves the public's need to be connected instantly. Consumers' daily interactions with digital media, technology, and content have dramatically altered the shopping experience. Apple's product and service offerings are the agents of such change.

Rank	Company	2014 Score	% Good Opinion	% Bad Opinion
1	Google	89.3	92.7	3.4
2	Tim Hortons	81.9	89.8	7.9
3	Shoppers Drug Mart	81.7	86.6	4.9
4	Sony	81.2	85.1	3.9
5	Canadian Tire	78.9	88.5	9.6
6	Heinz	78.8	86.0	7.2
7	Kraft	78.1	86.5	8.4
8	Samsung	78.0	82.9	4.9
9	FedEx	77.9	82.5	4.8
10	Kellogg	77.8	85.6	7.8

Figure 1.1   Best Brand Reputations in Canada

Shoppers Drug Mart and Apple demonstrate marketing initiative. These innovators don't sit still or rest on their laurels. They recognize the need to stay sharp and change with the times in order to always be a step or two ahead of their competitors. To do so, they constantly monitor their respective business environments and put marketing plans into place that meet the ever-changing needs of customers.

Video: National Lacrosse League: Gaining a Competitive Edge

THE NATURE OF MARKETING HAS EVOLVED

L03 Describe how marketing has evolved to become the driving force of business growth.

Marketing is based on a simple idea: identify a need and then satisfy it. To understand how this simple thought has grown into such a complex process, it is helpful to look at the evolution of marketing. Business organizations have moved through several stages of thinking with regard to how they approach customers. Initially the emphasis was on production, then on sales, then on marketing, and finally on societal or socially responsible marketing. More recently marketing has moved into an era we can call *social media marketing*. The philosophies behind marketing continue to change, as do the tools used to practise marketing.

Production Orientation

Organizations following a **production orientation** pay little attention to what customers need. Instead, they concentrate on what they are capable of producing. The basic premise of a production orientation is quite simple: if a company builds a quality product at an affordable price, the product will eventually sell itself. Businesses realize profits by producing and distributing only a limited variety of products as efficiently as possible. Henry Ford's classic statement, "They can have any colour of car as long as it's black" illustrates the philosophy behind the production orientation. Even today, some companies try to survive using this kind of outdated approach.

production orientation Occurs when organizations pay little attention to what customers need, concentrating instead on what they are capable of producing.

Selling Orientation

As manufacturers added new product lines, and more and more competitors entered the market, customers had a greater selection of products. Consequently, customers had to be convinced to buy products. The emphasis shifted from production to selling. The "hard sell" became the basic philosophy of doing business, and companies that adopted a **selling orientation** believed that the more they sold the more profit they would make. But companies that paid little attention to costs found that this was not always the case. At the same time, consumers increasingly demanded better product quality, performance, and dependability.

selling orientation Occurs when companies believe that the more they sell the more profit they will make.

Offering a wider range of goods was the earliest attempt to match potential customers' needs with products or services. In the automobile industry, competing firms, such as Ford and General Motors (GM), offered automobiles at different price points and then searched for a consumer market that would buy those models. For example, GM offered Chevrolet and Pontiac products in the lowest price range, Buick and Oldsmobile in a mid-level price range, and Cadillac in a high price range. The idea was to get customers into the GM family and move them up. The fact that more variety was available meant these companies had to "sell" their goods—their efforts focused on advertising and promotions to get customers into the dealer showrooms.

Marketing Orientation

When a marketing orientation exists, all business planning revolves around the customer. This organizational philosophy has been appropriately termed the

marketing concept The process of determining the needs and wants of a target market and delivering a set of desired satisfactions to that target market more effectively than the competition.

marketing concept and is expressed as follows: the essential task of the organization is to determine the needs and wants of a target market and then to deliver a set of satisfactions in such a way that the organization's product is perceived to be a better value than a competing product. The resources of the entire firm are directed at determining and satisfying customer needs and building ongoing relationships. Perhaps Burger King's famous slogan summarizes the essence of the marketing concept best: "Have it your way."

Firms applying the marketing concept realize profits by staying one step ahead of competitors in the delivery of desired satisfactions to customers. To do so, they must first implement sound marketing research programs to determine customer needs. Marketing research is an essential component of the marketing process (see Chapter 3 for details). Then they must concentrate on operating their production, sales, and distribution systems efficiently. There must be a close working relationship among the various departments of a business, and each must contribute to achieve common company goals.

Canadian Tire firmly believes in the marketing concept. Canadian Tire is a proven success story that has weathered intense competition from big box competitors that have moved in from the United States. It is based on a strong dealer network of 488 stores across Canada; effective marketing communications programs that have produced near universal (in Canada) brand awareness for the company name and logo (a red triangle); the offering of quality products and services in automotive, home, and leisure categories; and a rewards program that keeps customers coming back. Canadian Tire "money" is Canada's oldest loyalty program and awards more than $100 million annually to customers.[5] It's no coincidence that Canadian Tire is one of the most-shopped stores in Canada—a true reflection of customer satisfaction. Refer to the illustration in **Figure 1.2**.

There is a lesson to be learned from the Canadian Tire example: business organizations must adopt the marketing concept and reflect it in all their operations. If you give customers what they want you are on your way to operating profitably. To determine what customers want requires an organization that conducts marketing research to stay abreast of changing needs and expectations among customers. It must listen carefully to customers and react with appropriate marketing strategies.

For insight into how Ultima Foods applied the marketing concept, read the Think Marketing box **ÌÖGO: The New Way to Say Yogurt.**

Socially Responsible Marketing Orientation

socially responsible marketing The notion that business should conduct itself in the best interests of consumers and society.

Progressive business organizations are now at the stage where consideration for the environment and other worthwhile social causes has come to the forefront of strategic planning and decision making. This trend will continue. A **socially responsible marketing** organization is one that conducts all of its operations in an ethical manner

Figure 1.2 Canadian Tire is one of the most-shopped stores in Canada.

Think Marketing

İÖGO: The New Way to Say Yogurt

When Ultima Foods lost the distribution rights to Yoplait in Canada it had a choice to make. Either it vacated the yogurt market or it developed a new brand and product line of its own. The company decided on the latter.

Typically, the development of a new product is time-consuming, but a team effort at Yoplait produced a new line of yogurt under the brand name İÖGO in just 18 months. The product development process was guided by one primary objective—the products would offer a natural taste and simple ingredients that would be in keeping with the expectations of Canadian consumers.

Seven different product lines embracing 44 products were developed. Among the product lines were İÖGO 0% (a fat-free yogurt), İÖGO Probio (a new twist on probiotic yogurt), İÖGO Greko (Greek yogurt), İÖGO Nomad (a drinkable yogurt), and İÖGO Zip (a tube yogurt).

Branding and package design were unique elements of the marketing strategy. The three dots over the first two letters offer a European look and the colour scheme of the fruit on white packages clearly differentiates İÖGO from competitors.

The launch of İÖGO was a significant investment for Ultima Foods. The initial message to consumers was simple: "İÖGO is a new way to say yogurt." The multimedia campaign effort embraced traditional media such as television, print ads, outdoor boards, in-store displays, and coupon incentives. Social media efforts and experiential events also supported the launch.

From a financial perspective, Ultima Foods believed the benefits outweighed the costs of developing and marketing İÖGO. The Yoplait product line generated $60 million in sales revenue annually, about 20 percent of total company sales. For an investment of $70 million in product development and plant expansion, Ultima was back in business, and with a more exciting brand and greater revenue potential in the long term.

The investment and hard work by Ultima Foods and its external suppliers paid off. Within 10 weeks of launch,

Ultima Foods/ULTIMA FOODS/Newscom

brand awareness among Canadian consumers reached 74 percent and market share rose to 12 percent. The new brand disrupted the marketplace in a significant manner! It is off to a great start!

Question:

Some time has passed. What is the status of İÖGO in the yogurt market today?

Adapted from "Ultima Foods launches İÖGO: Development of one of the largest integrated marketing campaigns across Canada," September 20, 2012, www.newswire.ca/en/story/1039539/ultima-foods-launches-iogo; and Megan Haynes, "Verdict: İÖGO saves the day," Strategy, January 24, 2013, www.strategyonline.ca

and in the best interests of consumers and society. Refer to **Figure 1.3** for a visual illustration. Further, there is an obligation for marketing organizations to do no harm to the environment and to use their skills and resources to enhance the environment wherever possible.

Philosophically, conducting business in a socially responsible manner should be natural for all business organizations; after all, the planet's well-being is in everyone's best interest. One study conducted by the Canadian Democracy and Corporate

Figure 1.3   Elements
of Socially Responsible
Marketing

Accountability Commission determined that more than 50 percent of Canadians have
consciously chosen a company's product because they felt the company did business in a
socially responsible manner.[6] Despite this knowledge, business executives under pressure
often find it difficult to balance the demands of operating competitively, producing
profits, increasing shareholder value, and preserving the environment.

The scope of socially responsible marketing is expanding. Initially, being socially
responsible meant that an organization supported worthy causes and donated money
and services to needy groups. Such a practice was referred to as **cause marketing**. Cause
marketing is defined as an organization's support of causes that benefit society, such as
AIDS research, cancer research, help for underprivileged children, literacy programs, and
so on. Marketers are very aware that aligning their business activities with consumers'
social concerns has sales potential.

Bell Canada is a good example of an organization supporting a worthwhile cause.
Since 2010 Bell has been associated with mental health issues in Canada. Knowing that
one in five Canadians will experience some form of mental illness in their lifetime, Bell's
objective was to reduce the stigma attached to mental illness by encouraging dialogue.
Bell committed $50 million to the cause over a five-year period. To initiate dialogue, Bell
actively markets Let's Talk Day, an annual event, through a multimedia advertising
campaign. On Let's Talk Day, Bell donates five cents for every text or long distance call
made by Bell customers. In 2013, $4.8 million was raised in 24 hours. Sarah Hughes, one
of Canada's most distinguished female athletes, suffered from mental illness, and she
plays a cornerstone role in Bell's campaign.[7] Refer to the illustration in **Figure 1.4**.

cause marketing An
organization's support of
causes that benefit society.

Video: H&M: Our Models
are too Skinny

Bell Canada

Figure 1.4   Bell actively supports efforts to destigmatize mental illness in Canada.

Figure 1.5 Naya was the first bottled water company to introduce a bottle made of 100 percent recycled plastic.

Today, being socially responsible involves much more than just supporting good causes. It's about being green and being environmentally aware of the impact that a product (or an organization) has on the environment and society.

Food companies, for example, are now very sensitive to health and wellness trends in society. "There are common health and wellness trends across all age groups and some that are age and stage of life driven, but all of them are grounded in an increasing awareness of the role that food can play in enhancing overall well-being."[8] The challenge for food companies is to develop products that meet diverse consumer needs for meals that are tasty, convenient, and healthy. Companies such as Kraft, Campbell, and Heinz are either reducing the salt and sugar content in many of their products or launching new products with less of these harmful ingredients.

Wasteful packaging and its effects on the environment is another issue that manufacturers and retailers are dealing with. Naya Spring Water was the first bottled water company in the world to use 100 percent recycled plastic in its bottles. Recycled plastic is made from plastic previously used in packaging. It is reprocessed to create new bottles. Naya's 1.5 litre bottle represents a carbon footprint reduction of 30 percent compared to the same bottle made with virgin plastic.[9] Marketing decisions like this are good for the environment. Refer to the illustration in **Figure 1.5**.

Chemical-based cleaning products are also going green. The Clorox Company, a leader in this product category, launched a line of products under the GREEN WORKS® brand name in 2009. Within one year GREEN WORKS® cleaners, made mostly of coconut oil, corn, and lemon—and without bleach—became top sellers among natural cleaners. Refer to the illustration in **Figure 1.6**.

Figure 1.6 GREEN WORKS® markets naturally derived cleaning products to meet consumer demands for environmentally friendly products.

Social Media Marketing Orientation

In the age of digital communications, marketers have entered an innovative yet frightening era of marketing. Up until this point, marketers were in complete control of their marketing activities—they controlled the nature of the message and how it was delivered. The presence of social networks is changing things, and control of the message is shifting to consumers.

First, let's describe what a social network is. A **social network** connects people with different types of interests at one website. At the website, people become friends, develop relationships, and form communities—in effect, the community could be viewed as a potential market to pursue. When companies or products join these sites, an opportunity exists for the brand (company) to interact with people. The most popular social networks include Facebook, Twitter, YouTube, Pinterest, Instagram, and Vine.

In a social network environment, the nature of marketing has to be informal. For example, if a brand blatantly attempts to market itself, it may face rejection—and rejection can snowball quickly through word-of-mouth communications among online communities. Therefore, how a company utilizes social media requires careful thought and consideration. The objective of social network communications is to post interesting information about a brand so that people pass the information on to their network of friends. Through social networking sites, brands can have conversations and interactions with individual followers.

In the traditional mass media environment, marketers control the message; one-way communications are pushed upon consumers. In the online environment the situation is different. Communications are participative in nature—consumers can manipulate brand information, or they can create new information about a brand and distribute it freely among their network of friends or more openly on YouTube, a concept referred to as **brand democratization.**

Consumer-generated content refers to content produced by consumers for consumers. People create the content without being asked, and in many cases it presents the brand effectively. People who do this are often called *brand evangelists* and will do anything to promote their favourite brand. No doubt you have watched many brand-oriented videos on YouTube. Marketers are adapting to this shift in control and many are inviting consumers to participate in the creation of brand content. It is a way of generating buzz for a brand at no cost for the company.

Many organizations have jumped into social media marketing and met success while others have failed miserably. Keith Weed, chief marketing officer of Unilever Worldwide, sums things up this way: "We are in the middle of a digital revolution. Digital marketing is like high school sex. Everyone is talking about it, fewer are doing it, and those that are, aren't doing it very well."[10] For certain, an organization has to go on a steep learning curve if it is to maximize the potential of social media. Digital marketing and social media are becoming key components of marketing practice. Add in the growing significance of mobile communications and you can see the direction in which marketing is headed.

Those companies that have embraced social media have identified several key marketing benefits. The most important benefit is customer engagement (people willingly creating information about brands or transferring information about a brand to their friends). Other benefits include the ability to communicate directly with potential customers, securing feedback from customers, and learning about customer preferences—information that can be used to develop or refine marketing strategies.[11]

Social media has also led to a rise in what's now called **content marketing** or branded content. Content marketing is defined as any marketing format that involves the creation and sharing of relevant content in order to acquire customers. Simply stated, it is a different style of advertising, a style that involves communicating with consumers with more meaningful and engaging messages in a non-interruptive manner. To illustrate, Kokanee beer created a brand-centric movie about itself titled *The Movie Out*

social network A website that connects people with different kinds of interests for the purpose of socializing (e.g., Facebook or Twitter).

brand democratization A situation in which the customer can interact with a brand, giving the customer some control over the marketing of a brand (as in online user-generated content).

consumer-generated content Online content created by consumers for consumers (often the content is related to a branded good).

content marketing A marketing format that involves the creation and sharing of relevant brand-oriented content in order to acquire customers.

Here. Refer to the image in **Figure 1.7**. Randy Stein, a partner at Grip Limited (Kokanee's advertising agency) says, "If you can give [people] something they're genuinely interested in . . . then they'll happily engage, and watch that content."[12] As has been mentioned, engagement is the primary benefit of social media marketing.

Marketing has evolved through a series of stages with a different philosophy taking hold at each stage. For a summary of the evolution of marketing refer to **Figure 1.8**.

THE MARKETING PROCESS

LO4 Explain the fundamental process of marketing practised by organizations today.

The fundamental principle on which marketing programs are designed is that an organization anticipates unmet needs in the market and develops products to meet those needs. The organization then effectively communicates to customers the benefits of the product, the objective of which is to create awareness and interest in the product—so that they go out and buy it. It sounds very simple when put into words, yet it is a very complex process when put into practice.

Before proceeding, the term **market** should be defined. A market may be the ultimate consumer, an organizational buyer, or both. In consumer market terms, a market is a group of people who have a similar need for a product or service, the

Figure 1.7 Kokanee produced a movie about itself for distribution on social media networks.

Labatt Breweries of Canada; (background) Franz Pritz/Picture Press/Getty Images

market A group of people who have a similar need for a product or service, the resources to purchase it, and the willingness and ability to buy it.

Figure 1.8 Evolution of Marketing

Phase	Characteristics
Production Orientation	• Sell what you can make • Limited choice for customers • Profit from production efficiency
Selling Orientation	• More product choice to meet customer needs • Profits based on expanding sales • All activity revolves around customer needs
Marketing Orientation	• Very competitive since customer has wide choice of goods and services • Profit from efficient production and marketing • Fulfill society's expectations (e.g., for a safe environment)
Socially Responsible Marketing Orientation	• Informed consumers place increasing demands on organizations • Relationships between customers and organizations crucial to making profit (CRM) • Exchange of information among customers influences buying decisions (word-of-mouth)
Social Media Marketing Orientation	• Customers interact with brand; informally participate in marketing of a brand • Shift in control from marketer to consumer

Photo provided by Reebok

Figure 1.9 A socially oriented communications strategy fuelled by competition and camaraderie helps differentiate Reebok from competitors in the running-shoe market.

resources to purchase the product or service, and the willingness and ability to buy it. In business-to-business market terms, a market is an organizational buyer—such as a manufacturer or service organization, wholesaler, or retailer—that buys goods and services for its own use or for resale.

The goal of marketing is to attract, retain, and cultivate customers so that customers benefit from the goods and services they buy. In doing so, companies achieve their organizational objectives, such as profit, market share, and building a strong image and reputation. To achieve this goal, marketers develop innovative products and related marketing strategies that will provide value to customers. To devise products and related marketing strategies, marketers must anticipate consumer expectations and capitalize on trends in the marketplace. It is a complex process!

To quickly demonstrate the concept of providing value that meets consumer expectations, consider a product like Special K marketed by Kellogg's. Special K has always associated itself with healthier lifestyles and is very popular with adult women. Kellogg's has effectively expanded the brand into other product categories— the brand name giving instant credibility to a new product. One such product is Special K Cracker Chips. According to Andrew Loucks, then vice president, marketing at Kellogg's, "The popular new product was the answer to the needs of Special K women looking to satisfy her craving for something savoury without the guilt."[13]

In the highly competitive athletic shoe market, Reebok faces stiff competition from brands such as Nike, Adidas, and New Balance. All brands advertise heavily to convince consumers to buy. To break through the clutter Reebok realized a new strategy would have to be put into play. Reebok devised a new communications strategy with the tagline "The Sport of Fitness Has Arrived." The initial television commercial showed people training together; training would be a social activity where you compete with your peers but feel a sense of enjoyment and accomplishment when finished. Historically, athletic shoe commercials showed people training alone. Refer to the image in **Figure 1.9**.

The message in the new campaign differentiated Reebok from other brands. Michael Rossie, Reebok brand vice president, says, "Our brand of fitness is more social . . . the commercial showed people a new point of view on what fitness contributes to your lifestyle."[14]

Marketers must also be conscious of the price associated with attracting and retaining customers. The cost of getting a consumer to make an initial purchase is very high. Some researchers suggest that it is five times more costly to attract a new customer than to keep an old one. Therefore, it is in the firm's best financial interests to keep its current customers satisfied. The goods and services provided by a firm must live up to the expectations created by its own marketing efforts; otherwise, the firm will lose not only its credibility but its customer base.

The process of marketing embraces a host of activities designed to attract, satisfy, and retain customers. The essential elements of this process involve the following:

1. Assessing customer needs by doing marketing research. The purpose of research is to discover unmet needs among consumers and to determine the potential for new products.
2. Identifying and selecting a target market to pursue.
3. Developing a strategic marketing plan that embraces the components of the marketing mix.
4. Developing a customer relationship management program to encourage loyalty and maximize the value of each customer.
5. Evaluating marketing-mix strategies and customer relationship programs to ensure that goals set out in the plan are achieved.

Figure 1.10   Elements of the Marketing Process

The following section illustrates the essential elements of the marketing process and provides examples of these activities. Refer to **Figure 1.10** for a visual illustration of the marketing process in action.

Assessing Customer Needs

A needs assessment is the first stage in an organization's marketing planning process. In a **needs assessment** an organization collects appropriate information about consumer needs to determine if a market is worth pursuing. To do so, the company will use a variety of research techniques and examine various sources of information.

Typically, a company conducts market analysis and a consumer analysis. In a **market analysis**, the factors it considers include market demand, sales volume potential, production capabilities, and the availability of the resources necessary to produce and market the product or service. When an organization conducts a **consumer analysis**, it monitors social, demographic, and behaviour changes within Canadian society. Business organizations also use marketing research procedures to evaluate changes in consumers' tastes and preferences, attitudes, and lifestyles so that marketing strategies can be adjusted accordingly.

A few examples from the packaged goods industry demonstrate the needs assessment process. The trend toward healthier lifestyles in Canada has caused people to search for healthier alternatives in the food aisle. Carbonated soft drinks were losing ground to alternatives such as fruit juices and bottled water—consumers were concerned about the high calorie and carbohydrate content of products such as Coca-Cola and Pepsi-Cola.

Coca-Cola reacted and introduced a new soft drink called Coke Zero, a product that promises the Coca-Cola taste without any calories. Refer to the image in **Figure 1.11**.

needs assessment The initial stage of marketing planning in which a company collects appropriate information to determine if a market is worth pursuing.

market analysis The collection of appropriate information (i.e., information regarding demand, sales volume potential, production capabilities, and resources necessary to produce and market a given product) to determine if a market is worth pursuing.

consumer analysis The monitoring of consumer behaviour changes (tastes, preferences, lifestyles) so that marketing strategies can be adjusted accordingly.

Steve White/QMI

Figure 1.11   Coca-Cola Zero has been a big success—a product aimed at people leading healthier lifestyles.

Apparently, Coke Zero appeals to young males in the 18 to 34 age range. Maurice Cooper, senior brand manager says "It resonates with young men who are clear about what they want and live in a world where expectations are increasingly more difficult to satisfy. These young men don't want to compromise."[15] Through packaging (black graphics) and advertising, Coke Zero developed a bold and masculine personality that appeals to these males. Coke Zero is the company's most successful new beverage in a generation and is poised to break into the top 10 brands in the sparkling beverage category. Given the strong acceptance of the product, Coke Zero clearly meets consumer needs.

Detergent-buying consumers traditionally associate value with price, but in today's busy society of dual-income families with little family time to spare, people are defining *value* differently. Busy consumers are looking for products that are quick and convenient to use. Procter & Gamble recognized that need and launched Tide Pods in 2011 at a price point much higher than powdered and liquid detergents. Refer to the image in **Figure 1.12**.

Sales of Tide Pods literally took off and the company projected first-year retail sales in the $500 million range in North America—an incredible figure![16] Through effective communications, Tide Pods redefined value to mean efficiency more than price. Advertising focused on the concentrated cleaning power of the product compared to less expensive alternatives. Understanding what consumers were looking for certainly paid dividends for Procter & Gamble.

Identifying and Selecting a Target Market

target market A group of customers who have certain characteristics in common.

An organization cannot satisfy the needs of all consumers, so it concentrates its efforts on a segment of the population that offers the most promise. That specific segment of the population is referred to as a **target market**. A target market is a group of people to whom a company markets its products. Typically, members of a target group have something in common (e.g., they fall within a certain age range, they have similar educational backgrounds or occupations, they live in the same area, they share a common interest or activity).

Here's an example that illustrates the concept of targeting. You may already be familiar with some of the catchy phrases that describe Canada's population demographics—you are probably part of Generation X or Generation Y, and your parents are baby boomers. Each of these groups is a target market because they share things in common.

Let's examine Generation Y more closely. Members of this group were born between 1980 and 1996—perhaps you are among them. Generation Y is known by other names as well: Net Generation, Millennials, and Echo Boomers, to name a few. These descriptions associate the group with key events and cultural trends. They are the most tech-savvy of any generation and their media behaviour has and will continue to influence how marketers communicate with them. Generation Y quickly adopts new technologies, adapting them to fit their lifestyles. They do not read newspapers or watch television the way their parents do. Instead, they engage with social media, spending more time there than with traditional media. Facebook, Instagram, and YouTube are the most popular destinations.[17] Recognizing

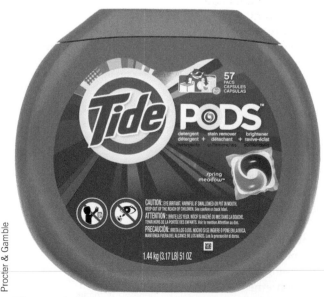

Procter & Gamble

Figure 1.12   Tide Pods effectively met consumers' need for convenience in the detergent market.

these behaviour differences, marketers are shifting their marketing dollars online in order to reach the next big generation of consumers.

In theory, the similarity of the target should mean that all people within the target would respond to a similar marketing strategy. But that is theory. In reality, marketing is extremely competitive, and numerous competitors battle it out for the same set of customers. The competitor with the best strategy—the strategy that has the most impact on the target market—wins the battle!

THE MARKETING MIX: DEVELOPING A MARKETING STRATEGY

L05 Explain the concept of the *marketing mix*.

An organization now shifts its focus to devising a marketing strategy or marketing plan. A well-defined strategy includes four key elements referred to as the **marketing mix**. The marketing mix refers to a set of strategic elements comprising product, price, distribution, and marketing communications. These elements are considered when planning a marketing strategy, with each element playing a unique role in the effective and efficient marketing of a product. When the elements are combined, the resulting strategy should satisfy the needs of a target market and achieve organizational objectives.

An additional factor, public image, also has an influence on the purchase intentions of customers. Generally speaking, if someone views a company positively there is a stronger likelihood he or she will buy its products. Therefore, companies strive to implement marketing strategies that enhance their images and reputations at both the corporate and brand level. Let us examine the four primary decision areas of the marketing mix along with the influence of public image. Refer to **Figure 1.13** for a summary of the marketing mix.

marketing mix The four strategic elements of product, price, distribution, and marketing communications.

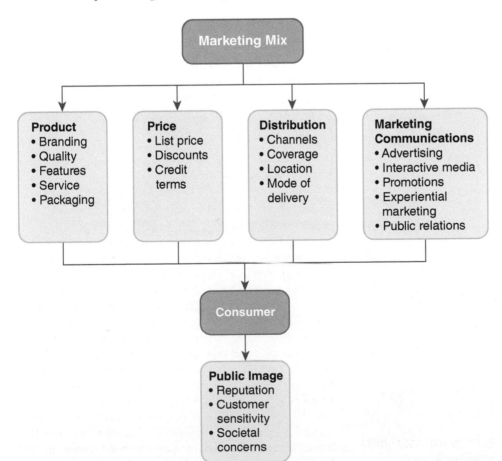

Figure 1.13
The Marketing Mix

Product Strategy

product strategy Making decisions about such variables as product quality, product features, brand names, packaging, customer service, guarantees, and warranties.

Product strategy embraces a variety of decisions. The most crucial decision a firm faces is determining what products or services to market. Once that decision is made, subsequent decisions may involve the setting of quality standards, sizes, brand name, packaging, guarantees, and level of service. For example, Quaker Oats markets great-tasting cereals that offer nutritious ingredients to health-minded consumers of all ages. The types of cereal and the variety of flavours Quaker offers are suitable for any household. The brand is identified by the Quaker name and the Quaker man that appear on all packages.

Earlier in the chapter it was mentioned that the Special K brand name was extended into product categories beyond cereal. Brand name decisions are an important aspect of product planning. Quaker Oats has successfully extended its brand name and the image of the Quaker man into categories such as cookie mixes, granola bars, and light snacks. Refer to the image in **Figure 1.14**. These actions are the result of good product decisions based on consumer needs identified by Quaker Oats.

Figure 1.14 Wise product decisions have expanded the Quaker brand into new cereal flavours and product categories.

PepsiCo Canada ULC

Product strategy involves **product differentiation**, which is defined as a strategy that focuses marketing practice on unique attributes, or differential advantages, of a product that are of value to customers in order to distinguish it from all other brands. With so many brands offering similar benefits it is important for a brand to get an edge on the competition. The goal is innovation—to invest considerable sums of money in developing products, resulting in a breakthrough product that will move the company forward. In the communications market Apple is strong on innovation. Apple products, for example, are technical in nature but are promoted as products that suit lifestyle needs of consumers. The iPhone and iPad are perceived as simple, sleek, and sexy—very different from their competitors.

Although Häagen Dazs was invented in the Bronx, New York, the name connotes a Danish image. That image, combined with the quality of the ice cream and effective marketing communications, has made Häagen Dazs a leader in the premium ice cream market. In the quick-serve restaurant market, Subway differentiates itself by offering fresh, healthy sandwiches: "Subway . . . Think fresh. Eat fresh."

product differentiation A strategy that focuses on the unique attributes or benefits of a product that distinguish it from another product.

Price Strategy

Price strategy involves the development of a pricing structure that is fair and equitable for the consumer while still profitable for the organization. Since most products are sold in a competitive market, organizations are free to establish prices according to what the market will bear. A host of factors are considered when a price strategy is established, including the cost of manufacturing the product, the location of the customer, the desired profit level, and the degree of competition. Generally, the less distinguishable a product is among its competitors (a condition referred to as *low differential advantage*), the less flexibility there is with price, because the product has no outstanding qualities to make it worth spending more on it than on its competitors' product. The inverse is also true. The Apple products cited earlier in the product section offer a high differential advantage (perceived or real) and as a result command a much higher price than their competitors' products—an enviable position to be in.

price strategy The development of a pricing structure that is fair and equitable for consumers and still profitable for the organization.

It should be pointed out that price is subject to regulation in certain markets and service sectors. In situations where a monopoly or near-monopoly exists, any planned increases in price must be approved by governments or government agencies. For example, in some provinces prices are controlled for hydroelectric power, cable television, and telephone services.

In addition to setting individual product prices, businesses can also establish comprehensive price policies that set company guidelines relating to trade allowances, discount programs, and credit terms. Businesses can provide these additional incentives, and customers can evaluate them while making their purchase decisions. A retailer such as Walmart, for example, buys the goods it resells in very large quantities. Therefore, it qualifies for larger discounts and allowances from suppliers, and in turn can pass on the savings to its customers. Walmart's price strategy is to offer the lowest possible prices on a regular basis. Walmart sums up its differential advantage with the advertising slogan "Save money. Live better." Refer to the image in **Figure 1.15**.

distribution strategy The selection and management of marketing channels and the physical distribution of products.

marketing channel A series of firms or individuals that participate in the flow of goods and services from producer to final users or customers.

Distribution Strategy

Distribution strategy refers to the selection and management of marketing channels and the physical distribution of products. A **marketing channel** is a series of firms or individuals that participate in the flow of goods and services from producer to final users or consumers, so decisions are based on the transactions between the various members of the channel. A product, such as packaged coffee, ice cream or cereal, moves from a manufacturer such as Nestlé or General Mills to a wholesaler such as National Grocers, to a retailer such as Valu-Mart or Your Independent Grocer, which in turn sells

Walmart >¦<
Save money. Live better.

Walmart Canada

Figure 1.15 Walmart's marketing strategy has always had an emphasis on price.

it to the consumer. These products may also bypass wholesalers entirely and be shipped directly to individual warehouse outlets, such as Costco.

Distribution decisions must be made as to which type of channel to use, the location and availability of the product, inventory (the amount of product stored at manufacturing or warehousing facilities), and transportation modes (air, rail, or water transport, pipeline, or digitally, as in the case of computer software products and video games). Developing effective and efficient distribution systems requires that an organization works closely and develops a harmonious relationship with distributors (wholesalers and retailers) who resell a product along the channel.

Distribution is about making the product available to customers. To demonstrate, consider how many Tim Hortons locations there are in Canada—about 3500 and counting. The fact that Tim Hortons is so accessible is one reason consumers visit it frequently.

Progressive companies now sell goods directly to customers via the Internet. In the automobile market consumers can buy products directly from manufacturers without setting foot inside a dealer location. At automotive websites for manufacturers such as Ford, Honda, and Mazda, consumers can design their own cars by adding various options and get the price of their cars instantaneously. They are then referred to their nearest dealer for delivery of the vehicle.

A change in consumer behaviour is fuelling direct distribution strategies to consumers. Among Canadian Internet users, 77 percent research goods and services online and 56 percent order goods and services for direct delivery. The total value of goods and services ordered online by consumers amounted to $18.9 billion in 2012, a 24 percent increase from 2010.[18]

Marketing Communications Strategy

marketing communications strategy The blending of advertising, sales promotion, event marketing and sponsorship, personal selling, and public relations to present a consistent and persuasive message about a product or service.

Marketing communications strategy involves unique yet complementary forms of communication: media advertising, which focuses on message and media strategies in traditional media (broadcast and print) and non-traditional media (online communications including social media networks, mobile communications, applications, and video games); direct-response communications (mail, telephone, and online); sales promotion (both consumer and trade promotions); public relations; experiential marketing; and personal selling.

Typically, marketing communications is the most visible aspect of an organization's marketing strategy. Since there are various methods of communication, it is important that a company or product present a clear and consistent message in each medium to achieve the highest possible impact. The coordination of all forms of marketing communications in a unified program that maximizes the impact on consumers and other types of customers is referred to as **integrated marketing communications (IMC)**.

integrated marketing communications (IMC) The coordination of various forms of marketing communications into a unified program that maximizes impact on consumers and other types of customers.

When considering marketing communications, marketing managers face two important decisions: what message to deliver, and what media and marketing communications alternatives to use in their mix. Rarely does a manager employ all components of the marketing communications mix at one time. The manager selects and uses those components deemed appropriate for resolving the situation at hand. For the components used, the message delivered must be complementary. In addition, a consistent message across all media has more impact on the audience it is intended to reach. With reference to the image in **Figure 1.16**, Ram trucks project an image of strength, power, and toughness regardless of the medium in which the message appears. Such imagery fits the lifestyle of hardworking males.

To demonstrate the importance of media choices, consider some basic differences in media consumption between younger and older Canadians. The younger generation has grown up with computers and mobile phones, whereas older Canadians have not; they learned how to use these tools along the way. The primary media of a younger tech-savvy generation would be the computer or smartphone. Among older Canadians the newspaper and television remain the primary media for information even though their use of computers, tablets, and smartphones is increasing. Marketers use this information to make decisions on where to place their ads.

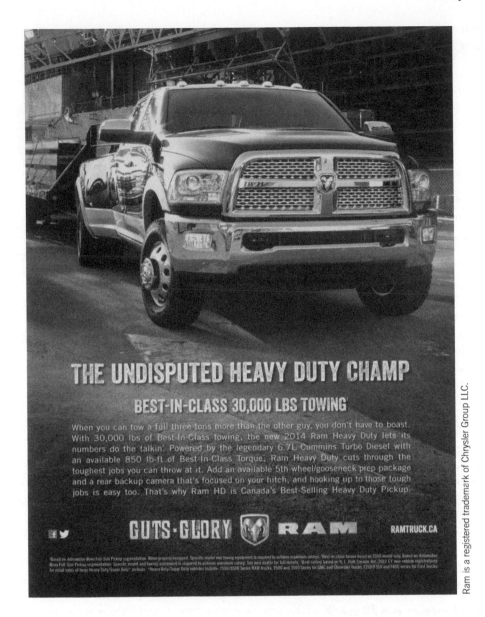

Figure 1.16
Advertising for RAM trucks reflects the lifestyle of hardworking males.

As you will learn later in the textbook, there is a general trend toward targeted media and marketing communications alternatives and away from mass media. Growing in popularity are online communications, social media network communications, and mobile communications. Social media are particularly interesting since consumers can manipulate a brand's message and share it with their friend network. Marketers (many of them reluctantly) are adapting to this shift in brand control.

Marketing managers now place more emphasis on complementary activities such as sales promotions, public relations, and experiential marketing. **Sales promotions** provide a means of offering consumers incentives to buy specific brands. For example, offering coupons and free samples is a good means of encouraging new customers to try a product for the first time. A well-planned contest involving big prizes is an effective means of encouraging repeat purchases. See **Figure 1.17** for an illustration of a sales promotion offer.

Public relations presents an opportunity to generate publicity for a brand. Public relations involves placing messages in the media via news releases. In effect, these messages generate "free" exposure for a product. Company-initiated stories about new products often appear on television newscasts and in newspaper and magazine articles. In today's technological environment, tools such as Facebook and Twitter get regular people communicating information (positive and negative) about products and companies. Online tools are now part of a good public relations strategy.

sales promotion Activity that provides special incentives to bring about immediate action from consumers, distributors, and an organization's sales force.

public relations A variety of activities and communications that organizations undertake to monitor, evaluate, influence, and adapt to the attitudes, opinions, and behaviours of their publics.

SPORTSNET™ MAGAZINE

☑ **YES,** send me 26 issues (1 year) of *Sportsnet* magazine for just $29*.
PLUS, when I pay – I will receive this **watch – as my bonus gift!**

Name

Address   Suite

City   Prov.   Postal code

Email Address: Email is the **fast, convenient, green** way to get information about your subscription, **digital access** and special offers.

Available on iPhone, iPad, Android tablet & Windows 8 devices

sportsnetmag.ca/5nsw

*Plus taxes. Offer valid only in Canada until June 30, 2014. Not valid with any other offer. *Sportsnet* magazine is published bi-weekly except for occasional combined, expanded or premium issues. Other organizations may ask to send offers to subscribers: if you do not wish to receive these offers, check here postal ☐ email ☐ ©2014 Rogers Publishing Ltd. #3101

BONUS GIFT!

Exclusive to Rogers customers:
You save when you add *Sportsnet* magazine to your monthly Rogers bill. Go to **sportsnet.ca/easy**

P4AAFLSG0    **ROGERS**™

80% SAVINGS
20 ISSUES FOR $20*

☑ **YES,** send me 20 issues of *Sportsnet* magazine for $20*. Includes access to iPhone, iPad, Android tablet & Windows 8 devices.

sportsnetmag.ca/5ns2

*Plus taxes. Offer valid only in Canada until June 30, 2014. Not valid with any other offer. *Sportsnet* magazine is published bi-weekly except for occasional combined, expanded or premium issues. Other organizations may ask to send offers to subscribers if you do not wish to receive these offers, check here postal ☐ email ☐ ©2014 Rogers Publishing Ltd. #3101

Name

Address   Suite

City   Prov.   Postal code

Email Address: Email is the **fast, convenient, green** way to get information about your subscription, **digital access** and special offers.

P41AFLSG0

Exclusive to Rogers customers: You save when you add *Sportsnet* magazine to your monthly Rogers bill. Go to **sportsnet.ca/easy**

 **ROGERS**™

Figure 1.17   A sales promotion offer can activate an initial consumer purchase.

experiential marketing A type of marketing that creates awareness for a product by having the customer directly interact with the product (e.g., distributing free samples of a product at street level).

Experiential marketing is a blend of communications disciplines that engages people with a brand in a more personal way. The goal of experiential marketing is to immerse consumers in a branded experience.

Reebok's shift in advertising strategy was mentioned earlier in the chapter. Part of that campaign included a partnership with CrossFit—a strength and conditioning program. The campaign included an experiential marketing effort in Toronto's downtown Dundas Square, a very busy public park. Using a crane, Reebok hoisted a 7000-kilogram shipping container above the square to raise public curiosity. A week later it was lowered to reveal a mobile CrossFit-branded gym and equipment that the public was encouraged to try. Events such as this allow consumers to engage and participate with a brand. A good experience could change their perception of a brand to the point where it activates a real purchase. Refer to the image in **Figure 1.18**.

Ryan Emberley/REEBOK CANADA INC/Newscom

Figure 1.18
Experiential marketing activities allow consumers to engage and participate with a brand.

Event marketing and sponsorships of events are key elements of experiential marketing. Experiential marketing is a growing component of the marketing communications mix. The key attraction of an event is the ability to reach a desired target audience directly.

event marketing The process, planned by a sponsoring organization, of integrating a variety of communications elements behind an event theme.

Public Image and Its Influences

Building a positive image and establishing a good reputation are important goals for a company. An organization can enhance its image by offering products and services of value to customers. Providing additional services in a manner that keeps customers satisfied over a long period helps build stronger relationships and enhances the trust a customer has in an organization. Every individual in an organization that has contact with customers and the public at large must share in the responsibility of representing the company in a positive light. This combination of activities strongly suggests that **public image** is an integral part of an organization's corporate strategy and marketing strategy. A firm's reputation is important enough to require special attention.

public image The reputation that a product, service, or company has among its various publics.

In an effort to develop a better public image, many firms are showing greater sensitivity to their customers. At the marketing level companies are implementing more comprehensive customer service programs and customer relationship management programs that are designed to encourage loyalty. A loyal customer is a profitable customer and profit is the ultimate goal of an organization.

Companies do make mistakes however, and those mistakes can take their toll on reputation and sales. To demonstrate, consider the situation Lululemon Athletic faced in 2013. Lululemon struggled when dealing with issues related to the sheerness of its Luon yoga pants. The pants were pulled from the shelves due to their see-through nature, but it took a long time to do so. The company ill-advisedly blamed the problem on style changes and production issues. Chip Wilson, the founder and CEO of the company then ignited a social media firestorm when he associated the problem with women's bodies. Wilson said "Some women's bodies just actually don't work for it. It's really about the rubbing through the thighs, how much pressure is there."[19] Sales began to plummet and ultimately Wilson was forced out of the company by the board of directors. The new CEO's immediate challenge is to persuade disenchanted customers to buy its pricey athletic wear in a market where rivals are offering cheaper alternatives. Restoring the reputation of the company is integral to future success!

At the corporate level, companies use corporate advertising campaigns to inform the public about what they are doing regarding social and environmental issues. Corporate advertising is not intended to directly sell a product, but since the objective is to enhance the image of the company and create goodwill, there could be some long-term and indirect effects on sales.

Simulation: Marketing Mix

MAXIMIZING CUSTOMER VALUE: BUILDING CUSTOMER RELATIONSHIPS

LO6 Explain how an organization maximizes the value of its customers.

As discussed earlier, the goal of marketing is to attract, cultivate, and retain customers. The tools used in the marketing mix create awareness and interest in products and make them available at a time and place when customers want them. Marketing today, however, is about building a solid relationship with individual customers in order to maximize the value of each customer. An organization forms a relationship with customers by collecting and analyzing information about customers and using the information when planning and implementing marketing strategies.

customer relationship management (CRM)
Strategies designed to optimize profitability, revenue, customer retention, and customer satisfaction.

loyalty (frequent buyer) programs Offer the consumer a small bonus, such as points or "play money," when they make a purchase; the bonus accumulates with each new purchase.

customer relationship management program
Analyzes data about customers' buying behaviour, their preferences when buying, and their likes and dislikes to create individualized marketing programs to meet unique customer needs.

An organization also forms relationships with members of the channel of distribution by planning and implementing partnership programs. Customer relationship management programs go beyond the marketing mix to focus on customers and relationships rather than markets and products, but it is the combination of these two concepts that contributes to an organization's success.

Customer relationship management (CRM) refers to strategies designed to optimize profitability, revenue, customer retention, and customer satisfaction.[20] Relationship management is not concerned with individual transactions, but with establishing, maintaining, and enhancing long-term relationships. The implementation of CRM strategies requires a firm to invest in software tools required to collect, analyze, and manage customer information. Information technology and database marketing and management techniques are the root source of customer information—the information needed about customers to devise better marketing strategies.

Customer retention strategies can be divided into two areas: **loyalty (frequent buyer) programs** that focus on retaining customers by offering rewards, and **customer relationship management programs** that analyze data about customers' buying behaviour, their preferences when buying, and their likes and dislikes. An effective CRM program uses information to create individualized marketing programs to meet unique customer needs.

Loyalty Programs

It is quite likely that you are familiar with the loyalty program concept. In your wallet you probably have a membership card for a loyalty program (e.g., Air Miles or Shoppers Drug Mart's Optimum card) or you have collected and redeemed Canadian Tire money at Canadian Tire stores. See the image in **Figure 1.19**.

Typically, a loyalty program offers incentives to customers to ensure repeat purchases—they are rewards for shopping at a retail establishment and are the starting point for establishing an ongoing relationship. McDonald's for example, introduced a coffee loyalty card that rewards customers with a free McCafe beverage after seven purchases. The loyalty card and coffee stickers for the card are on the side of each beverage cup. This rewards program is simple, and consumers readily see the value of participating in it—the sign of a good rewards program!

The Shoppers Drug Mart program is more complex since points are updated electronically. Member customers swipe their Optimum card each time they make a purchase. The points accumulate and the shoppers can convert their points to discounts on purchases made at a later date.

Figure 1.19   Rewards programs encourage repeat purchases by present customers.

Customer Relationship Management (CRM) Programs

A customer relationship management program can be divided into three distinct functions. First, the organization collects and analyzes the information. Second, the organization develops new marketing offers that should be of interest to its customers based on its analysis of the information. Third, a communications plan delivers the details of the new offer to the market.

The Shoppers Drug Mart Optimum program operates in such a manner. It is a rewards program but the data collected can be cross-referenced electronically in order to determine consumer buying preferences. Armed with such information, Shoppers Drug Mart can tailor offers and services to specific customers. The true benefit of a loyalty program is the information it collects for its database—the foundation for a good customer relationship management program. The Optimum card program has 10 million people registered in it.[21]

Where does the information come from? CRM programs are technology-based, and sophisticated software is used to collect and analyze customer information. Information is captured at the point of purchase—a computer automatically records what you purchase and when you purchased it. Perhaps the clerk asked for your address, postal code, or phone number. Personal information about customers is also collected through online surveys and from customer service centres. When seeking information online, how often have you been asked to fill in a short survey before gaining access to the information? Your personal information is now in a database.

To understand the application of a customer relationship management program, consider a plan implemented by Fairmont Hotels & Resorts. From customer feedback forms and surveys completed by guests, deep insights were identified regarding product and service expectations. The surveys revealed that travellers weren't interested in earning extra nights in a Fairmont Hotel (the typical perk offered by many competitors) as a reward for their loyalty. Their priorities focused on rectifying problems when they occurred, recognition of individual preferences, and flexibility regarding arrival and checkout times.

Based on this information, Fairmont examined each step in the guest experience—from check-in and valet parking to checkout—and set a standard of performance for each activity. The goal was to always satisfy customers with each and every thing they did. Internal systems were changed and the management structure was changed so that each hotel had someone available to ensure the hotel consistently met its customer commitments. After implementing these changes, Fairmont's share of the Canadian business travel market jumped 16 percent in a flat market.[22] That's more than a good return on investment!

EVALUATING MARKETING ACTIVITY

L07 Identify fundamental methods for measuring the effectiveness of marketing activities.

Marketing activity is planned on an annual basis. Every year a new marketing plan is created for each of the products a company markets. Such plans are essential because each product faces different marketing challenges. Once a plan is in progress it is reviewed throughout the year; a quarterly look at a marketing plan's performance is a common practice. The objective of the review is to determine if the current plan will achieve the objectives stated in the plan by the end of the planning cycle. In other words, is progress being made? Objectives are typically stated in terms of sales revenue, profit, and market share.

As part of the review, the manager evaluates the effectiveness of the marketing activities (the marketing mix) that have been implemented thus far and, if necessary, recommends changes to those activities. Conditions in the marketplace can change dramatically and on short notice so an organization has to make changes just as quickly. The review also includes an evaluation of competitors' marketing activities. What competitors are doing can influence a brand's marketing strategy for the balance of the year. Regardless of what situations arise and what changes are made to the plan, the

Simulation: What is Marketing?

marketing manager's responsibility is to achieve the objectives stated in the plan. If necessary, the objectives may also change during the course of the year.

ETHICAL CONSIDERATIONS FOR MARKETING

L08   Explain how ethical considerations impact marketing strategies.

It is important for business and the people who manage our business practices to lead the way in terms of ethical and moral conduct. That's an easy thing to say but sometimes business and industry fall short of consumer expectations in the way they conduct business.

business ethics The study and examination of moral and social responsibility in relation to business practices and decision making in business.

Business ethics is defined as the study and examination of moral and social responsibility in relation to business practices and decision making in business.[23]

Both the Canadian Marketing Association (CMA) and the American Marketing Association (AMA) have established certain standards that all marketers should adhere to. Both the CMA and AMA are guided by a set of norms and values. *Norms* are standards of conduct that are expected and maintained by society and business organizations. *Values* represent the collective conception of what communities find desirable, important, and morally proper.[24] Such values embrace characteristics that include honesty, responsibility, fairness, respect, transparency, and citizenship—all good things that a prudent marketing organization will abide by!

In Canada, the CMA's *Code of Ethics and Standards of Practice* guides marketing organizations. According to the code, marketers must establish and maintain high standards of practice showing responsibility to the public in winning and holding consumer confidence. Member organizations are obligated to the consumers and businesses they serve and must practise the highest standards of honesty, truth, accuracy, fairness, and professionalism.[25]

On a broader scale, businesses today strive for sustainability. Perhaps the simplest explanation of sustainability is the ability to sustain or the capacity to endure.[26] In terms of business practice, sustainability is about conducting business in a manner that helps the future of society. It's about balancing corporate growth and profitability while considering the impact of our decisions on the environment and society.

Socially responsible marketing (discussed earlier in the chapter) is part of the equation as is the trend toward conducting business in a green way. Many organizations today establish firm objectives and implement strategies that will reduce their carbon footprints. These objectives are just as important as sales, profit, and market share. For more insight into how organizations strike this balance between these objectives read the Think Marketing box **What's More Important, Profit or Sustainability?**

Industry leaders like Coca-Cola, Walmart, and SC Johnson lead by example in terms of sustainable business practice. Coca-Cola markets many of its products in bottles made of natural plant sugars that are fully recyclable. Walmart is the largest buyer of renewable energy in Canada. Some of their stores are testing geothermal energy and solar panels and new stores are 35 percent more efficient than stores built before 2006. Refer to the image in **Figure 1.20**. SC Johnson, a family-owned maker of household products has removed more than 61 million pounds of

Figure 1.20   Walmart's solar energy program is efficient and environmentally friendly.

ThinkMarketing

What's More Important, Profit or Sustainability?

Marketers today must deal with a generation of consumers that expect business organizations to consider the social and environmental impact of their activities. In the age of social media these organizations must practise what they preach or suffer the consequences from angry consumer groups.

Many organizations are truly doing good things. Unilever, a giant multinational company, is a clear leader when it comes to green marketing efforts and sustainable business practices. One of the first things Paul Polman did when he became CEO of the organization was to drop the emphasis on quarterly sales and profits and place more emphasis on social responsibility objectives. His benchmarks for success go well beyond achieving financial goals. He reports publicly on progress being made.

Unilever's goals focus on things like reducing manufacturing waste, reducing packaging, and removing transfats, salt, and calories from its processed foods. Unilever is also shifting agricultural practices toward sustainability by forcing suppliers to change their ways. In Canada, for example, Hellmann's mayonnaise is made with free-range eggs. The company's popular Dove soap brand is well known for its efforts to improve female self-esteem.

Walmart Canada is another organization that aligns its objectives with sustainability programs. It employs 95 000 people and pays nearly $18 billion to Canadian suppliers. Walmart is a financially giving organization, offering in the range of $180 million to charitable causes annually. On the business side of things Walmart has pioneered larger trucks to reduce the number of deliveries it makes and is rapidly

UNILEVER SUSTAINABLE LIVING PLAN 2013
MAKING PROGRESS, DRIVING CHANGE
Unilever

expanding its use of sustainable energy sources. Right now one-quarter of its energy comes from such sources.

Marketing has always been about dealing with change but in today's world it is more about making changes in how business is conducted—it is a top-down organizational philosophy that goes beyond marketing! It's no longer only about maximizing sales and profit. Perhaps the motto that Unilever operates by sums things up best: "Doing well by doing good."

> **Question:**
>
> **"Doing well by doing good." Is that the future of marketing and business practice or will financial goals prevail? What's your opinion?**

Adapted from Alec Scott, "How to save the world (and get richer trying)," Canadian Business, November 25, 2013, pp. 58–63.

volatile organic compounds from its products' environmental footprint—roughly the same amount produced by 656 000 cars in one year.[27]

Despite these efforts and those of many other organizations, consumers remain somewhat skeptical about green marketing claims. Many consumers believe that corporate claims are just marketing ploys to influence purchase decisions. One such study claimed 80 percent of Canadians felt that way.[28] The term for such skepticism is *greenwashing*—claims of environmental friendliness that may be unsubstantiated, vague, or misleading. For example, specific claims such as "100% recycled," "non-toxic," and "natural" or "all natural" try to portray a product as being green. Huggies Natural Care baby wipes contain "all natural" ingredients such as aloe vera and vitamin E, but they also contain chemicals like methylparaben and methylisothiazolinone—just how "natural" is this product?[29]

Another example of good intentions gone sour was the compostable Sun Chips bag launched by Frito Lay. Perhaps you will remember the bag. Once it was opened it made a rather noisy crackling sound. Many consumers found the bag irritating and the company eventually withdrew it from the market. Ontario's waste officials were very happy with

Video: Fact Check:
Organic Label

Simulation: Management
and Ethics

Frito Lay's decision since their industrial composting systems couldn't handle the bag. It didn't break down fast enough and was another contaminant to dispose of.[30] Was this greenwashing? You be the judge.

Companies that demonstrate corporate social responsibility must make the public aware of what they are doing. They must connect their brands to their environmental programs and the social issues they support. It's good for business and it's good for society! By the same token, companies that mislead consumers on ethical issues should be taken to task and suffer the consequences of consumer backlash.

✔ Experience Marketing

To experience marketing you must assess situations and make recommendations to change marketing strategies when necessary. What would you do in the following situation?

Coca-Cola is the best-selling soft drink in the world. Perhaps Coca-Cola is your favourite brand and you are passionate about it. So much the better! Have you ever thought about what Coca-Cola has done in terms of marketing to become the number one brand? It could be said that Coca-Cola has an effective marketing strategy that embraces all components of the marketing mix. The brand meets consumers' expectations better than any other brand. Coca-Cola is in an enviable position.

Now, put yourself in the role of marketing manager for Coca-Cola in Canada. You cannot be complacent with your number one position since Pepsi-Cola is always lurking, ready to challenge your position. A good marketing manager always wants to improve the brand's market position. What changes to Coca-Cola's marketing mix would you recommend?

In order to make any marketing mix recommendations you must first analyze what Coca-Cola is currently doing in Canada. Conduct some web-based secondary research to find out as much as you can about its marketing mix: product, price, marketing communications, and distribution. Try to summarize your findings under each component of the mix. Can you detect any weaknesses in Coca-Cola's strategy? Are there areas that Coca-Cola could improve upon? Be ready to provide some justification for your decisions and recommendations.

CHAPTER SUMMARY

L01 **Define the term** *marketing.*   (p. 3)

Marketing is defined as an organizational function and a set of processes for creating, communicating, and delivering value to customers and for managing customer relationships in ways that benefit the organization and its stakeholders.

L02 **Describe the importance of marketing in organizations today.**   (pp. 3–5)

Marketing is a vital business function, as it is the means by which an organization connects with customers. In terms of implementation, marketing is divided into two key areas. First, marketing attracts customers and encourages them to buy a good or service for the first time. Second, marketing programs encourage customer satisfaction and loyalty to maximize the lifetime value of customers.

L03 **Describe how marketing has evolved to become the driving force of business growth.**   (pp. 5–11)

The nature of marketing practice has evolved. It has moved from a production orientation to a sales orientation to a true marketing orientation. Contemporary marketing methods now revolve around social responsibility practices and new social media technologies. The manner in which an organization reaches and

influences potential customers continues to change how marketing is practised.

L04 **Explain the fundamental process of marketing practised by organizations today.**   (pp. 11–15)

Marketing can be described as a process that involves several key steps: assessing customer needs, identifying and selecting target markets, developing the marketing strategy by using elements of the marketing mix, developing customer relationship management programs that encourage loyalty, and finally, evaluating marketing mix and customer relationship management strategies for effectiveness. An organization devises independent marketing plans for each of its products. All products contribute to an organization's success in terms of sales, profit, and customer satisfaction.

L05 **Explain the concept of the** *marketing mix.*   (pp. 15–21)

The marketing mix is comprised of four distinct components: product, price, distribution, and marketing communications. When devising a marketing strategy decisions are made on each of these components. Although each component is separate in nature, it is the collective impact of all four variables that will ultimately influence a customer to buy a product.

LO6 Explain how an organization maximizes the value of its customers. *(pp. 22–23)*

To get full value from existing customers, marketing managers devise loyalty programs and use technologies to plan and implement customer relationship management programs. Loyalty programs offer customers incentives to maintain a good relationship. Customer relationship management programs consider the individual needs and behaviours of their customers. Information about customers is harnessed in a database that marketing managers access and analyze. Marketing today—and in the future—will depend upon how well an organization manages the relationship between itself and its customers. Technology is the driving force behind customer relationship management programs.

LO7 Identify fundamental methods for measuring the effectiveness of marketing activities. *(pp. 23–24)*

Marketing activity is planned on an annual basis. The plans are evaluated at predetermined intervals during the year to determine if the plan will meet its stated objectives. Objectives are typically stated in terms of sales revenue, profit, and market share. The reviewing manager will assess the effectiveness of the marketing activities (how the marketing mix is utilized), and if necessary make adjustments to the plan. Economic and competitive forces may also affect the direction a revised plan takes.

LO8 Explain how ethical considerations impact marketing strategies. *(pp. 24–26)*

It's important for businesses today to lead the way in terms of ethical and moral conduct. Both the Canadian Marketing Association (CMA) and American Marketing Association (AMA) have standards that marketing organizations should follow. These standards embrace characteristics such as honesty, responsibility, fairness, respect, transparency, and citizenship. On a broader scale, businesses are encouraged to operate in a sustainable manner so that they contribute to the well-being of society now and in the future.

In the age of heightened consumer awareness, there is increased expectation placed on companies to operate in an ethical manner. An organization must resist the temptation to mislead or misrepresent its actions to make itself look better than it is. A truly responsible organization must react to this awareness and consider the interests of customers, shareholders, communities, and the environment in everything it does. A positive imprint is good for society and good for business.

MyMarketingLab

Study, practise, and explore real marketing situations with these helpful resources:
- **Interactive Lesson Presentations:** Work through interactive presentations and assessments to test your knowledge of marketing concepts.
- **Study Plan:** Check your understanding of chapter concepts with self-study quizzes.
- **Dynamic Study Modules:** Work through adaptive study modules on your computer, tablet, or mobile device.
- **Simulations:** Practise decision-making in simulated marketing environments.

REVIEW QUESTIONS

1. What is the basic premise on which contemporary marketing is built? *(LO1)*
2. Briefly explain the significance of marketing in business organizations today. *(LO2)*
3. Identify the essential characteristics of successful marketing organizations. *(LO2)*
4. Briefly compare the operating philosophies of companies that have the following: a production orientation, a selling orientation, a marketing orientation, a socially responsible marketing orientation, a social media marketing orientation. (LO3)
5. Briefly explain the term *marketing concept*, and provide an illustration of how it is applied. *(LO3)*
6. What is content marketing? Briefly explain. *(LO3)*
7. Identify the essential steps in the marketing process. *(LO4)*
8. When a company "assesses customer needs," it conducts a market analysis and consumer analysis. Briefly describe what is involved in each area. *(LO4)*
9. What is a target market? *(LO4)*
10. Identify and briefly describe the four key elements of the marketing mix. *(LO5)*
11. What does *product differentiation* refer to? Provide two examples of brands in two different markets that are clearly differentiated from their competitors. *(LO5)*
12. What are the key components of the marketing communications mix? *(LO5)*
13. What is customer relationship management and what role does it play in contemporary marketing? *(LO6)*
14. What is the fundamental difference between a loyalty program and a customer relationship management program? *(LO6)*
15. Identify key criteria commonly used to evaluate the success of a marketing plan. *(LO7)*
16. Briefly explain how ethical considerations influence the development of contemporary marketing programs. Cite some specific examples to demonstrate this practice. *(LO8)*

DISCUSSION AND APPLICATION QUESTIONS

1. How do colleges and universities implement the marketing concept? Cite some examples of marketing activities at your college or university.
2. Investigate further the topic of socially responsible marketing. Provide some examples of what Canadian companies are doing to fulfill the mandate called for when marketing in a socially responsible manner.
3. What elements of the marketing mix are most important to each of the following companies or brands?
   a. Federal Express
   b. Toronto Raptors (or any other professional sports team)
   c. Canadian Tire
4. Select a brand or company and conduct some research to determine the nature and extent of the brand's [company's] social media marketing activities. Should the brand be doing more in this area of marketing?

2

The External Marketing Environment

REUTERS/Dado Ruvic

LEARNING OBJECTIVES

LO1 Identify the external forces that influence marketing. (pp. 29–30)

LO2 Explain the impact of the economy and various market structures on marketing practices. (pp. 30–33)

LO3 Describe the way various competitive forces influence marketing strategy development. (pp. 33–38)

LO4 Discuss how social, environmental, and demographic forces shape marketing strategies now and in the future. (pp. 38–46)

LO5 Identify and explain the effect technological trends and developments have on current and future marketing practices. (pp. 46–50)

LO6 Distinguish the role that laws, regulations, and self-regulation play in the practice of marketing in Canada. (pp. 50–52)

GOOGLE...

is the most visited site on the Web. While Google's core offering remains its search engine, the company has been expanding into services ranging from email and document storage to productivity software and mobile phone operating systems. Google has also acquired other Internet companies, from blogging services to the video-sharing site, YouTube. By paying close attention to trends and capitalizing on opportunities, Google has evolved from a two-man enterprise to a multibillion-dollar corporation in less than a decade.

Given that Google's main source of revenue is from advertising, the company has always been looking for ways to gain insight into our lives. The better Google knows us, the more efficient it can be in sending us relevant marketing messages. Google's recent purchase of Nest, a manufacturer of Internet-connected devices including smart home thermostats, is one more way for Google to extend its reach into our homes.

Google knows that consumers are very interested in these new smart gadgets that connect to the Internet and adapt to our lifestyle preferences. This trend sees the world becoming a place where everything around us is connected and smart—from laptops and mobile phones to refrigerators and even crockpots! Imagine being at your college campus on your way to class and being able to use your smartphone to turn on your crockpot so that you'll have a tasty warm dinner waiting for you when you get home. Picture your refrigerator making a shopping list for you—letting you know what's in the fridge and suggesting recipes based on your dietary requirements.

We're in the early stages yet, but in the near future you may even have a toothbrush that's able to sense a cavity and book a dental appointment for you! This interconnected world will change what we buy, how we buy it, and how we interact with one another—and Google plans to be a leader in this new marketplace.

But these innovations also bring privacy concerns. Just before Google bought Nest, Google was found in violation of Canada's privacy laws. And its move to get a foothold in the smart gadget market caused an outcry in the tech world. People and organizations will need to adapt to keep themselves and their data safe. Regulators will need to ensure privacy laws and regulations are up to date. Environmental lobbyists have also expressed concern over the impact technological changes have on our ecosystems.

The world around us is changing, and marketers need to pay attention and adapt. In this chapter we'll examine a variety of trends in the external environment and take a look at how these trends are influencing marketing practices.[1]

EXTERNAL FORCES THAT IMPACT MARKETING

LO1 Identify the external forces that influence marketing.

The environment in which marketing operates is constantly changing. Problems, opportunities, successes, and failures are largely dependent on an organization's ability to adapt to changing conditions. In this regard, a business must anticipate change and how it will affect its operations. To be successful, new strategies must evolve. To foresee and adjust to change, a company reviews and analyzes certain external forces that influence the nature of its marketing strategies. Trends that occur among consumers and in the economy, competition, technology, and laws and other regulations must be considered when developing a marketing strategy. Each of these external forces is examined in detail in this chapter.

Figure 2.1 highlights a few trends that marketers should be paying attention to. This partial list of trends shows the breadth of an environmental scan—from the increasing intensity of global competition, to the emphasis on corporate social responsibility, to the expanding use of new technologies.

Figure 2.1 Trends in the Canadian Marketplace

Environmental Force (C.R.E.S.T.)	Trends Revealed by an Environmental Scan
Competitive	• Price competition is intense as big U.S. retailers continue to enter the Canadian marketplace. • Mergers and acquisitions are occurring to create scale and improve competitiveness.
Regulatory	• There's an increased emphasis on free trade. • Regulators are introducing new legislation related to consumer privacy, intellectual property protection, and copyright.
Economic	• Canada's rate of economic growth is much lower than before the 2009 global recession. • Electronic commerce continues to grow. • There is concern about the high levels of personal and household debt.
Social, Environmental & Demographic	• Canadian society is more demanding of Canadian business practices and tends to reward those organizations that act in a socially responsible manner. • The population of Canada is more ethnically diverse than it used to be.
Technological	• Technological innovations are changing the way we communicate with each other and the way companies communicate with customers. • There has been a dramatic growth in open source or free software. • The "Internet of Everything" is connecting all aspects of our lives.

Individually or collectively, these trends (or forces) could have an impact on a company. Google's business situation in early 2014 was described in the opening of this chapter. Google gives careful consideration to all of these trends when devising its corporate and marketing strategies.

ECONOMIC FORCES

L02 Explain the impact of the economy and various market structures on marketing practices.

The economy has a significant impact on an organization's marketing activity. The federal government, through Statistics Canada, is continuously collecting and analyzing information that determines the relative health of the country's economy. Canada's economic situation is measured by such variables as the gross domestic product, imports and exports, retail sales, unemployment, interest rates, and the value of the Canadian dollar. An analysis of trends in these variables determines if the economy is in good or bad shape. How these variables interact with one another will influence how conservative or how aggressive an organization's marketing efforts will be.

gross domestic product (GDP) The total value of goods and services produced in a country on an annual basis.

Gross domestic product (GDP) refers to the total value of goods and services produced in a country on an annual basis. Positive growth in a year would reflect a productive economy and plentiful jobs. In terms of goods and services produced, Canada's economy is 30 percent goods and 70 percent services.[2] The rate of growth in Canada is often compared to that of other countries (particularly the United States), which offers an international perspective on how well our economy is doing.

Canada's economy has been recovering slowly since the 2008–2009 economic recession that affected not only Canada but also other countries around the world. After experiencing minimal gains in 2012 and 2013, Canada's real GDP growth is expected to improve over the next few years, with growth between 2 and 3 percent annually.[3]

Increased demand for Canadian goods and services at home and abroad, as well as low interest rates, improving consumer and business confidence, and a falling Canadian dollar, are key factors contributing to the economy's recovery.

The economic downturn had a more significant impact on the U.S. economy. Real growth in GDP has continued to be sluggish in recent years, averaging 2 percent in 2013. Important factors affecting the U.S. economy include a high debt load, lower government spending, political infighting, and an increase in long-term interest rates. The U.S. economic outlook, however, is fairly positive, with growth forecast to be about 3 percent in 2014. Even stronger gains are anticipated for 2015.[4]

Canada's international trade balance, determined by the amount of imports and exports each year, is another indicator of the economy's health. The objective is to have a positive trade balance where exports exceed imports. For years Canada enjoyed such a position. Climbing out of a recession, however, has affected Canada's trade balance of payments negatively. In 2009, 2010, and 2012 Canada's exports fell, and the country experienced a trade deficit. Canada's largest trading partner is the United States, a market that accounts for 73.2 percent of all exports and 62.5 percent of all imports.[5] Clearly, the state of economic affairs in the United States and other countries with which we trade affects the operational health and welfare of Canadian companies. Looking ahead, a healthier U.S. economy, as well as the recent free trade agreement between Canada and Europe (CETA), should help drive demand for Canadian goods and, as a result, boost exports.[6 & 7]

Refer to **Figure 2.2** for a summary of some economic indicators that influence marketing strategy in Canada.

The *value of the Canadian dollar* has a direct impact on the activities of Canadian organizations that export their products. When, for example, the Canadian dollar is worth less than the U.S. dollar, the demand for Canadian-produced goods in the United States rises as our goods can be priced below U.S.-produced goods. Conversely, if the Canadian dollar is higher in value than the U.S. dollar, demand for our goods decreases. The fact that the Canadian dollar is historically worth less

Indicator	2009	2010	2011	2012
Exports ($ billion) [1]	367.2	404.0	456.8	462.5
Imports ($ billion) [1]	373.9	413.7	456.0	474.5
Trade Balance (exports minus imports)	−6.7	−9.7	0.8	−1.2
GDP (annual growth rate; percent) [2]	−3.0	+3.5	+2.7	+1.8
Interest (annual average; percent) [3]	0.65	0.85	1.25	1.25
Unemployment rate (average percent) [4]	8.3	8.0	7.5	7.3

Figure 2.2
A Selection of Economic Indicators—Canada

Sources:
[1]Statistics Canada CANSIM Table 228 – 0058 Balance of Payments, Total of all merchandise http://www.statcan.gc.ca
[2]Statistics Canada CANSIM Table 379–0031 GDP All industries www.statcan.gc.ca
[3]Bank of Canada Bank Rates, www.bankofcanada.ca
[4]Statistics Canada CANSIM Table 109-5324 www.statcan.gc.ca

than the U.S. dollar contributes to Canada's positive trade balance with the United States.

The rise of the Canadian dollar to par or near par with the U.S. dollar, as we saw between 2010 and 2012, typically has a negative impact on trade with the United States. Since 2013, however the Canadian dollar has begun to depreciate in value and is expected to settle at around $0.90 U.S.[8] This situation should have a positive impact on demand for Canadian-made goods in the United States and boost industries such as tourism in Canada. In addition, higher demand for finished goods and goods used in production processes could contribute to much needed job creation in the manufacturing sector in Canada.[9 & 10]

The *level of employment or unemployment* from year to year also varies. A high level of employment reflects a vibrant economy, and vice versa. By the end of 2013, Canada's unemployment rate levelled off at 7.2 percent, down from a high of 8.1 percent in 2010. Despite a gradual decrease in the overall unemployment rate, employment gains in recent years show the slowest year-over-year growth rate since 2009, at just 0.6 percent in 2013. Furthermore, the unemployment rate among young people aged 15 to 24 years remains high at 14 percent as of December 2013.[11] Slower economic growth in Canada may make it difficult to return to pre-recession employment rates. On the bright side, though, healthier global economic growth is expected to stimulate Canada's export industries and positively impact employment numbers in 2014 and beyond. The health care and social assistance sector will also continue to drive employment growth due to growing demand from an aging population for health-care services.[12 & 13]

How much consumers spend in retail stores is another indicator of an economy's health. Consumer spending directly influences demand for goods and services, and influences production and manufacturing decisions among source companies. Retail sales have taken a hit following the 2009 recession, but are showing gradual improvement as the job market strengthens and consumers' disposable incomes increase. The most recent statistic from 2011 indicates 4.2 percent annual growth in retail sales.[14] Going forward, price competition among the big retailers like Walmart, Sobeys, and newly arrived Target, as well as a strengthening economy, should continue to encourage value-conscious consumers to spend.

Interest rates (the cost of borrowing money) are another factor influencing the economy. The Bank of Canada sets an interest rate based on how it interprets the health of the economy. For example, if rapid economic growth is anticipated, and the corresponding possibility of inflation, the bank may increase the rate to cool the economy down a bit. **Inflation** refers to a generally rising price level for goods and services, resulting in reduced purchasing power. In Canada, inflation has been running at around 1 percent annually in recent years and is expected to remain at this level through to 2016. This historically low level of inflation will likely mean interest rates will stay low, as well.[15] A lower bank rate helps boost the economy as it less expensive for businesses and consumers to borrow money. However, cheap lending rates offered by chartered banks (BMO, RBC, CIBC and others) encourage consumers to spend on credit. The Bank of Canada's concern now is for the amount of personal and household debt Canadians carry—a delicate balancing act!

The relationship among the economic variables described in this section is dynamic. It is wise for business organizations to stay abreast of economic trends and adjust their business strategies, including marketing, accordingly. Dollarama, for example, Canada's largest operator of dollar stores with 847 locations across the country, continues to expand, saying it has been benefiting from consumers' concern about household debt and the weak economy. The company's low-price strategy is very timely and Dollarama saw profits jump 20 percent in the third quarter of 2013 as a result.[16]

More people are turning to reselling sites like UsedEveryWhere.com, a network of 90 hyper-local free classified sites in Canada, the United States, and the United Kingdom, not just as way to make and save money, but because they offer more choice than is found in a typical mall. "UsedEveryWhere has positioned itself well by catering to consumers looking for great deals and innovative ways to save money on essentials so they can pay off debt. Traffic on our site is continuing to grow," says Director of Marketing Lacey Sheardown.

Lululemon has taken a more cautious approach with its marketing in recent years. According to former CEO Christine Day, "It's easy to make decisions and to be

inflation The rising price level for goods and services that results in reduced purchasing power.

good when everything is going well. It's far harder to protect the brand and live your values when the going gets tough."[17] Consequently, Lululemon, a very successful retailer, has reined in the pace of new store growth. Instead of adding locations, which was the original objective, the new objective has become to encourage consumers to visit existing stores more often by introducing new products with an edge and by offering special incentives, such as more free yoga classes and invitation-only shopping nights—two proven tactics that make customers feel good about this organization.

COMPETITIVE FORCES

LO3 Describe the way various competitive forces influence marketing strategy development.

The activity of competitors is probably the most thoroughly studied aspect of marketing practice, as competitors are constantly striving to find new and better ways of appealing to similar target markets. The competitive environment that an organization operates in must be defined and analyzed, and the strategies of direct and indirect competitors must be monitored and evaluated.

Market Structures

In Canada, a business operates in one of four different types of market structure: monopoly, oligopoly, monopolistic competition, or pure competition. Each market structure is unique and has a different impact on marketing strategy. **Figure 2.3** offers a summary of each market.

In a **monopoly**, one firm serves the entire market (there are no close substitutes) and therefore theoretically it controls most of the marketing mix elements: product, price, distribution, and marketing communications. In Canada, government regulates monopolies so market control is limited. Examples of monopolistic but regulated markets include cable television within geographic areas, electricity, and water. Since consumers do not have a choice in matters such as these, governments at all levels must regulate price and service availability, ensuring that customers are treated fairly. Canadian Blood Services (CBS), a not-for-profit organization responsible for managing the supply of blood and blood products in all provinces and territories except Quebec, is an example of a monopoly as there is no other blood service provider from whom blood products can be acquired. CBS performs a number of vital functions, such as collecting about one million units of blood each

monopoly A market in which there is a single seller of a particular good or service for which there are no close substitutes.

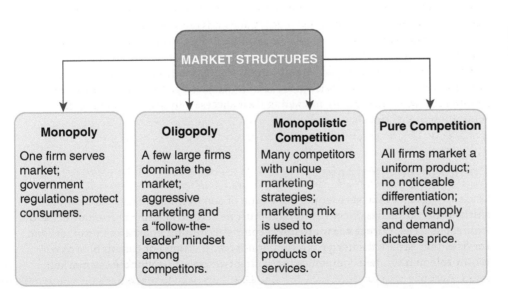

Figure 2.3   Market Structures in Canada

Monopoly	Oligopoly	Monopolistic Competition	Pure Competition
One firm serves market; government regulations protect consumers.	A few large firms dominate the market; aggressive marketing and a "follow-the-leader" mindset among competitors.	Many competitors with unique marketing strategies; marketing mix is used to differentiate products or services.	All firms market a uniform product; no noticeable differentiation; market (supply and demand) dictates price.

oligopoly A market situation in which a few large firms control the market.

year from over 430 000 active blood donors and serving every hospital from coast to coast.

In an **oligopoly**, a few large firms dominate the market. In the telecommunications industry, for example, three firms control the Canadian market: BCE, Rogers, and Telus. In the video game console category, Microsoft, Sony, and Nintendo dominate. In both industries it is very difficult for others to enter the market and be successful, unless they are satisfied with a very small piece of the action. New competitors typically do not have the marketing budgets to compete in terms of advertising and promotion.

In an oligopoly, firms generally compete on the basis of product differentiation and brand image. In an oligopolistic market, a "follow the leader" mindset prevails. When one company does something—say, increases its prices—the other company quickly follows. When such responses are so fast and predictable, it's difficult to get an edge on your competitor.

monopolistic competition A market in which there are many competitors, each offering a unique marketing mix based on price and other variables.

In a market characterized by **monopolistic competition**, there are many firms, large and small, each offering a unique marketing mix. Marketers use any of the mix elements to differentiate the product or service from competitors. Products are clearly distinguished by brand names. In effect, each competitor is striving to build its market share, but due to the presence of strong competition there are always substitute products for consumers to turn to. Most Canadian industries are best described as oligopolies or as monopolistically competitive.

In the restaurant market, for example, the quick-serve segment can be subdivided among hamburger chains, fresh-food chains, and coffee shops, but they all compete with one another when consumers are making meal choices. Well-known brands such as McDonald's, Harvey's, A&W, Burger King, Dairy Queen, Subway, KFC, and Tim Hortons give consumers a wide variety to choose from.

Both McDonald's and Tim Hortons are dominant market leaders due to the success of their respective marketing programs. Both companies offer products that their customers want at prices they are willing to pay, they outspend competitors on advertising and promotions, they are socially responsible, and they have locations virtually everywhere. The other brands do the best they can to compete using their available financial resources.

The automobile market is another market that is monopolistically competitive. Consumers choose from an array of makes and models produced and marketed by companies such as Toyota, General Motors, Ford, Honda, Nissan, Mazda, Mercedes-Benz, BMW, and many more. All these companies invest heavily in marketing to entice prospective customers in their direction.

pure competition A market in which many small firms market similar products.

In a market where **pure competition** exists, all firms market a uniform product—no single buyer or seller has much effect on the price. There are many buyers and sellers. In effect, the advantage of one product over another is at times unclear to consumers. Pure competition is common in the agriculture industry and in markets for financial assets such as stocks, bonds, and mutual funds. In the financial services market there is an endless array of companies, so it is often very difficult for customers to make decisions about which ones to use. Very often the deciding factor is performance and level of service provided. Consequently, financial services firms tend to differentiate themselves by marketing their success—their investment track record or reputation in the industry.

Competitive Strategies

Once an organization has identified the type of competition it faces, its attention shifts to the strategies of competitors. It must monitor competition from direct and indirect sources. **Direct competition** is competition from alternative products and services that satisfy the needs of a common target market. For example, in the toothpaste market, two companies marketing two brands dominate the market.

direct competition Competition from alternative products and services.

Procter & Gamble's Crest toothpaste and Colgate-Palmolive's Colgate Total toothpaste each control about one-third of the market. All other brands, and there are many of them, divide the remaining third of the market. To protect or build market share, each brand focuses on product innovation and extensive marketing communications programs to try to get an edge on its rival. Refer to the Crest illustration in **Figure 2.4**.

In the razor market, Gillette is the market leader with offerings such as the Gillette Fusion ProGlide razor, the Fusion Power razor, and the Mach3 Sensitive razor, but Gillette faces stiff competition from Schick, which markets the Quattro Titanium razor and the Quattro Midnight razor. Both brands invest significant sums of money in marketing communications to differentiate their offerings, attract new users, and encourage users to switch brands. Typically, both brands use advancements in technology to identify improved benefits for the customer.

Firms must also consider indirect competition. **Indirect competition** is competition from substitute products that offer customers the same benefit. For example, when someone is thirsty, he or she may reach for a soft drink such as Coca-Cola or Pepsi-Cola, two products that are direct competitors with each other, and with any other carbonated soft drink. However, consumers have a broader choice, and in the age of healthier living they are looking seriously at beverage alternatives. Other categories such as bottled waters, fruit juices, iced teas, sports drinks, and energy drinks are potential substitutes for soft drinks.

Figure 2.4   Product innovation and effective advertising help keep Crest toothpaste ahead of its competitors.

Therefore, brands such as Coca-Cola and Pepsi-Cola must consider the actions of an extended list of competitors when they develop marketing strategies for carbonated soft drinks. Both Coca-Cola and Pepsi-Cola understand and react to consumer trends in beverage consumption by introducing new products in the other beverage categories. Both companies describe themselves as "beverage" companies, not soft drink companies. Coca-Cola, for example, markets Dasani water, Minute Maid juices, Powerade sports drinks, and Full Throttle energy drinks. Pepsi-Cola markets Aquafina water, Tropicana juices, Gatorade sports drinks, and Amp Energy drinks. Both companies compete with many other brands in all of these beverage categories.

The nature of competition is changing and the lines between traditional competitors are becoming blurred. In the pharmacy market, for example, Pharmasave, Jean Coutu, and London Drugs are direct competitors and used to be concerned only about one another. Now, Target, Walmart, and Loblaws all offer pharmacy services and are indirect competitors with the major drugstores. In fact, the sale of prescriptions and over-the-counter drugs in supermarkets and general merchandise stores now accounts for about $6.1 billion annually, or 21 percent of all sales.[18] In the grocery business, Walmart has added a complete supermarket in its superstores and poses a real threat to established chains such as Loblaws, Sobeys, and Metro.

For additional insight into the influence of social and technological trends, and competitive activities on marketing strategies, see the Think Marketing box **Indigo Books and Music Inc. Transforms Itself**.

indirect competition
Competition from substitute products that offer customers the same benefit.

Video: New Coke Ads Defend Safety of Artificial Sweeteners

Think Marketing

Indigo Books & Music Inc. Transforms Itself

Heather Reisman, Indigo's chief executive officer, has global ambitions for Canada's biggest book chain. Indigo is going through a "fundamental transformation," explains Ms. Reisman. "Our intention is that the new Indigo will be a global company."

Given the current environment, however, achieving this goal will be a challenging task. The company has seen traditional book sales at its 236 stores slowly erode in recent years, given stiff competition from mass discounters and an increase in online book sales and digital books. Indigo's revenue slid 4.4 percent to $893 million from $934 million at 2013 fiscal year end. The book retail industry as a whole also saw sales fall 4.9 percent in Canada, to $973.8 million.

Booksellers such as Indigo are being forced to reinvent their businesses as digital trends squeeze their traditional sales and profit margins, prompting them to turn to new, higher-margin areas of growth. As Ms. Reisman points out, many customers browse in-store, only to go home to purchase the items they want online at the cheapest possible price. She says Indigo sells books online at cost while other retailers do so below cost to drive sales of other products.

People are also transitioning from paper books to e-readers and e-books. Digital reading now makes up about 20 percent of total book market sales. The e-book market in 2012 peaked at 17.6 percent of sales in the first quarter, but declined over the rest of the year to hit 12.9 percent in the fourth quarter, according to a recent study.

To continue navigating the changing book retailing landscape, Indigo is betting on an international push, as well as a repositioning of its Canadian stores. "As books are being cannibalized by e-readers and Amazon and online, we know we need to grow our business in other areas to really make up for that book decline," explains Tod Morehead, executive vice president, group general merchandise manager at Indigo.

The company has been on a multiyear journey to reimagine Indigo as the world's first "lifestyle" department store—a multichannel, multicategory retailer that is branching out into home goods, toys, children's clothing and now, Apple tech shops, while keeping books as a key offering. As part of its strategy to transform into a trend-setting retailer, Indigo has been reconfiguring its superstores into stores that house a number of small shops within the larger store. The first Indigo Tech boutique opened recently in Toronto and forty more are planned in 2014, within the

CNW Group/Indigo Books & Music Inc./Newscom

retailer's superstores, carrying items such as iPads and Apple TV. Indigo also plans to create an in-store boutique featuring American Girl, a popular doll brand with dolls that sell for over $100. These newest in-store boutiques will include a doll hair salon, apparel, books, and accessories.

The other major factor facing Indigo is rising competition from large generalist retailers, including U.S.-based discount giants Walmart, Costco, and now the recently launched Target. All of them are expanding in Canada, and are continuing to steal sales from Indigo. Indigo's management believes that by broadening its scope the company will be in a better position to take on deep-pocketed global rivals.

Indigo has invested time and money to better understand the changing market place and hopes that its new direction will pay dividends at the cash register. The company has developed unique marketing strategies to meet the changing expectations of consumers and remain competitive. Indigo isn't expecting to reap the benefits of its transformational efforts and investments much before 2016, says Reisman. "Early indications are trending very much in the right direction." Non-book sales of items now represent about 22 percent of overall sales at Indigo, compared with roughly 12 percent five years earlier. And those general merchandise sales are gaining momentum every month.

Question:

Do you think Indigo is making the right changes for long-term success? If not, what other opportunities should Indigo pursue?

Adapted from: M. Strauss, "American Girl dolls coming to Canada's Indigo stores," The Globe and Mail, *www.theglobeandmail.com/ report-on-business/american-girl-dolls-coming-to-canadas-indigo-stores/ article15133826/#dashboard/follows/; and M. Strauss, "Indigo's next chapter could be global,"* The Globe and Mail, *www.theglobeandmail. com/report-on-business/indigo-targets-global-market-in-fundamental-transformation/article12799375/*

The Competitive Position

A firm's market share indicates its competitive position in the marketplace. In a brand-marketing situation, **market share** is the sales volume of a brand expressed as a percentage of the total product category sales volume. For example, if a brand has $1 million in sales in a market valued at $10 million, its market share would be 10 percent. Market share may also be calculated on the basis of unit sales instead of dollars. Competing products are classified in many ways. Author Philip Kotler describes and classifies competitors as leaders, challengers, followers, and nichers.[19]

A **market leader** is the largest firm in a given industry and is a leader in strategic actions (e.g., new-product innovation, pricing and price increases, and aggressive promotion activity). Subway is an example of a market leader. It is the world's largest fast-food chain by store count. By January 2014 there were 41 217 Subway locations in 105 countries. Subway also enjoys the biggest bite in the "sub wars" with 62 percent market share. Its closest rivals are Mr. Sub with 14 percent and Quiznos with 6 percent. Subway's dominant position is the result of successful marketing—it was first to bring to market healthy products made with fresh ingredients, offers a good price proposition, maintains a strong presence in the social media community to attract and retain customers, and is readily available—there are 3034 outlets in Canada.[20, 21 & 22] No direct competitor is remotely close to that! See **Figure 2.5**.

A **market challenger** is a firm or firms (product or products) attempting to gain market leadership through aggressive marketing efforts. Perhaps the best example is the battle between Pepsi-Cola (the challenger) and Coca-Cola (the leader). While Coca-Cola retains leadership, Pepsi-Cola implements more aggressive marketing strategies. Pepsi-Cola has never been afraid of comparing the quality of its product to Coca-Cola in its effort to attract Coca-Cola drinkers to its brand.

In the smartphone category, Apple is challenging Samsung, the market leader, by launching the iPhone 5C into the affordable-price smartphone segment and ensuring the Apple platform delivers an overall exceptional experience to users.[23]

A **market follower** is generally satisfied with its market share position. Often, it has entered the market late and has not incurred the research and development costs that innovators do. As a result, it is content to follow the leaders on product, price,

market share The sales volume of one competing product or company expressed as a percentage of total market sales volume.

market leader The largest firm in the industry and the leader in strategic action.

market challenger Firm or firms attempting to gain market leadership through aggressive marketing efforts.

market follower A company that is generally satisfied with its market-share position.

Figure 2.5   Subway dominates the fresh sandwich market in Canada.

distribution, and other marketing actions. In a product category such as toothpaste, for example, Colgate in its various sizes and formats is the current market leader with Crest just behind as the challenger. Remaining brands, such as Tom's of Maine, Sensodyne, Oral B Rembrandt, Aquafresh, and others, have less than 5 percent market share and are followers. Brands such as these do not have the financial resources to compete with the leaders.

market nicher A firm that concentrates resources on one or more distinguishable market segments.

niche marketing Targeting a product line to one particular segment and committing all marketing resources to the satisfaction of that segment.

A **market nicher** practises niche marketing. **Niche marketing** refers to the concentration of resources in one or more distinguishable market segments. A market nicher specializes in serving niches that larger competitors overlook or are simply not interested in. A market nicher is the big fish in a small pond, as opposed to the little fish in a big pond. In order to niche market, a firm differentiates itself on the basis of specialization or an area of strength.

For example, Porter Airlines started by offering 10 round-trip flights between Toronto and Ottawa. Porter has been focusing on short-haul travel by offering customers convenience, speed, and a list of services not offered by the bigger airlines: complimentary in-flight food and beverages, free shuttle buses, and a complimentary espresso bar waiting lounge.[24] Bigger airlines such as Air Canada and WestJet, with much higher operating costs, would have a tough time competing in this market niche. Porter recently announced plans to broaden its service by opening up new destinations, such as Vancouver, Edmonton, Calgary, Winnipeg, Los Angeles, Florida, and the Caribbean. This growth strategy allows Porter to continue to serve its niche markets, while entering into direct competition with major airlines in other markets. Air Canada and WestJet have responded by launching their own discount subsidiaries, Rouge and Encore respectively. Competition is heating up in the Canadian airline industry![25]

SOCIAL, ENVIRONMENTAL, AND DEMOGRAPHIC FORCES

LO4 Discuss how social, environmental, and demographic forces shape marketing strategies now and in the future.

When developing marketing strategies, marketers must be aware of and react to certain social changes taking place. How Canadians perceive social issues is very important. For a variety of reasons, the lifestyle that Canadians enjoy is changing. As well, Canadians are showing deeper concern for issues related to ethical business practices and how corporations preserve and protect the natural environment. Successful companies are responding by focusing on a triple bottom line—people, planet, profits.

Lifestyles

Canadians live very hectic lifestyles. The conundrum for most families is how to balance work life with family life. Generally speaking, we are now a society that places a greater emphasis on quality of life rather than work. That said, work is essential to sustain the desired quality of life, and Canadians are working harder than ever. The traditional 40-hour workweek is a myth. People choose to work longer hours to get ahead.

Being pressed for time suggests a need for convenience. Many industries have reacted to this. For example, the home services industry has exploded as aging baby boomers that used to be do-it-yourselfers have become the do-it-for-me generation. They don't have time for house-related chores and repairs. This change has resulted in all kinds of new services being offered by retailers such as The Home Depot, Rona, and Lowe's. Drive-throughs at McDonald's, Wendy's, KFC, and other restaurants now generate as much as 50 percent of their revenue as they directly appeal to the on-the-go consumer. Grocery retailers have also capitalized on the convenience trend by expanding their deli sections to include offerings of fresh and ready-to-go meals. The deli section of a supermarket continues to be one of the biggest and most profitable areas. Pre-packaged lunches that are ideal for kids' lunchboxes are also popular with busy moms.

Consumers are expressing a stronger concern for health and welfare. Issues such as childhood obesity and the aging process are causing consumers to make wiser choices. As a result, people will continue to spend more for products and services related to a healthy lifestyle. Marketers are responding to these new demands. For example, in 2010 the world's largest food and beverage companies voluntarily agreed to remove billions of calories from the products they sell to help combat obesity. According to a study released in January 2014, the participating firms have already exceeded their five-year goal.[26] Kraft, one of the food companies participating in this initiative, has put a cap on portion size for single-serve packages and has implemented new guidelines to improve the nutritional characteristics of all of its brands. In its marketing communications, Kraft encourages appropriate eating habits and active lifestyles.

For many years Unilever has been committed to offering consumers choice, for instance, Hellmann's Original (80 percent fat), Hellmann's Light (37 percent fat) and Hellmann's Extra Light (7 percent fat). Unilever has also been ahead of the curve in terms of nutritional labelling and health claims, by incorporating more comprehensive front-of-pack information that make it easier for busy shoppers to make informed choices.[27] The illustration in **Figure 2.6** shows detailed nutrition and health information on the package of Unilever's Lipton Chicken Noodle Soup. All companies in the food industry must now meet Health Canada's new nutrition labelling regulations that are designed to provide consumers with the necessary information to make wise choices.[28]

Social Responsibility and the Natural Environment

The concept of socially responsible marketing was introduced in Chapter 1. To extend that discussion further it must be noted that Canadian consumers have a genuine concern for the environment, and they show a preference toward companies that act responsibly with regard to protecting the environment they live in. This attitude has a definite impact on how an organization plans and implements its manufacturing processes and marketing programs.

Video: Toms Shoes

Many companies embrace cause-related marketing and provide financial support to causes of interest to their customers. Well-publicized financial support for a worthwhile cause can have a positive effect on the consumer's perception of a brand. It can help form an emotional connection between the brand, the cause, and the consumer. Such is the benefit that CIBC derives from its ongoing title sponsorship of the Canadian Breast Cancer Foundation CIBC Run for the Cure, where the overall goal is to raise funds to help find a cure for breast cancer.

But companies now realize they must go beyond financial contributions and demonstrate ethical business practices that benefit society. Today, companies are much more socially responsible, and they communicate to the public what they are doing to try and make the world a better place The entrepreneurs behind Rumble, a highly nutritious single-serve drink, have taken this business

Figure 2.6   Comprehensive front-of-pack information makes it easier for busy shoppers to make informed choices.

Rumble

Figure 2.7   Companies like Groove Nutrition, makers of Rumble, are focusing on a triple bottom line: people, planet and profit.

Video: Ecoist: Analyzing The Marketing Environment

demographics The study of the characteristics of a population.

philosophy to heart. The company donates 1 percent of all sales to various charities that fight hunger. Says Paul Underhill, co-founder of Groove Nutrition, the company that makes Rumble, "We're mindful that hunger takes many forms. That's why we love the One Percent for Hunger initiative and the opportunity to be part of something greater than ourselves. We can all nourish the planet. With every sale of Rumble, we are hoping to do just that." Groove Nutrition considers the environment, too, by using a novel container for Rumble that is resealable, recyclable, and repurpose friendly. See **Figure 2.7** for an illustration.[29]

In the consumer electronics industry, Panasonic is demonstrating a commitment to preserving and protecting the environment. The company is committed to the principles of pollution prevention and operates in compliance with relevant environmental legislation and other voluntary requirements it establishes for itself. The company continually strives to improve its performance with regard to environmental issues. Panasonic has established an eco-conscious initiative called Green Plan 2018. The main objectives of the plan are to create products that have less impact on the environment, to design and manufacture new lines of green products, and to make its production facilities more environmentally friendly. Currently, all Panasonic products are built using lead-free soldering. By 2018, Panasonic plans to use at least 16 percent post-consumer recycled content materials in all its products.[30]

DEMOGRAPHIC FORCES

To keep abreast of the changing consumer, market planners analyze demographic and social trends. **Demographics** involve the study of the characteristics of a population. These characteristics include age, gender, income, occupation, education, marital status, family size, household formation, and ethnic background. Marketers define their target markets in terms of demographics, so it is important they understand and capitalize on key demographic trends.

The nature and composition of the consumer marketplace is changing. Today, marketers find they are dealing with consumers who are more educated and more technologically savvy. One of the biggest challenges marketers face is how to retain current customers who are getting older while attracting a new generation of younger customers. Another challenge is how to attract various immigrant populations, the numbers of which are growing rapidly.

A combination of education and technology has produced a more informed consumer: a consumer who evaluates options thoroughly before making buying decisions. For example, consumers can do much of their product research online and can access information that is delivered by the marketing organization (planned information) or from independent and more critical sources (unplanned information on social networks or blogs). They also rely on their social network and the word-of-mouth information that their friends pass on. Let us examine some of these trends.

Size and Age

The age distribution of Canada's population is changing. In 2013, Canada's population was 35 158 300.[31] Between 2006 and 2011, Canada's population growth rate (+5.3 percent) was the highest among the G8 countries. Since 2012, though, population increases have

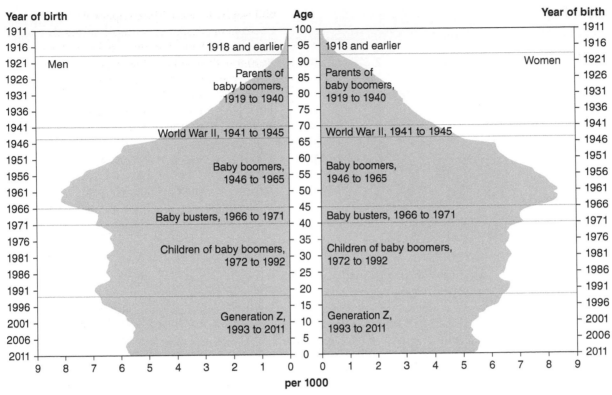

Figure 2.8   Canada's Population by Age

Source: Statistics Canada. (2011). Census of Population. Retrieved from http://www12.statcan.gc.ca/census-recensement/2011/as-sa/98-311-x/2011003/fig/fig3_2-2-eng.cfm

settled back down to average annual gains of around 1 percent a year, a rate comparable to that of the United States. Population growth is determined by four factors: birth rates, death rates, immigration, and emigration. Two-thirds of Canada's population growth in the most recent five-year period is attributable to immigration. Looking farther down the road, baby boomers are aging and death rates will be higher than birth rates. By 2030, Canada's entire population growth will come from immigration.[32]

Canada's population is aging. **Figure 2.8** shows that middle-aged Canadians (the group commonly referred to as baby boomers) comprise the largest portion of Canada's population. Certain age groups are growing much faster than average. Changes in the age distribution of the population are due to variations in the birth rates; the baby boom from 1946 to 1964 was followed by a "baby bust" in the late 1960s and the 1970s; a mini-boom then occurred in the 1980s. The latter group is often referred to as Generation Y, or Millennials, and includes Canadians in their twenties and thirties. This large group of young adults is a primary target for marketers now, and will continue to be in the future. The newest demographic cluster, often referred to as Generation Z, or digital natives, includes people born between 1993 and 2011. This tech-savvy generation is one that marketers will be paying close attention to as businesses try to learn more about this highly diverse group of consumers.[33, 34 & 35]

It's predicted that by 2020, 30 percent of all retail sales will be to Millennials.[36] Major brands like McDonald's, Walmart, and Budweiser are already focusing on Millennial consumers. In May 2013, McDonald's launched a McWrap, saying that its young adult customers who were asking for healthier menu options. In the United States, Walmart is opening smaller versions of its stores on college campuses and in untapped urban markets with large Millennial populations. On the other hand, the baby boomer segment of the market is projected to be 40 percent of Canada's population by 2021.[37] The aging population will also provide challenges and opportunities for marketing organizations. For instance, within a decade, seniors will outnumber children. The combination of aging boomers and seniors will alter the social landscape as more pressure is placed on the health-care

Figure 2.9 Projected Population in Canada by Age

Age Group	2013 (000s)	% of Population	2021 (000s)	% of Population	2026 (000s)	% of Population
0–19	7878.2	22.6%	8499.3	22.1%	8977.9	22.3%
20–34	7256.1	20.8%	7421	19.3%	7269.8	18.0%
35–49	7410.9	21.2%	7630	19.9%	8116.2	20.1%
50–64	7201.6	20.6%	7763.7	20.2%	7540.4	18.7%
65+	5175.1	14.8%	7091.5	18.5%	8383.5	20.8%

Source: Statistics Canada, CANSIM, table 052–0005.

system and the labour market.[38] Goods and services that encourage healthier lifestyles, security services and products, and products that extend vitality and longevity should have a bright future. The pharmaceutical industry has already tapped into this market with products such as Viagra and Cialis (remedies for erectile dysfunction), Lunesta (a product that makes people sleep better), and Lipitor (a product that lowers cholesterol levels). See **Figure 2.9** for details on age trends in Canada.

Location

More Canadians than ever before live in cities. According to the 2011 census data, 81 percent of the population lives in urban areas. Canada has six metropolitan areas with more than one million people—Toronto, Montreal, Vancouver, Ottawa-Gatineau, Calgary, and Edmonton. A total of 13.6 million residents, or 45 percent of Canada's population, live in these urban areas. Between 2006 and 2011 the population of Calgary grew by 12.6 percent and Edmonton by 12.1 percent, well above the Canadian average. In 2011, only one in five Canadians (six million people) lived in rural areas.[39]

In the largest metropolitan areas population growth has occurred mainly in the municipalities that surround the cities. These areas are called census metropolitan areas. A **census metropolitan area (CMA)** encompasses all urban and rural areas that are linked to a city's urban core, either socially or economically. In Toronto, for example, the CMA includes Mississauga to the west, Vaughan to the north, and Oshawa and Whitby to the east.

To further demonstrate the concentration of Canada's population in urban areas, the Greater Golden Horseshoe (a region that includes Toronto and extends to Kitchener in the west and Peterborough in the east), Montreal, and Vancouver share special demographic characteristics: their growth is largely due to international immigration and the pull that these large urban centres have on younger adults from other parts of the country.[40] The Greater Golden Horseshoe consists of more than 100 municipalities, 16 of which have a population of more than 100 000. In Western Canada, the populations of both Calgary and Edmonton now exceed one million, and these cities are Canada's fastest-growing urban areas.

Keeping track of where Canadians live is an important consideration when developing marketing strategies. In order for products and services to succeed in the future, there will have to be a greater concentration of marketing strategies in key urban areas. The trend toward urban living is expected to continue.

Family Formation and Household Size

The nature of Canadian families is changing. Essentially, families are getting smaller and becoming less traditional in structure. The traditional family was a married couple with a few children. Many Canadians now postpone marriage or dispense with it

census metropolitan area (CMA) An area that encompasses all rural and urban areas that are linked to a city's urban core, either socially or economically.

altogether. Common-law unions are increasing, while people who do marry are doing so later in life. Now, married couples comprise only 67 percent of all Canadian families, and common-law couples 16.7 percent. Lone-parent families (predominantly lone females) represent the remaining 16.3 percent of Canadian families. The number of same-sex married couples nearly tripled between 2006 and 2011, reflecting the first five-year period for which same-sex marriage has been legal. Same-sex common-law couples rose 15.0 percent, slightly higher than the 13.8 percent increase for opposite-sex common-law couples.[41] Refer to **Figure 2.10**.

Figure 2.10   The number of same-sex married couples is growing.

More and more children are born and raised outside marriage or experience the breakdown of their parents' marriage. As a result, we are witnessing an evolution in cultural values where there is a difference between younger and older people in terms of their attitudes, values, expectations, and assumptions about marriage. Canadians, many of whom have children, now have relatively high rates of separation and divorce. New forms of cohabitation have produced the **blended family**, which brings together children of previous marriages, and where kids may move back and forth between parents.

In the past decade, there was a back-to-the-family-unit trend as baby boomers, who had previously delayed marriage to pursue careers, started forming families. In fact, the baby boomers created a mini boom (Generation Y). What has emerged is the so-called **sandwich generation**, in which people are simultaneously trying to assume responsibility for dependent children and care for aging relatives. A growing number of Canadian grandparents are sharing homes with their grandchildren, many as part of three-generation households formed as a result of economic, social, or cultural needs.[42] This trend places an added burden on family finances. The burden is magnified by the fact that young adults between 20 and 29 years of age have decided to extend the period in which they live with their parents. Many members of Generation Y prefer the comfort, security, and convenience of their parents' homes.

It is estimated that as much as 10 percent of the population is gay or lesbian. Same-sex marriage partners are creating new kinds of families, and these households are of interest to marketers. Progressive-minded marketers see the gay market as an opportunity for growth. The gay community will spend over $800 billion this year. A large percentage are affluent, hip, and trendsetting.[43] Recent marketing research conducted by the Print Measurement Bureau reveals that gays and lesbians are more attentive to personal improvement. They are three times more likely to use a hair gel daily, 75 percent more likely to use a face moisturizer, and twice as likely to use bath additives—good information for marketers in the personal care products industry— Procter & Gamble, Unilever, L'Oreal, and others.[44]

Canadian households continue to shrink in size. Currently, the average Canadian family has 2.5 members, a reflection of the marriage trends described earlier. Since 2001 there has been a large increase in one-person households. The households with the slowest growth are those composed of couples with children aged 24 years and under.[45] The character of the family has changed for economic reasons. With each passing decade there are more women in the workforce. Two wage earners per household has become the norm, so it is expected that the number of members within each household will remain small.

Spending Power and Wealth

How much people earn has an impact on their spending patterns and priorities. The trend in recent years is for Canadians' **disposable income** (after-tax income) to grow at a lower rate than the cost of basic necessities required in a household (food, shelter, car,

blended family A family structure created by separation or divorce; two separate families merge into a single household as spouses remarry.

sandwich generation A generation of parents who are simultaneously caring for children and aging relatives.

disposable income Actual income after taxes and other expenses; it is income available for basic necessities and optional purchases.

© Carol Lundeen/Alamy

clothing, supplies, utilities, and so on). Canadians are working harder than ever, yet there seems to be less money for discretionary purchases such as vacations, sports, and recreational activities. Lower- and middle-income families (the masses) are more cautious about how and on what they spend their money.

Another trend in Canada is the concentration of wealth among upper-income groups. The old expression "the rich are getting richer and the poor are getting poorer" applies here. Census data from Statistics Canada verify a polarization of incomes at the upper and lower ends of the spectrum. The top one-fifth of Canadian families had an average after-tax income of $135 500 in 2010, while the lowest one-fifth of Canadian families earned $14 600, a gap of $120 900.[46]

How people spend their disposable income varies with the state of the economy. As discussed earlier in the chapter, the current economy is growing only modestly, so generally speaking consumers are more cautious about how they spend their money, or they continue to spend at a high level and accumulate significant personal debt. In contrast, people in the high-income groups tend to spend regardless of the economic situation. Refer to **Figure 2.11** for an illustration.

Figure 2.11
The entry-luxury CLA model Mercedes Benz appeals directly to affluent younger buyers.

Mercedes-Benz Canada Inc.

Marketing organizations that target the lower- and middle-income groups find it wise to stress value in their marketing strategies. Walmart is an expert at this. During the last recession, Walmart changed its slogan to "Save money. Live better." Walmart experienced monthly sales increases while competitors were losing business. Walmart always emphasizes price and value in its marketing communications.

Education

New jobs in North America have higher entry requirements than ever and are largely based on technology. More than ever before, education and training are key issues if Canada is to compete globally. It is imperative that Canadians possess the necessary skills to cope with ever-changing technology; shortages in basic skills would adversely affect Canada's ability to compete. So that we may have a well-trained workforce in the future, it is expected that governments and industries will have to cooperate to increase spending on quality education.

The Canadian population is now better educated than ever. Canada ranks highest among countries that are members of the Organisation for Economic Co-operation and Development (OECD) in terms of the proportion of its working-age population that has a college or university education. Currently, 51 percent of our working population has a post-secondary certificate, college diploma, or university degree. The OECD average is 38 percent.[47] The demand for higher education is a factor affecting marriage rates and household formations (discussed earlier). Young men and women who have opted for more education are more likely to extend their stay in the parents' home and delay marriage.

From a marketing perspective, customers are now more informed and they take more time deliberating on purchases. Consumers are using the Internet to search for goods and services that provide better value. Generations Y and Z have grown up with the technology required for this, such as tablets and smartphones. To effectively reach this group, marketers must adapt their marketing strategies to digital media or face rather harsh consequences.

Multiculturalism

Canada is a culturally diverse country. Aboriginal populations have grown by 20 percent over the past five years and represent 4.3 percent of Canada's population—up from 3.8 percent in 2006.[48] Also, immigration trends indicate that the makeup of the population is continuing to shift away from one of a predominantly European background. Existing within Canadian culture are many diverse **subcultures**—subgroups within a larger cultural context that have distinctive lifestyles based on religious, ethnic, and geographic differences.

subculture A subgroup of a culture that has a distinctive mode of behaviour.

Currently, Canada's foreign-born population represents 20.6 percent (one in five Canadians) of the total population, and it is expected to rise to as high as 23 percent by 2017.[49] Most immigrants come from the Philippines, China, and India, although Africans are also arriving in growing numbers. Canadians of Asian ancestry now comprise 58 percent of immigrants entering Canada, at 11 percent of the population (East Asians comprise 7 percent and West Asians 4 percent). As in the past, newcomers are settling in Canada's biggest cities and are generally younger than the established population (31.7 years compared to 37.3 years). Of Canada's 6.8 million immigrants, 63.4 percent live in the Toronto, Montreal, or Vancouver areas.[50] Refer to **Figure 2.12** for details.

Companies that recognize the importance of the diverse multicultural markets stand to profit. The sheer size of this developing market and the fact that unique groups tend to cluster in urban areas make them a reachable target for Canadian brands. The key to an organization's success is to spend time learning more about the target—their customs, beliefs, mores, and so on—and then formulate appropriate marketing strategies. Walmart is a leader in this area. It has identified the South Asian, Cantonese, Mandarin, Spanish, Portuguese, and Italian communities as priorities. Walmart adjusts its merchandising

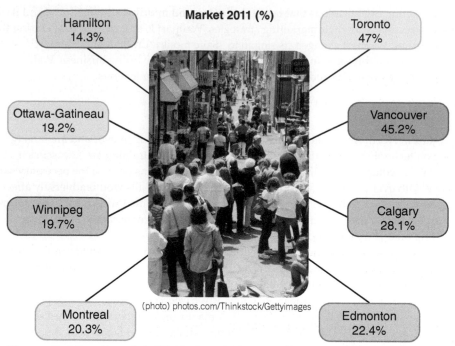

Market 2011 (%)

Hamilton
14.3%

Toronto
47%

Ottawa-Gatineau
19.2%

Vancouver
45.2%

Winnipeg
19.7%

Calgary
28.1%

Montreal
20.3%

Edmonton
22.4%

(photo) photos.com/Thinkstock/Gettyimages

Figure 2.12   Canada's Ethnic Population as a Percentage of Each Market's Overall Population

Source: Statistics Canada. (2011). National Household Survey.

strategies to meet local, culture-based market conditions and runs television ads featuring people belonging to the minorities listed.

For more insight into ethnically based marketing practices in Canada, read the Think Marketing box **Ethnic Diversity Presents New Marketing Opportunities**.

TECHNOLOGICAL FORCES

L05 Identify and explain the effect technological trends and developments have on current and future marketing practices.

The technological environment consists of the discoveries, inventions, and innovations that provide marketing opportunities. New products, new packaging, cost-reduced materials, and the emergence of electronic commerce and communications are all the result of technological advancement. Over the past decade the role and influence of the Internet has had a dramatic impact on the development of marketing and marketing communications strategies. In fact, it has forced many organizations to rethink and reshape their business models in order to take advantage of new opportunities.

Technology will continue to be the driving force for change in the next decade. From how a company collects and uses information, to the development of new products, to improving production and distribution processes, to how a company communicates with current and prospective customers, all are affected by technology. Perhaps the areas of marketing affected most are those that involve how customers will be managed to maximize revenue and profit, and how companies communicate with customers. To demonstrate the influence of technology, there is no better example than the ways in which people use mobile devices today. Examine your own behaviour with your cell phone. Try not using it for a few days—you will slowly suffer the pain of withdrawal! Products such as Apple's iPhone and the Samsung Galaxy are integral components of the daily routines of Canadian consumers. Digital habits are being formed at a very early age. According to a 2013 study, 25 percent of grade four students have cellphones.[51]

ThinkMarketing

Ethnic Diversity Presents New Marketing Opportunities

There's an old expression: "Sometimes numbers speak louder than words." Let's look at a few numbers that seem to speak volumes about a potential marketing opportunity:

- Over 6.2 million people in Canada belong to a visible minority.
- Immigrants account for over 25 percent of the population in metropolitan areas.
- Visible minorities make up around 20 percent of the population.
- The three largest ethnic groups, South Asians, Chinese, and Blacks, represent just over 61 percent of the visible minority population.

Are marketing organizations moving fast enough to take advantage of these numbers? In terms of size, Canada (in total) is perceived by many global organizations to be a small market, so to break down the market further and absorb the costs of definitive marketing strategies for various ethnic groups may not be profitable. A detailed cost–benefit analysis would be needed to determine a move in that direction. "It just comes down to the size of the market—it's that simple," says Ken Wong, marketing professor at Queen's University.

Clorox Company of Canada understands the importance of multicultural marketing. "As the consumer landscape in Canada is changing, we felt we had to make some fundamental changes to our business model," explains Kaery Lall, business lead—national shopper marketing and multicultural brand strategy. "We saw the country is letting in about 250 000 immigrants every single year. So we want to make sure we are talking to those consumers in a way that we maybe haven't done in the past."

Clorox started by doing some research to find out about the country's two largest ethnic groups—South Asians and Chinese. The Clorox marketing team wanted a detailed picture of their demographics and psychographics, including their tastes and preferences in relevant product categories as well as what the immigrant experience is like for them.

Clorox's first campaign was the launch of a limited-edition red water filter for its BRITA® water pitchers brand in

BRITA® water pitchers and the BRITA® water pitchers logo are registered trademarks of Brita LP. Used with permission.

celebration of Chinese New Year. The decision was made based on the fact that BRITA® water pitchers is a popular brand among Chinese consumers and red is associated with good fortune, especially during New Year celebrations. In just the first eight weeks of the launch, the red filter became one of the fastest-selling BRITA® water pitchers ever.

The company continues to invest in its multicultural strategy. "We have a full-blown multicultural strategy specifically targeted towards Chinese and South Asian Canadians," says Lall. "We're not just going to alter the packaging once and call that ethnic marketing. We're aiming to create a long-term, meaningful relationship with these customers. They have unique needs, especially in the first five to ten years of immigrating to Canada, in terms of their product education and usage."

Question:
What are some ways Clorox could further enhance its relationship with Chinese and South Asian Canadians?

Adapted from: Statistics Canada. (2011). National Household Survey, and C. Daniels,"Multicultural marketing: The visible majority," Marketing, March 12, 2012.

Managing Customers

Today's technology allows companies to deal with customers on an individual basis; that is, unique marketing strategies can be developed for each customer. This capability is based on database marketing technology and is referred to as customer relationship management (CRM). An effective customer relationship management program continually collects information about customers in the database (a computer-based information file), analyzes the information to predict how likely the customer is to buy again and what they are likely to buy, and then develops a marketing strategy precisely designed to meet the needs of the customer.

Customer relationship management programs (discussed in Chapter 1) are based on database technology. Companies such as Canadian Tire, Bell, Apple, Shoppers Drug Mart, Unilever, and Procter & Gamble realize the importance of customer relationship management and have successful database programs in place. These companies and many others employ toll-free telephone numbers, telemarketing, personal selling, and online communications to target messages directly to individual customers. They also use social media networks to seek feedback from consumers, to engage consumers with their brands, and to deliver unique offers. The concept of relationship marketing is based on the belief that it is less expensive and more profitable to hold on to current customers than to attract new ones. Databases and CRM will be discussed in more detail in Chapter 3.

Technology and Marketing Communications

Traditionally, marketers relied on the mass media (television, radio, newspapers, magazines, and outdoor advertising) to deliver messages to large audiences. However, technologies such as the Internet, laptops, tablets, and smartphones are changing the way customers use media. People today are busier and more mobile than ever; they travel with these electronic devices and use them to access information. The rapid growth in the development and use of these technologies means people are spending less time with television, radio, newspapers, and magazines. For the latest trend information on media consumption by Canadians refer to **Figure 2.13**.

Technology is changing how marketers think about the media. Terms such as *video-on-demand, rich media, blogs,* and *social media* highlight the environment in which marketers operate. The challenge for marketers is to figure out the best way of integrating individualized media with the more traditional mass media environment. As mentioned in Chapter 1, control has shifted from the marketer to the consumer, a significant change that marketers are adapting to.

Figure 2.13
Canadian Media Usage

Canadians are spending more time with the media. TV, radio, newspapers and magazines have all been hurt by the Internet. Share of weekly minutes per capita, adults 18+

Medium	2001 Minutes	2001 Share	2013 Minutes	2013 Share
TV	1531	46%	1728	36%
Radio	1282	38%	1065	22%
Internet (total for all devices)	311	9%	1735	37%
Newspaper	161	5%	189	4%
Magazine	77	2%	34	1%
Total	3362	100%	4751	100%

Source: The 2013 CMUST Report: Commissioned by IAB Canada.

In the past, younger people dominated digital communications. That's not the case any longer! A recent study by the Interactive Advertising Bureau of Canada "found that the Internet provides marketers with a mirror image of the age profile [for users] of other major media, particularly when comparing the Internet to television."[52] Thinking strategically, marketers now view the Internet and everything it offers as complementary to traditional media, and believe that when used together, the two media will more effectively achieve marketing objectives. Some organizations, such as Pepsi-Cola, are going a step further. Pepsi has transferred a full third of its advertising budget online and is using the Internet as a primary medium for launching new products. From Pepsi's perspective, the Internet and social media such as Facebook and Twitter are essential components of their marketing strategy.

Progressive-minded marketers are following their customers online. Shifting from mass-reach media campaigns, they are now implementing selective reach, highly targeted campaigns—a key benefit offered by the digital media. So sophisticated are these devices that the information collected from them allows marketers to track down the whereabouts of consumers and lets them send out offers that consumers can take advantage of immediately. This ability to directly target customers is referred to as location-based marketing, a concept that will be discussed in more detail in Chapter 6.

The Internet and E-Commerce

Internet users are quickly adapting their buying behaviour to embrace online buying. For some time, Canadians were concerned about privacy issues and about transferring credit card information online. While a certain amount of concern remains, the rampant use of tablets and smartphones on a daily basis makes it very convenient to research products online and then conduct purchase transactions if so inclined.

Companies that have integrated online and e-commerce strategies are now seeing the benefits. For the latest year statistics are available (2012), total online sales in Canada among consumers were $18.9 billion, a 24 percent jump from 2010. Although online shopping remains a small part of the total retail economy, accounting for just 4 percent of Canada's overall retail sales of $470 billion annually, it is growing rapidly.[53] Marketing organizations see a bright future in online commerce and are revising their marketing strategies accordingly. An informative and entertaining website with e-commerce capabilities combined with a brand page on a social network like Facebook allows the marketer to interact directly with customers and build relationships that will lead to purchases. For some additional facts and figures regarding e-commerce, see **Figure 2.14**.

More and more Canadian retailers are engaging in e-commerce activities. Online storefronts—such as those for Indigo, Sport Chek, The Home Depot, and many others—make it easy for consumers to browse and shop online or browse online and shop offline. All of the product research and perhaps the decision on what to buy can be done online. When the customer visits the store they know exactly what they want.

Some companies are capable of customizing products to meet the precise needs of customers, a concept referred to as mass customization. **Mass customization** is a system that can personalize messages, and ultimately products, to a target audience of one. At Element Bars, a successful online food company, customers are invited to pick and choose the elements (or ingredients) that they want in their custom nutrition bars or granola cereal. Shoppers can even make up a brand name for their product! The company owners believe nutrition should be personal and that creating a tasty nutrition bar or cereal should be fun and easy.[54]

mass customization The creation of systems that can produce products and personalize messages to a target audience of one.

Other organizations are being creative with customization as well. For example, The North Face has launched a gallery of designs created by customers for its Denali jacket. Helping consumers share their creations with friends and relatives creates a sense of community and inspires others to be creative as well. The *Globe and Mail*'s Dashboard now allows readers to customize their news experience on any type of digital device. Subscribers can create custom alerts, select topics or companies to follow, save stories for later reading, and watch breaking news as it unfolds.

Figure 2.14
Canadian E-Commerce
Facts and Figures

Simulation: The
Marketing Environment

> Canada is one of the most "connected" countries in the world. As of 2012, 86 percent of Canadians had Internet access from anywhere, and 80 percent had Internet access at home. Such high figures present ample opportunity for marketers to pursue e-commerce opportunities. Here are some facts and figures about the Canadian market in 2012.
>
> • Canadian consumers placed orders for $18.9 billion worth of goods and services, up 24% from 2010.
> • 56% of Internet users ordered goods or services online, up from 51% in 2010.
> • 77% of Internet users did research on goods or services or window shopped.
> • Young adults aged 25 to 34 were most likely to make a purchase online, with 69% purchasing online in 2012.
> • Of those Canadians who ordered online, the average online shopper made about 13 separate orders and spent approximately $1450.
> • 58% of online shoppers purchased travel, such as airline tickets or hotel reservations and 52% purchased event tickets online.
> • Online shopping is still a small part of the retail economy, making up just four percent of total retail sales of $470 billion.

Source: Statistics Canada. (2013, October 28). The Daily. Retrieved from http://www.statcan.gc.ca/daily-quotidien/131028/dq131028a-eng.htm and CBC News. (2013, October 28). Average online shopper spent $1,450 last year. Retrieved from http://www.cbc.ca

LEGAL AND REGULATORY FORCES

LO6 Distinguish the role that laws, regulations, and self-regulation play in the practice of marketing in Canada.

Yes, Canada is a free-enterprise society, but in any society of this nature the consumer can be subjected to unscrupulous business practices—practices that serve only the needs of the business using them. Just recently, two of the world's largest chocolate companies, Nestlé and Mars, were charged with conspiring to fix the price of chocolate treats across Canada.[55] In an age when ethics and corporate social responsibility are top-of-mind issues with Canadian consumers, it is difficult to believe that such practices occur. Regardless, an organization must face the wrath of the courts and the public if it steps over the line.

Numerous laws and regulations (some voluntary and some involuntary) have been put into place to protect both consumer and corporate rights and ensure that businesses compete on a level playing field. Generally speaking, laws and regulations are established for the benefit of Canadian society as a whole.

The legal environment for marketing and other business practices in Canada is the domain of **Industry Canada**. Its principal responsibility is to administer the **Competition Act**, an act that brings together a number of related laws to help consumers and businesses function in Canada. The purpose of the *Competition Act* is threefold:

1. To maintain and encourage competition in Canada
2. To ensure that small- and medium-sized businesses have an equitable opportunity to participate in the Canadian economy
3. To provide consumers with product choice and competitive prices

Within the Ministry of Industry, the Competition Bureau and the Office of Consumer Affairs administer laws, regulations, and policies that influence business and marketing activity. There are many laws in areas such as competition, advertising, packaging and labelling, environmental protection, and pricing that an organization must be familiar with. Canadian companies that market internationally must also be aware of foreign laws and regulations that will influence marketing strategies.

Canadian consumers are protected by various privacy laws, the *Privacy Act*, and the *Personal Information Protection and Electronic Documents Act* (PIPEDA). The *Privacy Act* respects the rights of Canadians by placing limits on the collection, use, and disclosure of

Industry Canada Regulates the legal environment for marketing and other business practices in Canada.

Competition Act Brings together a number of related laws to help consumers and businesses function in Canada.

personal information. It gives Canadians the right to access and correct any personal information about them held by government organizations.

PIPEDA sets the ground rules for how private-sector organizations may collect, use, or disclose personal information. For example, the law requires organizations to obtain customer consent before they undertake any marketing activities.[56] Such a law has direct implications for marketing organizations that accumulate data about their customers. It also has implications for the direct marketing industry, which relies heavily on direct-mail lists and email marketing lists to send offers to prospective customers. For more information about privacy laws, see the Privacy Commissioner of Canada website, Privacy Commissioner of Canada www.privcom.gc.ca/

Competition Bureau

This bureau enforces the rules that govern and promote the efficiency of a competitive Canadian marketplace. Its chief instrument for carrying out these functions is the *Competition Act*. The Bureau investigates anti-competitive activities such as price fixing, bid-rigging, false or misleading representations, abuse of dominant position, exclusive dealing practices, mergers, and deceptive marketing practices. Its role has been illustrated in decisions against several respected companies in Canada. Not long ago, the Bureau determined that Bell Canada was violating the National Do Not Call List (a set of regulations that all marketing organizations must follow) and fined the company a record-setting penalty of $1.3 million. The Canadian Radio-television Telecommunications Commission (CRTC), the body that regulates telecommunications companies such as Bell, Telus, and Rogers, had been besieged with calls from frustrated citizens complaining about calls that interrupt dinner conversations with unwanted sales pitches.[57]

Office of Consumer Affairs (OCA)

This office promotes a safe, orderly, and fair marketplace for consumers and businesses. In consultation with other government agencies and organizations that represent business groups, the mandate of the Office of Consumer Affairs is to establish regulations and programs that protect the interests of consumers and help ensure a more productive economy. To do so, the OCA works with consumers to ensure they have the information and tools needed to protect their interests, while encouraging industry to be more innovative. The OCA also works with business to develop consumer-friendly business practices through the development of voluntary codes and practices.[58]

The OCA ensures that dangerous products are identified and certain products that cause injury are removed from the market. The legislation under the jurisdiction of the federal Office of Consumer Affairs includes the *Consumer Packaging and Labelling Act*, the *Textile Labelling Act*, and the *Weights and Measures Act*.

In 2012, Health Canada changed the food labelling laws to address consumers' concerns about food allergies. Food manufacturers must now clearly list all common allergens such as peanuts, eggs, and soy on a product's label. The intention is to provide information on packages that allows consumers to make safer and better choices about the foods they buy. There are still some gaps in the legislation though, as foods sold in bulk and in delis and bakeries are exempt. It's up to the company selling those types of products to decide whether or not to follow the new guidelines. How a company and its brands are presented to consumers will largely depend on the corporate culture of an organization. Those that offend will be judged by their customers and face the consequences.

Self-Regulation

Self-regulation is an alternative to government regulation. Organizations such as the Canadian Marketing Association (CMA) and the Canadian Bankers Association have established policies and guidelines that their member companies agree to follow. The CMA's *Code of Ethics and Standards of Practice* is the foundation of the marketing community's self-regulation.

self-regulation A form of regulation whereby an industry sets standards and guidelines for its members to follow.

The mission of the CMA is to identify, plan, and react to issues affecting marketing in Canada. *The Code of Ethics and Standards of Practice* promotes ethical practices among member organizations. The CMA also takes an active role in ensuring compliance. The code is a thorough document covering such issues as ethical principles, protection of personal privacy, special consideration for marketing to children and teenagers, protection of the environment, and media-specific standards of practice. For complete details of the code refer to the CMA website, www.the-cma.org

In consultation with the government, the CMA established a privacy policy that identifies principles and policies regarding the protection of personal information collected by the CMA. The objective of the policy is to promote responsible and transparent personal information management practices that are consistent with the provisions of PIPEDA (described earlier). The CMA website has complete details of the privacy policy.

✔ **Experience**Marketing

To experience marketing you have to assess situations and make recommendations to change marketing strategies when necessary. What would you do in the following situation?

You are the marketing manager for Lipton Brisk Iced Tea, a popular brand marketed in Canada by PepsiCo. You are contemplating a unique marketing strategy for Canadians of Asian ancestry but have to determine if such a strategy is feasible. As a first step you want to examine the ethnic population trends in Canada, particularly in major urban markets (Toronto, Montreal, and Vancouver).

Your challenge is to identify the best ethnic opportunity for the brand and make a decision on whether or not you would proceed with the development of a marketing strategy to support it. You must offer enough evidence to justify your decision to proceed or not to proceed. Do the benefits outweigh the costs?

CHAPTER SUMMARY

L01 Identify the external forces that influence marketing. *(pp. 29–30)*

Decisions about the marketing mix are influenced by conditions that exist beyond the company's control. Essentially, there are six key external influences: the economy, competition, social trends, demographic trends, technology, and laws and regulations.

L02 Explain the impact of the economy and various market structures on marketing practices. *(pp. 30–33)*

The general state of the economy will influence how aggressive or how conservative an organization's marketing strategy may be. The marketer will adjust marketing strategies based on fluctuations in the economy (e.g., recession versus recovery). If the economy is in a recession the marketer will be more cautious and perhaps spend less on marketing. In recovery the manager may be more aggressive and spend more on marketing.

L03 Describe the way various competitive forces influence marketing strategy development. *(pp. 33–38)*

An organization's position or relative strength in a market (leader, challenger, follower, or nicher) also has an impact on marketing strategy. Leaders and challengers are typically aggressive with their marketing strategies. Followers and nichers tend to have fewer financial resources and spend only what is appropriate to maintain their market position.

L04 Discuss how social, environmental, and demographic forces shape marketing strategies now and in the future. *(pp. 38–46)*

Healthier lifestyles and a societal desire for environmental conservation impact marketing strategies. Products that promote healthier living will be successful. Organizations that demonstrate social responsibility will also succeed. Consumers and the public at large are more accepting of organizations that support worthwhile causes and implement programs that show a genuine concern for the environment. Smart marketing organizations tell people what they are doing in these areas.

Demographic trends must be monitored closely. An organization must be aware that Canada's population is aging, household formations are changing, the level of education is increasing, wealth and spending are concentrated among higher-income groups, the ethnicity of the population is increasingly diverse, and there is a trend toward living in urban areas. These trends present both opportunities and challenges for marketers and will guide the direction of future marketing strategy.

LO5 **Identify and explain the effect technological trends and developments have on current and future marketing practices.** *(pp. 46–50)*

Technology will have a strong and direct impact on marketing. More organizations will adopt database management techniques and implement customer relationship management programs. Marketing communications will shift in the direction of digital communications and away from the mass media. The growth of

e-commerce strongly suggests that web-based marketing strategies be integrated into an organization's marketing strategy.

LO6 **Distinguish the role that laws, regulations, and self-regulation play in the practice of marketing in Canada.** *(pp. 50–52)*

All marketers must be aware of and follow provincial and federal laws and the rulings of regulatory agencies. Marketers know that being socially responsible not only makes sense, it is good for business. Many companies are embracing a triple bottom line philosophy: people, planet, profit.

MyMarketingLab

Study, practise, and explore real marketing situations with these helpful resources:

- **Interactive Lesson Presentations:** Work through interactive presentations and assessments to test your knowledge of marketing concepts.
- **Study Plan:** Check your understanding of chapter concepts with self-study quizzes.
- **Dynamic Study Modules:** Work through adaptive study modules on your computer, tablet, or mobile device.
- **Simulations:** Practise decision-making in simulated marketing environments.

REVIEW QUESTIONS

1. What are the external environmental factors that impact marketing? (*LO1*)
2. In what way do the following economic variables influence an organization's outlook and marketing activities: trends in the gross domestic product, interest rates, and the value of the Canadian dollar? (*LO2*)
3. What are the basic components of the following markets: monopoly, oligopoly, monopolistic competition, pure competition? Identify an example of each. (*LO3*)
4. What is the difference between direct competition and indirect competition? Provide an example to demonstrate the difference between the two forms of competition. (*LO3*)
5. How do the marketing strategies differ between a market leader and a market challenger? (*LO3*)
6. What are the important social and demographic trends affecting marketing? What demographic trends will become more important in the future? (*LO4*)
7. How are environmental factors influencing marketing strategy? (*LO4*)
8. How are marketers using technology to build relationships and engage with their customers? Give specific examples. (*LO5*)
9. What role does self-regulation play in the practice of marketing? (*LO6*)
10. What are some important laws governing marketing in Canada? What regulatory bodies oversee these laws? (*LO6*)

DISCUSSION AND APPLICATION QUESTIONS

1. Provide some examples of companies that have a positive corporate image. What marketing activities have helped these companies achieve their image?
2. With reference to the Think Marketing box **Indigo Books and Music Inc. Transforms Itself**, what trends has Indigo capitalized on and how has it influenced its marketing strategies? Do some additional research to update yourself on more

recent Indigo activities and happenings before presenting your opinion.
3. Conduct some Internet-based secondary research to compile recent statistics on ethnic population trends and urban living trends. Discuss how the impact of these trends will influence the direction of future marketing activity.

3 Marketing Intelligence

rmnoa357/Shutterstock

LEARNING OBJECTIVES

LO1 Define marketing research and identify the ways in which marketing research findings are used. (pp. 55–56)

LO2 Outline the basic stages in the marketing research process. (pp. 56–58)

LO3 Describe secondary data sources available to marketing organizations. (pp. 59–62)

LO4 Explain the steps and methodologies used for collecting primary data. (pp. 62–71)

LO5 Describe the role and impact of information collection on customer relationship marketing strategies. (pp. 71–74)

LO6 Identify key issues associated with the collection and use of information about consumers. (p. 74)

COLLECTING, ANALYZING...

and using information is what marketing intelligence and customer relationship management is about. Nobody knows that better than retailers like Shoppers Drug Mart, Hudson's Bay Company, and supermarketers such as Loblaws and Metro. Giving customers what they want should be based on what they are currently buying. That kind of information, which is usually contained in a company's customer database, tells the retailer what items to stock and what not to stock.

Loyalty programs are now popular with big retailers such as Shoppers Drug Mart, Metro, and Loblaws, among many others. These programs provide an abundance of information on the buying tendencies of their shoppers. Careful utilization of the information allows for individualized offers to shoppers and ultimately gives a retailer an edge over its competition.

Shoppers Drug Mart is working to make its marketing more personalized and targeted at individuals and specific groups of shoppers. Shoppers' Optimum program rewards shoppers with points based on how much they spend and helps give the company insight into its customer needs.[1] For example, tailored offers can be delivered by email. Email is an efficient means of communication with customers, as opposed to mass media alternatives such as television and magazines.

A business organization will invest considerable sums of money in marketing programs. To protect this investment an organization must be knowledgeable about consumers' changing needs and must collect and utilize appropriate information. Carefully planned marketing research is the tool that provides organizations with insight necessary to take advantage of new opportunities.

There's an expression in marketing: "information is power." How to collect information and use it to advantage is what this chapter is all about.

MARKETING RESEARCH: DEFINITION, ROLE, AND SCOPE

LO1 Define marketing research and identify the ways in which marketing research findings are used.

The American Marketing Association defines **marketing research** as the function that links the consumer/customer/public to the marketer through information—information used to define marketing opportunities and problems; generate, refine, and evaluate marketing actions; monitor marketing performance; and improve the understanding of marketing as a process.

When companies conduct marketing research they specify the information required to address these issues, design the method for collecting information, implement and manage the information collection process, analyze the results, and communicate the findings and their implications.[2]

Collecting and Managing Information

Generally speaking, the collection of information via marketing research covers three main areas: **market analysis**, which produces information about the marketplace; **product research**, which produces information about how people perceive product attributes; and **consumer analysis**, which produces information about the needs and motivations of consumers.

The testing of new product concepts is the single most common task market research firms perform for their clients. Other uses of marketing research include testing advertising for impact and effectiveness, conducting attitude and usage studies, conducting surveys to measure customer satisfaction, tracking brand awareness versus the competition, and measuring the influence of pricing tests.

marketing research A function that links the consumer, customer, and public to the marketer through information—information used to define marketing opportunities and problems; generate, refine, and evaluate marketing actions; monitor marketing performance; and improve understanding of marketing as a process.

market analysis The collection of appropriate information (i.e., information regarding demand, sales volume potential, production capabilities, and the resources necessary to produce and market a given product) to determine if a market is worth pursuing.

product research Produces information about how people perceive product attributes.

consumer analysis The monitoring of consumer behaviour changes (tastes, preferences, lifestyles) so that marketing strategies can be adjusted accordingly.

Regardless of the nature of the research study, the information obtained will assist managers in their decision making.

In very broad terms, marketing research can be divided into two areas. First, information is collected about customers, competitors, and conditions in the market. Second, the information collected is housed in a database where it can be reviewed and managed on an ongoing basis in order to use the information in a manner that maximizes the value of customers. The expression "information is power" applies. Profitable organizations use their power wisely!

Marketing research is a vital marketing tool. It is used to help reduce or eliminate the uncertainty and risk associated with making business decisions. In many ways, marketing research is a form of insurance—it ensures that the action a company might take is the right action.

To demonstrate how risk can be eliminated, let's examine a situation in which a new package design is being considered—new shape, new colours, etc. Would you consider testing the design, or a few designs for that matter, with consumers, before making the decision to change? Explorer Shopping Solutions offers a lab facility that simulates a real store environment. Staged like a grocery store, it is equipped with eye-tracking technology on the shelves and on packaging that can determine what a shopper is and isn't looking at.[3] In other words, you will discover how your new package attracts a consumer's eye. Such information will aid in deciding the final design.

The collection of information is done in a scientific manner. Procedures are implemented to ensure the information obtained is both reliable and valid. **Reliability** refers to similar results being achieved if another study were undertaken under similar conditions. **Validity** refers to the research procedure's ability to actually measure what it was intended to. Prudent marketing decision makers then combine their intuition and judgment with the information to make better marketing decisions.

reliability Refers to similar results being achieved if another research study were undertaken under similar circumstances.

validity Refers to a research procedure's ability to actually measure what it is intended to measure.

Applying proper research procedure influenced a decision at E.D. Smith, a prominent marketer of jam products in Canada. Just a few years ago, E.D. Smith had to react to the low-calorie, low-carbohydrate craze that was sweeping the nation. Jam sales were falling. More than 3600 consumers were interviewed right in the jam aisle to find out what they liked, disliked, and wanted. The company discovered that jams were too sweet; consumers wanted more healthy alternatives—provided they couldn't taste the difference between healthy jams and regular jams. To meet this need E.D. Smith launched new products in three segments: traditional jams, low-sugar Fruit Lovers jams with 42 percent less sugar, and a no-sugar-added line. To the company, the three-tiered lineup made sense. As a result of the new products, sales of E.D. Smith products are modestly increasing while the product category is decreasing.[4]

Over the long term, an organization accumulates information about consumers, trends in the marketplace, business-to-business customer sales, brand market share, and so on. All this information is stored in a database management system referred to as a decision support system. A **decision support system (DSS)** is an interactive computer-based information system that marketers can access and manipulate to help make better decisions and devise more effective marketing strategies.

decision support system (DSS) An interactive information system that marketers can use to obtain and manipulate information that will assist them in the decision-making process.

The database is a key tool in the organization's customer relationship management program. From the data, a customer profile will emerge that outlines purchase preferences. It is an important tool for individually targeted marketing programs. These concepts are discussed in more detail later in the chapter.

THE MARKETING RESEARCH PROCESS

L02 Outline the basic stages in the marketing research process.

The marketing research process is best described as a systematic (step-by-step) process. There are many steps: problem awareness, exploratory research, primary research (which involves the collection and processing of data), data analysis and interpretation, and

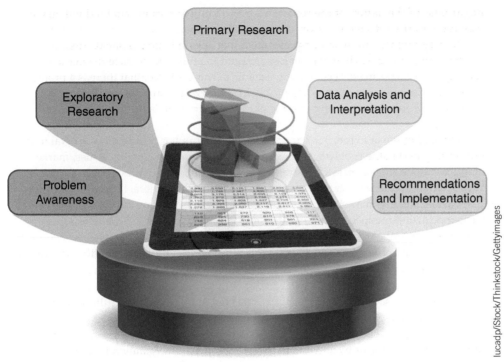

Figure 3.1 Marketing Research Process

recommendations and implementation. Refer to **Figure 3.1** for a summary of the steps in the research process.

Problem Awareness

In the problem awareness stage, an attempt is made to specify the nature of the difficulty. For example, a company or product may be experiencing declining sales (as in the E.D. Smith example). But the decline itself is not the problem. Instead, it is a symptom that makes marketers aware that there is a deeper problem that must be identified. Many practitioners of marketing research say that the proper identification of a problem is the first step in finding its solution. Therefore, it is essential that a problem be precisely defined. After all, an organization does not want to waste valuable time and money collecting information that will not lead to action.

It is common to commission a market research project that will address a specific decision that has to be made—a good research project is designed to address that decision alone. Defining a problem involves developing a clearly worded statement that provides direction for further research on the topic under investigation. To define a problem precisely, a company usually performs some form of exploratory research.

Exploratory Research

Exploratory research is research that helps define the precise nature of a problem through the use of informal analysis. This informal analysis is often referred to as the funnelling process. **Funnelling** is the process of dividing a subject into manageable variables and thereby narrowing down the field so that specifically directed research can be conducted. Funnelling is accomplished by means of a thorough situation analysis. In a **situation analysis** the researcher collects information from knowledgeable people inside and outside the organization and from secondary sources

exploratory research A preliminary form of research that clarifies the nature of a problem.

funnelling Dividing a subject into manageable variables so that specifically directed research can be conducted.

situation analysis Collecting information from knowledgeable people inside and outside the organization and from secondary sources.

such as government reports, census data, trade and industry associations, studies on related issues, and a variety of other sources. Many variables are analyzed as potential problem areas and, through the funnelling process, areas that appear to be unrelated are eliminated.

Figure 3.2 illustrates exploratory research and the funnelling process. Let's assume that the sales of a particular product are declining. This indicates that there is a problem (declining sales are a symptom of the problem). Finding the cause of the decline will identify the problem. Identifying the true nature of a problem is the task of exploratory research.

As the diagram in Figure 3.2 demonstrates, the researcher could follow several routes in order to pinpoint the problem, assessing product and product quality issues, marketing communications strategies, pricing strategies, availability, and distribution. In this case, the problem is identified as marketing communications. From there, the researcher looks into possible areas of marketing communications where the real problem might be, rejects some, and further pursues others—advertising, in our example. As this analysis unfolds, it should become apparent which elements are contributing to the sales decline. The eventual isolation of a creative problem in this illustration (a problem with the advertising message) assumes that other areas have been evaluated, at least informally, and rejected as the source of the problem.

It is possible that the problem could be resolved at this stage. Consulting with knowledgeable people in this particular area (message strategy) may yield a solution. Sometimes the problem is both pinpointed and resolved through discussions held with knowledgeable people or by analyzing relevant secondary information that may be available on the subject. If a solution is not available, the process continues with primary research. A study will be devised to focus on the specific nature of the problem—in this case the advertising message. Exploratory research has narrowed the scope so that primary research is possible.

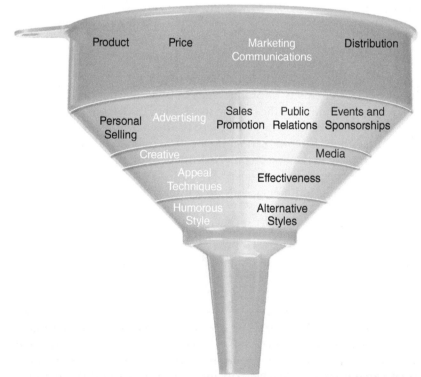

Exploratory research narrows the scope of an investigation until a specific problem is identified. In this example, a problem has been traced to the style of advertising. Potential problem areas were explored and discarded along the way. Primary research would be conducted on styles of advertising.

Achim Prill/iStock/Thinkstock/Gettyimages

Figure 3.2
Exploratory Research and the Funnelling Process

SECONDARY DATA COLLECTION

L03 Describe secondary data sources available to marketing organizations.

Exploratory research usually involves the use of secondary data. **Secondary data** are data that have been compiled and published for purposes unrelated to the specific problem under investigation, yet may have some significance to its resolution. They are available from sources both internal and external to the company.

secondary data Data that have been compiled and published for purposes other than that of solving the specific problem under investigation.

Internal Data Sources

Internal data sources are those that are available within the organization. Such information includes customer profiles (e.g., size and frequency of purchase), sales analysis reports (e.g., sales by region, nation, customer, or product), inventory analysis, production reports, cost analyses, marketing budgets (e.g., actual spending versus planned spending), and profit-and-loss statements. This information is incorporated into a company's database and is updated continuously for use in planning and decision making—the decision support system that was presented earlier in the chapter. For example, if a rise in raw material costs or packaging costs above what was anticipated is detected, a price increase will have to be implemented if desired profit levels are to be achieved.

External Data Sources

An organization refers to external data sources when internal information does not resolve the problem at hand. The primary sources of external data are government, business, and academia. In today's technological environment the Internet contains a wealth of information valuable to marketing organizations and the information can be accessed very quickly.

Federal, provincial, and municipal governments have an abundance of information that marketing organizations can access. The major source of government information is Statistics Canada, which provides census information (population and household trends, income, education, and occupation trends) and information on all aspects of the economy (employment, inflation, interest rates, domestic production, and international trade, to name a few) for free or a small fee. A selection of this information is readily available in summary form online from the Statistics Canada website.

At the federal and provincial levels, the department or ministry involved with industry, trade, and commerce is the most common source of business information. At the municipal level, departments of economic development publish reports relevant to their municipalities.

A company may also obtain market-related information from many commercial sources. One of the more prominent commercial providers of secondary information is Nielsen Canada. Nielsen's market measurement services track a variety of information for consumer packaged goods manufacturers. Their data are electronically retrieved at the point of purchase (in supermarkets, drugstores, and mass merchandisers) and are used to compile market share data, distribution data, retail inventory data, and retail price data. The information is available nationally, regionally, and by key markets within some regions. Access to such data allows an organization to understand trends and identify market opportunities. Nielsen sells this information to business clients on a subscription basis.[5]

Other ongoing services offered by Nielsen include the Nielsen TV Audience Analysis, which measures the audience size of all prime-time television shows. Nielsen also conducts an annual lifestyle study among Canadians called Nielsen Prizm. The study offers insights into consumer behaviour, shopping patterns, and

Video: Nielsen: Observing
and Predicting Consumer
Behaviour

media preferences. The study categorizes Canadians into various clusters based on lifestyle.

Environics Analytics, a division of Environics Research Group, is another Canadian research company that conducts surveys of interest to marketing organizations. The findings of the surveys are offered for sale to any organization that has an interest in them. One of Environics' flagship products is a market segmentation study (PRIZM C2) that classifies Canadians into 66 different lifestyle segments, such as Cosmopolitan Elite, Electric Avenues, and Lunch at Tim's.[6] The study successfully links demographic data with attitudes and social values expressed by Canadians—valuable insights about Canadians that can be used to develop better marketing strategies. For more insight into this study, refer to **Figure 3.3**.

A sound understanding of the attitudes and social values of a specific target market often has a direct impact on a marketing strategy. PRIZM C2 data is used by banks and insurance companies to develop new products, services, and messages that

Socioeconomic Groups	Demographic Description	% of Total Population
Urban Elite		
Cosmopolitan Elite	Very affluent middle-aged and older city dwellers	0.35
Urbane Villagers	Wealthy middle-aged urban sophisticates	1.02
Money & Brains	Upscale and educated professionals and family	1.74
Suburban Elite		
Suburban Gentry	Well-off middle-aged suburban families	1.36
Nouveaux Riches	Prosperous Quebec suburban families	0.71
Pets & PCs	Large upscale suburban families	5.22
Urban Upscale Ethnic		
Continental Culture	Successful multi-ethnic urban households	0.45
Cluttered Nests	Upper-middle-class multigenerational families	1.11
New Italy	Established Italian city families	0.89
Suburban Midscale		
Upward Bound	Middle-aged families in suburban comfort	1.43
Rods & Reels	Older and outdoorsy upper-middle-class families	1.67
Nearly Empty Nests	Successful suburban households starting to empty	1.51
Urban Francophone		
Les Chics	Sophisticated urban Quebec couples and singles	0.46
La Cité Nomad	Mix of young and old low-income Quebec singles	2.17
Jeunes et Actifs	Young and active students and singles in cities	2.64

Figure 3.3   A Sample of Selected Lifestyle Segments Identified by Environics Analytics

Source: © 2011 Environics Analytics. Selected PRIZM and PRIZMC2 nicknames from The Nielsen Company are used with permission.

increase client retention. Tourism marketers use the information to create highly targeted direct mail pieces that focus on the aspirational motives of vacationers. Governments use the data to ensure that the right services are available to constituents in the appropriate areas. There is endless opportunity for marketers to take advantage of this information.

Having access to good information about the attitudes and values of beer drinkers lead to a new advertising campaign for Dos Equis beer. "Consumer research revealed that import beer drinkers were tired of clichés and sophomoric humor that are the staple of the category," says Paul Smailes former senior brand manager.[7] That insight led to a new ad campaign: The Most Interesting Man in the World. The performer in the ad was journeyman actor Jonathan Goldsmith. Using a grey-haired, bearded man as a spokesman was an unlikely and risky decision in a market where younger drinkers are the key target. But it worked! In the first year of the campaign, sales for Dos Equis increased 20 percent in North America. New versions of the commercial have been added in recent years.

The presence of valuable information on the Internet has made it more convenient and often less expensive for an organization to track down the information it needs. The rapid development of online databases means that information can be transferred almost instantaneously, assuming access to electronic communication facilities.

Online databases are available from public and commercial sources. Among public sources available electronically is the federal government's census data (Statistics Canada). The information collected is very detailed and covers dozens of demographic and socioeconomic topics such as family and household structures, occupation, income, education, ethnicity, age, marital status, and so on.

From commercial sources, such as Dun & Bradstreet, organizations can access **directory databases**. These databases provide a quick picture of a company, its products and services, and its financial situation. Typical information includes ownership, size (dollar sales), and location of the company; number of employees; identification of key management personnel and officers; and basic revenue and profit data. This information helps identify potential customers that an organization may want to do business with. Dun & Bradstreet also provides list management services and can provide direct-mail lists and telemarketing lists to organizations that want to reach companies with specific characteristics.

Secondary data available from external sources offer a marketing organization numerous advantages and disadvantages. Refer to **Figure 3.4** for details.

For more insight into how information gained from research can influence the direction of marketing strategy see the Think Marketing box **Research Leads to Key Marketing Decisions**.

online databases A public information database accessible to anyone with proper communications facilities.

directory databases A commercial database that provides quick information about a company (e.g., size, sales, location, and number of employees).

Secondary Data

Advantages
1. Information is inexpensive or obtainable at no cost.
2. Information is readily available.
3. Possibly the only source of information (e.g., census data).
4. Useful in exploratory research stage where information is assessed to identify a problem.

Disadvantages
1. The data do not resolve the specific problem under investigation (e.g., data were compiled for another problem or purpose).
2. Reliability and accuracy of data are questionable.
3. Information can be outdated, even obsolete, for the intended situation.

Information from an Online Database

Advantages
1. Data are available very quickly (on the spot).
2. Identification of relevant data occurs quickly.

Disadvantages
1. Amount of data available is overwhelming (discourages use of data).
2. Hidden costs associated with retrieval and distribution of data (e.g., cost per hour for computer time).

Figure 3.4 Secondary Data and Online Database Information

ThinkMarketing

Research Leads to Key Marketing Decisions

When you dine at McDonald's the first thing that comes to mind might be burgers, chicken, and fries. Healthier options might be lower down on your list. Nonetheless, insights gained from the McDonald's Our Food. Your Questions social media campaign and a research study conducted by Environics produced some valuable insights about consumers' food expectations, which in turn led to some new products at McDonald's.

The survey research produced some key data:

- 76 percent of respondents wanted more vegetables in their diet
- 71 percent search for veggie-only items at least sometimes
- 51 percent of respondents feel fast-food veggie options are "fairly limited" to "terrible"

The data reveals that consumers do have an appetite for veggie options, but if they are offered, they'd better taste good.

McDonald's kitchens went to work, the result being the introduction of two veggie-based McWraps: Mediterranean Veggie and Sante Fe Veggie. The CEO of McDonald's, John Betts, sees nothing but future success for the McWraps. He says, "A key ingredient of our success has been our ability to remain relevant and consistently deliver what our customers are looking for. We listen and respond to their needs."

You've probably seen television ads for Scotiabank telling people, "You're richer than you think." The primary objective of the campaign is to spread a sense of optimism across the country during troubled economic times. The ads encouraged people to visit Scotiabank for a second opinion. When visiting the bank, people could learn that their position wasn't as bad as they thought.

The campaign is based on insights garnered from primary research that the bank conducted. The research revealed people were concerned about their financial struggles—struggles that don't necessarily depend on income level. That insight was the impetus for a new adver-

Richness is:
The moment everything changes.

Scotiabank's 5 Year Plan.
You define richness. With a 5 Year Plan that lets you adapt to anything, we can help with the money part.

To book an appointment please call: 1-800 551-8941

You're richer than you think.®   **S** Scotiabank®

(Ad) Scotiabank; (photo) Rhea Anna/Gettyimages

tising campaign to make people more comfortable and confident about their finances.

The campaign was successful. It raised the bank's recognition factor significantly and attracted new customers to the bank. Just recently, the bank altered the message of the advertising somewhat, again based on insights obtained from research. New research indicated that "richness" meant different things to different people. It had to do with the stage of life, such as getting married, having a baby, and sending children to college. The new advertising campaign showed people and scenes reflecting these events.

The moral of the story is a simple one. Good insights gained from marketing research will lead to profitable marketing decisions.

Question:
How important is marketing research when an advertiser is in the development stages of an advertising campaign? Explain.

Adapted from "Veggies? Canadians asked. McDonald's listened," press release, August 27, 2013, www.mcdonalds.ca; and Kristin Laird, "Scotiabank redefines 'Richer' campaign," Marketing, January 23, 2012, www.marketingmag.ca

PRIMARY RESEARCH

L04 Explain the steps and methodologies used for collecting primary data.

primary research Data collected and recorded for the first time to resolve a specific problem.

If secondary research does not resolve the problem, the research process moves to another stage: the collection of primary data. **Primary research** refers to the process of collecting and recording new data, called primary data, in order to resolve a specific problem, usually at a high cost to the sponsoring organization. Primary research is custom designed and focuses on resolving a particular question or obtaining specified information. A procedure is developed and a research instrument designed to perform the specific task.

In directing the primary research, the marketing organization identifies the precise nature of the problem, the objectives of the study, and the hypotheses associated with it. **Research objectives** are statements that outline what the research is to accomplish, while **hypotheses**, which are statements of predicted outcomes, are confirmed or refuted by the data collected. Consider the following example:

> *Research Objective:* To determine the impact of an emotional style of advertising on adults 25 to 49 years of age.
> *Research Hypothesis:* An emotional style of advertising will generate significantly higher recognition and recall scores than other types of message appeal techniques.

In this case, the findings of the research will be compared to the norms achieved in similar studies for other products using other styles of advertising. Such comparisons will determine the effectiveness or ineffectiveness of emotional messages. Research companies have access to such data and provide this type of comparison when needed.

The outcome of the research often leads to certain actions by the marketing organization. If the hypothesis is proven, the client may adopt a new style of advertising. Refer to **Figure 3.5** for a summary of the steps involved in primary research.

Conducting a marketing research study is beyond the scope and expertise of most marketing organizations in Canada. Consequently, independent market research firms are hired to perform the task. Usually a marketing research manager from the sponsoring organization is responsible for supervising the research study and works directly with the marketing research firm in designing the project.

Sample Design

Prior to implementing a research study, the researchers identify the characteristics of the population they would like to study so that they can create an appropriate sample group. A **sample** is defined as a representative portion of an entire population that is used to obtain information about that population. A sample must be an accurate reflection of the population if the information gathered is to be reliable. Some basic steps must be taken to develop a representative sample:

1. *Define the Population (Universe)*— It should be first pointed out that the terms *population* and *universe* are interchangeable in research terminology. A **population** is a group of people with certain age, gender, or other demographic characteristics. Defining a population involves identifying its basic characteristics. For the purposes of primary research, a description of a population might be *male golfers between the ages of 21 and 45 years living in cities with over 500 000 residents.* A proper research procedure will screen potential respondents for these characteristics.

2. *Identify the Sampling Frame*— The **sampling frame** refers to a listing that can be used for reaching a population. For example, the telephone directory could be used as a sampling frame for the golf population, as could a subscription list from *Score* or *Golf*

research objectives Statements that outline what the research is to accomplish.

hypotheses Statements of predicted outcomes.

sample A representative portion of an entire population used to obtain information about that population.

population A group of people with certain age, gender, or other demographic characteristics.

sampling frame A listing that can be used for reaching a population.

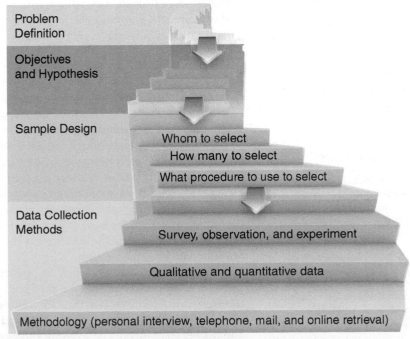

Figure 3.5　Primary Research Steps

magazines. Visitors to golf-oriented websites could also be given consideration. If Nike were trying to reach the golfers, it could also recruit people who visit its website to seek information about Nike golf equipment. Online research is a rapidly growing segment of the research industry. Such feedback is quick and convenient, and much less costly than traditional forms of information collection.

3. *Determine the Type of Sample*— The researcher has the option of using a probability sample or a non-probability sample. If a **probability sample** is used, the respondents have a known or equal chance of selection and are randomly selected from across the population. For example, the researcher may use a predetermined and systematic procedure for picking respondents through a telephone directory or other type of list. The known chance of selection enables statistical procedures to be used in the results to estimate sampling errors.

   In a **non-probability sample**, the respondents have an unknown chance of selection, and they are chosen based on such factors as convenience for the researcher or the judgment of the researcher. The researcher uses his or her experience to determine who would be most appropriate. For example, if a survey is conducted among golfers visiting the Nike website (as described previously) it would be a non-probability sample. It is very convenient for Nike to conduct this type of survey. Factors such as cost and timing are other reasons for using non-probability samples.

4. *Determine the Sample Size*—Generally, the larger the sample, the greater the accuracy of the data collected and the higher the cost. The nature of the research study is a determining factor in the number of participants required. Some researchers use a 1 percent rule (1 percent of the defined population or universe), while others state absolute minimums of 200 respondents. To illustrate the concept of sample size, Environics Analytics conducts an annual survey that collects information about the social values of Canadians. This study uses a sample of 2000 households but the data gathered are projected across the entire population. The accuracy of the sample is usually calculated statistically and stated in the research report. Therefore, a researcher takes into consideration the margin of error that is acceptable and the degree of certainty required.

probability sample A sample in which the respondents have a known or equal chance of selection and are randomly selected from across the country.

non-probability sample The respondents have an unknown chance of selection, and their being chosen is based on such factors as convenience for the researcher or the judgment of the researcher.

Data Collection Methods

There are three primary methods a researcher can use to collect data: surveys, observation, and experiments. The data collected can be either qualitative or quantitative in nature. See **Figure 3.6** for an illustration of the collection methods.

Survey Research   For **survey research**, data are collected systematically through some form of communication with a representative sample by means of a questionnaire that records responses. Most surveys include predetermined questions and a choice of responses that are easily filled in by the respondent. This technique is referred to as **fixed-response questioning**. Survey research is conducted by personal interview, telephone, mail, and online through company websites.

A survey is usually designed to be structured or unstructured. In a **structured survey**, the questionnaire follows a planned format: screening questions at the beginning, central-issue questions (those dealing with the nature of the research) in the middle, and classification (demographic) questions at the end. In the case of questions dealing with the specific nature of the issue, it is common to ask some general questions initially, progressing to more specific questions as the respondent proceeds through the questionnaire.

Fixed-response questions that list possible answers (e.g., multiple-choice questions or answers with check boxes) are the most popular. They permit the data to be easily transferred to a computer for tabulation and subsequent analysis. Computer software is now available that allows researchers to conduct surveys on electronic devices (laptops and pocket computers). The software allows researchers to skip the transfer step just

survey research Data collected systematically through some form of communication with a representative sample by means of a questionnaire.

fixed-response questioning Questionnaire used for a large sample that contains predetermined questions and a choice of answers that are easily filled in by the respondent or interviewer.

structured survey Follows a planned format: screening questions at the beginning, central-issue questions in the middle, and classification questions at the end.

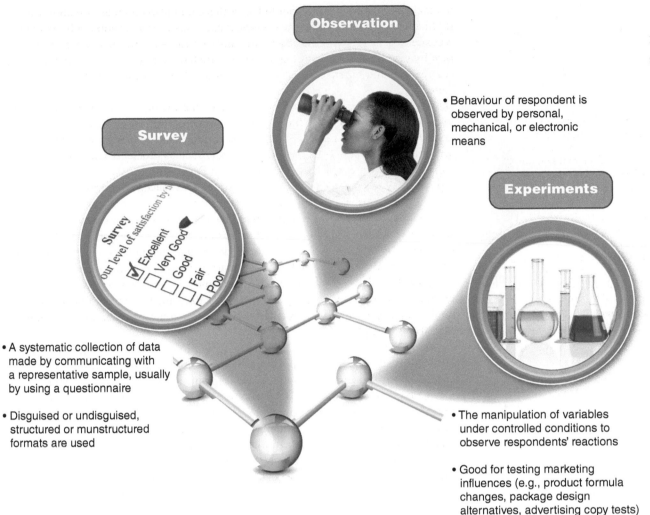

Survey

Observation

Experiments

- Behaviour of respondent is observed by personal, mechanical, or electronic means

- A systematic collection of data made by communicating with a representative sample, usually by using a questionnaire

- Disguised or undisguised, structured or munstructured formats are used

- The manipulation of variables under controlled conditions to observe respondents' reactions

- Good for testing marketing influences (e.g., product formula changes, package design alternatives, advertising copy tests)

Figure 3.6   Data Collection Methods

described, thus helping to avoid keying errors associated with transferring data from paper to a computer.[8]

In an **unstructured survey** the researcher has some leeway in determining how the questions are asked (for example, the sequence in which they are asked), and the questions may be of an open-ended nature, and the responses will be less structured. In this case, the researcher must be careful to record the responses accurately.

Observation Research   In **observation research**, the behaviour of the respondent is observed and recorded. In this form of research a person knowingly or unknowingly participates in a study. For example, the purchase behaviour of people in a supermarket can be observed in person or by electronic means. In other situations, respondents are usually aware of being observed, perhaps through a two-way mirror, by a hidden camera while being interviewed, by agreeing to be followed, or by electronic measurement of impulses.

Observation research in retail stores using hidden cameras or other devices is growing in popularity. Marketers tend to place high value on observation research because a natural shopping environment is being studied. Refer to the illustration in **Figure 3.7**. If not in the store, shoppers can be monitored in simulated retail environments where their eye movements and behaviour can be recorded electronically. The research facility of the Explorer Group that was briefly mentioned in the chapter introduction is a good example of observation research by electronic means.

unstructured survey Gives researcher some leeway in determining how the questions are asked; questions may be of an open-ended nature.

observation research A form of research in which the behaviour of the respondent is observed and recorded.

Figure 3.7 Shopping patterns that are observed by personal or electronic means provide input for in-store merchandising strategies.

Ethnographic research is a different form of observation research. **Ethnographic research** is the study of human behaviour in a natural setting. To demonstrate, many companies now hire anthropologists who go on "cultural digs," excavating the lives of real people. They will go shopping with people, follow them around, and watch how they interact with others. Such a practice is common among packaged goods marketers such as Procter & Gamble, Unilever, and Scott Paper.

Scott Paper placed an anthropologist in selected homes to observe women 25 to 54 years old. The goal was to build a brand idea by finding out what *really* goes on in the bathroom. Scott discovered that women view the bathroom as a place where they can have a moment of solitude and privacy.[9] Such knowledge led to a marketing decision! Cashmere toilet paper was positioned as a luxury brand. It was aligned with the idea that solitude can be a luxury in a hectic life.

ethnographic research The study of human behaviour in a natural setting.

experimental research Research in which one or more factors are manipulated under controlled conditions, while other elements remain constant, so that respondents' reactions can be evaluated.

test marketing Placing a product for sale in one or more representative markets to observe performance under a proposed marketing plan.

Experimental Research In **experimental research**, one or more factors are manipulated under controlled conditions while other elements remain constant, so that respondents' reactions can be evaluated. Test marketing is a form of experimental research. **Test marketing** involves placing a product for sale in one or more limited but representative markets in order to observe the product's performance under a proposed marketing plan.

Good test marketing provides a marketing organization with three main benefits: it allows the organization to observe consumers' reactions to the product, it enables alternative marketing strategies to be evaluated (e.g., different pricing options or advertising strategies can be tested in different geographic markets), and it helps determine the characteristics of consumers (age, income, and lifestyle) who will buy the product when launched regionally or nationally. From a test market, a manager gains valuable insights for refining marketing strategies.

Dairy Queen employed test marketing prior to launching its new DQ Grill & Chill restaurants in Canada. Dairy Queen had to evaluate customer response to a restaurant concept quite different from its ice cream and milkshake image. The DQ Grill & Chill includes updated store decor, table service, a premium burger patty, a new style of bun, and new grilled sandwiches—a dramatic change from the traditional Dairy Queen. Refer to the images in **Figure 3.8**. Test stores were opened in several locations, including Fredericton and Vancouver. Dairy Queen worked from the premise that the casual restaurant business was growing and that customers would be willing to pay more for a higher-quality offering.[10] The test markets were successful and Dairy Queen is expanding with updated franchise outlets across Canada.

Some experts believe test marketing is an optional step in the marketing process, noting that this kind of research tips off competitors about what a company is doing and gives them time to react. If a product stays too long in the test market, a competitor could launch its product first. That said, proceeding with an expensive marketing campaign—like a new restaurant concept—without careful testing could lead to a financial disaster.

Qualitative Data and Quantitative Data

qualitative data Collected from small samples in a controlled environment, the data result from questions concerned with *why* people behave as they do and from in-depth questioning of the participants.

Research data are classified according to the nature of the information sought—as qualitative or quantitative. There are significant differences between these classifications.

Qualitative data **Qualitative data** are usually collected from small samples in a controlled environment. They result from questions concerned with *why* people behave as they do and from in-depth questioning of the participants. Typically, such data are gathered from focus group interviews. A **focus group** is a small group of people (8 to 10) with common characteristics (e.g., a target market profile), brought together to discuss issues related to the marketing of a product or service.

The word "focus" implies that the discussion concentrates on one topic or concept. A trained moderator usually conducts the interview. The role of the moderator is to get the participants to interact fairly freely in order to uncover the reasons and motivations underlying their remarks. Probing reveals the hidden interplay of psychological factors that drive a consumer to buy one brand rather than another. The major drawback of using focus groups concerns the reliability of the data. The sample size is too small to be representative of the entire population, and most people in a focus group do not like to show disagreement with a prevailing opinion.

To compensate for the small sample size, interviews are often held in several locations. A typical session lasts about two hours and costs between $4500 and $5500. A major packaged-goods company can spend $40 000 for one eight-session study, which is considered the minimum needed to find out anything important. Sessions are typically planned in various regions and cities to obtain a cross-section of perspectives.

Marketers see several key benefits of focus groups. First, participants can interact with each other, and this usually produces new and meaningful discussion. People can share their views without having to agree or disagree. Second, the client can be involved by observing the discussion from behind a one-way mirror. Actually seeing the participants respond makes the findings more believable. Finally, the respondents get involved in the discussion. They are there to discuss one topic for an extended period of time.

While most marketers acknowledge that focus groups aren't scientific, the participants' offhand reactions sometimes influence key marketing decisions. The focus group yields a better understanding of customers' needs and expectations. However, marketing decisions involving considerable sums of money are very risky if based on such limited research.

There are some drawbacks to focus groups. Marketers should be aware that focus groups are exploratory in nature and sometimes the discussion can be dominated by a small number of participants. The moderator must be very good at moving the discussion along and ensuring that all members participate. The attitudes revealed in a focus group can be used as a foundation for formulating questions and questionnaires if and when quantitative research is required.

Many organizations now conduct online focus groups. Participants are recruited and brought together online under the direction of a moderator. All communication in such a group is done by typing responses to the moderator and other participants. The participants can be from any location, one of the benefits of this form of focus group.

Advancing technology now allows organizations to use chat and web conferencing software to conduct focus groups. Web conferencing programs include tools such as chat and messaging technology, webcams that can stream video content, and screen sharing that allows participants to view information on the moderator's screen. New technologies

Figure 3.8 The DQ Grill & Chill—a concept quite different from traditional Dairy Queen—was test marketed for acceptance.

(top) Francis Vachon/CP Images; (bottom) Photo by Keith J. Tuckwell

focus group A small group of 8 to 10 people with common characteristics, brought together to discuss issues related to the marketing of a product or service.

Qualitative Research	Quantitative Research
• Collected from a small sample group • Question format is unstructured • Questions deal with why people act, do, purchase, etc. • Small sample poses reliability (of data) problems	• Collected data from a truly representative sample (e.g., 200–300 people who represent a specified target market) • Structured format (e.g., questionnaire with predetermined responses) is common • Questions deal with "what," "when," "who," "how many," and "how often" • Data are statistically reliable; degree of error can be calculated

Figure 3.9   Comparing Qualitative and Quantitative Research

allow companies to bring focus groups together at a lower cost and in a faster time frame than do traditional face-to-face focus groups.[11]

quantitative data Collected using a structured procedure and a large sample, the data provide answers to questions concerned with *what, when, who, how many,* and *how often.*

Quantitative Data   **Quantitative data** provide answers to questions concerned with *what, when, who, how many,* and *how often.* This research attempts to translate feelings, attitudes, and opinions into numbers and percentages. The data are gathered from structured questionnaires and a large sample to ensure accuracy and reliability. The interpretation of results is based on the numbers compiled, not on the judgment of the researcher. For this reason, it is a tool that is used for measuring and evaluating rather than investigating and exploring.

Quantitative research will statistically confirm the attitudes and feelings that arose in qualitative research, enabling a marketer to have more confidence in the decisions that are made based on the research. A brief comparison of qualitative and quantitative research is provided in **Figure 3.9**.

In today's marketplace, the respective roles of qualitative and quantitative research are changing. Companies tend to do more qualitative research, as it yields information quickly and cheaply. But for complex marketing decisions involving significant sums of money (say a multimillion-dollar new product launch or advertising campaign) the value of quantitative research should not be downplayed. Reliable information helps eliminate some of the risk when making decisions. Quantitative data is the marketing manager's insurance policy.

personal interviews
Face-to-face communication with groups or individuals, usually done through quantitative questionnaires.

Survey Methodology   There are four primary means of contacting consumers when conducting surveys to collect quantitative data: personal interview, telephone interview, mail interview, and online interview. **Personal interviews** involve face-to-face communication with groups (e.g., focus groups) or with individuals and are usually done through quantitative questionnaires. Popular locations for interviews are shopping malls and homes of respondents. Trained interviewers provide guidance and explain difficult questions to respondents if necessary.

telephone interviews
Communication with individuals via the telephone, usually conducted from central locations.

Telephone interviews involve communication with individuals via the telephone. Usually, the interviews are conducted from a central location where there is supervised control over the interview process. Generally speaking, telephone interviews yield higher response rates than the other data collection methods.

Market researchers are finding it increasingly difficult to locate Canadians who are willing and available to take part in telephone surveys. A recent survey by the Marketing Research and Intelligence Association (MIRA) concluded that high refusal rates are the result of deceptive telemarketing practices by unscrupulous direct sellers and fundraisers. "These fraudulent marketers use the survey research industry's good reputation to sell goods or services or to solicit money under the guise of legitimate marketing research." MIRA refers to this fraudulent practice as **mugging**—marketing under the guise of interviewing.[12]

Mail interviews are a silent process of collecting information. Using the mail to distribute a survey means that a highly dispersed sample is reached in a cost-efficient manner. In a mail interview there is no interviewer present, so there is a tendency for respondents to provide more honest answers. The main drawbacks are the lack of control and the amount of time required to implement and retrieve the surveys. As a result, response rates tend to be lower.

Online surveys allow an organization to be much less invasive in collecting information. Some companies have actually found that consumers seem more willing to divulge information over the Internet compared with the more traditional means of surveying. As well, it takes less time and money to get results.

Online research is proving effective in terms of testing new product concepts, uncovering consumer attitudes about products, and getting feedback on new advertising ideas. Coca-Cola used online concept testing to determine what new flavours to add to the Fruitopia single-serving product line. A **concept test** determines what new-product ideas are worth pursuing before a significant investment is made in product development. In the Fruitopia test, more than 3000 respondents took part online. When the new flavours were launched, overall Fruitopia sales increased by 30 percent.[13]

The use of online surveys is growing. Online research now accounts for about 20 percent of research-industry revenue. Marketers are concerned about time, and traditional research methods take a great deal of time relative to online methods. With online research a manager can quickly access and analyze information. On the downside, recruiting participation can be a lot like fishing—participation is left up to the fish. Therefore, the validity of the information is questionable. The information collected may not truly represent the feelings of the target market the company is trying to reach.

A fraud factor exists with online research and it can have an impact on how the results of any particular survey are analyzed. One study by ComScore found that 0.25 percent of respondents account for 30 percent of online surveys and 20 percent account for 80 percent of surveys—extraordinary figures! Some survey cheaters have developed software bots to automate the process of filling in surveys.[14] The research industry is developing its own software to detect fraud and eliminate fraudulent respondents (that is, the computers that are associated with those filling in the surveys). While this helps, no software can detect if someone representing themselves as a 35-year-old mother is really an 18-year-old male.

The decision about which of these survey techniques to use is based on three primary factors:

1. *Nature of Information Sought*— The amount of information to be collected and the time it will take to complete the survey are considerations. For example, if discussion or explanations are necessary to get the answers needed, personal or telephone interviews may be best. If large amounts of information are required, the best option may be the mail.
2. *Cost and Time*— When time is critical, certain options are eliminated. The telephone and the Internet are the best means of obtaining quick, cost-efficient information. Costs must also be weighed against benefits. The net financial gains expected to result from the research may determine which method is to be used.
3. *Respondent*— The selection of a survey method can be influenced by the location of the respondents and how easily they can be reached. For example, if the participant is to be reached at home, any method—personal interview, telephone, mail, or online—can be used. Responding online is very convenient for people. In contrast, if the participant has to be reached in a central location, such as a shopping mall, a personal interview is the only choice.

Refer to **Figure 3.10** for a summary of the advantages and disadvantages of each survey method.

mugging Fraudulent marketing under the guise of interviewing, in which sellers pretend to be conducting a marketing research interview.

mail interviews A silent process of collecting information; reaches a highly dispersed sample in a cost-efficient manner.

online surveys Surveys conducted via the Internet.

concept test The presentation of a product idea in some visual form, with a description of the basic product characteristics and benefits, in order to get customers' reactions to it.

PERSONAL INTERVIEW

Advantages	Disadvantages
• Higher rates of participation • Visual observations possible by interviewer • Flexibility (e.g., inclusion of visuals possible) • Large amounts of data collected	• Higher cost (time needed) • Reluctance to respond to certain questions • Interviewer bias is possible

TELEPHONE INTERVIEW

Advantages	Disadvantages
• Convenience and control • Costs less • Timely responses • Geographic flexibility	• Lack of observation • Short questions and questionnaire • Can be viewed as an invasion of privacy

MAIL SURVEYS

Advantages	Disadvantages
• Geographic flexibility in selecting target • Cost-efficient • Large sample obtainable • Respondent in relaxed environment • Impersonality results in more accurate responses	• Lack of control • The time between distribution and return is long • Potential for misinterpretation by respondent • Low response rates

ONLINE RESEARCH

Advantages	Disadvantages
• Efficient and inexpensive reach (elimination of telephone and humans) • Less intrusive than traditional methods • Convenient for respondent • Fast turnaround of information (2–3 days versus 4–5 weeks)	• Respondent voluntarily participates, so respondent authenticity is questioned • Limited sample frame (Internet users only) • Research via bulk email associated with spam (Internet junk mail) • Reliability of information is questionable

Figure 3.10 Survey Methodology for Collecting Quantitative Data

---

Data Transfer and Processing

editing In marketing research, a stage when completed questionnaires are reviewed for consistency and completeness.

data transfer A process whereby data from a marketing research questionnaire is transferred to a computer.

tabulation Counting the various responses for each question and arriving at a frequency distribution.

frequency distribution In a survey, the number of times each answer was chosen for a question.

cross-tabulation Comparison and contrast of the answers of various subgroups or of particular subgroups and the total response group.

Once the data have been collected, editing, data transfer, and tabulation take place. In the former age of paper and clipboards, transferring information was more complicated than it is now in the age of pocket computers and other electronic devices. Regardless of how the information is collected, certain steps must occur to ensure the accuracy of the information.

In the **editing** stage, completed questionnaires are reviewed for consistency and completeness. Whether to include questionnaires with incomplete or seemingly contradictory answers is left to the discretion of the researcher. In the **data transfer** stage, answers to questions (for example, from a paper-based personal interview) are transferred to a computer. Most questions are closed ended (require fixed-response answers), and all answers are pre-coded to facilitate the transfer. In the case of telephone surveys or online surveys, the data is collected electronically, essentially eliminating the data transfer stage.

Tabulation is the process of counting the various responses for each question and arriving at a frequency distribution. A **frequency distribution** shows the number of times each answer was chosen for a given question. Numerous cross-tabulations are also made. **Cross-tabulation** is the comparison and contrasting of the answers of various subgroups, or of particular subgroups and the total response group. For example, a question dealing with brand awareness could be analyzed by the age, gender, or income of respondents.

Data Analysis and Interpretation

Data analysis refers to the evaluation of responses on a question-by-question basis, a process that gives meaning to the data. At this point, the statistical data for each question are reviewed, and the researcher makes observations about them. Typically, a researcher makes comparisons between responses of subgroups on a percentage or ratio basis.

data analysis The evaluation, in market research, of responses on a question-by-question basis, a process that gives meaning to the data.

    Data interpretation, on the other hand, involves relating the accumulated data to the problem under review and to the objectives and hypotheses of the research study. The process of interpretation uncovers solutions to the problem. The researcher draws conclusions that state the data's implications for managers. For example, Nestlé Canada conducted extensive consumer research before it introduced new flavours of its Coffee Crisp brand. The research was designed to learn how chocolate and snacks fit into consumers' lives. As former brand manager Mark Wilson jokingly acknowledges, "We found out—surprise, surprise—that Coffee Crisp is about the taste of coffee, not a dark rich taste but a light, fun taste." The research determined that Coffee Crisp owns the coffee position. It is a unique attribute that creates equity for the brand. The research was the impetus for launching two new flavours: Triple Mocha and French Vanilla.[15]

data interpretation Relating accumulated data to the problem under review and to the objectives and hypotheses of the research study.

Recommendations and Implementation

The recommendations identify courses of action the organization should take in view of the data collected. Once a research project is complete, the research company will present its findings in a written report. Frequently, a verbal presentation of the key findings is made to the client. Very often senior management is informed as the data become known, so that the managers are better prepared for possible actions or changes in strategic direction. Preparing senior managers in this way is important, particularly if the proposed actions are in conflict with their personal views and feelings. The managers most likely to implement research findings are those who participate in research design, have the flexibility to make decisions, and see research findings that confirm their intentions.

    In the age of advanced technology market research is more streamlined, with clients expecting solid decision-making results—yesterday. Voluminous research reports often referred to as "doorstoppers" have been replaced with PowerPoint presentations that display the objectives, analysis, and recommendations in an easy-to-digest format.

MANAGING INFORMATION AND CUSTOMER RELATIONSHIP MANAGEMENT

L05 Describe the role and impact of information collection on customer relationship marketing strategies.

This section of the chapter focuses on how an organization manages all the information it collects. As stated earlier in the textbook, it is far more costly to attract a new customer than to secure additional revenue from a current customer. Therefore, wise organizations have integrated software technologies that facilitate the collection and management of customer information. The objective of a customer relationship management program is to devise efficient marketing strategies that will attract customers, retain customers, and extend the value of customers over the lifetime of the relationship.

    The scope of a good customer relationship management program can be very broad. For example, at an operational level it supports anyone who comes in direct contact with customers. Any time there is interaction with the customer the details are added to the customer's history. Others in the organization will have access to that history. The technology also provides a means to communicate directly with customers. For example,

cross-selling Customer campaign that includes selling related products and services.

up-selling Customer campaign that includes selling more expensive products and services.

data mining The analysis of information so that relationships are established between pieces of information, and more effective marketing strategies can be identified and implemented.

a company may utilize the Internet, automated emails, and automated telephone calls. Companies generally have to be careful how they communicate using technology, as many customers do not appreciate automated (self-serve style) forms of communications—they prefer the human touch!

The heart of a good customer relationship management (CRM) program lies in the analysis of the data, so sophisticated analysis software is required. With proper analysis the true benefits of CRM materialize. For example, an organization should be able to design and execute highly targeted marketing campaigns, design and execute specific customer campaigns that include **cross-selling** (selling related products and services) and **up-selling** (selling more expensive products and services) that are in the best interests of the customer, and analyze customer behaviour to assist with product and service decisions for each customer. A visual illustration of a customer relationship management model appears in **Figure 3.11**.

Essentially, customer relationship management is the means by which an organization develops more effective and efficient marketing programs. And, like marketing, to be effective it must be a key element of an organization's overall philosophy and part of an organization's policies and processes. All employees have an impact on how a customer perceives an organization so they must participate in customer relationship management.

For additional insight into how information technology is used to a company's advantage, read the Think Marketing box **Retailers Track Every Move You Make**.

The Database and Data Mining

The electronic era has resulted in an information explosion that allows for the storage and transfer of great amounts of business data in a short time. What has emerged is **data mining**. In a marketing context, data mining is used to establish relationships between pieces of information so that more effective marketing strategies can be identified and implemented. Rather than looking at an entire data set, data mining techniques attempt to locate informational patterns and nuggets within that database.[16]

The goal of data mining is to lower marketing costs and increase efficiency by identifying prospects most likely to buy, or buy in large volume; the availability of CRM software programs provides this opportunity.

Walmart is a company adept at data mining. Don't be fooled by the folksy greeters; Walmart controls one of the largest data collection systems in the world, capable of tracking sales on a minute-by-minute basis. It can also quickly detect regional and local market trends. Such knowledge allows Walmart to customize each store's offerings while keeping suppliers abreast of how well their products are selling.

Shoppers Drug Mart has amassed information about its customer demographics and shopping patterns, so it can pinpoint what people are likely to buy. Through its Optimum Rewards card, Shoppers has one of the largest databases in the country (10 million members and counting), and it provides a means to communicate offers directly to loyal customers. In fact,

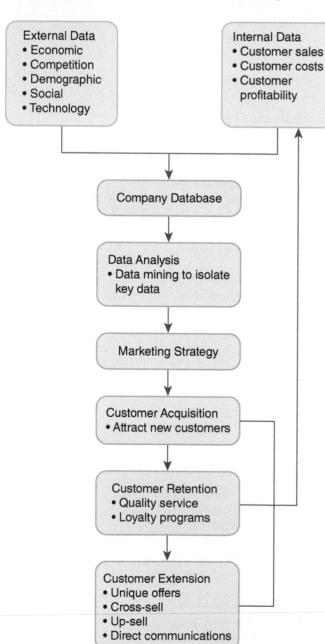

Figure 3.11 Customer Relationship Management Model

ThinkMarketing

Retailers Track Every Move You Make

So, just what do retailers know about you? It boils down to what you buy, how much you spend, and how often you visit. When information like that accumulates in a database, a retailer can develop an individualized customer profile for everyone in its database. Further, if the retailer has the means to communicate with you (email is very popular) it can send you offers of interest based on your profile.

Every large retailer in Canada is doing some form of information collection, and they are mining the data to find ways to get customers to buy more products in the future. Data mining is about predicting what you *will* buy based on what you *do* buy. In data management terms, it's called customer DNA.

Determining a customer's DNA can create a picture that is as sophisticated as it needs to be. For example, purchase preferences and purchase patterns can indicate that someone is an adventurous traveller, a photography enthusiast, or an avid recreational runner. The goal of data mining is to determine what is relevant to individual customers. Once that's known, the marketing to a customer can begin.

Canadian Tire uses data to plan what products to carry and where to carry them, and to determine the best merchandising and display strategies to sell more goods. If it finds that two products are purchased together, the company may decide to merchandise them together on the shelf or in a separate display. A key source of information is the loyalty program originally based on Canadian Tire money. That program is now in full electronic mode with all purchases recorded at the checkout when you pay by Canadian Tire MasterCard. Canadian Tire can also combine automotive service information with in-store purchase information to further develop a customer profile.

Robert Hoetink/Shutterstock

Customers do see the benefit of information collection while expressing some concerns about privacy. But a recent research study revealed that 62 percent of Canadians are not offended and are neutral to retailers analyzing their shopping and purchase behaviour, and 26 percent are willing to share more personal information in return for preferential treatment or special offers.

In a hypercompetitive retail marketplace, retailers are constantly looking for anything that will give them an edge on their rivals. The retailer that collects and mines data effectively and offers its customers a good value proposition, by means of incentives or simply by presenting customers with new products and services that are meaningful to them, stands to gain the most.

Question:

Is collecting information in the manner described here a good way of doing business? Should consumers be concerned about this practice? What is your opinion on this issue?

Adapted from Dave McGinn, "Retail of the tape: How stores keep track of your shopping DNA," The Globe and Mail, December 23, 2013, pp. A1, 14.

database management has led Shoppers to place less emphasis on mass-distributed flyers and television advertising and more emphasis on direct mail and email campaigns. The Optimum program has been successful: cardholders spend 60 percent more on their purchases than non-members and two-thirds of front-of-store sales (non-prescription items) come from card holders.[17] Such results verify the impact a good database management system can have on sales.

To get maximum benefit from a database management system, it must be relatively easy for a manager to use. In that respect, the systems that exist today tend to be interactive, flexible, discovery-oriented, and easy to learn and use. A good system not only allows managers to ask *what if* questions but also enables them to manipulate the data to give them the information they need. It is a useful tool for sales forecasting,

Simulation: Market Research

planning marketing campaigns, and financial analysis. Database technology and customer relationship management programs can be integrated into an organization of any size.

INFORMATION COLLECTION AND CONSUMER PRIVACY

LO6 Identify key issues associated with the collection and use of information about consumers.

An ongoing and rather hot issue in marketing revolves around the collection of information about consumers and how it is being used. It may be information collected electronically at a retailer's checkout or information collected about your online behaviour when using the Internet.

The key concern is: what do marketers know about people and how do they use this information? Consumers must recognize (many do) that, when online, every activity is tracked and logged and has potential value for marketers. For many people this is a frightening thought, and it should be, if the information is not used for legitimate purposes. The manner in which retailers collect information was discussed in the Think Marketing box **Retailers Track Every Move You Make**.

In marketing today, data is king and marketers are good at collecting and interpreting data. Marketers have always done this, but in the age of technology the data is available in a fast and furious manner. The collection of online data provides marketers with an opportunity to devise unique advertising messages based on personal interests (as expressed by online surfing behaviour) that can be delivered directly to the individual's computer or mobile device. Similarly, retailers can develop an individual customer profile and deliver offers of interest to that individual. It is an efficient way to market.

So what do consumers fear? One recent survey found that 64 percent of respondents found the idea of targeted advertising invasive, with 40 percent saying they would change their online behaviour if advertisers were collecting data. A survey by the Public Interest Advocacy Centre found that 75 percent of respondents were either "not very comfortable" or "not comfortable at all" with tracking-based advertising. In the social media world 70 percent of Facebook users and 52 percent of Google users are "somewhat" or "very concerned" about their privacy.[18]

There are regulations in place to ensure consumers are aware of their rights with regard to how information is used. Various opt-in and opt-out clauses are found in agreements people sign when dealing with online organizations, but there is a fear that marketers disregard the regulations. Privacy law does exist in Canada through the *Personal Information Protection and Electronic Documents Act* (PIPEDA). The Act does not offer rules but does offer a list of guiding principles for businesses to follow. For example, an organization must obtain consent for the use or disclosure at the time of collection, and purposes for the collection of information must be limited, well defined, and stated in a clear and understandable manner. The degree to which organizations abide by these principles fuels the ongoing debate with consumers.

✔ ExperienceMarketing

To experience marketing you have to assess situations and make recommendations on what actions need to be taken to solve a problem or pursue an opportunity. What would you do in the following situation?

You are the marketing manager for Degree deodorants (women's line) in Canada. Degree offers four different products: Degree Dry Protection, Degree Clinical, Degree Motion Sense, and Degree Ultra Clear. You can visit the degreedeodorant.ca website for more insight into these products.

You have been asked to evaluate the opportunity to launch a new line of Degree body washes for women in Canada. Body washes tend to be more popular with male users. Degree is a strong brand name so the company believes it can be expanded into other women's product categories.

Your challenge is to develop a fundamental marketing research proposal that will uncover information to shed light on the decision to proceed or not proceed with the product. What information do you need and how will you get it? To assist with the development of your proposal you should respond to the following questions:

1. Will qualitative or quantitative research be necessary?
2. If quantitative research is necessary, what will the sample design be?
3. What data collection techniques should be used to collect the information?

CHAPTER SUMMARY

LO1 Define marketing research and identify the ways in which marketing research findings can be used. *(pp. 55–56)*

Marketing research is a function that links consumer, customer, and public to the marketer through information. Information is used to define marketing opportunities and problems; generate, refine, and evaluate marketing actions; monitor marketing performance; and improve understanding of the marketing process.

Marketing research can be divided into two key areas: the collection of information and the management of information. Information is collected and managed to make better marketing decisions. The collection of information usually falls into three key categories: market analysis, product analysis, and consumer analysis. Once the information is collected it is stored and managed from a database. Marketers access and manipulate information from a computer-based decision support system (DSS), which allows them to make better decisions and to develop marketing strategies.

LO2 Outline the basic stages in the marketing research process. *(pp. 56–58)*

The marketing research process involves five distinct stages: problem awareness (clearly identifying a topic to research), exploratory research (investigating areas of concern to eliminate factors contributing to the problem), primary research (developing a process for collecting first-hand information to resolve a problem), data analysis (giving meaning to the data collected in relation to the problem being researched), and formulating recommendations based on how the data is interpreted (altering marketing strategies accordingly).

LO3 Describe secondary data sources available to marketing organizations. *(pp. 59–62)*

Secondary data are data compiled by another source which can be used to help resolve a marketing problem. Secondary data is available from internal sources (any information available in an organization's database) and external sources (data available from research surveys conducted by other organizations such as Nielsen Canada and Environics Analytics, Statistics Canada, provincial and local government bodies, and online databases).

LO4 Explain the steps and methodologies for collecting primary data. *(pp. 62–71)*

The initial phase, primary research, involves clearly stating the problem and establishing research objectives and hypotheses. Primary research involves gathering new data from a representative sample. Researchers must define the population to obtain data from, identify a means of reaching the population, determine the size of the sample (how many people to include), and choose the type of sample (both probability and non-probability techniques are options).

Primary data are collected from surveys, observation, and experiments. Survey data are qualitative or quantitative in nature. Qualitative data are collected by focus group interviews or by one-on-one interviews, to answer the question *why?* Quantitative data are obtained by questionnaires through personal and telephone interviews, and mail or online surveys, and involve translating thoughts and feelings into measurable numbers. Once the data are secured, they are entered into a computer for analysis and interpretation by the researcher.

The research process is complete when the marketing research company presents its findings to the client. Clear recommendations that resolve the problem are included in the report and the presentation to the client.

LO5 Describe the role and impact of information collection on customer relationship management practices. *(pp. 71–74)*

Customer relationship management and database management technologies are tools that offer meaningful insights into the needs and preferences of customers. A database is the nucleus of the marketing organization's management information system. This system ensures the continuous and orderly flow of information to the decision makers, who use the information to make better choices and to develop more effective marketing strategies. Simply understanding customers better provides valuable input for developing unique and individualized marketing programs.

LO6 Identify key issues associated with the collection and use of information about consumers. *(p. 74)*

What marketers do with the information they collect is a controversial topic. The key concern is what marketers know about people and how marketers use this information. People, generally, are concerned for their privacy. Various research studies reveal that consumers are uncomfortable with targeted advertising—they say they would change their behaviour if they knew so much information were being collected about them. There are regulations in place to protect consumers, and most business organizations have opt-in and opt-out clauses in any agreements they have with consumers. Privacy laws do exist in Canada (the *Personal Protection and Electronic Documents Act* or PIPEDA) that marketers should abide by. The degree to which organizations adhere to these principles remains an issue with consumers.

MyMarketingLab   Study, practise, and explore real marketing situations with these helpful resources:
- **Interactive Lesson Presentations:** Work through interactive presentations and assessments to test your knowledge of marketing concepts.
- **Study Plan:** Check your understanding of chapter concepts with self-study quizzes.
- **Dynamic Study Modules:** Work through adaptive study modules on your computer, tablet, or mobile device.
- **Simulations:** Practise decision-making in simulated marketing environments.

REVIEW QUESTIONS

1. Briefly define the term *marketing research* and describe its primary role in marketing. (*LO1*)
2. What is a decision support system (DSS)? (*LO1*)
3. What are the key steps in the marketing research process? Briefly explain each step. (*LO2*)
4. What is exploratory research? Briefly explain. (*LO2*)
5. What is secondary data, and by what means does an organization collect it? (*LO3*)
6. What are the basic steps for conducting a primary research study? Briefly explain each step. (*LO4*)
7. What are the basic steps for developing a representative sample in a research study? Briefly explain each step. (*LO4*)
8. What are the three basic methods for collecting primary research data? Briefly explain each step. (*LO4*)
9. What is the difference between qualitative data and quantitative data? Briefly explain. (*LO4*)
10. What is a focus group? (*LO4*)
11. What are the four primary methods for collecting quantitative data? Briefly explain each method. (*LO4*)
12. What is the difference between data analysis and data interpretation? Briefly explain. (*LO4*)
13. What are the primary objectives of a customer relationship management program? (*LO5*)
14. What is data mining? Briefly explain. (*LO5*)
15. What are the key issues raised by consumers about how marketers collect and use information about them? (*LO6*)

DISCUSSION AND APPLICATION QUESTIONS

1. "Decisions based on qualitative data are not risky." Discuss this statement by examining the nature of information collected by qualitative research.
2. Many experts doubt the reliability and validity of online research surveys, but many marketing organizations see online research as a quick and convenient means of securing information from customers. Conduct some secondary research on the usefulness of online surveys and form a position on the issue. Will online surveys continue to grow in importance?
3. Many experts believe online research will replace the need for focus groups as well as methods for collecting quantitative information. Conduct some secondary research on this issue and formulate a position on this trend. Are the experts right in their assessment?

4 Consumer Buying Behaviour

Agence Quebec Presse -Pierre Roussel/Newscom

LEARNING OBJECTIVES

LO1 Explain why it is important for marketing managers to understand consumer behaviour. (pp. 78–79)

LO2 Describe the steps a consumer goes through when buying a product or service. (pp. 79–83)

LO3 Discuss the main psychological and personal influences on consumer buying behaviour. (pp. 83–90)

LO4 Describe the key social and cultural influences on consumer buying behaviour. (pp. 90–96)

THE U.S. RETAIL GIANT...

Target Corporation, has been busy opening its first Canadian stores—a total of 124 locations in all 10 provinces as of January 2014. Given that nine of these new stores are in Quebec, Target may want to consider a study just released on the very distinct consumer attitudes of *la belle province*.

Research by Headspace Marketing Inc. surveyed 3000 people to identify consumer sentiment in Quebec versus the rest of Canada. It found that brand loyalty—and an intense resistance to switching brands—is far more pronounced in Quebec than anywhere else. Quebecers are also far less welcoming of things that are considered foreign, making it a particularly tricky market for companies expanding there from elsewhere.

Target seems well aware of the challenges, though. "We recognize that Canada is made up of a variety of culturally diverse markets and we look forward to engaging with these great communities," said Tony Fisher, former president of Target Canada. "Our goal is to offer a brand that's true to both Target and the uniqueness of Canada."

Currently, Target's own research shows that brand awareness is 92 percent in Canada, versus the high 70s in Quebec. According to Livia Zufferli, vice president, marketing, "We spent a lot of time ensuring that we are entering Quebec in a way that is appropriate and genuine for that market. It's taken a lot of research, a lot of team members, and a lot of new organizational structures designed to support this new multi-language capacity that we have."

As Target begins to win over brand-loyal Quebecers, it may also want to focus on how it speaks to Quebec. Research shows that "taking measures to simplify my life" is rated far higher by francophone Quebec consumers than by anglophones in the rest of Canada. "If Target is looking to push their private labels, then they'll need to help consumers in Quebec understand very simply and quickly what value they offer," says Headspace President, Éric Blais. "There's a tendency in marketing to identify all these value propositions and tell the whole story. Quebecers won't pay attention. They won't dig deep. They won't give you much time. Don't tell your whole story; make it super simple."[1 & 2]

Understanding consumer behaviour is essential for developing the right marketing strategy. Canada is a big country geographically, and there are significant cultural differences across regions. For Target the rewards are greater than the costs when it comes to developing customized marketing strategies for the unique needs and preferences of the Quebec market. That's what this chapter is about: understanding consumers and creating appropriate marketing strategies that will influence a target audience!

The behaviour of Canadian consumers evolves over time. The expression "the only constant in life is change" holds true here. It is this change that marketing organizations must recognize and act on. Organizations must anticipate changes among consumers and develop marketing strategies to meet the challenges of a dynamic marketplace. To keep abreast of change, an organization will implement many of the research procedures that were discussed in the previous chapter.

Marketers must also keep close watch on the various external forces that were presented in Chapter 2, because they also have an impact on the marketplace. Trends such as the aging population, different family formations, the growth of ethnic households, and advancing technologies have an effect on consumer behaviour and will shape marketing decisions.

Simulation: Understanding
Consumer Behaviour

consumer behaviour The acts of individuals in obtaining goods and services, including the decision processes that precede and determine these acts.

UNDERSTANDING CONSUMER BEHAVIOUR

L01 Explain why it is important for marketing managers to understand consumer behaviour.

Consumer behaviour is defined as "the acts of individuals in obtaining goods and services, including the decision processes that precede and determine these acts."[3] An organization must have a firm understanding of how and why consumers make purchase decisions so that appropriate marketing strategies are planned and implemented.

To quickly understand how companies react to changes in consumer behaviour, consider a voluntary pledge made by 16 of the biggest food and beverage firms, from Coca-Cola Co. to Kraft Foods, to remove 1.5 trillion calories from their products by 2015. The companies said they would substitute lower-calorie products, re-engineer existing products to cut their calories, and reduce portion size, such as with the popular 100-calorie packs of cookies and other snacks. They are also shifting advertising to lower-calorie options. These initiatives are in response to society's desire for lower-calorie food options and concern about childhood obesity.[4]

From a purely competitive viewpoint, marketers must have access to information on consumer buying motivation in order to develop persuasive strategies— they have to know "what buttons to press." Consequently, large sums of money are allocated to marketing research to determine who makes the buying decision and what factors play a role in making the decision. Refer to the illustration in **Figure 4.1**.

Before examining the different factors that influence buying decisions, we will first look at the steps consumers go through when buying products and services.

© Mediablitzimages / Alamy

Figure 4.1   Consumers, concerned about high obesity rates, are demanding lower-calorie food choices. Companies are continually adapting to changes in buying behaviour.

CONSUMER PURCHASE DECISION PROCESS

L02 Describe the steps a consumer goes through when buying a product or service.

Knowing exactly how purchase decisions are made is difficult. While we know that certain variables influence behaviour, there are so many contributing variables that we cannot be certain which ones actually trigger a response. The purchase of a particular brand or product could be the result of an endorsement by a celebrity or a friend (as in the case of word-of-mouth endorsements that circulate in social media networks), it could be based on past experience with the product, or it could be due to the delivery of a free sample or an in-store encounter. Every purchase situation is unique.

When making a buying decision, consumers process a lot of information from the media, family, friends, and their own personal experiences. A recent marketing research study among adults revealed that past contact with a brand is the most important factor in a purchase decision (83 percent response rate). Other factors that are important, but with lower response rates, include quality comparisons with other brands, price, recommendations from others, manufacturer's reputation, and how well known and well advertised a product is.[5] This list reinforces the idea that a product must live up to the promise made in any form of marketing communication.

There are five steps in the consumer purchase decision process (see **Figure 4.2**). Whether or not a consumer follows all steps depends on the nature of the purchase. *Routine* purchases such as toothpaste, coffee, razor blades, and deodorant are usually based on product satisfaction—there is no need to follow a prescribed buying procedure.

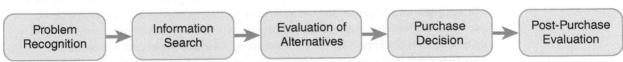

Figure 4.2   The Consumer Purchase Decision Process

In contrast, *complex* purchase decisions such as an automobile, laptop computer, smartphone, or major household appliance require a lot of time, effort, money, and a proper evaluation of alternatives. In this case, it is likely that all steps in the buying process are followed.

Let us examine each step in the decision-making process in detail.

Problem Recognition

problem recognition In the consumer buying process, a stage in which a consumer discovers a need or an unfulfilled desire.

The process begins with **problem recognition**. At this stage, a consumer discovers a need or an unfulfilled desire: for example, the engine of a 10-year-old automobile finally gives out, or a child outgrows a bicycle. In both cases there is a need to replace the product. A person could also simply decide she wants something, such as an ultra-high-definition television or a new smartphone. The problem, however, is which brand to buy?

Information Search

information search Conducted by an individual once a problem or need has been defined.

Once the problem or need has been defined, the individual conducts an **information search** to solve the problem. The extent of the search varies with the nature of the purchase. If it is a routine purchase, no information may be sought. If it is a complex decision, numerous sources of information may be investigated. Generally, as the price and associated risks of the purchase increase, the extent of the search for information also increases.

Sources of information may be internal or external. For example, personal experiences with a product may be sufficient to make a new decision. A person will spend little time on the decision to replace a tube of toothpaste or bottle of mouthwash. However, the ultra-high-definition television or smartphone problem requires information and an evaluation of alternatives.

Very likely, numerous external sources would be consulted. As mentioned, some of those may include personal contacts (e.g., relatives and friends), public resources (e.g., ratings organizations such as Consumer Reports), blogs (that critique products and services), and commercial sources (e.g., the marketing activities of companies, including their websites and Facebook brand pages, where an abundance of information is available).

Today's consumers use the Internet to search for information about products they may purchase. Statistics Canada reports that over 83 percent of adults rely on the Internet for personal reasons, and 77 percent of adult Internet users search for information about products and services before making buying decisions.[6]

Social media are becoming more important as consumers search for product information. One study concluded that 66 percent of online users rely on social media to learn about products and services, and 33 percent follow companies or brands on social networking sites such as Facebook, Twitter, and Pinterest. Further, consumers are increasingly looking to their smartphones (43 percent) and tablets (16 percent) to access social media. Time spent on mobile apps and mobile websites increased by over 63 percent from 2012 to 2013.[7 & 8] These data suggest marketers maintain a strong online presence through their own websites and on social media networks such as Facebook. Adapting content for mobile devices should also be a top priority for marketers.

The importance of the purchase plays a key role in the time and effort a consumer will spend searching the marketplace for information. For example, a young married couple in the midst of decorating their first home (their first big purchase) have all kinds of decisions to make about furnishings. Do they buy traditional-looking white appliances or do they opt for something more contemporary and expensive, such as stainless steel? The couple's lifestyle and how much they are willing to pay for that lifestyle will influence the decision. Regardless, the couple will seek information on brands they may purchase. Refer to **Figure 4.3** for an illustration of the different types of consumer purchase decisions.

With information in hand, the consumer will move to the next stage.

Consumer

Low ← **Involvement** → High

Factors That Influence a Purchase Decision	Routine Decision	Limited Decision	Complex Decision
Time needed to make purchase decision	Minimal	Moderate	Extensive
Number of alternatives evaluated	Minimal	Several	Many
Brand preferences	Existing familiar product	Open to new products	Very open to new product information
Purchase frequency	Frequent	Occasional	Infrequent
Risk	Low	Medium	High
Experience with product/product category	A lot	Some	Very little

Figure 4.3
The Consumer Purchase Decision Continuum

Evaluation of Alternatives

Let us use the example of buying a new automobile. At this stage, a consumer will establish some kind of criteria against which the attributes of the vehicle will be evaluated. The evaluation criteria may include how economical the car is to run, the look and style of the car, customer satisfaction ratings for reliability, the warranty, and the price (there could be many more criteria). For a marketer, this is a crucial stage, since the quality of a marketing strategy is being tested. Will the advertising deliver the right message? Will the message be convincing and actually motivate an individual to act on it?

To illustrate the concept of evaluation, we'll assume that a young couple is contemplating the purchase of an economical, entry-level vehicle. With such a car, they have established certain criteria: it must get good gas mileage; be comfortable to sit in, even though it will probably be small; and it must look somewhat sporty. The criteria determines the makes of cars that will be in the consumer's **evoked set**. The evoked set is a group of brands that a person would consider acceptable among competing brands in a class of products. In this case, the evoked set may include a selection of compact cars such as the Honda Civic, Mazda2, Toyota Yaris, Ford Focus, and Chevrolet Cruze. All these cars are priced somewhere between $15 000 and $25 000. The couple would evaluate each car against the criteria described.

evoked set A group of brands that a person would consider acceptable among competing brands in a class of product.

Purchase Decision

Once the best alternative has been selected, a consumer is ready to make the purchase decision. In the case of the car purchase, the young couple will visit a few dealers and more than likely test drive the models that are under consideration.

In addition to buying a specific make and model, the couple will go through another decision-making process, as they must decide who to buy the car from and when to buy it. These decisions will be based on such factors as price, convenience, availability of credit, the level and quality of service, and dealer reputation. The couple could also decide to buy the car online, avoiding the perceived hassle of negotiating with a dealer.

The simultaneous evaluation of the car and the dealer influences the final decision. For example, the couple may forgo their first choice—say, the Honda Civic—to take advantage of an extended warranty, better service, or incentive package offered by the Mazda dealer or from the manufacturer. Incentives are now a very common technique in this industry to attract prospective buyers.

Post-Purchase Evaluation

Purchases involve risk, and the higher the cost of the purchase, the greater the risk for the consumer. Once the decision to purchase has been made, the delivery order signed, and the bank loan secured, certain common questions arise. Did I make the right decision? Do I feel good, bad, or indifferent about the purchase?

The purchase of routine items is based on past experience and satisfaction; therefore, there is a positive, secure feeling after the purchase that says, "I trust this product." Conversely, other purchases may result in dissatisfaction leading to brand switching, a process involving more purchases and evaluations. Such dissatisfaction is the result of **cognitive dissonance**, which is defined as the unsettled state of mind experienced by an individual after he or she has taken action. Its presence suggests that the consumer is not confident that he or she has made the right decision. The consumer can overcome cognitive dissonance by taking certain actions. In the example of the automobile purchase, the couple could reread favourable consumer reports, get out the brochures again and review all the positive attributes, or perhaps talk to a friend about the purchase.

From a marketing perspective, the organization should initiate appropriate follow-up activities to put the consumer's mind at ease. In the automobile purchase decision, simply keeping in touch through service reminder notices may be all that is required. Progressive companies understand the importance of satisfaction and realize that the sale is simply the first step in what they hope will be a long-term relationship.

cognitive dissonance An individual's unsettled state of mind after an action he or she has taken.

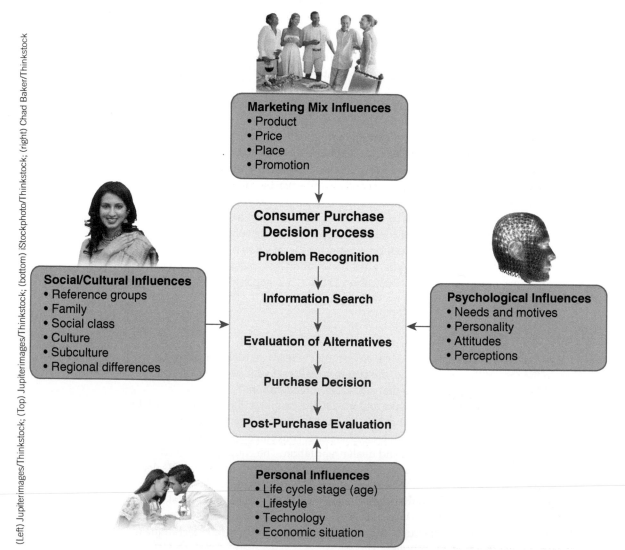

(Left) Jupiterimages/Thinkstock; (Top) Jupiterimages/Thinkstock; (bottom) iStockphoto/Thinkstock; (right) Chad Baker/Thinkstock

Marketing Mix Influences
• Product
• Price
• Place
• Promotion

Consumer Purchase Decision Process

Problem Recognition

Information Search

Evaluation of Alternatives

Purchase Decision

Post-Purchase Evaluation

Social/Cultural Influences
• Reference groups
• Family
• Social class
• Culture
• Subculture
• Regional differences

Psychological Influences
• Needs and motives
• Personality
• Attitudes
• Perceptions

Personal Influences
• Life cycle stage (age)
• Lifestyle
• Technology
• Economic situation

Figure 4.4 Influences on the Consumer Purchase Decision Process

Influences on Consumer Behaviour

The purchase decisions of Canadian consumers are primarily influenced by psychological, personal, social, and cultural factors. Collectively, these variables represent a dynamic consumer situation that has a dramatic influence on if, how, and when consumers will buy. Understanding the customer is essential if an organization is to maximize the effectiveness of the marketing strategies it develops and implements. Decisions about product, price, availability, and marketing communications are designed to positively influence consumers. Refer to **Figure 4.4** for a summary of influences on consumer behaviour.

PSYCHOLOGICAL AND PERSONAL INFLUENCES

LO3 Discuss the main psychological and personal influences on consumer buying behaviour.

Psychological Influences

Needs and Motives Let's clearly distinguish between needs and motives. The term **need** suggests a state of deprivation or the absence of something useful, whereas **motives** are the conditions that prompt the action necessary to satisfy a need (the action stimulated by marketing activities). The relationship between needs and motives is direct in terms of marketing activities. Needs are developed or brought to the foreground of consumers' minds when products' benefits are presented to them in an interesting way (e.g., in conjunction with a lifestyle that the targeted consumers associate themselves with) so that they are motivated to purchase the product or service.

Needs are classified in an ascending order, from lower to higher (see **Figure 4.5**). In this **hierarchy of needs**, developed by psychologist Abraham Maslow, an individual progresses through five levels:

1. *Physiological Needs*—Food, water, sex, and air (basic survival needs)
2. *Safety Needs*—Security, protection, and comfort
3. *Social Needs*—A sense of belonging, love from family and friends
4. *Esteem Needs*—Recognition, achievement, and status; the need to excel
5. *Self-Actualization Needs*—Fulfillment, realization of potential (someone achieves what they believe they can do)

need A state of deprivation or the absence of something useful.

motives The conditions that prompt the action necessary to satisfy a need.

hierarchy of needs The classification of consumers' needs in an ascending order from lower-level needs to higher-level needs.

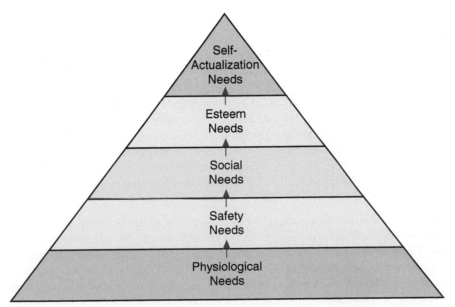

Figure 4.5 Hierarchy of Needs

Figure 4.6   The Burton brand appeals to young adults on the basis of individuality and empowerment.

Burton

There are two principles at work in this hierarchy:

1. When lower-level needs are satisfied, a person moves up to higher-level needs.
2. Satisfied needs do not motivate. Needs yet to be satisfied influence behaviour.

Understanding consumers' needs is essential for a marketing organization. Numerous examples can be cited to demonstrate marketing applications of Maslow's needs theory. Safety needs are used to motivate people to purchase life insurance or certain brands of cars, like Volvo. The desire to be accepted by peers and the need for social satisfaction (to fit in with peers) is the heart of marketing communications campaigns for personal-care products and clothing. To illustrate, the skateboarding and snowboarding crowd are into individuality and empowerment. Popular brands like Quiksilver and Burton tapped into the social needs of this group with their advertising. Refer to the illustration in **Figure 4.6**.

Esteem needs are addressed in messages that show people in successful roles and occupations, or people enjoying life to its fullest. The products they buy are a symbol of their success and the status they have achieved.

personality Distinguishing psychological characteristics of a person that produce relatively consistent and enduring responses to the environment in which that person lives.

Personality and Self-Concept   **Personality** refers to a person's distinguishing psychological characteristics, those features that lead to relatively consistent and enduring responses to the environment in which that person lives. Personality is influenced by self-perceptions that, in turn, are influenced by physiological and psychological needs, family, culture, and reference groups. Why do people buy designer-label clothing at high prices and in upscale boutiques when low-priced items performing the same functions are available? Such purchases are based on the images we desire of ourselves. To appreciate this principle, we need to understand the self-concept theory.

self-concept theory States that the self has four components: real self, self-image, looking-glass self, and ideal self.

Self-concept theory states that the self has four components: real self, self-image, looking-glass self, and ideal self.[9]

1. *Real Self*—An objective evaluation of yourself. You as you really are. Your perception of your real self is often distorted by the influence of the other selves.
2. *Self-Image*—This is how you see yourself. It may not be your real self, but rather a role that you play with yourself.
3. *Looking-Glass Self*—How you think others see you. Your view of how others see you can be very different from how they actually see you.

4. *Ideal Self*—This is how you would like to be. It is what you aspire to be.

Marketers use this self-concept theory to their advantage. They know that, human nature being what it is, many important decisions are based on the looking-glass self and the ideal self. Goods and services that help fulfill the ideal self appeal to the consumer.

The men's grooming market presents a good illustration of the self-concept. Today's men are concerned about body image and feel insecure about aging. They are spending money on manicures, skin treatments, and many are pursuing cosmetic surgery. Males are being influenced by the body images presented in magazines such as *Maxim* and *Men's Health*. Marketers have responded by launching face scrubs, moisturizers, cleansing products, and body sprays for men. See **Figure 4.7** for an illustration. Brands such as Biotherm Homme, L'Oréal Men Expert, and Nivea for Men understand how contemporary men feel about themselves and are offering a range of health-care products that were once only available to women.

Marketers must stay abreast of such changes among consumers. A shift in emphasis with regard to the various elements of the self should result in new or different marketing strategies. Based on the grooming example, many experts are forecasting that the male skin-care category could grow as large as the women's category—what an opportunity for companies that market personal-care products!

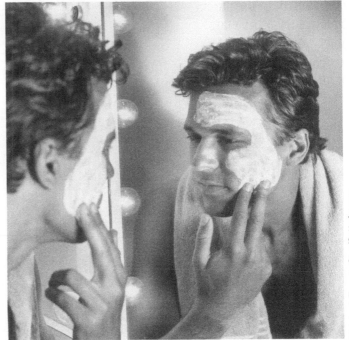

Figure 4.7 Contemporary males are purchasing skin-care products that will help them look and feel good about themselves.

Attitudes and Perceptions **Attitudes** are an individual's feelings, favourable or unfavourable, toward an idea or object (the product or service). Generally, marketing organizations present their products to consumers in a way that agrees with prevailing attitudes. Marketers have found that it is expensive to try to change attitudes. Considering how difficult it is for parents to understand their teenagers, do marketers have a chance of understanding them? Yes, if they consider some basics about teen attitudes.

If teens see themselves on the edge of what the rest of the world considers *normal* they will be attracted to products for which the advertising message pushes the boundaries. Apple, for example, has been successful with products like iTunes, iPod, iPhone, and iPad. Apple's advertising positions the products as sleek and sexy, and relevant to the lifestyles of people of all ages. It's not by accident that Apple is a leader in these markets.

While it is difficult for a marketing organization to change attitudes, it must be prepared to act when consumers' attitudes do change. For example, parents with young daughters have been complaining that toys marketed to girls are all about beauty or taking care of something. Toy manufacturers are taking note. A new line of toys called GoldieBlox, designed to spark young girls' interest in building and inventing, launched in 2013. The brand's tagline is "More than just a princess." Parents have embraced the GoldieBlox message of inspiring girls to enter the science, technology, engineering, and math fields, making the brand one of the hottest-selling new toy items on the market.[10] Refer to the GoldieBlox image in **Figure 4.8**.

The moral in these examples is simple: products must first be aligned with the psyche of the consumers before they will be considered for purchase. Further, if a company decides to launch a new product, it must take into account consumers' attitudes before proceeding too far with a project.

Perception refers to how individuals receive and interpret messages. Marketers know that different individuals perceive the same product differently and accept only those messages that fall in line with their needs, attitudes, and self-concepts. They tend to ignore other messages. A variety of marketing actions influence consumer

attitudes An individual's feelings, favourable or unfavourable, toward an idea or object.

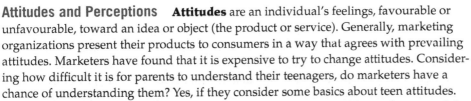

Video: New Toy Company Inspires Little Girls to Build Houses

perception How individuals receive and interpret messages.

Figure 4.8   Parents embrace GoldiBlox and other new construction-related products aimed at girls.

perceptions—advertising, pricing, packaging, and place of purchase—but perceptions differ because consumers are quite selective about the messages they receive. Selectivity is based on their level of interest and needs. There are three levels of selectivity:

1. *Selective Exposure*—Our eyes and minds notice only information that is of interest.
2. *Selective Perception*—We screen out messages and information that conflict with previously learned attitudes and beliefs.
3. *Selective Retention*—We remember only what we want to remember.

To understand how perception works, consider a common perception held by consumers about the automobile industry. For years the major domestic manufacturers such as General Motors, Ford, and Chrysler have been losing market share to Japanese manufacturers. Why? There is a perception that foreign models offer better quality and are more reliable. As a result, consumers may tune out messages for cars made by General Motors and Ford (selective exposure). Over the last three decades, Toyota has risen to become the world's largest automobile manufacturer, surpassing General Motors. Even though Toyota issued massive recalls due to sticky gas pedals and braking problems in 2010, the company remains the top-selling automaker in the world. Toyota sold a record 9.98 million vehicles worldwide in 2013—beating General Motors by 270 000 vehicles.[11] As we can see from this example, consumers' perceptions are difficult to change. And it is perceptions held by consumers that marketers must deal with.

Consumers will quickly tune in to messages for items they are thinking about purchasing. For example, consumers who are interested in purchasing healthier food products will be more likely to notice advertisements that include expressions such as "lighter," "less," "zero trans-fats," "all natural," "no additives or preservatives," and so on. These are relevant messages—consumers notice them!

This selective nature of perception helps explain why only some people respond to certain marketing activities while others do not. The challenge for marketers is to penetrate the perceptual barriers—they must design messages and strategies that will command attention and compel the reader, listener, or viewer to take action.

Personal Influences

lifestyle A person's pattern of living as expressed in his or her activities, interests, opinions, and values.

Lifestyle is a "person's pattern of living as expressed in his or her activities, interests, opinions, and values."[12] Marketing organizations try to determine who buys their product on the basis of demographic variables such as age, income, gender, and education. Nevertheless, individuals with these variables in common, even if they look alike and live side by side, can be entirely different in their lifestyles. It is the psychographic profile that indicates differences between people and why similar people buy different products.

In Chapter 3 we mentioned that research companies conduct annual surveys to collect information about Canadian consumers in order to categorize them into various lifestyle segments. A list of the consumer segments was included in the chapter. Since many organizations conduct lifestyle research, there is a tendency for each company to describe the segments differently. Look up your lifestyle segment profile on the Environics Analytics website: www.environicsanalytics.ca.

Psychographic research determines the activities (work, sports, and hobbies), interests (family, friends, social situations), and opinions (social issues, business, or politics) of consumers. Activities, interests, and opinions are commonly referred to as AIOs. When information about a person's lifestyle is combined with demographic data, a more complete picture of an individual emerges—a picture that allows marketers to understand how someone interacts with others and their surroundings.

Psychographic information shows how an individual's interest in a particular product depends on his or her lifestyle. Automakers produce and market a range of vehicles to satisfy the requirements of various lifestyle groups. For example, trendy sports cars with European or Japanese styling appeal to outgoing, ambitious individuals with materialistic values and instant gratification needs. In contrast, the redesigned Acura MDX sport wagon is targeting affluent female drivers using ads that show women hiking a mountain ridge, dancing, and interacting with a robot.[13] Refer to **Figure 4.9** for an illustration of the redesigned Acura MDX sport wagon.

Psychographics allow the marketing organization to position its products effectively in the marketplace and to communicate better with its target buyers. To illustrate, consider the change that is occurring among adult males. It used to be "men and their tools"—men fixed things up around the house. Today, the phrase also describes men fixing up meals in the kitchen. According to a recent study, 47 percent of men said they are responsible for at least half of their household's grocery shopping and meal preparation. Of this group 59 percent check store websites for sales and 74 percent clip or print coupons. Procter & Gamble has responded by placing ads for many of its household and personal care products on NFL football games.[14] Kitchenware marketers have taken note and are designing utensils that are bigger, heavier, and faster. Larger handles, for example, are more suited to the male hand.

Figure 4.9   The Acura MDX sport wagon has been redesigned to suit active and outgoing female drivers.

David Paul Morris/Bloomberg/Getty Images

ThinkMarketing

Men Are from Sears, Women Are from Bloomingdale's

When it comes to retail shopping, most of us know that what women look for in a store and what men want are about as different as, well, Sears and Bloomingdale's. Typically, for men, shopping is a mission. They like to go in, get what they need and leave. They're not major comparison shoppers and they're more willing to pay a little more to speed up the process than they are to spend time hunting down bargains. They also like convenient parking. Most women, on the other hand, require more details before making a purchase and like to have help from store personnel. Women consider shopping a social experience and tend to meander, looking in a variety of stores.

But do the same differences between the sexes hold true when it comes to online purchases? Here are some interesting findings based on recent research:

- Men tend to stick to their mission when shopping online, while women browse among products and categories.
- Males and females differ in how they move through a product page. Males intensely research the page, viewing all the product details and pictures, while women quickly scan the product page and go to the next product they want.
- Males tend to search by product while females search by brand.
- Fifty-four percent of men browse the Web every few days for shopping research purposes compared to 47 percent of women.
- Forty-seven percent of females search for coupons as their primary use of social media, compared with 33 percent of men.
- Females are more likely to recommend a brand, product, or service to their friends and family through a social network.

Fuse/Thinkstock/Gettyimages

One exception is 18-to-24-year-old males as, according to one study, young men are defying most male shopping patterns by browsing—both in retail stores and online—shopping with friends and rivalling women in the number of impulse purchases.

Marketers need to understand the distinctive shopping patterns of men and women so they can tailor their marketing strategies and entice consumers to buy.

Question:

Think about your purchase behaviour. What are the retailers where you shop (either in-store or online) doing to entice you to buy?

Adapted from: T. O'Reilly, "Men are from Sears: Women are from Bloomingdale's," Under the Influence, *January 14, 2012, www.cbc. ca/undertheinfluence/season-1/2012/01/14/men-are-from-sears-women-are-from-bloomingdales/; R. Lesonsky, "Online male shoppers are from Mars, women are from Venus,"* Small Business Trends, *August 15, 2013, http://smallbiztrends.com/2013/08/male-vs-female-shopping-behavior-survey.html; and M. Kaplan, "Behavioral differences between men and women influence shopping,"* Practical Ecommerce, *December 9, 2011, www.practicalecommerce.com/articles/3222-Behavioral-Differences-Between-Men-and-Women-Influence-Shopping*

For more insight into buying behaviour differences between men and women, read the Think Marketing box **Men Are from Sears, Women Are from Bloomingdale's**.

Age and Life Cycle   Individuals and families progress through a series of stages, starting with being a young single adult, progressing to marriage and parenthood, and ending as an older single individual. Understanding the stages in the life cycle offers insight into household purchase decisions. Life-cycle theory is based on the changing needs of a family as its members progress through the various stages. For example, as a person grows older, tastes in such things as food, clothing, travel, and sports activities change.

An individual who is a sports enthusiast may shift from a competitive mode to a recreational mode, or their travel desires may shift from being adventurous to seeking relaxation-oriented vacations.

Marketers tend to define their target markets on the basis of age and life cycle, and devise appropriate marketing strategies suited to particular stages. Certainly the needs of a young working family with children will be quite different from those of an older married couple with no children living at home. Different types of buying occur in each stage. Marketers must also consider the needs of non-traditional families, as the needs and buying motivations of unmarried couples, childless married couples, same-sex couples, and older married couples are quite different.

The trends in Canada's population indicate that baby boomers and Generation Y will be key customer groups in the next 20 years. Companies will launch new products geared specifically to an older demographic. At the same time, firms must attract new, younger customers—a real marketing dilemma. Microsoft's recent advertisement for Internet Explorer, "Child of the 90s," is an example of a mature brand that is attempting to win over Millennials—a generation that grew up with Internet Explorer but is now loyal to Chrome and Firefox. Given that Millennials and Internet Explorer are children of the 1990s, the ad uses nostalgia to create trust in the brand, featuring scenes of yin and yang necklaces, Tamagotchi, and pogs—products that were part of a 1990s childhood.[15] Refer to the illustration in **Figure 4.10**.

Figure 4.10   Microsoft's Internet Explorer uses nostalgia to build trust with Millennials.

Technology   Several factors are combining to dramatically change the way in which consumers buy goods and services. These factors include the growing numbers of time-pressed consumers, the availability of information through the Internet and social media networks, and our growing obsession with mobile devices such as smartphones and tablets.

Certainly, the Internet is a vital aspect of daily life for Canadians. According to a recent study, Canadians are the heaviest users of the Internet in the world.[16] Over 83 percent of the population 16 and older (22.8 million people) now uses the Internet regularly and for a variety of activities that include researching products, online banking, and accessing social networking sites.[17] A global study of how young kids are using the Internet shows that three- to five-year-old Canadian children know how to use a mouse and play computer games before they can ride a bike or write their names.[18] Marketers have always wanted to know about their customers. Now, the amount of data and available technology allows retailers to monitor where consumers are and what they are purchasing. This information is being used to reconfigure store layouts and make staffing decisions. Retailers can also create detailed consumer profiles and target individual customers. For example, Tesco, a large British retail chain, has started using facial recognition technology in its stores to detect a customer's age and gender. The retailer then presents tailored ads to the shopper. The ads are further customized by time of day and number of other people in the store.[19]

Clearly, marketers who can take advantage of the technology–convenience combination stand to prosper in the future. The Internet and social media networks offer an effective and efficient means to communicate directly with people and are an essential component of the marketing communications mix. Mobility is the newest wave in marketing communications. As of 2013, 56 percent of Canadian adults were using a smartphone. Further, about 77 percent of smartphone users search for products or businesses on their phones, and one in four have made online purchases with their device.[20] With such huge growth in cell phone usage, companies are creating five- or ten-second ads specifically for the mobile platform.[21] There also are opportunities for marketers to locate consumers as they move around and communicate directly with them, a concept referred to as *location-based targeting*. This form of targeting will be examined in Chapter 6.

Economic Situation   The economy directly or indirectly influences the attitudes, values, and lifestyles of people in Canada. There is little doubt that the cyclical nature of the economy shapes purchase decisions. When the economy is in recession, for example, unemployment may be on the rise, and the discretionary income of consumers may be low. Consequently, major purchases will be delayed, and consumers will make products they do have last longer; new purchases of items such as a larger house, a renovation, a car, or a major appliance may be placed on hold.

Conversely, if the economy is booming, consumers are more likely to purchase more goods and services. The construction and housing industries are good examples of markets that reflect Canada's economic shifts. When mortgage rates decline, the cost of carrying a mortgage drops; therefore, there is a frenzy as first-time buyers enter the market and current homeowners consider trading up to larger accommodations even though the steady demand forces the price of housing up. An organization will adjust its marketing strategies based on changes in the economy. Generally, a business organization remains conservative in hard times and is more aggressive in good times.

SOCIAL AND CULTURAL INFLUENCES

LO4 Describe the key social and cultural influences on consumer buying behaviour.

Social Influences

The social factors that influence the purchase decision process include reference groups, the family, and social class.

reference group A group of people with a common interest that influences the members' attitudes and behaviour.

Reference Groups   A **reference group** is a group of people with a common interest that influences its members' attitudes and behaviour. Common reference groups include fellow students in a class, co-workers, sports teams, hobby clubs, and civic and recreational associations. A reference group can also be the immediate *peer group*—the friends people hang out with. A member of a group experiences considerable pressure to conform to the standards of the group, to "fit in." The desire to fit in influences the type of products a member will purchase.

The influence of reference groups is quite strong among younger people. For example, adolescents and teens share a desire to have the latest technological gadgets, shop at the trendiest stores, or have parts of their bodies tattooed or pierced. It's all part of their social scene and their desire to satisfy social needs. They may also start experimenting with drugs as a means of rebelling against their parents and other adults. They turn to their peers for information on what behaviour is desirable. With the right strategy, a marketer need only associate its brand with a certain situation and the target will become interested in the brand. For example, Google, YouTube, and Amazon.com are the top three most-loved brands within the youth market.[22]

Family   The members of a family think and act as individuals, and the decisions they make can influence household purchases. The actual impact each member has on the decision depends on the type of product or service under consideration. In the past, the effect each person had on the purchase decision was related to the traditional roles of household members, where purchase decisions were classified as husband dominant, wife dominant, or shared equally. Today, however, the lines are blurring between the sexes, and the decision makers are not who they once were. This is partly due to women's increased financial influence—31 percent of wives earn more than their husbands and 20 percent earn about the same. Further, 92 percent of Canadian women are solely or jointly in control of family finances and 55 percent say they make the daily financial decisions.[23] Major retailers that have traditionally targeted men, like Canadian Tire and The Home Depot, have redesigned their store layouts and implemented new merchandising strategies to be more female-friendly.

Men, on the other hand, now have much more influence on household purchases and are taking responsibility for tasks like grocery shopping. Supermarket chains and consumer packaged goods companies have responded and are looking for ways to entice male shoppers, trying out more masculine colour schemes and writing slogans aimed at men.[24] Marketers cannot make assumptions anymore about who the primary buyer is. They must consider both the buyers and the influencers, and the fact that major decisions are often shared by people who live together (in any type of household formation). Changing roles and responsibilities between male and female heads of households are changing how marketers view target marketing. Consequently, some marketers are double targeting. **Double targeting** involves devising a single marketing strategy that reaches both of the partners effectively. Financial institutions, automobile manufacturers, and retailers recognize the influence of women in major buying decisions and are designing campaigns that reflect contemporary decision making. At one time Mark's (formerly Mark's Work Wearhouse) marketed only to men. Then the company discovered that women shopping for men were the store's primary customer. Mark's now devotes half of its space to women's clothing and targets both genders with its advertising. Their slogan, "Clothes that work," appeals to both genders and aptly portrays the key benefit that Mark's offers. See the illustration in **Figure 4.11**.

double targeting Devising a single marketing strategy for both sexes.

The role of children also has to be considered by the marketer. A recent study by Viacom's Nickelodeon has found that family decision making in general is more inclusive these days; more than half of parents seek their kids' input, and just under half say their family discusses and makes major decisions together. Kids even get a say when the purchase is something they won't directly use. Nearly three out of five parents consult with their kids before they buy a car—an increase of almost 20 percentage points in just three years.[25]

In many households, it is the children who are the tech experts. Therefore, it is quite common for parents to seek their advice when purchasing the latest electronic gadgets. In addition, marketers are realizing that activity directed at children now will help form impressions and habits that will influence their buying patterns as adults. See **Figure 4.12** for more details about the influence of children on household purchase decisions.

Figure 4.11   Mark's adopted a double targeting strategy when it discovered that 50 percent of shoppers were female.

Figure 4.12
Marketers must react to the power children have in family buying decisions.

We know that children have a lot of influence on their parents and their family's buying decisions. Take this short quiz to find out just how much influence kids really have.

1. What percent of household purchases do children influence?
2. What percent of the time do kids influence family entertainment choices?
3. What percent of parents talk to their children before buying a new vehicle?
4. At what age do children start to become brand loyal?
5. What percent of grade 4 students own a cell phone?

Answers: 1. 80%[1] 2. 98% 3. Nearly 60%[2] 4. Age 2[1] 5. 25%[3]

Sources:

[1]Goodwin, B. (2013, October 16). The undeniable influence of kids. Packaging Digest. Retrieved from: http://www.packagingdigest.com

[2]White, M. (2013, April 11). American families increasingly let kids make buying decisions. Time Magazine. Retrieved from: http://business.time.com

[3]Oliveira, M. (2014, January 22). 25 percent of grade 4 students have their own cell phone: survey. The Hamilton Spectator. Retrieved from: http://www.thespec.com

social class The division of people into ordered groups on the basis of similar values, lifestyles, and social history.

Social Class   A person's social class derives from a system that ranks or classifies people within a society. **Social class** is the division of people into ordered groups based on such variables as income, occupation, education, and inherited wealth. In Western society, class groups are divided as follows: upper-upper, lower-upper, upper-middle, lower-middle, upper-lower, and lower-lower. Individuals may move in and out of the various social classes as they go through life. As an example, the young business executive on the rise in the corporate world could move rapidly from, say, a lower-middle-class background to a lower-upper-class level as he or she gains more power, responsibility, and salary in an organization. Conversely, a senior executive accustomed to a certain style of living and a certain social circle could suffer socially if he or she loses a job. The fallout might affect the social position of the entire family.

A person's place in the class structure influences his or her purchases of housing, automobiles, clothing, travel, and entertainment. The lower-upper-class executive, if single, is likely to live downtown, drive a trendy automobile that reflects achievement, and wear custom-tailored suits. Such purchases help create or maintain the image that goes with the corporate position.

Cultural Influences

culture Behaviour learned from external sources that influences the formation of value systems that hold strong sway over every individual.

Culture   **Culture** refers to behaviour learned from external sources, such as the family, the workplace, and education, which help form the value systems that hold strong sway over every individual. Over time, people's values can change. For example, our current value system has been influenced by the attitudes, opinions, and customs of the baby boom generation. But that generation is aging and the attitudes of younger generations, such as Generation X and Generation Y, are starting to shape our value system. Witness the changes that have occurred on issues such as Aboriginal rights, racism, and same-sex marriage.

An irony of Canadian culture is our tendency to define ourselves not by who we are but by how we differ from Americans. When asked in research polls, Canadians often self-identify as less patriotic than Americans, less proud of their achievements, and more modest about their accomplishments. Regional differences also affect our values. For example, a vast majority of Canadians (81 percent) agree strongly that they are proud to be Canadian. But in Quebec fewer than half of the French-speaking population agree strongly that they are proud to be Canadian.[26]

Culture is also influenced by where a person lives. For example, non-urban Canadians place a greater emphasis on family goals, while urban dwellers tend to have goals that are more individually focused. Non-urban Canadians place greater emphasis on family life, and on average they are more conservative about issues such as violence, homosexuality, and nudity.[27]

Values change over time. As people grow older they acquire different needs and adopt different attitudes that, in turn, influence buying behaviour. To demonstrate, consider that in the years between 2000 and 2008, when the economy was relatively strong, materialism prevailed among Gen Xers and baby boomers as individuals constantly strove to possess more and better things—a larger house, an exotic vacation, an expensive automobile, and so on. More recently, partly due to aging as well as the economic downturn in 2009, these two demographic groups have been turning to a simpler way of living. As a result, collaborative consumption, where people barter, swap, or trade, is now flourishing. Businesses have responded to make connecting and exchanging easy, no matter what product or service is needed, from travel accommodation (AirBnB) to transportation (Zipcar), and crowdfunding (Kickstarter) to skills (Kutoto).[28]

Another trend is that many Canadians are working both ends of the consumption spectrum. Middle-class Canadians are trading up to more expensive products in some cases and trading down in other cases. An emerging category of consumers referred to as "new luxury" willingly pay more—in some cases thousands of dollars more—for what they view as premium products and services. That same consumer will also look for the absolute best buy (lowest price) in product categories such as groceries and small household durable goods.

The trading up–trading down phenomenon has created marketing problems for retailers such as Sears, which traditionally catered to the middle class. Sears has lost ground to high-end specialty retailers and boutique-style retailers that market upscale fashion goods and offer better personal service. At the lower end of the spectrum, warehouse operations such as Costco and mass merchandisers such as Walmart have also benefited.

These examples show how the values of the Canadian society can change. Marketers monitor the changing values of society and subgroups in society to identify the new needs that the change produces. A firm's ability to adapt marketing strategies to the changing personality of the Canadian marketplace ultimately determines success or failure.

Subculture Many diverse subcultures exist within the Canadian culture. A **subculture** is a subgroup of a culture that has distinctive attitudes and values that set it apart from the larger culture. Canada's subcultures are evident in cities, where parts of urban and suburban neighbourhoods contain large populations of one ethnic group. Canada has long prided itself on this diversity in ethnic composition. Very often, these ethnic groups are served by their own media, which provide marketers with an effective means of reaching them.

Prudent marketers are recognizing the opportunities that these markets represent. By 2017 it is estimated that visible minorities could comprise half the population of Toronto and Vancouver.[29] In both Toronto and Vancouver, Chinese-Canadians and South Asians are the largest visible minority groups. Marketers must pursue ethnic markets more aggressively if the objective is to grow a business. Mainstream marketers who ignore ethnic populations do so at their peril.

RBC Financial knows that 15 percent of its customers (about 1.6 million people) are immigrants and visible minorities, and it has responded accordingly. Much of the bank's future growth will come from immigrants. RBC is developing new products specifically for immigrants and new, more lenient procedures to help them build a credit history. The bank's ads have an ethnic flavour. In a series of RBC Financial television ads, an immigrant couple and their children are shown navigating their way through open houses, car lots, and job interviews. The family then meets with an RBC banker who is from the same ethnic group. As the ads say, "It's another way RBC is putting us first." The ads were created in the English, Punjabi, Hindi, Mandarin, and Cantonese languages.

In assessing cultures and subcultures, marketers must decide if a national marketing strategy is suited to everyone or if subcultures should be isolated and appropriate strategies developed for them. A prudent manager may conclude that consumers across the country need the same products, but the way in which the products are presented will vary. This concept is discussed in greater detail in the next section.

Before an organization approaches an ethnic community it must fully understand the attitudes, beliefs, and values that community holds. For some insight into the Chinese community, read the Think Marketing box **Multicultural Marketing 101.**

subculture A subgroup of a culture that has a distinctive mode of behaviour.

ThinkMarketing

Multicultural Marketing 101

Before a marketer can approach any ethnic group with a marketing message, it's best they go to school first. Their goal is simple: make sure they fully understand the target so they can approach the consumers on their own terms. Anything short of that will probably fail.

Some of the differences the marketer should be aware of include visual cues, traditional values, what motivates buying, language, and preferred media. To illustrate, here are some key points about the Chinese community in Canada.

Visual Cues

There is a tendency to be superstitious. Red and gold colours are good—red meaning good luck and gold denoting riches and wealth; white should never be used as it implies death. In Mandarin, the numbers two, three, and eight are good—when spoken, "two" 2 sounds like "easy," "three" sounds like "lively," and "eight" sounds like "prosperous." Number four is unlucky as it sounds like "death."

Traditional Values

Relationship, harmony, and status are very important. Individuals must look respected among peers, friends, and family.

Motivation for Buying Behaviour

Chinese society is based on group harmony. Members of this culture like to form relationships with people, and that translates to relationships with products and services. Immigrants are here for a better future and are driven by success, dreams, and aspirations. The Chinese are very status conscious. It is important to own a luxury good, for example, a Lexus automobile. Chinese restaurants often appeal to the status instinct by using phrases such as "abundantly prestigious and expensive dishes made from rare ingredients" to attract customers.

Language

Language is fragmented into Hong Kong Chinese who speak Cantonese, Mainland Chinese who speak Mandarin,

Home Depot Canada

and Taiwanese who speak a dialect of Mandarin. Canadian-born Chinese tend to speak English.

Preferred Media

There is a preference for print media. TV works only if there is an all-Chinese cast for the ad and the language is impeccable.

Spending Preferences

Chinese tend to be rational on expensive purchases and are more likely to pay up front in cash and pay off credit cards monthly. Faster payment features (e.g., double-up payments on mortgages) are attractive.

This is just a sampling of what marketers must consider. Marketers who proceed without proper knowledge do so at their own peril.

Question:

What would a similar analysis look like for South Asians, Blacks, or another subculture in Canada?

Adapted from Jeromy Lloyd, David Brown, and Tom Gierasimczuk, "The Chinese Consumer Primer," Marketing, *March 28, 2011.*

Regional Differences   Are regional cultural differences in Canada significant enough to warrant unique marketing strategies? As we saw in the opening vignette, Target thinks so and has developed strategies to reflect differences between English-speaking and French-speaking regions in Canada. The company knows that simply adapting its English advertising for the French-Canadian market would likely fail. French Canadians do not respond to the same cues and triggers as do English-speaking Canadians, nor do they watch typical Canadian television programming. As consumers, francophone Quebecers as a whole tend to be characterized by the positive cultural values of family loyalty and pride, emotional rather than rational decision-making behaviour, and unique social- and community-driven leisure behaviour.[30] Marketers must recognize such differences and develop marketing programs that lend themselves to Quebecers' value structure.

In the context of marketing, francophone Quebecers, by and large, tend to be more emotional than English Canadians and to respond to different stimuli. Brand, service, and selection are decided on an emotional basis more than on a purely rational one. Marketers who understand that the values of Quebecers are different recognize that these consumers seek different benefits from a product. Therefore, a solid advantage must be established first, and then, to maintain loyalty, the advantage must be communicated in a manner that will have an impact on the francophone Quebec consumer. Quebecers want products that reflect their sense of uniqueness within Canadian culture.

Quebec, it seems, is a society that thrives on local heroes, whether they are from the world of sports, arts, business, or even politics. And they are influenced by these figures when they appear in advertisements. Quebecers will elevate to hero status anyone who is seen as contributing in a substantial way to their uniqueness.

Marketing managers who, from the outset, understand Quebecers and plan strategies that are culturally relevant will garner success. "You've got to understand the sensibilities, the sense of humour," says David Yost, former creative director at Marketel, a Quebec-based advertising agency.[31] For example, when Durex sought to launch a campaign that stamped Wednesday—commonly referred to as hump day—as a day for sex, it discovered that the word *hump* had no currency in Quebec as a reference to the middle of the week *or* a term for sex. Durex developed a Quebec-specific campaign with the tagline "Cinque a sexe"—a play on *cinq a sept*, a phrase Quebecers use to refer to the 5 p.m. to 7 p.m. post-work happy hour.[32]

The differences in lifestyle between French Canadians and English Canadians result in differences in buying behaviour. For example, French Canadians make a larger portion of their family food purchases in specialty stores, and they spend more on food and beverages for home consumption than do English Canadians. French Canadians also like to take their chances on the lottery and are avid purchasers of Loto-Québec tickets. Refer to **Figure 4.13** for a summary of the French Quebec market's unique characteristics.

What about the rest of Canada? Is Western Canada different from Central Canada and Eastern Canada? There are differences, but it's the significance of the differences that dictates the need for unique regional marketing strategies. From an annual survey conducted by the Print Measurement Bureau it appears that Westerners are closer to Torontonians than either group would like to admit, but what distinctions there are seem to hark back to pioneer stereotypes.

To illustrate, consider the nature of alcohol and beer consumption. In Western Canada more rye whisky (21 percent of the population) is consumed compared to Toronto (16 percent of the population). Slightly more Westerners partake of beer, but what they drink beer *from* is revealing. In the West the sheer practicality of canned beer is embraced by 30 percent of the population compared to only 12 percent in Toronto. Such knowledge could play a role in the development of new advertising campaigns for beer brands, at least in terms of the type of container displayed in the ads.[33]

In the age of global marketing strategies, a multicultural country such as Canada poses a challenge for global marketers. Marketers gain greater efficiencies when they can implement a global strategy to communicate a brand's benefits; however, investing in a Canadian-specific ad campaign that portrays the multicultural diversity of the population can reap huge dividends. AV Communications, a Canadian advertising and marketing agency, specializes in developing multicultural ad campaigns for its global clients. Recently AV Communications developed a campaign for Disney on Ice to attract the growing multicultural population in Toronto. In the Chinese community, marketing focused on grass-roots activities and family events. In the South Asian community, grass-roots activities were combined with print, cinema, and community-based ticket outlets to make the purchase more convenient. Every year, an increasing percentage of total ticket sales are attributed to the multicultural markets due to this focused campaign.[34]

Figure 4.13 The French Quebec market has unique characteristics.

Many marketing executives must decide whether to develop unique marketing strategies for the Quebec market. Are the language and cultural differences significant enough to justify such an investment? This sampling of some French Quebec characteristics suggests a need for unique marketing communications.

1. Living in the moment
The old adage "live for today, for tomorrow may never come" is embraced by Quebecers. They seize the day and give less thought to the future.

2. Chez nous
Quebecers' sense of place is central to their identity. They're closer to home, to the land, and to people like them. They'll enthusiastically support all that reinforces their local pride.

3. Joyful living
It's the proverbial "joie de vivre" that compels Quebecers to seek pleasure in all aspects of their lives. Quebecers typically take this joyful approach to life to more intense levels than other Canadians. They want to live experiences more fully, and are more adventurous.

4. All about me
Quebecers look after number one. This makes them ask, "What's in it for me?" It's a trait that may make them appear self-centred at times, but it's also what makes them relentless at getting what they want. For example, they give less to charities than other Canadians, but they give to causes that are close to them, locally.

5. Life, uncomplicated
Citizens of *la belle province* want to keep things simple, short, and sweet to help reduce complexity in their lives. They seek simplicity in everything and will reward those who deliver simpler solutions.

Source: Fortin, C. (2013, May 16). Headspace says it knows what Quebec consumers want. *Marketing Magazine*. Retrieved from http://www.marketingmag.ca/news/marketer-news/what-do-quebec-consumers-want-78693

 # ExperienceMarketing

To experience marketing you have to assess situations and make recommendations to change marketing strategies when necessary. What would you do in the following situation?

You are the manager of media relations and communications for Colleges Ontario. After reviewing the latest enrolment statistics, it's clear that Aboriginal peoples (including Aboriginal, Indian, Métis and Inuit) remain under-represented in post-secondary education.

Aboriginal students face distinct issues when they are considering post-secondary education. For example, students living on reserves may face the challenge of moving to a new community where nothing is familiar.

Your role is to raise awareness of the supports and opportunities available to students, as well as the career opportunities available through higher education. Ontario's colleges seek to provide a welcoming environment with support services to help students succeed—a good fit for Aboriginal students.

Advertising has always been an important way for Colleges Ontario to reach prospective students. You are sure that if the right message is communicated—one that is appropriate to Aboriginal cultures and traditions, and communicates the unique supports available—more Aboriginal students will be encouraged to pursue college education.

Your immediate challenge is to compile a general profile of this target audience. You must learn more about Aboriginal culture in Ontario and what might influence members to attend college or not. Conduct some research online and see what you can learn about this audience. What are the key insights that will help you develop a relevant advertising campaign? Summarize your findings in a brief report.[35 & 36]

CHAPTER SUMMARY

LO1 **Explain why it is important for marketing managers to understand consumer behaviour.** *(pp. 78–79)*

The study of consumer behaviour deals with why people buy the products and services they do and explains why two or more people behave differently or similarly. Since organizations cannot control consumers, it is essential that they understand them so that they can adapt their strategies to consumers' thinking and behaviour.

LO2 **Describe the steps a consumer goes through when buying a product or service.** *(pp. 79–83)*

The consumer decision-making process involves five distinct stages: problem recognition, information search, evaluating alternatives, the purchase decision, and post-purchase behaviour. A consumer doesn't necessarily follow all of these stages each time he or she buys something. Factors such as the cost of the purchase (less expensive or expensive) often dictate how much time and effort a person puts into the decision-making process.

LO3 **Discuss the main psychological and personal influences on consumer buying behaviour.** *(pp. 83–90)*

Psychological influences include needs and motives, personality and self-concept, and attitudes and perceptions. Personal influences include lifestyle considerations, age and life cycle, how consumers adapt to technology, and the economic circumstances faced by individuals.

LO4 **Describe the key social and cultural influences on consumer buying behaviour.** *(pp. 90–96)*

Social factors include reference groups, family, and social class. Cultural influences embrace Canadian culture as a whole while considering various subcultures based on ethnic background, values, and language differences.

For the marketer, it's a matter of knowing what's going on in the customer's mind. Marketing organizations that understand what influences behaviour are adept at developing target-market profiles and using these profiles to prepare marketing strategies that trigger a response from the target markets.

MyMarketingLab   Study, practise, and explore real marketing situations with these helpful resources:

- **Interactive Lesson Presentations:** Work through interactive presentations and assessments to test your knowledge of marketing concepts.
- **Study Plan:** Check your understanding of chapter concepts with self-study quizzes.
- **Dynamic Study Modules:** Work through adaptive study modules on your computer, tablet, or mobile device.
- **Simulations:** Practise decision-making in simulated marketing environments.

REVIEW QUESTIONS

1. Why is it important for marketers to understand consumer buying behaviour? *(LO1)*
2. Briefly explain the steps in the consumer purchase decision process. *(LO2)*
3. What is the difference between a routine purchase and a complex purchase? *(LO2)*
3. Briefly explain *cognitive dissonance*. *(LO2)*
4. Identify the five levels of the hierarchy of needs. Provide two examples that demonstrate the application of needs and motivation theory. *(LO3)*
5. Briefly explain the four components of the self-concept theory and illustrate how they have an influence on marketing strategy. Provide two new examples that demonstrate the application of this theory. *(LO3)*
6. Explain the difference between selective exposure, selective perception, and selective retention. *(LO3)*
7. Explain how an understanding of consumer attitudes is essential before developing a marketing strategy. Provide an example that takes into account the importance of understanding consumer attitudes. *(LO3)*
8. What is a reference group? Give an example of one of your own reference groups and explain how this reference group has influenced your purchases. *(LO4)*
9. What is double targeting? Provide an example of a brand or company that practises double targeting. *(LO4)*
10. What is the difference between culture and subculture? What are the implications of culture and subculture on marketing activity? *(LO4)*

DISCUSSION AND APPLICATION QUESTIONS

1. Compare and contrast your own behaviour when deciding whether or not to make the following purchases:
   a. A new business suit for an important job interview
   b. An electronic communications device such as a smartphone or tablet
   c. A case of beer

2. On the basis of your knowledge of the hierarchy of needs and the theory of motivation, what level of needs do the following brands appeal to? (Consider the slogan and anything you may know about the product's advertising.)

   a. Nike: Just do it.
   b. L'Oreal: Because you're worth it
   c. Apple: Think different
   d. Harley-Davidson: Things are different on a Harley.
   e. McDonald's: I'm lovin' it.
   f. HSBC: The world's local bank.

3. How important will it be to market directly to subcultures in the future? Are Canadian marketing organizations adequately addressing this issue with their marketing strategies? Discuss, and provide relevant examples to substantiate your position.

4. Can a brand survive by simply associating with the lifestyle of a prospective target market? Do lifestyle appeals influence consumers to buy? Examine the issues surrounding lifestyle marketing, and provide relevant examples to substantiate your position on its effectiveness or ineffectiveness.

5 Business-to-Business Marketing and Organizational Buying Behaviour

Level Ground Trading

LEARNING OBJECTIVES

LO1 Identify the types of customers that make up business-to-business markets. (pp. 101–103)

LO2 Discuss the unique characteristics of organizational buying behaviour. (pp. 103–107)

LO3 Describe how the business-to-business buying process works. (pp. 107–112)

LO4 Explain the steps in the business-to-business buying decision process. (pp. 112–114)

LEVEL GROUND TRADING LTD. ...

is a fair trade importer, wholesaler, and specialty coffee roaster based in Victoria, B.C. Level Ground began in 1997 by trading with a single coffee cooperative in Colombia. Today, the company is trading with over 5000 small-scale farming families in 10 countries. In dealing directly with small-scale producers, Level Ground's goal is to benefit communities where food is grown and processed. The result? Level Ground's trading initiatives now (2014) put over $2 million in the pockets of small-scale farmers annually and have helped fund health care, education, and other producer-initiated programs. "Direct fair trade is about relationships. More than the business transaction, it's about the people involved," says Hugo Ciro, company CEO.[1]

In the past couple of years, Level Ground has been looking for opportunities to diversify its product line. Just recently the company has established fair trade agreements with producers for products such as tea, coconut oil, vanilla, spices, rice, and cocoa. Level Ground is also expanding distributor relationships across Canada and the United States.[2]

Now, think about all the raw ingredients and packaging materials a company like Level Ground would need to prepare its coffee and other products for market. As well, think about the coffee bean roasting process, the roasting equipment that would be required, the assembly and maintenance of packaging lines, and all of the business goods and supplies that would be required to simply operate the company—anything from paper clips to photocopiers to laptop computers to cell phones. Also, consider the distributor agreements that enable Level Ground to get its product to consumers. Often in the coffee business, suppliers such as Level Ground are asked to provide coffee brewing equipment, as well as supply coffee, to cafes and restaurants.

How does a company like Level Ground go about sourcing what it needs to operate its business while staying true to its core value of sustainable fair trade? How do suppliers or marketers approach a company like Level Ground with their products or services and become an approved vendor? The simple answer is that it's a process that involves careful planning and negotiation between buyers and suppliers or marketers. This chapter outlines the details of that process.

In business-to-business (B2B) marketing, companies market goods and services to other organizations. Marketing strategies used in the business-to-business market are quite different from strategies used in the consumer market, and firms succeed in the B2B market when they fully understand the complex buying process that is involved and the criteria used to evaluate purchase decisions. For example, many B2B organizations require, as a condition of doing business, that suppliers demonstrate social responsibility by adopting policies and practices to reduce their impact on the environment. **Figure 5.1** illustrates the triple bottom line philosophy—people, planet, profit—that businesses like Level Ground are embracing.

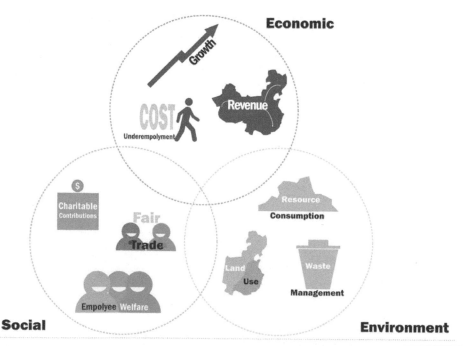

Figure 5.1   Businesses like Level Ground are embracing the triple bottom line philosophy – social (people), environment (planet), economic (profit).

BUSINESS-TO-BUSINESS MARKETS

L01 Identify the types of customers that make up business-to-business markets.

The **business-to-business (B2B)** market comprises individuals and organizations that acquire goods and services that are then used in the production of different goods or services that are sold or supplied to others. The B2B market also includes resellers who purchase products for resale to other organizations in the channel of distribution.

The business-to-business market can be divided into five distinct buying groups: manufacturers or producers, governments, institutions, wholesalers and retailers, and professions. In serving these diverse markets, organizations must identify the unique demands and needs of each and then develop responsive marketing strategies showing how their products or services will resolve a special problem or satisfy a particular need. Refer to **Figure 5.2**.

business-to-business (B2B) Markets comprising individuals and organizations that acquire goods and services that are then used in the production of other goods or services that are sold or supplied to others.

Manufacturers or Producers

Much of Canada's economic progress in the twentieth century was due to growth in manufacturing. However, since the 1960s services have contributed an increasing share of total output and employment. Currently, service-producing industries represent 70 percent of economic production and goods-producing industries account for 30 percent.[3] Among service industries, the largest in terms of annual revenue are financial services (finance, insurance, and real estate), wholesale and retail trade, public administration, and health care and social assistance.[4]

Much of the decline in the goods-producing industry is directly related to various external factors that organizations must deal with (value of the Canadian dollar, labour rates, interest rates, and so on). In good economic times manufacturers benefit, but the reverse is also true. For the past decade, the manufacturing sector has been in decline. To become more efficient many manufacturers adopted an outsourcing strategy.

Outsourcing is defined as the contracting out of services or functions previously done in-house. For example, most companies at one time planned their own shipping schedules and had to deal with a multitude of transport companies. Now this is a service that companies such as Purolator, FedEx, and UPS provide. They are experts at shipping and delivery and are able to provide clients with an efficient and cost-effective means of transportation. Other services that are now commonly outsourced include information processing, payroll, advertising, legal services, and e-commerce

outsourcing The contracting out of services or functions previously done in-house (e.g., a firm contracts out its computer services function).

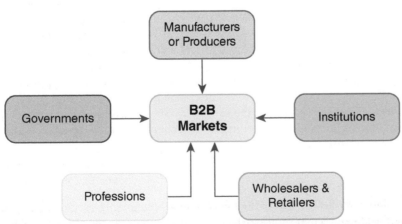

Figure 5.2   The B2B market can be divided into five distinct buying groups.

Trends in Outsourcing

1. Cost savings is not the only reason firms are outsourcing. More and more, companies are outsourcing to: a) gain competitive agility, b) manage fluctuations in demand, and c) gain access to talent.
2. Increasingly, firms are outsourcing strategic activities. As a result, organizations are contracting out with 'local' or domestic firms for high talent – higher cost labour – a term called "near-shoring".
3. It is more common now for outsourcing solutions to be customized by industry.
4. Global revenues for business process outsourcing is continuing to rise, and will reach $191 billion US in 2015.
5. Privacy and protection of data is increasingly a key priority for all organizations.

Figure 5.3   Trends in Outsourcing

Source: The Talent Project. (2013, September 24). Six key trends in outsourcing. Kelly OCG. Retrieved from http://www.kellyocg.com/Knowledge/Ebooks/6_Key_Trends_in_Outsourcing/.

transaction services. The demand for specialists in these and other service areas has grown immensely. **Figure 5.3** summarizes key trends in outsourcing.[5]

Governments

Collectively, the federal, provincial, and municipal governments form Canada's largest buying group. Governments tend to have a specialized buying procedure involving detailed order specifications and tender submissions from potential suppliers. Government contracting opportunities are advertised online through MERX Canadian Public Tenders service. Through MERX, Canadian manufacturers and service providers can access billions of dollars in contract opportunities.

Institutions

This market includes hospitals, restaurants, and educational institutions. Buying motivation is somewhat different from one institutional sector to another. For example, hospitals base buying decisions on improving health care or quality of life while working within the budgets they are granted. However, cutbacks in health spending by governments have forced hospitals to search for cost-effective solutions. For example, the largest hospital in Kingston, Ontario, now buys its meals for patients from a company in Ottawa that specializes in food production and distribution.

Wholesalers and Retailers

Businesses use wholesalers and retailers to resell their goods and services. Typically, a wholesaler purchases finished products (e.g., a grocery wholesaler, such as Loblaws or Sobeys, will purchase goods from suppliers, such as Kraft, General Mills, and Procter & Gamble), holds those goods in inventory in its warehouse, and then ships them to retailers (e.g., Real Canadian Superstore, Valu-Mart, Thrifty Foods) as demand dictates. In the grocery industry, it is quite common for national food suppliers, such as Kraft or Procter & Gamble, to present sales plans to their key account customers (e.g., Loblaws, Sobeys, or Metro) at the start of a year. At that time, marketing support from the selling organization and volume commitments from the customers are negotiated and agreed to.

Professions

The professional market consists of doctors, lawyers, accountants, architects, engineers, and so on. The products that professionals buy usually improve the efficiency of their practices; for example, the purchase of computers and other communications equipment enhances productivity in an accounting or law office.

It should be recognized that these five buying groups (manufacturers, governments, institutions, wholesalers and retailers, and professions) may require the same or similar products and services, but their needs and the reasons they buy are quite different. For this reason, marketing organizations must develop precise marketing strategies for each segment of the market.

CHARACTERISTICS OF ORGANIZATIONAL BUYING BEHAVIOUR

L02 Discuss the unique characteristics of organizational buying behaviour.

When a marketing firm develops a marketing mix that it can use to approach business customers, it should understand the elements that influence the decision-making process in organizations. **Organizational buying** may be defined as the decision-making process by which firms establish what products they need to purchase and then identify, evaluate, and select a brand and a supplier for those products.

Business markets are quite different from consumer markets (see **Figure 5.4** for an illustration of these differences). The principal distinctions are that they have fewer buyers than consumer markets, the buyers tend to be concentrated near each other, the market presents different kinds of demands, the buying criteria are practical, and a formal buying process is used. Organizations involved in business-to-business marketing are heavily involved with customer relationship management (CRM) programs. Maintaining close and productive relationships with suppliers and customers is essential to success today.

Let us examine the characteristics of organizational buying behaviour in detail.

organizational buying The decision-making process that firms follow to establish what products they need to purchase, and then identify, evaluate, and select a brand and a supplier for those products.

	Consumer Marketing	Business-to-Business Marketing
Product	Products are standardized, purchased frequently, and marketed by brand name.	Products are complex and marketed on the basis of a combination of price, quality, and service. Products are purchased less frequently.
Price	Distributors are offered a list price and a series of discounts. Savings are passed on to consumers.	The same as consumer marketing, plus extensive price negotiation or contract bidding.
Marketing Communications	Mainly advertising, with support from sales promotion and direct marketing techniques. Personal selling used in the channel of distribution.	Mainly personal selling, with support from sales promotion, direct marketing, and Internet communications. Mass advertising is now more common than in previous times.
Distribution	Mainly traditional channels—manufacturer to wholesaler to retailer to consumer.	Short, direct channels due to need for personal selling and high dollar value of transaction.
Purchase Decision	Made by an individual or household members.	Made by influence centres (users and non–users) and buying commitees.
Buying Behaviour	Consumers more subject to emotional appeals that play on concerns about image, status, prestige.	Organizational buyers are more rational due to the formality of the purchase decision process.

Figure 5.4   Differences between Consumer and Business-to-Business Marketing

Number of Buyers

There are fewer buyers or customers in the business-to-business market than there are in consumer markets, but those buyers have immense buying power. To illustrate, automobile manufacturers such as General Motors, Ford, and Toyota dominate their industry. These firms are few in number but purchase enormous quantities of products (e.g., tires, windshields, engine parts, and so on). Therefore, parts manufacturers that have supply contracts with these companies plan much of their production around consumer demand for automobiles and are subject to shifts in the economy that affect demand for cars and trucks. When the automobile manufacturers pressure suppliers to reduce the costs of parts it often places pressure on the supplier—to the point of bankruptcy in some cases. It can be a feast-or-famine situation, with the buyers calling the shots. For insight into the balance of power between buyers and suppliers in the retail industry, read the Think Marketing box **Canadian Grocery Suppliers Fight Back.**

Think Marketing

Canadian Grocery Suppliers Fight Back

A grocery war is heating up in store aisles across Canada. Loblaw Companies Limited Executive Chairman Galen Weston calls the environment "intensely competitive" as non-traditional players, such as Walmart and Target, continue to drive down grocery prices. Amazon.ca is also entering the market with its plan to sell 15 000 non-refrigerated food products like soup and granola bars on its website.

All three major Canadian grocers, Loblaws, Sobeys, and Metro, have been slashing prices to attract bargain-hungry customers. As margins are being squeezed, grocery retailers have been pressuring suppliers to cut prices.

This time, though, suppliers are fighting back. Makers of food and consumer goods are acting to prevent heavy discounting of their products by setting minimum advertised prices. Their aim is to stop retailers from using their merchandise as loss leaders.

Over the past several months, major suppliers of items ranging from Coke to Delissio pizza, Folgers coffee, and Chef Boyardee spaghetti have told grocers they will pull funding for flyers and other promotions for the products—and in some cases suspend or limit product shipments—unless the retailer agrees to the new pricing policy. "Some of the pricing dynamics have gotten so aggressive that they're detrimental and inconsistent with what we're trying to do," says Stephen Kouri, vice-president of sales and trade marketing at Smucker Foods of Canada Corp.

In January 2014, Smucker implemented a "minimum feature selling price" of $6.97 or higher for its 642- to 975-gram packages of Folgers decaffeinated roast and ground coffee—items grocers have often promoted for less than $6. "We are investing millions of dollars in building our brands," Mr. Kouri explains. "To have them sold at prices sometimes that are well below our strategies and leave consumers wondering about our brands makes us feel vulnerable."

Aaron Vincent Elkaim/THE CANADIAN PRESS

Another supplier, ConAgra Foods Canada Inc., has set a $1.20 minimum advertised price for its 410- to 425-gram cans of Chef Boyardee pasta meals. According to Ian Roberts, vice president sales at ConAgra, the company is introducing its new policy "in order to reduce supply chain volatility, protect brand equity, maintain our commitment to deliver value to our end consumers and retailer partners, and better compete in the market."

It's a difficult situation in the grocery business and still too early to assess the effects of this latest move by suppliers to bolster prices at retail. Some industry analysts say it may be time for a code of conduct, modelled on codes in Britain and Australia where the grocery sector is also controlled by a few big retailers. Canada's federal government has introduced codes of conduct in the wireless as well as credit and debit card payment sectors in the past. In the meantime, as the major grocery retailers battle for market share, consumers will continue to benefit at the till.[6 & 7]

Question:

What are the pros and cons of introducing a code of conduct for the grocery industry in Canada?

Organizations that pursue the business market must invest in marketing communications to create awareness for the company and its products. Both personal selling and online communications are vital. Today virtually all procurement officers use the Internet to identify and communicate with potential suppliers.

Location of Buyers

Business markets tend to concentrate by area; the Quebec City–Windsor corridor is a popular location for manufacturers. Ontario and Quebec account for 69 percent of the nation's manufacturing sales and employ 71 percent of people working in manufacturing industries.[8 & 9] This area is also the centre of banking and financial services in Canada. Resource-based industries, such as agriculture, forestry, and fishing, dominate other regions.

To identify and locate potential target markets, marketing firms utilize the North American Industry Classification System (NAICS). This is a numbering system established jointly by the United States, Canada, and Mexico (post–North American Free Trade Agreement) that provides statistical information about business activity across North America.

The classification system subdivides the main classifications into major industry segments; for example, a major classification may be retail trade. The system then subdivides retail trade into categories such as general merchandise stores, department stores, variety stores, and miscellaneous general merchandise stores. Further subdivision will identify firms by sales volume and number of employees. NAICS is useful for tracking down prospective customers and obtaining basic information about them.

The combination of a small number of buyers with higher dollar value purchases and more geographic concentration makes personal selling an attractive and practical way to market goods and services to these markets, despite the high costs of such activity. However, other promotional techniques such as online communications, social media, telemarketing, and direct mail now play a more important role in helping firms penetrate the business-to-business marketplace. The growth of e-commerce and its impact on supply chain management continues, so business marketing organizations must be prepared for this form of buying and selling.

Demand Characteristics

There are two types of demand in the business-to-business market: derived demand and joint (shared) demand. **Derived demand** is demand for products sold in the business-to-business market that is actually driven by consumer demand, or demand ultimately created by the final user. The example cited earlier in this section about automobiles applies here. If consumer demand for small electric cars rises (due to increases in gasoline prices or other economic factors), parts suppliers must be ready to gear up production to meet the rising demand. At the same time, if sales of larger vehicles drop, suppliers must reduce their production of parts for these vehicles. For suppliers in both segments of the automobile market it becomes a delicate balancing act.

Joint or shared demand occurs when industrial products can be used only in conjunction with others—when the production and marketing of one product is dependent on another. This happens when the various parts needed to create a finished product arrive from various sources to be assembled at one central location. To manufacture Level Ground fair trade Colombian coffee, for example, Level Ground Trading would need coffee beans (imported from Colombia), foil-lined paper bags (from a packaging manufacturer that produces the bags to Level Ground's specifications), and a cardboard shipping case (from a paper products supplier). If any of these components is unavailable, production of Level Ground coffee would be adversely affected, and demand for the other components would decrease.

derived demand Demand for products sold in the business-to-business market that is actually driven by consumer demand.

joint or shared demand A situation in which industrial products can be used only in conjunction with others, when the production and marketing of one product is dependent on another.

The Buying Criteria Are Practical

In business and industry, the buying criteria tend to be practical and rationally pursued. Criteria such as quality, price, and service are the basis for buying decisions in business and industry.

Central to the buying procedures of organizations is a vendor analysis. A **vendor analysis** entails an evaluation of potential suppliers. They are assessed based on technological ability, consistency in meeting product specifications, overall quality, capacity for on-time delivery, ability to provide needed quantities, and their reputation in their industry. How well a supplier rates in these areas affects its chances of selection, but price also plays a key role in the decision. With reference to the ad in **Figure 5.5**, Sage advertises that its software is a leader in accounting and business management software; software that manages everything from finances to inventory to customer relationships. Such diverse benefits would be important to a business buyer.

Let us examine these criteria in more detail:

1. *Price*—Price is usually evaluated in conjunction with other buying goals. The lowest price is not always accepted. A company will consider the differential advantages offered by vendors and evaluate price in the context of other purchase criteria. Typically, a buyer will evaluate cost savings in the long term against higher costs in the short term. The pressure to reduce costs, however, has led

vendor analysis An evaluation of potential suppliers based on an assessment of their technological ability, consistency in meeting product specifications, delivery, ability to provide needed quantity, and price.

Figure 5.5   Sage software appeals to the rational side of the organizational buyer.

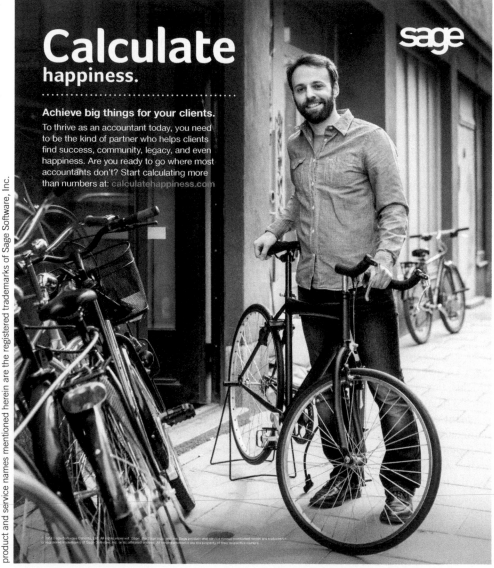

many buyers to offshore suppliers that provide goods at much lower cost than domestic manufacturers.

2. *Quality*—Business customers look for sources of supply that can provide consistent quality with each order. Since a supplier's goods become part of a new product during manufacturing, it could affect the quality of the final product if the supplier's goods are inconsistent in quality. Business buyers must assess the price–quality relationship carefully.

   Assessing the quality of a good from a foreign country may be difficult. The importance of quality became an issue for Menu Foods, a Canadian pet food manufacturer, when it had to recall tainted products. Some dogs actually died from eating its food. Menu Foods was unaware of the content of certain ingredients it was buying from East Asian suppliers (a risky situation to be in at any time). Having to recall dog food products damaged the company's reputation and had a significant financial impact on the company.

3. *Service and Services Offered*—Customers frequently review a supplier's reputation for keeping its current customers satisfied. They do so by contacting other customers to see how well the supplier performs the service function. The primary concern of the buying organization is that repair and replacement services be readily available when needed. The sales representative will play a key role in managing the customer relationship.

4. *Continuity of Supply*—Customers are concerned about the long-term availability of a product or service. They want to know how reliable the supplier is in meeting customer demand. To maintain a steady source of supply, customers often deal with numerous suppliers, knowing that such factors as strikes could halt the flow of a product from any one supplier. The location of potential suppliers is now less important in the decision-making process. Having online capabilities, companies will search the world for suppliers that can best combine the features of price, quality, and delivery. In the automobile industry, North American suppliers must compete for contracts with suppliers from East Asia and Europe.

BUSINESS-TO-BUSINESS BUYING PROCESS

L03 Describe how the business-to-business buying process works.

Buying Committees and Buying Centres

In many business organizations, one individual has the authority to sign the purchase order, but many other individuals may influence the purchase decision. There are two primary reasons for this situation in modern business. First, businesses today often utilize **buying committees**, which bring individuals together to share the responsibility of making the purchase decision. Second, businesses may hold meetings of various stakeholders in order to arrive at a purchase decision. This informal approach, involving several people in the organization, is called a **buying centre**.

1. *Buying Committees*—To illustrate this concept we will assume that a firm is considering the purchase of a million-dollar piece of production-line equipment. Since the financial ramifications are significant, it is imperative that the best possible decision is made. Consequently, the firm appoints a committee consisting of key personnel from various departments—production, engineering, finance, marketing, and purchasing—so that the decision can be evaluated from a variety of angles. Theoretically, such a decision-making process is very rational, and the participants are comforted to know that a costly purchase decision is a shared one.

2. *Buying Centres*—In buying centres, which are more informal than buying committees, the individuals involved have certain roles. Researchers have identified five specific roles:

   - *Users:* Those who use the product (e.g., a Samsung Galaxy tablet or Apple iPad used by travelling sales people).

buying committee A formal purchasing group involving members from across a business organization who share responsibility for making a purchase decision.

buying centre An informal purchasing group in which individuals with a variety of roles influence the purchase decision but may not have direct responsibility for the decision to purchase.

■ *Influencers:* Those who assist in defining specifications for what is needed (e.g., the head of the information technology department who outlines technology requirements for the sales force).

■ *Buyers:* Those with the authority and responsibility to select suppliers and negotiate with them (e.g., a purchasing agent).

■ *Deciders:* Those with formal or informal power to select the actual supplier (e.g., a high-dollar-value purchase of electronic devices for the sales team may ultimately be the responsibility of a vice-president of sales).

■ *Gatekeepers:* Those who control the flow of information to others in the centre (e.g., a purchasing agent may block certain information from reaching influencers and deciders).

From a marketing perspective, it must be determined who on the committee or within the buying centre has the most influence. Once that is known, the best means of communicating with that person must be determined. What role should personal selling, sales promotion, marketing communications, and direct marketing each have in reaching and influencing customers to buy?

Centralized Purchasing

In today's economic environment, buying organizations are looking for the best possible prices and value for dollars spent. Consequently, many firms have developed centralized purchasing systems in order to secure better price discounts based on volume purchases. For example, Walmart Canada does all of its national and regional buying from its head office in Mississauga, Ontario. Becoming a Walmart supplier—having your product sold in its stores—is not easy. To become a supplier a company must fill in an application form available on the Walmart website. Potential suppliers must meet requirements such as having financial information listed with Dun & Bradstreet, having a Universal Product Code (UPC), and having applicable liability and workers' compensation insurance. And the odds of getting a product listed with Walmart are slim—only about 2 percent of new suppliers are accepted.

Once Walmart starts selling a product it can quickly assess how successful it is. Decisions about how much inventory to carry are based on sales that are tracked electronically at the point of purchase on a daily basis. If a product isn't moving, it won't be there for long! Automatic computer re-ordering measures product movement, desired inventory levels, and delivery time. Where customer relationship management (CRM) models exist, an order request from a buyer will automatically trigger delivery from a supplier.

Personal Characteristics

Business buyers are just as human as other consumers; the more knowledge a marketer has about the specific buyer, the more impact the marketing message can have. To address the needs of certain personalities, emotional appeals centred on status and prestige may be included in overall marketing strategies, along with ordinary rational appeals. Marketers also recognize that many business decisions are influenced or made in social settings, such as on the golf course, over a drink after a squash game, or at a sports or theatre event of some kind. Entertaining customers is an essential aspect of business-to-business marketing.

Relationships Are Sought

In today's marketplace, organizations that deal directly with one another (suppliers, manufacturers, and distributors) are doing so in a more co-operative, less competitive way. Partnership marketing programs are being established to evaluate the flow and use of goods and services through the channel of distribution. The aim of a partnership is to devise and implement strategies that will produce mutual benefits for all participants. The concept of building relationships is discussed in detail in the next section.

Refer to **Figure 5.6** for a summary of organizational buying criteria and the buying decision process.

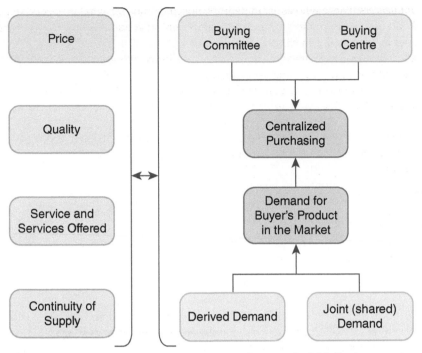

Figure 5.6   Buying Criteria and Buying Process in B2B Environment

Integration and Partnering in Business-to-Business Marketing

The manner in which business-to-business organizations do business with each other is changing. What is becoming increasingly common is partnership marketing. **Partnership marketing** involves cooperation and collaboration among members of a channel of distribution that do business with one another. Data are exchanged electronically between partners so that all partner members can make better business decisions. These partnerships are part of a supply chain management system (see Chapter 12 for more details on supply chain management). For an example of how one company plans to work with supply chain partners to reduce its impact on the environment, read the Think Marketing box **Monk Office's Path Toward Sustainability**.

Movement toward the formation of partnerships is desirable because it helps organizations to operate more efficiently. As well, the increasing level of competition between similar products has influenced companies to form partnerships, since it can give an otherwise undistinguished product an edge in the marketplace. For example, a supplier that secures a long-term commitment from a buyer would hold a secure position in the partnership model. Producers of competitive products that perform the same function would find it difficult to dislodge such a supplier from the partnership.

The essential ingredient in the partnership marketing model is an integrated tie between customers and their suppliers. There is a closer relationship between the manufacturer and its suppliers and between manufacturers and distributors (resellers). All their production and marketing decisions could be influenced by derived demand, a concept discussed earlier in this chapter. In the partnership model, a decision made by one company could automatically trigger a decision at another company. For example, if a distributor decides to order less volume of product, that decision will automatically affect the level of production at the source manufacturer. While this system has always existed in B2B marketing, the presence of technology and direct electronic links between partners makes the system more formal and efficient.

In order to be considered as a partner, a supplier must understand the nature of a manufacturer's operation and the markets that organization is selling to. A view of the entire

partnership marketing A process that involves cooperation and collaboration among members of a channel of distribution that do business with one another.

Think Marketing

Monk Office's Path Toward Sustainability

Monk Office has been a family-owned business on Vancouver Island for over 60 years. The company's office interiors division markets ergonomic eco-friendly furniture and office equipment. Its technology services department helps business customers maximize efficiency, while its ten retail locations carry thousands of office products and services—from paper to printers, pens to Post-it notes.

Monk Office started on its path towards sustainability in 2006 when a group of passionate employees decided to form what they called an ECO Team. Since then, the company has taken action in every area of the business where it had an environmental impact including waste, water, energy, paper, and fuel. By 2014, they had reduced carbon emissions by nearly 80 percent. "We look at sustainability from a triple-bottom-line perspective, assessing not only the financial, but the environmental and social impacts. These values and new standards for operating with a lower footprint extend throughout our retail locations, technical services, distribution centres, and offices," explains James McKenzie, co-owner of Monk Office.

The sustainable changes that Monk has made are being noticed. The company has received nine awards for environmental business practices. It has also become ISO 9001:2008 (quality management) and ISO 14001:2004 (environmental management) certified. These awards and ISO certifications enable Monk Office to differentiate itself as an eco-friendly organization. "I can say that the effort of the past seven years has had a positive impact on our business. I feel good about stewarding a company with strong values, and in the process we have also reduced costs and are able to donate and contribute more to the local community. We appreciate our customers and our customers appreciate what we do and how we do it," says McKenzie.

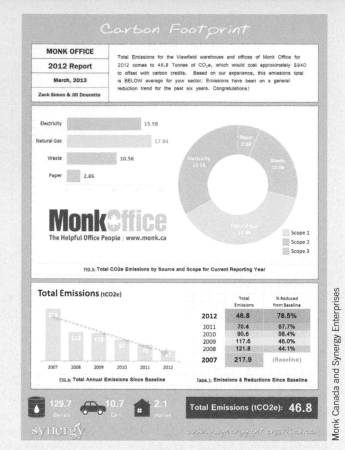

Monk Canada and Synergy Enterprises

Looking forward, the company is now in a position to help its partners, customers, and other businesses reduce their environmental impact. By working with its partners, McKenzie believes Monk Office can make an even greater impact and reduce the environmental impact of its whole supply chain.[10]

Question:
What are some advantages of having ISO 9001 and ISO 14001 certification?

---

picture is needed that works backward from the consumer. Collecting vital information about customers and their operations is an essential input element in the marketing process.

Partnering is also changing the nature of communications with customers. Salespeople still play a key role, but rather than calling on customers individually, **project teams** are being formed to deal with customers' needs more effectively. Under the leadership of an account manager (sales representative), the team may include customer service people, engineers, distribution specialists, information systems specialists, and so on. Essentially, a team from the marketing organization is dealing with a team (buying committee) representing the customer. The two teams work together to achieve common goals. They devise programs that are compatible so that all parties benefit.

project teams Groups of sales representatives formed to deal with customers' needs more effectively.

officemaxcanada.com

› Shop More Than 100,000 Products
  (Office Supplies | Interiors & Furniture | Print & Documents | Facility Resources | Technology)

› **FREE** Shipping On Most Items With Orders Of $50 Or More*

› Big Deals On Day-To-Day Office Supplies

› Enhanced Search To Help You Find What You Are Looking For Faster

› Great Features Like Order Notifications And Tracking

*For our complete terms and conditions, visit officemaxcanada.com/termsandconditions.

Figure 5.7   OfficeMax Grand & Toy rebrands itself as part of a marketing strategy to form strategic partnerships with customers and suppliers.

To demonstrate the concept of partnering, consider the transition that occurred within OfficeMax Grand & Toy. OfficeMax Grand & Toy has restructured itself into a completely e-commerce operation with five different business units (technology, interiors, office supplies, imaging, and professional services).[11] Through a rebranding effort, OfficeMax Grand & Toy has moved from being a supplier of commodities to a strategic partner with its customers. By partnering, OfficeMax Grand & Toy is able to combine the orders of its largest customers and deliver a more efficient procurement process from its suppliers. To appeal to small- and medium-sized customers, OfficeMax Grand & Toy is partnering with firms in services fields such as human resources, design, and web hosting, thus providing access to large business value and solutions. Refer to **Figure 5.7**.

In the partnership process, companies can seek partners anywhere in the world. General Motors, for instance, uses a global supply-sourcing policy to improve and change the way its cars are made, and as a result, reduce the industry's environmental footprint. The company has completed an analysis to better understand the impact of greenhouse gas emissions of its products throughout the supply chain so it can make broader improvements. For example, GM Canada has been working with its supplier partners to replace outdated, inefficient chillers at its St. Catharines powertrain facility and upgrade its waste water treatment plant— all steps to reduce its environmental impact. GM and the communities in which it operates continue to benefit from ongoing energy, water, and waste reduction. As of 2014, the company has met its commitments to reduce total waste and volatile organic compound emissions by 10 percent each and to establish 25 non-manufacturing landfill-free facilities. In Canada, the St. Catharines plant sends no waste to a landfill.[12]

General Motors understands that industry transformation does not come from one company's actions alone. Partnering with competitors such as Honda to develop fuel cell systems and technology, and with non-governmental organizations such as the BlueGreen Alliance, Union of Concerned Scientists, World Wildlife Fund, and Ceres, help GM to create a greener economy and conserve the resources vital to the industry.

Another form of partnering is frequently referred to as reverse marketing. **Reverse marketing** is an effort by organizational buyers to build relationships that allow them to influence the specifications of suppliers' goods and services to fit the buyer's (and, by extension, the customers') needs. In other words, the buyer sets the product specifications and

Video: CH2MHill: Ethics and Social Responsibility

reverse marketing An effort by organizational buyers to build relationships that allow them to influence the specifications of suppliers' goods and services to fit the buyer's (and, by extension, the customers') needs.

the supplier produces the goods to those specifications. Private-label products, such as President's Choice (or PC), sold at various Loblaws, Valu-Mart, and Real Canadian Superstore outlets, and Mastercraft products, sold at Canadian Tire, are examples. The products are designed to meet buyer specifications, and suppliers must meet those standards continuously. The concept of private-label marketing is discussed in more detail in Chapter 8.

E-Procurement

As mentioned earlier in the chapter, the federal government engages in online procurement practices, and any interested supplier can take advantage of the opportunity. The entire process of bidding for a job, processing orders, and making payments for goods and services rendered can be exchanged electronically. The concept of electronic buying exchanges in the private sector was also mentioned earlier in the chapter. The purpose of a buying exchange is to allow buyers from similar organizations to combine forces to purchase in larger quantities and secure better prices.

e-procurement An Internet-based business-to-business marketplace through which participants are able to purchase goods from one another.

E-procurement provides buying organizations with several benefits. First, buyers are able to source products at lower cost from suppliers anywhere in the world. Second, purchases are easier to track because they are done electronically. Third, it saves an organization time (and time is money). There are no delays in placing orders and suppliers can fulfill, ship, and receive payment for orders much faster than with traditional procurement methods.

From a marketing perspective, e-procurement methods allow an organization to reach new customers and offer a means to better coordinate the decisions and actions of suppliers, customers, and partners. In such a system, partners freely transfer information to each other through a system referred to as an electronic data interchange (EDI).

Combining customer relationship management practices with e-procurement models fosters long-term relationships with buyers and sellers and presents a situation in which participants are directly influenced by the decisions and actions of other participants.

STEPS IN THE BUYING DECISION PROCESS

LO4 Explain the steps in the business-to-business buying decision process.

Organizational buyers generally exhibit rational buying behaviour. That behaviour is reinforced by electronic buying procedures in place at many organizations. In some organizations the human element has been removed completely from the buying equation. There is a fairly standard process for evaluating and selecting potential suppliers. See **Figure 5.8** for a summary of the steps in this process. Let us examine each of these steps.

Problem Recognition

problem recognition In the consumer buying process, a stage in which a consumer discovers a need or an unfulfilled desire.

The initial stage, **problem recognition**, describes the fact that a change has occurred in the organizational environment that reveals a problem or a new need to be resolved. For example, perhaps an automated inventory system signals that it is time to reorder, plant personnel become dissatisfied with production capacity, or purchasing is not satisfied with some of the current suppliers because of their slow, unreliable delivery.

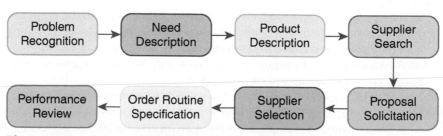

Figure 5.8   Steps in B2B Buying Decision Process

Need Description

For the **need description**, the buying organization identifies the general characteristics and qualities of the needed item or service. It may start to look at potential solutions by reviewing some alternatives that have been successful in the past.

Product Description

With a general solution in mind, the buying organization now establishes precise **product descriptions**, or specifications of the item needed. The process of formally describing the characteristics of the product ensures that needs are clearly communicated both within the organization and to potential suppliers. It is now common for this information to be posted online for members of the current supply chain management system to consider, or it can be posted separately to attract new vendors.

The quantity required is usually stipulated at this time, which assists suppliers in submitting bids. Specifications may consist of blueprints for a new production line, document copy quality and maximum run length for a photocopier, or stipulations on temperature tolerances for a machine tool. The specifications are key criteria against which a potential supplier's products are evaluated. At this stage the buying organization usually determines who will be responsible for the buying decision (e.g., an individual or buying committee). The marketing organization must be ready to identify those with the most influence and direct its communications appropriately.

Supplier Search

During the **supplier search** stage, the buying organization looks for potential suppliers. Usually, two key decisions need to be made in the purchase process: first, which product or service the organization should buy, and second, from what particular supplier it should buy. Buying organizations, at this point, search for and qualify acceptable suppliers, using the vendor analysis discussed earlier in this chapter. To qualify a supplier means that the buying organization determines that the supplier can provide the good or service in a consistent, reliable manner. In many cases, a company has to apply to be a potential supplier so that the buying organization has an opportunity to fully assess their financial status and reputation. In the age of partnership marketing organizations like to have a good fit among members.

To ensure that they are considered seriously, potential suppliers must make themselves known to buyers through various forms of marketing communications. B2B buyers visit websites searching for prospective suppliers; therefore, a marketing organization must have an easy-to-navigate yet information-rich website where potential buyers can evaluate products and services. A company's reputation (as communicated across an industry by positive word of mouth) also plays a role in the supplier selection process.

Proposal Solicitation

In **proposal solicitation**, the buying organization seeks and evaluates detailed written proposals from acceptable suppliers. Depending on the complexity of the purchase, the proposal could consist of a formal bid, a written quotation, or a price catalogue reference.

1. *Formal Bid*—A **bid** is a tender submitted by a specified deadline. There are two forms of bids:
   - A **closed bid** is a written, sealed bid submitted by a supplier for review and evaluation by the purchaser on a particular date. It is now common for bids to be submitted by electronic means. The bid is based on specifications, or precise descriptions of what is required, published by the purchaser. Usually, the bid from the lowest acceptable supplier is accepted.
   - An **open bid** is less formal and may involve only a written or oral price quotation from a potential supplier. The quotation usually specifies how long the price will be in effect. Typically, during an open bidding process buyers and sellers negotiate a price.

need description In business-to-business marketing, a stage where a buying organization identifies the general characteristics of the items and services it requires.

product descriptions (specifications) In a B2B context, a description of the characteristics of a product an organization requires. The description is used by potential suppliers when preparing bids to supply the product.

supplier search A stage in the business-to-business buying process in which a buyer looks for potential suppliers.

Video: CH2MHill: Innovation

proposal solicitation A procedure whereby a buying organization seeks and evaluates written proposals from acceptable suppliers.

bid A written tender submitted by a specific deadline.

closed bid A written, sealed bid submitted by a supplier for review and evaluation by the purchaser on a particular date.

open bid An informal submission of a price quotation in written or verbal form by a potential supplier.

quotation A written document, usually from a sales representative, that states the terms of the price quoted.

2. *Quotation*—A **quotation** consists of a written document, usually from a sales representative, that states the terms of the price quoted.
3. *Price Catalogue Reference*—In this situation, the price is obtained by referring to a catalogue where all prices are listed. Buyers usually maintain current supplier catalogues on file. This procedure is common for routine orders of standard products and supplies.

Supplier Selection

supplier selection The stage in the business-to-business buying process in which the buying organization evaluates the proposals from various suppliers and selects the one that matches its needs.

At the **supplier selection** stage, the buying organization evaluates the proposals of qualified suppliers and selects the one that matches its needs. Each proposal is assessed with reference to the purchase criteria. In a complex buying situation, the supplier's proposal might be judged on such factors as price, quality, delivery, technical support service, warranties, and trade-in policies.

While weighing these many variables, buyers may attempt to negotiate a better price with the short-listed suppliers. The bargaining process between buyers and sellers is now at its most intense, and there may be pressure on suppliers to lower their prices. As mentioned earlier in the chapter, dominant retail chains and automobile manufacturers place significant price pressure on potential suppliers, to the point where the supplier must evaluate the viability of the sale.

The influence of buying centres (informal) or buying committees (formal) must be considered and their members addressed by the marketing organization during this phase. Another option for the buying organization is to select several sources of supply for its own protection, assuming there are equal alternatives to choose from.

Order Routine Specification

order and reorder routine In business-to-business marketing, the placing of an order and the establishment of a repeat order process with a supplier.

After the supplier has been selected, the buying organization and marketing organization (the successful supplier or suppliers) agree on an **order and reorder routine** stipulating such matters as the procedure for accepting orders, delivery times, return policies, quantities to be ordered, repair and service policies, and any other factors judged important by the buyer. However, now that ordering is done electronically, automatically, and without any human input, many of the administrative tasks and much of the paperwork associated with traditional ordering procedures have been eliminated.

Performance Review

Since businesses are constantly looking for products and services to improve the efficiency of their operations, there is no guarantee that the relationship between a buyer and seller will be a lasting one. In fact, the relationship may last only until the next price quotation. Once the purchaser receives a lower quotation, a new supplier may replace the existing one, even if the current supplier has been satisfactory in other respects. General Motors, for example, implements price reviews on automobile parts every 30 days. It does not wait for a contract to expire. Current suppliers must offer prices that are very close to the lowest prices GM finds at that time or risk losing the business.[13]

performance reviews The final step in the buying process, where the buying organization establishes a system of obtaining and evaluating feedback on the performance of the supplier's products.

To ensure that their operations remain as efficient as possible, businesses implement **performance reviews**. As the final step in the buying process, the buying organization establishes a system of obtaining and evaluating feedback on the performance of the supplier's products. The purchasing manager will design an internal system for securing responses from user groups. Depending on whether the feedback is positive or negative, a decision to continue with or to drop a supplier is made. New price negotiations could also occur at this stage.

To marketers, this procedure demonstrates that the sale is never over. To avoid being dropped as a supplier, marketing organizations must accept criticisms and adapt their strategies, when necessary, to ensure that customers' needs are continuously satisfied. It has been shown that strong personal and business relationships develop when marketing organizations take fast, corrective action to resolve customer problems. This aspect of business reinforces the importance of a sound customer relationship management program that is designed to build customer loyalty.

✔ ExperienceMarketing

To experience marketing you have to collect information, assess situations, and make recommendations to change marketing strategies when necessary. What would you do in the following situation?

You are the marketing manager for a medium-sized manufacturing company. You supply airtight storage bags to many food and pharmaceutical companies and have a good reputation within your industry. Your bags have two separate layers—an outer layer of recycled paper and an inner layer of aluminum foil. The fact that the outer layer of the bag can be removed and recycled makes it better for the environment than your competitors' bags, which are non-recyclable.

Currently, your customer list does not include any companies involved in the coffee roasting business in Canada, but you recognize that your environmentally friendly storage bags would be a key component for products like coffee beans and ground coffee. You see significant opportunity for growth if you can secure a supply contract with some coffee roasters.

Before you can do anything you need information. Answers to the following questions will get you started.

1. What companies roast coffee in or near your community?
2. Which of these companies would be most interested in environmentally friendly storage bags?
3. Who is the initial contact person at one of the local coffee roasting companies you identified?
4. How do they buy packaging supplies?
5. What buying decision process do they use?

Conduct a brief audit of the coffee roasting market in your area and profile a company in that market based on your answers to the five questions. A phone call to the company will be beneficial.

CHAPTER SUMMARY

LO1 Identify the types of customers that make up business-to-business markets *(pp. 101–103)*

The business-to-business market comprises five primary buying groups: manufacturers or producers, governments, institutions, wholesalers and retailers, and professions, all of which require a vast array of products and services.

LO2 Discuss the unique characteristics of organizational buying behaviour *(pp. 103–107)*

The business market has fewer buyers than consumer markets, the buyers tend to be concentrated near each other, and the market presents different types of demand. The buying criteria are practical and include factors such as price, quality, service and services offered, and continuity of supply.

LO3 Describe how the business-to-business buying process works. *(pp. 107–112)*

The decision-making process in organizations is quite formal. The dollar value of the transaction often dictates what procedure will be used. The more expensive the decision, the more formal the process will be. It is common for an organization to use a buying committee that is a formal group within the organization. They may also use a buying centre, which is an informal group within an organization.

Personal or lifestyle influences must be considered in the business-to-business seller–buyer relationship. Including lifestyles in the marketing equation is based on the notion that new, younger managers with different attitudes are taking over management positions from older, more traditionally oriented managers. Within an organization all buying decisions may be centralized. In the age of technology it is also common for organizations to form partnerships with suppliers (marketers) in order to ensure consistency of supply and cost certainty. E-procurement models are used in such partnerships.

LO4 Explain the steps in the business-to-business buying decision process. *(pp. 112–114)*

Organizations frequently use a predetermined procedure for soliciting suppliers. A typical buying procedure would include the following steps: problem recognition, need description, product description, supplier search, proposal solicitation, supplier selection, order routine specification, and performance review.

Marketing organizations have to be flexible when approaching business customers. Different customers in various markets have unique needs. Marketers must adapt their marketing strategy to meet specific needs and buying situations. Tailored marketing strategies tend to be more successful in business-to-business marketing.

MyMarketingLab   Study, practise, and explore real marketing situations with these helpful resources:
- **Interactive Lesson Presentations:** Work through interactive presentations and assessments to test your knowledge of marketing concepts.
- **Study Plan:** Check your understanding of chapter concepts with self-study quizzes.
- **Dynamic Study Modules:** Work through adaptive study modules on your computer, tablet, or mobile device.
- **Simulations:** Practise decision-making in simulated marketing environments.

REVIEW QUESTIONS

1. What are the five major buying groups comprising the business-to-business market? (*LO1*)
2. How is buying behaviour in the business market different from that in the consumer market? (*LO2*)
3. Explain the influence the following characteristics have on organizational buying behaviour: (*LO2*)
   a. Number of buyers
   b. Location of buyers
   c. Derived demand and joint demand
   d. Centralized purchasing
4. Briefly describe the primary buying criteria in business-to-business buying situations. (*LO2*)
5. What is NAICS, and how do marketers use NAICS to segment B2B markets? (*LO2*)
6. Distinguish between a buying committee and a buying centre. (*LO3*)
7. What role do gatekeepers have in a buying centre, and how do they influence the purchase decision? (*LO3*)
8. Explain the concept of e-procurement. What benefits does the e-procurement model offer a participating company? (*LO3*)
9. Briefly describe the steps in the decision-making process that organizations follow to make purchases. (*LO4*)
10. Does every B2B purchase decision need to go through all steps of the buying decision process? Give examples of B2B buying situations that would not go through all steps of the buying decision process. (*LO4*)

DISCUSSION AND APPLICATION QUESTIONS

1. Find an example of each of the five main types of B2B organizations.
2. How important is price (cost) in the B2B marketing equation today? Is it the most important variable that influences buying decisions, or must buyers consider other aspects of the mix as being equally important? Assess the situation and present an opinion.
3. "Developing partnerships with suppliers and customers is crucial to the success of business-to-business marketing organizations." Do you agree or disagree with this statement? Justify your position.
4. Should lifestyle considerations be factored into the marketing of business-to-business goods and services? Are today's new and younger managers any different from their predecessors? Conduct some research on this topic and develop a position on it. Provide relevant examples or illustrations to substantiate your position. Refer to the appropriate section of the chapter for initial discussion on the issue.
5. Viking Air, a small aircraft manufacturer on the west coast, has designs for a new aircraft that it would like to sell to some of its existing customers as well as new customers. You are part of the sales team. How would your approach to selling to an existing customer be different from selling to a new customer?

6

Market Segmentation and Target Marketing

© P Cox/Alamy

LEARNING OBJECTIVES

LO1 Explain market segmentation and differentiate among the different forms of market segmentation. (pp. 118–123)

LO2 Describe the process used and information needed to identify and select target markets. (pp. 123–132)

LO3 Explain the concept of market positioning and its role in contemporary marketing practice. (pp. 132–140)

A REDESIGNED...

Ford Focus and a new innovative communications strategy was exactly what Ford needed to compete in the small-car segment in Canada. What's different about this campaign is the way in which Ford approached the situation. This new Focus was the first true global car for Ford, as it is to be sold in many countries around the world.

While the TV campaign was created by a global marketing team to be broadcast in many markets, Ford of Canada extended the campaign heavily into the digital and social worlds, marketing spaces that are both crucial to reaching the Focus target.

The key to the new campaign lies in Ford's understanding of the target market it was pursuing. They like music, consumer electronics, and socializing online. New message and media techniques would be needed to get the attention of the key demographic.

Ford decided to concentrate on a technology-themed activity that aligns with the fact that Focus is the first to offer Ford's MyFord Touch in-dash infotainment system. While television commercials and print ads were part of the media mix, the campaign had a web-heavy component that showed the benefits of the MyFord Touch system as much as the car itself.

The campaign included a multiple screen approach (TV, mobile, and computer) delivering custom content such as immersive digital product demonstrations and in-show TV content on popular TV shows as well as custom video content on Facebook and MSN.

Did the change pay off? You bet! Ford of Canada's Focus Facebook fan page quickly became #3 in the world, up from #11 before the campaign launched. Sales, brand health, and earned media all increased measurably as a result of the multifaceted launch. Good results based on good input about customers! That's what this chapter is about.

Before discussing market segmentation let us review what a market is. A market is a group of people who have a similar need for a product or service, the resources to purchase the product or service, and the willingness and ability to buy it. The reality of this explanation is that most products and services are marketed to smaller groups (called segments) that fall within the larger mass market. This practice is referred to as *market segmentation*.

Essentially, a firm adopts a market segmentation strategy that is best suited to achieving its goals and objectives while staying within the financial resources that are available. Organizations now have the ability to reach individual consumers with unique marketing strategies. This is the ultimate form of market segmentation, a concept that will be discussed in detail in this chapter.

MARKET SEGMENTATION

L01 Explain market segmentation and differentiate among the different forms of market segmentation.

Marketers choose among four basic segmentation alternatives: mass marketing, market segmentation, niche marketing, and direct (one-to-one or individual) marketing. Depending on the size of an organization and the resources available, an organization may employ several of these alternatives at one time. By no means are these strategies exclusive.

Mass Marketing

mass marketing The use of one basic marketing strategy to appeal to a broad range of consumers without addressing any distinct characteristics among them.

An organization practising **mass marketing** isn't really segmenting the market. Instead, the organization implements one basic marketing strategy to appeal to a broad range of consumers. It does not address any distinct characteristics among the consumers. In effect, the nature of the product or service is such that it enjoys widespread acceptance.

Perhaps the best example of mass marketing today is Walmart. While positioned as a discount department store, Walmart offers everyday prices and product selection that attracts a wide cross-section of the North American population. It seems that people of all income brackets like a bargain! And talk about success—Walmart is the largest private retailer in Canada with sales in the range of $22.3 billion annually—well ahead of competitors such as Costco Wholesale, Sobeys, and Hudson's Bay Company.[1]

The presence of Walmart has created financial hardship for many established Canadian retailers. Zellers, once the largest discount mass merchandiser in Canada, is out of business and Sears faces declining sales revenue. Sears has been forced to close some of its largest stores and sell the properties in order to remain financially viable.

In the retailing sector, consumers are either trading up or trading down in terms of the quality of goods they are buying and the stores they are shopping in. Consumers shopping for fashion goods, for example, will shop less frequently at stores such as Hudson's Bay and Sears, and more often at upscale boutiques and mid-range specialty stores where there is a better selection of goods and better service. Stores such as Harry Rosen or Holt Renfrew are more to their liking. Such a distinction refers to the concept of market segmentation and a firm's ability to distinguish itself from its rivals.

At the lower end Walmart markets fashion goods of reasonable quality and low prices—a value proposition that brings in customers. The sheer variety and selection that Walmart provides across an endless array of product categories makes it a destination of choice for most Canadians—the concept of mass marketing at its best!

Market Segmentation

Market segmentation is the division of a large market (mass market) into smaller homogeneous markets (segments or targets) on the basis of common needs and/or similar lifestyles. Segmentation strategies are based on the premise that it is preferable to tailor marketing strategies to distinct user groups, where the degree of competition may be less and the opportunities greater. For example, the automobile market is divided into many different segments: sub-compact, compact, mid-size, luxury, sport utility, and so on, based on the needs and lifestyles of different groups of people.

market segmentation The division of a large market (mass market) into smaller homogeneous markets (targets) on the basis of common needs and/or similar lifestyles.

When utilizing market segmentation, a company specializes by concentrating on segments of the population.

In the coffee market, manufacturers of coffee brands such as Maxwell House and Nescafé consider the preferences and lifestyles of various customers and market a host of products to meet their needs. The at-home coffee market segments embrace roast and ground coffee, instant coffee, coffee beverage mixes, and coffee discs that are suitable for use with Tassimo and Keurig coffee makers. A well-known brand such as Nescafé offers a variety of products in many of these segments. Refer to the image in **Figure 6.1**.

Reitmans, a prominent Canadian fashion retailer, operates under banners such as Reitmans, Smart Set, RW&Co., Penningtons, Addition Elle, and Thyme. Product offerings cover virtually every segment of women's fashion. The product lines and styles in their stores appeal to women in different age groups and with different needs. For example, Addition Elle appeals to plus-size women wanting flattering and fashionable clothing

Figure 6.1　Nescafé offers product lines in most segments of the at-home coffee market.

Figure 6.2   The Ashley Graham signature lingerie collection marketed by Addition Elle is aimed at a specific segment of the female fashion market.

Courtesy of Addition-Elle. Model: Ashley Graham. Photographer: Jean-Claude Lussier

that allows them to express their femininity. These women want to feel confident, beautiful, and included in the fashion world.[2] A specific illustration of this is the Ashley Graham line of lingerie, which combines affordable, sexy luxury (intricate embroideries, luxurious lace, and sultry mesh) with incredible comfort and fit for women of all ages and sizes.[3] Ashley Graham is a famous plus-size model whose star quality is featured in television and print ads. The slogan for the Ashley Graham campaign—"Sexy is a state of mind"—aptly summarizes the needs and mindset of the target market described above. An illustration of Addition Elle advertising appears in **Figure 6.2**.

To maximize profits, a firm may operate in many different segments. A successful segmentation strategy enables a firm to control marketing costs, allowing it to make profits. As well, the organization may be able to develop products for many different segments of a market. For example, PepsiCo is a beverage company with prominent brands in many different segments: Pepsi-Cola, Diet Pepsi, 7Up, and Mountain Dew in the soft drink segment; Aquafina in the bottled water segment; Tropicana, Dole, and Ocean Spray in the juice segment; Gatorade and G2 in the sports drink segment; and AMP and SoBe in the energy drink segment.

On the downside, organizations employing market segmentation must be alert to shifting consumer trends and the cyclical patterns of the economy or suffer the consequences. For example, the sale of regular carbonated soft drinks has fizzled lately as consumers show preference for healthier beverages. As illustrated by the PepsiCo example cited above, the company has reacted by offering lines of bottled waters, fruit juices, and energy drinks. Coca-Cola has similar offerings in each segment of the market. Both companies get your beverage dollar through one brand or another!

A combination of demographic, psychographic, geographic, and behaviour information is commonly used to segment a market. These concepts are discussed in detail in the next main section of the chapter—Identifying and Selecting Target Markets. Refer to **Figure 6.3** for an illustration of the levels of market segmentation and a brief explanation of each level.

Niche Marketing (Sub-Segmentation)

niche marketing Targeting a product line to one particular sub-segment of a segment and committing all marketing resources to the satisfaction of that sub-segment.

Niche marketing takes market segmentation a step further. Initially, **niche marketing** strategies focused on subgroups within a market segment. The subgroup has unique and identifiable characteristics, and even though the sub-segment is small it presents sufficient opportunity and profit potential. This strategy is ideal for small companies that have limited resources and large companies wanting to target a specific sub-segment with specialized

1. Mass Marketing	2. Market Segmentation	3. Niche Marketing	4. Direct or One-to-One Segmentation
One marketing strategy appeals to a broad range of consumers. Distinct characteristics of consumers are not considered when devising strategies.	Unique marketing strategies are devised based on the unique characteristics of specified customer groups. The customer groups are identified based on similarities in demographics, psychographics, geographics, and behaviour responses.	Unique strategies are devised for a particular segment of a bigger market. All marketing strategies are dedicated to this one particular segment.	Unique marketing strategies are devised for the unique needs and preferences of individual customers.

Figure 6.3   The Levels of Market Segmentation

products. Often the sub-segment pursued is quite small, so the key to success is in finding opportunities that do not require large economies of scale in production and distribution.

An organization using a niche strategy finds opportunities to customize products and services to the narrow interests of each niche. It is kind of an optimized form of segmentation.[4] Hat World has chosen to operate in a narrow niche within the sports apparel market. Its focus is strictly on hats: branded sports caps featuring teams and schools from the NBA, MLB, NCAA, NFL, and NHL; ski hats; and pop culture–related hats. The company operates more than 1000 stores in North America under names such as Lids, Hat Shack, Hat Zone, Head Quarters, and Cap Connection. Sunglass Hut, a retailer specializing only in sunglasses, is another example of a company being successful with a niche marketing strategy. Refer to the image in **Figure 6.4**.

In the beer market, Molson and Labatt offer a variety of beers in the mainstream market and use market segmentation (described above) to differentiate brands for people of different age groups and interests. Over the past ten years or so, beer drinkers have slowly moved away from mainstream brands toward premium brands and brands brewed by microbrewers. Microbrewers have carved out their niche and now control about 5 percent of Canada's beer market. Examples of successful microbrewers include Granville Island Brewing in Vancouver, Big Rock Brewery in Calgary, and Steam Whistle Brewery in Toronto, among many others. Steam Whistle's slogan about how it operates makes a clear statement about successful niche marketing—do one thing really well! Refer to the image in **Figure 6.5**.

Niches start out small in size or narrowly defined, but niches become larger in scope as more mainstream consumers are attracted to them. As the niche expands, new competitors enter and the niche becomes more of a market segment than a niche. If the microbrewery niche described above suddenly controlled 10 percent of the market (a reflection of changing consumer preferences) it would no longer be considered a niche, it would truly be a segment of the market and a more significant threat to mainstream brewers such as Molson, Labatt, and Sleeman.

direct segmentation (or *one-to-one marketing* or *individual marketing*) A situation in which unique marketing programs are designed specifically to meet the needs and preferences of individual customers.

Direct Segmentation and Behavioural Targeting

In the context of market segmentation, **direct segmentation** (or *one-to-one marketing* or *individual marketing*) refers to a situation in which unique marketing programs are designed specifically to meet the needs and preferences of individual customers. Advancing technology encourages and enables such a definitive marketing practice. Marketers are empowered by more detailed consumer data that allow for a much higher degree of intimacy and frequency of contact with customers—

Figure 6.4   Sunglass Hut operates in a narrow niche of the sports apparel market—eyewear.

Steam Whistle Brewery

Figure 6.5   Successful niche marketing involves doing one thing really well.

this is the concept of customer relationship management that was discussed earlier in the textbook.

Sophisticated computer systems collect and process information from a variety of sources. Through marketing research, a company collects demographic, psychographic, and media consumption information on customers in order to target them more effectively with messages. Electronic meters in homes track television viewing, software cookies in computers monitor surfing behaviour, and electronic checkout counters capture all kinds of purchase information (what, when, how much was spent, and so on) that can be attributed to individuals. If you think big brother is watching you . . . he is!

Technology has fuelled the use of behavioural targeting. In an online environment, **behavioural targeting** is a database-driven marketing system that tracks a consumer's behaviour to determine his or her interests and then serves ads to that person relevant to those interests. For example, if someone spent time on a financial website looking up mortgage rates it could be inferred that that person is in the market for a new home. He or she could receive ads from a mortgage company or real estate company on whatever webpages he or she visits. If someone were searching for a new car, ads for automobiles would appear.

Behavioural targeting has forced marketers to rethink their media strategies. They are shifting away from traditional media (television, radio, newspapers, magazines, and outdoor) that reach a mass audience and toward media that reach consumers directly and more efficiently—media such as the Internet, direct mail, and text and video messaging via smartphones.

Marketers have the ability to target customers individually based on where they live. When online, an individual's physical location can be determined and messages can be sent to a website visitor based on his or her location. The result is a new marketing technique referred to as geo-targeting. **Geo-targeting** is the practice of customizing an advertisement for a product or service to a specific market based on the geographic location of potential buyers (country, province, city, or postal code). Geo-targeting allows a marketer to specify where ads will or won't be shown on a website based on the searcher's location. Such technology allows local marketers and smaller marketers with limited financial means to compete more effectively with larger marketers who have far greater resources.

Mobile technology is also shaping individual targeting practices. Your smartphone takes geo-targeting a step further by tracking down individuals while they are on the move. Essentially, a person's location information (available through GPS chips in smartphones) is factored into a marketing communications strategy. Let's assume a fast-food restaurant such as McDonald's or Dairy Queen Grill & Chill knows where you are; they can instantly send you an incentive (coupon) to encourage you to visit a nearby location. It is unexpected but you might take advantage of the offer.

behavioural targeting A database-driven marketing system that tracks a consumer's behaviour to determine his or her interests and then serves ads to that person relevant to those interests.

geo-targeting The practice of customizing an advertisement for a product or service to a specific market based on the geographic location of potential buyers.

The McDonald's and Dairy Queen illustration illustrates a new technique referred to as location-based targeting. **Location-based targeting** is an effort to integrate consumers' location information into the marketing strategy. Location-based targeting is relatively new but the growth of smartphone penetration, and the dependence that people have on them, bodes well for highly targeted marketing practices in the future. In 2012, 12.4 million Canadians had a smartphone and 79 percent of them will not leave home without it![5]

Check-in services such as Groupon and Foursquare have capitalized on this phenomenon. Both services bring special deals to people in real time on their mobile devices. People agree to have these offers sent to them—the concept of checking in.

Figure 6.6 Consumers search for daily deals online.

Groupon uses the power of scale to negotiate sizeable discounts for shoppers and takes a cut of the revenues from retailers that participate. Their location-based services have proven popular, with restaurants, spas, exercise classes, and automotive repair shops, among others, offering considerable savings—in the neighbourhood of 50 percent—to attract new customers. Technology has had a significant and positive impact on the coupon business in North America. According to Andrew Sloss, former vice-president at Indigo Books and Music, "Finding good deals online is not a trend but rather an expectation of Canadian consumers."[6] Refer to the image in **Figure 6.6**.

With so much useful information available, companies are adopting a new concept called mass customization. **Mass customization** refers to a marketing system that can produce products and personalize messages to a target audience of one. This concept is not new to marketing, but its potential use by so many marketing organizations is a dramatic change from the past. Tailor shops, for example, have always offered ready-made suits while also providing made-to-measure suits for customers seeking the perfect fit and better quality. Mass customization is an extension of this way of doing business.

Nike capitalized on the online buying trend and customization by telling customers to "Just do it . . . yourself." Nike launched a website on which shoppers can design their own shoes, choosing everything from the colour of the famous Nike swoosh to personalizing the tongue with a word or phrase. This bid to target customers who want to stand out is part of the growing trend toward customization. It's also about building a relationship with customers. Nike is connecting with customers by giving them the power to put their personal stamp on their shoes.

The Nike example indicates that a brand liberation process is underway. Some experts have coined a phrase for this process, calling it brand democratization. With **brand democratization**, a company seeks opinions from customers, and lets the consumer interact with and make changes to the brand (as in the Nike customization illustration), giving the customer the power to take some control over the brand. According to Mitch Joel, president of ad agency Twist Image (Montreal), "By soliciting consumer opinion and participation online, companies not only give their customers a constructive outlet through which to express themselves but can 'educate' them about a brand to encourage a deeper connection."[7] This truly is what relationship building and direct segmentation is about.

location-based targeting An effort to integrate consumers' location information into a marketing strategy.

mass customization The creation of systems that can produce products and personalize messages to a target audience of one.

Video: Jean Machine Promises a Perfect Pair of Jeans

brand democratization A situation in which the customer can interact with a brand, giving the customer some control over the marketing of a brand (as in online user-generated content).

IDENTIFYING AND SELECTING TARGET MARKETS

LO2 Describe the process used and information needed to identify and select target markets.

Segmentation involves three steps: (1) identifying market segments, (2) selecting the market segments that offer the most potential (e.g., profit or future competitive position), and (3) positioning the product so that it appeals to the target market. Once these steps have been taken, an organization shifts its attention to developing a marketing mix strategy. Typically, a company pursues those target markets that offer the greatest profit potential.

When identifying target markets, an organization must consider various social and demographic trends. Some of the key trends occurring in Canada that marketers should be following include:

- *The Aging Population* Baby boomers are a key market segment, but equally important are the large numbers of consumers, referred to as Generation X and Generation Y, who followed them.
- *Social Responsibility* Canadian consumers have a genuine concern for the environment and they show preference toward companies that act responsibly with regard to protecting the environment we live in.
- *New Household Formations* Traditional households have been replaced with single households (people are getting married later in life), same-sex households, and empty nest households, with each type of household having different needs and expectations of marketers.
- *Ethnic Diversity* In urban markets, ethnic communities are growing at a rate much higher than traditional English-language and French-language communities.

A marketer will examine these trends and identify new marketing opportunities, anything from developing new products for profitable niche markets (such as ethnic markets), to repositioning a brand's image to appeal to new groups of consumers (say, making a brand attractive to Generation X and Generation Y), to developing smaller package sizes to meet the needs of single or empty nest households. Refer to the illustration in **Figure 6.7**.

A target-market profile emerges from this kind of analysis. A **target-market profile** describes the ideal customer around which the marketing strategy will be devised and delivered. The customer is carefully described based on demographic, psychographic, geographic, and behavioural characteristics. Refer to **Figure 6.8** for a visual illustration. Let us examine each one of these segmentation variables.

Demographic Segmentation

Demographic segmentation is defined as the division of a large market into smaller segments on the basis of combinations of *age, gender, income, education, occupation, marital status, household formation,* and *ethnic background*. Marketers analyze demographic characteristics and what emerges is a target-market profile embracing those characteristics judged to be relevant for the purpose of developing a marketing strategy.

target-market profile
Describes the ideal customer around which the marketing strategy will be devised and delivered.

demographic segmentation
The division of a large market into smaller segments based on combinations of age, gender, income, occupation, education, marital status, household formation, and ethnic background.

Figure 6.7 Attractive target markets based on factors such as age, gender, and ethnicity present opportunities for marketers.

Digital Vision/Th nkstock/Gettyimages

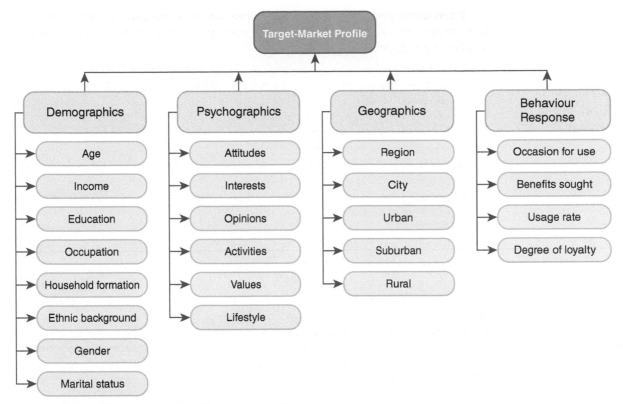

Figure 6.8   Variables for Identifying Target Markets

To demonstrate, if an organization looked only at age trends they would quickly understand that Canada's population is aging. This trend was discussed in detail in Chapter 2 in the section on demographic forces. By age, the population is divided into segments based on common characteristics. These segments include Generation X and Generation Y (younger age groups), baby boomers (middle-aged consumers), and greys (people in their senior years).

Each generation has a different outlook, different values, and different needs. Even within these generations there are sub-groups with different psychographic and behavioural profiles. A different marketing strategy (how the brand is presented to potential consumers) would be needed for each of the different segments.

For example, brands such as Mercedes-Benz and Acura market luxury automobiles. Both are successful in attracting customers in the 35- to 54-year-old age bracket—working professionals with higher education levels and healthy incomes. Consumers with this demographic profile, who are looking for a car that combines expressive design, power, and a sporty look, would probably be interested in the new Mercedes-Benz CLS or an Acura RLX. Refer to **Figure 6.9** for an image of this automobile.

A marketer must be aware of how different segments of the population consume the media. When approaching a young audience, such as Generation X and Generation Y, the Internet and cell phones are appropriate media channels, as this audience is a heavy consumer of these media. Some traditional media can then be added to the media mix. In contrast, baby boomers are also frequent users of the Internet, but newspapers and magazines remain media of choice and a fixture in most of their lives. The shift to digital media consumption among all age groups has an impact on how an advertiser allocates its media budget.

Social media networks such as Facebook, YouTube, Twitter, and Instagram are attractive media for reaching younger consumers, so you would think all companies and brands would be actively trying to engage consumers on social networks. Many have jumped in and enjoyed success while others remain reluctant or have struggled trying to figure out the medium. One study revealed that 71 percent of executives feel it is "somewhat challenging" to stay abreast of social media trends and consequently feel unprepared to meet the changes that are happening.[8]

Harley riders tend to be older, but that didn't stop Harley-Davidson from using social media effectively. In fact, a successful Twitter campaign was sourced from a member of the brand's Facebook-based Fan Machine. The fan suggested that having real riders show off

Figure 6.9 The new Acura RLX appeals to a target customer described as managerial or professional, with higher education and a healthy income.

Print advertisement provided courtesy of Honda Canada Inc.

their own chrome would provide instant credibility to potential customers. Harley-Davidson agreed and developed a campaign that challenged assumptions about Harley riders and showcased the Harley community's surprising diversity. According to Dino Bernacchi, director of marketing, "Many of Harley's 3.3 million Facebook fans don't yet own bikes. All it takes is a little push to awaken the hog within."[9] Since entering the social media arena, Harley's unit sales have been much higher than the industry average.

Gender trends are another factor marketers consider when developing a target market profile. With more and more women in the workforce (a significant change from earlier generations) and the changing roles of men and women in Canadian households, the marketing orientation is becoming increasingly "unisex" in nature.

Prudent marketers are aware of gender trends. They know that 31 percent of women earn more than their husbands and 20 percent earn about the same. Further, within the context of the average Canadian family, women control 51 percent of private wealth, make 58 percent of the investment decisions, and control 80 percent of household spending.[10] Marketers have to capitalize on these numbers! Statistics such as these justify a unisex targeting notion, mentioned previously, or individualized targeting for such an important group.

Progressive-minded marketing organizations have reacted positively to the gender trend. Home Depot leads the way in Canada's home improvement market, largely based on its understanding of both men and women. A Home Depot survey revealed that 80 percent of women prefer to do their own home projects. It gives them a sense of accomplishment, pride, and expression, and helps them save money while improving their homes. To help women, Home Depot runs Do-It-Herself workshops on a range of subjects including tiling floors, installing fixtures, and bathroom renovations.[11]

When communicating with such an empowered woman, an organization must be very careful not to portray women in stereotypical situations—and should be ready to suffer the consequences if it does. A message will have an impact if it communicates to a woman based on how she sees herself or wants to see herself. Nike Inc. is often cited as a brand that does it right with women. Nike communicates intelligently with women while recognizing they lead multidimensional lives. Advertising messages hit the mark by focusing on women's inner confidence and self-esteem.[12]

Canada's *ethnic diversity* presents new target-marketing opportunities for Canadian marketers. According to Statistics Canada, visible minorities will account for one in five citizens by 2017. Further, minorities will account for 70 percent of the growth in consumer spending.[13] The largest visible minorities are South Asians, Chinese, and Blacks. These people tend to live in large cities. In Toronto, visible minorities comprise over half of the population.

Marketers must consider the size and profit potential of an ethnic marketing strategy. On the surface, such a strategy seems to make sense, but many multinational companies view Canada as a small market. Therefore, to subdivide the market further and absorb the costs of a distinctive marketing campaign for various ethnic groups may not be practical.

Some of the leaders in ethnic-oriented marketing include Walmart, The Home Depot, McDonald's, Loblaws, RBC Financial, and Scotiabank. Loblaws was quick to react to the ethnic trend by acquiring T&T supermarkets in 2009. T&T was the top Asian supermarket chain (23 stores) in Canada. Since then, Loblaws has started carrying more ethnic merchandise in its mainstream stores. Home Depot has drawn overflow crowds to workshops at its stores that are offered in Cantonese (in Richmond, B.C.) and in Hindi and Punjabi (in Brampton, Ontario).

Quick-serve restaurants have been quick to target visible minorities, particularly the Asian communities. Not so long ago, the only choices were Chinese and Japanese restaurants. Now Thai, Szechwan, Vietnamese, Malaysian, and Korean cuisines are widely available. Restaurants such as Teriyaki Experience and Manchu Wok are expanding quickly.

Since there is a tendency for immigrants to migrate to large urban areas, the location characteristic of demographics is an important targeting issue. The concentration of ethnic communities in Canada's three largest cities (Toronto, Montreal, and Vancouver) gives national marketing organizations an opportunity to develop local marketing strategies to reach ethnic populations.

Walmart was among the first to see this trend developing and took appropriate action to capitalize on it. Walmart airs television commercials using real people (not actors) telling their own stories, in their own languages, about their relationships with Walmart. For more insight into how Walmart and Scotiabank are reaching out to ethnic markets read the Think Marketing Box **Ethnic Markets: A Golden Opportunity**.

In summary, demographic trends present challenges and opportunities for marketers, assuming they are keeping track of the trends. Understanding the differences in people as they age, knowing the differences in buying behaviour of males and females, and being versed in ethnic nuances are but some of the keys to successful marketing practice.

Psychographic Segmentation

Psychographic segmentation is market segmentation on the basis of the attitudes, interests, opinions, values, and activities (the lifestyles) of consumers. Psychographic segmentation is multidimensional: it considers a variety of factors that affect a person's purchase decision. Such information is advantageous to marketers because it tells them not only who buys, but also *why* they buy. When this information is combined with demographic information, a more complete portrait of a target market emerges.

psychographic segmentation Market segmentation based on the activities, interests, and opinions of consumers.

ThinkMarketing

Ethnic Markets: A Golden Opportunity

The ethnic market is a big market in Canada. Statistics Canada reports that a vast majority of Canadians belonging to a visible minority live in major cities. In Toronto they represent 63 percent of the population, in Vancouver 59 percent, and Montreal 31 percent. Those numbers are significant! The largest visible minority group comprises people of South Asian descent, followed by Chinese, Black, Filipino, and Hispanic.

Emma Fox, when senior vice president of marketing at Walmart Canada, understood it was absolutely vital that Walmart pursue the ethnic market. "It's really important to win a share of that market. It's a necessity because all the future market growth in terms of spending is coming from new population growth." She's right. The number of new Canadians is growing at five times the rate of the overall population.

Walmart Canada is a leader in ethnic marketing. The company developed a "store of the community" concept that caters to local needs and tastes. A store in the east end of a city carries different merchandise than one in the west end. The location of various ethnic groups in a city is a determining factor in what merchandise a store carries.

Scotiabank holds similar views and is pursuing niche markets that competitors may be neglecting. Scotiabank recently focused on the Hispanic market in Toronto and Montreal. Fabiola Sicard, director, multicultural banking at Scotiabank, says, "They are a smaller market than other immigrant communities, they are fragmented geographically, and no significant research has been done on their needs."

In demographic terms the population of the Hispanic community is 600 000+. They are highly educated—50 percent have at least a bachelor's degree and another 12 percent have a college diploma. Scotiabank sees Hispanic

Canadians as a growth market for its StartRight bank accounts, which are tailored to the needs of newcomers.

In terms of marketing communications, Scotiabank stays away from mainstream media, preferring a more targeted grassroots approach. The bank targets professional associations, street festivals, and blogs aimed at people living in Latin American countries who are mulling a move north. To reach recent arrivals, the bank gives seminars in Spanish—as many as 150 people show up. Scotiabank does not neglect the larger Chinese and South Asian communities, but the other banks are aggressively pursuing them, as well. Scotiabank is going into areas nobody else is targeting. A wise move on its part.

Question:

How significant will ethnic marketing in Canada be in the future? Do the benefits of ethnic marketing outweigh the costs?

Adapted from Marina Strauss, "Walmart aims to cater to a more diverse palate," The Globe and Mail, April 17, 2012, p. B7; and Simon Houpt, "Unknown, ignored and invisible," The Globe and Mail, November 18, 2011, p. B7.

Many of the variables that comprise psychographic segmentation were discussed in Chapter 4. Variables such as needs and motivation, attitudes and perception, personality and self-concept, and reference groups combine to influence lifestyle. When organizations target psychographically, they present products in line with the lifestyle of the target market so that the personality of the product matches the personality of the target.

Various lifestyle segments were discussed in Chapters 3 and 4. The lifestyle segments are the result of studies conducted by various marketing research organizations. Marketers today are astute at using psychographic (lifestyle) profiling to market products to satisfy the requirements of the Canadian lifestyle groups. The advertisement for Acura that appeared in Figure 6.9 appeals to the "bold achiever" or the "up and comer" lifestyle segments. These are people who reward themselves with some luxury goods—a reflection of their status, perhaps, in their careers. The advertisement for chocolate milk that appears in **Figure 6.10** appeals to a younger generation of consumers who firmly believe in living a healthy, active lifestyle. Brand messages that portray that lifestyle will have an impact on that target.

Figure 6.10
A message that appeals to Canadians wanting to live healthier, active lifestyles.

Even product categories such as appliances are getting into lifestyle marketing for their products. At one time, appliances were functional kitchen items, and usually white. Now, they have the industrial look and many are stainless steel—their design is European and they exude luxury. A well-designed kitchen adorned with such appliances is now a key aspect of lifestyle. Refer to the image in **Figure 6.11**.

Geographic Segmentation

Geographic segmentation refers to the division of a large geographic market into smaller geographic or regional units. Canada can be divided into five distinct areas: the Maritimes, Quebec, Ontario, the Prairies, and British Columbia. Geographic considerations used in conjunction with demographics and psychographics provide the marketer with a clear description of the target market, and from this description marketing strategies can be developed.

It is possible that different strategies may be required for different regions, provided those differences are significant and the potential returns profitable. The most obvious difference is in Quebec, where the language and cultural characteristics require the use of

geographic segmentation
The division of a large geographic market into smaller geographic or regional units.

Figure 6.11 A well-designed kitchen that includes the latest in contemporary appliances is a key aspect of lifestyle.

iStockphoto/Thinkstock/Gettyimages

original marketing strategies. Many companies simply adapt their English market campaigns into French and expect them to work. Their expectations are far from reality. The uniqueness of the French Quebec market demands unique marketing strategies. As many would say, "You get what you pay for!"

Wise marketers devise unique marketing campaigns that will resonate with French-speaking Quebecers. For example, a campaign for Dr. Pepper was successful in Quebec because it understood the sensibilities and sense of humour of French Quebecers. Here's the scenario of a Dr. Pepper television commercial: Two guys are moving a pinball machine down a staircase, when one of them is bothered by a sudden pain. A doctor arrives and offers a Dr. Pepper, which his patient enjoys before being struck by pain once again. A voiceover in thick Quebec accent says, "Dr. Pepper, c'est juste de la liqueur (it's only a soft drink)," poking fun at the brand's medicinal connotation. Bernard Yeung, brand manager at Canada Dry Mott's, says "We know that Quebec, like Dr. Pepper, is one of a kind, that's why we wanted to have an original approach there, to make sure we would have immediate impact."[14]

Geographic regions are subdivided into urban and rural areas. Within urban metropolitan areas, the market can be divided further on the basis of location: urban downtown, suburban, and regional municipalities that surround large cities. More Canadians than ever before are living in urban metropolitan areas—in fact, close to 80 percent of Canadians. There is also a concentration of population in four broad urban regions: the extended Golden Horseshoe area of southern Ontario, Montreal and environs, British Columbia's lower mainland and southern Vancouver Island, and the Calgary–Edmonton corridor. These four areas account for about half of Canada's population.

geodemographic segmentation The isolation of dwelling areas through a combination of geographic and demographic information, based on the assumption that people seek out residential neighbourhoods in which to cluster with their lifestyle peers.

Geodemographic segmentation combines demographic characteristics with geographic characteristics and refers to the isolation of dwelling areas (e.g., areas within a city) based on the assumption that people seek out residential neighbourhoods that include their lifestyle peers. For example, younger, higher-income households may cluster in redeveloped downtown areas, and dual-income, traditional families may reside in suburbia. Sophisticated database marketing techniques allow marketers an opportunity to target neighbourhoods if they so desire.

Whether it's a region or a neighbourhood, when a marketing strategy is developed to reach that target, the marketer is practicing micro-marketing. **Micro-marketing** involves the development of marketing strategies on a regional or local basis, giving consideration to the unique needs of the area being targeted. Many Canadian marketing organizations are moving away from "broad strokes" national marketing strategies toward strategies based on regional considerations and opportunities.

micro-marketing The development of marketing strategies on a regional or local basis, giving consideration to the unique needs of a small group of highly targeted customers.

Behaviour Response Segmentation

Behaviour response segmentation involves dividing buyers into groups according to their occasions for use of product, the benefits they require in a product, the frequency with which they use it, and their degree of brand loyalty. It is used in conjunction with other segmentation variables.

behaviour response segmentation The division of buyers into groups according to their occasions for use of a product, the benefits they require in a product, the frequency with which they use the product, and their degree of brand loyalty.

Occasions for Use   In order to increase the consumption of the product, marketers using the occasion-for-use segmentation strategy show how the product can be used on various occasions. For example, advertisers show such products as breakfast cereals, orange juice, and milk being consumed at times other than the traditional mealtimes. The advertisement for chocolate milk in Figure 6.10 presents milk as an alternative to water or an energy drink when a person is working out. Other products are associated with special occasions and are promoted heavily at these times. Flowers and chocolates, for example, are associated with Valentine's Day, Mother's Day, Easter, and Christmas. Branded advertising campaigns are more visible during these special time periods.

Benefits Sought   Benefit segmentation is based on the premise that different consumers try to gratify different needs when they purchase a product. For example, people of all ages eat breakfast cereal, and there is much overlap in the types of cereal people buy based on the benefits they are looking for. Post Foods Canada Corporation markets a variety of cereals that offer unique benefits to consumers of all ages. For the sweet tooth there's Post Alpha-Bits, Sugar Crisp, and Honeycomb. Those wanting a healthier experience can choose from Shredded Wheat, Great Grains, Shreddies, and 100% Bran.

A shampoo buyer may be looking for shinier hair, wavier hair, curlier hair, and so on. To meet such a variety of benefits a brand such as Garnier Fructis offers many variations under one brand name. Among them are Garnier Sleek & Shine, Garnier Body & Volume, Garnier Curls & Shine, and Garnier Anti-Dandruff. Why people buy one variety or another has little to do with demographics or psychographics. The key issue is the benefit the consumer is seeking.

Usage Rate   Frequency of use is an important segmentation variable. Marketers will conduct research to distinguish the characteristics of a heavy user from those of a medium or light user. Very often, an 80/20 rule applies; that is, 80 percent (or some figure close to that) of a product's sales volume comes from 20 percent of its users (heavy users). The trick is to identify the profile of the heavy users and then attract more of them. Beer marketers are very familiar with this principle. They know that younger male adults account for the most per-capita consumption and that the popularity of beer declines as consumers age. Therefore, beer marketers focus much of their advertising on younger audiences (think Coors Light, Budweiser, Molson Canadian, Blue, and so on). The battle rages on to attract the 19- to 25-year-old beer drinker!

Loyalty Response   The degree of brand loyalty a customer has also influences segmentation strategy. As with usage-rate segmentation, the marketing organization should conduct research to determine the characteristics of brand-loyal users and what motivates them to buy a particular brand. Strategies would then be developed to attract users with similar profiles and behaviour tendencies. Consideration must be given to users with varying degrees of loyalty. For example, defensive activities (for defending or retaining market share) are directed at medium and heavy users to maintain their loyalty. Distributing coupons on the package for use on the next purchase is an example of a defensive activity. Offensive tactics, such as trial coupons delivered by the media, are employed to attract new users and users of competitive brands. Because brand switching does occur, marketers must be conscious of customers at both ends of the loyalty spectrum.

Much marketing activity is devoted to building brand loyalty, for a loyal customer is a profitable customer. Generally speaking, truly loyal customers have a strong relationship with a brand and they are unlikely to switch to another brand. Perhaps this explains why brands such as Nike and Coca-Cola remain leaders in their respective markets. Nike presently controls 40 percent of the active-wear market and is well ahead of any other competitor. Its rivals have to work very hard to convince people to switch to their brand.

To summarize the discussion about target marketing, the marketing manager must carefully describe who the primary customer will be. The customer profile is based on any combination of demographic, psychographic, geographic, and behaviour response variables deemed to be relevant. For example, the following profile might represent the target market for an upscale (luxury) automobile or watch:

- *Age:* 35 to 49 years old
- *Gender:* Male or female
- *Income:* $100 000 plus annually
- *Occupation:* Executives, owners, and professionals
- *Education:* College or university
- *Location:* Cities with a population of 500 000 plus
- *Lifestyle:* Progressive thinkers and risk takers who like to experiment with new products; they are interested in the arts, entertainment, and adventure travel.
- *Behaviour Response:* Present users are extremely brand loyal and were attracted to the brand based on its heritage, image, and reputation. Potential users will be attracted to the brand based on similar intangible characteristics—image is very important.

This profile represents a good fit for an automobile like a Mercedes-Benz or a watch like a Rolex. Refer to the image in **Figure 6.12** for details.

MARKET POSITIONING CONCEPTS

L03 Explain the concept of market positioning and its role in contemporary marketing practice.

positioning Designing and marketing a product to meet the needs of a target market, and creating the appropriate appeals to make the product stand out from the competition in the minds of customers.

Once a target market has been identified and a product developed to meet the needs of the target, the next step is to position the product. **Positioning** refers to the place a product occupies in the customer's mind in relation to competing products. It involves (1) designing and marketing a product to meet the needs of a target market, and (2) creating the appropriate appeals to make the product stand out from the competition in the minds of the target market (through marketing mix activities). How a consumer perceives a product is initially influenced by image (pre-purchase stage) and actual experience with a product (post-purchase stage).

Marketers describe how a brand will be positioned in a *positioning strategy statement*. It is an important statement around which all marketing activities revolve. The positioning strategy statement includes the essential benefits offered to customers and the desired image or brand personality the brand hopes to instill in the customer's mind. A good positioning strategy statement is fairly short and written in easy-to-understand language. The positioning strategy should be attractive to customers, distinctive from the competition, deliverable by the company, and durable over time.[15]

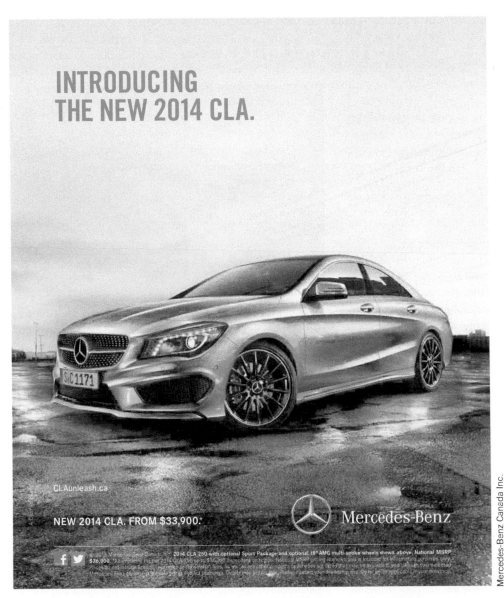

Figure 6.12   Mercedes Benz targets an upscale audience.

An advertising slogan is often the execution of a brand's positioning strategy statement. A brand such as Nike is positioned on the basis of empowerment. Advertising messages encourage consumers to try new things, to meet new challenges, to do the best they possibly can. The now famous slogan "Just do it" aptly captures the essence of Nike's positioning strategy.

Considered conceptually, a *position* is a mental space that a marketer can own with an idea that is compelling to the target audience. Here is a potential positioning statement for Apple-branded products:

> The core of Apple's brand is innovation, beautiful design, and an ability to bring warmth and passion to those customers who may be averse to technical gadgetry, but need it nonetheless to survive in today's world.

Now think of the way Apple markets its products: clear, simple images for innovative products such as the iMac, iPhone, iPod, and iPad. Refer to the image in **Figure 6.13**.

Figure 6.13   Innovation, design, and simplicity are core components of Apple's positioning strategy.

Think Marketing

Soul of a Sports Car

A sound positioning strategy is the foundation upon which a marketing strategy is built. Its importance cannot be overstated. At Mazda, the positioning statement is very clear: "The soul of a sports car is built into every car we make." Where did this positioning strategy come from?

The spirit stems from the popularity of the Mazda MX-5 Miata, a classic model in the Mazda franchise. The tagline Mazda uses in its communications—"Zoom-Zoom"—captures the essence of the brand's positioning. The MX-5 was an inexpensive little sports car people enjoyed driving; it was a vehicle that connected with people. In fact, there is a network of Miata clubs in North America, a sure sign of brand loyalty.

The company developed the Zoom-Zoom mantra as a way to extend the MX-5's equity to the rest of the brand. The sleek and sporty designs of models such as the Mazda3, Mazda6, and Mazda CX-7 exude the same spirit. While Mazda no longer advertises the MX-5 (it has a loyal following in a niche segment of the market), its design and spirit has influenced all other vehicles in the lineup.

Internally, Mazda refers to the MX-5's impact as a *halo* effect. All Mazda vehicles appeal to people who desire excitement and want to have some fun when they drive. In contrast, competitors may offer a sports car that is fun to drive, but few can claim that their other models offer the same enjoyment.

The positioning strategy is working. Success is often measured on the age of buyers. Any car company that is

Courtesy of Mazda Canada Inc.

attractive to younger buyers is in good shape moving forward. The median age of Mazda buyers is 40, one of the youngest in the industry. Smaller cars like the Mazda2 and Mazda3 appeal to Generations X and Y—Zoom-Zoom has had an impact on them. The Mazda6 appeals to the 55-year-old guy who loves to drive—Zoom-Zoom has had an impact on him. Mazda has a common strategy that appeals to young and old, an enviable position to be in. The moral of the story is clear: a sound positioning strategy truly is the foundation of a successful marketing strategy.

Question:

Is a solid positioning strategy absolutely necessary before developing a marketing strategy? Explain.

Adapted from Karl Greenberg, "Mazda's Miata MX-5 still magnetic north for brand," Media Post Marketing Daily, *November 3, 2010,* www.mediapost.com

For more insight into the importance of having a sound positioning strategy, read the Think Marketing box **Soul of a Sports Car**.

Brands are positioned within the context of competing brands. Marketers collect information about a brand's attributes and the attributes of its competitors. Such attributes may include quality, variety, price (high or low), services offered, and so on. Marketers can plot all brands on a positioning map (sometimes referred to as a perceptual map). Once plotted, a marketer can see where changes in marketing strategy are necessary if a brand is to improve or alter its image with consumers. As well, gaps on the map (places not occupied by any existing brands) may show where new marketing opportunities exist.

To understand the concept of a positioning map, consider the Canadian hotel market. Refer to **Figure 6.14** for an illustration. For simplicity's sake, let us assume that the market can be segmented into three broad categories: top-end (high price and quality), middle-of-the-road (average price and quality), and low-end (lower price and quality).

Competitors are plotted on a two-dimensional axis that considers the attributes of price and quality. In the higher-price and higher-quality quadrant are brands such as Four Seasons, Intercontinental, and Hilton. In the middle segment where price and quality are somewhat lower are brands such as Holiday Inn, Radisson, and Best Western.

Figure 6.14
A Positioning Map of the
Canadian Hotel Market

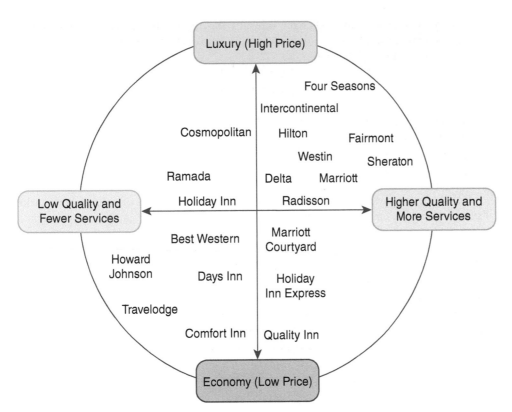

In the lower-price or economy quadrant are brands such as Comfort Inn, Quality Inn, and Holiday Inn Express. Both Comfort Inn and Holiday Inn Express have been successful by offering good quality at a reasonable price. This segment of the market is growing faster than the other segments, as both leisure and business customers are looking for better value when they travel.

Types of Positioning

When developing a marketing strategy, the positioning strategy is determined first and it acts as the foundation. All marketing activities revolve around what a company or brand wants the customer to understand about itself. Volvo wants to be known as a safe automobile, Mountain Dew wants to be known for its edgy attitude, Ford wants its trucks to be known for their rugged durability—this is what the consumer learns about these brands when exposed to their marketing and marketing communications activities. Refer to the image in **Figure 6.15**.

head-on positioning A marketing strategy in which one brand is presented as an equal or better alternative to a competing brand.

The impression or perception a consumer holds about a product is directly influenced by the impact of the marketing strategy. Tangible factors such as price, quality, where a product is available, and the style of advertising influence consumers' perceptions positively or negatively. In the implementation stage, several common strategies are used to position a product. Following are a few of them.

Head-On Positioning In **head-on positioning**, one brand is presented as an alternative equal to or better than another brand. It may not be the leader in the market but it wants to instill that thought in the customer's mind. This strategy is

Figure 6.15 Mountain Dew presents an "edgy" image to better identify with the attitude and lifestyles of the youth market.

usually initiated by a brand challenger, typically the number-two brand in the market. One approach for this strategy is to show people who declare they regularly use one brand actually choosing another brand.

The Pepsi Challenge is now a classic example of such head-on positioning. In the television commercials for this campaign, non-believers were challenged to a taste test. Once they experienced the taste of Pepsi, their conclusion was rather obvious. In one television commercial, a Pepsi truck driver and a Coke truck driver are sitting at a diner counter. The Coke driver tries a sip of Pepsi, not knowing that the Pepsi driver is taking his picture and uploading it to the Internet for the world to see. A fight ensues between the two. Pepsi effectively delivered its message in the commercial.

Challenger brands are often brands with an attitude. In terms of volume and market share they may be far behind other brands, but they do what they can to attain *thought leadership* in the customer's mind. They typically have something innovative to offer consumers. For example, Apple's iMac computer is positioned as being intuitive and easy to use, it is a sleek tool compared to a PC. Refer back to the image in Figure 6.13.

Head-on positioning requires financial commitment, because the brand leader is likely to react with increased marketing spending. In the past, a direct counterattack by the brand leader was unlikely. A brand leader preferred to let its number-one position and product benefits speak for it. In many markets today, the level of competition is so intense even brand leaders resort to using head-on strategies.

Brand Leadership Positioning Brands that are market leaders can use their large market share to help position themselves in the minds of consumers. Their marketing communications are designed to state clearly that the product is successful, a market leader, and highly acceptable to a majority of users. Coca-Cola has successfully used the leadership approach to build the world's most recognized brand. "Coke is it," "Can't beat the real thing," "Always Coca-Cola," and, more recently, "Open happiness" are examples of universally recognizable signatures. The brand name, unique bottle, and popular slogan are a deadly combination for Coca-Cola—they are instantly recognizable by consumers everywhere.

Figure 6.16 Visa communicates its brand leadership position by using phrases such as "More people go with Visa" in its advertising.

Imaginechina via AP Images

Brand leaders usually share some common characteristics over competing brands: they have greater consumer awareness and household penetration, are readily available, and have significant marketing budgets to protect their position. In the debit and credit card market, Visa positions itself as a leader. Its most recent effort involves a global positioning strategy that is summed up in the tagline, "More people go with Visa." Refer to the image in **Figure 6.16**.

Product Differentiation Positioning Product differentiation is a strategy that focuses squarely on the unique attributes or benefits of a product—those features that distinguish one brand from another. BAND-AID® brand adhesive bandages compete with many other brands. BAND-AID®'s unique attribute is a super-stick adhesive. The benefit to the consumer is that the bandage stays on longer, even in the toughest, wettest conditions, offering better protection.

BAND-AID® brand adhesive bandages compete with many other brands. One of BAND-AID®'s unique attributes is Quiltvent technology. As stated in the advertisement in **Figure 6.17**, this technology wicks away fluids and offers superior breathability—benefits of interest to consumers.

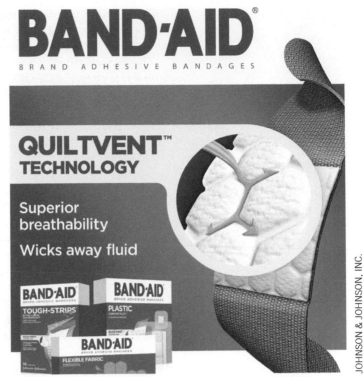

Figure 6.17 Offering a significant benefit to consumers helps differentiate BAND-AID® brand bandages from competitors.

Technical Innovation Positioning Technical innovation is often more important for a company as a whole than for individual products. Of course an innovative company markets innovative products! Companies seeking to project an image of continued technical leadership will use this strategy to position themselves as representing the leading edge of technology.

Apple is one such company—it is well known for designing easy-to-use yet technologically advanced products. Apple has had its share of innovative products, including the Macintosh computer, iMac computers (the first product marketed in the trendy "i" line of products), iTunes (digital music store), iPod, iPhone, and iPad. Apple is also a market leader in these product categories. Producers of competing products in all these categories have to be concerned about the technological advances Apple is making.

In the razor-blade market, the battle has been traditionally waged through advertising messages showing how various blades perform their functions. Gillette just recently launched the new Gillette Fusion ProGlide razor with flexball technology, which promises men a smoother, closer shave. The flexball innovation offers an additional benefit to current and potential customers. As part of the launch, men in Boston were invited to an executive trial event at a Boston barbershop. Refer to the image in **Figure 6.18**.

Figure 6.18 Innovations such as new flexball technology help keep Gillette at the forefront of the male razor market.

A TRUCK AS STRONG AS THE MAN WHO DRIVES IT.

ALL-NEW CHEVY SILVERADO   THE MOST FUEL-EFFICIENT V8 IN A PICKUP (23 MPG HWY*); 355 HP; AVAILABLE BEST-IN-   CLASS TOWING.**STRONG. FOR ALL THE ROADS AHEAD.

FIND *NEW* ROADS

Figure 6.19   Chevy Silverado trucks are positioned to appeal to hardworking, adventurous males.

Lifestyle Positioning

In crowded markets where competing-product attributes are perceived to be similar by the target market, firms must look for alternative ways of positioning their products. The addition of psychographic information has allowed marketers to develop marketing communications on the basis of the lifestyle of the target market. Essentially, the product is positioned to "fit in" or match the lifestyle of the user, or to appeal to potential users on the basis of satisfying esteem needs. Brand messages appeal to consumers on an emotional level and are delivered using sex, love, fear, and adventure. Coors Light uses such a strategy—young guys, beautiful girls, party situations, and cottage country (the desired lifestyle of the 20-something target audience) are common backdrops for television commercials.

In the truck market all of the major brands such as the Ford F-150, Chevrolet Silverado, and Ram appeal to the lifestyle of hardworking, outdoor-oriented, adventurous males. The message focuses on the strength and toughness of the vehicle. Advertisements for Silverado use phrases such as "Strong . . . for all the roads ahead" to establish the desired brand image. Refer to **Figure 6.19**. The image of the truck exudes strength and power.

Simulation: Segmentation, Targeting and Positioning

Repositioning

repositioning Changing the place a product occupies in the consumer's mind, relative to competitive products.

In a competitive marketplace, marketing organizations must be ready to alter their positioning strategies. It is unrealistic to assume that the positioning strategy adopted initially will be appropriate throughout the life cycle of a product. Therefore, products will be repositioned on the basis of the prevailing environment

Figure 6.20   The launch of the Buick Verano and the advertising associated with it helped position the Buick brand in the minds of younger female customers.

in the marketplace. **Repositioning** is defined as changing the place that a product occupies in the consumer's mind in relation to competitive products. There are two primary reasons for repositioning or adapting a product. One, the marketing activities of a direct competitor may change, and two, the preferences of the target market may change. Marketers must continuously monitor these changes.

Out of necessity, Buick (a vehicle marketed by General Motors Canada) launched a new vehicle called the Verano with a completely new image in 2013. Buick, traditionally, is the preferred ride of older men. While GM can't ignore its older target, the path to future success lies with the brand's ability to attract new, younger customers. For more insight into this story read the Think Marketing box **Melina: Buick's New Target**. Also, refer to the image in **Figure 6.20**.

The concepts of positioning and repositioning are important to understand. Potential marketers must realize that marketers do not position brands, consumers do. Once a brand's basic positioning has become set in the customer's mind, there is little marketers can do to influence it, and any change that can be effected tends to happen extremely slowly. Therefore, if a positioning strategy is working a company should avoid the temptation to change things. Perhaps the old expression should apply: "If it ain't broke, don't fix it." For a summary of the steps involved in market segmentation, identifying target markets, and positioning, see **Figure 6.21**.

Identify Segments (Target) Based on
- Demographics
- Psychographics
- Geographics
- Behaviour response

↓

Select Target(s) with Greatest Potential (Profit)
- Accurately describe the characteristics of the target

↓

Devise Positioning Strategy

↓

Devise Marketing Strategy
- Product
- Price
- Marketing communications
- Distribution

Figure 6.21   Steps Involved in Market Segmentation, Target Market Identification, and Positioning

Think Marketing

Melina: Buick's New Target

When a brand is facing declining sales and its primary target market is aging, what must it do to get things back on track? Many marketers try to reposition their brand so that it appeals to a younger target market. That said, can the same product appeal to diverse age groups? Making it happen is more difficult than it sounds.

Buick, a product line marketed by General Motors, faced this very situation. The brand had always been popular with older men and image-wise it had become rather stale. While Buick cannot ignore its primary target, future success depends on attracting new, younger customers. The product and the marketing behind it had to change.

The solution was Melina, the internal name GM gave to the new target market Buick would pursue. Melina is a tech-savvy urbanite making a good salary who likes to treat herself to nice things—spa treatments, nice clothes, and nights out with the girls.

For Melina, Buick launched a completely new vehicle called the Verano. A new style of advertising featured young women enjoying fine coffee, relaxing in beach settings, and driving the new compact, fuel-efficient vehicle. A well-balanced, traditional media buy, combined with a campaign using new social media and experiential marketing, introduced the vehicle to the market. Buick actually lent the Verano to young people who had high Klout scores—people who had influence on social media. The goal was to get the influencers to spread the word via Facebook, Instagram, and Twitter.

General Motors LLC. Used with permission, GM Media Archives.

General Motors is happy with the results. Buick sales are trending upward with the increase fully attributed to the launch of the new Verano. As well, the buyers are younger, and non-GM buyers—a sure sign that the advertising campaign had an impact on the new target market.

In more general terms, GM has its eye on younger targets moving forward. Rob Assimakopoulous, director of marketing and communications for Buick, says, "The products we're building for Buick today reinforce the needs of a modern consumer, in many cases a younger consumer."

Question:
Pursuing a new target worked for Buick. Are there any other options Buick could have considered to reverse the declining sales trend?

Adapted from Susan Krashinsky, "There's something about Melina," The Globe and Mail, November 23, 2012, p. 5.

Experience Marketing

To experience marketing you have to assess situations and then make changes to marketing strategy when necessary. What would you do in the following situation?

You are the marketing manager for 7Up, a reasonably popular soft drink among Canadian adults. The product is not on the radar of younger age groups who prefer brands like Coca-Cola, Pepsi-Cola, and Mountain Dew. For 7Up to grow in the market, you have determined that you must attract a younger customer. You have also determined the only way to do so is to market some new flavours that will appeal to the new target group. The tentative plan is to market two new flavours: raspberry and tangerine. You envision a brand name like 7Up Razzle Dazzle Raspberry to get the attention of the younger age group.

The specific market you are going after is the *tween* market. You lack information on this market segment. Your immediate challenge is to conduct a Web-based search to uncover relevant demographic, psychographic, and behaviour information about tweens.

On the basis of the information you uncover how will you position the new flavours of 7Up? What marketing strategies would you recommend to market the new flavours?

CHAPTER SUMMARY

LO1 Explain market segmentation and differentiate among the different forms of market segmentation. *(pp. 118–123)*

A market was defined as a group of people having a similar need for a product or service, the resources to purchase the product or service, and the willingness and ability to buy it.

When an organization offers a product or service to a wide range of consumers it is practising *mass marketing*. Market *segmentation* involves the division of a large market into smaller segments (or targets) based on common need and/or similar lifestyles. The marketer concentrates on segments of the population by marketing different products to segments with different characteristics. Other market segmentation alternatives are niche marketing, where an organization targets a very small or narrow segment of the market, and direct segmentation, where the organization targets customers on an individual basis.

With marketing segmentation the goal is to reach customers effectively. Advancing technologies have enhanced the marketer's ability to do so. Marketers can target customers individually and send messages to where they live, a practice referred to as geo-targeting. Through smartphones and GPS technology a marketer can track an individual's whereabouts and send messages to them as they move around, a practice referred to as location-based targeting.

LO2 Describe the process used and information needed to identify and select target markets. *(pp. 123–132)*

Segmenting a market involves three steps: identifying market segments, selecting the most attractive segments to pursue, and positioning the product to appeal to the target market. The marketer will use his or her knowledge of demographic trends in the population when identifying potential markets to pursue. The marketer will identify a profile of the target customer. The profile is based on demographic, psychographic, geographic, and behaviour response characteristics—whatever information is relevant to the situation.

Demographic characteristics include age, gender, income, education, occupation, marital status, household formation, and ethnic background. Psychographic characteristics relate to the lifestyle of the target and consider the target's attitudes, interests, and opinions. Geographic characteristics relate to where the target lives: urban, suburban, or rural locations. Behaviour response segmentation considers the target's occasion for using the product, the benefits they require in the product, the frequency with which they use it, and their degree of brand loyalty.

The marketer develops a target market profile that considers relevant demographic, psychographic, geographic, and behavior response characteristics. The target market profile is a key element of a marketing plan, since all marketing strategies are based on how well a marketer understands the customer.

LO3 Explain the concept of market positioning and its role in contemporary marketing practice. *(pp. 132–140)*

Positioning involves designing a product or service to meet the needs of a target market and then creating the appropriate marketing appeals so that the product stands out in the minds of consumers. The goal is to plant a desirable image of the product in the customer's mind. Marketers describe how a brand is positioned in a positioning strategy statement, another key element of a marketing plan. Many experts believe a sound positioning strategy is the foundation of a marketing plan. Its importance is demonstrated by the fact that all marketing mix strategies (product, price, distribution, and marketing communications) must fit with the positioning strategy. Such integration is what creates the desirable image for the brand in the customer's mind.

Some common positioning strategies include head-on comparisons with competitors, brand leadership, product differentiation, technical innovation, and lifestyle approaches. As a product matures, such factors as competitive activity and changing consumer preferences will force the re-evaluation of positioning strategies.

MyMarketingLab

Study, practise, and explore real marketing situations with these helpful resources:
- **Interactive Lesson Presentations:** Work through interactive presentations and assessments to test your knowledge of marketing concepts.
- **Study Plan:** Check your understanding of chapter concepts with self-study quizzes.
- **Dynamic Study Modules:** Work through adaptive study modules on your computer, tablet, or mobile device.
- **Simulations:** Practise decision-making in simulated marketing environments.

REVIEW QUESTIONS

1. What is the difference between mass marketing and market segmentation? Briefly explain. *(LO1)*
2. What is niche marketing and what are the risks associated with this form of market segmentation? *(LO1)*
3. What is direct segmentation? Briefly explain. *(LO1)*
4. What is the relationship between behavioural targeting and the concept of mass customization? Briefly explain. *(LO1)*
5. What is a target-market profile? *(LO2)*
6. What is the difference between demographic segmentation, psychographic segmentation, and geographic segmentation? Briefly explain. *(LO2)*
7. Why it is important for marketing organizations to monitor demographic and social trends in Canada? Briefly explain. *(LO2)*
8. What is geodemographic segmentation and how may it be applied in marketing practice? *(LO2)*
9. Briefly describe the four types of behaviour response segmentation, and provide an example of each. *(LO2)*
10. Explain the relevance of positioning and repositioning in marketing practice. *(LO3)*

DISCUSSION AND APPLICATION QUESTIONS

1. Can one branded product be successfully positioned to be attractive to several different target markets (e.g., Generation Y and baby boomers) at the same time? Discuss and provide examples to strengthen your position.

2. How important is it for an organization to devise specific marketing strategies for the Quebec market? Should unique strategies be developed for other regions and other cultural groups that exist in major urban areas? Discuss and offer an opinion on the issue.

3. Conduct some secondary research to update the status of location-based marketing in Canada. Has this marketing tool benefited Canadian companies? Provide some examples to verify the benefits of this form of marketing.

4. Provide a new example of a company or brand that employs a brand leadership positioning strategy. With regard to the consumer they are trying to reach, and their competition, how effective is this strategy? Assess and offer an opinion.

7 Strategic Marketing Planning

Stan Behal/Toronto Sun/QMI Agency

LEARNING OBJECTIVES

LO1 Identify the key elements of strategic business planning. (pp. 144–146)

LO2 Identify the nature of corporate planning and its impact on marketing planning. (pp. 146–150)

LO3 Outline the process of creating a marketing plan. (pp. 150–151)

LO4 Describe the content of a typical marketing plan. (pp. 152–157)

LO5 Describe fundamental marketing strategies employed by organizations. (pp. 157–161)

LO6 Explain the control and evaluation procedures used in marketing planning. (pp. 161–163)

HIGH LINER FOODS...

is a Canadian company that is North America's largest processor and marketer of prepared frozen seafood. The High Liner brand is one of the most recognized food brands in Canada. From humble beginnings in 1899 with the founding of W.C. Smith & Company, a salt fish operation in Lunenburg, Nova Scotia, High Liner Foods now generates annual revenues in the neighbourhood of US$947 million. Its branded products are also sold in the United States and Mexico. Other brand names include *Fisher Boy*, *Sea Cuisine*, and *Mirabel*.

High Liner products are marketed in all regions of Canada and in all major supermarkets across the country. The company attributes its strength to the fact that it successfully satisfies changing consumer tastes through new products. It also prides itself on its worldwide procurement practices, proficiency in frozen food logistics, and its strong relationships with every supermarket, club store, and food service operation in North America.

High Liner Foods has a vision statement that guides its planning process. "To be the leading supplier of frozen seafood in North America."[1] High Liner Foods is guided by three key values: customer focused, innovative, and responsible. In recent years, innovation has been a priority, particularly in the areas of new products and operational efficiency—both of which have improved the company's bottom line.

Effective strategic planning has helped High Liner Foods grow over the years. This chapter examines how companies much like High Liner Foods set objectives and put corporate strategies and marketing strategies in place to build their brands and their business.

marketing plan A plan that is short-term and specific, and combines both strategy and tactics.

Before developing a **marketing plan**—a document that outlines the direction and activities of an organization, product, or service—a marketer must consider the plan for the rest of the organization. Marketing strategies are directly influenced by the overall business plan or corporate plan. A corporate plan provides direction to all the operational areas of a business, from marketing and production to human resources and information systems. To understand marketing planning, therefore, it is imperative that we know the planning process of an organization and appreciate the interaction of plans at different levels of the organization.

THE BUSINESS PLANNING PROCESS

LO1 Identify the key elements of strategic business planning.

Strategic business planning involves making decisions about three variables: objectives, strategies, and execution or tactics. All corporate plans and functional plans in an organization (e.g., marketing, human resources, operations, information technology, and so on) formulate plans by clearly identifying objectives, strategies, and execution details. Let us first define these planning variables.

objectives Statements that outline what is to be accomplished in a corporate plan or marketing plan.

1. **Objectives** are statements that outline what is to be accomplished in the corporate plan or marketing plan. For example, they outline how much sales revenue, profit, or market share is to be achieved over a one-year period. Objectives are specific, measurable, and time based.

strategies Statements that outline how objectives will be achieved.

2. **Strategies** are statements that outline how the objectives will be achieved. Strategies usually identify the resources necessary to achieve objectives, such as money, time, people, and type of activity.

execution (tactics) Action plan that outlines in specific detail how strategies are to be implemented.

3. **Execution**, or *tactics*, refers to the plan of action that outlines in specific detail how the strategies are to be implemented. Tactical plans usually provide details of an activity's cost and timing.

A diagram of the business planning process as it applies to marketing is provided in **Figure 7.1.**

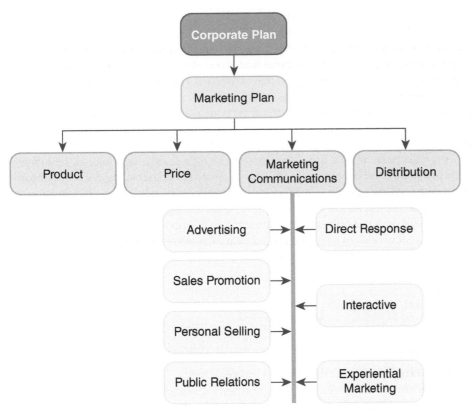

Figure 7.1 Business Planning Process: Marketing and Marketing Communications Orientation

Strategic Planning

When a company embarks on a plan, it anticipates the future business environment and determines the courses of action it will take in that environment. For example, a firm will look at trends in the areas of the economy, competition, demography, culture, and technology and then develop a plan that will provide for growth in such changing times. A typical plan considers long-term (three to five years) and short-term (one year) situations. For example, a firm devises a five-year plan that sets the guidelines and the direction the company will take. This is the long-term plan. Each year, the plan will be evaluated and, where necessary, revisions made on the basis of economic and competitive circumstances. This is the short-term plan.

Strategic planning is the process of determining objectives (stating goals) as well as identifying strategies (ways to achieve the goals) and tactics (specific action plans) that will help achieve the objectives. It is a comprehensive process done at most levels of an organization. A **corporate plan** originates at the top of the organization and is largely based on input from senior executives, such as the president and the vice-presidents.

Such plans are usually not elaborate documents, since their purpose is to identify the corporate objectives to be achieved over a specified period. The corporate plan plots the future course of an organization and acts as a guideline for planning in the various operational areas of the company.

Business planning throughout the organization begins and ends at the corporate or senior management level. The senior management formulates the overall strategic direction for the organization and establishes the financial objectives the company should aspire to (sales, profits, return on investment, and social responsibility, among other objectives). Then, in accordance with the objectives and directions passed down from the senior management level, the marketing department develops marketing plans that embrace objectives, strategies, and tactics for individual products, divisions, or target markets.

strategic planning The process of determining objectives and identifying strategies and tactics within the framework of the business environment that will contribute to the achievement of objectives.

corporate plan Identifies the corporate objectives to be achieved over a specific period.

Marketing plans consider such matters as the marketing mix (product, price, distribution, and marketing communications), target-market characteristics, and control and evaluation mechanisms that determine the effectiveness of the implemented strategies. Essentially, the plan outlines how the various components of the marketing mix will be utilized to achieve marketing objectives. The content of a marketing plan is presented in more detail later in this chapter.

The phrase "a chain is only as strong as its weakest link" is an appropriate description of the relationships between various elements of a plan. Strategic planning attempts to coordinate all the activities so that the various elements work harmoniously. Whether it's marketing for the entire company or for a particular brand, all activities must present a consistent message in order to create a favourable impression in the minds of consumers. One weak link in the chain can create conflict or confuse the target market. For example, a product's selling price could be set too high in relation to the customer's perception of quality. Or the product could fail to live up to the promises made in advertising. Inconsistent activities spread over numerous company products could seriously disrupt attempts to achieve marketing and corporate objectives.

CORPORATE PLANNING

L02 Identify the nature of corporate planning and its impact on marketing planning.

The corporate plan sets the direction for an organization. The plan is developed by senior executives and usually includes three variables: a vision statement and/or mission statement, a statement of corporate objectives, and a statement of corporate strategies. A corporate plan provides direction for all the functional areas of the company, including marketing; therefore, it is long-term in nature and broad in scope, and considers the overall well-being of the organization.

Mission, Vision, and Values Statements

mission statement A statement of purpose for an organization reflecting the operating philosophy and direction the organization is to take.

vision statement A statement that defines plans for the future, what the company is and does, and where it is headed.

values statement A statement (or set of statements) that reflects an organization's culture and priorities.

An organization may include some or all of these statements in its strategic plan:

- **Mission statement** A statement of an organization's purpose and a reflection of the operating philosophy and the direction an organization will take.
- **Vision statement** A statement of what an organization would like to be and where it would like to be in the future.
- **Values statement** A statement or set of statements that reflect an organization's culture and priorities. Such statements guide an organization's progression.

These statements may be quite detailed or very brief in content. From one company to another there may be different titles on the statements, as well. Nonetheless, the intentions of the statements remain the same. Refer to **Figure 7.2** for an illustration of these statements.

PepsiCo Canada ULC

Our Mission

Our mission is to be the world's premier consumer products company focused on convenient foods and beverages. We seek to produce financial rewards to investors as we provide opportunities for growth and enrichment to our employees, our business partners, and the communities in which we operate. In everything we do, we strive for honesty, fairness, and integrity.

Our Vision

Our vision is put into action through programs and a focus on environmental stewardship, activities to benefit society, and a commitment to build shareholder value by making PepsiCo Canada a truly sustainable company.

Figure 7.2 An Illustration of Mission and Vision Statements from PepsiCo

Corporate Objectives

Corporate objectives are statements of a company's overall goals; they take their direction from the mission statement. They may state how much return on investment or what level of sales or market share is desired of a particular market segment. Objectives may also include statements about where the company might diversify, what businesses to acquire, what social responsibility initiatives to pursue, and other goals. Good objective statements are written in quantifiable terms so that they can be measured for attainment. Consider the following examples:

- To increase total company sales revenue from $500 million to $550 million (in a specified period)
- To increase market share from 25 percent to 30 percent (in a specified period)
- To demonstrate leadership in the areas of social responsibility and corporate citizenship

Objectives like these provide the framework for the development of detailed plans in the operational areas of the organization, with marketing being one of those areas. Typically, the marketing plans for various divisions of a company or the various brands set financial and market-share objectives. The success or failure of individual products has an impact on whether or not overall corporate objectives are achieved.

corporate objectives Statements of a company's overall goals.

Corporate Strategies

The next step is to identify corporate strategies. **Corporate strategies** are plans outlining how the objectives are to be achieved. When devising strategies an organization considers several factors: marketing strength, degree of competition in markets the company operates in, financial resources (e.g., the availability of investment capital or the ability to borrow required funds), research and development capabilities, and commitment (i.e., the priority the company has placed on a particular goal). PepsiCo, for example, is committed to business and financial success while leaving a positive imprint on society. The company grows by addressing social and environmental issues when making business decisions. See **Figure 7.3** for details.

corporate strategies Plans outlining how the objectives are to be achieved.

Performance with Purpose

At PepsiCo Canada, we're committed to achieving business and financial success while leaving a positive imprint on society—delivering what we call *Performance with Purpose*.

Performance with Purpose is at the heart of every aspect of our business. We believe financial achievement can and must go hand-in-hand with social and environmental performance. By addressing social and environmental issues, we also deliver on our purpose agenda, which consists of human, environmental, and talent sustainability.

- **Human Sustainability**
  Nourish consumers with a broad range of high-quality food and beverage products that deliver great taste, convenience, and affordability, from simple treats to healthful offerings.

- **Environmental Sustainability**
  Conserve our natural resources and operate in a way that minimizes the impact that our business has on the environment.

- **Talent Sustainability**
  Develop our employees by creating a diverse and inclusive culture and make certain our company is an attractive destination for the world's best people.

PepsiCo Canada ULC

Figure 7.3   PepsiCo achieves business and financial success by delivering what they call Performance with Purpose.

A company can achieve growth through any one, or combination of two or more, of the following corporate strategies.

Penetration Strategy

penetration strategy A corporate strategy that calls for aggressive and progressive action on the part of an organization—growth is achieved by investing in existing businesses.

A **penetration strategy** calls for aggressive and progressive action on the part of an organization. Growth is achieved by building existing businesses (either company divisions or product lines). PepsiCo implements a penetration strategy across its various product lines in its two operating divisions in Canada. PepsiCo Beverages Canada includes brands such as Pepsi and Diet Pepsi, Gatorade, and Tropicana. PepsiCo Foods Canada includes all Quaker brands and salty snack foods such as Doritos, Tostitos, Sun Chips, and Frito Lay. Marketing managers devise annual marketing plans that are designed to improve the business performance of all of these brands and to penetrate the market further by increasing market share. PepsiCo wants to stay ahead of its competitors and maintain a strong presence among consumers.

Acquisition Strategy

acquisition strategy A corporate strategy in which a company decides to acquire other companies that represent attractive financial opportunities.

An **acquisition strategy** involves the purchase of another company or parts of another company. A strategy based on acquisition allows a company to enter an attractive market quickly, and it may be less costly in the long term. It may also be a strategy to gain more market share in the industry an organization presently competes in. In contrast, the time required to develop new products can be extensive and the financial commitment considerable.

Several big acquisitions occurred in Canada's retailing sector in recent years. Sobeys, the second-largest supermarket chain, acquired Safeway's Canadian operations at a cost of $5.8 billion. With the acquisition Sobeys became the leading grocer in western Canada. The acquisition included 200 in-store pharmacies and 62 gas stations on the Safeway properties.[2] What was Sobeys motivation for such a large acquisition? The answer revolves around being competitive. Sobeys ranked second behind Loblaws in Canada and was facing increased competition from U.S.-based retailers such as Walmart, Target, and Costco. By broadening its geographic reach and by increasing its purchasing power it can keep prices down. Their eye is on the consumer and how they make buying decisions. Longer term, the company can look for improved cost efficiencies in its distribution system to improve profit margins.

In the home furnishing industry Leon's acquired The Brick in a $700 million transaction. Again, the motivation for the acquisition was about remaining competitive in a market being affected by the presence of more American retailers. According to CEO Terry Leon, "The acquisition of The Brick strengthens Leon's position in the home furnishings marketplace. Our combined team will have access to national buying opportunities in merchandising and marketing, and a national distribution network will enable us to enhance our online shopping capabilities."[3]

A company will acquire another company because they see it as a good corporate "fit." Both examples cited above appear to be good fits for the acquiring organization. The acquisitions were in industries where the acquiring organizations were firmly established and highly experienced.

New-Products Strategy

new-products strategy A corporate strategy that calls for significant investment in research and development to develop innovative products.

A **new-products strategy** requires considerable investment in research and development. Such a strategy also requires financial commitment over an extended period, as it takes considerable time to develop a new product. And the odds of successfully marketing a new product remain low.

To demonstrate, Kraft developed and successfully launched a completely new "liquid water enhancer" called Mio. Mio is packaged in a squeezable container small enough to carry in a purse or pocket. Refer to the image in **Figure 7.4**. Users squeeze as little or as much as they like into a glass of water. With some good

Figure 7.4 Mio was one of Kraft's most successful new products ever.

advertising, Mio skyrocketed out of the gate. North American sales were expected to reach $200 million in 2013. Mio was specifically targeted at millennials, a generation of consumers who like to personalize things. Mio was a good fit for their lifestyle—it embraced their sense of individuality. Kraft CEO Tony Vernon called Mio "One of our most successful new products ever."[4] Eyeing the success of Mio, Coca-Cola launched a similar beverage called Dasani Drops, a zero-calorie liquid beverage enhancer.

New products also come in the form of new varieties or flavours of existing products. Kraft provides a good example of this, as well. Kraft peanut butter is a dominant leader in its market but the market is relatively flat in terms of growth potential. Kraft added some new, intriguing flavours to the product line to generate interest in the category—honey, banana granola peanut, cinnamon granola raisin, and cranberry peanut. The flavor extensions were sparked by consumer behaviour. According to Jori Lichtman, "Consumers mix things with their peanut butter . . . peanut butter and honey, and peanut butter and banana . . . and putting it together in a package that's convenient and delicious was the next step for the brand."[5]

Procter & Gamble, the world's largest packaged-goods company, is looking at new service opportunities—instead of more packaged goods—as a means of delivering growth. To demonstrate, two of its more popular brands, Mr. Clean and Tide, have expanded into franchised service operations in the car wash and cleaning businesses—Mr. Clean Car Washes and Tide Dry Cleaners. Their motivation is clear: car washes represent a $20 billion industry and dry cleaners are a $9 billion industry in North America. The power of established brand names will help market these new ventures.[6]

Vertical and Horizontal Integration Strategies

In a **vertical integration strategy**, one organization in the channel of distribution owns and operates organizations in other levels of the channel. For example, Apple Computer traditionally marketed its range of computer products and accessories through an independent dealer network and various catalogue merchants, but in an attempt to get closer to its customers, the company decided to open its own retail network. Owning and operating retail stores was not Apple's area of expertise. The venture would be costly and the company risked alienating existing retailers who had been loyal to the brand.

Nonetheless, Apple saw the benefit of getting closer to its customers. Apple opened its first store in 2001. By 2010 Apple retail stores had reached $9.1 billion in sales revenue and $2.3 billion in profit. The retail division contributes significant value to the overall success of the company. The stores are well designed (much like their products) and offer daily exposure to Apple's products in an inviting environment, an environment that is more socially oriented than sales oriented.[7]

In a **horizontal integration strategy**, one organization owns and operates several companies at the same level in the channel of distribution. The objective of horizontal integration is to control greater market share within a certain segment of a market. For example, Cara Operations, a Canadian restaurant chain, owns and operates many different restaurant chains in Canada that embrace fast food and casual dining experiences. Its original stable of restaurants included Harvey's, Swiss Chalet, Kelsey's, Montana's, and Milestones. Just recently Cara merged with Prime Restaurants, a division of Fairfax Financial Holdings. Prime operates East Side Mario's, Casey's, Fionn MacCools, and BierMarkt.

As a result of the merger, one company now operates at many different price points, offering different customer experiences to diverse target markets. It's an enviable position to be in. One way or another they will get your restaurant dollar! On speaking about the merger John Rothschild, CEO of Prime says, "This broadens our offering to Canadian families and moves us further towards our vision of becoming the undisputed leader of the restaurant industry in Canada."[8]

Strategic Alliance Strategy

Strategic alliances are now very popular among companies wanting to find ways of reducing costs or improving operating efficiencies. A **strategic alliance** is a relationship between two or more companies that decide to work cooperatively to achieve common goals. Alimentation Couche-Tard (a convenience store

vertical integration strategy A corporate strategy in which a company owns and operates businesses at different levels of the channel of distribution.

horizontal integration strategy A corporate strategy in which one organization owns and operates several companies at the same level in the channel of distribution.

strategic alliance A partnering process whereby two firms combine resources in a marketing venture for the purpose of satisfying the customers they share; the firms have strengths in different areas.

CP PHOTO/Andre Forget

Figure 7.5   A strategic alliance between Chapters and Starbucks improves the shopping experience for Chapters customers and provides additional revenue for Starbucks.

chain that includes Mac's and a variety of other banners) formed alliances with a variety of food-service providers in an effort to stay ahead of competitors. The alliance involves food-service counters for Subway, A&W, and Timothy's World Coffee.

Alliances are a means of reducing costs and improving operating efficiency. A successful alliance between Target and Starbucks in the United States was introduced to Canada when Target opened its stores in 2013. The in-store Starbucks-licensed stores serve the usual customized beverages along with breakfast items and lunch sandwiches. Target says the relationship brings the true Target experience to Canadian shoppers.[9] Starbucks also has a successful strategic alliance with Chapters in Canada. Refer to the image in **Figure 7.5**.

To demonstrate the cost savings benefit of a strategic alliance, consider the relationship that was formed between Nestlé and General Mills, competitors in the food business. The two companies recently opened a new $50 million innovation centre that will focus on innovations that deliver "nutrition, taste, and quality benefits" in the breakfast cereals they manufacture and market. The centre will also focus on packaging and technology as platforms for future growth.[10] This would have been a costly venture for either company had they done it alone.

Divestment Strategy   Bigger is not always better! Rather than expanding, some companies are consolidating their operations by **divesting** themselves of unprofitable operations or operations that no longer fit strategically with the direction a company is heading. Divestment alternatives include downsizing, closing, or selling parts of a company.

divesting Removing an entire division of a company through sale or liquidation.

Procter & Gamble decided food was no longer a strategic fit and over the past five years has been divesting itself of a variety of product lines, all of which were attractive acquisitions for smaller companies in the food business. The latest product to go was Pringles chips, which sold to Kellogg's for $2.3 billion. Kellogg's looked at the situation differently. Its core business is cereal, a market that is facing limited growth due to changes in consumer behaviour around the breakfast table. Kellogg's operates in a small way in the snack business but sees Pringles as a path to revenue and profit growth in the future.[11]

The examples cited throughout the corporate strategy section illustrate how companies use different kinds of strategies to grow and prosper. They also indicate how strategies can change based on factors such as the degree of competition, the availability of financial and marketing resources, and an organization's profitability. The underlying principle is related to an organization's mission and vision. If an organization knows where it is and where it wants to go, it will define the right corporate strategy for getting there. As the examples demonstrate, there is no right or wrong way—simply different ways of doing business.

Video: Rudi's Bakery: Strategic Management

MARKETING PLANNING

L03 Outline the process of creating a marketing plan.

The nature and direction of the corporate plan will have an impact on marketing plans. For example, if a new products strategy is called for in the corporate plan, the marketing plans for new products will be *launch* oriented, supported by a significant budget to create awareness and interest, and be aggressive in nature. If the corporate plan calls for a penetration strategy, existing products will be given priority and the marketing plans will be designed to build brand market share. To build market share, a brand's benefits must be clearly communicated to the target market to attract users of competitor brands; to penetrate the market, especially a mature market, is to steal market share from competitors.

The marketing department operates under the direction of a chief marketing officer (or similar title) within the guidelines established by the senior management or executive branch of the organization. The objectives, strategies, and action plans developed by marketing are designed to help achieve the overall company objectives. Where planning is concerned, the major areas of marketing responsibility include the following:

1. Identifying and selecting target markets
2. Establishing marketing objectives, strategies, and tactics
3. Evaluating and controlling marketing activities

Marketing planning is the analysis, planning, implementation, evaluation, and control of marketing initiatives in order to satisfy target-market needs and achieve organizational objectives. It involves the analysis of relevant background information and historical trend data and the development of marketing objectives and strategies for all products and services within the company. The integration of the various elements of the marketing mix is outlined in the marketing plan of each product. Other elements of marketing planning include target-market identification, budgeting, and control mechanisms.

marketing planning The analysis, planning, implementation, evaluation, and control of marketing initiatives in order to satisfy target-market needs and organizational objectives.

Marketing plans are short term in nature (one year), specific in scope (they deal with one product and outline precise actions), and combine both strategy and tactics (they are action oriented). They are also subject to change on short notice, as a result of economic shifts or competitive activity. **Figure 7.6** summarizes the stages of marketing planning.

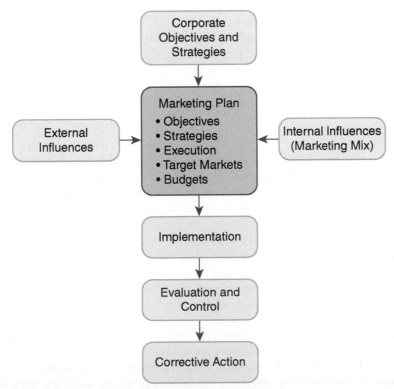

Figure 7.6 The Marketing Planning Process

THE MARKETING PLAN

L04 Describe the content of a typical marketing plan.

While there is no typical format for a marketing plan (i.e., the content and structure vary from company to company), it is usually subdivided into two major sections: background information and plan information. In terms of background, the company conducts a **situation analysis** (sometimes called an *environmental analysis* or *scan*) in which data and information about external and internal influences are compiled. External considerations include economic trends, social and demographic trends, and technology trends. As well, information is compiled about the market, competition, and customers.

Using this information, a SWOT analysis (an evaluation of a brand's strengths, weaknesses, opportunities, and threats) is undertaken. The SWOT helps crystallize the current situation and provides guidance for developing marketing strategies. In the marketing plan, the objectives, strategies, and tactics for the brand or company are clearly delineated. The following is a description of the various elements of a marketing plan.

situation analysis (environmental analysis/scan) The collecting of information from knowledgeable people inside and outside the organization and from secondary sources.

Marketing Plan Background—Situation Analysis

As a preliminary step to marketing planning, a variety of information is compiled and analyzed and summarized in the front section of the marketing plan. These trends and this information were discussed in detail in previous chapters.

External Influences

1. *Economic Trends*—Basic economic trends dictate the nature of marketing activity (e.g., if the economy is healthy and growing, more resources are allocated to marketing activity; if the economy is less than healthy—as in a recession—a more conservative approach is often adopted).
2. *Social and Demographic Trends*—Basic trends in age, income, immigration, and lifestyle influence decisions about which target markets to pursue. For example, the Canadian population is aging, and there is a steady migration of the population to urban areas. Ethnic population trends, particularly in larger cities, must also be considered. These factors necessitate changes in marketing strategy.
3. *Technology Trends*—The rapid pace of change (e.g., the manner in which people communicate with each other and the way they seek information) influences the development of new products, shortens product life cycles, and influences the communications strategies used to reach customers.

Market Analysis

1. *Market Size and Growth*—A review is made of trends in the marketplace over a period. Is the market growing, remaining stable, or declining?
2. *Regional Market Importance*—Market trends and sales volume trends are analyzed by region to determine areas of strength or weakness, and areas to concentrate on in the future.
3. *Market Segment Analysis*—The sales volume for a total market and for segments within a market are reviewed. For example, the cold beverage market is analyzed in terms of soft drinks (regular and diet varieties), fruit juices, bottled waters, sports drinks, and energy drinks. The different market segments experience different growth rates. In the hotel market, what are the growth trends among upscale hotels, mid-market hotels, and budget hotels?
4. *Seasonal Analysis*—An examination is conducted of seasonal or cyclical trends during the course of a year. For example, special holidays, such as Christmas, Thanksgiving, Halloween, and others, often have an impact on sales volume.
5. *Consumer Data*—Current users of a product are profiled according to such factors as age, income, gender, lifestyle, and location.

6. *Consumer Behaviour*—A review is made of the degree of loyalty customers exhibit toward a product or brand. Are customers loyal, or do they switch brands often? Other factors considered are benefits consumers seek in the product and how frequently they purchase.

7. *Other Factors*—Factors such as pack-size trends (regular size, single size, family size, etc.); colours, scents, or flavours; analysis of products sold; and other relevant areas play a role in the planning process.

8. *Media*—Trends in competitive spending on media advertising will influence marketing communications decisions and budgeting. Media consumption trends (as in the movement away from mass media toward digital) by consumers also influence marketing strategy.

Product (Brand) Analysis

An assessment of a brand's marketing mix strategy is reviewed at this stage. An attempt is made to link marketing activities undertaken in the past year with the sales volume and market share that was achieved—did the plan work? Is the brand meeting consumers' expectations?

1. *Sales Volume*—Historical sales trends are plotted to forecast future growth.

2. *Market Share*—Market share success is the clearest indicator of how well a brand is performing. Market share is examined nationally and regionally to identify areas of strength and weakness.

3. *New-Product Activity*—The success or failure of new product lines introduced in recent years is highlighted (e.g., new pack sizes, flavours, product formats, and so on).

4. *Distribution*—The availability of a product nationally or regionally is reviewed. Distribution is also assessed based on the business size or type (e.g., chains versus independents, and the successes or failures of online distribution initiatives).

5. *Marketing Communications*—An assessment of current activities will determine if strategies are to be maintained or if new strategies are needed. A review of media spending and utilization (e.g., television, newspaper, magazines, outdoor, online communications, experiential programs, and promotions) assesses the impact on brand performance, nationally and regionally.

Competitive Analysis

Major competitors are identified and their performance is analyzed. Essentially, a competitive product is reviewed much like a company's own brand. A manager will want to know a competitor's sales volume trends and market-share trends and what marketing activities they have undertaken to produce those trends. A review of the competitor's marketing mix activities is undertaken.

SWOT Analysis

Once the market, product, and competitor information is assembled, the next step is an appraisal of it. Such an appraisal is referred to as a **SWOT analysis**. The acronym SWOT stands for strengths, weaknesses, opportunities, and threats. A SWOT analysis examines critical factors that have an impact on the nature and direction of a marketing strategy. Strengths and weaknesses are internal factors (e.g., resources available, research and development capability, production capability, and management expertise), while opportunities and threats are external factors (e.g., economic trends, competitive activity, and social and demographic trends).

> **SWOT analysis** The examination of critical factors that have an impact on the nature and direction of a marketing strategy (strengths, weaknesses, opportunities, and threats).

The end result of a SWOT analysis should be the matching of potential opportunities with resource capabilities. The goal is to capitalize on strengths while overcoming weaknesses. A SWOT analysis can be conducted at any level of an organization—product, division, or company. For a summary model of the background section of a marketing plan, refer to **Figure 7.7**.

Background Information

External Influences
- Economic trends
- Social and demographic trends
- Technology trends

Market Analysis
- Market size and growth rates
- Regional market importance
- Market segment analysis
- Seasonal analysis
- Consumer data (target user)
- Consumer behaviour (category and brand loyalty)
- Product trends
- Media expenditure trends

Product Analysis
- Sales volume trends
- Market share trends
- Distribution trends
- New-product activity
- Marketing communications activity

Competitive Analysis
- Market share trends
- Marketing activity assessment
- Competitive innovations

SWOT Analysis
- Strengths
- Weaknesses
- Opportunities
- Threats

Figure 7.7   Content of a Marketing Plan—Background Section

Marketing Plan—Plan Section

Positioning Strategy Statement   The concept of positioning strategy was discussed in Chapter 6. There, it was stated that positioning attempts to place a desirable image of a product, service, or company in the minds of customers. In the context of the marketing plan, a **positioning strategy statement** acts as a focal point for the development of marketing strategies and the utilization of the marketing mix.

Effective positioning strategy statements are realistic, specific, uncomplicated, and they clearly distinguish what the brand has to offer. To illustrate, consider the positioning statement that has guided Visa Canada recently:

Visa gives you the confidence that you are able to do anything.

The benefits of having and using a Visa card are successfully portrayed in ads that say, "More people go with Visa."

Marketing Objectives

Marketing objectives are statements identifying what a product or service will accomplish over a one-year period. Typically, marketing objectives concentrate on sales volume, market share, and profit (net profit or return on investment), all of which are quantitative (as opposed to qualitative) in nature and measurable at the end of the plan cycle. Qualitative objectives could include new-product introductions, new additions to current product lines, product improvements, and packaging innovations. To illustrate the concept of marketing objectives, consider the following sample statements:

1. *Sales Volume:* To achieve a unit volume of 200 000 units by the end of the year, an increase of 10 percent over the current-year sales
2. *Market Share:* To achieve a market share of 30 percent in 12 months, an increase of four share points over the current position
3. *Profit:* To generate an after-budget profit of $600 000 in the next 12 months
4. *Product:* To launch a new package design in the fourth quarter of this year

Objectives should be written in a manner that allows for measurement at the end of the year. Were a particular set of objectives achieved or not?

Marketing Strategies

Marketing strategies are the *master plans* for achieving marketing objectives. Marketing strategies usually include three main elements: a description of the target market,

positioning strategy statement Statement that acts as a focal point for the development of marketing strategies and the utilization of the marketing mix.

marketing objectives Statement outlining what a product or service will accomplish in one year, usually expressed in terms of sales volume, market share, or profit.

marketing strategies Strategies that identify target markets and satisfy the needs of those targets with a combination of marketing mix elements within budget constraints.

discussion about how the various elements of the marketing mix will be used, and a budget. All marketing strategies must fit with the positioning strategy described in the previous section.

Target Market

When developing a marketing plan, the planner identifies, or targets, markets that represent the greatest profit potential for the firm. A **target market** is a group of customers who have certain characteristics in common: similar needs, ages, incomes, habits, and lifestyles. As discussed in Chapter 6, the customer is described in a target-market profile that considers demographic, psychographic, geographic, and behaviour response characteristics. To demonstrate, the following profile might represent the *primary target market* for a compact or subcompact automobile such as the Mazda2 or Ford Fiesta. Refer to the image in **Figure 7.8**.

Figure 7.8 The Mazda2 is targeted at young males and females with a socially active, urban lifestyle.

target market A group of customers who have certain characteristics in common.

- *Age:* 21 to 34 years old
- *Gender:* Male or female
- *Income:* $45 000+ annually
- *Occupation:* Entry-level business or professional occupation; staff as opposed to management
- *Education:* High school and post-secondary
- *Location:* Mainly urban; cities of 50 000+
- *Lifestyle:* Video generation; social media plays a key role in their daily routine; interested in the arts and entertainment; nightlife and socializing essential on weekends

Additional targets—or *secondary targets,* as they are referred to—will have a different profile. Pursuing secondary targets offers the potential for incremental sales and profit. For example, when Nivea launched Nivea for Men, the primary target market was defined as urban males, 20 to 35 years old. Granted, other males would buy the product, as well. However, Nivea knew that females often purchase their mate's personal care products. Consequently, when Nivea for Men was launched females were specifically targeted with advertising messages in media they consume. The female target helped introduce the Nivea for Men brand to men.

Kraft peanut butter is a well known and firmly established brand in its product category, but being a mature product, some new marketing strategies were needed to spur growth. Managers responsible for the brand carefully assessed market trends, the brand's position in the product category, and opportunities for pursuing a new, younger target market. For insight into this campaign read the Think Marketing box **Reaching Millennial Moms**.

Marketing Mix

At this stage of the planning process, the role and importance of each component of the marketing mix and those activities that comprise every component are identified. The task is to develop a plan of attack so that all the elements combine to achieve the marketing objectives. For example, in the soft drink business, both Coca-Cola and PepsiCo offer products of comparable quality and price. Therefore, it is the strength of their advertising and promotional activities (a marketing communications strategy) and their availability (distribution strategy) that determines competitive advantage. Both brands will invest heavily in these two areas. They will also introduce new beverages (product strategy) to meet the changing needs of consumers.

Different brands facing different situations may utilize the various elements of the marketing mix in different ways. At Walmart, for example, some combination of product

ThinkMarketing

Reaching Millennial Moms

What does an established leading brand do when its primary target market is aging? Kraft peanut butter faced this dilemma and decided it was time to pursue a new, younger target with a new message and media strategy.

Baby boomers grew up with Kraft peanut butter and they are genuinely loyal to the brand. Such loyalty has helped Kraft maintain a dominant position in this product category. But the times are changing. Simply stated, baby boomers are starting to retire and they are not purchasing peanut butter like they used to.

Millennials are broadly defined as those born between 1980 and 1994. This cohort is currently the second-largest segment of the population and by 2030 it will be the largest segment. Future growth for Kraft peanut butter and any other Kraft product depends on how effectively they reach this target.

Here are a few facts about millennials that marketers must consider:

- 64 percent see themselves as being as brand loyal as their parents, so it is essential for marketers to reach them early.
- 60 percent say social media advertising has the most influence over them in how they perceive a brand.
- 32 percent say social media lends the most credibility to influencing brand decisions.
- 55 percent say a recommendation from a friend is one of the strongest influences in getting them to try a brand.
- 52 percent say they want brands that are willing to change based on consumer opinion.
- Key criteria for selecting a new brand for trial include value/price (62 percent), recommendation by a friend (55 percent), brand reputation (47 percent), and quality (35 percent).
- Among traditional media, television is by far the most important option.

These data strongly suggest that a combination of television and social media is the route to follow when pursuing the millennial target. The focus of the message should be on value, reputation, and quality, all factors that marketers have some control over.

In terms of message, younger mothers believe advertisers are out of touch. They say the typical advertising message is not geared to women like them. These moms are not the prototypical mom of the past wearing a cardigan and talking to the camera about how good a product is. They are moms leading a hectic and messy lifestyle and want to be depicted as such. They want to make an emotional connection with a brand without being beaten over the head with product claims.

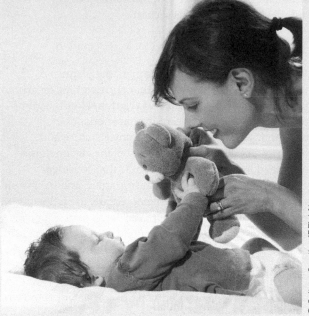

© Cultura Creative (RF) / Alamy

Kraft's priority was to reach new millennial moms in a manner that would resonate with them. The launch commercial for the new campaign shows a new mother giving a teddy bear to her new baby. As the baby grows, she takes the bear everywhere. Moving through her teen years and then into motherhood herself, her new baby gets a bear, as well—an emotional tug at the heartstrings! Teddy bears are a central figure in the package design of Kraft peanut butter and play a key role in experiential marketing activities.

Leisha Roche, senior director of marketing for grocery brands at Kraft Canada says, "Companies that will win in the future are those that humanize their brands. You can't just push your brand anymore." She goes on to say how significant the broader digital media environment is and how people are posting and sharing watchable human content all the time. Kraft has to fit into that environment.

The second phase of the campaign will involve more research. Kraft is hiring an anthropologist to explore the concept of distracted living. Insights gained will lead to more changes in how the company pursues the millennial target. The company also plans to implement social events that will bring this important target market together.

Question:
Are there other message strategies and media alternatives a marketer should consider when trying to reach the millennial target?

Adapted from Susan Krashinsky, "A new generation of moms meets an old favourite," The Globe and Mail, April 18, 2004; and "Tech savvy millennials take over spending from boomers," research brief from the Centre for Media Research, April 22, 2014.

quality and low price (a value proposition) tends to be more important. Walmart's slogan, "Save money. Live better." summarizes their marketing strategy effectively.

Canada Goose is a made-in-Canada success story—success based on a combination of quality and price (high price). The company is famous for its high-end parkas made with goose down sourced in Canada and coyote-fur-lined hoods. Some coats cost upward of $1200. How consumers perceive the Canada Goose brand has contributed to its success. People see the brand as authentic, real, and made in Canada.[12] In an age of rampant outsourcing by fashion manufacturers to foreign countries, such a positive image for a Canadian brand is refreshing.

Marketing Plan
Positioning statement

Marketing Objectives
• Sales volume
• Market share
• Profit
• Other

Marketing Strategies
(strategic priorities)
• Target market description
• Marketing mix strategies
  • Product
  • Price
  • Marketing communications
  • Distribution
• Marketing research
• Budget

Marketing Execution
(specific action plans)
• Product
• Price
• Marketing communications
• Distribution
• Marketing research
• Profit improvement

Marketing Budget
• Allocation by activity
• Allocation by time (e.g., month, quarter, etc.)

Marketing Calendar
• Activity schedule by month

Figure 7.9   Content of a Marketing Plan—Plan Section

Budget

The corporate plan has already identified a total marketing budget for the company, giving consideration to the overall profit concerns for the forthcoming year. The budget must be allocated across all company products on the basis of the firm's analysis of current priorities or profit potential. Managers responsible for product planning must develop and justify a budget that allows for enough funds to implement the strategies identified in their marketing plan and to achieve the financial objectives identified for the product. The final stage of the budgeting process is the allocation of funds among the activity areas in the plan (product development, marketing research, advertising, sales promotion, personal selling, event marketing, direct marketing, and online marketing). It should be recognized that there is much competition internally among brand managers for budget resources.

Marketing Execution   **Marketing execution**—or *marketing tactics*, as it is often called—focuses on specific details of activities that were identified in the strategy section of the plan. In general terms, a tactical plan outlines the activity, how much it will cost, what the timing will be, and who will be responsible for implementation. Detailed tactical plans for all components of the plan—product improvement, advertising, sales promotion, distribution expansion, marketing research, and so on—are included here.

A summary of the information that is usually included in the plan section of a marketing plan appears in **Figure 7.9**.

marketing execution
(marketing tactics) Planning that focuses on specific program details that stem directly from the strategy section of the plan.

SOME FUNDAMENTAL MARKETING STRATEGIES

L05 Describe fundamental marketing strategies employed by organizations.

As discussed earlier in the chapter, corporate strategies plot the basic direction an organization will take for an extended period—it may follow an acquisition strategy, a penetration strategy, a new-product development strategy, or a diversification strategy, among many potential alternatives.

Once the basic direction is established, marketing strategies that will be implemented over a one-year period must be developed for individual products. The collective success or failure of the products influences the overall health of the organization and whether or not corporate objectives are achieved. Some of the fundamental product marketing strategies have labels similar to the corporate strategies discussed earlier. Refer to **Figure 7.10** for a visual illustration of these strategies.

	Existing Product	New Product
Existing Market	Market Penetration	Product Development
New Market	Market Development	Diversification

Figure 7.10   Some Fundamental Marketing Strategies

market penetration A strategy whereby a company attempts to improve the market position of existing products in existing markets.

Market Penetration

Strategies that focus on **market penetration** are aimed at improving the market position (building market share) of an existing product in existing markets. These strategies attempt to increase sales to current users while stealing market share from competitors. In this respect, the marketing mix elements are modified to develop a better formula for convincing current and new customers to buy. Among the options available to a marketing manager might be to improve the product, lower the price, change the style of advertising, add new distributors to make the product more available, or any combination of these.

The key to success with this strategy is to get an edge by reacting to changes in the marketplace more quickly or by clearly differentiating a product from competitors. In the quick-serve restaurant market, McDonald's offers an array of products at different price points. To appeal to budget-minded customers McDonald's offers the best value menu in the industry—their egg-based breakfasts are inexpensive, they offer a coffee and muffin combination for $1.59, and their lunch and supper value menu has a selection of sandwiches and side dishes for $1.39 each. A quality product at a good price and that is readily available in a comfortable environment is an effective penetration marketing strategy—one that competitors have a difficult time matching.

In the fresh sandwich segment of the quick-service restaurant market, Subway is very aggressive. Subway offers quality sandwiches that are readily available—they have over 2600 locations across Canada! Subway has competitive prices and invests significant sums of money in consumer advertising to entice people to their restaurants. Their tagline, "Subway . . . eat fresh," is engrained in the minds of Canadians. This combination of marketing activities makes Subway a leader. It is difficult for Mr. Sub and Quiznos to compete with such a giant. Refer to the image in **Figure 7.11**.

market development A strategy whereby a company attempts to market existing products to new target markets.

Market Development

A company pursuing a strategy based on **market development** attempts to market existing products to new target markets. Such strategies attempt to attract consumers of different demographic categories, different lifestyles, or different geographic areas.

La Maison Simons, a popular Quebec-based fashion retailer, is expanding geographically. The retailer is betting its cheap-chic styles and expensive designer lines will resonate with the rest of Canada. Its marketing plan considers product and merchandising modifications based on local tastes and preferences. The first store outside Quebec opened in 2013 in Edmonton (West Edmonton Mall) and offered more casual lines, including jeans, and less high-end dressy clothing. It also stocked larger sizes: the company's research found that people in Edmonton are on average two sizes bigger than Quebecers. Future stores are planned for Ottawa (Rideau Centre in 2015) and Toronto (Yorkdale and Square One Shopping Centres in 2016). On the horizon are locations in Vancouver, Calgary, and Winnipeg.[13]

Many large retailers, including Walmart, Home Depot, and Best Buy, plan to expand

THE CANADIAN PRESS/Richard Buchan

Figure 7.11   Subway employs a penetration marketing strategy; it offers a competitively priced, quality product that is readily available and well supported with advertising and promotions.

geographically, but they are also considering lifestyle changes in their plans. Smaller, neighbourhood stores about half the size of the stores they currently operate are targeted at smaller communities with populations of 20 000 to 40 000 as well as the downtown areas of bigger cities where the needs and lifestyles of consumers are different. Different needs require a different range of product and service offerings in these stores.

For more insight into how companies apply a market development strategy read the Think Marketing box **The Rise of the Small Box Store**.

Product Development

In the case of a strategy involving **product development**, new products are offered to current target markets. Such initiatives may include the introduction of completely new products with new brand names or new versions of an existing product—for example, a new size, colour, flavour, and so on. The latter involves the use of the same brand name on the related products, which creates a family of products.

product development A strategy whereby a company markets new products or modifies existing products to current customers.

Think Marketing

The Rise of the Small Box Store

Keeping pace with changes in the marketplace is the key to business success. Retailers have noticed a trend toward Canadians living in smaller spaces, such as downtown apartments and condominiums. As well, they see consumers who are more pressed for time than ever—they are seeking convenience and faster ways to shop.

Many of Canada's biggest retailers have responded to these trends and are opening smaller stores in downtown areas of our biggest cities. It's almost a retreat to the way things used to be a long time ago, well before there was urban sprawl into the suburbs—sprawl that produced shopping malls and ultimately big box stores.

Loblaws is test marketing a new discount format called The Box by No Frills. For a grocery store, it's small—10 000 square feet. Regular No Frills stores are 25 000 square feet. The selling proposition is "hard discounts and everyday low prices." Loblaw's objective is to attract more customers in urban areas.

Canadian Tire is also testing smaller stores in urban malls. Facing intense competition from other big box stores and new competition from Target, the objective with smaller stores is to provide additional revenue in underserviced areas of a city. The urban stores, called Canadian Tire Express, are small—10 000 square feet—about one-quarter the size of a conventional store. The urban store will stock most product categories but fewer items.

Canadian Tire is also adjusting its product mix to meet the smaller living spaces of downtown residents. Canadian Tire will stock down-sized furniture, appliances, barbecues, and smaller household appliances such as microwaves,

Canadian Tire

toaster ovens, and other products. Applying a geo-targeting strategy, Canadian Tire distributes a separate flyer for areas with a lot of condominiums.

Canadian Tire is looking at other options for the future. It is considering standalone specialty stores that focus on kitchenware and home goods, and possibly an outdoor recreation store focused on hunting and fishing supplies. Canadian Tire is a successful company. Keeping pace with change is essential to their success.

Question:

Moving forward, are there any other marketing strategies that Canadian Tire should consider?

Adapted from "Loblaws testing smaller discount format for urban areas," Marketing, June 19, 2013, www.marketingmag.ca, and Marina Strauss, "Downsizing the big box? Canadian Tire's shrinking vision," The Globe and Mail, March 7, 2013, pp. B1, B7, and Marina Strauss, "Retailers race to downsize product offerings," The Globe and Mail, September 20, 2012, p. B9.

Canada Bread

Figure 7.12   An example of a new product that offers hidden nutritional benefits.

If you were asked to identify a leading brand of cookies, no doubt Oreo would come to mind. Oreo stands out in a crowded and competitive market, and to remain a leader it recently launched four new varieties: chocolate crème, mint crème, peanut butter, and golden. The new flavours will appeal to current and new users, producing incremental sales volume for the Oreo brand.

Maple Leaf Foods is one of Canada's biggest meat and bread producers. The company develops new products around three core trends occurring in the marketplace: changing demographics (such as single-person households), emphasis on health and nutrition, and convenience. All new products must address one or more of these trends. The company's Natural Selections pre-packaged meats were facing marginal decline due to concerns consumers have for processed meats. To combat that concern Maple Leaf launched a line of no-preservative meat products, and sales increased significantly over the next two years. Maple Leaf now markets four of the top ten sliced meat products in Canada.[14]

Canada Bread Company Limited, which used to be a division of Maple Leaf Foods, recently launched Dempster's Garden Vegetable bread, flecked with pieces of carrot and pumpkin. This innovative product responds to a new trend—that of promoting products with nutritional extras inside. As consumers become more pressed for time, food companies like Canada Bread see value in offering products that add nutritional benefits into a person's day. Refer to the image in **Figure 7.12**.

In the retail market, companies are expanding their product mix to offer shopping convenience. Shoppers Drug Mart, for example, is no longer just a drugstore. It is a one-stop shopping destination for women. It now offers a wider range of health and beauty products, food, and electronics items. Refer to the image in **Figure 7.13**, the new food section in Shoppers Drug Mart.

Diversification

diversification A situation in which a company invests its resources in a totally new direction (e.g., a new industry or market).

Diversification, as it applies to products, refers to the introduction of a new product to a completely new market. In effect, the company is entering unfamiliar territory when it uses this strategy. Such a strategy requires substantial resources for research and

Shoppers Drug Mart

Figure 7.13   Shoppers Drug Mart added new product lines to become a one-stop shopping destination.

development, initially high marketing expenses, and a strong commitment to building market share. To illustrate, consider Apple Computer's recent marketing adventures.

Apple Computer—always a niche player in the computer market, and always a company that does things differently—opted for diversification when it decided to open up its own retail stores. Apple's main selling points are that its products are cool and sexy—a good fit for retail. Apple believed that the stores would attract both current and new customers—and it was right! Apple stores became the fastest-growing chain in history, reaching $1 billion in sales in just three years—besting the record previously held by the Gap, which took four years to reach the same level.[15]

Apple ventured into the music business with its iTunes music service and the iPod portable music player, both of which are innovations that dramatically changed the music industry and the way people listen to music. As of 2013, Apple accounted for 75 percent of all digital music sales and it produces $6.9 billion in revenue for the company.[16] In the tablet market Apple was once the dominant player, but intense competition has reduced its market share somewhat. Nonetheless, the iPad is the market leader with 29.6 percent market share.[17] Diversification of product lines has moved Apple from being a computer company to being an entertainment company.

MARKETING CONTROL AND EVALUATION

LO6 Explain the control and evaluation procedures used in marketing planning.

Since clearly defined and measurable objectives have been established by the organization and the marketing department, it is important that results be evaluated against the plans and against past performance. This evaluation indicates whether current strategies need to be modified or whether new strategies should be considered. **Marketing control** is the process of measuring and evaluating the results of marketing strategies and plans, and taking corrective action to ensure that the marketing objectives are attained. Marketing control involves three basic elements:

1. Establishing standards of marketing performance expressed in the form of marketing objectives
2. Periodically measuring actual performance (of the company, division, or product) and comparing it with the established objectives
3. Taking corrective action (e.g., developing new strategies) in those areas where performance does not meet the objectives

marketing control The process of measuring and evaluating the results of marketing strategies and plans, and taking corrective action to ensure that marketing objectives are attained.

Refer to **Figure 7.14** for a diagram of the control process. The nature of an organization's control process can vary and the frequency of evaluation is left to the discretion of the management. For evaluating the effectiveness of marketing strategies, there are three primary measures or indicators: *marketing activity reviews, financial reviews,* and *strategic control reviews.*

Marketing Activity Reviews   The effectiveness of a marketing plan is measured against a few key indicators: *sales volume, market share,* and *profit.* Activity reviews typically occur on a quarterly basis and often involve a gathering of brand managers, sales managers, and some senior marketing executives. Planning cycles that have activity reviews built in give an organization the opportunity to make strategic adjustments during the course of a year.

For any of the three indicators (sales, market share, and profit), the managers will compare *actual results* versus *planned results* and *actual results* versus *results for the same period a year ago.* Understanding why sales are up or down is the responsibility of the sales managers and marketing managers, so naturally there is much discussion among these managers to figure out the results and agree on how to proceed. By reviewing performance and customer feedback together they can mutually agree on revised figures and marketing activities for the balance of the year.

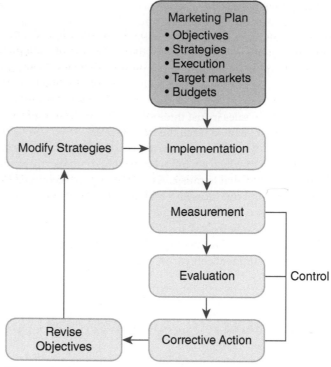

Figure 7.14   Marketing Control Process

Part of the marketing activity review should also include a review of competitor activity. What are the competitors doing? Are they gaining or losing market share? Such analysis attempts to link marketing activities to share performance in an effort to determine which activities are effective and which are ineffective.

Financial Reviews   As part of the organization's marketing control process, periodic profit reviews are conducted for all product lines and divisions. Key variables in a profit review are up-to-date *sales forecasts*, *costs*, and *marketing budgets*.

Because senior executives are largely evaluated on the profit the organization generates and the value of a company's stock, the financial review process can be challenging for the marketing department. For example, if it is forecast that profit will fall short of expectations by the end of the fiscal year, marketing budgets will have to be trimmed. Such reductions could occur by product, division, or region. For example, the advertising budget could be slashed to protect other marketing activities. A financial review forces managers to establish priorities and withdraw funds from those activities that will feel the effects the least.

Strategic Control Reviews   Strategic control is more long term in nature than marketing control. Since conditions in the marketplace (economy, technology, competition, and governments) change rapidly, marketing strategies soon become outdated. An organization must be ready for change! Therefore, strategic reviews are intensive and are conducted every three to five years. Within this framework, marketers reassess marketing strategies for all products annually, during the preparation of the marketing plan. For example, technology is changing the very nature of marketing communications today, and many firms are struggling with how to deal with the situation. Business organizations know they must invest in interactive communications and social media but they struggle to understand these media, the benefits they offer, and the analytics that measure success or failure of the communications. Therefore, expertise from external agents that specialize in this area is called upon. This is a big issue facing senior marketing executives today.

Keeping Pace with Change

In contemporary marketing, an organization must be flexible in order to take advantage of new developments in the marketplace. Throughout the planning cycle, a firm is presented with new threats and opportunities that can make a plan obsolete rather quickly. Consequently, the wise marketing manager builds a contingency plan into the master plan. A contingency is the possibility of something happening that poses a threat to the organization. A **contingency plan** identifies alternative courses of action that can be used to modify an original plan if and when new circumstances arise.

A contingency plan is based on "what if" or "worst case" situations. If these situations develop, the organization is ready to implement alternative strategies. Some events that would require alternative action would be the following:

1. The competition unexpectedly increases its level of media spending.
2. The competition reduces its price to build market share.
3. A new competitor enters the market.
4. A strike in your own plant halts production of your product.
5. A new trend emerges that changes market conditions.
6. The economy unexpectedly takes a turn for the worse.

Such situations add a dimension of foresight to strategic marketing planning and force the manager to plan for the unexpected at all times.

contingency plan
Alternative courses of action that can be used to modify an original plan if and when new circumstances arise.

✔ **Experience**Marketing

To experience marketing you have to assess situations and make recommendations to change marketing strategies when necessary. What would you do in the following situation?

You are the marketing manager for Red Bull in Canada. Red Bull is marketed in 120 countries and is the leader in the energy drink segment. In Canada it is the market leader in the energy drink market segment with a 50 percent market share and annual sales revenue of approximately $22 million.

Red Bull is a product designed to combat mental and physical fatigue. Red Bull promises to improve performance during times of stress or strain, to increase concentration and improve reaction speed, and to stimulate metabolism. Red Bull claims to revitalize the body and mind.

The energy drink market is now more competitive than ever in Canada. Red Bull must contend with PepsiCo brands such as Mountain Dew Amp and SoBe No Fear, and Coca-Cola brands such as Rock Star and Full Throttle. Red Bull has been able to hold its ground because

consumers show preference for niche brands. In this segment there is a certain cachet associated with the name Red Bull.

Most brands, including Red Bull, target young urban males 16 to 29 years old (Generation Y), though others in need of a boost do consume the drink. In terms of marketing, Red Bull avoids mass marketing, preferring to focus on buzz-marketing strategies and word-of-mouth to build the brand. Red Bull also associates itself with adventure and risk-taking sports. Red Bull's advertising efforts have been restricted to a campaign using the theme and slogan "Red Bull gives you wings." The slogan aptly summarizes the primary product benefit.

As the marketing manager, you are contemplating changes in marketing strategy in order to protect your position in the Canadian market. Before you can make any changes you need answers to several questions. Should you target an older market? Should the brand positioning strategy be changed? If the positioning strategy changes, what new marketing strategies should be implemented?

You must quickly audit the market, key competitors, and the brand to gain insights on what to do. What will you recommend? Be prepared to justify your recommendations.

CHAPTER SUMMARY

L01 Identify the key elements of strategic business planning.   *(pp. 144–146)*

Strategic business planning is a problem-solving and decision-making effort that forces management to look at the future and develop courses of action that are appropriate for the external conditions the organization faces. Strategic planning is a process in which objectives, strategies, and execution details are clearly identified. Objectives outline what is to be accomplished (e.g., sales growth, market share growth, and so on); strategies indicate how the objectives will be achieved (e.g., time and resources required); and execution outlines the tactical details of the strategy (e.g., specific activities, their costs, and timing). Strategic business planning typically starts and ends with the senior executives of an organization.

L02 Identify the nature of corporate planning and its impact on marketing planning.   *(pp. 146–150)*

In a business organization, two separate but related plans work together to achieve growth objectives. A corporate plan provides direction to a marketing plan; a marketing plan provides direction to the various components of marketing, such as product strategy and marketing communications strategy. Each plan has its own objectives, strategies, and execution details. Corporate planning starts with the development of a mission and vision statement, followed by corporate objectives and strategies. These plans consider both the short term and the long term, and their objectives are financial in nature. The objectives are stated in terms of growth in sales, profit, return on investment, and market share.

Some of the more common corporate strategic alternatives include penetration strategies that focus on more aggressive marketing, acquisition strategies, new-product development programs, forming strategic alliances, vertical and horizontal integration strategies, and divestment strategies. Large business organizations often combine several of these strategies.

L03 Outline the process for creating marketing plans.   *(pp. 150–151)*

Marketing planning is the analysis, planning, implementation, evaluation, and control of marketing initiatives in order to satisfy target market needs and organizational objectives. The strategic marketing planning process involves reviewing and analyzing relevant background information, establishing appropriate marketing objectives, devising a positioning strategy, identifying target markets, devising marketing strategies (utilization of the marketing mix) and marketing executions (specific action plans to implement the strategies), accessing budget support, and implementing control procedures.

L04 Describe the content of a typical marketing plan.   *(pp. 152–157)*

Marketing plans are typically developed on an annual basis. The plan is divided into two major sections: the background section and the plan section. The background section includes relevant information about various external influences (such as economic, social, and demographic trends), a thorough review of the market a brand competes in, an assessment of the brand's most recent performance, and a review of key competitor activities. All information is then consolidated in a SWOT analysis that portrays the brand's current position in the market.

The plan section plots the brand's future. It includes a positioning strategy statement, identifies key objectives for the forthcoming year, portrays the target market to be pursued, and outlines how the various components of the marketing mix will be employed to accomplish the objectives. A budget to support all activities is also identified in the plan.

L05 Describe fundamental marketing strategies employed by organizations.   *(pp. 157–161)*

The more commonly used product marketing strategies include market penetration, market development, product development, and diversification. Market penetration is a strategy that attempts to improve the current position of existing products. Market development is a strategy in which existing products are marketed to new target markets. A product development strategy involves developing new products for current customers or modifying current products for existing customers. Diversification is a situation in which a company invests its resources in a totally new direction—new products for new target markets.

L06 Explain the control and evaluation procedures used in marketing planning.   *(pp. 161–163)*

Once the marketing plan is implemented, it is subject to evaluation. The evaluation and control process attempts to draw relationships between strategic activities and results. The organization determines which activities are effective or ineffective and then alters its strategy as needed. The marketing plans (the performance of the product based on the plan) are reviewed at predetermined intervals during the course of a year. Corrective action is implemented when necessary. Due to uncertainty in the marketplace, wise marketing planners build contingency plans into the overall marketing plan. Such plans force planners to consider in detail the environments that influence marketing activities.

MyMarketingLab   Study, practise, and explore real marketing situations with these helpful resources:
- **Interactive Lesson Presentations:** Work through interactive presentations and assessments to test your knowledge of marketing concepts.
- **Study Plan:** Check your understanding of chapter concepts with self-study quizzes.
- **Dynamic Study Modules:** Work through adaptive study modules on your computer, tablet, or mobile device.
- **Simulations:** Practise decision-making in simulated marketing environments.

REVIEW QUESTIONS

1. What is strategic planning? Briefly explain. *(LO1)*
2. In planning, what are the basic differences among objectives, strategies, and tactics? *(LO1)*
3. What is the role of a mission statement and a vision statement in the corporate planning process? *(LO2)*
4. What is the relationship between a corporate plan and a marketing plan? *(LO2)*
5. Briefly differentiate among the following corporate strategies: acquisition, strategic alliance, vertical integration, and divestment. *(LO2)*
6. What is marketing planning? Briefly explain. *(LO3)*
7. What is the difference between a situation analysis and a SWOT analysis? Briefly explain. *(LO3)*
8. What is the relationship between a positioning strategy statement and the marketing strategies and executions of a brand or company? *(LO4)*
9. What are the key components of a marketing strategy? (LO4)
10. At the product planning level what is the difference between a penetration strategy, market development strategy, and a new product development strategy? *(LO5)*
11. What is the difference between a marketing activity review and a financial review? *(LO6)*
12. What is a contingency plan, and why is such a plan necessary? *(LO6)*

DISCUSSION AND APPLICATION QUESTIONS

1. Provide additional examples of the following corporate strategies:
   a. Strategic alliance
   b. Acquisition
   c. Divestment
   d. Vertical integration
   e. Horizontal integration
2. Identify a product (a good or a service) or a retail organization that uses the following marketing strategies. Provide an explanation of each strategy as it applies to the brand and company.
   a. Market penetration
   b. Market development
   c. Product development
   d. Diversification (product)
3. Marketing evaluation and control procedures tend to be quantitative in nature. Is this the best approach for measuring the effectiveness of marketing strategies? Can you suggest any alternatives?
4. The chapter discusses the importance of identifying primary and secondary target markets. Provide some additional examples of products and services that have expanded their sales and market shares by pursuing secondary targets. How did these companies target these markets (e.g., new product lines, new advertising messages)?

8

Product Strategy

© chainsaw75/Alamy

LEARNING OBJECTIVES

LO1 Explain the total product concept and product mix. (pp. 167–169)

LO2 Describe how consumer and business goods are classified. (pp. 169–173)

LO3 Explain the role and importance of branding strategies. (pp. 173–177)

LO4 Discuss the role of packaging and labelling in the development of product strategies. (pp. 178–184)

LO5 Explain the benefits of branding. (p. 184)

LO6 Describe the various stages of brand loyalty and how brand equity is created. (pp. 185–186)

DAVID'S TEA ...

has put a fresh, North American twist on tea. The company opened its first store in Toronto in 2008, and has since expanded its colourful and modern shops to neighbourhoods and communities across Canada and the United States. The brand strategy is simple—delight customers with great-tasting teas and exceptional customer service. "It seems like a basic idea, but there wasn't anyone else that was doing it at the time," explains owner David Segal.

With over 150 types of tea, including exclusive blends like Read My Lips, a delicious chocolate mint dessert tea, and Movie Night, a combination of apple pieces, maple, and popcorn, David's Tea has built a loyal following. "Our customers come in to sample our teas and talk to our staff—they feel like they've travelled around the world without even leaving the store," says Segal. Over time, David's Tea has expanded its product mix to include a line of innovative tea accessories designed in-house, from spoons and infusers to tea sets and travel mugs, as a way to help ensure customers are able to make the best cup of tea possible.

David's Tea makes tea fun and accessible. According to Segal, "Tea had a stereotype for being a bit stodgy, a bit off the beaten track, either highly British or Asian. If one of our customers hasn't tried loose-leaf tea before, we take them by the hand and show them how easy it is." The company's branding strategy is working, as tea sales are soaring. And it appears the trend is going to continue, as Canadians' tea consumption is expected to rise 40 per cent by 2020, according to a government agency report on food trends published by Agriculture and Agri-Food Canada.[1 & 2]

Effective branding strategies and a continuous effort to improve the quality of a product are essential ingredients for success. That's what this chapter is about.

Product strategy is just one element of the marketing mix, but it is an important one because decisions about other mix elements are based on the attributes and benefits the product offers. For example, the price charged is related to the product's quality, and an advertising campaign is responsible for communicating a product's benefits in a manner that will influence the target market to try the product. Advertising and other marketing communications help distinguish products from one another. The key elements of product strategy—decisions that are made that help distinguish one brand from others—are presented in this chapter.

TOTAL PRODUCT CONCEPT AND PRODUCT MIX

L01 Explain the total product concept and product mix.

A **product** is "a bundle of tangible and intangible benefits that a buyer receives in exchange for money and other considerations."[3] In effect, the consumer purchases much more than the actual object. To demonstrate, consider the purchase of a luxury automobile such as a Porsche. The decision to purchase is not based on transportation needs. This is a car you do not really need; you buy it in order to display your achievements and success. Such a purchase is bound up with the intangibles of prestige, status, and image.

This example illustrates that a product is more than the actual physical object. There are several elements that a marketer can emphasize when attempting to attract consumers; those elements comprise the benefits that a buyer receives. This package of benefits is referred to as the **total product concept**. It includes the physical item as well as the package, brand name, label, service guarantee, warranty, and image presented by the product. A marketing manager makes crucial decisions in each of these areas. That's what product strategy is about. A manager more than likely makes decisions about a mix of products that all fall under the same brand name.

product A bundle of tangible and intangible benefits that a buyer receives in exchange for money and other considerations.

total product concept The package of benefits a buyer receives when he or she purchases a product.

The Product Mix

The **product mix** is the total range of products offered for sale by a company. It is the collection of product items and product lines that a firm tries to market. Each of the

product mix The total range of products offered for sale by a company.

products or product items in the mix appeals to a particular segment, and in a way that makes it distinct from the offerings of the competition. Most, if not all, large consumer packaged-goods companies have a complete product mix: that is, they offer for sale a variety of different products that appeal to different user segments. For example, Kraft Foods markets products in a variety of categories that include beverages, cereals, convenient meals, cheese, grocery products, and snacks.

A **product item** is defined as a unique product offered for sale by an organization. The key word in this definition is *unique*. Marketers refer to the distinguishing product characteristic or primary benefit of a product or service, the one feature that distinguishes it from competing products, as the **unique selling point (USP)**. Such a feature may be the format of the product, the sizes and variety available, or the ingredients. To illustrate, consider the following examples.

Tide is a laundry detergent that offers different varieties to meet the unique needs of customers. Generally, the message is that Tide keeps your clothes beautiful: it cleans thoroughly, protects colour, preserves shape, maintains finish, enhances softness, prevents pilling, and fights stains.

Tom's of Maine all-natural toothpaste offers different varieties to address five different issues: cavity prevention, plaque, sensitivity, whitening, and bad breath. The issues are addressed individually under the Tom's of Maine brand name. For example, the company markets Tom's Cavity Protection, Tom's Simply White, and Tom's Wicked Fresh! Each product item has a unique selling point. See **Figure 8.1** for details.

With so many brands and varieties of energy drinks to choose from, how do consumers know which brand to buy? Typically, energy drink brands focus on the function of the drink (that energy boost factor) as the key benefit. Rockstar, the number three brand in the category behind Red Bull and Monster, goes in a different direction with a very bold tagline in its promotions: "Party like a Rockstar!" This tagline is suggestive of celebrity and sex appeal, and makes the brand all about how consumers perceive themselves when they're drinking it.

A product item often grows into a line of products. A **product line** is a grouping of product items that share major features but may differ in terms of attributes such as size, function, or style. For example, Lululemon's original products included women's yoga pants and tops. Since opening its first store in Vancouver in 1998, the company has expanded its niche product line to include athletic clothing for running, tennis, and dance, as well as a line of men's athletic wear. The expanded product line is part of Lululemon's overall brand positioning in the market: offer high quality garments manufactured from technical fabrics and functional designs. Lululemon's loyal customers not only love the clothing, they have bought into the company's healthy living, positive lifestyle, and yoga culture.[4 & 5] Refer to the image in **Figure 8.2**.

A firm's product line is described in terms of width and depth. **Product line width** is the number of lines in the mix. **Product line depth** refers to the number of items in the

product item A unique product offered for sale by an organization.

unique selling point (USP) The primary benefit of a product or service, the one feature that distinguishes a product from competing products.

product line A grouping of product items that have major attributes in common but that may differ in size, function, or style.

product line width Number of lines in the mix.

product line depth Number of items in the line.

Figure 8.1   Tom's of Maine offers a variety of toothpaste products to meet the diverse needs of consumers.

line. All items and lines collectively form a firm's product mix. Nestlé markets products in many categories—baby foods, water, coffee, frozen meals, pet foods, and ice cream among them. Within each category there is product line width and depth. See **Figure 8.3** for a listing of a small selection of Nestlé product lines.

The width and depth of a product mix depend on the firm's overall marketing strategy. The idea is to balance risks and offset seasonal sales fluctuations. As well, the firm must constantly address consumers' ever-changing needs when managing the product mix.

PRODUCT CLASSIFICATIONS

Figure 8.2   Lululemon offers a range of yoga and casual wear product lines to meet the needs of consumers.

L02 Describe how consumer and business goods are classified.

Products are divided in two basic ways. First and most important, a product is classified according to the target market it is intended for. Second, it is classified according to the durability and tangibility it offers.

Products are also broadly classified into two groups on the basis of who buys them and why: consumer goods and industrial (business) goods. **Consumer goods** are products and services purchased by consumers for their own personal use or benefit. **Industrial (business) goods** are those products and services purchased by businesses,

consumer goods Products and services ultimately purchased for personal use.

industrial (business) goods Products and services purchased to be used directly or indirectly in the production of other goods for resale.

Figure 8.3 An Illustration of Product Line Width and Depth

Source: Adapted from www.nestle.ca

Product Line Width

Nestlé Canada offers a wide range of lines that include the following:

- Baby foods
- Sports nutrition
- Chocolates
- Waters
- Coffee
- Other beverages
- Frozen meals
- Ice cream and frozen treats
- Pet foods

Product Line Depth

Listed below is a sample of Nestlé product line depth in the chocolate category.

Kit Kat	Aero	Smarties
Regular	Regular	Regular
Snack Size	Snack Size	King Size
Minis	King Size	Giant Box
Chunky	Chunky	Holiday Shaker Bag
Chunky Xtra Chocolate	Caramel	Holiday Stand up Bag
Chunk MAX	Peppermint	Holiday Giant Tube
Chunky Peanut Butter	Singles–Dark	Stand up Bag Regular
Singles–Dark	Singles–Milk	Stand up Peanut Butter
Singles–Milk		

industries, institutions, and governments that are used directly or indirectly in the production of another good or service that is resold, in turn, to another user (possibly a consumer).

nondurable good A tangible good normally consumed after one or a few uses.

durable good A tangible good that survives many uses.

A **nondurable good** is a tangible good normally consumed in one or a few uses. Examples include everyday products such as toothpaste, coffee, milk, and detergent. These products are replenished frequently. A **durable good** is a tangible good that survives many uses. Examples include automobiles, appliances, personal computers, and consumer electronics. These items are purchased infrequently.

Consumer Goods

Consumer goods are commonly classified into three categories: convenience goods, shopping goods, and specialty goods (see **Figure 8.4**). This classification is based on consumer buying behaviour.

convenience goods Those goods that consumers purchase frequently, with a minimum of effort and evaluation.

Convenience Goods **Convenience goods** are those goods purchased frequently, with a minimum of effort and evaluation. Typical examples include food items such as bread, milk, cookies, and chocolate bars, and personal-care products such as soap, deodorant, and shampoo. Convenience goods fall into the routine decision-making process discussed in Chapter 4.

Generally, consumers do not spend much time purchasing convenience goods (e.g., price comparisons from store to store are unlikely). Therefore, it is in the best interests of the marketing organization to inform the consumer of the merits of the product through marketing communications as well as making sure that the product has an attractive, eye-catching package and is readily available when consumers need it.

shopping goods Goods that the consumer compares on such bases as suitability, quality, price, and style before making a selection.

Shopping Goods **Shopping goods** are goods that the consumer compares on such bases as suitability, quality, price, and style before making a selection. Other factors of concern to the shopper include dependability, service, functionality, guarantees, and warranties. Examples of shopping goods include automobiles, clothing, major appliances,

Type of Consumer Good

Basis of Comparison	Convenience	Shopping	Specialty
Examples	• Bread • Cookies • Shampoo • Deodorant	• Automobiles • Clothing • Home furnishings • Cleaning services	• Michael Kors hand bags • BMW automobiles • Rolex watches
Product	• Attractive package • Proven performance • Brand name	• Quality • Style • Reliability	• Brand name • Brand image • Reputation • Superior quality
Price	Relatively inexpensive	Fairly expensive	Usually very expensive
Distribution	Widely available in many outlets	Available in a large number of selective outlets	Only available at a few resellers
Marketing communications	Focus on price and availability	Personal selling at point-of-sale	Focus on brand status and quality
Consumer buying behaviour	• Purchase often • Little time spent in researching purchase	• Purchase infrequently • Some time and effort made to compare alternatives	• Purchase infrequently • A lot of time and effort is put in to purchase decision process

Figure 8.4 Marketing Considerations for Consumer Goods

household furnishings, decoration services, and major repairs around the house. The price of shopping goods tends to be higher. Buying behaviour tends to be more rational in nature—people often shop and compare alternatives before they buy.

Marketing considerations deemed important for shopping goods include being located near competitors where comparisons can be easily made, having a consistent and attractive image (proven performance has an advantage over little-known brands), and having effective communications so that awareness among consumers is high when their need for the product arises. Marketers know that consumers do their product research online before making a major buying decision. It is therefore imperative that makers of shopping goods have a strong online presence, and even endorsements by satisfied customers and other influencers—for example, bloggers who may report on their particular industry.

To illustrate these principles, consider how Maytag's new macho Maytag Man builds on the traditional old and bored Maytag Repairman character and reinforces Maytag's benefits to a younger clientele. Instead of stressing reliability, the new strong and masculine Maytag Man actually represents the strength of a Maytag machine. Over time, such a focused brand message builds on Maytag's excellent reputation and gives customers a basis for comparison with other brands.

Specialty Goods **Specialty goods** are goods that consumers make an effort to find and purchase because they possess some unique or important characteristic. In effect, the consumer has already decided what item to buy; it is simply a matter of making the shopping excursion to buy it. Generally speaking, the marketing considerations that are important for specialty goods include the image and reputation resulting from communications, product quality, and the availability of goods in the appropriate stores (e.g., selective locations that make the product special). The price, usually a high one in keeping with the product quality and the prestigious image created by other marketing activities, is also a consideration in marketing specialty goods. A Michael Kors handbag, for example, could be classified as a specialty good on the basis of these criteria. Even in a major metropolitan market, Michael Kors handbags may be offered by only a very select group of upscale retailers. Refer to the image in **Figure 8.5**.

specialty goods Goods that consumers will make an effort to find and purchase because the goods possess some unique or important characteristic.

Industrial (Business) Goods

By definition, industrial (or business) goods are products and services that have a direct or indirect role in the manufacture of other products and services. These goods are classified not on the basis of consumer behaviour but by the function the good has in the

Figure 8.5
A purchaser of a Michael Kors handbag or another Michael Kors fashion accessory seeks the status and prestige associated with the brand.

Figure 8.6   Categories of Industrial (Business) Goods and Services

Category	Type	Examples
Capital Items	• Installations	• Buildings • Production line equipment • Computer systems
	• Accessory equipment	• Computers • Photocopiers • Office furnishings
Parts and Materials	• Raw materials	• Crude oil • Lumber • Farm goods (wheat, milk, fruit)
	• Processed materials	• DuPont Nylon
	• Component parts	• Glass windows • Tires • Steel frames
Supplies and Services	• Office supplies • Consulting • Other services	• Paper and stationery • Tax or legal counsel • Office cleaning services

production of another good. The major marketing considerations for industrial goods are price (low price based on price negotiation and bidding), personal selling, ability to meet customer specifications, and the reliability of supply when direct channels of distribution are used.

Typically, industrial (business) goods are subdivided into three categories: capital items, parts and materials, and supplies and services. See **Figure 8.6** for an illustration of these categories.

capital items Expensive goods with a long lifespan that are used directly in the production of another good or service.

Capital Items

Capital items are expensive goods with a long lifespan that are used directly in the production of another good or service. Whether an item has a direct or indirect role in the production process determines which of the two types of capital item it is.

installations Major capital items used directly in the production of another product.

Installations are major capital items used directly in the production of another product. Examples of installations include buildings, production line equipment (e.g., robots in assembly plants), and computer systems. These goods are characterized by their high price, long life, reliance on strong personal selling programs to gain customer acceptance, technical sales and support service, and direct channels of distribution. A lengthy and complex decision-making process confronts the marketer of installations.

accessory equipment Items, such as computers and power tools, that facilitate an organization's operations.

Accessory equipment refers to items that facilitate an organization's operations. Their role is indirect. Typically, these goods are much less expensive than installations and include such products as computers, photocopiers, power tools, and office furnishings. These goods are characterized by their reasonably long life, the significance of price negotiation in the marketing process, and the unique features of the product that appeal to rational buying motives.

parts and materials Less expensive goods that directly enter a manufacturer's production process.

Parts and Materials

Parts and materials are less expensive goods that directly enter a manufacturer's production process. These goods are an integral part of the customer's product and affect its quality. Parts and materials are subdivided into three categories: raw materials, processed materials, and component parts.

raw materials Farm goods and other materials derived directly from natural resources.

Farm goods and other materials derived directly from natural resources are **raw materials**. Raw materials from natural resources include crude oil, lumber, and iron ore. Farm goods include wheat, livestock, fruits, vegetables, and milk, all of which are used by food processors in the manufacture of packaged consumer food products such as bread, cheese, and jams.

Processed materials are materials used to create another product, but that are not readily identifiable with the product. Examples include DuPont nylon, a synthetic fibre used in clothing and other fabrics, and other yarns that become part of cloth fabrics. In each example, the original material is further processed or used in the manufacturing process of another good so that it changes form.

Component parts are goods that are used in the production of another product. They do not change form as a result of the manufacturing process. Typically, these items are part of an assembly-line process. For example, component parts such as glass windows, steering columns, radios, tires, and steel frames arrive at an automobile manufacturing facility ready for assembly. Price negotiation and continuity of supply are important considerations in the purchase of component parts.

Supplies are standardized products that are routinely purchased with a minimum of effort. Typically, they are divided into three categories: maintenance, repair, and operating supplies. Paint is an example of a maintenance supply; bearings and gears are examples of repair supplies; writing instruments, paper and stationery, toner cartridges, and fastening devices are examples of operating supplies. Consumers of such items look for quality at a good price. Purchasing agents also perceive service by the supplier's sales representatives to be important.

processed materials Materials that are used in the production of another product but that are not readily identifiable with the product.

component parts Goods that are used in the production of another product but do not change form as a result of the manufacturing process.

supplies Standardized products that are routinely purchased with a minimum of effort.

BRANDING STRATEGIES

L03 Explain the role and importance of branding strategies.

While a marketing manager makes many decisions about a product, some of the more crucial decisions involve branding, packaging, and labelling. If the product doesn't come in a package—for example, a kitchen appliance or automobile—the crucial decision involves the design of the product. The styling and how an appliance or automobile looks are important inputs in the consumer buying decision process.

To develop a brand strategy, a manager makes decisions in unique yet closely related areas. First, decisions must be made regarding the brand name and logo. Second, decisions are made about the design of the package (if it is a packaged good) and what information the label must communicate. Product decisions, in turn, influence decisions about other marketing mix strategies—price, marketing communications, and distribution.

Defining the Brand

The *Dictionary of Marketing Terms* defines a **brand** as an identifying mark, symbol, word(s), or combination of the same that separates one company's product from another company's product.

The key components of a brand are the following:

- *Brand Name* The **brand name** is that part of a brand that can be spoken. It may consist of a word, a letter, or a group of words and letters. Examples include such names as Axe, Dove Sensitive Skin, Fido, Google, Lexus, Red Bull, Roots, Starbucks, and WD40.
- *Brandmark or Logo* The unique design, symbol, or other special representation of a company name or brand name is referred to as a **brandmark** or logo. Examples include Target's bullseye; the blue Ford oval that appears on the front or back of Ford cars, on dealer signs, and in advertising and promotional literature; and Starbucks' famous green-and-white mermaid. **Figure 8.7** offers a selection of well-known logos.
- *Trademark* A **trademark** is the part of a brand that is granted legal protection so that only the owner can use it. The symbol ® is the designation of a registered trademark. Trademarks include the brand names and brandmarks (logos) described above.

brand A name, term, symbol, or design, or some combination of these, that identifies a good or service.

brand name That part of a brand that can be vocalized.

brandmark (logo) That part of a brand identified by a symbol or design.

trademarks That part of a brand granted legal protection so that only the owner can use it.

Figure 8.7   A Selection of Well-Known Brand Logos

Sources: (left to right) Shoppers
Drug Mart; Canadian Tire; WestJet;
All Tim Hortons trademarks
references herein are owned by
Tim Hortons. Used with permission

"Coke" and "Coca-Cola" are registered trademarks of the Coca-Cola Company. The Nike swoosh is a trademark of Nike. The swoosh is so well known it can stand alone in advertisements and communicate a message about the brand. In some cases, trademarks become so well known they become household words. When this happens the trademark holder is a victim of its own success, because the trademark loses its distinct nature. Such is the case of famous trademarks such as Xerox, Kleenex, and Band-Aid.

patent A provision that gives a manufacturer the sole right to develop and market a new product, process, or material.

■ *Patent* A **patent** protects a manufacturing process or product design from being copied by competitors. It gives a manufacturer the sole right to develop and market a new product, process, or material as it sees fit. An industrial design registration protects appearance, while a true patent protects function. Under Canada's *Patent Act*, the maximum life of a Canadian patent is 20 years from the date on which the application is filed.

The explanations above describe a brand in tangible terms, but a brand also possesses intangible characteristics. How an individual perceives a brand depends on the brand name and what it stands for—that is, on the image that marketing has developed for it over an extended period. For example, the image that appears in Figure 8.5 for Michael Kors suggests high quality, status, and prestige. Apple stands for sleek, user-friendly products. Nike sells shoes, but it is known for bringing out the power within people—the power to do better! Brands like these are more than just physical products. Their image is such that they have formed a special relationship with their customers.

Video: Pirate Joe's
Resells Trader Joe's
Popular Products

Brand Names

Many types of brands exist and they can be grouped according to who names them. Most of the brands mentioned in this section so far are manufacturers' brands or national brands. These brands are usually supported with their own marketing strategies to make them competitive and distinctive in the marketplace.

National Brands
A national brand organization has two branding options: an individual brand strategy or a family brand strategy, both of which offer advantages and disadvantages.

individual brand strategy
The identification of each product in a company's product mix with its own name.

Individual Brand Strategy
An **individual brand strategy** means that each product in a company's product mix has its own name. This brand name strategy is common among large packaged-goods manufacturers such as Procter & Gamble and Kraft Canada. Some Procter & Gamble names include Scope (mouthwash), Secret (deodorant), and Crest (toothpaste). Kraft names include Cool Whip (dessert topping), Philadelphia (cream cheese), Oreo (cookies), and Jell-O (gelatin and pudding). As shown using the example of Lululemon earlier in the chapter, individual brands can expand into a family of brands, which will be covered in more detail in the next section.

multibrand strategy The use of a different brand name for each item a company offers in the same product category.

Very often, a marketing organization operates several brands in one product category or in different segments of a market. In this case, a multibrand strategy is used. The term **multibrand strategy** refers to the use of a different brand name for each item a company offers in the same product category. Nestlé offers a wide range of options in the chocolate snack market: Aero, Butterfinger, Coffee Crisp, KitKat, Mirage, Rolo, Smarties, and Turtles, among many others (refer to Figure 8.3). In effect, the brands compete against one another, but the revenues they generate all return to the same source.

Family Brand Strategy   A **family brand** exists when the same brand name is used for a group of related products. Family brand names are usually steeped in tradition and quickly come to mind because they have been on the market for a long time. Family brands may embrace the company name or may be a name that a company has popularized over an extended period. For example, Procter & Gamble uses a family brand strategy for Old Spice. Some examples of products in this line include: Old Spice Body Wash, Old Spice Body Spray, Old Spice Hair Care and Styling, and Old Spice Trimmers and Shavers. In the soup business, Campbell's (a corporation and a family brand name) markets Campbell's Condensed Soup, Campbell's Chunky Soup, Campbell's Ready to Enjoy, Campbell's Créations, and Campbell's Gardennay among its soup product lines.

A family brand strategy offers two advantages to a marketing organization. First, promotional expenditures for one product will benefit the rest of the family by creating an awareness of the brand name. Second, consumers and distributors accept new products more readily because the products capitalize on the success and reputation of the existing family products. This is referred to as the halo effect. For example, Lululemon's plan to become a big player in men's wear by 2016 involves keeping its brand at the forefront, as the company's line of men's clothing carries the Lululemon name. Existing Lululemon stores are dedicating more space to the men's lines, with some outlets having separate entrances. Standalone Lululemon men's wear stores are also being opened.[6 & 7]

A family brand strategy has a disadvantage as well. The failure or poor quality of a new product could tarnish the image of a family of products; for that reason, such products are usually removed from the market quickly by the marketing organization.

In deciding what brand strategy to use, a company analyzes its own situation in relation to its corporate and marketing strategies. Nike and Apple use their company name as the primary brand name, and for good reason. Both names are highly recognized globally and are associated with quality products with a good reputation. In contrast, packaged-goods companies like Unilever and Procter & Gamble opt for individual brand names. Each company offers a wide variety of products in countless product categories. For them, the individual brand strategy helps differentiate their products from those of competitors.

Co-Branding   A brand strategy now gaining popularity among national brand manufacturers is **co-branding**. Co-branding occurs when a company uses the equity in another brand name to help market its own brand name product or service. The marketer feels that using multiple brand names in conjunction with a single product or service offering provides greater value to demanding customers. Recently, Google and Nestlé created some buzz by announcing the Android KitKat, the name of Android's next operating system. Both companies see the agreement as an opportunity to shape the way customers think about their brands. For example, in Nestlé's press release, Nestlé states that the co-branding partnership is a good opportunity to connect with their customers with digital technology. They want to show that they care about people who buy their brands and that they're a creative company. The press release goes on to say that Google chose KitKat because Google's engineers love the chocolate bar. Google comes across as a very cool employer—they even know what kind of chocolate their staff likes.[8 & 9] See **Figure 8.8** for an illustration of Android KitKat co-branding.

When using a co-branding strategy, a key issue to consider is "fit." It is essential for the brands to complement each other. As just described, the transfer of KitKat's brand name to Android's operating system is unique and a good fit.

family brand The use of the same brand name for a group of related products.

co-branding Occurs when a company uses the equity in another brand name to help market its own brand-name product or service (two brand names on a product); also applies to two organizations sharing common facilities for marketing purposes (e.g., two restaurants in one location).

Figure 8.8   Google and Nestle's co-branding agreement resulted in the Android KitKat, the name of Android's new operating system.

private-label brand A brand produced to the specifications of the distributor, usually by national brand manufacturers that make similar products under their own brand names.

Private-Label and Generic Brands   A **private-label brand** is a brand produced to the specifications of the distributor (wholesaler or retailer), usually by national brand manufacturers that make similar products under their own brand names. Some examples of these brands are shown here:

Company	Brand Name
Canadian Tire	Mastercraft, Motomaster
Costco	Kirkland Signature
Loblaws	President's Choice, Joe Fresh
Sobeys	Compliments
Walmart	George, Great Value

The private-label brand was originally conceived as a means by which a retailer could provide the price-conscious consumer with a product of reasonable quality as an alternative to national brands. Recently, they have proven to be a hot commodity with consumers when the economy takes a turn for the worse—savvy shoppers scoop up the savings that are to be had on such products!

Loblaws is a leader in private-label branding with its President's Choice (PC) brand, which is marketed in all Loblaws-owned outlets (Loblaws, Provigo, Zehrs, Super Value, and others). The Loblaws strategy is to position its PC brand between national brands and its own generic (no-name) brands (see the no-name discussion in the next section). Prices for private-label brands can be significantly lower than national brands yet yield better profit margins for the retailer. The goal for Loblaws is to continue to increase its private label business to more than 30 percent of sales.[10]

Private-label brands have taken business away from national brands. Consequently, many manufacturers have adopted a *three-and-out* approach: either you are among the top three brands in a given category or you're out. Several manufacturers once marketed second-tier brands, but many of these have been withdrawn from the market. Private-label brands were killing them!

generic brand A product without a brand name or identifying features.

A **generic brand** is a product without a brand name or identifying features. The packaging is kept simple: a minimum of colour is used, and label text simply identifies the contents—for example, Corn Flakes or Chocolate Chip Cookies. Generic brands are common in such product categories as cereals, paper products, canned goods (fruits, vegetables, and juices), and pet foods, among others. Consumers who purchase generic brands may sacrifice a little in quality but appreciate the savings they can obtain. In Canada, it was Loblaws and its related supermarkets (Super Value and Zehrs, to name two) that popularized the use of generic brands. They encouraged shoppers to look for "yellow label" products to save money. Competitors quickly followed suit.

Private-label and generic brands intensify competition. Shelf space is limited, so it is more difficult for national brands to compete for space. As indicated in the private-label section, some manufacturers have voluntarily withdrawn products that can no longer compete.

Licensed Brands   Brand image is a powerful marketing tool and a valuable asset to marketing organizations. The use of one firm's established brand name or symbol on another firm's products can benefit both firms financially. To create such an arrangement, the owner of the brand name or symbol enters into a licensing agreement with a second party. Licensing is a way of legally allowing another firm to use a brand name or trademark for a certain period (the duration of the contractual agreement). The licensee usually pays a royalty to the company that owns the trademark. When a brand name or trademark is used in this manner, it is called a **licensed brand**.

licensed brand Occurs when a brand name or trademark is used by a licensee.

Clothing and fragrance products are well known for licensed brands. Just think of the number of entertainment and sports celebrities who have lent their name to fragrances: Jennifer Lopez, Katy Perry, Beyoncé, and David Beckham among them. For consumers who don't know much about scents, celebrity-branded versions offer an established image and something people feel they can understand and identify with.

Sports leagues, such as the NHL, NBA, and Major League Baseball, also license the rights to their team logos and trademarks to clothing manufacturers. Putting brand names on clothing provides moving advertisements for the owners of the brand name or trademark and ready-made promotion for the owners of the licensed product.

Cult Brands   Unique in the world of branding is the cult brand. A **cult brand** is a brand that captures the imagination of a small group of devotees who then spread the word, make converts, and help turn a fringe product into a mainstream name. Cult brands are not fads; instead, they start out small and build a steady following, sometimes over many years. Many cult brands decide to stay small, seeing that as the key to their success; they are hard to get. In contrast, other cult brands opt for growth and eventually become leading national brands—Apple being the perfect example.

There have always been cult brands, mostly smaller brands unknown to the masses. But in today's marketing environment, where social media networks play an important role, developing strong communities (a band of loyal and passionate followers) has become a widespread strategy. It is now common for average everyday people to actively promote their favourite brands to others; these consumers are dubbed *brand evangelists* by the marketing organizations they are supporting.

An example of a cult brand is Vans, an action sports brand that positions itself as a lifestyle company. Vans is a leader in skate and snowboarding culture, promoting events like Go Skateboarding Day and sponsoring its famous Warped Tour, an extreme sports and music festival.[11] See the Vans image in **Figure 8.9**.

Do cult brands share anything in common? According to Matt Ragas, author of *The Power of Cult Branding*, "Cult brands dare to be different. They sell lifestyles and marketers behind them are willing to take big risks; they understand the potential pay-off." Zappos, an online retailer, and Lululemon have also achieved cult status. Zappos sells over $1 billion in shoes and apparel every year and the company is known for its customer focused, fun, and quirky culture; Lululemon's loyal followers are drawn to the brand's focus on healthy living.[12]

cult brand A brand that captures the imagination of a small group of devotees who then spread the word, make converts, and help turn a fringe product into a mainstream name.

Figure 8.9 Vans enjoys cult brand status; Vans owners become brand evangelists and promote the ownership experience.

PACKAGING AND LABELLING STRATEGIES

LO4 Discuss the role of packaging and labelling in the development of product strategies.

How important is a package? Very important! Packaging has become an essential element in building a brand's image. In fact, many package designers now believe the thirst for fresh designs has accelerated among marketing organizations. They say "you lose relevance if the package doesn't evolve every three years."[13]

It is true that a package must change with the times, but it also must not lose touch with the identity that gave it a special appeal to loyal customers. Coca-Cola, for example, has kept its signature alive by using the original handwriting of a company accountant from nearly a century ago. Today's white-on-red logo is recognizable even in other alphabets. Coke has not had to change. But then, other brands do not have the same stature as Coca-Cola. Refer to the image in **Figure 8.10**.

Package designers understand that 40 percent of communication is visual, and 80 percent of visual communication is conveyed through colours and shapes. Coca-Cola, for example, is associated with the colour red, Pepsi-Cola is blue, and Tide detergent is orange. In a crowded retail setting the package must capture the attention of consumers in the blink of an eye.

A recent packaging innovation by British firm, Vivid Water, has resulted in a more environmentally friendly alternative for bottled water—Water in a Box! Instead of plastic, Vivid Water's box uses recyclable paperboard from responsibly managed forests. While you can't see the water itself, the carton has a simple clean design and uses a blue and white colour palette for the main product and a water drop icon, aiming to make the packs easily identifiable as a water product.[14 & 15] Refer to **Figure 8.11** for a Water in a Box image.

The Role and Influence of Packaging

packaging Those activities related to the design and production of the container or wrapper of a product.

Packaging is defined as those activities related to the design and production of a product's container or wrapper. But more than that, it is the combination of the package (which attracts the consumer's attention), the product (the quality inside the package), and the brand name that contributes to the image held by consumers. Package design decisions are an integral part of product strategy.

Some recent statistics reveal how important packaging is in the marketing of a product. More than 80 percent of purchase decisions at a supermarket are made within the store, and 60 percent of those are made on impulse. During the average 22-minute shopping trip, a consumer spends only 12 seconds in front of any product category and views an average of 20 products.[16] A product's marketing life is thus reduced to seconds!

Marketers now see packages as having a growing influence on purchase decisions amid ongoing media fragmentation—the package itself is an increasingly important selling medium. Therefore, it is important for a brand to create and maintain a consistent brand identity. The "look" of the brand must be consistent across all shapes, sizes, and formats, as that is what the customer is watching for. Successful brands such as Tide, Olay, and Coca-Cola are good illustrations of package design consistency.

Steve White/QMI

Figure 8.10   Coca-Cola's signature is one component of the brand's marketing strategy that does not change. Coca-Cola packaging presents a consistent "look" for the brand.

As suggested earlier, the power of colour cannot be underestimated. Many brands actually own a colour, a concept referred to as brand blocking. In the hair-care aisle, for instance, Garnier Fructis owns a not-so-subtle bright green. Colours are emotional triggers—and, consequently, powerful marketing tools. The colour red, for example, demands attention and is a sign of power. In the soft drink market, Coca-Cola is the market leader. The brand's package designs have always been based on a specific shade of red that distinguishes Coke from other brands. Dark colours project richness (think about coffee brands such as Maxwell House and Nescafé). Refer to the Colour Emotion Guide in **Figure 8.12**.

Many factors are considered when designing a package—the objective is always to break through the shelf clutter. Expert designers offer several tips for marketers when contemplating potential designs. Among their recommendations are the following: own a colour (the concept of brand blocking discussed earlier); stand out (do not blend in with colours that are common in a product category); be different (if everyone is round and tall, be short and angular); and consider the power of white space (simplicity pays off when other packages are cluttered with information).[17] When these principles are used correctly, packages do stand out. When Unilever launched Dove Men+Care it used a medium grey colour—a colour unique to the product category. Refer to the image in **Figure 8.13**.

Vivid

Figure 8.11 'Water in a Box' is a more environmentally friendly alternative to plastic bottles.

Components of a Package

The package is what consumers look for when they are thinking of a purchase; marketers, therefore, spend considerable time and money developing effective, functional, and eye-catching designs. There are four basic components of a package. The **primary package** contains the actual product (e.g., the jar containing the jam, the tube of toothpaste, and the plastic bottle holding shampoo or liquid soap).

primary package The package containing the actual product (e.g., the jar that contains the jam).

Figure 8.12 Colour Emotion Guide

COLOUR EMOTION GUIDE

peaceful, growth, health — Tropicana

optimism, clarity, warmth — YellowPages

creative, imaginative, wise — YAHOO!

trust, dependable, strength — Bell

balance neutral, calm — (Wikipedia)

excitement, youthful, bold — STAPLES MAKE more HAPPEN

diversity — ebay

friendly, cheerful, confidence — (Firefox)

Figure 8.13   Dove Men+Care uses grey packaging with white lettering to present a consistent image to consumers.

secondary package An outer wrapper that protects the product, often discarded when the product is used the first time.

labels Printed sheets of information affixed to a package container.

shipping carton Packaging that can be marked with product codes to facilitate storage and transportation of merchandise.

The **secondary package** is the outer wrapper that protects the product, often discarded once the product is used for the first time. The box that tubes of toothpaste are packed in is an example. Even though these outer packages are discarded, they are important to the marketer as it is their design that attracts the customer's eye to the product.

Labels are printed sheets of information affixed to a package container. A label can be wrapped around a jar of coffee, a can, or a cardboard canister, or glued to a flat surface at the front or back of a rigid surface. Labelling is discussed in detail later in this chapter.

Packages are packed in cartons, usually corrugated cardboard cartons, to facilitate shipping from one destination to another. The **shipping carton** is marked with product codes to facilitate storage and transportation of merchandise. Today, more products are being shrink-wrapped, a process of encasing a product packed on a cardboard tray (e.g., fruit juices and soft drinks) in plastic wrap.

Functions of a Package

Essentially, a package has four basic functions: it must protect the product, market the product, offer convenience to the consumer; and, in this era, be environmentally friendly.

Protect the Product   Because products may pass through many warehouses on their way to the consumer, and be loaded onto and unloaded from trucks several times, they require protection. The degree of protection needed depends on how long the products will be in storage, how they will be transported, what kind of handling they will experience, and how much protection from heat, light, and moisture they will need.

Market the Product   In its communications function, the package does everything a medium such as a television or a magazine should do: the package is loaded with psychological implications. For this reason, a package design should be researched with consumers. It is the "look" of the package that helps the consumer form opinions about quality, value, and performance. As indicated earlier, a package should undergo changes in design periodically to keep the look fresh while maintaining core elements that are familiar to current users. Many packaged-goods products, for example, are now available in easy-to-open stand-alone packages (outer boxes have been eliminated).

The package also communicates information about promotional offers such as coupons, contests, and giveaways. Such promotions are of a temporary nature, so a *package flash* is usually added to the face of the package to draw attention to the offer. Refer to the illustration in **Figure 8.14**.

Marketers must remember that the package is the last chance to make a strong impression on customers. All package design elements must blend together effectively to plant a positive impression in the customer's mind.

Provide Convenience to Consumers   A package should be easy to carry, open, handle, and re-seal. For example, if the product is a liquid, it should pour without spills or drips (e.g., squirt tops on dish detergent containers and no-drip spouts on liquid laundry detergent containers). If the product is heavy or bulky, handles often become an important aspect of the package design. Examples of convenience in packaging include

Figure 8.14   A Selection of Package Designs that Include Temporary Promotional Offers

re-sealable plastic lids for jars and cans, twist-off caps, easy-pour spouts, and portable-sized prepared-food packages that are ideal for lunch boxes.

Be Environmentally Friendly   Marketing organizations that have adopted socially responsible business practices demonstrate their commitment to the environment by making packaging changes. Less packaging means less waste in landfill sites and less work and lower costs at recycling stations. As indicated above, simply eliminating an outer package or reducing the size of a package points a company in an environmentally friendly direction. Consumers who are environmentally conscious view such companies in a positive light.

Puma, the German shoe and sports-apparel company, has introduced a shoe bag that provides a more convenient and environmentally friendly option to the traditional shoe box. The bag is made from 100 percent cornstarch and will decompose in a compost pile in three months. The company estimates that the new compostable bag will save 192 tons of plastic and 293 tons of paper annually.[18 & 19] Refer to the image in **Figure 8.15**.

Method, an innovative soap company, has combined convenience and environmental responsibility in its 2-in-1 dish and hand soap. The dual-purpose soap is packaged in bottles made with a blend of recovered ocean plastic and post-consumer recycled plastic. To find out more about Method's innovative approach to packaging, read the Think Marketing box **Too Much Plastic!**

Labelling

Labels are those parts of a package that contain information. A label serves three functions: it identifies the brand name and the owner of the brand; it provides essential information to the buyer; and it satisfies legal requirements where applicable. In the case of food products, labels may also communicate nutritional information.

The typical components of a label include the brand name, usually in a distinctive font, an illustration that represents the product (e.g., a delicious looking pizza on a Delissio pizza box), directions for use, a universal product code, and information mandated by law. The universal

Figure 8.15   Puma's shoe bag provides a more convenient and environmentally friendly option to the traditional shoe box.

Think Marketing

Too Much Plastic!

Did you know that almost 80 percent of the 3.5 million tons of trash in the ocean is plastic? Or that every year at least a million sea birds and 100 000 sharks, turtles, dolphins, and whales die from eating plastic?[20] Well, Method, a small soap company, has decided to do something about this problem by creating innovative bottles made from waste plastic found in the ocean. "Plastics are a valuable material that we should use, but when we're done using it, we should recapture it and use it again," says Adam Lowry, Method co-founder and Chief Greenskeeper.

Method employees, with the help of local beach clean-up groups and volunteers, collect plastic from beaches and, with recycling partner Envision Plastics, turn it into bottles. This new and innovative use of recovered ocean plastic shows how package design can be used to tackle environmental problems. "We're not saying that the solution to the ocean plastic problem is making bottles out of trash, but by doing so we can prove that there are alternatives to using virgin materials, and that is the first, most important step toward improving the state of our oceans," explains Lowry.[21]

Method Products

Question:

What are some other ideas you could suggest to companies to help reduce the amount of plastic that ends up in our landfills or oceans?

---

product code, or UPC symbol as it is commonly called, is a series of black lines that appear on virtually all consumer packaged goods. These bars identify the manufacturer and product item (brand, size, variety, and so on). Electronic scanners at the point of sale read these codes. For retailers, the UPC symbol offers an electronic system to monitor inventory turnover and triggers re-orders when inventories are reduced to a predetermined level.

The mandatory information includes the volume or weight of the product and the company name and address. If the item is a packaged food product, identifying common allergens such as egg, dairy, and soy is mandatory.[22] Canadian marketers can now trumpet the health benefits of their products in three areas: nutrition labelling, nutrient content claims, and health claims. Nutritional information appears in a Nutrition Facts box on the package or as a package flash that draws attention to any claim. Becel margarine, for example, "helps lower cholesterol." The product is available in a variety of formats including salt-free, vegan, and reduced-calorie. Becel sums up its health proposition in its advertising tagline: "Becel. Love your heart."

Video: Vitamin Water Maker Accused of "Misleading" Marketing

BRAND DESIGN

Not all products are sold in a package; therefore, the design of the product itself must attract the attention of consumers. Think about it—what attracts you to a particular automobile, laptop computer, cell phone, or television? It's the design of the product.

brand design Designing the brand experience into the product or service.

Brand design means designing the brand experience into the product or service. It's about creatively designing innovative approaches in order to create a unique brand experience.[23] Ask yourself why the Apple iPad has been such an overwhelming success and you are bound to think about the sleek and sexy appearance of the product. According to a 2014 report by *Media Technology Monitor*, Apple's iPads have the lion's share of the tablet market, accounting for about two-thirds of the tablets Canadians own.[24] There is a lot of psychological satisfaction in owning and using such a product!

When people buy an automobile, what are they actually buying? Yes, they are getting a vehicle that will take them from here to there, but more than that they are buying an experience and that experience should be enjoyable. Many experts on the subject often comment, "You are what you drive." We are either attracted to a car and like it, or look at a car and say, "I would never drive that." Quite simply, it has something to do with the design and the perceived potential experience we expect to have with the car.

Figure 8.16   Brand design thinking for Joe Fresh considered lighting and fixtures, merchandising concepts, dressing rooms, and service areas to tempt customers to buy.

Loblaws effectively used brand design when it devised a strategy to attract consumers to its Joe Fresh line of clothing. Why, they asked, would anyone shop in a supermarket for clothes? The design team quickly realized it needed something more compelling than what Walmart offered via its line of clothing under the George brand name. The solution was Joe Fresh—a name based on the real name of the designer (Joe) and the food spin (Fresh). All elements of the brand would be consistent, from the product, to the marketing, to the store design, to the fixtures. Refer to the image in **Figure 8.16**. "Every element was considered, from erecting dressing rooms to developing the cash desk areas with registers, to creating a merchandising system that flowed with the grocery store environment" explains Joseph Mimran, lead designer. [25] It's worked—Joe Fresh has become a fashion leader in Canada. Loblaws is now planning a major international expansion for its Joe Fresh discount clothing line—adding 141 stores in 23 countries beyond North America by 2018.[26 & 27]

Brand design has influenced many products in the kitchen. Traditional white appliances have been replaced with new colours and surfaces such as stainless steel, rust, and red, and the physical design of stoves, refrigerators, and microwave ovens has become more contemporary or trendy. The kitchen is a key room in any household and how it looks reflects the personality of the inhabitants. The image in **Figure 8.17** demonstrates how design concepts have changed the look of modern household kitchens.

The brand design process has four stages: imagination, innovation, operationalization, and renovation.[28] Through these four stages, a designer interprets the soul of the brand, bringing it to life for the customers to experience. Mazda is a good example. All Mazda's television commercials remind people of one simple yet important attribute of Mazda: "The spirit of a sports car is built into every car we make." That reference stems from the success of the Mazda MX-5 (Miata) sports car and the passion owners display for their cars. Zoom-Zoom!

In the design process, *imagination* means being able to generate insightful and creative brand ideas. Starbucks founder Howard Shultz had imagination. He changed the definition of the coffee experience by making Starbucks a place (other than home or work) where people could

Figure 8.17   Brand design in appliances helps create brand image and facilitates the consumer's brand experience.

Figure 8.18 The
Stages of Brand Design

> **Brand design incorporates the brand experience into the product or service. The brand design process has four stages:**
>
> **1. Imagination**
> Generating insightful and creative brand ideas
>
> **2. Innovation**
> Making the idea a reality
>
> **3. Operationalization**
> Offering the product in a consistent manner
>
> **4. Renovation**
> Commiting to continuous innovation and improvement; staying ahead of competitors

relax and enjoy coffee. Innovation occurs when the creative idea becomes reality—a product is invented. The implementation of the innovation is the *operationalization* stage. The Starbucks experience is available in a consistent manner throughout thousands of locations. As you will learn in the next chapter, all products have a life cycle, and throughout the cycle attempts are made to breathe new life into a product. This is the *renovation* stage of brand design. With reference to Starbucks again, the company is now at the stage where it is marketing more products and wants to be seen as more than just a coffee experience. The key is to never stand still—competitors will eat you alive!

A summary of the brand design stages appears in **Figure 8.18**.

BENEFITS OF BRANDS

LO5 Explain the benefits of branding.

From the marketer's perspective, there are several benefits to be achieved from good branding strategies. First, a good brand name accompanied by an attractive, attention-getting package (for a non-durable good) or good brand design (for a durable good or service) will effectively communicate the point of difference (USP) and highlight the distinctive value added. For example, a brand name such as Lean Cuisine addresses two strategic issues: *lean* communicates the low-calorie benefit, and *cuisine* implies that it tastes good. The name is pleasant-sounding and meaningful. Branding distinguishes one brand from other brands.

Second, good branding strategy enables the marketer to create and develop an image for the brand. Through brand design and marketing communications the brand experience comes to life. For example, Volvo is known for safety, Nike is known for empowerment, and Apple is known for ease of use.

As discussed earlier in the textbook, a good slogan often summarizes the brand experience. Here are a few examples that are among the top 10 slogans of all time according to *Advertising Age* magazine:

- Avis: "We Try Harder"
- M&Ms: "M&Ms melt in your mouth, not in your hand"
- Nike: "Just do it"

Finally, if the goal is brand loyalty, consumers remain loyal to brands that consistently meet their expectations. The brand name is the stamp of quality that people look for; it is what they know, understand, and trust. Branding is the mechanism that keeps the relationship between the consumer and the brand humming!

Creating a meaningful brand name, designing an attractive and tempting package, and providing a brand experience that consumers will enjoy are crucial aspects of product strategy. Product decisions in all these areas directly influence the nature of other marketing activities—the price of the product, the style of marketing communications, and where the product will be available.

BRAND LOYALTY AND BRAND EQUITY

LO6 Describe the various stages of brand loyalty and how brand equity is created.

Brand loyalty is defined as the degree of consumer attachment to a particular brand of product or service. This degree of attachment can be weak or strong and varies from one product category to another. Brand loyalty is measured in three stages: brand recognition, brand preference, and brand insistence.[29] Refer to **Figure 8.19** for an illustration of these stages.

In the early stages of a product's life, the marketing objective is to create **brand recognition**, which is customer awareness of the brand name, package, and/or design. Media advertising and social network communications play a key role in creating awareness. Once awareness is achieved, a brand may offer customers incentives such as free samples or coupons to tempt them to make the first (trial) purchase.

In the **brand preference** stage of a product's life, the brand is in the ballpark—that is, it is an acceptable alternative and will be purchased if it is available when needed. If it is unavailable, the consumer will switch to an equal, competitive alternative. For example, if Pepsi-Cola is requested at McDonald's and the order cannot be filled because the product is unavailable there, the consumer will usually accept the substitute, in this case Coca-Cola.

At the **brand insistence** stage, a consumer will search the market extensively for the brand he or she wants. No alternatives are acceptable, and if the brand is unavailable, the consumer is likely to postpone purchase until it is. Such a situation is a marketer's dream, but a dream rarely achieved. Some critics insist that the original Coca-Cola product reached a level beyond brand insistence. So strong was the attachment that the product could not be changed. When it was changed (to New Coke), the backlash from consumers was so strong that the company had no alternative but to bring the original product back under the name Coca-Cola Classic. Some 22 years later (in 2007), the Classic name was dropped and Coca-Cola returned to its original brand name.

The task of the marketer is to keep customers loyal. Study after study has shown that it is many times more difficult and expensive to convert a new customer than it is to retain a current customer. In preserving loyalty, companies cannot take their customers for granted. Many brands are instituting customer relationship management (CRM) programs that are specifically designed to keep a customer as a customer. The concept of CRM was discussed earlier in the textbook. For more insight into brand loyalty, read the Think Marketing box **Brand Loyalty Starts Young.**

The benefits of brands and the various levels of brand loyalty are what marketers refer to as brand equity. **Brand equity** is defined as the value a consumer derives from a product over and above the value derived from its physical attributes. Equity is the result of good marketing, and it is measured in terms of four variables: name awareness, a loyal customer base, perceived quality, and the brand's association with a certain attribute. When Canadian brands are ranked on these criteria some familiar names pop up. The top five brands in 2013 were Tim Hortons, WestJet, McCain Foods, Canadian Tire, and Jean Coutu Group.[30]

Another explanation of brand equity is directly related to monetary value. Brand equity is defined as the value of a brand to its owners as a corporate asset.[31] When Canadian brands are ranked on this basis a different set of names emerges. Among the brand equity leaders are TD Bank, RBC Financial Group, Scotiabank, Bank of Montreal, and Bell. Compared to the list above, only McCain Foods (ranked 16th) and Canadian Tire (ranked 19th) cracked the top 20 in terms of value.[32]

On a global scale the undisputed brand equity leader in terms of value is Apple, valued at $98.3 billion. Google ranks second with a value of $93.3 billion. Coca-Cola, IBM, and Microsoft round out the top five global brands.[33]

Brand Recognition
Consumer is aware of the name, benefit, and package.

↓

Brand Preference
Brand is top of mind and considered a good alternative. Consumer will buy if available.

↓

Brand Insistence
Consumer buys one brand only. If brand is not available, the purchase is postponed.

Figure 8.19 The Stages of Brand Loyalty

---

brand loyalty The degree of consumer attachment to a particular brand, product, or service.

brand recognition Customer awareness of the brand name and package.

brand preference The stage of a product's life at which it is an acceptable alternative and will be purchased if it is available when needed.

brand insistence At this stage, a consumer will search the market extensively for the brand he or she wants.

brand equity The value a consumer derives from a product over and above the value derived from its physical attributes.

Think Marketing

Brand Loyalty Starts Young

Children's spending power has never been higher. According to marketing consultant Martin Lindstrom, children's global purchase influence is over $1.88 trillion.[34] In addition,

David L Ryan/The Boston Globe/Getty Images

a growing body of research shows that if children are exposed to a brand early in life, they are much more likely to respond favourably to that brand as adults.[35]

Lululemon understands the importance of appealing to customers when they're young. "Kids represent a huge niche market that was missing," says former Lululemon CEO Christine Day. As a result, in early 2014, the company announced that it would continue to invest heavily in Ivivva Athletica, its brand of yoga clothing targeted at the 6-to-12-year-old age group. In terms of brand strategy, market analysts believe creating a separate brand, Ivivva Athletica, has made sense "as some young girls may not want to be seen shopping in the same store as their moms."[36]

Like the Lululemon stores for adults, the 11 Ivivva store locations in Canada and 22 in the U.S. feature dance, yoga, and athletic classes, and the retailer's blog posts motivational advice, and fan pictures. By creating a sense of community and by being first to market, Lululemon hopes to create loyal customers—for life. And, given Ivivva Athletica's track record of double-digit sales growth, the company's investment appears to be a good one.[37]

> **Question:**
> **What are some ethical issues around marketing directly to children?**

Experience Marketing

To experience marketing you have to assess situations and make recommendations to change marketing strategies when necessary. What would you do in the following situation?

Eco-conscious consumers care about buying environmentally friendly products for their homes. These shoppers are more likely to buy products with labels claiming "natural ingredients" or that they are "biodegradable" and "non-toxic," because they perceive them to be safer and better for the environment. Typically, a "green" claim on a label can help boost sales of a brand. But are these green

household products really as eco-conscious or as safe as we think? Most are, but occasionally, some companies' brands claim to be green and safe when they really aren't. This practice of making a misleading or unsubstantiated claim about the environmental benefits of a product or service is called *greenwashing*.

Go online and find examples of companies or brands that you feel are making misleading claims about environmental benefits. (Hint: CBC's Marketplace is one good source: www.cbc.ca/marketplace/).

Do you think the practice of greenwashing makes consumers' sceptical about so-called green products in general? What can consumers do to ensure the products they are buying are really ecologically friendly?

CHAPTER SUMMARY

L01 Explain the total product concept and product mix. *(pp. 167–169)*

When consumers make a purchase, they are buying a physical product—a bar of soap, a can of coffee, a new automobile, and so on—but they are really buying a lot of intangibles associated with the product. One of those intangibles is the psychological satisfaction gained by purchasing a brand that has a desirable image. In product strategy terms, a product is a combination of tangible and intangible benefits. Marketing organizations develop and market a total product concept. This concept includes the physical item, the image, the brand name, the level of sales support, and other marketing activities.

The total range of products offered for sale is referred to as the product mix. The product mix comprises product items and product lines that are available in various shapes, sizes, and formats.

L02 Describe how consumer and business goods are classified. *(pp. 169–173)*

Products are classified as either consumer goods or industrial (business) goods. Consumer goods are intended for the personal use of the customer, and are commonly classified into three categories: convenience goods, shopping goods, and specialty goods. Business goods, on the other hand, are generally used in the production of other goods and services. These goods are subdivided into three groupings: capital items, parts and materials, and supplies and services.

L03 Explain the role and importance of branding strategies. *(pp. 173–177)*

Marketing organizations use branding as a means of identifying products and developing an image. Branding strategies involve decisions on the brand name and logo, the package design, and the product design if it is a durable product. Core decisions in these areas affect marketing decisions on price, marketing communications, and distribution.

In determining the brand name there are three options: an individual brand strategy, multi-brand strategy, or a family brand strategy. Other brand name strategies include co-branding, in which two brand names share equal billing on one product; private-label branding; and generic-label branding (both are strategies employed by retailers). A brand name phenomenon is the cult brand. Such a brand is supported by a passionately loyal

group of customers who act as brand evangelists to further promote the product.

L04 Discuss the role of packaging and labelling in the development of product strategies. *(pp. 178–184)*

Packaging plays an integral part in the product mix. Decisions that must be made about packaging concern the type of package to use and the design of the package. Packages selected must fulfill four basic functions: they must protect the product, market the product, provide the consumer with convenience in handling and using the product, and be environmentally safe. For durable goods and services, product design is important. The product must communicate the brand experience to the customer.

Labels are those parts of a package that contain information. A label serves three functions: it identifies the brand name and the owner of the brand, it provides essential information to the buyer, and it satisfies legal requirements, where applicable.

L05 Explain the benefits of branding. *(p. 184)*

Branding has three main benefits. First, a good brand name and effective package or brand design communicate the product's unique point of difference. Second, a good branding strategy enables the marketer to create and develop an image for the brand. Finally, consumers tend to remain loyal to brands that consistently meet their expectations.

L06 Describe the various stages of brand loyalty and how brand equity is created. *(pp. 185–186)*

Consumers come to trust what a brand stands for and, if they derive satisfaction from the brand, certain levels of brand loyalty develop. Brand loyalty is measured in three stages: recognition, preference, and insistence—the latter being the goal! Marketers must constantly deliver satisfaction and ensure that their brands meet changing preferences of consumers. Managers also encourage loyalty by implementing customer relationship management programs.

Brand equity is the value a consumer derives from a product over and above the value derived from its physical attributes. One way to measure brand equity is in terms of four variables: name awareness, a loyal customer base, perceived quality, and the brand's association with a certain attribute. Another measure of equity is the monetary value of the brand.

MyMarketingLab Study, practise, and explore real marketing situations with these helpful resources:
- **Interactive Lesson Presentations:** Work through interactive presentations and assessments to test your knowledge of marketing concepts.
- **Study Plan:** Check your understanding of chapter concepts with self-study quizzes.
- **Dynamic Study Modules:** Work through adaptive study modules on your computer, tablet, or mobile device.
- **Simulations:** Practise decision-making in simulated marketing environments.

REVIEW QUESTIONS

1. What is the difference between product line depth and product line width? Provide some examples other than those in the text to illustrate the difference. (*LO1*)
2. Describe the characteristics of the following goods: (*LO2*)
   a. Convenience goods
   b. Shopping goods
   c. Specialty goods
3. What are the three classifications of industrial (business) goods? (*LO2*)
4. What is the difference between an individual brand strategy and a family brand strategy? (*LO3*)
5. What does a multibrand strategy refer to? (*LO3*)
6. What are the basic functions of a package? (*LO4*)
7. What are the three functions of a label? *LO4*
8. What are the benefits of branding? (*LO5*)
9. Distinguish among brand recognition, brand preference, and brand insistence. (*LO6*)
10. What is brand equity? How is it determined? (*LO6*)

DISCUSSION AND APPLICATION QUESTIONS

1. Many Canadians are trying to make healthier food choices. But, how much can they rely on the health information on food labels? Conduct some secondary research to find out what information must be included on labels of packaged food products in Canada. Should manufacturers of packaged foods be required to include additional information on their labels, such as identifying genetically modified ingredients? Why or why not?
2. Examine the phenomenon of cult brands. Identify a cult brand and present an opinion on why the brand is so popular with the loyal consumers who buy it.
3. Select any two packages on the market. Choose one you think is good and one you believe is not so good. Discuss the marketability of each package.

9

Product Management

Deborah Baic The Globe and Mail/CP Images

LEARNING OBJECTIVES

LO1 Explain the different organizational structures used to manage brands. (pp. 190–193)

LO2 Describe the steps in the new product development process. (pp. 193–196)

LO3 Discuss key decisions involved in managing current products. (pp. 196–199)

LO4 Identify the stages in a product's life cycle and discuss how a brand manager's decisions are influenced at each stage. (pp. 199–206)

LO5 Explain how the product adoption process influences the length and shape of a product's life cycle. (pp. 206–208)

MARKETERS KNOW...

that growth over time often involves repositioning a brand to attract new customers. For example, Mountain Equipment Co-op, a national outdoor retailer, was formed in Vancouver in 1971 to sell hard-to-find climbing, mountaineering, and hiking gear to sports enthusiasts. Today, 71 percent of its members are city dwellers. In order to interest a broader clientele, MEC management knew it needed to shed its image as a store just for the "granola-eating, sandal-wearing, mountaineering type."[1]

A major rebranding in 2013 resulted in a revitalized store concept, fresh product lines, a new logo, and the tagline, "We are all outsiders." The redesigned logo refers to the retailer simply as MEC and does away with the image of a mountain. "The rebrand reflects the reality of the new MEC," says Anne Donohoe, MEC's chief marketing officer. "We've grown from six members to 3.5 million members over the last 40 years, many of whom live in urban centres."

In any rebranding it's important to remain relevant to traditional clientele, as well as to appeal to new customers. MEC has been able to do this successfully by continuing to provide equipment for back-country hiking, skiing, and paddling, while introducing new product lines for cycling, running, and yoga. "MEC has stayed true to its values, yet is able to broaden its offering to more Canadians," explains Ms. Donohoe. "Truly, our mission is to inspire Canadians to be active outdoors."

This chapter focuses on product decisions and how to devise effective marketing strategies as a product moves through its life cycle. MEC's success story demonstrates the importance of adapting to changing market demands in order to stay relevant over time. To manage a brand successfully, the right marketing strategies have to be put in place.

Product management concerns three key areas: (1) the internal organization structure for managing current products, (2) the allocation of resources for the development of new products, and (3) dealing with changing market needs, especially as products progress through their life cycles. In this third area, the firm must be aware of the need to change its marketing strategies during the various stages of the product's life cycle. Organizations realize that demand for the products they offer for sale now will not last forever. Adapting to the external trends discussed earlier in the textbook is essential.

ORGANIZATIONAL STRUCTURES USED TO MANAGE BRANDS

LO1 Explain the different organizational structures used to manage brands.

The trend in contemporary marketing practice is to combine various organizational structures so that products may be developed and marketed more efficiently than before. In packaged-goods companies, an organizational structure called the *brand management system* was traditionally the norm, but recently it has given way to *category management, regional management,* and *target-market management* systems. There is a trend toward "customer-centric" management structures.

Companies in business-to-business marketing are moving toward target-market management systems. For example, business-to-business organizations develop new products and manage existing products to meet the needs of particular market segments (e.g., communications, health, transportation) or particular industries (e.g., chemicals, banking). The type of management system used often depends on three factors: an organization's size, growth objectives, and resources.

brand manager An individual assigned responsibility for the development and implementation of effective and efficient marketing programs for a specific product or group of products.

Brand Management

A **brand manager** (product manager) is an individual who is assigned the responsibility for the development and implementation of marketing programs for a specific product or

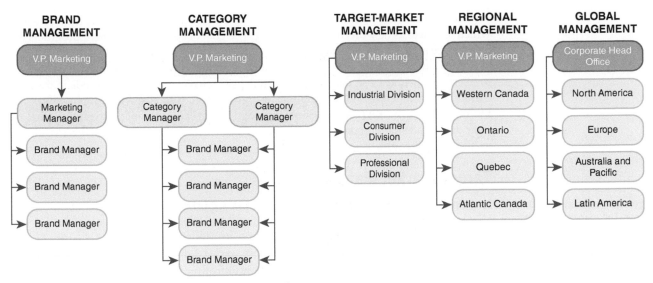

Figure 9.1 Alternative Product Management Systems

group of products. For example, Procter & Gamble sells brands in the beauty and grooming, and household care markets. Among its leading beauty and grooming brands are shampoos such as Pantene, Head & Shoulders, and Herbal Essences. A brand manager would be assigned to each individual brand—the manager becomes the "expert" on the brand. A similar situation exists for detergent brands such as Tide, Cheer, and Ivory Snow.

The brand manager works closely with others in the organization and with external suppliers in such areas as marketing communications, package design, and marketing research. For multi-product companies, this system ensures that all products receive equal attention in planning, even though some products may have a higher marketing profile when plans are implemented. A diagram of the brand management system is presented in **Figure 9.1**. In this system, it is assumed that the manager is ultimately responsible for all marketing mix elements. In many organizations, the manager may also be responsible for the profitability of the brand.

Category Management

A **category manager** is an individual who is assigned ultimate marketing responsibility for a portfolio of brands in a particular product category. As described above, several brand managers are responsible for a selection of beauty and grooming, and household care products at Procter & Gamble. A category manager would be responsible for the entire line of shampoos or the entire line of detergents, and also would be responsible for managing the brand managers—the category manager would be the immediate superior of the brand manager in the organizational structure.

The category management system is a management structure that groups products according to their similarity to one another. In addition to those already mentioned, prominent categories at Procter & Gamble include cosmetics, shaving products, deodorants, and pet care products.

In this system, the category manager adopts a more generalized view of the business than would an individual brand manager. In Canada, the system has become popular as manufacturers realize they must work more closely and cooperatively with retailers (relationship marketing) who have significant buying power and who organize their shelves according to the sales volume of brands within each product category.

Leading retailers such as Loblaws, Sobeys, and Pharmasave work with suppliers cooperatively and manage categories of products instead of individual brands. Buyers at these and other chain stores deal with all suppliers within a category (e.g., pet food, oral-care products, soft drinks, juice beverages). Electronic scanning determines which

category manager An individual assigned responsibility for developing and implementing marketing activity for a group of related products or product lines.

products are moving well. This information tells the retailer which products to carry and which to delete as new products come along. The goal of space-management programs is to improve sales in each category.

With category management there is much negotiation between manufacturers and retailers for shelf space. A company such as PepsiCo, which has leading brands in the soft drink market (all Pepsi and Mountain Dew branded soft drinks) and leading brands in the snack foods market (Doritos, Sun Chips, and Lay's) can recommend to retailers that their drink and snack brands be merchandised close to one another or displayed together to maximize the sales of both product lines.

Target-Market Management

target-market management system The management of marketing activity based on the requirements of different customer groups (e.g., industry, government, consumers).

In a **target-market management system**, the organization recognizes that different customer classes with different needs require different marketing strategies (see Figure 9.1). Such a strategy makes sense for multi-divisional companies dealing with diverse target markets. A company with both industrial and consumer customer bases would utilize different strategies when communicating with those targets. For example, Bell Canada manages its products and services in the following customer categories: personal, small business, and enterprise. Each category of customer has unique needs that Bell's marketing strategies must address.[2]

Bell's personal division segments the market even further: Bell Mobility, Bell TV, and Bell Internet. Bell Mobility has a youth-oriented marketing team that develops and implements marketing strategies specifically for the youth target. Bell Mobility understands that the way in which young consumers use cell phones deserves special attention. The company also organizes its marketing planning around other unique consumer targets such as First Nations groups.[3 & 4]

Regional Management

regional marketing management system The management of marketing activity based on the needs of customers in different geographical locations (e.g., Ontario, Western Canada, Quebec).

Geography plays a key role in a **regional marketing management system**. In this management structure, decision making is decentralized. Instead of dividing an *organization* by function (production, marketing, finance) and by products, a *country* is divided up geographically into regions. Molson Coors Brewing Company, for example, has established separate companies to manage three regions: Western Canada, Ontario/Atlantic, and Quebec.

A national marketing team manages a group of brands, referred to as "strategic national brands." Canadian, Coors Light, and Export are in this group. Each region has a staff of marketing and sales personnel who develop regional strategies for these national brands. Regional managers also develop marketing strategies for brands marketed only in their regions. According to Molson, such a system allows a company to build on its strengths and chip away at its weaknesses. The closer the decision makers are to the action, the quicker is the response time for planning and implementing new marketing strategies.[5]

Continental and Global Management

Companies with growth aspirations now view the world as one market. What has emerged are management systems that group various regions of the world together for the purposes of planning and decision making, or systems in which companies plan and implement strategies on a global scale.

Some companies group countries together on a continental basis. For example, a company may develop marketing plans for North America, for South America, for Europe, and so on. Under this system the uniqueness of each large region is given consideration. Kraft Foods Inc. has moved in this direction. Previously, Kraft Canada operated separately from its U.S. parent and there were separate marketing plans for all brands sold here. Now, Canadian managers report directly to U.S. managers. This realignment is part of a continental strategy to reduce costs and streamline the corporation.[4] Marketing plans are now North American in scope.

Other companies seek economies on a global scale. In this system, ideas that are developed in one country may be considered for another, so that economies of scale are achieved. The often-used expression "Think globally, act locally" is now a common salute among multinational marketers. In other words, while brand managers and marketing managers in Canada are responsible for marketing in Canada, they are also influenced by the decisions of managers elsewhere. In extreme cases, managers in small countries can be eliminated entirely.

Airbnb, the Craigslist of apartment rentals, makes marketing decisions globally. Airbnb's online marketplace allows people to list and book accommodations—from inexpensive to luxury—in 192 countries around the world. The company's website is available in 21 languages and has consistent information, style, and personality to appeal to like-minded users across cultures. The brand tweaks its content to best suit the culture, but it's still obvious which brand you're interacting with regardless of language. Having a strong, consistent voice across countries is working for Airbnb, as the company has opened nine overseas offices within the past four years to keep up with demand. See **Figure 9.2** for an illustration of Airbnb's mobile app page in English.[6 & 7]

Figure 9.2   Airbnb's Mobile App in English

NEW PRODUCT DEVELOPMENT PROCESS

LO2 Describe the steps in the new product development process.

Some of the product decision areas were introduced in Chapter 8. Let's discuss those decisions from the perspective of a brand manager. You should note that organizations use various titles for this position (*product manager* and *brand leader* among them). For consistency, we will use the term brand manager.

A brand manager is responsible for all areas of the marketing mix. A brand manager must establish profitable and fair prices; decide on marketing communications elements, such as advertising, sales promotion, and experiential marketing; and determine where the product should be available to customers.

With regard to the product, the brand manager's decisions occur in several key areas: developing new products, modifying the product, altering the product mix, introducing a new package design or product design, and maintaining and withdrawing a product from the market.

Video: Google Glass: A First Real Life Look

new product A product that is truly unique and meets needs that have previously been unsatisfied.

knock-off A look-alike product that often is a copy of a patented product.

New Product Decisions

In the truest sense of the word, a **new product** is a product that is truly unique and meets needs that have previously been unsatisfied. An example of such an innovative product is Google Glass—a small stamp-sized computer screen attached to a pair of eyeglass frames. Google Glass, a wearable technology device, can record video, access email, and retrieve information from the Web by connecting wirelessly to a user's cell phone. See **Figure 9.3**.

In Canada, innovations can be protected by patent if the innovation is registered in accordance with the *Patent Act*. Some organizations choose to ignore patent protection laws, and produce and market copies of patented products, though doing so is illegal. These look-alike products are referred to as **knock-offs**. The presence of knock-offs shortens the innovation's life cycle. Consequently, there is less opportunity to recover development costs associated with the innovation.

Figure 9.3   Sergey Brin, Co-founder of Google, Wearing Google Glasses

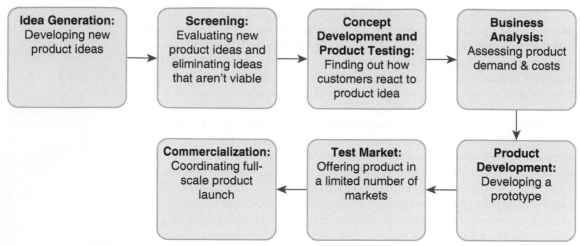

Figure 9.4 New Product Development Process

The development of innovative products involves seven steps: idea generation, screening, concept development and product testing, business analysis, product development, test marketing and marketing planning, and commercialization. See **Figure 9.4** for an illustration of this process. The prudent organization must spend adequate time in each stage of development to ensure that the ideas that move forward are the right ones. They want to avoid costly mistakes! Let's examine each step in the new product development process.

Idea Generation   All products stem from a good idea. Where do these ideas come from? Contemporary organizations are receptive to ideas from any source—customers, suppliers, employees, or marketing intelligence about competitors. Internally, a company may have a research and development department in place, with the sole responsibility for researching and developing ideas. Other companies may schedule regular meetings of executives and cross-sections of employees to brainstorm potential opportunities. It is common for a brand manager to coordinate the activities of a new product development team.

Starbucks taps into the creativity of its customers through MyStarbucksIdea.com— an online community for people to share, discuss, and vote for ideas on how to enhance the Starbucks experience. The company has received close to 200 000 ideas from customers leading to over 300 new product and service innovations. Innovations range from digital rewards and new coffee flavours, to splash sticks and a refreshed iPhone app that allows for digital tipping. "For over six years, our passionate customers and partners have been sharing their ideas with us on My Starbucks Idea, and we have listened and acted upon many amazing innovations that we have received from this online community," says Alex Wheeler, vice president of global digital marketing for Starbucks. "Our customers have incredible ideas that we can bring to life in stores worldwide." [8 & 9]

screening An early stage in the new product development process in which new ideas are quickly eliminated.

Screening   The elimination of ideas begins with product **screening**. The purpose of screening is to quickly eliminate ideas that do not appear to offer financial promise for the company. Senior executives typically make screening decisions. They must decide if the product is a good fit for the strategic direction the company is taking. They may evaluate the idea against certain criteria such as patent protection, sales potential, threat of competition, compatibility with current products, marketing investment required, anticipated life cycle, degree of uniqueness, expertise in production, and capital investment required.

The design firm IDEO, is recognized around the world for its innovative and creative product designs. After new ideas are generated through a brainstorming process, session participants are given a set of small circular stickers to place on the posted ideas that look most promising. Participants are able to put more than one sticker on a given idea or spread out their "sticker votes" across many ideas. The ideas with the most stickers are the ones selected to go forward to the next step, concept development and testing.[10] Refer to **Figure 9.5.**

Concept Development and Testing

A **concept test** involves the presentation of a product idea in some visual form (usually a drawing or photograph) with a description of the basic product characteristics, the benefits, and the anticipated price. The purpose of a concept test is to find out early how consumers react to the product idea and if they would be interested in buying it if it were available on the market. In line with research procedures, the test (survey) could be conducted by personal interviews, online surveys, or focus group sessions.

Figure 9.5   IDEO employees generate new ideas through a prototyping process.

Companies proceed only with ideas consumers indicate to be of high interest. To gauge the level of acceptability, a firm may show different information about the same concept. It may, for example, test different prices in order to determine how price influences the level of interest in the concept and to see at what point the concept becomes uninteresting. Such information is important for the sales and profit projections in the next stage.

Nissan, for example, has spent more than a year canvassing dozens of people aged 39 or younger to discover the kinds of vehicles that would most appeal to young drivers. The result is the company's IDx concept car, which Carlos Ghosn, Nissan's president, describes as "an out-of-the-box, epoch-making vehicle that is bound to excite new and younger consumers."[11] See **Figure 9.6.**

Business Analysis

A **business analysis** entails a formal review of a possible new product's potential. The analysis is conducted by a brand manager, and those ideas with limited financial promise will be eliminated. By this time, the company is dealing only with product ideas that have been judged positively by potential customers. The business analysis will assess the market demand for a product, calculate the costs of producing and marketing the product, and forecast expected sales revenue and profit. If competitors are already on the market, their presence will be factored into the decision to proceed or not.

Product Development

In this stage, the idea or concept is converted to a physical product. The purpose is to develop a prototype or several prototype models for evaluation by consumers. The **prototype** is a physical version of a potential product. The prototype is refined on the basis of feedback obtained in consumer research. In effect, the research and development department experiments with design and production capability to determine what type of product can be produced within the financial constraints established in the business analysis stage.

Kellogg's operates a pilot plant, a research and development facility that is one-tenth the scale of an actual manufacturing facility, where the company runs test batches of cereals and snacks. Issues that must be resolved at this stage include

concept test The presentation of a product idea in some visual form, with a description of the basic product characteristics and benefits, in order to obtain customers' reactions to it.

business analysis A formal review of some of the ideas accepted in the screening stage, the purpose of which is again to rank potential ideas and eliminate those judged to have low financial promise.

prototype A physical version of a potential product—that is, of a product designed and developed to meet the needs of potential customers; it is developmental in nature and refined according to feedback from consumer research.

Figure 9.6   Nissan's IDx concept car is the result of extensive marketing research with young drivers.

the type and quality of materials available to use for manufacturing; the method of production and any additional capital requirements; the package configuration and its influence on production, shipping, and handling; and the time required for startup (the time needed to have all equipment and materials in place, ready for production).

At this stage, various functional areas of the firm must work together to ensure that the product is what the customer wants. What the engineering and production departments can provide may not be what the marketing department would like. The brand manager in charge of the project must delicately manage the politics of the situation and arrive at a solution that will benefit the company. Creating the prototype is an expensive phase of the development process. If they receive a positive consumer reaction to the prototypes, the organization moves to the next stage.

Test Marketing and Marketing Planning

test marketing Placing a product for sale in one or more representative markets to observe performance under a proposed marketing plan.

At this point, an introductory marketing plan is devised to support test marketing. **Test marketing** is the first real acid test for the product. It is the stage at which consumers have the opportunity to actually purchase the product instead of simply indicating that they would buy it. The test market allows the company to gain feedback in a relatively inexpensive way. Many marketers view the test market stage as mandatory; without it, a significant financial risk is faced. A test market helps determine if and when the company will proceed with market expansion and a full-scale marketing plan. The rate of consumer acceptance and the forecasted financial viability of the product are the determining factors in such a decision.

Some managers believe test marketing is a step that can be bypassed. They say it gives competitors time to react and develop imitations, or plan defensive strategies for products already on the market. Skipping the test market stage is risky.

Software developers worldwide are using Canada as a testing ground for apps before rolling them out to other markets. The Canadian test market allows bugs to be worked out before introducing software in other countries. Although Canada's population is one-tenth that of the United States, WiFi access and smartphone and tablet usage are similar. "Canada is a good test market for several reasons," says Thorbjorn Warin, CMO of Finnish gaming company GrandCru. "Canada is big enough to get the number of users needed for reliable data, but also small enough that you don't lose too much by testing there. Canadians also tend to be very friendly and when asked, provide great feedback."[12]

Commercialization

commercialization The full-scale production and marketing plan for launching a product on a regional or national basis.

Commercialization is the concluding step in the new-product development process. The brand manager puts together a full-scale production and marketing plan for launching a product on a regional or national scale. All the refining, adjusting, and tinkering with product design characteristics, production considerations, and marketing strategies is over at this point. The product should meet the needs and expectations of the target market. The product has now entered the introduction stage of the product life cycle (a discussion of life cycle can be found later in this chapter). Future success of the product will depend upon how well the product fits with and reacts to trends that occur in the marketplace—for example, economic trends, demographic and social trends, and technology trends. For insight into a successful new product launch, read the Think Marketing box **Can't Get Enough of East Coast Lifestyle!**

Video: Fruit Breeder Invents Cotton Candy Flavoured Grapes

MANAGING CURRENT PRODUCTS

L03 Discuss key decisions involved in managing current products.

The key decisions in product management concern the development of new products and the rejuvenation of current products. Decisions about current products revolve around product modifications and design changes, alterations to marketing mix strategies, and whether to keep a product in the market or withdraw it. Let's take a look at each type of decision.

ThinkMarketing

Can't Get Enough of East Coast Lifestyle!

Launching a new product isn't for the faint of heart, given that over 75 percent of new consumer packaged goods and retail products fail in their first year.[13] This is why 22-year-old Alex MacLean's brand, East Coast Lifestyle, is such a sweet success story.

As part of an Acadia University entrepreneurship course, the marketing student started East Coast Lifestyle, a line of casual clothing and accessories. The products have become so popular that in less than a year the brand has 104 000 Facebook likes, 20 000 Instagram fans, 31 000 Twitter followers, and over $250 000 in sales.

MacLean's idea for the business started as a hunch that east coasters would get behind a brand meant to show off their regional pride, especially if it promised to give back to the community. Alex did some research and found that there wasn't a clothing line specifically aimed at the east coast market . . . yet.

Product development involved selecting core products as well as developing a logo. The brand's stylized anchor logo, which MacLean designed on a flight home from a family vacation, evokes memories of summer days spent on the water. "The brand stands for more than just a logo, more than just a company. It represents where we're from. If you wear it, you wear it proudly if you're a Maritimer," explains MacLean.

Alex borrowed $800 from his father to produce the first 30 hoodies. While waiting for them to arrive, he prepped his social media channels and posted East Coast Lifestyle stickers all around campus to create some buzz. The first 30 hoodies were sold mostly to friends, but the next orders sold swiftly to strangers. Photos of Sidney Crosby and Nathan MacKinnon wear-

East Coast Lifestyle

ing the brand have been posted on Instagram, giving East Coast Lifestyle the type of publicity that usually costs big money.

The company isn't all about sailing and surfing though—it's about giving back, too. Alex has donated money to Acadia's S.M.I.L.E. foundation and to support shelters for the homeless. Now a graduate, Alex is devoting all his time to the business, and sales are continuing to soar.[14 & 15]

Question:

What are some things you would recommend Alex do to grow his business?

Product Modification Decisions

Products are modified in many ways and for a variety of reasons. For example, Unilever's new roll-on deodorant packaging uses 18 percent less plastic, which helps reduce the amount of waste going to landfill.[16] Changes in style are often implemented to give a product a contemporary look, such as automobiles that are redesigned to appeal to changing consumer tastes and preferences. Electronic devices, like smartphones and tablets, are modified to incorporate the latest technological features and maintain interest in the category.

Functional modifications make a package easier or safer to use. A no-mess pour spout added to a container for a liquid product is an example of a functional modification. Tropicana, for example, changed the pour spout on its large plastic juice packages from a circle to an oval to facilitate "no spill" pouring. Quality modifications include increasing product durability (e.g., gel nail polish), improving taste (a beverage or food product), and improving the speed of operation (e.g., a tablet or laptop).

Product Mix Expansion Decisions

As discussed in the previous chapter, product mix decisions concern the *depth* and *width* of a product line. The addition of new products and the creation of extended versions of existing products are the lifeline of growth-oriented marketing organizations. To foster growth, a manager looks for gaps in the marketplace (perceived opportunities) and recommends developing products for the opportunities with the highest potential.

This procedure is referred to as **product stretching** and is defined as the sequential addition of products to a product line so that its depth or width is increased. Stretching can occur in several ways. Colgate-Palmolive Canada makes eight types of Colgate toothpaste: toothpaste for cavity protection, sensitivity relief, children, whitening, tartar control, long-lasting fresh breath, and plaque and gingivitis protection. There are a total of

Figure 9.7   Stretching a Branded Product Line into New Product Categories

product stretching The sequential addition of products to a product line to increase its depth or width.

41 different items in this product mix marketed under brand names such as Colgate Total, Colgate Optic White, Colgate Sensitive Pro-Relief, Colgate Cavity Protection, and My First Colgate for infants and toddlers. Does Colgate need to market this many items? By meeting the unique needs of different customers, new items drive sales growth.

At Unilever, Dove was once a bar of beauty soap well known for its gentle characteristics. Today, the brand name appears on antiperspirants, body washes, moisturizers, hand lotions, facial cleansers, and shampoos. It is the flagship brand of Unilever's personal-care portfolio and the world's number-one cleansing brand.[17] Refer to the illustration in **Figure 9.7**.

Packaging and Brand Design Decisions

Packaging often creates the first impression consumers have of a brand, which is why the most successful companies always try to keep their merchandise wrapped in something fresh, eye-catching, and unique. Reese's, for example, has boosted sales by modifying its packaging, as well as its product, to match a seasonal holiday or event, like Halloween. Reese's stays true to the brand by keeping its traditional colours and just adding a new holiday twist to the product. See **Figure 9.8** for an example of Reese's seasonal packaging.

It is also common for consumer brands to undergo one or more logo design changes throughout their lives. As we saw with MEC earlier in the chapter, a refreshed logo helps to reposition a brand in the minds of consumers. Any modification to a brand needs to be supported by marketing communications in order to create awareness of the changes and maintain trust in the brand.

Figure 9.8   Reese's fun seasonal packaging keeps consumers interested in the brand.

Product Maintenance or Withdrawal Decisions

One of the toughest decisions facing a manager is whether or not to cut the lifeline of a product. Such a decision should be based on profit or loss and strategic fit, but other factors, such as sentiment and emotion (attachment to long-established products), enter into the decision as well. It is unrealistic to think that products will remain profitable indefinitely, particularly in today's fast-paced marketplace. Traditional GPS devices made by Garmin and TomTom, for instance, have been very successful. Whether they'll continue to be useful, though, is questionable, now that so many people own a smartphone with Google Maps. The iPhone has turn-by-turn directions and so does Android, which means there isn't a compelling reason to buy a standalone GPS system any more.

Many companies practise planned obsolescence. **Planned obsolescence** involves deliberately outdating a product before the end of its useful life by stopping its supply or introducing a newer version. The objective is to get the consumer to abandon the current item in favour of the new item. Such a practice is very common in the computer hardware and software industry—faster computers and upgraded software are the lifeblood of the industry. In the smartphone market, think of the innovations brought to market by Apple. The iPhone 5 model was firmly entrenched, but was soon followed by the 5s. Shortly after the 5s launch rumours started spreading about the iPhone 6. Each generation of phone brings product improvements that tempt consumers to buy.

planned obsolescence Deliberately outdating a product before the end of its useful life by stopping its supply or introducing a newer version.

THE PRODUCT LIFE CYCLE

L04 Identify the stages in a product's life cycle and discuss how a brand manager's decisions are influenced at each stage.

Products go through a series of phases known collectively as the **product life cycle**. The term refers to the stages a product goes through from its introduction to the market to its eventual withdrawal. See **Figure 9.9** for a graph of the product life cycle. According to the life cycle theory, a product starts with slow sales in the introduction stage, experiences rapid sales increases in the second (growth) stage, undergoes only marginal growth or even some decline when it reaches maturity, and then enters the decline stage, where sales drop off at a much faster rate each year. The variables of *time, sales,* and *profits* are the determinants of a product's stage in the life cycle. The life cycle concept is popular in strategic marketing planning. Since the conditions of each stage are quite different, the life cycle suggests that different strategies, or marketing mixes, should be used in each phase. This section of the chapter examines the four stages of the life cycle and discusses some of the marketing implications that each stage presents to the manager.

product life cycle The stages a product goes through from its introduction to the market to its eventual withdrawal.

All products do not have the same life cycle; some are quite long (Levi's Jeans—invented in 1873, and Kraft Macaroni and Cheese—introduced in 1937), while others are quite short (Microsoft Zune). The Zune was Microsoft's answer to the hot new iPods that Apple was pushing. But the Zune failed to gain enough market share as it was clunky to use and didn't have an easy-to-access music

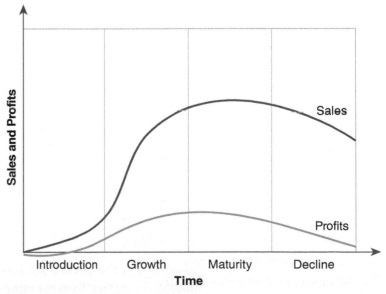

Figure 9.9   The Product Life Cycle

Scott Olson/Getty Images

Figure 9.10   Microsoft Zune's life cycle was relatively short.

introduction stage The period after the product is introduced into the marketplace and before significant growth begins.

growth stage The period of rapid consumer acceptance.

Procter & Gamble

Figure 9.11   Crest 3D White Glamorous White Rinse

store. After several years, Microsoft discontinued all Zune hardware and encouraged users to transition to Windows Phone.[18] See **Figure 9.10**.

Introduction Stage

As its name suggests, a product's **introduction stage** is the period after it has been introduced into the market-place. At introduction, the brand manager tries to create awareness of and interest in the product among the primary target market. It is a period of slow sales growth, because the product is new and not yet widely known. Losses are frequently incurred in this stage because research and development expenses must be recovered and a heavy investment in marketing is needed to achieve awareness, interest, and trial-purchase marketing objectives. This marketing investment is a reflection of the company's commitment to building a viable market position.

The manager allocates a sizeable budget for marketing communications (media advertising, websites, and social media). It is common for advertising to include incentives, such as coupons, that reduce the consumer's financial risk in making the first purchase. Through public relations and experiential marketing activities there is an attempt to generate buzz for the new product in the media and through online viral marketing campaigns. Apple, for example, typically announces a new product about three months in advance of its being available. The media buzz that precedes the launch creates pent-up demand and people line up at the stores for the product the day it is launched—a great strategy by Apple! When Apple opened its very first South American store in Rio de Janeiro on February 15, 2014, over 1700 people lined up to be among the first customers.[19]

When launching an entirely new product, price is a major decision for the manager. If too high, consumers could reject the product; if too low, financial objectives may not be achieved. Many marketers believe a higher price is preferable since it is much easier to lower the price if things aren't going well. IKEA was forced to change its pricing strategy for the China market—slashing prices by an average of 50 percent across all product lines. "When we came to market [in China], we realized that our prices had been too expensive," explains Angela Zhu, IKEA China's retail manager. "It took years for us to continuously reduce our retail prices, to really let many people afford them." IKEA's strategy in China is finally starting to pay off. Sales were up 17 percent in 2013, making China one of the retailer's fastest growing markets.[20]

At introduction the brand manager devises strategies to secure distribution. Financial incentives in the form of discounts and allowances are the norm. Obtaining distribution for new products with new brand names is challenging. For this reason, many new products are brought to market bearing established brand names. When P&G launches new oral care products, the Crest name is used. The Crest name provides instant credibility for the product with distributors and consumers. **Figure 9.11** shows an example of a new P&G mouthwash and whitener under the Crest brand name.

The length of time a product stays in the introduction stage depends on how quickly or slowly consumers adopt the product and on the degree to which sales increase annually.

Growth Stage

As indicated by the sales curve in Figure 9.9, the **growth stage** is a period of rapid consumer acceptance. Sales rise rapidly, as do profits. Several competitive brands generally enter the market at this stage, each seeking a piece of the action for itself;

therefore, the manager of the original product must continue to market aggressively to protect and build market share.

The emphasis of the activity in this stage shifts from generating awareness to creating preference. Many of the activities implemented are designed to encourage consumers to prefer a particular product or brand. Depending on the degree of competition, the organization maintains or perhaps increases its marketing investment at this point. Advertising messages focus on product differentiation (unique selling points) and are intended to give consumers a sound reason why they should buy a particular brand. Since more information about the target market is known at this point, messages and media selection become better suited to the target; therefore, the marketing activities tend to be more efficient at this stage. A greater variety of promotional incentives are also used, because it is important to get people to make both trial purchases (by continuing to generate awareness of the product) and repeat purchases (by encouraging preference and loyalty). Incentives such as contests, coupons, and refund offers are commonly used to stimulate purchases.

Price strategies at this stage remain flexible; that is, they are often determined by competitive prices. If competitors have entered the market with lower prices, the manager of the original product might adjust price downward. How consumers perceive the product and the benefits it offers also influences pricing strategy. If one brand is perceived to offer better value (for example, it is a dominant brand leader in the market), a higher price is possible. Since consumer demand is higher in the growth stage than it is during the introduction stage, distribution is now easier to obtain. In effect, the combination of consumer demand and trade incentives offered by the manufacturer makes the product attractive to new distributors and help move the product through the channel of distribution.

Mature Stage

In the **mature stage** of a product's life cycle the product has been widely adopted by consumers; sales growth slows, becoming marginal, and eventually a slight decline develops. Profits stabilize and begin to decline because of the expenses incurred in defending a brand's market share.

When a product is in the mature stage there is less emphasis on marketing communications. Rather than spend a lot of money in this area, the objective is to spend only what is needed in order to maximize profit. Profit generated by mature products provides funds for investment in new product opportunities. See **Figure 9.12** for an illustration of this process.

There are exceptions to every rule, however, as this is a period when the only way to grow is to steal business from competitors. For insight into how the changing nature of the market place can determine how much is invested in marketing in the mature stage, read the Think Marketing box **For Coke, the Challenge Is Staying Relevant**.

Generally, most products remain in the mature stage for a long period of time, so brand managers are accustomed to implementing marketing strategies for mature brands. The mature stage is a stage where rejuvenation can occur. Maintaining customer loyalty becomes a priority. The marketing objective is to extend the life cycle of the product.

In the mature stage, retail distributors carefully monitor the sales volume of the products they sell. It is a stage where slow-moving products are eliminated from the shelves. The concept of category management that was discussed earlier in this chapter comes into play. Wholesalers

mature stage The stage of a product's life cycle when it has been widely adopted by consumers; sales growth slows and eventually declines slightly.

Figure 9.12   The Product Life Cycle and New-Product Development

Think Marketing

For Coke, the Challenge Is Staying Relevant

Coca-Cola has been the world's number one ranked brand for years, but in 2013 both Apple and Google overtook it in Interbrand's Best Global Brands report. This is not surprising, though, given that soft drink sales by volume in North America have been declining for nine straight years. The reasons for the downward sales trend are varied and complex. In addition to concerns about rising obesity rates and growing consumer demand for healthier food and beverage products, Coke drinkers are getting older. Research shows that the average age of a Coke drinker is 56. Studies also find that young people tend not to like highly carbonated drinks. "Coke is more heavily carbonated than Pepsi, and roughly twice as carbonated as the energy drinks Red Bull and Monster, which are rapidly gaining market share, especially among the young," explains Martin Lindstrom, a brand and marketing consultant.

As products mature, brand managers must adopt strategies to extend a product's life cycle. Coca-Cola has done this by creating a venturing and emerging brands team, whose goal is to develop new billion-dollar brands. An example of a recent new brand is Coca-Cola Life, a naturally sweetened, reduced-calorie sparkling beverage, that was introduced in Argentina and Chile. "It's another example of how we are working to be part of the solution to the obesity problem, giving consumers a blend of sugar and natural zero-calorie sweeteners," explains a company spokesperson. Coca-Cola is also investing heavily in promotion to keep its brands top of mind with consumers and to prevent the products from slipping into decline. Just

Eric Lafforgue/age fotostock

recently the company has announced plans to increase media spending by up to $1 billion by 2016.

Coca-Cola has thrived for over 127 years and has survived countless passing health fads. No doubt, the brand has many loyal followers. But, in order to remain successful in the future, Coca-Cola must connect with a younger market through product innovation and continue to invest in marketing.[21]

Question:

Take a look at some recent Coca-Cola marketing communications. Do you think the company is doing a good job of connecting with a younger market? Why or why not?

and retailers want to carry only product lines that are moving at a desired pace. At the same time, manufacturers start to ponder the possible withdrawal of brands from the market sometime in the future if they enjoy only second-tier status among distributors.

Extending the Product Life Cycle

Many brand managers attempt to rejuvenate brands and extend their life cycles for as long as possible. The three most commonly used strategies for extending the life cycle of a brand are to look for new markets, to alter the product in some way, and to experiment with new marketing mix strategies. The effect of life cycle extensions is illustrated in **Figure 9.13**. Let us examine each of these options in more detail.

Attract New Markets   Increasing the number of product users can be accomplished by entering new market segments. Consideration is given to attracting people with a different demographic profile or expanding on a geographic basis. For example, the successful regional brand East Coast Lifestyle, has already been adapted for the west coast. The logo's anchor is replaced with a snow-capped mountain, and the line extension, West Coast Lifestyle, has rolled out.

Several packaged-goods companies have taken aim at new demographic targets by launching micro-sized versions of their products. For example, Cadbury Adams Canada introduced a 100-calorie chocolate bar called Cadbury Thins (a thinner version of a regular Cadbury bar). Cadbury believes it is reaching consumers who weren't buying chocolate or weren't buying very much. The new option allows these consumers to indulge just a little.[22]

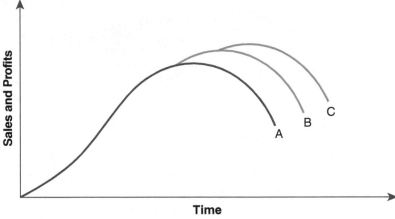

A: **Traditional product life cycle**
B and C: **Desired life cycle, achieved by appealing to new targets and by altering the product or the marketing mix**

Figure 9.13   Life Cycle Extensions

Alter the Product   In a product altera-tion strategy, the brand manager changes certain characteristics of the product to attract new users. There could be improvements in quality, features, and style in order to encourage customers to purchase more of the product.

Consumers are used to the expression "new and improved" but often question the validity of it. Be assured, if it's on the package some kind of change has occurred. Frito Lay is a leader in the salty snack market. The company sees product improvements as absolutely essential in order to stay ahead of competitors. Their brands include Doritos, Tostitos, Lays, and Ruffles. Frito Lay reformulated its offerings using cottonseed oil with new frying technologies. The result was a better-tasting, crispier, and crunchier chip—benefits other competitors were not offering. Standing still in a mature and competitive snack market is not an option for Frito Lay.

Feature improvements could involve a change in the packaging—something that makes the product easier to use. Last year, Danone did just that under the Danino brand when it introduced easy to hold dinosaur-shaped bottles of drinkable yogurt for kids.[23] See **Figure 9.14**.

What's referred to as a *bonus pack* may also attract new customers. A **bonus pack** offers customers more volume or weight for the same price as the original size. A package flash announcing "25 percent more" on the package grabs shoppers' attention.

For durable goods such as appliances and cars, style changes are a sound rejuvenation strategy. In the context of brand design concepts that were presented in Chapter 8, changing the look of a product has an impact on how consumers will perceive it. General Motors completely revamped Cadillac with new models to counter consumer perceptions that it was "grandpa's car." The objective is to attract an upscale buyer who is looking for luxury, but also one who is much younger than their traditional customer. Refer to the Cadillac image in **Figure 9.15**.

Add New Products   Another way of rejuvenating a mature brand is to add new products—to stretch the line into new areas. These products are referred to as product **line extensions**. Often, the line extensions meet new needs in the market. For example, chewing gum manu-facturers like Mars (Juicy Fruit, Big Red, and Double-mint) and Mondelez (Bubbalicious, Dentyne, and Trident) are growing sales by offering new lines of enhanced gum, called nutraceuticals. According to

bonus pack Offers customers more volume or weight for the same price as the original size.

line extensions Products added to rejuvenate a mature brand by stretching the line into new areas.

Figure 9.14   Danino drinkable yogurt comes in small dinosaur-shaped bottles that are easy for kids to hold and carry with them wherever they go.

Figure 9.15 Cadillac appeals to younger buyers seeking luxury in their ride.

Global Industry Analysts, Inc., a research firm, "Gums offer many benefits to consumers beyond the simple pleasure of chewing and are gaining recognition as an innovative platform for nutritional dosage delivery systems, on par with pills and capsules. With growing awareness, gum is emerging as a substitute to regular pills, hence widening the scope of the gum industry."[24]

Greek yogurt has become so popular that it is now considered a super trend, on par with gluten-free foods and antioxidants. Affinnova, a consumer research firm, conducted a study recently and found that possible line extensions might take Greek yogurt beyond the dairy case. Among the top new product ideas listed in the report are: Greek yogurt vitamin chews, which consumers perceive as "easy on the stomach"; frozen Greek yogurt; and Greek yogurt anti-wrinkle cream, which scored high with people 55 and older.[25]

Change Other Marketing Mix Elements Brand managers must look beyond the product when making strategy decisions in the mature stage of the life cycle. Other variables such as price, marketing communications, and distribution play a role in the success of the brand. Since there are many competitors in the mature stage, the time is right to contemplate lowering the price. Cost-conscious shoppers could suddenly show interest in a national brand they had not tried before.

There's also the option of temporary price in the form of cash rebates and discount financing; both strategies are frequently used by automobile manufacturers when the economic situation is uncertain and when gasoline prices escalate. There is a drawback to such a strategy—consumers have grown accustomed to rebates and will postpone purchases until one is offered.

With regard to marketing communications, changes to the message are common in the mature stage. Even if the product does not change, an attempt to reposition the brand in the minds of consumers is possible by communicating a different message. Sales promotion incentives can be employed to encourage current customers to buy more frequently or buy in greater quantity. Cash refunds and premium offers, for example, may require multiple purchases for the consumer to qualify for the offer. The impact of promotions can be significant. Promotion incentives are discussed in detail in the marketing communications chapters.

Where the product is available is another consideration for building a brand. Among cafes and fast-food retailers, location decisions are crucial to success. At this stage, retailers look for cost-effective ways to expand the availability of their products. Building a stand-alone café or restaurant is costly. A much less expensive option is to form a partnership with another retailer that has similar objectives. Both parties will benefit from the partnership. Starbucks, which saw a slowdown in Canada during the recession and closed some cafes, is back in growth mode with a licensed Starbucks installed in the vast majority of the 124 new Canadian Target stores. "If your target demographic is someone looking for a bit more premium quality, but also the good deal on home essentials, like the Target consumer is—the moms—Starbucks ties really nicely into that," says Robert Carter, executive director of food and fashion trends at NPD Group, a market research company. "They're looking for quality experience as well as deal-finding."[26]

Decline Stage

decline stage Stage in the product's life cycle when sales begin to drop rapidly and profits are eroded.

In the **decline stage** of the product life cycle sales begin to drop rapidly and profits are eroded. Products become obsolete as many consumers shift to innovative products entering the market. Price cuts are a common marketing strategy in a declining market, as competing brands attempt to protect market share.

Stage in Life Cycle			
	Introduction	**Growth**	**Maturity**	**Decline**
Competition	None or a few	More (3–5)	Many (late entrants)	Fewer as brands drop out
Marketing objective	Awareness and trial purchase	Preference via product differentiation	Encourage brand loyalty (extend the life cycle); potential rejuvenation	Potential withdrawal
Product	Initial product	Line extensions	Complete product mix	Some items dropped; maintain core product
Price	Tends to be high (easier to drop price if necessary)	Competitive pricing based on intensity of competition	Potentially lower price to protect market share	Lower price but attempt to remain profitable
Distribution	Limited; hard to obtain initially	Expanded based on consumer acceptance	Peak distribution; potential to lose distribution if not among top sellers	Much less; distributors drop unpopular products
Marketing communications	Emphasis on advertising and social media for brand exposure; high budget expenditure	Emphasis on product benefits to differentiate; high budget expenditure to remain competitive	Reminder-oriented advertising; promotions to encourage loyalty; spend only what is necessary	Reduce or cut expenditures completely; preserve profits

Figure 9.16   How each stage of the product life cycle relates to a firm's marketing objectives and marketing mix decisions.

Because the costs of maintaining a product in decline are quite high, the brand manger will start thinking about planning the withdrawal of the product from the market. This is the time to cut advertising and promotion expenditures to maximize profit or minimize potential losses, and to generate funds that can be invested in new products with greater profit potential. Companies do not have the resources to support all products equally, and the wise ones have products at various stages of the product life cycle so that the marketing strategies can be effectively managed within financial constraints.

A summary of the key marketing influences on the product life cycle is included in **Figure 9.16.**

THE LENGTH OF THE PRODUCT LIFE CYCLE

All products do not follow the same life cycle. So far, this chapter has presented what may be called the traditional product life cycle so that marketing strategies associated with each stage can be described. Let us examine some of the common variations in the length and shape of the product life. Refer to **Figure 9.17** for an illustration.

Instant Bust   The term **instant bust** applies to a product for which a firm had high expectations and perhaps launched with a lot of marketing fanfare but which, for whatever reason, consumers rejected very quickly. Some of the best marketing companies in the world have had their share of instant busts. PepsiCo has failed miserably with some new products. Among its misfortunes were Pepsi A.M., a breakfast cola that offered more caffeine and less carbonation, and Crystal Pepsi, a product positioned as a "clear" cola. While marketing

instant bust A product that a firm had high expectations of and launched with marketing fanfare but that consumers rejected very quickly.

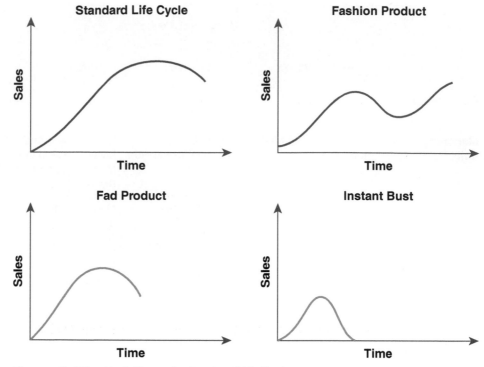

Figure 9.17   Variations of a Product Life Cycle

research showed both concepts to be acceptable to consumers, the early failures show what consumers say they will do and what consumers actually do can be two different things.

fad A product that has a reasonably short selling season, perhaps one or a few financially successful seasons.

Fad   The cycle of the **fad** is reasonably short, perhaps one selling season or a few seasons, and usually financially successful for the organization. A fad could have something to do with clothing (leisure suits, miniskirts, bell-bottom pants), collectibles (Beyblades and mood rings), or lifestyle activities (fad diets). Crocs, those ugly but comfortable rubber shoes with goofy holes, are a fad. Crocs achieved enormous success quickly. But, where there is a spectacular rise in sales, there is also a spectacular fall. Crocs failed when lower-priced knock-offs moved in. But the company sold 120 million pairs and made a fortune in the process.

fashion A cycle for a product that recurs through many selling seasons.

Fashion   The cycle of a **fashion** is a recurring one. What is in style now will be out of style later, and perhaps back in style at an even later date. Product categories subject to fashion cycles include clothing (items such as business suits, skirts, and bathing suits), cosmetics, and automobiles. In the fashion industry, casual clothing (business casual) has been popular for quite a while but very recent trends indicate a strong return of the traditional business suit. The urban business professional is sprucing up his or her wardrobe, and custom tailoring businesses like Indochino are reaping the benefits. Refer to the illustration in **Figure 9.18**.

These variations indicate that marketers must not be satisfied with passing through the various stages of the conventional product life cycle. Instead, strategies must be implemented that will initiate growth as the product matures. In this regard, many of the product and marketing mix decisions discussed in this chapter will come into play.

Simulation: Product Life Cycle

PRODUCT ADOPTION PROCESS

L05 Explain how the product adoption process influences the length and shape of a product's life cycle.

The degree to which consumers accept or reject a product is the measure of its success or failure. Consumers adopt products at different speeds and in doing so have an influence on the length and shape of a product's life cycle. Product acceptance is

Indochino Apparel Inc.

Figure 9.18   Young urban males are sprucing up their wardrobes with custom tailored suits and shirts.

concerned with two areas: *adoption* or individual acceptance, and *diffusion* or market acceptance.

Adoption is defined as a series of stages a consumer passes through on the way to purchasing a product on a regular basis. The adoption process has up to five distinct steps: awareness, interest, evaluation, trial, and adoption (see **Figure 9.19**). The gradual acceptance of a product from introduction to market saturation is referred to as the **diffusion of innovation**. Everett M. Rogers has conducted intensive research into the diffusion process, and he makes three conclusions. First, individuals require different amounts of time to decide to adopt a product. Second, consumers can be classified on the basis of how quickly or how slowly they adopt a product. And third, there are five categories of adopters.[27]

The five categories of adopters are *innovators, early adopters, early majority, late majority,* and *laggards.* Innovators and early adopters are trendsetters and opinion leaders who adopt new products quickly. The early and late majority categories represent mass market acceptance of a product, and the laggards are the last to buy. Mass market acceptance occurs once the product is recognized as a proven commodity. Refer to **Figure 9.20** for a visual image and brief description of each adopter category.

It should be noted that innovators and early adopters have moved on to new innovations by the time the mass market starts buying a product. For example, the price of LCD flat-screen televisions has dropped in the wake of newer television technologies that are now available. The laggards will be buying the LCD flat-screen TVs while innovators and early adopters discard them. Innovators want products that fit with their ambitious, trend-setting lifestyle.

adoption A series of stages a consumer passes through on the way to purchasing a product on a regular basis.

diffusion of innovation The gradual acceptance of a product from its introduction to market saturation.

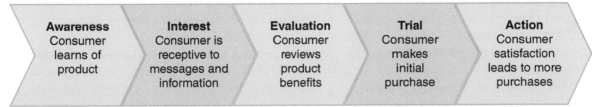

Figure 9.19   The Adoption Process

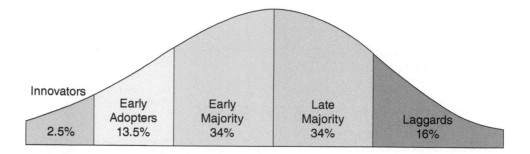

Innovators
Risk takers and trendsetters eager to try new products; they seek new products to be separate from mainstream (2.5% of population)

Early Adopters
Opinion leaders affected by status and prestige; they want new products early (13.5% of population)

Early Majority
People who like to buy a proven commodity; mid-range social and economic status; they represent the initial phase of mass market acceptance of product (34% of population)

Late Majority
People who only buy established products that have been around a while; lower in social and economic status (34% of population)

Laggards
People who do not like change; they buy the same old things; the last group to buy the product (16% of population)

Figure 9.20 Adopter Categories

 ExperienceMarketing

To experience marketing you have to assess situations and make recommendations to change marketing strategies when necessary. What would you do in the following situation?

You may be familiar with Rumble Supershake, a product that was successfully pitched on the CBC's Dragons' Den. Rumble is a nutritious, protein-rich drink chock full of all-natural ingredients like organic cherries, pomegranate, beet juice, and walnut oil, just to name a few. A perfect energy boost for active and health-conscious people!

Rumble is sold in a 12-ounce reusable bottle and comes in two flavours, Dutch cocoa or vanilla maple. Positioning is an issue, though, says Paul Underhill, company founder. "It's not a meal replacement or a natural energy drink or a smoothie, but it has elements of all three." The Canadian Food Inspection Agency has labelled Rumble as a "nourishing drink," the first brand in this new beverage category.

Rumble lasts for 12 months on the shelf, which is a great advantage for shipping and storage, but is also found in refrigerated display cases. Distribution is continuing to grow with Sobeys, Thrifty Foods, and Longo's recently listing the brand. Rumble is also carried by Whole Foods and natural food stores across Canada, as well as in fitness clubs and cycling shops. Suggested retail price is $3.99 a bottle, and sales in 2013 were about $500 000.

The company would like to expand to the United States, using the same strategy as in Canada—start in natural foods stores and then follow with conventional grocery stores. With a consumer marketing budget of only $75 000, which includes a U.S. launch, the company isn't sure what to do.

What marketing recommendations do you have for Rumble over the next 12 months? Your recommendations should consider basic planning principles that include a review of the market, competition, and brand; a precise description of the target; a product positioning strategy; and a marketing mix strategy that fits the positioning strategy.[28 & 29]

CHAPTER SUMMARY

LO1 **Explain the different organizational structures used to manage brands.** *(pp. 190–193)*

There are many different organizational structures for managing brands. Factors such as company size, financial resources, and growth expectations usually determine which structure to use. The basic structures include brand management, category management, target market management, regional management, and continental and global management.

LO2 **Describe the steps in the new product development process.** *(pp. 193–196)*

The brand manager oversees seven steps in the process of developing and marketing a new product: idea generation, screening, concept development and testing, business analysis, product development, test marketing and marketing planning, and commercialization.

LO3 **Discuss key decisions involved in managing current products.** *(pp. 196–199)*

The key decisions in product management concern the development of new products and the rejuvenation of current products. Regarding current products, decisions revolve around product modifications and design changes, alterations to marketing mix strategies, and whether to keep a product in the market or withdraw it.

LO4 **Identify the stages in a product's life cycle and discuss how a brand manager's decisions are influenced at each stage.** *(pp. 199–206)*

The product life cycle refers to the stages a product passes through, from its introduction to its withdrawal from the market. The life cycle involves four stages: introduction, growth, maturity, and decline. The marketing strategies employed by the firm vary considerably from stage to stage. The brand manager tends to be aggressive with his or her marketing strategies in the intro-

duction and growth stages. Marketing objectives in these stages focus on creating awareness and interest in a brand and encouraging trial and repeat purchases. Competition forces each brand to clearly differentiate itself from the others. Marketing spending tends to be high in the introduction and growth stages.

In the mature stage, the brand manager is more concerned with protecting a brand's position. Marketing strategies focus less on expensive advertising and more on promotional incentives that encourage brand loyalty. It is also a time when managers look at strategies to rejuvenate their brand. The objective is to extend the product's life cycle. Strategies to extend the life cycle include attracting new markets; altering the product by making quality, feature, or style improvements; adding line extensions; or changing the other components of the marketing mix.

In the decline stage the brand manager begins planning a product's withdrawal from the market. The manager will cut advertising and promotion expenditures to maximize profit or minimize potential losses and to generate funds that can be invested in new products with greater profit potential.

LO5 **Explain how the product adoption process influences the length and shape of a product's life cycle.** *(pp. 206–208)*

The length of a product's life cycle can vary. Some cycles are short (fads), while others are long (fashions). Regardless of the length of the cycle, the manager's primary objective is to generate profits. Profits are maximized in the late growth and mature stages of the product life cycle; hence, organizations initiate strategies for extending these phases.

The speed at which consumers accept a product has an influence on the length and shape of the product's life cycle. This gradual acceptance of a product from introduction to market saturation is called the diffusion of innovation. Purchasers can be divided into five groups according to how soon they buy the product after it has been introduced: innovators, early adopters, early majority, late majority, and laggards.

MyMarketingLab   Study, practise, and explore real marketing situations with these helpful resources:
- **Interactive Lesson Presentations:** Work through interactive presentations and assessments to test your knowledge of marketing concepts.
- **Study Plan:** Check your understanding of chapter concepts with self-study quizzes.
- **Dynamic Study Modules:** Work through adaptive study modules on your computer, tablet, or mobile device.
- **Simulations:** Practise decision-making in simulated marketing environments.

REVIEW QUESTIONS

1. What are the four different organizational structures or systems used to manage brands? *(LO1)*
2. Which management system or structure is the business-to-business market moving toward? *(LO1)*
3. List the steps in the new product development process. What are some ways companies generate ideas for new products? *(LO2)*
4. Which step in the new product development process involves assessing market demand for a product, calculating the costs of producing and marketing the product, and predicting sales revenue and profit? *(LO2)*
5. What are the specific marketing decisions a brand manager is responsible for? *(LO3)*
6. What is a reason a company might practise planned obsolescence? *(LO3)*
7. What is the product life cycle? Describe strategies an organization could use to extend the life cycle of a mature product. *(LO4)*
8. What is the difference between a fad and a fashion life cycle? *(LO4)*
9. Outline the five distinct steps in the adoption process. How might an understanding of this process influence marketing strategies and decisions? *(LO5)*
10. What are the characteristics of each of the five adopter categories? *(LO5)*

DISCUSSION AND APPLICATION QUESTIONS

1. Provide examples of brands or companies that are using the following strategies to extend their life cycles: (a) entering new market segments, (b) altering the product, and (c) adding line extensions. Explain the strategy in each case.
2. In the continental and global product management section of the chapter, the concept of using strategies from other markets was discussed. Based on what you know about Canada and Canadian consumers (e.g., language and cultural backgrounds), is it practical to think that an advertising campaign devised elsewhere will work in Canada? What are the costs and benefits of utilizing such campaigns? Provide real examples to strengthen your position on the issue.
3. Test marketing is a step in the new product development process. In the chapter it was stated that some marketers see test marketing as an essential step, almost a mandatory step. Other marketers see it as a step that can be eliminated because it tips off competitors about an organization's pending actions. What is your opinion on this issue?

10 Price Strategy and Determination

Vince Talotta/Toronto Star/Getty Images

LEARNING OBJECTIVES

LO1 Explain the importance of price in the development of marketing strategy. (pp. 212–214)

LO2 Describe the impact of internal and external forces on price decisions. (pp. 214–218)

LO3 Explain the differences among profit, sales, and competitive price objectives. (pp. 218–221)

LO4 Calculate basic prices using a variety of pricing methodologies. (pp. 222–226)

LO5 Describe how legal issues can affect pricing strategy. (pp. 226–228)

AFFORDABLE LUXURY...

is the name of the game as upscale retailer Holt Renfrew tries to attract a new, younger shopper. Holt Renfrew has been in business for 175 years and has always been positioned as the store for affluent shoppers. From clothes, to accessories, to handbags, Holt Renfrew is the place to shop if you are seeking brand names such as Cole Haan, Kate Spade, and Ralph Lauren.

Holt's desire to pursue a younger target was triggered by the looming entrance of Nordstrom stores to Canada. Sensing much stiffer competition for upscale shoppers, Holt decided to initiate preemptive strategies to protect its position. Even without the presence of Nordstrom, the upscale baby boomer market is aging; Holt's future success rests with its ability to attract a new target.

The marketing solution involved a mixture of product and price. Holt's launched its first location of HR2 in 2013. HR2 offers designer label products at discounted prices. Both Holt Renfrew and HR2 stores will carry similar brand name products but the product assortment will not overlap. Conceivably, that justifies the different price structure.

With regard to targeting, Holt's move is wise. Generation Y is the next big group of shoppers. It is important to strike a relationship with them while they are young. They may not have the same disposable income as older shoppers but if they shop HR2 now, they may trade up to Holt Renfrew later on. "To have a brand that becomes more accessible to a wider net of consumer makes a lot of sense," says Alyssa Huggins, vice-president retail at Bimm Direct & Digital.[1]

The new strategy does pose a potential problem. Might the discounted prices at HR2 upset existing customers shopping at Holt Renfrew? Will the presence of HR2 dilute the image and reputation of the Holt brand? Core customers could revolt if they felt the high-end brands they covet were being shared with the masses. Apparently, this is a gamble Holt Renfrew is willing to take.

This chapter introduces some of the basic pricing concepts used in marketing strategy. The discussion initially focuses on the variety of markets that Canadian firms operate in and the implications these markets have for pricing strategy. The external and internal factors influencing pricing strategy are then discussed. Finally, the issues of how pricing strategy is used to achieve marketing objectives and what specific methods are available for determining prices are addressed.

THE DEFINITION AND ROLE OF PRICE

LO1 Explain the importance of price in the development of marketing strategy.

price The exchange value of a good or service in the marketplace.

Price is defined as the exchange value of a good or service in the marketplace. The key word in this definition is "value." The value of a good or service is derived from its *tangible and intangible benefits* and from the perception a consumer has of it once he or she has been subjected to other marketing influences. Let us use an example to explain what tangible and intangible benefits are.

A young male decides to buy a pair of top-of-the-line Nike basketball shoes. The shoes are endorsed by LeBron James, perhaps the biggest NBA star today, and they are called LeBron X. The shoe has a very high price (various models available in the $200–$300 range) because it is made of the best materials using the finest technology that Nike is known for. Those are the tangibles the young buyer might look at. More than likely, however, the young male is more impressed with the style of the shoe and the aura that surrounds the endorsement by LeBron James. The shoe will impress his friends—and that's what he really wants. Those characteristics are the intangibles—intangibles that justify a higher price for the shoes.

Prices take many forms and terms. Consider the following examples of price:

- Your college tuition fees
- A club membership
- The rate of interest on a loan
- Admission charged at a theatre
- Rent charged for an apartment
- A fare charged on a bus or train
- A bid at an online auction site

From a marketing organization's perspective, price is the factor that contributes to revenues and profits. An organization must consider a multitude of variables in order to arrive at fair and competitive prices in the marketplace while providing reasonable revenues, profits, and return on investment internally.

Price is only one element of the marketing mix, but it can be the most important. For example, a prominent retailer such as Walmart relies on price to establish and maintain its image with consumers. Many experts believe that Walmart has set the price bar so low that it has actually caused competitors who couldn't match their prices to go out of business. Zellers literally gave up the battle and was taken over by Target, and Sears Canada has resorted to closing stores in its bid to remain financially viable.

Walmart currently uses the slogan, "Save Money. Live Better." The slogan reinforces Walmart's positioning strategy, which is ideal for a lacklustre economic environment and extremely competitive retail marketplace, a marketplace where shoppers are searching for value. Even Walmart faces competitive pressure when it comes to price. Bargain stores such as Dollarama, Dollar Tree, and Dollar Store with More offer incredibly low prices. Dollarama generates $2.2 billion in revenue in Canada annually—about 10 percent of Walmart's annual revenue. Refer to the image in **Figure 10.1**.

At the opposite end of the scale there are specialty retailers such as Harry Rosen, an upscale men's clothing emporium. Customers of Harry Rosen view price as an unimportant variable in the purchase decision. Customers may not buy as much at Harry Rosen when the economy takes a turn for the worse, but it is the image created by the high prices that attracts the upscale clientele when they do buy. Harry Rosen's customers get some psychological satisfaction knowing they are wearing a quality suit!

In a relatively free market economy such as Canada's, price is also a mechanism for ensuring adequate levels of competition. In a free and open market, where competition is strong, supply and demand factors influence price. Thus, when demand for a good

Figure 10.1 Price sensitive shoppers are attracted to retail stores such as Dollarama.

The Canadian Press Images-Mario Beauregard

increases, marketing organizations have the flexibility to increase price. When demand for a product drops, organizations tend to lower prices to entice consumers to continue to buy the product. For example, when gasoline prices rise, demand for larger vehicles declines. The impact on car manufacturers and dealers is enough to warrant an array of financial incentives to keep people buying cars. Cash rebates and low-interest financing—key elements of pricing strategy—kick in when needed.

EXTERNAL AND INTERNAL INFLUENCES ON PRICE

L02 Describe the impact of internal and external forces on price decisions.

Both external and internal forces are considered when establishing the price of a product. External forces are beyond the control of an organization and include the nature of the market the product competes in, consumer demand for the product, and the financial expectations of distributors. Internal forces include production and marketing costs incurred by the firm, both of which an organization has control over.

Nature of the Market

Video: Rudi's Bakery: Management in the Global Environment

pure competition A market in which many small firms market similar products.

law of supply and demand The law declaring that an abundant supply and low demand lead to a low price, while a high demand and limited supply lead to a high price.

A firm's ability to establish price depends on the type of market it operates in. In the Canadian economy, there are several different types of markets: pure competition, monopolistic competition, oligopoly, and monopoly. See **Figure 10.2** for an illustration of these markets.

In a market environment of **pure competition**, there are many small firms marketing the same basic product; therefore, no single firm can dictate or offset the market. Commodities such as wheat, barley, and sugar fall into this category, as do financial securities such as mutual funds. The firm has no choice but to charge the going market price, because buyers can buy as much as they need at that price.

The market in this situation controls the selling price. The basic **law of supply and demand** applies: an abundant supply and low demand lead to a low price, while a high demand and limited supply lead to a high price. Often, it is simply *expectations* about supply or demand that have an impact on price. For example, if the supply of gasoline were expected to dwindle below normal demand, there would be a rush to buy the

Factor	Pure Competition	Monopolistic Competition	Oligopoly	Monopoly
Competition and product	Many sellers with same or similar product	Many sellers with differentiated product	Few large sellers with some product differentiation	Single seller with unique product
Price decision criteria	Price based on open market. How much should be produced?	Price based on competition and brand loyalty. How much should be produced and invested in marketing?	Price based on competition. Quick reaction to price changes. How much should be invested in marketing?	Price based on fair and reasonable profit for supplier
Controls	None. Dictated by market dynamics	Some	Some (e.g., uniform beer pricing in retail outlets in some provinces)	By government or other regulatory body (e.g., CRTC)

Figure 10.2   Market Structures and Their Price Implications

resource and its price would be driven up, at least temporarily. In other cases, it is the actual supply and demand that influences prices. The demand for stocks on the stock market influences the rate at which they are traded.

If a market is characterized by **monopolistic competition**, there are many competitors selling products that, although similar, are perceived to be different by consumers. Companies marketing packaged-goods items such as coffee, cereal, and household cleaners operate in this kind of market, as do consumer electronics companies. The consumer always has lots of choice. Marketing strategy is designed to distinguish one brand from the others. Such variables as product quality, service, style, function, and packaging are used to convey a difference to the consumer. Advertising is employed to present a certain image for the brand.

So why can some products charge more than others? Smart marketing. A brand such as Red Bull, for example, applies a premium price strategy. Red Bull's price is much higher than the price for competitors' offerings even though the can is much smaller—less actual product. In this market, consumers are willing to pay more for Red Bull due to the quality of the product and the benefits it offers. It is perceived as being superior to the alternatives. Add to the mix some significant image-building experiential marketing campaigns and you can see why Red Bull is the world's best-selling energy drink. Refer to the image in **Figure 10.3**.

The effectiveness of the marketing mix strategy determines a brand's fate and explains why leading bands are perceived to be better than other brands. These brands can charge a higher price for their products.

If the consumer thinks there are differences among the brands, brand loyalty can be created. Traditionally, consumers who are loyal to a brand are less likely to be influenced by price; that is, they are willing to pay a little more for the brand of their choice than for other brands.

In an **oligopolistic market**, there are a few large sellers of a particular good or service. Industries traditionally associated with oligopolies are the commercial airline industry, dominated by Air Canada and WestJet; the retail gasoline industry, dominated by Petro-Canada, Imperial Oil, and Shell; and the telecommunications industry, dominated by Bell, Rogers, and Telus. Collectively, these brands control significant portions of their respective markets. In the wireless phone market, Rogers, Bell, and Telus are loosely referred to as "the big three," and for good reason. Latest statistics on the industry reveal they hold 90 percent of Canadian subscribers.[2]

In an oligopoly, a competitor's actions are monitored closely. The competition is so intense that if one firm raises or drops its price, other firms will quickly do the same. For example, if Esso raises its prices, Petro-Canada and Shell are likely to follow quickly. In fact, in a matter of hours, usually overnight, the price at every gas station in a city will change to exactly the same figure. This reaction is especially pronounced in markets where the products are essentially the same.

To many consumers, this practice hints at collusion and price fixing, though independent investigations by Industry Canada (a federal government agency) have never proven this to be so. Sometimes, price wars erupt between competitors, and consumers temporarily enjoy bargain-basement prices. In a price war, the consumer is the only winner. Very often, the price war places financial hardship on the companies involved.

In a **monopoly**, a single seller of a good or service for which there are no close substitutes serves the market. With so much control, a company can manipulate supply and demand for the good or service and influence prices to the detriment of the public. In Canada, monopolies are not common, but they do exist in the service-industry sector as regulated monopolies. For example, utilities and power corporations such as SaskPower and Hydro-Quebec are provincially regulated monopolies. Cable television companies such as Rogers and Cogeco that have protected market areas (e.g., the local communities that each serves) are also monopolies. In the case of cable providers, however, they face competition from satellite providers and other services, such as Netflix. The competitive landscape of that market changes with the technology that is available.

© Aurora Photos/Alamy

Figure 10.3 Red Bull is the leader in the energy drink market, in spite of a price that is much higher than that of the competition.

monopolistic competition A market in which there are many competitors, each using a unique marketing mix based on price and other variables.

oligopolistic market A market situation in which a few large firms control the market.

monopoly A market in which there is a single seller of a particular good or service for which there are no close substitutes.

In a regulated monopoly, the government allows the supplier to set prices to ensure a reasonable amount of profit is earned so that the company can maintain and expand its operations when needed. Price increases must go through an approval process before they are implemented. The CRTC, for example, approves the rates of all cable television suppliers.

Consumer Demand for the Product

The number of consumers in a target market and the demand they have for a product has a bearing on price. Essentially, there are two common principles at work. First, consumers usually purchase greater quantities at lower prices. Second, the effects of a price change on volume demanded by consumers must be factored into the pricing strategy. To illustrate, if price is increased and demand drops significantly, the objective of the price increase (higher sales revenue or profit) will not be achieved. This principle is referred to as **price elasticity of demand**.

There are two types of demand: elastic demand and inelastic demand. **Elastic demand** describes a situation in which a small change in price results in a large change in volume (e.g., price increases by 5 percent and volume drops by 15 percent). If demand is elastic, the firm's total revenues go up as price goes down (because total sales increase), and revenues go down when price goes up (because total sales decrease). **Inelastic demand** is a situation in which a price change does not have a significant impact on the quantity purchased. In this case, total revenues go up when prices are increased and go down when prices are reduced. For example, the Toronto Maple Leafs increase ticket prices every year. Every ticket for every game is always sold regardless of how well the team performs. In comparison, some American NHL teams have to discount their ticket prices to generate a sellout. These demand concepts are illustrated in **Figure 10.4**.

Canada's two most common markets are monopolistic competition and oligopoly. In these markets demand is based on the need in the marketplace and the availability of substitute products. If demand for a product category is high, all competing firms can maintain high prices and reap the financial benefits. However, once a major competitor changes prices—say, lowers the price significantly—demand in the market can change.

price elasticity of demand Measures the effect a price change has on the volume purchased.

elastic demand A situation in which a small change in price results in a large change in volume.

inelastic demand A situation in which a change in price does not have a significant impact on the quantity purchased.

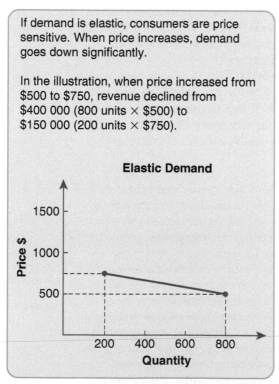
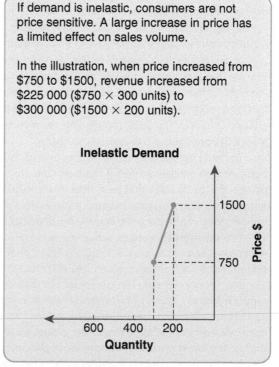

Figure 10.4 The Differences Between Elastic and Inelastic Demand

Such would be the case if a prominent brand such as Apple suddenly dropped the price of its phones for an extended period. Apple traditionally leads the market on price. Such a move could catch competitors like Samsung, Nokia, and BlackBerry off guard and place some financial pressure on these brands. If their unit sales start to drop they may have no alternative but to drop their prices, as well. Such a situation could occur if an economy slows down and sales of all phone brands begin to stagnate.

Consumer behaviour also has an impact on pricing strategy. A consumer may compare the price and quality of one product with other similar products; to other consumers, such matters as image, status, and prestige may be so important that the actual price of the product is ignored (a product such as a Rolex watch would be in this category). In the first case, the consumer behaves rationally, so the price of the product is important. In the second case, the consumer acts less rationally and is influenced by other factors, so price is less important. Thus, products aimed at status-seekers are apt to be priced high to convey prestige, while products targeted to the price-conscious would logically be priced low.

Consideration of Channel Members

The ultimate price a consumer pays for a product is influenced by markups in the channel of distribution. Once the product changes hands, pricing is determined at the discretion of the new owner. Like manufacturers, however, the distributors (wholesaler and retailer) who resell products usually have competition. They are concerned about moving the merchandise. Hence, their markup usually conforms to some standard in the industry that provides a reasonable profit margin.

To encourage channel members to charge prices that are in agreement with a manufacturer's overall marketing strategy, manufacturers consider several factors. They provide for an adequate profit margin (e.g., they consider the distributor's operating and marketing costs), they treat all customers fairly (e.g., all distributors are offered the same list price), and they offer discounts to encourage volume buying or marketing support (e.g., a portion of a discount offered by a manufacturer is passed on to the consumer by the distributor). In the latter case, the objective of the discount is to influence consumer demand during the discount period. Some examples of distributor markups are included in the Pricing Methods section of this chapter.

Even distributors show concern for higher prices that consumers must pay for products in retail stores. In Canada's supermarket industry, an industry controlled by three large companies—Loblaws, Sobeys, and Metro—there is pressure on suppliers (manufacturers such as Procter & Gamble, Kraft, and Coca-Cola, among many others) to keep prices down. Sobeys recently requested (January 2014) that its suppliers shave their prices by 1 percent retroactive to November 1, 2013 and scrap any planned increases for 2014. Their demands reflect the competitive nature of the grocery market, which has been squeezed even further by the expansion of Walmart in Canada and the launch of Target stores.[3]

Production and Marketing Costs

Costs that have a direct effect on price include the costs of labour, raw materials, processed materials, capital requirements, transportation, marketing, and administration. A common practice among manufacturing firms is to establish a total product cost, taking into consideration these elements as well as a desirable and fair gross profit margin. The addition of the profit margin to the cost becomes the selling price to distributors. Such a practice is based on the assumption that the resulting retail price will be acceptable to consumers. See **Figure 10.5** for an illustration.

The pricing decisions of an organization become increasingly difficult as costs rise. If cost increases are gradual and the amounts are marginal, a firm can usually plan its strategy effectively; it can build prices around projected cost increases for a period of time, using, say, a one-year planning cycle. Unforeseen increases (those that happen quickly and unexpectedly) are a different matter. In such cases, a firm may choose to absorb the cost increases and accept lower profit margins, at least for the short term, in the hope that the situation will correct itself. If it does not, there is little choice but to pass

Cost Items	Actual Cost
Ingredients	$15.75
Packaging (inner/outer)	1.79
Shipping case	0.68
Labour	1.48
Manufacturing	0.20
Warehousing	0.34
Total Plant Cost	**20.24**
Add: Freight cost	1.36
Total Product Cost	**21.60**
Add: Gross profit margin (40%)	8.64
List Price	**30.24**
Add: Retail profit margin (25%)	7.56
Retail price (per case of 24)	37.80
Selling Price at Retail	**1.57**

This example assumes a desired profit margin of 40% for the manufacturer of the product and a 25% markup at retail. The manufactured item is a case good that contains 24 packages in a shipping case. After all costs and profit margins are considered for the manufacturer and distributor, the price at retail is $1.57.

Figure 10.5 Cost Components of a Packaged-Goods Product

cost reductions Reduction of the costs involved in the production process.

the increase to channel members in order to ensure long-term profitability.

To illustrate, consider a situation recently faced by Kellogg's. The company announced price increases for many of its cereal lines, such as Frosted Flakes, Froot Loops, and Apple Jacks, due to rising prices it pays for ingredients and fuel. At the same time, Kellogg's also announced it was reducing the size of the boxes. Reducing the size of the box is an indirect way of raising prices. Consumers tend to balk less at quantity reductions than they do at price increases. In fact, a survey in Walmart stores revealed that this box-reduction strategy went virtually unnoticed by consumers.[4]

Kellogg's is not alone when it comes to reducing the content of food packages. Perhaps you have noticed that chocolate bars are getting smaller, there are fewer cookies in a package than before, and the size of a large coffee tin isn't quite as big as it used to be. It may seem sneaky, but the practice is becoming common and for good reason—in financial terms a manufacturer can only absorb so many cost increases before action is necessary. They do consider what consumers actually pay for the product.

As described in the cereal price increase example, an alternative to increasing price is to search for and implement **cost reductions**, which are reductions of the costs involved in the production process. Examples of some cost-reduction measures include improving production efficiency (e.g., achieving lower long-term costs by adding automation), using less-expensive materials (e.g., lower-priced ingredients and packaging materials), shrinking the size of a product (e.g., baking smaller cookies while maintaining the same pricing or putting fewer cookies in the package), and relocating manufacturing facilities to a region where production costs are lower (e.g., the migration of production from Canada to Mexico or East Asia). All of these practices are quite common but they do come with some risk. The company must be certain that the quality of the product isn't compromised. If consumers do notice a difference they could switch brands.

Generally, a firm tries to remain competitive and move prices, when necessary, to protect the profitability of the firm. Should costs actually decline, the company has the option of lowering prices or taking advantage of higher profit margins. An example of an industry in which cost reduction has resulted in lower prices is the consumer electronics industry. Advancing technologies have led to reductions in the price of computers, televisions, and other electronic appliances. The reduced prices opened the market to lower-income consumers, resulting in an expanded market that all manufacturers benefited from.

For more insight into how costs affect prices, see the Think Marketing box **Sound Strategy or Deceptive Strategy?**

PRICING OBJECTIVES INFLUENCE PRICE DECISIONS

LO3 Explain the differences among profit, sales, and competitive price objectives.

In a pure business environment, the primary goal of the organization is to produce the highest possible rate of return for the owner (shareholders, partners, sole proprietor, and so on). Pricing strategies are part of a marketing strategy that must be in line with this overall company strategy.

Think Marketing

Sound Strategy or Deceptive Strategy?

A national brand of ice cream is wrestling with a rise in ingredient costs and energy costs associated with production. To protect profit margins a decision is made to reduce the size of the package and increase the price—a double whammy, so to speak. The consumer winds up paying more for less. Is this a sound pricing strategy or simply a deceptive strategy that will ultimately cause consumer unrest?

Before making a decision on the matter, consider a few more details. Product downsizing is nothing new. Cookie manufacturers have been slowly reducing the number of cookies in a package for years—the bags are getting much smaller. Gum manufacturers have been reducing the number of pieces in their packages, and paper towel manufacturers have been reducing the number of sheets in their rolls. Cereal manufacturers have been downsizing their packages in the wake of rising ingredient costs. In all of these examples the consumer winds up paying more for less. These are just a few examples. Does the consumer notice these changes? Do they care?

A recent situation for Hellmann's mayonnaise demonstrates why marketers do what they do. Hellmann's options were to increase the price or find a way to absorb increases in costs. Instead of increasing the price, they decided to shrink the size of the jars from 950 mL to 850 mL and change the containers from glass to plastic, which drastically cut manufacturing costs. But because of the reduced pack-

iStockphoto/Thinkstock/Gettyimags

age size, the price of the mayonnaise has effectively gone up for the consumer. The increase is simply hidden.

The reality of the situation dictates these kinds of practices. Consumers are generally fed up with continual price increases and they simply rebel by switching to less expensive brands in the same product category. Consumers may switch to private label brands such as President's Choice or even buy generic (no name) store brands to save money. Today's consumers seek value in a variety of ways.

Question:
You be the judge. Is this practice sound marketing strategy or deceptive strategy? Are there risks associated with such a practice?

Adapted from David Hutton, "Consumer gets less bang for the buck," The Globe and Mail, *July 8, 2008, p. B2.*

A firm is not locked in to one particular pricing strategy. In fact, each product or product line (a category of products) will be assessed independently, and appropriate objectives will be established for each. With regard to pricing objectives there are three basic options: maximizing profit, maximizing sales volume, and establishing a competitive position. Pricing objectives are often influenced by the current stage of the product's life cycle.

Maximizing Profit

The goal of **profit maximization** is to achieve a high profit margin, a high return on investment, and a recovery of any capital invested. In this case, a company sets some type of measurable and attainable profit objective based on its situation in the market. Consider the following example.

> **Objective:** To achieve a net profit contribution of $2 000 000 and a return on investment (ROI) of 20 percent in fiscal year 20XX

While we cannot assess how conservative or how aggressive this objective is, it is certain that the organization will implement a marketing strategy to accomplish it. At the end of the year, the degree of success can be measured by comparing actual return to planned return. The profits obtained are redirected into new-product development projects, which facilitate the organization's expansion into new markets. Historical trends

profit maximization To achieve this, an organization sets some type of measurable and attainable profit objective on the basis of its situation in the market.

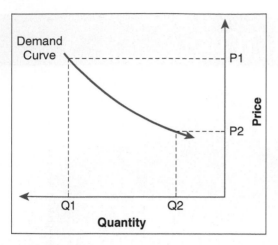

Figure 10.6 Relationship Between Price and Quantity

sales volume maximization
A firm strives for growth in sales that exceeds the growth in the size of the total market so that its market share increases.

competitive pricing Placing prices above, equal to, or below those of competitors.

pertaining to such ratios as a firm's return on investment or return on sales are also a factor in attracting potential new investors to the firm.

Maximizing Sales Volume

The objective of **sales volume maximization** is to increase the volume of sales each year. A firm strives for growth in sales that exceeds the growth in the size of the total market so that its market share increases. Here is an example of a sales volume objective.

> **Objectives:** To increase sales volume from $15 000 000 to $16 500 000, an increase of 10 percent, in 20XX
> To increase market share from 25 percent to 27.5 percent in 20XX

Sales levels, as we have seen, are affected by price; an increase in price can result in a decrease in demand and, therefore, a reduction in the quantity sold. In **Figure 10.6**, we see that when price goes down (P_1 to P_2), volume (quantity) goes up (Q_1 to Q_2); when prices go up, volume goes down.

An organization also develops the appropriate marketing strategies, including price strategy, for achieving sales objectives. In establishing these objectives, a firm considers the type of market it operates in and its elasticity of demand. Generally, brand leaders have the most flexibility in establishing sales and market-share objectives. Brands with a small share of the market tend to follow the trend established by the leader. To achieve market-share objectives a firm often sacrifices profit, at least temporarily.

Establishing a Competitive Position

The aim in this case is to minimize the effect of competitors' actions and provide channel members with reasonable profit margins. To attain such an objective, an organization assesses the competitive situation, including its own position in the market, and adopts a strategy termed *status quo pricing*— or, simply, **competitive pricing**—that puts its prices above, equal to, or below those of competitors. In effect, each competitor uses a pricing strategy to position itself in the consumer's mind. For example, Walmart is positioned in the customer's mind based on its discount pricing strategy—its prices are perceived to be lower than major competitors.

Above Competition
To set a price above a competitor, a product must be perceived as being of higher quality than the competitor's products or must offer customers an intangible benefit, such as prestige or status, otherwise it will fail. Other elements of the marketing mix, such as product quality and the brand image created by advertising, establish this position. Such a strategy provides a higher profit margin on each unit sold and is usually reserved for market leaders in a product category. Q-tips, for example, controls about 65 percent of the cotton swab market. Consumers view the brand with a high level of trust and confidence. As a result, Q-tips can charge more than competing brands.

Equal to Competition
A firm that uses this strategy adopts a conservative position because it does not want to be caught in price wars. In effect, the company is satisfied with its volume, market share, and profit margin and is content to follow the lead of others. Other elements of the marketing mix will differentiate one brand from another.

Below Competition
Here, a firm uses price to secure and hold a certain position in the market. To accomplish this objective, the company must accept lower profit margins (unless it is producing so efficiently that profit margins are maintained despite the reduction in price). If the volume of sales rises significantly because of the low prices, production efficiency will increase, thus lowering costs further and improving profit margins.

Walmart effectively demonstrates how a low-price strategy can work. Walmart's combination of everyday low prices and good product selection has produced a leadership position in Canada's department store market. While other elements of its

ThinkMarketing

Manufacturers Cease Operations in Canada

You have learned that companies establish different pricing objectives in the management of their brands. A company will assess various factors when establishing its prices, including fixed and variable costs, consumer demand for the product, and the degree of competition in the market. Some costs affect the entire operation of the company, and when those costs get too high some drastic business decisions have to be made.

Nick Brancaccio/The Windsor Star

Over the past eight years Ontario has been hit particularly hard with plant closings in the manufacturing sector. More specifically, food companies have been shuttering production facilities at an alarmingly high rate. Among the fatalities are Campbell's Soup in Listowel (500 jobs lost), E. D. Smith in Seaforth (180 jobs), Hershey in Smiths Falls (600 jobs), Bick's in Dunnville (150 jobs), Kellogg's in London (500 jobs), and Heinz in Leamington (740 jobs). A total of 2670 jobs lost in one industry alone.

There is always also a trickle-down effect when plants close. The suppliers of goods and services to these plants are no longer needed so layoffs among suppliers could also occur. Such action by manufacturers is cause for concern, but as potential marketers you must understand that the overriding objective of any business is to maximize profit and generate a positive return on investment for shareholders. When a business determines that the cost of doing business in Canada is too high, and it is beyond their control, they may choose to go elsewhere.

The recent decisions by Heinz and Kellogg's were shockers. Heinz had operated in Leamington for 104 years and Kellogg's in London for 89 years—they were institutions in the community and good corporate citizens. But, regardless of all the good that these companies did, the sheer economics of the situation drove the decisions each company made.

The key factors behind the decisions to close were energy and labour costs. Energy costs, which are relatively high in Ontario, are going up. So are labour costs relative to other countries like the United States and Mexico. A bigger factor was the strong Canadian dollar (it has since dropped) that was at or near par with the American dollar. The elevated dollar puts manufacturers at a competitive disadvantage in terms of exporting to the U.S.—our biggest trading partner.

Both Heinz and Kellogg's reviewed their operations with an eye to reducing costs. Heinz said they were looking at ways to maximize efficiencies and leverage scale. It didn't matter that its Leamington facility was the second-largest Heinz plant in the world. What was produced there could be produced somewhere else more efficiently. The actions by Kellogg's were triggered by stagnating profits and falling sales of breakfast cereals. Busy lifestyles and a switch to more convenient breakfast items played a role in the company's decision.

Question:

Closing a manufacturing facility is a major decision. Are there any other options that could be considered before doing so? Does it make sense to continuously increase the price of goods to cover cost increases?

Adapted from Eric Atkins and Tavia Grant, "Kellogg plant a casualty of changing tastes," The Globe and Mail, December 11, 2013, pp. B1, B10; and Vanessa Lu, "Heinz to close Leamington plant, 740 employees affected," The Toronto Star, November 14, 2013, www. thestar.com/business

marketing mix have also played a role, the focus on low price is the one that drives traffic to the stores.

For more insight into how managing costs affect pricing decisions and ultimately have an impact on key business decisions read the Think Marketing box **Manufacturers Cease Operations in Canada**.

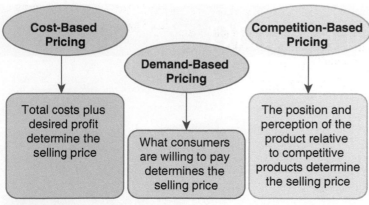

Figure 10.7   Pricing Methods

cost-based pricing A type of pricing whereby a company calculates its total costs and then adds a desired profit margin to arrive at a list price for a product.

fixed costs Costs that do not vary with different quantities of output.

variable costs Costs that change according to the level of output.

full-cost pricing A desired profit margin is added to the full cost of producing a product.

target pricing A pricing strategy designed to generate a desirable rate of return on investment and based on the full costs of producing a product.

PRICING METHODS

L04 Calculate basic prices using a variety of pricing methodologies.

A firm may use one or any combination of three basic methods in calculating prices for the products and services it markets: cost-based pricing, demand-based pricing, and competitive bidding. See **Figure 10.7** for an illustration of pricing methods.

Cost-Based Pricing

In the case of **cost-based pricing**, a company arrives at a list price for the product by calculating its total costs and then adding a desired profit margin.

The costs usually included in this calculation are as follows:

1. **Fixed costs** are those costs that do not vary with different quantities of output (e.g., equipment and other fixed assets, such as light, heat, and power).
2. **Variable costs** are costs that do change according to the level of output (e.g., labour and raw materials). Variable costs rise and fall depending on the production level—up to a point, per-unit variable costs frequently remain constant over a given range of volume. Generally, the more a firm is producing, the greater the quantities of raw materials and parts it buys, and this increased volume leads to lower unit costs; therefore, the variable costs should be lower.

For an illustration of these cost concepts refer to **Figure 10.8**, which shows how fixed, variable, and total costs vary with production output. In the long term, the firm must establish prices that recover total costs (i.e., fixed costs plus variable costs). To recover total costs the firm has a few options: *full-cost pricing, target pricing*, and *break-even pricing (break-even analysis)*. All three consider the variables of costs, revenues, and profits. Refer to **Figure 10.9** for the mathematical formulas and an example of each pricing method.

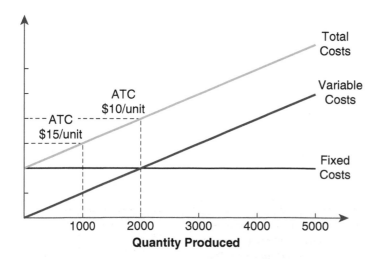

The total cost per unit declines as the quantity produced increases. At 1000 units of production, the average total cost (ATC) is $15/unit. At 2000 units of production, the average total cost (ATC) is $10/unit.

Figure 10.8   The Concept of Fixed, Variable, and Total Costs

Full-Cost Pricing   In **full-cost pricing**, a desired profit margin is added to the full cost of producing a product. In such a system, profits are based on costs rather than on revenue or demand for the product. When a firm establishes a desired level of profit that must be adhered to, the profit goal could be interpreted as a fixed cost (see Figure 10.7).

Target Pricing   **Target pricing** is designed to generate a desirable rate of return on investment (ROI) and is based on the full costs of producing a product. For this method to be effective, the firm must have the ability to sell as much as it produces. The major drawback of this method is that demand is not considered. If the quantity produced is not sold at the target price, the objective of the strategy—to achieve a desired level of ROI—is defeated (see **Figure 10.9**).

Figure 10.9 Pricing Methods: Examples

1. Cost-Plus Pricing

A manufacturer of colour televisions has fixed costs of $100 000 and variable costs of $300 for every unit produced. The profit objective is to achieve $10 000 based on a production of 150 televisions. What is the selling price?

$$\text{Price} = \frac{\text{Total Fixed Costs} + \text{Total Variable Costs} + \text{Projected Profit}}{\text{Quantity Produced}}$$

$$= \frac{\$100\,000 + (\$300 \times 150) + \$10\,000}{150}$$

$$= \frac{\$155\,000}{150}$$

$$= \$1033.33$$

2. Target Pricing

A manufacturer has just built a new plant at a cost of $75 000 000. The target return on investment is 10 percent. The standard volume of production for the year is estimated at 15 000 units. The average total cost for each unit is $5000 based on the standard volume of 15 000 units. What is the selling price?

$$\text{Price} = \frac{\text{Investment Costs} \times \text{Target Return on Investment\%}}{\text{Standard Volume}}$$

$$+ \text{Average Total Costs (at Standard Volume/Unit)}$$

$$= \frac{\$75\,000\,000 \times 0.10}{15\,000} + \$5000$$

$$= \$5500$$

3. Break-Even Pricing

A manufacturer incurs total fixed costs of $180 000. Variable costs are $0.20 per unit. The product sells for $0.80. What is the break-even point in units? In dollars?

$$\frac{\text{Break-Even}}{\text{in Units}} = \frac{\text{Total Fixed Costs}}{\text{Price} - \text{Variable Costs (per unit)}}$$

$$= \frac{\$180\,000}{\$0.80 - \$0.20}$$

$$= 300\,000$$

$$\frac{\text{Break-Even}}{\text{in Dollars}} = \frac{\text{Total Fixed Costs}}{1 - \dfrac{\text{Variable Costs (per unit)}}{\text{Price}}}$$

$$= \frac{\$180\,000}{1 - \dfrac{\$0.20}{\$0.80}}$$

$$= \$240\,000$$

Break Even Analysis **Break-even analysis** has a greater emphasis on sales than do the other methods, and it allows a firm to assess profit at alternative price levels. Break-even analysis determines the sales in units or dollars that are necessary for total revenue (price times quantity sold) to equal total costs (fixed plus variable costs) at a certain price. The concept is quite simple. If sales are greater than the *break-even point* (BEP), the firm yields a profit; if the sales are below the BEP, a loss results (see Figure 10.9 and **Figure 10.10**).

break-even analysis
Determining the sales in units or dollars that are necessary for total revenue to equal total costs at a certain price.

Demand-Based Pricing

As the name suggests, the price that customers will pay influences demand-based pricing. For example, how much is the consumer willing to pay for a personal care

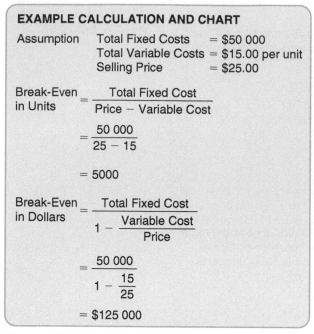

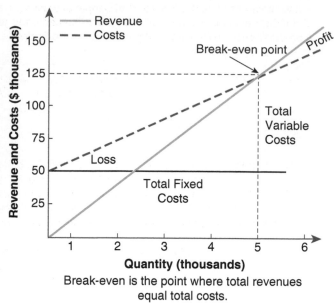

Figure 10.10 Standard Break-Even Chart

product, say, a deodorant or body wash, in a retail store? In determining price a company can proceed in two directions. One direction is to establish all costs and profit expectations at the point of manufacture, adding appropriate profit margins for various distributors, thus arriving at a retail selling price that the marketing company hopes is in line with consumer expectations. This approach is referred to as **forward pricing**.

The alternative is to work backward by first determining what the consumer will pay at retail. The profit margins for the various distributors are deducted to arrive at a total-cost price at the point of manufacture. The goal is a price that will be sufficient to cover the manufacturer's desired profit margin and costs. If there isn't enough profit the manufacturer will have to find ways of reducing costs or perhaps forgo producing and marketing the product. This approach is referred to as **backward pricing**. Examples of these demand-based price calculations are included in **Figure 10.11**.

Price Skimming

Price skimming involves the use of a high price when a product enters the market, which enables a firm to maximize its revenue early. Typically, such a product is an innovation or is significantly better than anything already on the market. The product may also have patent protection, so with no direct competition a high price can be charged. In either case, the company has an opportunity to recover research and development costs quickly.

Apple uses a price skimming strategy when it launches new products. Apple is well known for producing innovative products, and even though their products may not be better than competitors such as Samsung, Nokia, LG, and others in terms of quality and performance, the image and reputation that Apple has built up over the years helps justify the higher price. Apple dominates the tablet market with its iPad, and its iPhone is the world's second-best-selling phone.

Apple announces its product launches well in advance of the item being available. Effective marketing communications creates pent-up demand for the product—another factor that justifies a higher price. Prescription drug manufacturers invest heavily in research and development to develop new products. They price their products very high while they are still under patent protection, since they know lower-priced generic drug competitors will be on the market once their patent expires.

forward pricing A pricing strategy where all costs and profit expectations are established at the point of manufacture, with appropriate profit margins added for various distributors, thus arriving at a retail selling price that the marketing company hopes is in line with consumer expectations.

backward pricing An organization determines the optimum retail selling price that consumers will accept and then subtracts the desired profit margin and marketing expenses to arrive at the cost at which the product should be produced.

price skimming Establishing a high entry price so that a firm can maximize its revenue early.

Figure 10.11
Demand-Based Pricing
Methods

1. Backward Pricing

A CD distributor has determined that people are willing to spend $30.00 for a three-CD set of classic rock "n" roll tunes. The company estimates that marketing expenses and profits will be 40 percent of the selling price. How much can the firm spend producing the CDs?

Product Cost	= Price × [(100 − Markup %)/100]
	= $30.00 × [(100 − 40)/100]
	= $30.00 × (60/100)
	= $18.00

2. Forward Pricing

A manufacturer of blue jeans has determined that its total costs are $20.00 per pair of jeans. The company sells the jeans through wholesalers who in turn sell to retailers. The wholesaler requires a markup of 20 percent and the retailer requires 40 percent. The manufacturer needs a markup of 25 percent. What price will the wholesaler and retailer pay? What is the selling price at retail?

a) Manufacturer's Cost and Selling Price	= $20.00 + 25% Markup
	= $20.00 + $5.00
	= $25.00

b) Wholesaler's Cost and Selling Price	= Manufacturer's Selling Price + 20% Markup
	= $25.00 + $5.00
	= $30.00

c) Retailer's Cost and Selling Price	= Wholesaler's Selling Price + 40%
	= $30.00 + $12.00
	= $42.00

A possible hazard of skimming is that competitors who see a product enjoying high profit margins, mainly due to the lack of competition and a skimming pricing strategy, are likely to bring similar products to the market very quickly. Users of a skimming strategy recognize that it is easier to lower prices than it is to raise prices during the life cycle of a product.

Companies known for innovation (as in the case of Apple) have a pricing advantage. The fact that consumers are willing to pay more for their products certainly has an impact on sales revenue and profitability. Competitors must enter the market at a much lower price, which affects their ability to recover development costs and pay for marketing expenses.[5]

Price Penetration

A **price penetration** strategy establishes a low entry price to gain wide market acceptance for a product quickly. In this situation, price is typically an important factor in the buying decision; for example, a market may be segmented into various price points (budget brands, competitively priced brands, and expensive brands). The market is also one in which demand is elastic, meaning that any change in price has a direct impact on the quantity purchased. The objective of price penetration is to create demand in a market quickly, to build market share, and to discourage competitors from entering if the product is new.

When Netflix entered the market it used a price penetration strategy. Initially, Netflix was an online, mail order, and streaming movie rental company. It offered movie rentals at discounted prices. Its objective at the time was to take customers away from Blockbuster, the largest retail renter of movies. The penetration price strategy was a success. It enlisted subscribers and was a contributing factor in Blockbuster's demise.

Netflix evolved and now offers TV shows and movies streamed instantly online or to a television via an Xbox, Wii, PS3, Mac, or mobile operating system. Refer to the image in

price penetration Establishing a low entry price to gain wide market acceptance quickly.

Figure 10.12   Netflix entered Canada using a price penetration strategy.

Figure 10.12. Netflix maintained a penetration pricing strategy and is placing pressure on cable providers such as Rogers and Shaw—people are cutting their cable cord! A survey by the Convergence Consulting Group found a quarter of a million Canadians pulled the plug on their cable subscriptions in 2012 and they forecast the number to grow by 400 000 in 2013. Consumers cite convenience and price as the reason for the switch—they want to watch specific shows according to their schedule, not the schedule of a network. Statistics show 40 percent of young adults aged 17 to 24 mainly watch television online, using Netflix as well as Apple and Google TV consoles to stream movies and TV shows.[6]

Walmart was cited earlier in the chapter for its low price strategy. It has been successful with a price-penetration strategy over the long term. Using such slogans as, "Always low prices" and "Save money. Live better." has had a significant impact on their success. Several factors allow Walmart to offer low prices. Sheer buying power—the actual amount of product they buy from a supplier—gives Walmart an edge on other distributors. They can negotiate better discounts from suppliers. Walmart also operates one of the most efficient supply chains in the industry. By keeping operating costs as low as possible, it can pass on the savings to its customers. Walmart is in an enviable business position! Many of its direct competitors could not duplicate their success and have gone out of business.

Competitive Bidding

competitive bidding A situation in which two or more firms submit written price quotations to a purchaser on the basis of specifications established by the purchaser.

Competitive bidding involves two or more firms submitting to a purchaser written price quotations based on specifications established by the purchaser.

Due to the dynamics of competitive bidding and the size, resources, and objectives of potential bidders, it is difficult to explain how costs and price quotations are arrived at. For example, if several firms are submitting bids for the opportunity to construct a new building there will be a great variation among price quotations if one firm considers all its costs and then adds a profit margin, while another firm sets its price at the break-even point. The objectives of firms submitting bids differ; some businesses simply want to win the contract, while others expect to earn a certain profit. Thus, if a firm builds a high profit margin into its bid, the likelihood of its being accepted by the purchaser diminishes.

Simulation: Pricing

PRICING AND THE LAW

L05 Describe how legal issues can affect pricing strategy.

The federal government oversees price activity in Canada through the *Competition Act*. The act covers many important areas that organizations must be aware of. Ignorance of the law is not a defence in a court of law should a firm find itself violating any rules and regulations. Some of the key legal issues are discussed in this section.

Ordinary Price Claims

A common practice among retailers is to quote sale prices using comparisons with the ordinary selling price of an article. For example, "Save up to 50 percent off the regular price." For the purposes of the law, no person or business shall

> make a materially misleading representation to the public concerning the price at which a product or like products have been, are, or will be ordinarily sold.[7]

The following general test can be used to determine whether an expression is in violation of the law:

> Would the use of the expression lead a reasonable shopper to conclude that the comparison price quoted is that at which the product has been ordinarily sold?[8]

When a comparison price is used to communicate the offer, it should be a recent and relevant price: the price at which the product has normally been sold over an extended period of time. To comply with the law the definition of *regular price* means that an item must have been sold at that price 50 percent of the time in the six months before running a sale advertisement, with 50 percent of the sales volume occurring at the regular price.

Companies that violate this law are subject to legal proceedings and significant fines if found guilty. It should be noted that in the age of frequent discount pricing, Canadian retailers are lobbying the government to change the laws. They see pricing law as being outdated and unsuitable for meeting current consumer expectations for value. Consumers are now more accustomed to looking at sale prices than regular prices. The regular price is largely irrelevant to consumers.

Manufacturer's Suggested List Price

It is common for manufacturers to suggest that retailers charge a certain price for their products; this amount is called the **manufacturer's suggested list price (MSLP)**. Such prices usually provide adequate profit margins for retailers and help manufacturers protect the image of their brands. However, manufacturers cannot force distributors to sell goods at the prices they suggest. Retailers can charge more or less if they want to.

manufacturer's suggested list price (MSLP) The price manufacturers suggest retailers should charge for a product.

The laws on how retailers use MSLP are somewhat vague. If a retailer has never charged the MSLP but uses it to suggest that a sale price offers a greater saving than it actually does, that retailer has broken the law. In this case, the message is misleading because the retailer has customarily sold the product at another price, a lower price. If both the regular selling price and the MSLP are quoted in a sales message, the intent to mislead is less pronounced.

Double Ticketing and Bar Code Price Variances

Double ticketing occurs when more than one price tag appears on an item. When this situation occurs, the product must be sold at the lower price. This provision of the law does not prohibit the practice but requires that the lower of the two prices be collected from consumers.

double ticketing A situation in which more than one price tag appears on an item.

Double ticketing is now less of a problem because prices are scanned electronically at the point of sale. However, that doesn't mean that the price scanned is the correct price. Consumers should closely check items passing through electronic checkouts. There are remedies if errors are found. The Competition Bureau has endorsed a voluntary code of practice developed by members of the Retail Council of Canada. The Scanner Price Accuracy Voluntary Code provides for consumer protection as follows:

> If the scanned price of a non-priced ticketed item is a higher than the shelf price or any displayed price, the customer is entitled to receive the item free, up to a $10 maximum. When the item is price-tagged the lower price applies. If the item is more than $10 the retailer will give the customer a $10 discount off the corrected price.

It pays to bring any error to the attention of the store. This code is supported by national and regional drugstore chains, grocery chains, leading department stores, and mass merchandisers. Error rates are monitored by various industries and it is generally accepted that a 2 percent error rate is acceptable. If consumers don't complain that leaves a lot of money on the table for retailers.

bait and switch A situation in which a company advertises a bargain price for a product that is not available in reasonable quantity; when customers arrive at the store they are directed to another product, often priced higher than the product advertised.

Bait and Switch

Bait and switch selling is the practice of advertising a bargain price for a product that is not available in reasonable quantity. A customer arrives at a store expecting to buy one product but is directed to another, often at a higher price. If the lack of supply is beyond the control of the store or agent, and this can be proven if challenged, the firm running this advertisement is not liable for penalty. Offering rain cheques is a way to avoid liability. A **rain cheque** guarantees that the original product or a product of comparable quality will be supplied within a reasonable time to those consumers requesting the product. Bait and switch selling tactics are illegal and any retailer using the practice is subject to heavy fines by the Competition Bureau.

rain cheque A guarantee by a retailer to provide an original product or one of comparable quality to a consumer within a reasonable time.

Predatory Pricing

Periodically, an organization employs a pricing strategy that is judged to be unfair because it violates the spirit of competition. One such practice is **predatory pricing**, which occurs when a large firm sets an artificially low price in an attempt to undercut all other competitors and place them in a difficult financial position or even drive them out of business.

Walmart is often accused of predatory pricing because of the success of its "everyday low price" policy. Walmart's pricing policies have caused much hardship for competitors such as Zellers, Kmart, and Eaton's, all of which have disappeared from the retail landscape in Canada. But their failure to compete could be blamed on marketing strategies that go well beyond price competition. In Walmart's defence, the company is simply giving consumers what they want—good value for the money they spend. It's nothing more than a competitive price situation.

While predatory pricing is against the law, it is very difficult to prove legally and would be a very expensive undertaking for any company to pursue. To get a conviction, the Competition Bureau must establish that prices are unreasonably low, as well as prove that the company had an explicit policy of using predatory pricing to eliminate competition. While the law acts as a deterrent, it does not shield companies from competitors able to set lower prices because they are genuinely more efficient. Canada is a free market. Shouldn't companies be able to price their products wherever they want?

predatory pricing A situation in which a large firm sets an extremely low price in an attempt to undercut all other competitors, thus placing them in a difficult financial position.

Price Fixing

Price fixing refers to competitors banding together (conspiring) to raise, reduce, or stabilize prices. While such a practice is common and relatively easy to implement, it is illegal under the *Competition Act*. Price fixing usually occurs in markets where price is the most important variable in the marketing mix. When implemented, there is an agreement between the participants that, if followed, will result in benefit for them all. As mentioned earlier in the chapter, oil and gasoline companies are often accused of price fixing as prices at the pump are perceived to be increased by all firms simultaneously. Despite the perception, such charges have not been found to be true.

To discourage price fixing, the anti-conspiracy provisions of the *Competition Act* are clear—companies and their executives are accountable for illegal actions and could face stiff fines and jail terms if charged and found guilty.

To illustrate, Hershey Canada was fined $4 million for its involvement in a conspiracy to fix prices in the chocolate industry. Hershey pleaded guilty in the case while three other companies (Nestlé, Mars, and Itwal) pleaded not guilty and chose to contest the charges against them. These companies and their top executives were charged with conspiracy under the *Competition Act* to fix the prices of chocolate in Canada. Hershey acknowledged that it entered into a conspiracy to lessen competition and the supply of everyday chocolate, including chocolate bars. At the time (2007) four companies controlled 75.3 percent of chocolate sales in Canada. Hershey executives involved in the conspiracy have since been fired.[9]

price fixing Competitors banding together to raise, lower, or stabilize prices.

✔ ExperienceMarketing

To experience marketing you have to assess situations and make recommendations to change marketing strategies when necessary. What would you do in the following situation?

You are the brand manager for Aquafresh toothpaste at GlaxoSmithKline Canada. You are in the not-so-enviable position of being a brand follower in a mature market. The toothpaste market in Canada is dominated by two brands: Colgate and Crest. Each of these brands offers a wide and deep product mix that satisfies virtually all of the oral needs of consumers.

Colgate is the market leader with 40 percent market share. Crest is the challenger with 37 percent market share. Aqua Fresh follows in third place with a 10 percent market share. As a follower, the pricing strategy for

Aquafresh has traditionally been to be lower in price than the market leaders. Aquafresh offers a product that satisfies the basic oral needs of consumers, so to have a price advantage was seen as an attractive proposition to consumers.

Just recently, pressure has been mounting within the company to maximize profits. Wherever possible, brand managers have been asked to evaluate potential price increases in order to improve profit margins. Your immediate challenge is to examine the conditions that prevail in the toothpaste market. How competitive are brand prices in retail stores? How would consumers react to an increase in price? Would they accept a price increase or reject it? Would a price increase negatively affect sales and market share? You don't know how elastic demand is in this market. Will you recommend a price increase, or recommend that price remain as it is? Be prepared to defend your recommendation.

CHAPTER SUMMARY

L01 Explain the importance of price in the development of marketing strategy. *(pp. 212–214)*

Price refers to the exchange value of a good or service in the marketplace. While price is only one component of the marketing mix, it plays a key role, combined with other mix components, in creating an image for a product or company. For example, at Walmart price is the focal point of the entire marketing strategy. Consumers perceive Walmart to offer lower prices and that's why they shop there. Higher prices also have an impact on a brand's image. Male consumers expect to pay much more for a suit at Harry Rosen. In both cases it is the combination of price and quality (a value proposition) that attracts customers to the brand.

L02 Describe the impact of external and internal forces on price decisions. *(pp. 214–218)*

Several external factors must be considered, including the market structure the brand or company operates in (monopoly, oligopoly, monopolistic competition, or pure competition). In a monopoly, prices are regulated, in an oligopoly and monopolistic competition, an organization controls its pricing but the price is influenced by the intensity of competition.

Other factors that influence pricing decisions include consumer demand for the product, giving due consideration to profit expectations of distributors, production costs, and marketing costs. Marketers must closely monitor their production and marketing costs, and consider implementing cost reduction programs as a means of protecting profit margins.

L03 Explain the differences among profit, sales, and competitive pricing objectives. *(pp. 218–221)*

The pricing objectives of an organization influence price decisions. The primary goal of an organization is to produce the highest return possible for the owner or shareholders. In this regard there are three basic pricing objectives. If profit maximization is the objective an organization will firmly establish a quantitative profit margin. Total cost plus the profit margin equals the selling price. If sales volume maximization is the objective an organization may be more flexible on price in order to achieve higher unit sales and market share objectives. A well-balanced marketing strategy that considers the nature of competition helps achieve the objective. If competitive pricing is the objective an organization will decide to price its goods above the competition, equal to the competition, or below the competition. Brand leaders tend to be priced above the competition. Other brands tend to be priced somewhat lower.

L04 Calculate basic prices using a variety of pricing methodologies. *(pp. 222–226)*

Specific methods for calculating price include cost-based pricing, demand-based pricing, and competition-based pricing (competitive bidding). The method a firm uses is chosen according to the nature and degree of competition in the markets it operates in. An organization using a cost-based methodology has several options. The full-cost price method considers fixed and variable costs and the desired profit margin when arriving at a selling price. A second option involves determining a desired return on investment and the full costs of the product.

If demand-based pricing is applied, an organization considers the final price consumers are willing to pay for the product as well as the profit expectations of distributors and their own company. A company may approach this method two ways. Forward pricing views things from the manufacturer to the consumer and considers all costs and profit margins of the manufacturer and distributors in order to arrive at a final price consumers will pay. Backward pricing views things from the consumer backward to the manufacturer. It involves determining a price consumers will pay, and then considers the profit margins for distributors and the costs and profit margins of the manufacturer. If the manufacturer is satisfied with the profit margin it will proceed. If not, the organization must consider other marketing options.

Should an organization be known for innovative products, it may adopt a price skimming strategy in which a high price is charged for the product. In contrast, products of lesser quality or products that enter a market late will adopt a price penetration strategy whereby a low price is charged for the product.

LO5 **Describe how legal issues can affect pricing strategy.** *(pp. 226–228)*

Organizations must be aware of legal implications stemming from improper price decisions. Companies that violate laws and regulations suffer the wrath of angry consumers and can be penalized financially in a court of law. Some of the key issues involve ordinary price claims, how a company uses manufacturer's suggested list price when quoting sale prices, double ticketing and price scanning violations, bait and switch techniques, and price fixing.

In all of these cases, except price fixing, the onus is on the marketing organization not to mislead consumers or misrepresent the product being sold. For example, exaggerating a sale price based on an original price that was never used is illegal. Price fixing typically involves members of an industry collaborating on price strategy—they agree amongst themselves what the price of their respective products will be. The price charged may not be in the best interests of distributors or consumers; hence, such a practice is illegal.

MyMarketingLab   Study, practise, and explore real marketing situations with these helpful resources:
- **Interactive Lesson Presentations:** Work through interactive presentations and assessments to test your knowledge of marketing concepts.
- **Study Plan:** Check your understanding of chapter concepts with self-study quizzes.
- **Dynamic Study Modules:** Work through adaptive study modules on your computer, tablet, or mobile device.
- **Simulations:** Practise decision-making in simulated marketing environments.

REVIEW QUESTIONS

1. What role does price play in attracting customers to a product or retail establishment? *(LO1)*
2. Briefly explain how operating in (a) an oligopoly and (b) a monopolistic competition market affects the pricing activity of an organization. *(LO2)*
3. What are the differences between elastic demand and inelastic demand? How does each type of demand influence price decisions? *(LO2)*
4. Briefly explain how channel members influence price decisions. *(LO2)*
5. Briefly explain how cost reduction programs influence price decisions. *(LO2)*
6. What is the difference between a profit maximization pricing objective and a sales volume maximization pricing objective? *(LO3)*

7. Explain the concept of competitive pricing. Provide some new examples of companies or brands that practice *above competitor* pricing and *below competitor* pricing. *(LO4)*
8. Explain the difference between fixed and variable costs. *(LO4)*
9. What is full-cost pricing? Briefly explain. *(LO4)*
10. What is demand-based pricing? Briefly explain. *(LO4)*
11. Briefly explain the usefulness of break-even analysis. *(LO4)*
12. What is the difference between a price skimming strategy and a price penetration strategy? *(LO4)*
13. In terms of pricing, explain the tactics of bait and switch, and double-ticketing. *(LO5)*
14. What is predatory pricing? Briefly explain. *(LO5)*

DISCUSSION AND APPLICATION QUESTIONS

1. Given the following information, calculate the unit price, using the cost-plus pricing method:
   Fixed Costs = $350 000
   Variable Costs = $65.00 per unit of production
   Profit Objective = $29 500 based on a production level of 600 units
2. Calculate the break-even point in units and dollars, given the following information:
   Fixed Costs = $300 000
   Variable Costs = $0.75 per unit
   Selling Price = $2.50 per unit
3. Visit a few fast-food restaurants in your area (e.g., McDonald's, Burger King, Wendy's) and assess the pricing strategies that each restaurant uses. Briefly analyze the pricing strategies for effectiveness. Are their strategies appropriate? Are there other pricing strategies that they should consider?

4. Ace Manufacturing produces refrigerators. The fixed costs amount to $250 000, and the variable costs are $175 for each unit produced. The company would like to make a profit of $20 000 on the production of 200 units. What selling price must the company charge?
5. A manufacturer has total fixed costs of $54 000. Variable costs are $2.50 per unit. The product sells for $8.00. What is the break-even point in units?
6. A manufacturer of dress belts estimates that consumers will pay $22.00 for one of its belts. The company sells the belts through wholesalers that in turn sell to retailers. The manufacturer takes a markup of 25 percent in selling to wholesalers, and the wholesalers take a markup of 15 percent in selling to retailers. What price will the wholesalers and retailers pay for the belts? Use the forward pricing method to arrive at a solution.

11 Price Management

THE CANADIAN PRESS IMAGES/Denis Beaumont.

LEARNING OBJECTIVES

LO1 Describe the various pricing policies practised by marketing organizations. (pp. 232–238)

LO2 Explain adjustments made to price based on factors such as geography, discounts, and allowances. (pp. 239–243)

LO3 Explain the role and impact of leasing as a pricing option. (p. 243)

WHEN YOU SELL...

something for a dollar you had better be operating your business efficiently, and right now no other company does that better than Dollarama. Dollarama's mission is clear—it offers great value to the customer. According to the company's website (www.dollarama.com): "Our goal is to exceed our customers' expectations of the quality and variety of products they can purchase for up to $3."

Dollarama has experienced significant growth in the past decade. It now operates 800 locations coast-to-coast in Canada and generates approximately $2.0 billion in revenue each year. Consumers know exactly what they are getting when they shop there—great value!

Dollarama offers a broad range of products, including general merchandise items, consumable products that are typically sold in supermarkets and drug stores, and seasonal products for special occasions like Christmas, Halloween, and Valentine's Day. Dollarama's well-balanced product mix at such low prices is an attractive value proposition. In marketing terms, Dollarama is ideally positioned to meet the needs of customers seeking value and convenience. For true bargain hunters, Dollarama is a stand-alone destination store.

Dollarama's success is attributed to many aspects of its marketing strategies, but nothing stands out more than how it manages its prices—its everyday low prices. That's what brings the shoppers in!

The focus of this chapter is on how an organization manages its pricing activity. The various pricing policies a firm may adopt are discussed, along with the types of discounts commonly offered in the marketplace. It is common for an organization to quote a list price and then offer discounts as part of its overall marketing strategy to reduce the price for customers. Finally, the practice of leasing goods as an alternative to selling goods is examined.

PRICING POLICIES

LO1 Describe the various pricing policies practised by marketing organizations.

Pricing policies are the basic rules about pricing that enable a firm to achieve its marketing objectives. The policy options available are classified into four primary categories: psychological pricing, promotional pricing, geographic pricing, and flexible pricing. A firm may use one or any combination of these pricing policies, depending on the objectives established for the product or the nature of the market that the product competes in.

Psychological Pricing

psychological pricing Pricing strategies that appeal to tendencies in consumer behaviour (other than rational ones).

In the case of **psychological pricing**, the organization establishes prices that appeal to tendencies in consumer behaviour. It is a practice used more often by retailers than by manufacturers. There are several types of psychological pricing strategies.

prestige pricing A high price charged for a luxury good that enhances the image of the product and the status of the buyer.

Prestige Pricing   **Prestige pricing** is the practice of setting prices high to give the impression that the product is of high quality. This practice is strongly associated with luxury goods. The fact that the price is high contributes to the image of the product and the status of the buyer. For example, there is a one-year waiting list for the Porsche 911 Turbo in Canada even though the price starts at $160 000. The pursuit of prestige is quite expensive, it seems, but buyers of these cars don't seem to care. People who own and wear a Rolex watch do so for a variety of reasons, but certainly the price of the watch is not a factor in the buying decision. People are buying the status and prestige associated with brand names such as Porsche and Rolex. Refer to **Figure 11.1** for an illustration.

Odd–Even Pricing   For psychological reasons, an odd number is more effective with consumers than a rounded-off number. Thus, a flat-screen television is priced at $499

Video: Target to Sell 99 Dollar Wedding Dresses

because it is then perceived as costing less than $500 by a good many consumers. Research has shown that consumers register and remember the first digit more clearly than they do subsequent ones (in this case the 4, which puts the price in the $400 range).[1] Setting prices below even-dollar amounts is called **odd–even pricing**. The sales tax in most provinces puts the price into the next range—over the *even barrier*—but does not have a major influence on purchases because consumers are accustomed to these mandatory additions to most of the items they purchase.

Customary Pricing A **customary pricing** strategy matches prices to a buyer's expectations; the price

Figure 11.1 Buyers of a Porsche willingly pay a higher price for the prestige associated with the brand name.

reflects tradition or is a price that people are accustomed to paying. For example, chocolate bars of average size and weight are expected to have the same price, regardless of the different brand names. Research indicates that people are knowledgeable about price ranges in a category and they will buy products as long as they are in that price range. For example, a cup of coffee ranges from $1.00 to $3.00, with an average price of $1.50. If a customer visits Starbucks for a coffee, he or she would expect to pay a price at the top end of the range; at Tim Hortons the price should be at the low end of the range.[2] In other words, there is an expectation (based on knowledge and effective marketing) of what the coffee should cost before paying for it. Refer to the image in **Figure 11.2**.

If prices go beyond the customary price, consumers may not buy. An option for the marketer, when faced with cost increases that could take the retail price beyond expectations, is to cost-reduce the product or tinker with the size of products it markets (a concept discussed in Chapter 10). Tim Hortons faced this situation recently and decided to add a new extra-large size to its coffee lineup. Since consumers tend to order based on size, many traded up to the new size, which leads to more coffee sold and more profit for Tim Hortons. In the confectionary market chocolate bars are now smaller. Selling a slightly smaller chocolate bar at a customary price is less objectionable to consumers. For more insight into the psychology behind pricing decisions read the Think Marketing box **Sizing Up for Profits**.

Price Lining **Price lining** refers to the adoption of price points for the various lines of merchandise a retailer carries. Thus, in the case of a clothing store, the retailer establishes a limited number of prices for selected lines of products rather than pricing the items individually. For example, price ranges for business suits could be set in the $300 range ($399), the $500 range ($599), and the $700 range ($799). Customers entering the store are directed to an assortment of suits that fall within their price range, once it is known. In each range, the retailer may have purchased suits from different suppliers at different costs but is satisfied with an average markup within each price range because it saves the consumer any confusion over price. Assuming the retailer understands the needs and expectations of its customers and how much they are willing to pay, it can establish its price lines (price ranges) accordingly.

odd–even pricing A psychological pricing strategy that sets prices below even-dollar amounts.

customary pricing The strategy of matching prices to a buyer's expectations: the price reflects tradition or is a price that people are accustomed to paying.

price lining The adoption of price points for the various lines of merchandise a retailer carries.

Figure 11.2 Consumers have preconceived notions about how much a cup of coffee should cost; it may be less expensive at Tim Horton's compared to Starbucks.

ThinkMarketing

Sizing Up for Profits

Tim Hortons added a new, larger-size cup to its coffee lineup. At 24 fluid ounces, the new cup is large enough to hold two cans of Coca-Cola. Joking about the size of the cup, one customer said, "You may as well order the pot."

What's the motive behind such a large size? It might have something to do with the psychology of how people make buying decisions and it might have something to do with profit. When Tim Hortons launched the new size it had a trickle-down effect on existing cup sizes—the old extra-large became large, the large became medium, and so on down the line. The standard eight-ounce cup was now an extra small. Who orders an extra-small coffee in a coffee shop?

The new cup sizes mean customers ultimately wind up buying more coffee. For example, if a person always buys a medium, that medium is now a little bit bigger than before and the customer will pay more at the till. It may only be pennies more, but when you consider that Tim Hortons serves eight out of every ten coffees in the industry you quickly see how these pennies accumulate into a pile of profit! This has to be judged as smart marketing.

Tim Hortons recognized that people order based on size; they are more familiar and comfortable with size than with the price they actually pay. Psychologically, consumers tend to view larger sizes as more economical on a cost per volume basis. Therefore, Tim's large cup appeals to this perception of value.

Psychology aside, there were good marketing reasons behind the decision, as well. Looking for revenue growth potential in a very competitive market, the new cup size

was test marketed in Sudbury and Kingston. The test results exceeded expectations by far. The larger size offers some protection against customer loss to McDonald's, which is aggressively marketing its McCafé line of coffees.

Is there a risk associated with the larger size cup? A customer may drop in twice a day for two 12-ounce cups of coffee. It's conceivable that the 24- ounce cup could be enough to satisfy a person's coffee fix. If a person visits less frequently there is less opportunity to sell something else—like a donut or muffin. The profit made on coffee could be lost elsewhere.

The names of our hot cup sizes have changed.

The names of our hot cup sizes have shifted to accommodate our brand new **24oz Extra Large cup.** For example, a **large** Double-Double is now a **medium** Double-Double. There isn't a change in the price or actual amount of beverage – it's only the name of the size that's changed.

If you have any comments please call Guest Services at 1-888-601-1616.

At participating restaurants. © Tim Hortons, 2011

Tim Hortons, the Tim Hortons logo, Tim Card Design, and RRRoll up the Rim to Win are trademarks of Tim Hortons. Used with permission.

Question:

The new cup size presents an interesting proposition to consumers. Will the new size have the impact the company is looking for? What's your opinion on this product and price strategy?

Adapted from "Tim Hortons' new coffee cup: Why the supersize?" Canadian Business, *February 14, 2012, www.canadianbusiness.com/ business-strategy/tim-hortons-new-coffee-cup/*

unit pricing The expression of price in terms of a unit of measurement (e.g., cost per gram or cost per millilitre).

Unit Pricing

Unit pricing is a policy adopted by retailers—particularly grocery retailers—that lists the cost per standard unit of a product to let shoppers compare the prices of similar products packaged in different quantities. Typically, this is done by posting bar code price tags on shelf facings. Refer to the illustration in **Figure 11.3**. The bar codes allow consumers to determine per-gram prices in different-sized containers and to compare the prices of competing brands in a product category. Comparisons are made based on the weight (grams) or volume (millilitres) of the item. With consumers generally being very value-conscious today, comparison shopping has become more common. The shopper gets to see which brand offers the best value without having to do the math.

Promotional Pricing

Promotional pricing is defined as lowering prices temporarily to attract customers (i.e., offering sale prices). In a retail environment, the objective of this practice is to attract people to (build consumer traffic in) the store; retailers know that while the customers are in the store, they could purchase other merchandise at regular prices. Common types of promotional pricing used by retailers include loss leaders and multiple-unit pricing strategies.

Loss leaders are products offered for sale at or slightly below cost. The consumer recognizes the item as a true bargain and is attracted to a store by the offer. Shoppers may be attracted to such offers not knowing they are loss leaders. For example, consider the retail price of a home printer. With the manufacturer's approval, big box retailers will sell printers at very low prices (even below cost). Here's the catch. The retailer and manufacturer make their money on replacement cartridges that tend to be quite expensive—the real profit is in the ink cartridges. Built-in microchips inhibit the use of less-expensive third-party replacement cartridges. How about free peanuts in the bar? Think about it. They make you awfully thirsty. Another drink, please!

Multiple-unit pricing offers a good for sale in multiples (pairs are quite common), at a price below the combined regular price of each item. Such a practice is often used when selling goods in supermarkets and discount department stores. Stores such as Safeway, Metro, and Sobeys offer such deals in their weekly flyers (e.g., soup at two for $1.99). Other variations include such deals as "two for the price of one" specials, or "buy one get one free," or "buy one at regular price and get the second at half price." Refer to the illustration in **Figure 11.4**. These types of offers are more frequent in segments of the retailing industry such as clothing and sporting goods stores.

In a manufacturing environment, companies offer a variety of price incentives to attract new users (often users who purchase competing brands). For example, when branded items are on sale in a supermarket or drugstore, it is likely the result of a discount being offered to the retailer by the manufacturer of the product. They are designed to build sales of the item in the short term. (For more information, see the Source Pricing and Offering Discounts section in this chapter.)

Geographic Pricing

Geographic pricing is a pricing strategy based on the answer to the question, "Who is paying the freight?" In a business-to-business situation, does the seller pay the freight costs of delivering the merchandise to the buyer, or does the buyer absorb these charges? Are freight charges averaged to all customers and included in the price? These are geographic pricing questions, and their answers are largely based on the practices of the industry in which the firm operates. In some industries the seller customarily pays, while in others the buyer generally pays.

Several geographic pricing possibilities exist, including F.O.B. pricing (free-on-board pricing), uniform

Figure 11.3   Retail price tags tell consumers the unit price of a product by size or weight; this allows consumers to compare brands for the best value.

promotional pricing The temporary lowering of prices to attract customers.

loss leaders Products offered for sale at or slightly below cost.

multiple-unit pricing Offering items for sale in multiples, usually at a price below the combined regular price of each item.

geographic pricing Pricing strategy based on the question, "Who is paying the freight?"

Figure 11.4   An illustration of multiple-unit pricing—a two-for-one deal at a fast food restaurant.

Who Pays the Freight?

F.O.B. Origin, or Plant	Buyer	The buyer takes title when the product is on a common carrier (e.g., a truck).
F.O.B. Destination, or Freight Absorption	Seller	The seller pays all freight necessary to reach a stated destination.
Uniform Delivered-Price	Buyer	The buyer's price includes an average freight cost that all customers pay regardless of location.
Zone-Pricing	Buyer	All customers within a designated geographic area pay the same freight cost.

Figure 11.5   Who Pays the Freight?

F.O.B. origin pricing A geographic pricing strategy whereby the price quoted by the seller does not include freight charges (the buyer assumes title when the goods are loaded onto a common carrier).

F.O.B. destination pricing A geographic pricing strategy whereby the seller agrees to pay freight charges between point of origin and point of destination (title does not transfer to the buyer until the goods arrive at their destination).

uniform delivered pricing A geographic pricing strategy that includes an average freight charge for all customers regardless of their location.

phantom freight The amount by which average transportation charges exceed the actual cost of shipping for customers near the source of supply.

zone pricing The division of a market into geographic zones and the establishment of a uniform delivered price for each zone.

flexible pricing Charging different customers different prices.

delivered pricing, and zone pricing. See **Figure 11.5** for a summary of geographic pricing.

F.O.B. Origin (Plant)   In an **F.O.B. origin pricing** arrangement, the seller quotes a price that does not include freight charges. The buyer pays the freight and assumes title (ownership) of the merchandise when it is loaded onto a common carrier—a truck, a train, or an airplane. This practice is satisfactory to local customers, but distant customers are disadvantaged. Under such a pricing system, a customer in Vancouver would pay much more for merchandise shipped from Montreal than would a customer in Toronto.

F.O.B. Destination (Freight Absorption)   To counter the impression that distant customers are being penalized, under the terms of **F.O.B. destination pricing** the seller agrees to pay all freight charges. How much of the charges the seller actually absorbs is questionable, however, because the freight costs are built into the price that the buyer is charged. In any event, the title does not transfer to the buyer until the goods arrive at their destination—the buyer's warehouse. Such a strategy is effective in attracting new customers in distant locations.

Uniform Delivered Pricing   In the case of **uniform delivered pricing**, the price includes an average freight charge for all customers regardless of their locations. To develop a uniform delivered price, a firm calculates the average freight cost of sending goods to the various locations of its customers. This practice is more attractive to distant customers than to nearby customers, who pay more than they would under a different pricing system. Local customers pay **phantom freight**, or the amount by which average transportation charges exceed the actual cost of shipping for customers near the source of supply.

Zone Pricing   In the case of **zone pricing**, the market is divided into geographic zones and a uniform delivered price is established for each zone. For these purposes, the Canadian market is easily divided into geographic zones: the Maritimes, Quebec, Ontario, the Prairies, British Columbia, and the Territories. Each of these zones may be subdivided further. The Ontario zone could be divided into Northern Ontario, Eastern Ontario, South-Central Ontario, and Southwestern Ontario. For an illustration of geographic pricing strategies and calculations, see **Figure 11.6**. Air-freight carriers, such as Federal Express and UPS, use zone pricing. The distance a parcel travels determines the rate charged. For example, one price is charged for zero to 599 kilometres, another for 600 to 1199, and so on.

Flexible Pricing

Flexible pricing refers to charging different customers different prices. While such a practice initially seems unfair, its actual effect is to allow buyers to negotiate a lower price than that asked by the sellers. It means that the price is open to negotiation. Such negotiations are typical in the purchase of something expensive—say, a house or an automobile. In the case of a house purchase, the buyer submits an offer and then back-and-forth negotiations begin. When buying a car, negotiations are commonly referred to as *dickering*. The salesperson and the buyer dicker back and forth until a mutually agreeable price is arrived at, usually a price well below the sticker price.

F. O. B.	Maritimes	Quebec	Ontario	Prairies	B.C.
F.O.B. origin (Toronto)	$10.00	$10.00	$10.00	$10.00	$10.00
Add: Profit margin and freight to each customer	2.75	1.75	1.10	2.00	3.25
Customer pays	12.75	11.75	11.10	12.00	13.25
Uniform Delivered Price:					
Zone price:	16.50	15.50	15.00	16.50	17.00
Multiply by:					
Volume importance of each region	5%	25%	40%	15%	15%
Uniform delivered price			$15.72		
Zone Price:					
F.O.B. origin (Toronto)	$10.00	$10.00	$10.00	$10.00	$10.00
Add: Profit margin (40%)	4.00	4.00	4.00	4.00	4.00
	14.00	14.00	14.00	14.00	14.00
Add: Average freight to each region	2.50	1.50	1.00	2.50	3.00
Zone price for each customer	16.50	15.50	15.00	16.50	17.00

Figure 11.6 Examples of Geographic Pricing Calculations: Uniform Delivered Price and Zone Pricing

According to the Automobile Protection Association, price dickering is an experience many consumers don't like. Consequently, many consumers go online to buy their car. Most manufacturers now offer a website where people can custom build their car and get the price instantaneously. The buying experience is much more pleasant.

Prices for hotel rooms booked online (often through a third-party service such as Travelocity, Expedia, or Priceline) can vary considerably based on time. A person booking a room at the last minute may get a much better rate than someone booking well in advance. The objective for the hotel is to get people into the hotel so they can spend their money elsewhere in the hotel.

Product-Mix Pricing

When a product is part of a larger product mix, setting prices is more difficult. The goal in this situation is to set prices so that profits are maximized for the total mix. Some products may be priced low while others are high. On balance, profit objectives are achieved and customers are generally satisfied with the price they pay.

Product-mix pricing embraces the following situations.

Optional-Feature Pricing This involves offering additional products, features, and services along with the main product. Specific option packages are common with cell phone plans. As more options are added, the price of the plan will increase. Consumers often find these plans confusing and in many cases wind up paying for services they rarely use.

Product-Line Pricing Companies normally develop product lines rather than single products. For example, Sony offers its W802 LED Internet TV in various sizes and prices. The 47-inch model is priced at $1299.99; the 55-inch model at $1699.99 and the 65-inch model at $2599.99. As you know from earlier discussion in the chapter, this pricing structure is also an example of odd-even pricing.

Captive-Product Pricing   Some products and services require the use of ancillary—or captive—products. If so, a company must price the captive product appropriately in order to encourage use. Rogers Communications or Bell Mobility may sell a telephone at a relatively low price to attract customers. They will make their money from the monthly fees and on the frequency with which the customer uses the phone. In this example, the phone could also be called a loss leader.

Fixed-Variable Pricing   Service firms commonly offer two-part pricing consisting of a fixed fee plus a variable usage fee. For example, fees charged for basic and long-distance telephone service by firms such as Bell or Rogers work this way. Fees are established for a certain number of minutes, with the fees increasing once a user goes beyond specified limits.

Product-Bundling Pricing   In this situation the seller bundles its products and features at a set price. Both Bell and Rogers Communications practise this option when selling their digital bundles. For example, Bell offers its Internet, satellite television, and cell phone services in one bundle. The bundling of the various services makes the package look attractive to potential customers. Refer to **Figure 11.7** for an illustration.

Figure 11.7
Bell bundles its digital services to attract potential customers.

SOURCE PRICING AND OFFERING DISCOUNTS

L02 Explain adjustments made to price based on factors such as geography, discounts, and allowances.

Part of price management involves offering discounts to customers. The firm first establishes a **list price**, which is the price normally quoted to potential buyers. Then, a host of discounts and allowances that provide savings off the list price are commonly offered. In effect, price discounts and allowances become part of the firm's promotional plans for dealing with trade customers—wholesalers, for example—who, in turn, pass on all or some of the savings to the retailers they supply. Very often, it is the combination of allowances that convinces customers to buy a new product or to buy in large volumes. In business buying situations, the buyer rarely pays the list price. Typically, a buyer is eligible for some of the discounts given by a manufacturer. Various types of discounts exist.

list price The rate normally quoted to potential buyers.

Cash Discounts

Cash discounts are granted when a bill is paid promptly, within a stated period. An example is "2/10, net 30." In this case, the buyer may deduct 2 percent from the invoice price if the charge is paid within 10 days of receipt of the invoice. The account is due and payable within 30 days at invoice price. While this discount appears to be small, it adds up to considerable savings for such mass merchandisers as Canadian Tire, Walmart, and The Bay.

cash discounts Discounts granted for prompt payment within a stated period.

Quantity Discounts

Quantity discounts are offered on the basis of volume purchased in units or dollars and can be offered non-cumulatively (i.e., during a special sale period only) or cumulatively (i.e., so that they apply to all purchases over an extended period—say, a year). Normally, eligible purchases are recorded in an invoicing system, and a cheque from the supplier is issued to cover the value of the discounts earned by the buyer at the end of the discount period. Refer to **Figure 11.8** for an illustration of a quantity discount schedule.

quantity discounts Offered on the basis of volume purchased in units or dollars.

The supplier establishes quantity discounts but they are sometimes negotiable. For example, Holiday Inn or any other major hotel chain may offer corporations a 25 percent discount if they commit to 5000 room nights a year (the total number of rooms booked by all employees). If Holiday Inn is anxious to attract new business it may offer a slightly higher discount to get the business. It is common for a corporation to pool the travel of employees in all subsidiaries in order to earn a better discount.

slotting allowance Discount offered by a supplier to a retail distributor for the purpose of securing shelf space in retail outlets; such allowances are commonly associated with product introductions.

Trade or Functional Discounts

There are several types of trade discounts.

Slotting Allowances A **slotting allowance** is a discount offered by a supplier to a retail distributor for the purpose of securing shelf space in retail outlets. These allowances are commonly offered with the introduction of new products. Since shelf space is scarce, it is often difficult to motivate distributors to carry new products. Given the number of new products introduced each year, retailers can be selective and are more receptive to suppliers that offer discounts to help defray the costs associated with getting a new product into their system (e.g., warehousing costs, computer costs, and redesigning store shelf sections).

Schedule Based on Volume Purchased over One Year		
Volume		Discount
Units	Dollars	
100–1000	200 000–2 000 000	10%
1001–2000	2 000 001–4 000 000	15%
2001–3000	4 000 001–6 000 000	20%
3001–4000	6 000 001–8 000 000	25%

Figure 11.8 An Illustration of a Quantity Discount Schedule

The practice of offering and accepting slotting allowances is a controversial issue. Critics argue that such a practice puts small suppliers at a disadvantage because they cannot afford them, and therefore getting a new product into distribution is difficult for them. Large suppliers do not necessarily like to offer these allowances but, as retailers have control in most markets (oligopolies exist in most cases) over the channel of distribution, the alternatives are few if guaranteed distribution is the goal.

off-invoice allowance A temporary allowance that is deducted from the invoice at the time of customer billing.

Off-Invoice Trade Allowances

An **off-invoice allowance** is a temporary allowance applicable during a specified time period and is deducted from the invoice at the time of customer billing. The invoice indicates the regular list price, the amount of the discount, and the volume purchased. Consider the following example:

Product (24 units in case)	$36.00 per case
Off-Invoice Allowance	$7.20 per case
Net Price	$28.80 per case
Volume Purchased	10 cases
Amount Due	$288.00
Terms	2/10, net 30

Manufacturers offer an off-invoice allowance to distributors as an incentive to purchase in greater volume in the short term and to encourage distributors to pass on the savings to their customers. In the example above, as much as $0.30 per unit ($7.20/24 units) could be passed on. Instead of allowing for such discounts on the invoice, a manufacturer sometimes offers them on the basis of a **bill-back**, in which case the manufacturer keeps a record of the volume purchased by each customer and reimburses them at a later date for the amount they earned over the term of the offer.

bill-back A discount in which the manufacturer records sales volume purchased by a customer and then pays the customer the total accumulated discount at the end of a deal period.

performance allowance Discount offered by a manufacturer to a distributor who performs a promotional function on the manufacturer's behalf.

Performance (Promotional) Allowances

A **performance allowance** is a price discount given by a manufacturer to a distributor that performs a promotional function on the manufacturer's behalf. These discounts are frequently made available in conjunction with off-invoice allowances. When the discounts are combined, a wholesaler that purchases in larger volumes will achieve greater savings. The performances that qualify for the allowances may take some or all of the following forms:

seasonal discounts Discounts that apply to off-season or pre-season purchases.

- There is guaranteed product distribution to all stores served by the distributor (e.g., Canadian Tire, Shoppers Drug Mart, or Sobeys agrees to ship a certain quantity of the product to each of its stores in a certain region), rather than a system whereby the distributor waits for individual stores to place orders.
- In-store displays are set in a prominent location (see **Figure 11.9**).
- The product is mentioned in retail advertising flyers or newspaper advertisements that announce weekly specials.

Performance allowances are usually negotiated between a manufacturer and a distributor, and an agreement is signed. The distributor is paid on proof of performance at the end of the term of the offer. Refer to **Figure 11.10** for an illustration of promotional discount calculations that a manufacturer may use to promote its product and their effect on the price customers pay.

Seasonal Discounts

Seasonal discounts apply to off-season or pre-season purchases. They are typical of products and services that sell strongly only in a certain

Steve White/QMI

Figure 11.9   Performance allowances encourage product displays at point of sale.

season or during certain times. For example, downtown hotels are busy during the week with business travellers but require family package plans to attract customers on weekends. Summer resorts and vacation retreats often offer 20 to 30 percent discounts before and after their prime season. Television viewing is much lower in the summer months. Therefore, networks such as CTV and CBC offer discounted rates to advertisers during this period.

Rebates

Rebates are temporary price discounts that take the form of a cash return made directly to a consumer, usually by a manufacturer. Periodically, car and appliance manufacturers offer cash rebates to customers who buy their models. Frequently, the rebate program becomes the focal point of advertising campaigns. Such programs are commonly used to reduce inventories or to stimulate sales in traditionally slow selling seasons, or at times when the economy is weak. For more insight into rebates, read the Think Marketing box **Price Incentives: Short-Term Gain for Long-Term Pain.**

Information:	
Cost of product	$40.00 per case
Trade discount	$4.00 per case
Quantity discount	2% for each 100 cases
Performance allowance	5%
Cash discount	2/10, n30
Customer purchases	500 cases

Calculation of Price to Customer:	
List price	$40.00
Less: Trade discount (10%)	4.00
	32.00
Less: Quantity discount (2% × 5)	3.60
	32.40
Less: Performance allowance (5%)	1.62
	30.78
Less: Cash discount (2%)	.62
Net price	30.16
Total discount	9.84
Total percentage discount ($9.84/40)	= 24.6%

Figure 11.10 List Price and Discount Calculations

Trade-In Allowances

A **trade-in allowance** is a price reduction granted for a new product when a similar used product is turned in. Trade-ins are common in the purchase of automobiles, industrial machinery, and various types of business equipment. If a supplier wanted a company to trade up to a more sophisticated photocopying machine, that supplier might have to offer a high trade-in value on the buyer's existing equipment. Trade-in allowances are a means of providing customers with a better price without adjusting the list price of the item.

The Dilemma of Discounts

Retail leaders such as Loblaws (supermarket retailing) and Shoppers Drug Mart (pharmacy retailing) that hold dominant positions in the channel of distribution exercise considerable control over their suppliers; they can pressure suppliers for deeper and more frequent discounts. Essentially, these and other retailers purchase products under a system known as forward buying. **Forward buying** involves buying discounted merchandise (merchandise bought when various trade allowances are offered) in quantities sufficient to carry a retailer through to the next deal period offered by the manufacturer. In effect, the retailer doesn't buy goods at the regular price. In such cases, even though the item was bought at a discount it doesn't mean the retail price will be lower for the item. Simply stated, the retailer may pocket the discount—it boosts its profit margin on every item sold!

The Legalities of Offering Discounts

Marketing organizations must be careful about how they offer discounts and allowances to channel customers. Customers must be treated fairly: that is, if discounts are offered, the same offer must be made to all customers. For example, if cereal is offered at $20 off per case for a four-week period, all customers must receive the discount. In the case of a volume discount, the rate is graduated to accommodate

rebates Temporary price discounts in the form of cash returns made directly to consumers, usually by manufacturers.

trade-in allowance Price reduction granted for a new product when a similar used product is turned in.

forward buying The practice of buying deal merchandise in quantities sufficient to carry a retailer through to the next deal period offered by the manufacturer.

Think Marketing

Price Incentives: Short-Term Gain for Long-Term Pain

In the automotive industry, price incentives are a huge hit with consumers. They get customers into the showroom and help keep the industry running, from one end to the other. Let's take a closer look at the auto industry and see what the real benefits are. What happens when the incentives are removed?

To put things into perspective, factors such as economic cycles, market elasticity of demand, and inventory levels often conspire against the industry. To keep production lines going they have little alternative but to offer incentives—cash incentives! Automobile manufacturers are convinced that cash is the most effective way to sell vehicles, mainly due to its universal appeal. The result is an endless array of cash-back offers, low- or no-interest financing, and bundling option packages at no extra charge. In recent years these types of programs have hit frenzy levels.

To make the incentives sound more attractive, automakers began touting "employee discount plans" to the general public. Ford called its plan the Ford Family Plan. It was downright folksy but proved to be a powerful connector with consumers. General Motors quickly followed suit. Psychologically, the phrase *employee pricing* has greater impact on consumers than *rebates*, but in real terms the price of the vehicle is higher. Understanding consumer behaviour goes a long way in this business.

In financial terms, incentives are not a *spend* but rather a reduction of profit margin, and that poses a problem for the manufacturers. Profit ultimately dictates how successful an organization is in its ability to attract investors, to expand facilities, and to develop new vehicles. A manufacturer must have a long-term view of where the company is going and how it's going to get there.

According to General Motors the amount of incentive money in the market is not sustainable. The general feeling, however, is that incentives are essential to maintain short-term growth. More simply put, among the components of the marketing mix, pricing has evolved as the major strategy for achieving short-term objectives.

Andre Kudyusov/Photographer's Choice RF/Getty Images.

Why, then, do they offer so many rich deals to customers? For certain they would like to put an end to incentives, but their own marketing programs have caused consumers to wait for an incentive. Consumers will postpone a purchase until the right incentive comes along. They will also compare the incentives of one manufacturer with another.

Now, let's examine the situation. Would it be preferable for carmakers to concentrate on other elements of the marketing mix to build brand image? Would they benefit more by focusing on key brand attributes to differentiate themselves from competitors? If so, would the presentation of a price/value relationship have more impact on potential buyers?

What's your opinion of price incentives? Is it a good strategy or a bad strategy? Do the benefits outweigh the costs?

Question:
Should carmakers shift their focus away from incentives?

Adapted from Greg Keenan, "GM Canada cuts prices amid slow sales," The Globe and Mail, *June 25, 2010, p. B3; "Incentives and the Automotive Industry, 2008, www.incentivecentral.org; and Jeremy Cato, "The risky business of discount pricing,"* The Globe and Mail, *August 25, 2005, p. G12.*

both small and large customers (refer to Figure 11.10). In this situation, a manufacturer such as Kellogg's or General Mills offers a higher discount to Metro or Sobeys than it does to a local independent grocer because the national chain stores buy in much greater quantity. Customers are usually categorized by size on the basis of the volume of product purchased from the manufacturer. The volume discount scale is in proportion to the size of each customer or buying group. Discounts of this kind are legal.

LEASING AS A PRICING OPTION

L03 Explain the role and impact of leasing as a pricing option.

A **lease** is a contractual agreement whereby a lessor (owner), for a fee, agrees to rent an item (e.g., equipment, house, or land) to a lessee over a specified period. In recent years, certain industries have increasingly used leasing in place of buying and selling. When considering the purchase of expensive capital equipment, buyers now frequently assess the lease option.

Expensive capital equipment such as computers, farm equipment, manufacturing machinery, office equipment and furnishings, and automobiles are often purchased on a lease agreement. Colleges and universities, for example, often lease computer equipment so that they have access to the latest technology when a lease expires.

The leasing industry in Canada has grown significantly in the past few years. As of 2010, the value of assets under management by equipment finance companies was $100.7 billion, which includes equipment financing, vehicle fleet financing, and consumer vehicle financing.[3]

Leasing is a common practice in the automobile industry. It accounted for 20 percent of new vehicle sales in 2011.[4] Leasing becomes an attractive proposition for consumers when they compare the purchase price of a good used car with the leased price of a new car. It could sway them in the direction of the new, leased option.

The main advantage of the car lease is that the customer pays only for the use of the vehicle versus the entire car. This can mean payments that are 20 to 30 percent less than bank financing payments. This is due to an equity benefit remaining in the car that belongs to the leaseholder at the end of the term. Generally, the more high-tech a piece of equipment is, the more likely it is that companies will lease it. Another standard guideline is often cited: If it appreciates, buy it; if it depreciates, lease it. A good many car owners just don't get it!

There are two types of leases. An **operating lease** is usually short term and involves monthly payments for the use of the equipment, which is returned to the lessor after a specified period. The lessee does not pay the full value of the equipment, so after the lease term is up the residual value belongs to the lessor. This is a standard arrangement if a consumer is leasing an automobile. A **full-payout lease** is a longer-term lease, and the lessor recovers the full value of the equipment's purchase price through monthly payments. It operates much like a bank loan, with the leased goods as collateral. In effect, it is like 100 percent financing with no down payment. This type of lease is more common for items classified as capital goods (e.g., heavy construction equipment, manufacturing equipment).

Leases provide advantages for buying organizations and marketing organizations. For the buying organization, a lease preserves working capital for other ventures, and it allows the company to keep pace with technology (e.g., trade up to new equipment at the end of the lease period). This is a good option for companies that want to keep pace with computer technology, a market in which products become obsolete quickly. Payment schedules are usually lower than those financed by a standard bank loan. For the marketing organization, a lease provides a sale that otherwise would have been lost if the purchaser had to buy it. Financially, the same amount of money is collected, but over a longer period. This helps the cash flow in the marketing organization.

lease A contractual agreement whereby a lessor, for a fee, agrees to rent an item to a lessee over a specified period.

operating lease A short-term lease involving monthly payments for use of equipment, which is returned to the lessor.

full-payout lease A type of lease where the lessor recovers the full value of the goods leased to a customer.

✔ Experience Marketing

To experience marketing you have to assess situations and make recommendations to change marketing strategies when necessary. What would you do in the following situation?

You are the marketing manager at Harvey's restaurants. Harvey's has been operating in Canada for over 50 years and is well known for its charbroiled burgers cooked on an open-flame grill. Over the years Harvey's has managed to maintain a relatively good position in the market despite intense competition from McDonald's, Wendy's, and A&W.

Much of Harvey's success is attributed to the quality of the product and the fact that each burger is customized to the individual taste of each customer. Harvey's likes to say to its customers "you get your burger just the way you want it." In addition to hamburgers, the menu includes chicken burgers, veggie burgers, hotdogs, and fries. Harvey's operates 240 restaurants in Canada and is owned by Cara Operations, a $1.2 billion restaurant business. Cara also owns Swiss Chalet, Kelsey's, Montana's, and Milestones.

Participants in the fast-food restaurant market have to respond to changes in consumer behaviour. While fast food is relatively cheap, customers are less loyal now and are searching for the best deals when contemplating a restaurant visit. Both McDonald's and Wendy's offer a value menu that has increased store traffic. The economics of the Canadian marketplace have made value menus quite popular. At the present time Harvey's does not offer a value menu. It occasionally runs specials on its core items when a meal package is assembled (e.g., burger, fries, and a soft drink).

You have been asked to investigate the potential of offering a value menu. Before you make any recommendations you must quickly audit the competition to see what they offer. The question you must answer is this: Will a value menu benefit Harvey's? Be prepared to justify your recommendation, whether you go in that direction or not.

CHAPTER SUMMARY

L01 **Describe the various pricing policies practised by marketing organizations.** *(pp. 232–238)*

An organization's pricing policies are the rules it establishes for setting prices that will enable it to achieve marketing objectives. Price policies are generally divided into four categories: psychological pricing (pricing concerned with tendencies in consumer behaviour), promotional pricing (pricing concerned with the availability of discounts and allowances for attracting potential customers), geographic pricing (pricing that takes into account freight and shipping costs and whether the seller or the buyer is to absorb such costs), and flexible pricing (charging different prices to different customers).

An organization may also utilize some form of product-mix pricing, which involves establishing low and high prices for various combinations of product offerings so that, on balance, profits are maximized. For example, a telecommunications company may bundle all of its offerings (phone, television, and Internet) into a bundle price to make it look attractive to customers.

L02 **Explain adjustments made to price based on factors such as geography, discounts, and allowances.** *(pp. 239–243)*

The marketing organization starts with a list price and then offers discounts and allowances to potential buyers. The discounts commonly offered to distributors include cash discounts for prompt payment; slotting allowances for securing distribution of new products; quantity discounts, which are meant to encourage volume purchases; performance allowances, which are paid to customers for performing a promotional function; seasonal discounts; rebates, which are temporary discounts intended to stimulate demand; and trade-in allowances.

All discounts offered must be made available to all competing distributors and must be offered, where applicable, on a proportionate basis: that is, distributors must be treated fairly in accordance with their size.

L03 **Explain the role of leasing as a pricing strategy.** *(p. 243)*

A lease is a contractual agreement between a seller and a buyer covering a specified period. Leasing is a popular pricing practice in the Canadian marketplace. Certain industries—computer, automobile, manufacturing machinery, and aircraft, for example—now frequently use leasing to generate new business. For the marketer, the primary advantage of leasing is that it preserves a sale that would have been lost had the lease option not been available. For customers, leasing a product allows them to avoid any potential debt load that would result from buying the product outright. With a leased automobile, for example, a person only pays for the use of the vehicle versus the entire car.

REVIEW QUESTIONS

1. Identify and briefly explain the various types of psychological pricing. (*LO1*)
2. What is a loss leader, and what role does it play in pricing strategy? (*LO1*)
3. What does multiple unit pricing refer to? Briefly explain. (*LO1*)
4. What is the difference between F.O.B. origin pricing and F.O.B. destination pricing? (*LO1*)
5. Briefly explain the difference between uniform delivered pricing and zone pricing. Under what conditions is one option better than the other? (*LO1*)
6. Briefly explain the nature of the following product-mix price policies: (*LO1*)
   a. Optional-feature pricing
   b. Captive-product pricing
   c. Fixed-variable pricing
   d. Product-bundling pricing
7. Briefly explain the nature and role of the following discounts: (*LO2*)
   a. Quantity discounts
   b. Trade discounts
   c. Performance allowances
   d. Rebates
8. What objectives do the following types of allowances achieve? (*LO2*)
   a. Slotting allowance
   b. Off-invoice allowance
   c. Performance allowance
9. What is forward buying? Briefly explain. (*LO2*)
10. What is the difference between an operating lease and a full-payout lease? (*LO3*)
11. What is the primary benefit of leasing for the marketer? For the consumer? (*LO3*)

DISCUSSION AND APPLICATION QUESTIONS

1. Conduct some secondary research to determine the regular-season ticket prices for the Toronto Maple Leafs and the price for another Canadian or American team in the NHL of your choosing. Why can the Maple Leafs charge so much more for tickets? Are its prices justifiable?
2. Refer to the Think Marketing box **Price Incentives: Short-Term Gain for Long-Term Pain.** Evaluate the dilemma that automobile manufacturers are facing. Are there other marketing solutions that you can offer?
3. Visit a car dealer in your area. Select a particular model of car and examine the pros and cons of leasing the car versus buying the car. Which method is best, and why?

12 Distribution and Supply Chain Management

AP Photo/Damian Dovarganes

LEARNING OBJECTIVES

LO1 Define distribution planning and describe the role of intermediaries in the distribution channel. (pp. 247–248)

LO2 Describe the structure of different types of distribution channels. (pp. 249–252)

LO3 Evaluate new channel strategies as a means of gaining competitive advantage. (pp. 252–255)

LO4 Describe the influences that are considered when selecting a distribution channel. (pp. 255–257)

LO5 Describe the nature of relationships between members of a channel of distribution. (pp. 257–259)

LO6 Explain the concept of integrated marketing systems. (pp. 260–261)

LO7 Explain how supply chain management systems are improving operational efficiency in the channel of distribution. (pp. 262–263)

LO8 Describe the key logistics marketing functions in a supply chain. (pp. 263–267)

FROM HUMBLE BEGINNINGS...

as a discount store in Rogers, Arkansas, in 1962, Walmart now operates 9230 stores under 60 different banners in 15 countries. Annual sales revenue exceeds $470 billion. Walmart has built its business on the premise that "saving people money helps them live better."[1] That was Sam Walton's goal when he opened that first store, and it remains the goal today.

You can imagine how difficult it is to effectively manage such a large and complex business. Distribution planning has played a key role in Walmart's success. The company's entire distribution system is driven by customer demand. What goes on at the cash register triggers action across the entire distribution channel. Walmart operates 10 700 stores and accommodates 245 million weekly shoppers. The stores, combined with best-in-class capabilities in online, mobile, and social media, offer customers seamless access to the products they want anytime, anywhere.

Another factor contributing to Walmart's success is the harmonious relationships or partnerships it has with supplier companies. Solid relationships provide business stability to suppliers and low prices to customers based on volume buying practices. Walmart's logistics management system is the envy of the retail industry. The system reduces costs and accelerates inventory turnover, and is the core of Walmart's competitiveness in the marketplace. Walmart firmly believes in the benefits of effective supply chain management and was the first retailer to openly exchange information with suppliers. The supply chain management system simplifies buying procedures and reduces operating costs for Walmart and its suppliers—a win–win situation for all partners. Distribution strategies are a key component of any marketing mix. That's what this chapter is about.

Distribution involves all the functions and activities related to the transfer of goods and services from one business to another, or from a business to a consumer. Given the competitive nature of the market today, business organizations constantly strive to improve the efficiency of their distribution systems. Very often, the goals of an organization include reducing the costs of distribution to improve profit margins and finding new channels of distribution to gain competitive advantage.

distribution Includes all activities related to the transfer of goods and services from one business to another, or from a business to a consumer.

DISTRIBUTION PLANNING

L01 Define distribution planning and describe the role of intermediaries in the distribution channel.

Distribution planning is "a systematic decision-making process regarding the physical movement and transfer of ownership of goods and services from producers to consumers."[2] The physical movement and transfer of ownership include activities such as order processing, transportation, and inventory management. These activities are carried out among members of the channel of distribution, which include suppliers, manufacturers, wholesalers, retailers, agents, and brokers. In marketing terminology, these organizations are called *channel members, intermediaries,* or *middlemen.* An effective distribution strategy calls for a firm understanding of the role of intermediaries and the structure of various channels of distribution.

distribution planning A systematic decision-making process regarding the physical movement and transfer of ownership of goods and services from producers to consumers.

Basic Role of Intermediaries

An **intermediary** offers producers the advantage of being able to make goods and services readily available to target markets. A manufacturer located in Winnipeg, Manitoba, would have difficulty contacting retail customers in all parts of Canada if it did not have a direct sales force of its own, and even if it did have such a sales force, it would

intermediary Offers producers of goods and services the advantage of being able to make goods and services readily available to target markets.

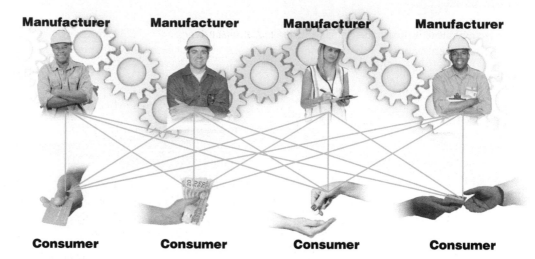

Option A. With no distributor, 16 transactions occur.

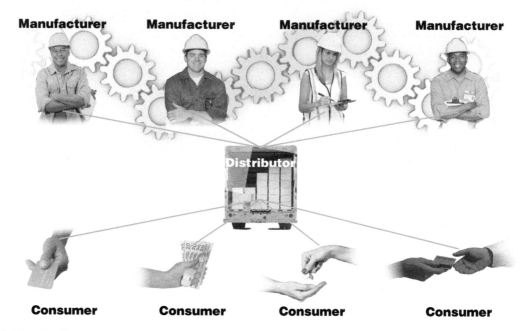

Option B. The inclusion of a distributor reduces the number of transactions to 8.

Figure 12.1 Economies of a Distribution System

not be able to contact its customers frequently. To address this difficulty, the manufacturer sells to a wholesaler that, in turn, contacts retail customers and supplies the product to them. The wholesaler is performing a marketing function on behalf of the manufacturer. In option A of **Figure 12.1**, 16 transactions occur when four different manufacturers attempt to reach four consumers. In option B, in which an intermediary is used, the transactions are reduced to eight. Option B provides a more economical transfer of goods.

Intermediaries, such as a wholesaler, purchase goods from a variety of different suppliers (manufacturers) and store them in inventory until retailers place orders for particular goods they wish to stock in their outlets. Once the retailer's order is placed, the goods are assembled on shipping pallets, transferred to a loading dock, and readied for shipping to the customer.

The Structure of Distribution Systems

L02 Describe the structure of different types of distribution channels.

Channels of distribution are either direct or indirect. A **direct channel** is a short channel, one in which goods move from producers to consumers without the use of intermediaries. Companies now sell goods through electronic channels directly to customers, bypassing traditional channel members in the process. You rarely buy music from retail stores anymore; you download music from Apple's iTunes store! You buy goods from Amazon.com instead of a traditional retailer. Perhaps you paid less for the goods on Amazon.com. Online buying is slowly becoming more popular with consumers; consequently, retailers must move in this direction to remain competitive.

direct channel A short channel of distribution.

An **indirect channel** is a long channel, one in which goods are moved through a series of intermediaries before reaching the final customer. Goods manufactured in one location in Canada (for example, everyday packaged goods that are relatively inexpensive) may pass through many intermediaries before they reach their final destination. See **Figure 12.2** for an illustration of direct and indirect channels.

indirect channel A long channel of distribution.

Manufacturer to Consumer The manufacturer-to-consumer channel of distribution is a *direct* channel. In this structure the manufacturer is responsible for contacting customers and distributing goods directly to them. It may take the form of a business-to-business transaction, or a transaction in which a business sells directly to a consumer. Software companies, for example, sell their products directly to consumers online and then distribute the products electronically.

The growth of online marketing is changing the nature of direct distribution. Organizations that traditionally did not sell directly to consumers are finding ways to do so via the Internet. If you want to buy Apple's latest iMac computer you needn't leave home to do so. You could go to an independent Apple dealer or an Apple store, or you could visit Apple.ca and place an order directly. If you choose the website your iMac will arrive at your doorstep a few days later.

Manufacturer to Retailer to Consumer The inclusion of a retailer makes the channel somewhat indirect. The retailer provides consumers with convenient access to goods. Apparel manufacturers such as Levi Strauss (blue jeans and leisure wear) and Nike (sport shoes and leisure clothing) sell to retail buyers of department stores and corporate chain stores. Retailers often store the merchandise in their own central warehouses so that it can be distributed to retail stores at a later time.

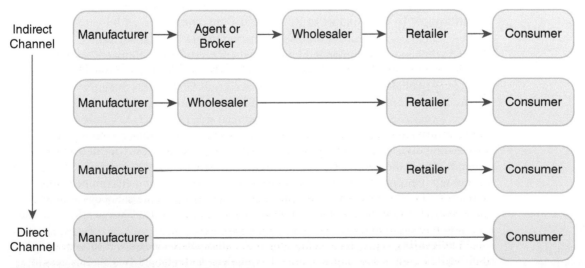

Figure 12.2 The Channels of Distribution

© B.O'Kane/Alamy

Figure 12.3   Apple exercises some marketing control by operating its own stores.

Sometimes the manufacturer will open its own stores to sell goods. Sony, for example, operates a chain of Sony stores to sell its consumer electronics products and Apple sells all of its products and services in Apple retail stores. In this structure, the retailer may be an online entity (a virtual store). For example, there was a time when tickets for Air Canada or any other carrier were purchased at a travel agent (a bricks-and-mortar retailer) but now they can be purchased at Travelocity.ca or Flyforless.ca, among many websites offering such a service.

In a direct channel the manufacturer of the product maintains more control of the marketing effort. In the case of Sony or Apple, each company can plan and control the merchandising strategy, the store environment, and the sales personnel. The desired image they wish to project is within their control. Such control does not exist when a third-party retailer such as Best Buy sells their products. In the case of Apple retail, the stores have a distinct advantage over its rivals—the experience is second to none. Apple now operates 416 stores globally. Retail sales revenue amounted to $20 billion in 2013.[3] Refer to **Figure 12.3** for an example of a manufacturer's retail outlet.

Manufacturer to Wholesaler to Retailer to Consumer   The addition of channel members increases the number of transactions and makes the channel indirect. The addition of a wholesaler is common in industries where products are ultimately sold through numerous types of retail outlets—convenience goods such as food, household cleaning products, personal-care products, and pharmaceuticals fall into this category.

A manufacturer such as Colgate-Palmolive (personal-care products) or S.C. Johnson (waxes and household cleaning products) ships its goods to wholesalers, which in turn ship to retailers they serve. Sobeys Inc., for example, operates its own wholesaling division in the form of distribution centres strategically located across Canada. Two of these warehouses use a fully automated warehouse and picking technology that provides superior product selection accuracy and customized store deliveries. These warehouses distribute goods to all Sobey retailers: Sobeys, IGA and IGA Extra, Thrifty Foods, Safeway, Foodland, FreshCo, and Price Chopper. Refer to the illustration in **Figure 12.4**.

wholesaling Buying or handling merchandise and subsequently reselling it to organizational users, other wholesalers, and retailers.

Wholesaling is the process of buying or handling merchandise and subsequently reselling it to organizational users, other wholesalers, and retailers. It is big business in Canada. In 2011, the total value of transactions by wholesalers across all trade groups was

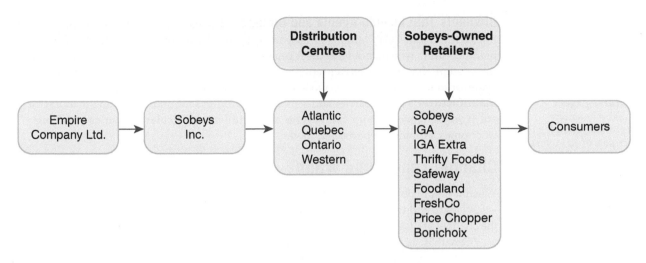

Products ordered by Sobey's Inc. from suppliers are delivered to regional distribution centres. The distribution centres perform the wholesaling function and redistribute to company-owned and -operated retail outlets. This is an example of corporate vertical marketing integration.

Figure 12.4   An Indirect Channel of Distribution in the Grocery Industry

$830.4 billion.[4] Wholesalers of petroleum products were the largest wholesale trade sector, followed by the "other products" group, which consists of wholesalers of agricultural fertilizers and supplies, chemicals, recycled materials, and paper products.

The following list describes the basic functions performed by wholesalers. They may perform some or all of these functions.

Providing Market Coverage—Manufacturers produce and market their goods from one or several manufacturing facilities. Since their customers tend to be geographically dispersed, a wholesaler provides the means to reach them efficiently. The wholesaler takes possession of the goods for redistribution to retail customers. In distributing goods, a wholesaler's sales force can complement a manufacturer's own sales force.

Holding Inventory—In many cases, the title to the merchandise is transferred to the wholesaler, who then holds the goods in inventory. For the manufacturer, this reduces the financial burden of carrying inventory and improves its cash flow to other operational costs.

Processing Orders—Wholesalers represent many manufacturers of similar products. Unlike manufacturers, wholesalers ship small quantities of a variety of merchandise to their customers. A wholesaler processes smaller orders for the manufacturers' products it represents. The costs associated with order processing are spread across all manufacturers' products.

Performing Market Intelligence—Wholesalers are in frequent contact with their customers, so they have a good understanding of customer needs (e.g., product requirements, service expectations, and price). This information is passed on to manufacturers to assist in improving marketing strategies.

Providing Service—After goods have been transferred to the next level in the channel—to another wholesaler, retailer, or organizational customer—the wholesaler can address any problems that arise. Such service takes the form of returns or exchanges, installations, adjustments, general repairs, technical assistance, and training users in how to use equipment.

Providing Assortment—Wholesalers carry a wide variety of manufacturers' products. The amassing of various items is called *assortment*. The assortment function simplifies customers' ordering tasks. In certain cases, customers can order from one wholesaler instead of many. A few general-line wholesalers can provide customers with most of the products they need.

Breaking Bulk—Breaking bulk refers to the delivery of small quantities to customers. Very often, small customers do not meet the minimum shipping-weight requirement established by the transportation companies that deliver the goods. Wholesalers will divide their bulk orders into smaller quantities to meet the needs of smaller retailers they supply goods to.

Channels That Include Agents and Brokers The inclusion of agents and brokers makes the channel very long. Typically, an agent or a broker represents a host of small manufacturers who do not have the resources to sell through the channel themselves. In this system, the agent or broker represents the manufacturer to the wholesale and retail trade, or to the final consumer, and earns a commission based on the sales generated. A **manufacturer's agent** carries and sells similar products for non-competing manufacturers in an exclusive territory. Such agents are common in particular industries including electronics, automotive parts, and food.

Channel Length and Width

When trying to develop an appropriate channel, a producer must consider two characteristics: length and width. **Channel length** refers to the number of intermediaries or levels in the channel of distribution. As indicated earlier, channels are direct (short) or indirect (long).

Generally, as products increase in price, sell less frequently, and require more direct forms of communication to keep customers informed, the channels become shorter and contain fewer intermediaries. The direct communication of accurate, often technical, product information between a seller and a buyer is more important under these conditions. For lower-priced products purchased frequently by consumers and supported with marketing communications campaigns, the channel tends to be longer and includes many intermediaries.

As channels become longer, control shifts from the producer to others in the channel. In this situation the producer of the good often implements marketing communications strategies directed at final users. Creating demand for the product among consumers helps move the product through the channel.

Channel width refers to the number of intermediaries at any one level of the channel of distribution. The width of the channel depends on how widely available a producer wants its product to be. Convenience goods, such as milk, bread, soft drinks, candy and gum, toothpaste, and deodorant have wide channels of distribution at both wholesale and retail levels. All of these products are readily available in any supermarket, drug store, or mass merchandiser such as Walmart.

Shopping goods, such as clothing, furniture, and appliances, require a narrower or more selective list of retailers to sell to consumers. Specialty goods are generally available in only a limited number of locations for any particular geographic market. For example, a market the size of Regina (Saskatchewan) or Kitchener (Ontario) would need only one Mercedes-Benz dealer. Vancouver's much larger market has seven dealers.

DISTRIBUTION CHANNELS AND COMPETITIVE ADVANTAGE

L03 Evaluate new channel strategies as a means of gaining competitive advantage.

The identification and pursuit of new channels of distribution is now the battleground for companies wishing to expand or gain advantage over competitors. Organizations are pursuing new opportunities presented by the Internet (online channel), multi-channelling, and contract marketing. These opportunities represent ways of gaining competitive advantage over rivals. Let us examine each of these practices.

Electronic Marketing Channels and Multi-Channelling

The e-commerce market in Canada is growing. In 2012 the total value of orders placed online by Canadians reached $18.9 billion. As well, Internet usage by all age groups continues to grow. More than half of Internet users (56 percent) ordered goods or services online. Some experts project online buying to reach $50 billion by 2016.[5] These figures indicate the need for business organizations to embrace the Internet and pursue direct distribution strategies. Future success will depend upon how well an organization meets the changing buying behaviour of its customers.

manufacturer's agent Carries and sells similar products for non-competing manufacturers in an exclusive territory.

channel length Refers to the number of intermediaries or levels in the channel of distribution.

channel width Refers to the number of intermediaries at any one level of the channel of distribution.

The online channel is a good complement to an organization's traditional channels. Companies that have already moved online are multi-channelling. **Multi-channelling** involves using different types of intermediaries at the same level of a channel to reach various customer groups. See **Figure 12.5** for an illustration.

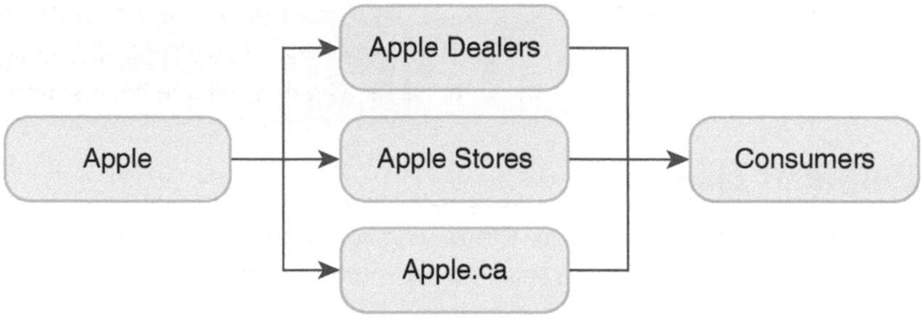

As mentioned earlier, Apple sells its products in traditional channels but chose to open its own stores as a means of attracting new customers and building relationships with present customers. The company also operates a very busy website from which consumers can buy Apple products directly. Chapters–Indigo has bricks-and-mortar retail locations but consumers can just as easily—or perhaps more easily—go online to the company's website to order a book.

In the automotive market, the traditional channel for companies such as General Motors and Ford was manufacturer to dealer to consumer. Now there are online options such as Autobytel.com, Cars4u.com, and AutoTrader.ca. Most manufacturers also offer direct buying at their websites. A customer can build the car of her dreams, secure the price, and complete the transaction online. She will have to visit the nearest dealer to pick up the car, but many customers like this no-hassle kind of convenience. Refer to the illustration in **Figure 12.6**.

A multi–channel system requires careful coordination between the various distribution channels.

Figure 12.5 Apple uses multiple channels of distribution to reach consumers.

multi-channelling A type of distribution for which different kinds of intermediaries are used at the same level in the channel of distribution.

Mazda Canada Inc.

Figure 12.6
Consumers can build a vehicle to their own specifications, obtain the price, and place the order online.

ThinkMarketing

Online or Else

In an era where technology is the driving force behind many business decisions you would think more Canadian companies would be actively involved in e-commerce— they would have established websites with transaction capabilities and they would have devised a system, be it their own system or that of a third party, to deliver goods to consumers. That is not the case.

E-commerce is growing in Canada. The latest figures show the business-to-consumer e-commerce market is valued at $18.9 billion, but in reality that only accounts for about 4 percent of total retail sales. As a comparison, online sales in the United Kingdom account for 23 percent of retail sales, in Germany it's 11.7 percent, and in the United States it's 8 percent. Canada is well down the list.

Some retailers jumped into e-commerce early, had a bad experience, and pulled out. Their systems did not meet consumer expectations. Canada is a land of unsatisfied online shoppers. Shoppers claim higher prices, poor selection, high shipping costs, and duty and customs expenses for items ordered from abroad drive up total costs. Nonetheless, Canadians do shop online. In 2012 the average online shopper placed 13 separate orders and spent about $1450. Further, most shoppers (82 percent) bought their goods from a Canadian company.

Many companies have resisted e-commerce due to the investment required. They see Canada as a vast country that lacks the population density required to make e-commerce work. Shipping costs to distant locations almost defeat the purpose of having e-commerce capabilities, and customers often expect free shipping in such a competitive environment.

For many Canadian retailers this situation spells trouble. When Canadian consumers become comfortable ordering from American online retailers more

firmly entrenched in e-commerce, that's business lost, pure and simple! Our bricks-and-mortar retailers already face enough American competition and American retailers are opening stores in Canada. Sooner, rather than later, Canadian companies must enter the e-commerce arena.

One of Canada's most successful retailers is very active online. Canadian Tire's website attracts 2.6 million unique visitors who are there to peruse merchandise and check out prices. Sears also has a busy website with 2.5 million unique visitors. Their visitors are there for a reason—to buy goods! Canadian Tire has plans to expand its transaction capability.

Companies now have an option to enter the e-commerce market on a shared cost basis. A new company called SHOP.CA is positioning itself as a Canadian retail solution. It has signed up some 850 retailers and suppliers to offer their goods through its website, and claims to offer wide selection—more than millions of items and 5000 brands including Tag Heuer, Canon, Nine West, and Samsung.

SHOP.CA is a startup company and it faces long odds at being successful. It's immediate challenge is to attract masses of customers and, in the longer term, develop strategies to keep them coming back. Their prices have to be competitive and they must offer the level of service that demanding consumers expect.

Question:

Is SHOP.CA a viable solution for companies that have resisted entry into the e-commerce arena? Examine the SHOP.CA website before offering an opinion.

For more insight into e-commerce growth, consumer buying behaviour and their impact on marketing and distribution strategy read the Think Marketing box **Online or Else**.

Direct Marketing and Electronic Marketing

Advancing technologies are fuelling interest in all aspects of electronic marketing. In terms of communications, organizations are investing more money in all forms of digital media, whether it's online, on a tablet or other mobile device, or with social media. The message can be delivered directly to a target market that has expressed some interest based on their online behaviour. From a distribution perspective, the product can be purchased directly (assuming web purchase capabilities at an organization's site), and the goods can be shipped directly to the customer in a reasonable time frame.

Some organizations only operate in a web-based environment. Amazon.com is an overwhelming success in this area. Mind you, a very elaborate distribution system is the backbone of Amazon.com. Once an order is placed, the product has to be found, packed, and shipped very quickly. Their customers expect prompt delivery.

In the music industry, the Internet has become the primary channel to get music from the source companies (record labels) to consumers. The intermediary in this process is Apple's iTunes music store. For a fee, consumers download music through Apple's iTunes service. Apple is now a major distributor of music and is much bigger than any single record label.

The Internet has changed the very nature of distribution. Organizations that have invested in online communications and distribution strategies are a step or two ahead of their competitors. All organizations that have done so have embarked on a steep learning curve to fully take advantage of the opportunities that online distribution presents.

Contract Marketing

In business-to-business marketing, selling directly to another organization via a contract offers significant advantage. With the contract come *exclusive rights*. A typical contractual agreement covers price policies, conditions of sale, territorial rights, service responsibilities, and contract length and termination conditions. More specifically, a supplier agrees to provide goods at certain prices or with certain discounts, and at a guaranteed quality level. To illustrate, if Fruit of the Loom has an exclusive rights clause in its agreement with Walmart, it will have a competitive advantage over competing national brands. Walmart's private label brand may be its only competitor.

In a contract marketing agreement the buyer limits the duration of such a contract in order to maintain control. The buyer also specifies conditions that could lead to the termination of the contract.

Many companies rely heavily on contractual arrangements with Walmart. Walmart currently accounts for 25 percent of Clorox company product sales and 40 percent of Fruit of the Loom underwear sales. What happens if Walmart does not renew its contract with either of these companies? It's not wise for any supplier to have too many eggs in the Walmart basket. If they lose the business they may have to close factories and lay off employees—the fallout could be significant. Walmart does not want its suppliers in such a situation and has been shortening the length of its contracts with suppliers.[6]

FACTORS INFLUENCING CHANNEL SELECTION

LO4 Describe the influences that are considered when selecting a distribution channel.

To determine what type of channel or channels are best for an organization, a number of factors are considered: the characteristics of the product or service, the nature of the competition, the financial resources available, and the intensity of market coverage that is desired. Let's examine each factor in more detail.

Product and Service Characteristics

Perishable goods such as fruits and vegetables require direct channels, or channels in which the goods are transferred quickly, to avoid spoilage. Products requiring installation and frequent maintenance, such as photocopiers and plant machinery, also require direct channels. Companies such as Xerox and Canon use a variety of channels, but they ship directly to other business organizations. The technical information communicated by their sales force to potential buyers necessitates the direct approach. For frequently purchased, inexpensive convenience goods, such as confectionery products and household cleaning supplies, indirect channels are used.

Technology is reshaping distribution decisions in organizations. As mentioned earlier, many companies are in direct contact with customers online. For packaged goods companies like Procter & Gamble, retailers such as Sears, and manufacturers like Dell, the Internet is proving to be a natural mode of getting products into the hands of consumers.

Sears has an aggressive multi-channel system embracing stores, catalogues, and online ordering. While Sears' distribution strategy is effective and efficient, other aspects of its marketing mix are not performing as well. The recent influx of American retailers to Canada has not helped their situation.

Competition

It is appropriate to employ the same channels as competitors and to employ channels that are common to a particular industry, because that is how and where customers look for products. However, an organization can gain competitive advantage by developing a new channel of distribution. For example, having a product available in a nontraditional location could result in purchases by new consumers.

When Procter & Gamble launched Febreze scented air freshener vent strips for automobiles it looked beyond traditional channels. Because it is a Procter & Gamble product, securing distribution in grocery stores was relatively easy; there, the vent clips are shelved next to Febreze in the air freshener section. But because the strips are a product for cars, convenience stores with gas stations seemed a natural fit. New distribution was secured at 7/11, Shell, Esso, Husky, and Ultramar locations. In-store display stands and promotional material was provided to these retailers to promote the brand.[7]

Well-known retailers looking for a competitive edge are also expanding into non-traditional areas through strategic alliances, a concept discussed earlier in the textbook. Tim Hortons' products are available in Esso stations across Canada; Subway has outlets in Mac's convenience stores; and Starbucks is in Target stores. Being available when the customer needs you is the name of the game in the fast-food business!

Company Resources

Size and financial resources determine which marketing functions a firm can or cannot handle. Small firms with customers located from coast to coast generally need to transfer the distribution function to intermediaries who can perform the task with greater efficiency. For example, small food-products manufacturers that do not have their own sales forces rely on food brokers to contact wholesalers and retailers on their behalf. Brokers represent many non-competing companies and work on a commission basis, usually an agreed-upon percentage of sales.

Large companies with more financial resources have more flexibility and can employ their own direct sales force or use a combination of direct and indirect channels, depending on the customer segments they are going after. The Internet is proving to be a cost-efficient way for small and large businesses to reach customers. With proper online marketing communications, a smaller business can create awareness for its products and ship goods directly to customers. Digital distribution levels the playing field for small companies competing with larger companies.

Intensity of Distribution

A producer has to consider what sort of coverage of the market is needed. The degree of market coverage or the availability of a product can be intensive, selective, or exclusive. See **Figure 12.7** for an illustration.

intensive distribution The availability of a product in the widest possible channel of distribution.

Intensive Distribution   An **intensive distribution** strategy is used by a company that wants to reach as much of the population as possible. This usually applies to low-priced, frequently purchased, branded convenience goods requiring no service or limited service. Personal-care products such as deodorant, body wash, shampoo, and so on are readily available in supermarkets, drugstores, convenience stores, and mass merchandisers such as Walmart. Among retailers, Tim Hortons' competitive advantage is availability—much of its success is directly attributed to the huge number of locations coast-to-coast in Canada. By comparison, outlets of direct competitors such as Country Style and Coffee Time are few and far between.

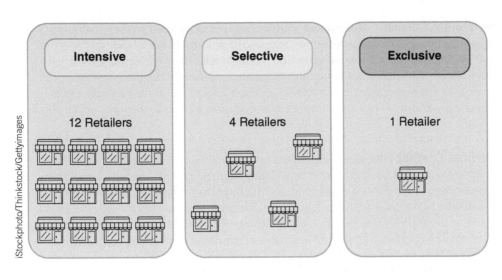

iStockphoto/Thinkstock/Gettyimages

Figure 12.7 Intensity of Distribution

Selective Distribution A **selective distribution** strategy is suitable for goods that are purchased less frequently and for industrial goods such as accessory equipment. By limiting the number of retailers, the marketing organization can reduce marketing costs while establishing better relationships with channel members. The number of Ford or GM dealerships in a city is an example of selective distribution. Typically, dealerships—for example, GM dealerships—are strategically located to battle competing dealerships (Ford, Chrysler, Toyota, and others) instead of their own dealerships.

selective distribution The availability of a product in only a few outlets in a particular market.

Exclusive Distribution An **exclusive distribution** strategy is sought for high-priced shopping or specialty goods that offer the purchaser a unique value. Typically, the product is purchased infrequently and is associated with prestige and status. In any given geographic area, only one dealer or retail outlet exists—a circumstance that helps protect the brand's image. Typically, the producers and retailers cooperate closely in decisions regarding advertising, promotion, inventory carried by the retailer, and prices. The producer's goals are to present a prestigious image and maintain channel control. High profit margins on every unit sold compensate for lower-volume sales. Such is the case for luxury categories such as premium watches and upscale jewellery. For example, Rolex watches are only sold in five stores in the Greater Toronto Area (an area with a population of 6.1 million people); two retailers serve all of Montreal and one dealer serves all of Ottawa.

exclusive distribution The availability of a product in only one outlet in a geographic area.

CHANNEL RELATIONSHIPS

L05 Describe the nature of relationships between members of a channel of distribution.

All channel members have the same basic objectives of making a profit, providing efficient distribution, and keeping customers satisfied. However, the strategies used by an organization can lead to problems or conflict between members. Potential sources of conflict often revolve around disagreements about distributor functions or a desire to retain control by a particular member of the channel.

In Canada, the balance of control or power in some markets has shifted from manufacturers to retailers due to the convergence and consolidation of retailing empires. Right now, three large grocery distributors, Loblaw Companies, Sobeys, and Metro control about 70 percent of traditional food store sales—therefore, they control the most valuable commodity in retail marketing: shelf space. Walmart and Costco Wholesale also play a dominant role in this industry. Such control breeds conflict and also worries manufacturers who need access to consumers through these retailers. The most common types of conflict are horizontal conflict and vertical conflict.

horizontal conflict Conflict between similar organizations at the same level in the channel of distribution.

Horizontal Conflict

Horizontal conflict stems from competition between similar organizations at the same level in the channel of distribution. For example, if Best Buy and Leon's are selling the same make and model of television, each store may strive to have a more attractive price policy. But if one store constantly has the lower price, the store with the higher price may begin to ask the manufacturer if the other retailer is receiving preferential treatment. Were better discounts offered to the store with the lower price?

vertical conflict Conflict that occurs when a channel member feels that another member at a different level is engaging in inappropriate conduct.

Vertical Conflict

Vertical conflict occurs when a channel member believes that another member at a different level is engaging in inappropriate conduct. For example, if wholesalers do not pass on manufacturers' discounts to retailers, friction between the wholesaler and retailer will develop. A manufacturer may pressure a retailer to keep prices at a certain level to protect a brand's image, but the action desired by the manufacturer may be contrary to the profit objectives of the distributors; there is conflict between the manufacturer and retailer.

Similarly, manufacturers such as Nike, Sony, and Apple, who establish their own retail stores or start selling directly to consumers through an online store, can expect negative reactions from their existing retail distributors. Established retailers stand to lose business, which could be a source of conflict between them and the manufacturer. The FGL Sports Group, a division of Canadian Tire, operates retail stores under banners such as Sport Chek, Atmosphere, and National Sports. Athletic shoes contribute about 70 percent of the sales revenue at Sport Chek, so manufacturer-operated retail stores are worrisome to other retailers.

Channel Control

channel captain A leader that integrates and coordinates the objectives and policies of all other channel members.

A **channel captain** is a leader that integrates and coordinates the objectives and policies of all other members of the channel. Depending on the circumstances, leadership and control may be held by the manufacturer, the wholesaler, or the retailer.

Manufacturer Control

When the manufacturer is in control, the channel is usually a direct one. Goods are distributed directly to the industrial user or consumers, or they are distributed through a company-owned or -sponsored retail outlet (e.g., a dealer). For example, General Motors and Toyota control the distribution of their automobiles through their dealer networks. In 2009, General Motors demonstrated its control when it eliminated some 200 Pontiac and Saturn dealers across the country. Those product lines were eliminated at a time when General Motors was facing bankruptcy protection. Streamlining the number of dealers in the system was one means to regain solvency.

In the automotive industry, the manufacturers require dealers to maintain quality standards for service and ensure that the physical environment of the showroom and service facilities meet specified criteria. The dealership must project the desired image the manufacturer wants. Failure to do so could result in the end of the manufacturer–dealer relationship.

Distributor (Wholesaler) Control

Wholesalers can also control a channel. Mentioned earlier in the chapter was the fact that three large grocery distributors control 70 percent of grocery sales (a $90 billion industry) in Canada. Each of these companies operates its own wholesaling division. For a manufacturer to gain access to retail shelf space controlled by these wholesalers, it must sell its goods to the central buying office of each wholesaling group. For example, Loblaws wholesaling division supplies goods to stores under numerous retail banners including Valu-Mart, No Frills, T&T, Zehrs, and Provigo among many others. Refer to **Figure 12.8** for a complete listing of the retailers that Loblaws wholesaling division supplies. This is also an example of a vertical marketing system, a concept discussed later in the chapter.

Loblaws is Canada's largest retailer, with more than 2300 stores across the country under many different banners. Over 14 million customers shop at their stores each week.

Western Canada	Ontario	Quebec	Atlantic Canada
Extra Foods	Loblaws	Loblaws	SaveEasy
Liquorstore	Zehrs	Provigo	Atlantic Superstore
No Frills	Your Independent	Maxi	No Frills
Superstore	Grocer	Club Entrepot	Wholesale Club
T&T	Valu-mart	Pharmaprix	Shoppers Drug
Wholesale Club	Fortinos		Mart
Shoppers Drug	Superstore		
Mart	No Frills		
	Wholesale Club		
	Shoppers Drug		
	Mart		

Figure 12.8   A wholesale-controlled distribution channel supplies stores under many retail banners.

The control exhibited by prominent grocery wholesalers places pressure on manufacturers to provide greater price discounts in order to retain distribution and shelf space in their stores. Not wanting to lose any distribution, manufacturers often succumb to their demands. Costco actually cut its ties with Coca-Cola due to a dispute over pricing. Coca-Cola was unwilling to sell product to Costco at the price Costco was demanding. Coca-Cola was removed from all stores. In advising customers of the situation the company stated, "Costco is committed to carrying name brand merchandise at the best possible prices. Coca-Cola has not provided Costco with competitive pricing so that we may pass along the value our members deserve."[8] In the aftermath, Coca-Cola relented—it realized the volume of product that Costco bought was too much to lose.

Retailer Control   Sometimes one retailer or a select group of retailers control the channel. Walmart is known to place considerable pressure on suppliers to keep prices down. If suppliers cannot meet the price demands, they risk losing Walmart's business. A specific case of retailer control involves Walmart and Rubbermaid. When Rubbermaid (a maker of plastic toys and containers) faced skyrocketing resin prices (a key ingredient in plastics), the company tried to pass on the cost increases to Walmart. Walmart immediately dropped Rubbermaid products in favour of another company adept at making Rubbermaid look-alikes at lower cost. Since Walmart represented 20 percent of Rubbermaid's business, Rubbermaid incurred financial losses and was forced to close many U.S. manufacturing facilities.

Walmart is the 800-pound gorilla of retailing that can place a lot of pressure on suppliers. To reduce its own merchandising costs, "Walmart is now pressuring suppliers for more marketing funds, demanding that all in-store displays be customized for their stores, and requires marketers to disclose the environmental impact of their products."[9] These mandates will place undue financial hardship on smaller suppliers. Through no fault of their own, their products could be ousted from Walmart.

It should be noted that the impact of social media networks and online marketing are changing the power equation. Consumers now have unprecedented access to information about products, competitive pricing, and sourcing options. If they are not satisfied with what one business is offering, they will move to another business. Information and a potential buying transaction are simply a mouse click away. It is now common for consumers to physically check out products in retail stores and then search the Internet for a source offering a better price for the same product. This practice is referred to as **showrooming**. Organizations that still think they are in control of their marketing might take a new look at the situation. It is the customer who is in control—a fundamental marketing concept at work!

showrooming A situation in which consumers physically review a product in a retail store and then search the Internet for a supplier offering the same product at a lower price.

INTEGRATED MARKETING SYSTEMS AND PARTNERSHIPS

LO6 Explain the concept of integrated marketing systems.

In order to gain control of a channel of distribution or to foster cooperation among its members, a firm develops a planned integrated marketing system. There are two types of integrated marketing systems: vertical marketing systems (or vertical integration) and horizontal marketing systems (or horizontal integration).

Vertical Marketing System

vertical marketing system (VMS) The linking of channel members at different levels in the marketing process to form a centrally controlled marketing system in which one member dominates the channel.

In a **vertical marketing system (VMS)**, channel members are linked at different levels in the marketing process to form a centrally controlled marketing system in which one member dominates the channel. A channel captain has control in a vertical marketing system. There are three types of vertical marketing systems: administered, contractual, and corporate.

administered VMS A cooperative system in which the organization with the greatest economic influence has control of planning the marketing program and identifies and coordinates the responsibilities of each member.

Administered VMS

In an **administered VMS**, the flow of goods in the distribution channel is controlled by the power and size of one member of the channel. This firm has a significant impact on the marketing programs of each member of the channel and often coordinates their responsibilities. For example, the wholesaling and retailing operations controlled by Loblaws and Sobeys (discussed earlier) is an administered VMS. Manufacturers such as Procter & Gamble, Kraft, and Nestlé have to manage their brands according to shelf-space guidelines established by Loblaws and Sobeys.

contractual VMS A legal agreement that binds the members in the marketing channel.

Contractual VMS

A **contractual VMS** is governed by a legal agreement that binds the members in the channel. Three forms of contractual vertical marketing systems are possible: retail cooperatives, wholesale-sponsored voluntary chains, and franchises.

retail cooperatives Retailers that join together to establish a distribution centre that performs the role of the wholesaler in the marketing channel.

Retail cooperatives are composed of independent retailers that join together to establish a wholesaling operation (e.g., a large distribution centre). Retail cooperatives may also be referred to as *buying groups*. The system is initiated by retailers and designed to allow them to compete successfully with chain stores. Each retailer owns a share of the operations and benefits from economies of scale in terms of buying and marketing goods. For example, lower prices are available to members in the form of discounts and allowances due to the higher volume of goods purchased collectively.

Calgary Co-op is a key player in Alberta, operating retail outlets that market food, petroleum, pharmacy, wine, spirits, beer, and travel products. It employs 3500 people, has more than 450 000 members, and generates annual sales of $1.1 billion.[10] It is one of the largest co-operatives in North America. Co-op Atlantic offers food, agriculture, and energy products to 150 communities in the Maritimes. It is the second-largest retail co-operative in Canada. Refer to the illustration in **Figure 12.9**.

Courtesy of Co-op Atlantic

Figure 12.9   Co-op Atlantic is an example of a retail co-operative.

A **voluntary chain** is a wholesaler-sponsored group of independent retailers organized into a centrally controlled system. Retailers agree to buy from the designated wholesaler. As in the case of the retail cooperative, the increased buying power results in lower prices for all retailers. Voluntary chains were originally established by independent grocers to compete more efficiently with large chains. Home Hardware and Western Auto are examples of voluntary chains. The voluntary chain implements inventory management programs and merchandising, and advertising programs that benefit all members. You may be familiar with Home Hardware's advertising slogan: "Home owners helping homeowners." Their advertising campaign features the owners of the hardware stores from across Canada.

In a **franchise agreement**, the franchisee (retailer), in exchange for a fee, uses the franchiser's name and operating methods in conducting business. The success of franchises is based on the marketing of a unique product or service concept and on the principle of uniformity—franchisees conduct business in a manner consistent with the policies and procedures established by the franchiser. Examples of franchise operations include McDonald's, Swiss Chalet, Property Guys, Snap-On Tools, Apple Auto Glass, and Instant Imprints. Franchise opportunities cover a diverse list of industries. Typically, franchise dealers receive a variety of marketing, management, and financial services support in return for a fee.

Corporate VMS A **corporate VMS** is a tightly controlled arrangement in which a single corporation owns and operates each level of the channel. The ownership and control of the channel can be located at either end: manufacturers may own wholesalers and retailers, or retailers may own the source of supply. In Canada, George Weston Limited (one of Canada's largest bread and dairy products producers) is at the helm of a corporate VMS. Weston is both a manufacturer and a distributor of the products it makes. Its various manufacturing divisions include Weston Bakeries (makers of Wonder, D'Italiano, Country Harvest, and Weston breads) and Neilson Dairy (the largest milk producer in Ontario under the Neilson brand name). These products are readily available in all the distribution outlets owned by Weston. Among the retail distributors are Loblaws, No Frills, Atlantic Superstore, Fortinos, Zehrs, Provigo, Real Canadian Superstore, and Your Independent Grocer.

Horizontal Marketing Systems

In a **horizontal marketing system**, many channel members at one level in the channel have the same owner. In the Canadian hotel business, Choice Hotels operates under a variety of banners: Comfort Inn, Comfort Suites, Quality Inn, Sleep Inn, Clarion, Rodeway Inn, and Econo Lodge. Refer to the image in **Figure 12.10**. Choice Hotels is a leader in the value segment of the hotel industry.

In the convenience store industry, Alimentation Couche-Tard Inc., a large Quebec-based convenience store chain, is the largest in North America operating under the banners of Couche-Tard, Mac's, and Circle K. In Europe, Couche-Tard operates Statoil fuel and convenience stores. Total global revenue is in the range of $23 billion annually.[11]

voluntary chain A wholesaler-initiated organization consisting of a group of independent retailers who agree to buy from a designated wholesaler.

franchise agreement A franchisee (retailer) conducts business using the franchiser's name and operating methods in exchange for a fee.

corporate VMS A tightly controlled arrangement in which a single corporation owns and operates in each level of the marketing channel.

horizontal marketing system A situation in which many channel members at one level in the channel have the same owner.

Simulation: Retailing/ Wholesaling

Figure 12.10
An illustration of a horizontal marketing system, Choice Hotels operates under various banners in Canada.

Choice Hotels International

SUPPLY CHAIN MANAGEMENT

LO7 Explain how supply chain management systems are improving operational efficiency in the channel of distribution.

supply chain management The integration of information among members of a supply chain to facilitate efficient production and distribution of goods to customers.

supply chain A sequence of companies that perform activities related to the creation and delivery of a good or service to consumers or business customers.

Technology is changing the nature of logistics marketing. Traditionally, producers of goods would evaluate and then implement the most efficient method of delivering goods to customers. Today, however, it is the customer, not the producer, who is the centre of the distribution universe. Essential planning starts with the customer and works backward in the channel to the manufacturer and even to the suppliers of raw materials and parts. This method of planning is called supply chain management. **Supply chain management** involves integrating and organizing information and logistical activities across all members of a supply chain in order to deliver goods and services efficiently to customers.

A **supply chain** is a sequence of companies that perform activities related to the creation and delivery of a good or service to consumers or business customers. The companies in this description include those mentioned earlier in the chapter: source suppliers of materials, wholesalers, and retailers, as well as warehouse and transportation companies that store and move goods from one location to another.

Essentially, supply chain management is a partnering of companies in the channel of distribution. It is a system that involves collaboration among channel members so that all members operate efficiently and profitably. All participants must be willing to make a financial investment (time, people, and money) in the system for it to work effectively. They must also openly pass information to one another so that all members can make sound business decisions regarding the production and delivery of their goods. Supply chain management spans all movement and storage of raw materials, work-in-process inventory, and finished goods from point of origin to point of consumption.[12] Refer to the illustration in **Figure 12.11**.

In a supply chain management system there are *outbound distribution* decisions involving the movement of goods from the point of manufacture to customers, and *inbound distribution* decisions involving the movement of goods from suppliers to the point of manufacture. See **Figure 12.12** for an illustration. From a marketing perspective, there are specific goals for a supply chain management system. An efficient system will serve customers better by providing lower prices and better service when goods are delivered or returned. It will also provide cost savings that trickle down to the bottom line—improved profit margins. Finally, the use of sophisticated planning software and other technologies such as point-of-sale scanners, satellite tracking devices, and electronic data interchanges facilitate ordering, delivery, and payment.

Raw Material Suppliers	Component Parts Suppliers	Sub-Assembly Suppliers
Steel	Transmission	Engine
Aluminum	Brakes	Chassis
Rubber	Wheel rims	Suspension
Plastic	Tires	
Fabric	Windows	

Ford Assembly Plant

Ford Dealer | Ford Dealer | Ford Dealer

Consumer Marketplace

Ford Website (Ordering Online)

Numerous materials, component parts, and assembled parts must be available at the assembly plant at the right time. This indicates the importance of just-in-time inventory management practices and electronic order processing and delivery procedures. All partners in the channel of distribution must work toward the same goal.

Figure 12.11 A Seamless Supply Chain

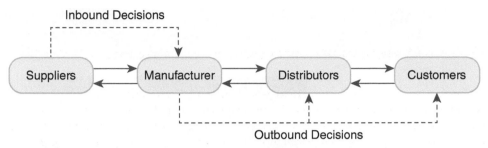

Figure 12.12
A Supply Chain
Management System

Information, materials, and finances flow both ways in an effective supply chain management system.

Advancing electronic technology brings members of a supply chain together to work cooperatively through an **electronic data interchange (EDI)**. The practice involves using computer technology to exchange information or data between two organizations; it is a set of standards that defines common formats for the information so that it can be exchanged in this way.[13]

The interchange acts much like a private communications channel among business participants. Information and data such as product sales, product inventory status, demand forecasts, and other metrics are shared with suppliers and their suppliers. The system offers significant benefits in terms of inventory management, transport and distribution, administration, and cash management. The three North American automakers—General Motors, Ford, and Chrysler—use electronic data interchange systems, as do big retailers such as Walmart and manufacturers such as Procter & Gamble.

Supply chain management practice has also benefited from **radio frequency identification (RFID)** technology. RFID is an automatic identification method that allows users to remotely retrieve data using *tags* or *transponders*. The tag can be incorporated into a product for the purpose of identification through radio waves. Each tag uniquely identifies the object to which it is attached, even if that object is one of a multitude of items. In the context of supply chain management, the use of RFID means that any member of the supply chain can monitor the flow of goods from raw materials through to finished product, and from manufacturer to consumer.

Some of the promised benefits of RFID technology include improved forecast accuracy, better inventory management and loss prevention in stores, reduced administration costs, and savings on labour costs due to automated scanning at shipping and receiving points. All partners in a supply chain are interested in these benefits.

The key distribution functions, such as warehousing, inventory management, transportation, and order processing (see next section for details), will be more efficient, and increased efficiency should mean increased profit margins for all participants. For a retail organization it means that buyers are able to concentrate on determining product mixes and keep up with the latest trends in the marketplace rather than having to worry about when and how much to order to order. Much of Walmart's business success is attributed to its supply chain management system, which incorporates the latest technologies. When its distribution operations are efficiently run, Walmart can pass the savings on to its customers.

Supply chain management is complex, sophisticated, and costly. Consequently, many organizations outsource many of the functions associated with it. For more insight into supply chain management read the Think Marketing box **UPS to the Rescue**. The various activities that are associated with supply chain management are discussed in the following section.

LOGISTICS FUNCTIONS IN A SUPPLY CHAIN

L08 Describe the key logistics marketing functions in a supply chain.

Logistics marketing involves a range of activities or functions that facilitate the movement of goods through supply chain (a channel of distribution). These functions include order processing, warehousing, inventory management, transportation, and

electronic data interchange (EDI) The computerized transfer of information or data among business partners to facilitate efficient transfer of goods.

radio frequency identification (RFID) The next wave of intelligent technology to impact inventory planning: RFID tags are placed on goods so they can be instantly tracked anywhere in the world.

logistics marketing The range of activities involved in the flow of materials, finished goods, and related information from points of origin to points of consumption to meet customer requirements at a profit.

ThinkMarketing

UPS to the Rescue

There was a time when manufacturers would simply call a transportation company to pick up goods at their warehouse for delivery to customers. But things are more complex today. With the movement to supply chain management systems, companies are searching for cheaper goods on a global scale, and that has complicated the warehouse and transportation process for manufacturers.

Rather than deal with such complicated issues, manufacturers have turned to transportation experts for a solution: UPS (and its competitors) to the rescue! UPS (United Parcel Service) is the largest express carrier and package delivery company in the world. It is also a leader in transportation, logistics, capital, and e-commerce services.

UPS offers customers many of the activities associated with supply chain management. Key services include logistics and distribution design and planning, transportation and freight (air, sea, ground, and rail), freight forwarding, international trade management, and customs brokerage. UPS employs 10 000 Canadians. UPS is a big company; it is a leading member of the $60-billion-a-year logistics industry in Canada.

A state-of-the-art warehouse at its Canadian headquarters in Burlington, Ontario, has 246 000 square metres (about 12 football fields) of storage space. It is one of 936 warehouse facilities that UPS runs worldwide. The Canadian warehouse is strategically located near Canada's busiest highways, 45 minutes from the U.S. border, and within 50 kilometres of three international airports. It receives 250 000 shipment units daily on behalf of 25 major clients—primarily major retail chains.

When the goods arrive, the universal product codes (UPCs) are scanned electronically and the goods are

The Canadian Press Images/Bayne Stanley

moved by forklift into storage—the entire inventory of the facility is turned over every five weeks. Shipments are sent by trucks and tractor-trailers to retail outlets, other UPS depots, and directly to homes.

The movement to logistics outsourcing stems from the rise of just-in-time inventory practices. Just-in-time was one of the initial ways to lower manufacturing costs by reducing inventory. Since the supply chain is a company's second-highest expense (estimated to be 32 percent of all costs for Canadian manufacturers), it seems logical to look at the system for efficiencies. UPS claims it can cut warehouse and distribution costs by 10 to 20 percent. Fewer headaches and higher profit margins—manufacturers are in favour of that!

> **Question:**
>
> **A manufacturing company is considering using a third-party distribution and logistics company. What are the key benefits of such an arrangement?**

Adapted from UPS, www.ups.com; and David Dias, "Just one word: It keeps you running," Financial Post Business, June 2007, pp. 14–23.

---

customer service. Refer to **Figure 12.13** for an illustration of the key functions of logistics marketing. The objective of logistics marketing is to deliver products to the right destination in a timely manner at the lowest possible cost.

Order Processing

order processing A distribution activity that includes checking credit ratings of customers, recording a sale, making the necessary accounting entries, and then locating the item for shipment.

stockout Items that are not available when a customer's order is received.

Order processing involves accepting an order from a customer, and includes checking credit ratings of customers, recording a sale, making the necessary accounting entries, ensuring that sufficient stock is available, and then shipping the order through established procedures. Sometimes, not all items that a customer orders are available for shipment. This situation is referred to as a **stockout**. Customers must be advised of stockout situations so that they will know if the item will be shipped automatically at a later date or if a new order must be placed for the item.

Warehousing

The role of a **warehouse** is to receive, sort, and redistribute merchandise to customers. There are two types of warehouses: storage warehouses and distribution warehouses. A **storage warehouse** holds products for long periods of time in an attempt to balance supply and demand for producers and purchasers. Generally, these facilities are not specialized; they handle a variety of items, such as tires, equipment, appliances and other hard goods, and case goods.

A **distribution warehouse**, or distribution centre, assembles and redistributes merchandise, usually in smaller quantities and for shorter periods of time. A variety of goods ordered by a customer are assembled into a truckload by the distribution centre for shipment to the customer. Sobeys warehouses, for example, receive shipments from a variety of manufacturers (refer to Figure 12.4). These warehouses store, assemble, and redistribute the same merchandise in smaller quantities to their retail locations. An efficiently run distribution centre has a direct impact on an organization's profitability.

Modern warehousing operations are very sophisticated; some are fully automated, with orders being placed electronically. The use of hand-held scanners to place orders is commonplace in many retail operations. Orders are then processed from a fully automated warehouse that can read computerized orders, determine the correct quantity of each product, and move them in the desired sequence to the loading dock. The automated system then determines how much stock is needed from producers.

E-commerce growth in Canada is creating a need for more high-tech distribution centres. Currently, e-commerce is only 4 percent of retail sales in Canada compared to 8 percent in the United States. If Canada's sales were to reach 8 percent, industry analysts project that the number of distribution-based warehouses in Canada would have to triple or quadruple simply to accommodate the demand.[14]

Inventory Management

Inventory management is a system that ensures a continuous flow of needed goods by matching the quantity of goods in inventory to sales demand so that neither too little nor too much stock is carried. The goal is to have just enough supply to meet the demands of customers.

Many firms have adopted a system called the **just-in-time (JIT) inventory system**, the objective of which is to reduce the amount of inventory on hand by ordering small quantities frequently. Rather than ordering large quantities at low costs, only to store the goods, just enough inventory is produced (if a manufacturer) or ordered (if a distributor) to meet current demand. As discussed in the preceding section about supply chain management, efficient inventory management is a benefit of technology utilization.

Transportation

Transportation tends to be the most costly item in physical distribution. The goal of a transportation system is to be efficient so that the producer has a competitive advantage. Hence, a logistics manager evaluates the basic modes of transportation available for the delivery of goods. The manager considers the location of the customer and then selects the most efficient mode of transportation. The modes of transportation are trucks, railways, air carriers, waterways, and the Internet.

Trucks are used to make small shipments over short distances. Deliveries within a local area or a certain region are made by truck. Truck transportation is also used for

The Key Functions of Logistics Marketing

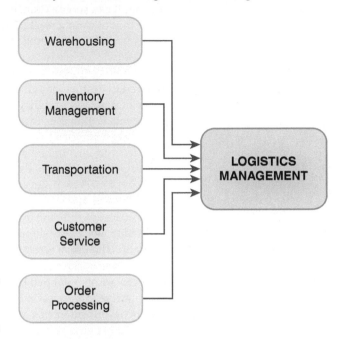

Figure 12.13   The Various Functions of Physical Distribution (Logistics Marketing)

warehouse A distribution centre that receives, sorts, and redistributes merchandise to customers.

storage warehouse A warehouse that holds products for long periods of time in an attempt to balance supply and demand for producers and purchasers.

distribution warehouse (distribution centre) A warehouse that assembles and redistributes merchandise, usually in smaller quantities for shorter periods of time.

inventory management A system that ensures continuous flow of needed goods by matching the quantity of goods in inventory to sales demand so that neither too little nor too much stock is carried.

just-in-time (JIT) inventory system A system that reduces inventory on hand by ordering small quantities frequently.

Video: Toyota: Outsourcing and Logistics

very long hauls when time is not a consideration. The main advantages of truck delivery are that it can serve a number of locations, particularly distant and remote locations that other modes cannot reach. Truck transport is significant. In terms of value it accounts for 61 percent of trade with the United States, Canada's biggest trading partner.[15]

Railways are the most efficient mode of transporting bulky items over long distances (e.g., farm equipment, machinery, steel, and grain). From Ontario, new automobiles are shipped to destinations all over Canada and the United States. Trains can carry a wide range of products, and they serve a large number of locations. The frequency of shipments is, however, low.

Air carriers commonly carry expensive items that can absorb the high freight costs (e.g., technical instruments and machinery). It is also common to ship perishable goods and urgently needed goods by air. The appeal of this method lies in its speed and in the number of markets it serves, particularly major urban markets in Canada and around the world. The high cost is its major disadvantage.

Waterways shipping involves moving goods by ocean tankers and inland freighters. In Canada, waterway shipping through the St. Lawrence Seaway and the Great Lakes is common. The use of water transportation is widespread for bulky items, such as coal, iron ore, grain, chemicals, and petroleum products. High-value finished goods from overseas are also shipped by water. For example, automobiles from Japan and South Korea arrive in Vancouver by water carrier. Water transportation moves products at lower cost but shipments are slow and infrequent.

As discussed earlier in the chapter, e-commerce initiatives by business organizations are resulting in more electronic distribution of goods. The Internet acts as an invisible distribution system for products such as software and music, as well as media content from newspapers, magazines, and television and radio stations. Most financial institutions distribute their services online. Tangerine (a direct banking subsidiary of Scotiabank) provides customers with convenient access, offering its products and services directly to consumers via the Internet, a call centre, mobile channels, and in their cafés. Refer to **Figure 12.14** for an illustration.

Transportation Coordination   To increase efficiency, more and more firms are employing a combination of transportation modes to ship their products. When several modes of transportation are used, containerization plays a key role. **Containerization**

containerization The grouping of individual items into an economical shipping quantity that is sealed in a protective container for intermodal transportation to a final customer.

Figure 12.14
Tangerine makes banking convenient by offering its products and services directly to customers through the Internet.

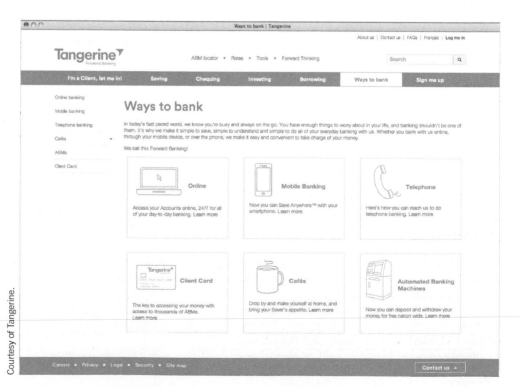

Courtesy of Tangerine.

Figure 12.15
Delivery specialists now play a more important role in the delivery of manufacturers' goods.

The Canadian Press Images/Bayne Stanley

groups individual items into an economical shipping quantity that is sealed in a protective container for intermodal transportation to a final customer. **Intermodal transportation** involves two or more modes of transportation, with goods being transferred from one mode to another (e.g., air to truck or rail to truck).

The most common form of intermodal transportation is piggybacking. **Piggybacking** is a system in which the entire load of a truck trailer is placed in a rail flatcar for movement from one place to another. The railway performs the long haul, and the truck performs the local pickup and delivery. Other combinations for intermodal transportation are possible: for example, containers from East Asia arriving in Vancouver by ship are directly transferred to trucks or flatbed rail cars for delivery to their Canadian destinations.

The combination of air and truck transportation is common for cargo carriers, such as UPS and Federal Express. These companies combine truck fleets for ground travel with air cargo for overnight delivery to distant locations. Due to the growth of online marketing, business has been booming for third-party cargo carriers such as UPS. Companies that have embraced the Internet as a means of marketing goods require the specialized services that UPS and others provide. See **Figure 12.15** for an illustration.

intermodal transportation Moving goods using two or more modes of transportation, with goods being transferred from one mode to another.

piggybacking A system in which the entire load of a truck trailer is placed in a rail flatcar for movement from one place to another. In retailing, piggybacking also means the sharing of facilities for marketing purposes.

✔ **Experience**Marketing

To experience marketing you have to assess situations and make recommendations to change marketing strategies when necessary. What would you do in the following situations?

You are the marketing manager at Chapters bookstores and have been assigned the task of reviewing the distribution channel strategies of the company.

Chapters sells books in big box-style stores located in major Canadian cities. It now operates Chapters.Indigo.ca to capitalize on the trend of online book buying and offers e-readers to customers who prefer to read digital editions

of books. This is an industry where technology is forcing a lot of changes to marketing practice.

In the longer term you are concerned about the impact of the online business on your retail store business and how it will affect your distribution strategy. You know that Blockbuster, once the largest distributor of home video content, went out of business. Will bookstores face a similar fate?

Your immediate challenge is to evaluate the external influences that could have an effect on your distribution strategies. Are there some new distribution strategies that Chapters should be considering as it moves forward? Be prepared to justify any new recommendations.

CHAPTER SUMMARY

LO1 **Define distribution planning and describe the role of intermediaries in the distribution channel.** *(pp. 247–248)*

Distribution planning entails making decisions regarding the physical movement of merchandise and its transfer between producers and consumers. Activities such as order processing, transportation, inventory management, and customer service are the responsibility of members of the channel of distribution. Channel members (or intermediaries) include wholesalers, retailers, agents, and brokers. Their primary role is to facilitate the transfer of merchandise in an efficient, economical manner.

LO2 **Describe the structure of different types of distribution channels.** *(pp. 249–252)*

In planning a distribution strategy, a company may use an indirect (long) channel or a direct (short) channel. If an indirect channel is used the wholesaler plays a key role on behalf of the source company. Wholesalers buy and resell merchandise to organizational users and retailers. The functions of a wholesaler include providing direct sales contact, holding inventory, processing orders, and offering sales support. Wholesalers resell goods to retailers who in turn sell goods to consumers. In an indirect channel some control over marketing shifts to the wholesalers and retailers.

If a direct channel is employed, a business will market directly to consumers. Very likely they will communicate directly with consumers to create awareness and interest in their products and offer a means (website) whereby a buying transaction can occur. The goods purchased are shipped direct to the customer. In a direct channel the manufacturer maintains control over the marketing function.

LO3 **Evaluate new channel strategies as a means of gaining competitive advantage.** *(pp. 252–255)*

The evolution of e-commerce in Canada should stimulate manufacturers and retailers to be more active with electronic channels. E-commerce in the business-to-consumer market is presently $18.9 billion and it is growing steadily each year. Embracing the Internet as a means to conduct business—to market and distribute goods—presents significant opportunity for a business. Employing non-traditional channels (e.g., seeking different outlets to sell a product) presents another opportunity. The key to growth lies in multi-channelling—combining traditional channels with new electronic channels

Manufacturers may also pursue contract marketing opportunities to gain competitive advantage. A contractual supply agreement with a large retailer such as Walmart may include an *exclusive supplier* clause that would lock out key competitors. Such a contract would generate significant revenue for a company. Companies must be cautious not to have too much of their business tied to one reseller. When the contract is up for renewal a competitor could replace the existing supplier.

LO4 **Describe the influences that are considered when selecting a distribution channel.** *(pp. 255–257)*

The influences a firm considers when designing channel strategy include product characteristics, competition, company resources, and the intensity of market coverage desired. Usually a company that wants to maintain control over marketing programs and customer contact will use direct channels. Companies that are more flexible about control will use indirect channels.

LO5 **Describe the nature of relationships between members of a channel of distribution.** *(pp. 257–259)*

In any distribution system, an organization must assume that conflict will occur among channel members. Conflict can be horizontal (i.e., between similar members at the same level) or vertical (i.e., between members at different levels). The channel captain implements strategies that encourage cooperation between channel members. The channel captain may be the manufacturer, an intermediary such as a wholesaler, or the retailer; it depends on which organization has more economic clout in the channel or if the channel structure dictates who the captain should be.

LO6 **Explain the concept of integrated marketing systems.** *(pp. 260–261)*

Integrated marketing systems are a means of gaining increased control over channel operations. There are two types of integrated marketing systems: vertical and horizontal. In a vertical marketing system, a manufacturer, wholesaler, or retailer could be in control. Control in a vertical marketing system can be administered, in which case the member with the most economic influence holds control; contractual, where control is maintained through a legal agreement; and corporate, in which case one company operates at each level of the channel. In a horizontal marketing system, one firm has many members at one level of the channel.

LO7 **Explain how supply chain management systems are improving operational efficiency in the channel of distribution.** *(pp. 262–263)*

Supply chain management involves an integrated flow of information (electronically), materials, and finances among channel members. It involves much collaboration and cooperation among members of the channel to optimize the efficiencies of the system. Effective supply chain management is crucial and in that regard technology plays a key role. Supply chain management has embraced technologies such as EDI (electronic data interchange), in which information is exchanged electronically between channel members, and RFID (radio frequency identification), which allows members to track the location of goods anywhere in the channel. The objective of supply chain management is to reduce costs while maintaining the most efficient and productive distribution system possible.

LO8 **Describe the key logistics marketing functions in a supply chain.** *(pp. 263–267)*

Logistics marketing refers to the activities involved in the ordering, storing, and delivery of merchandise. The major components of logistics marketing include order processing (accepting and filling orders), warehousing (receiving, storing, and redistributing goods to customers), inventory management (managing the supply of goods so they meet customer demand), and transportation (the actual delivery of goods by truck, rail, air, water, or the Internet). Many firms are calling upon external expertise in logistics management and are outsourcing this responsibility to companies such as UPS and FedEx.

MyMarketingLab
Study, practise, and explore real marketing situations with these helpful resources:
- **Interactive Lesson Presentations:** Work through interactive presentations and assessments to test your knowledge of marketing concepts.
- **Study Plan:** Check your understanding of chapter concepts with self-study quizzes.
- **Dynamic Study Modules:** Work through adaptive study modules on your computer, tablet, or mobile device.
- **Simulations:** Practise decision-making in simulated marketing environments.

REVIEW QUESTIONS

1. What is distribution planning? (*LO1*)
2. What is the basic role of intermediaries in the channel of distribution? (*LO1*)
3. What is the difference between a direct channel and an indirect channel? Under what conditions would a company select one option or the other? (*LO2*)
4. What are the basic functions associated with wholesaling? Briefly explain. (*LO2*)
5. What is meant by the terms *multi-channelling* and *contract marketing*? Briefly explain. (*LO3*)
6. Briefly describe the factors a firm considers when designing a channel of distribution. (*LO4*)
7. Under what conditions are the following types of distribution appropriate? (*LO4*)
   a. Intensive
   b. Selective
   c. Exclusive
8. What is the difference between horizontal conflict and vertical conflict in the channel of distribution? (*LO5*)
9. What is a channel captain, and what role does the channel captain play in the distribution channel? (*LO5*)
10. What is a vertical marketing system? Briefly explain. (*LO6*)
11. What is a horizontal marketing system? Briefly explain. (*LO6*)
12. Briefly explain the concept of supply chain management and explain the terms *outbound distribution* and *inbound distribution*. (*LO7*)
13. What are the key functions of logistics marketing? Briefly explain. (*LO8*)

DISCUSSION AND APPLICATION QUESTIONS

1. What type of channel of distribution would you recommend for the following products?
   a. Axe deodorants and body sprays
   b. Goodyear tires
   c. Rolex watches
2. What degree of distribution intensity is appropriate for each of the following?
   a. Toyota's Lexus dealerships
   b. Adidas athletic shoes
   c. Colgate Total toothpaste
   d. TAG Heuer watches
3. Conduct some secondary research on e-commerce in Canada. Compared to other countries, where does Canada rank in terms of e-commerce development and what impact will e-commerce have on future distribution strategies? iStockphoto/Thinkstock

13 Retailing

Deborah Baic/The Globe and Mail/CP Images

LEARNING OBJECTIVES

LO1 Explain the importance of retailing in Canada and identify key trends influencing the industry. (pp. 271–272)

LO2 Define the functions associated with contemporary retailing. (pp. 272–273)

LO3 Describe the various types of retailers based on ownership, products and services offered, and method of operation. (pp. 273–279)

LO4 Describe the roles and functions of the major components of the retail marketing mix. (pp. 280–286)

LO5 Describe retailing's transition into the digital marketing environment. (pp. 287–290)

SHOPPERS DRUG MART...

is one of the most-shopped stores in Canada. In fact, Shoppers attracts 87 percent of adult shoppers at least once in any given year, ranking second only to Canadian Tire in popularity. What is the secret to its success?

A combination of marketing strategies has worked well for Shoppers. Being a dominant player in the pharmacy market, the company has locked up the best locations in most urban and suburban markets. Now it is building super-sized stores designed to engage consumers in key product categories. One of Shoppers' biggest moves was in cosmetics. The company worked out deals with many high-end cosmetics brands that were formerly sold only in department stores. New beauty boutiques staffed by trained cosmeticians showcase the new products and the beauty section is the first thing a woman sees when she enters the store.

To provide more of a focus on current customers, its marketing communications strategy has shifted from mass media to highly targeted direct communications and customer relationship management programs. Shoppers has capitalized on the information it collects via the Shoppers Optimum Rewards Program—one of the largest databases in Canada. Shoppers can quickly identify precise targets—such as young mothers who will receive special offers around mother and baby needs.

Retail strategy consultant Chris Lund sums up Shoppers Drug Mart's success best: "Women today view Shoppers Drug Mart the same way men view Canadian Tire."[1] The future looks bright indeed for Shoppers Drug Mart!

RETAILING AND ITS POSITION IN THE ECONOMY

LO1 Explain the importance of retailing in Canada and identify key trends influencing the industry.

Retailing refers to those activities involved in the sale of goods and services to final consumers for personal, family, or household use. In Canada, overall retail sales have increased steadily. In 2012, the latest year for which statistics were available, retail sales in Canada amounted to $486 billion. Retailing accounts for 6.2 percent of Canada's gross domestic product and employs 12 percent of Canada's workforce. The largest categories of retailers include motor vehicle and parts dealers (23.4 percent), food and beverage stores (21.9 percent), and general merchandise stores (12.6 percent).[2]

retailing Activities involved in the sale of goods and services to final consumers for personal, family, or household use.

The retail landscape has been changing in recent years. Shifts in consumer behaviour and technology have had the greatest impact on retailers. Value-conscious consumers have migrated away from traditional department stores to other options. Consumers concerned with price have moved to discount retailers; consumers less concerned about price have moved upward to specialized retailers and boutique-style stores. E-commerce has become a key factor (almost a necessity) in the retailing equation. Consumers today are very comfortable conducting transactions online. The ownership of smartphones by so many consumers has created a behaviour known as showrooming (a concept introduced in Chapter 12). While looking at a product in a store, the consumer will use their smartphone to track down the same product at a lower price from an online supplier. Such behaviour places pressure on bricks and mortar retailers to alter their pricing strategies.

Traditional department store retailers that appeal to a wide cross-section of the population have been losing ground to specialized retailers and discount retailers. In the discount segment, Walmart is taking all kinds of business from mid-market competitors. Walmart is Canada's largest mass merchandiser, with annual sales in the $23.5 billion range. Consumers are attracted to Walmart based on its value proposition, which others just can't match—everyday goods of reasonable quality at an affordable price. The combination of price and selection has been the hallmark of Walmart's success. The entrance of even more American retailers into Canada will place added pressure on Canadian retailers—new strategies will be needed to hold their position.

The shopping behaviour of Canadians is changing. Time-pressed consumers are spending less time shopping. They want to shop in a timely, convenient manner. Rather than visiting traditional malls, shoppers are more likely to visit power malls, where many of the big-box retailers are located, or they are buying their goods online. The convenience of online shopping, combined with a potentially lower price for the same item, are motivators that trump bricks-and-mortar shopping.

The specialists include membership warehouse outlet stores such as Costco. Costco is a $15.9 billion a year business in Canada. Costco operates with a no-frills appearance, featuring cement floors and goods displayed on shipping pallets. Consumers must buy a membership to shop at Costco. Costco appeals to value-conscious consumers across all income groups.

The growth of retailers that focus on price (lower prices than traditional competitors) illustrates the changing values of shoppers today. More than ever before, retailers must understand how, when, and why customers buy the products they do, and they must adjust their marketing practices accordingly. For example, the shift to online buying necessitates some form of e-commerce capability. The impact of these trends will be discussed in more detail throughout this chapter.

RETAILING AND ITS FUNCTIONS

L02 Define the functions associated with contemporary retailing.

Generally, retailers perform four key functions. See **Figure 13.1** for a visual breakdown of these functions:

1. Retailers are part of the *sorting process*: the store buys an assortment of goods and services from a variety of suppliers, stores them in inventory, and offers them for sale.
2. They *market* goods by establishing selling prices, devising marketing communications programs, and effectively merchandising goods on the sales floor.
3. They complete a *transaction* by offering credit terms, convenient hours, and store locations, and other services such as debit card and credit card purchasing, and delivery.
4. They offer *e-commerce services* to consumers seeking the convenience of online buying.

When shopping for goods at retail, the consumer usually has a number of retailers to choose from. A retail store is chosen on the basis of such factors as store image, hours of

Figure 13.1 The Functions of a Retailer

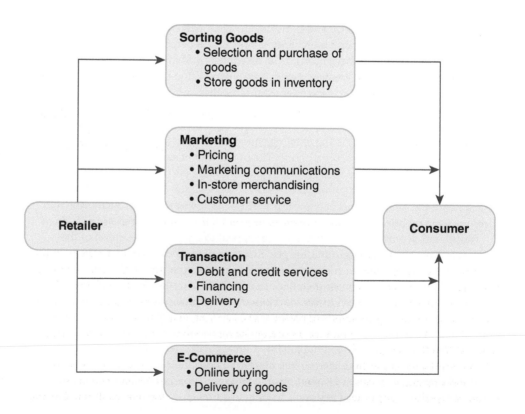

> In a changing retail environment, the companies that will succeed are those that understand consumer needs and realize they can't be all things to all people.
>
> Successful retailers are the ones that focus on only a few core strengths. All consumer transactions can be reduced to five elements—**price, product, service, access,** and **experience.** The best retailers understand this and devote their resources to the one or two elements where they feel they can compete. Here are a few examples:

IKEA	McDonald's	Tim Hortons	Golf Town
Price and Product	Access and Service	Access and Product	Product Selection and Customer Experience

Figure 13.2
Understanding consumers pinpoints strategic focus for retailers.

operation, availability of parking, quality of products carried, additional services provided, store location, and the environment of the store. In planning a strategy, retailers consider these factors and develop a **retailing marketing mix** to attract customers to the store. Retail marketing strategies are discussed in detail later in the chapter.

Successful retailers adapt to changes in consumer shopping tendencies and to changes in economic conditions; they revise their marketing strategies accordingly. Typically, a successful retailer sticks to what it does best—straying too far from its roots can be financially harmful! For example, Walmart is focused on lower prices for a range of popular products; Starbucks charges high prices for an enjoyable customer experience; Golf Town sells a wide selection of golf equipment and apparel and offers customers an enjoyable in-store shopping experience. Golf Town is a national chain of 54 stores. At Golf Town customers can expect expert customer service and can take advantage of unique offers such as customized golf clubs, a Try Before You Buy program, and a Trade In, Trade Up program. Refer to **Figure 13.2** for more examples showing the strategic focus of some other retailers.

retailing marketing mix The plan a retailer uses to attract customers.

Video: Things Your Grocer Won't Tell You

RETAILER CLASSIFICATIONS

L03 Describe the various types of retailers based on ownership, products and services offered, and method of operation.

There are many different kinds of retail operations. Canadian retailers are classified into groups according to form of ownership, products and services offered, and method of operation. The different types of stores have different characteristics and, therefore, diverse marketing strategies.

Ownership

In terms of ownership, there are two prevalent forms: chain stores and non-chain stores.

Chain Stores   A **chain store system** is a group of retail stores of essentially the same type, centrally owned and with some degree of centralized control. In Canada, stores are classified as **chain stores** if there are four or more stores in the system. Chain stores dominate the Canadian retail marketplace. Examples of large chain store systems include La Senza, Tip Top Tailors, Shoppers Drug Mart, Canadian Tire, Harry Rosen, and Lululemon. Collectively, chain stores account for 48 percent of retail operating revenues in Canada (some $230 billion in 2012).[3]

As mentioned earlier, there is a trend in shopping behaviour toward discount department stores and warehouse outlets, both of which are types of chain stores. Walmart is a mass merchandiser and Costco a warehouse outlet. They are among the top five retailers in Canada

chain store system A group of retail stores of essentially the same type, centrally owned and with some degree of centralized control.

chain store An organization operating four or more retail stores in the same kind of business under the same legal ownership.

Rank	Retailer	Revenue 2012 ($ billion)
1	George Weston Limited (Loblaws)	$32.8
2	Walmart	$23.4
3	Alimentation Couche-Tard	$23.0
4	Empire Company Limited (Sobey's)	$16.3
5	Costco Wholesale Canada	$15.7
6	Canadian Tire	$11.2
7	Metro Inc.	$12.1
8	Shoppers Drug Mart	$10.8
9	Home Depot	$7.2
10	Canada Safeway	$6.7

Note: In 2013 George Weston Limited (Loblaws) acquired Shoppers Drug Mart and Empire Company (Sobey's) acquired Canada Safeway.

Source: Canada's 100 Biggest Companies by Revenue, June 27, 2013, *Report on Business Magazine*, www.theglobeandmail.com

Figure 13.3 Canada's Top Retailers Based on Annual Revenue

warehouse outlets (big-box stores) No-frills, cash-and-carry outlets that offer customers name-brand merchandise at discount prices.

retail franchise A contractual agreement between a franchiser and a franchisee.

co-branding Occurs when a company uses the equity in another brand name to help market its own brand-name product or service; also applies to two organizations sharing common facilities for marketing purposes.

independent retailer A retailer operating one to three stores, even if the stores are affiliated with a large retail organization.

in terms of revenue generated annually. Refer to **Figure 13.3** for additional details. Canada is also a market where franchised retail operations flourish. Based on the number of stores and sales revenues, franchises are also classified as chain stores.

Warehouse outlets are no-frills, cash-and-carry outlets that offer consumers name-brand merchandise at discount prices. They are commonly referred to as *big-box stores*. Examples of warehouse outlets include Home Depot and Rona (both of which are building supply and home improvement stores), and Costco (which markets groceries and general merchandise).

Warehouse outlets are somewhat hybrid operations; they actually perform many wholesaling (refer to Chapter 12 for details) and retailing functions in one operation, because their size and buying power allow them to buy in large volume and manufacturers deliver directly to each outlet. They carry anything from Mont Blanc pens to Michelin tires to Doritos chips, so they are competing with all kinds of traditional retailers. Typically, these stores offer limited selection and a minimum of services—but their prices are lower, and that's what brings the customers in!

In response to the growth of warehouse stores, some general merchandisers and supermarkets such as Canadian Tire and Loblaws are opening their own warehouse stores and are adding new and non-traditional product lines. As mentioned earlier in the textbook, Loblaws introduced its Joe Fresh line of fashion goods and it has become a $1 billion a year business. Just a short time ago, few people would have thought about buying their clothes at Loblaws! Shoppers Drug Mart has expanded into grocery products. Loblaws recently acquired Shoppers Drug Mart, so Shoppers' transition into grocery products could conceivably expand further.

Retail Franchising

A **retail franchise** is a contractual agreement (a franchise) between a franchisor (a manufacturer, wholesaler, or service sponsor) and a franchisee (the independent business person). In a franchising arrangement, the franchisee purchases the right to own and operate a certain line or brand of business from the franchisor for a specific location. Further, the franchisee agrees to subscribe to a certain set of rules and business practices—a franchisor requires that the product be prepared in a certain way, and management practices and accounting systems must be consistent among all franchisees. Some of the more common names in franchising include Canadian Tire, McDonald's, Pizza Pizza, Tim Hortons, and Dairy Queen.

The typical franchise arrangement requires that an initial franchise fee and a percentage of sales (a royalty) be returned to the franchisor. Some franchisors also require that a percentage of sales be returned in order to build a fund for advertising, from which all franchisees benefit. For example, a Dairy Queen Grill & Chill franchise carries an initial franchise fee of $45 000, which covers initial training, opening, and support services. In addition, the franchisee pays a monthly royalty of 4 percent of gross sales and a monthly advertising fee of 5 percent to the franchisor. The total cost to open ranges from $800 000 to $1.3 million. Construction and land costs have an impact on the startup costs. Refer to the image in **Figure 13.4**. The initial franchise fee for a Harvey's is $25 000 for a 20-year agreement. The royalty and

Photo by Keith J. Tuckwell

Figure 13.4 Opening a well-known franchise is costly but potential investors benefit from the image of the franchise system.

advertising fees are similar to Dairy Queen's. Total startup costs range from $575 000 to $975 000.[4]

To become a partner in a successful franchise is a costly venture! For an entrepreneur, a franchise offers several benefits: franchises have significant buying power, which keeps costs down, and each franchisee benefits from the image of the total franchise system. Is owning a Tim Hortons franchise a licence to print money? Many outsiders think so! But there are also some drawbacks: franchisees have no flexibility or very limited flexibility to plan and implement their own ideas, and they are not expected to be innovative—innovation comes from the head office. Franchising is not for everyone.

A recent trend in franchising is **co-branding**. This involves two or more separate franchise operations sharing one facility. Yum Brands, for example, often places two or three of its restaurants together in one location: KFC, Taco Bell, and Pizza Hut. See the illustration in **Figure 13.5**. In theory, co-branding works best when stores offer complementary products. For example, Couche-Tard, Canada's largest operator of convenience stores, has evolved to include other retailers such as Subway and Timothy's coffee.

Figure 13.5 Co-branding of franchised outlets is a popular strategy.

Independent Retail Stores An **independent retailer** is a retailer operating one to three stores, even if the stores are affiliated with a large retail organization. Independent retailing is dominant among dealers of domestic and imported cars, local pharmacies, automotive parts, and locally owned food stores.

Independent retailers contrast greatly with chain stores. Competing with large chains is difficult. The chain store is a large-scale operation, and because it buys in large quantities, it can offer customers lower prices than the independent retailer can (although chains do not always choose to offer low prices). The risk of financial loss is spread across many stores in a chain operation; successful stores compensate for the unsuccessful ones. To survive as an independent requires adequate financial resources and good management skills. Slowly but steadily many independent retailers are closing their doors, citing stiff price competition from the big-box stores as the reason. Independent retailers, typically located on a town's main street, are closing; their business has suffered due to the growth and popularity of newer chain stores located at the edge of town.

Products and Services Offered

Stores are also classified based on the extent of products carried and services offered. Essentially, a store offers a full range of services, or a limited range of services, or is a self-serve operation.

Product Lines Stores classified by product line are differentiated by the variety of items and the assortment of each item they carry. A **specialty store** carries a variety of products in a single product line: for example, Aldo carries shoes, La Senza carries lingerie, and Sunglass Hut carries sunglasses. See **Figure 13.6** for an illustration of a specialty store. A **limited-line store** carries a large assortment of related lines: for example, Best Buy sells a variety of consumer electronics products and Golf Town sells golf equipment, clothing, and related accessories.

Finally, a **general-merchandise store** (also referred to as a *mass merchandise* store) offers a wide variety of product lines and a

specialty store A store selling a single line or limited line of merchandise.

limited-line store A store that carries a large assortment of one product line or a few related product lines.

general-merchandise store A store offering a wide variety of product lines and a selection of brand names within those product lines (e.g., a department store).

Figure 13.6 La Senza is a specialty store in a highly specialized market.

selection of brand names within these product lines. Stores such as Sears, Walmart, Target, and The Bay fall into this classification.

self-serve store A retailer characterized by the limited number of services offered. Such a store tends to rely on in-store displays and merchandising to sell products.

full-serve store A retailer that carries a variety of shopping goods that require sales assistance and a variety of services to facilitate the sale of the goods (such services may include fitting rooms, delivery, and installations).

limited-service stores A type of retailer that offers only a small range of services in order to keep operating costs to a minimum.

Services Offered   In a **self-serve store**, the retailer provides minimum services. The stores rely heavily on in-store displays, merchandising, and reasonable prices to attract customers. Warehouse stores, such as Costco, are self-serve operations, as are supermarkets, hardware stores, and drugstores. In contrast, a **full-serve store** offers customer assistance and a greater variety of in-store services, including fitting rooms, delivery, installations, and alterations as part of the service mix. Specialty stores such as Holt Renfrew and Harry Rosen are full-serve stores. Stores such as IKEA, Target, and Walmart offer some personal services but their goal is to keep services minimal so they can maintain lower prices for shoppers. Stores such as these can be classified as **limited-service stores**.

NON-STORE RETAILING

The previous sections described retailing in the traditional sense: that is, the purchase of goods in retail stores. There are other ways a retailer can market goods to consumers. Today there is a trend toward marketing to consumers directly. A retailer will consider direct response communications (e.g., catalogues and email communications to current customers) as potential options for selling goods and services. Vending machines are another form of non-store retailing.

Many retailers employ catalogues to display and sell their merchandise. Sears is the largest catalogue retailer in Canada, issuing two major catalogues each year (Fall/Winter and Spring/Summer), a Christmas Wish catalogue, and a series of sale catalogues throughout the year (see **Figure 13.7**). Canadian Tire publishes hard copy and digital

(top & left) Sears Canada;(bottom right) Steve White/QMI

Figure 13.7   Sears effectively combines catalogues and online communications with traditional retailing.

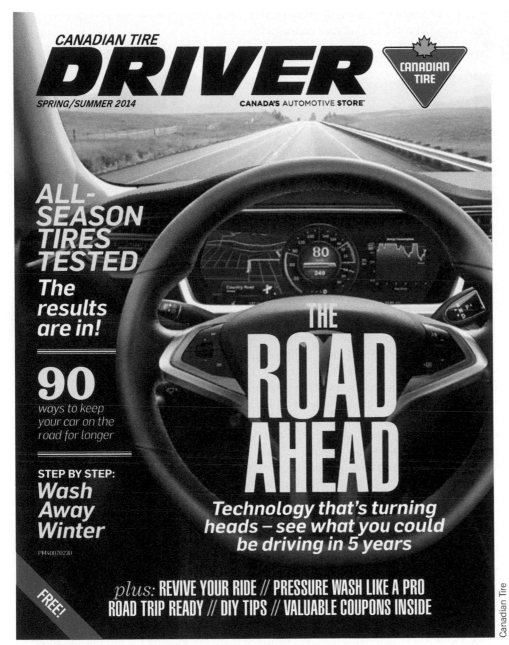

Figure 13.8
Canadian Tire distributes *Driver* magazine to customers classified as "automotive enthusiasts."

catalogues by season (e.g., an outdoor summer catalogue) as well as by product categories such as cooking and bakeware, car care, sports and recreation, and tools. Home Hardware offers an annual catalogue featuring the broad range of products it sells. Both Sears and Canadian Tire have effectively combined catalogues and web-based marketing to serve their customers better. The following section examines e-retailing in more detail.

Canadian Tire also publishes a *magalogue* in print and online. Titled *Driver*, it showcases automotive and related product lines, such as tools. The magalogue combines elements of a catalogue (product details and prices) and a magazine (articles about how to tackle automotive repairs and maintenance). Some 600 000 copies are distributed in stores across the country and another 1.5 million are distributed to targeted customers—customers interested in do-it-yourself repairs. The company's database identifies suitable customers. "Canadian Tire's objective with *Driver* is to showcase a broader range of products than those found in its weekly flyer in a higher quality environment," says Andrew Davies, vice president, automotive retail, at Canadian Tire.[5] Refer to the image in **Figure 13.8**.

We do not usually think of a vending machine as a form of retailing, but it is. Vending machines often sell soft drinks, coffee, and confectionery products. These

Courtesy of PepsiCo Canada ULC

Figure 13.9 Vending machines offer expanded distribution and trigger impulse buying.

Ken James/Bloomberg via Getty Images

Figure 13.10 Pop-up retail locations instill a sense of urgency and excitement about something new.

machines generate annual sales of approximately $650 million each year.[6] Manufacturers are looking at vending machines as a way of increasing market penetration and brand recognition. Vending machines are an important element of the marketing mix for companies such as Coca-Cola, PepsiCo, and Nestlé. See **Figure 13.9** for an illustration.

Non-store retailing is expected to grow in the years ahead. This form of retailing appeals to consumers seeking convenience and better prices. Consumers are shopping differently today. Earlier it was mentioned that shoppers today visit retail stores to physically look at products but then go online to find a cheaper source for the item. For more insight into this behaviour pattern and how retailers are responding to it, read the Think Marketing box **Retailers Retaliate: New Strategies to Keep Customers Coming Back.**

Temporary Displays and Kiosks Traditional manufacturers and retailers are showing interest in concepts such as temporary carts, kiosks, and "pop-up" retail locations. Telecommunications companies such as Rogers, Telus, and Bell utilize kiosks in shopping malls in an attempt to stop busy shoppers passing by. In some cases a store and a kiosk are located in the same mall. It's simply a matter of making the buying situation more convenient for consumers. It's not uncommon for all phone suppliers to have kiosks in the same mall—talk about intense competition!

pop-up stores (flash retailing) A retail trend where stores open for sales in a temporary space and then disappear anywhere from one day to a few weeks later.

Pop-up stores (also referred to as *flash retailing*) are a hot trend. A pop-up store involves opening a temporary sales space. The trend involves opening up one day and then disappearing anywhere from one day to a few weeks later. A pop-up store creates a unique environment that engages customers; there is a feeling of relevance and urgency to them. They are a good option for introducing new products. Both Sony and Microsoft used pop-up locations to launch their new game consoles in 2013.

The challenge for an online retailer is getting people to the website. Setting up a pop-up location gives shoppers an experience with the brand. With proper marketing communications strategies supporting a pop-up store, it is a means by which a new retailer can establish a presence in a new market. Consumers visiting the pop-up as well as potential media coverage can generate word-of-mouth buzz for the retailer. It could lead to a potential visit to a website and ultimately a purchase.

Some of the biggest retail brands—including Gap, Target, Urban Outfitters, and Marc Jacobs—use pop-ups to instill a sense of urgency around something new that is about to happen. Refer to the image in **Figure 13.10**. In retailing, being part of a trend is essential.

💡 **Think**Marketing

Retailers Retaliate: New Strategies to Keep Customers Coming Back

Almost 60 percent of Canadians admit to some form of showrooming behaviour—the practice of visiting a bricks and mortar store to see an item, but then using a mobile device to search for a better price and ultimately making an online purchase. Such behaviour has a negative impact on a retailer's bottom line.

The primary reasons consumers buy online instead of in a store are price and free shipping. Retailers are concerned about this and find it extremely difficult to compete with online companies that have designed and implemented better direct distribution systems, websites such as Amazon.com among them.

But the news isn't all bad. Some recent research reveals that mobile shoppers who buy online while they are in a store are just as likely to buy from the retailer's own online store as a competitor's. Another factor that encourages buying a product right in the store is the appeal of getting the item immediately—people just don't want to wait! They also cite familiarity with the retailer and rewards programs as other factors that encourage in-store buying.

So how does a retailer interpret this mixed set of information? Best Buy and Future Shop (both are owned by the same company) have devised unique strategies to keep customers buying in their stores. First and foremost, both retailers offer an offline and online option for their customers. Beyond that, Future Shop focuses on price and provides consumers with easy access to locations, reviews, and prices on its mobile app. It actually encourages showrooming but in a very controlled manner. Future Shop has an aggressive price-matching strategy—it will beat any competitor's prices by 10 percent.

AP Photo/Microsoft Corp

Best Buy is focusing on the in-store experience and is partnering with key suppliers such as Apple, Microsoft. and Samsung to establish and staff in-store boutiques for their product lines. Best Buy believes that expert and personalized service and the ability to test drive products before buying are crucial drivers of a consumer purchase.

Regarding e-commerce, Best Buy provides a Reserve and Pick Up service. Customers can order a product on the Web and pick it up at the nearest store. Best Buy's own research indicates that 85 percent of its customers do research on its website before coming into a store. Ron Wilson, president of Best Buy in Canada, says, "Customers want to come in to the store to experience the product, especially as product is changing as quickly as it is."

Question:

Should Best Buy be concerned about showrooming, and if so, what other marketing strategies should it consider to combat it?

Adapted from Marina Strauss,"Best Buy bets on bricks-and-mortar," The Globe and Mail, October 24, 2013, p. B4; and Jeff Fraser,"Infographic: Aimia says retailers shouldn't be worry about showrooming,"Marketing, September 13, 2013, www.marketingmag.ca

Effective marketing communications is also essential for a pop-up program. Since the time frame is short, communications is done guerilla style, through e-mail blasts, Twitter, and postings on fashion and design blogs.

Nike operates a more permanent version of a pop-up store. The Nike Runner's Lounge initially started as a temporary location where athletes gathered for a run. There they could get free massages, drinks, and snacks and, more importantly, test-run Nike's line of running shoes. The lounges were successful at engaging consumers with the brand. The Nike lounges have evolved into permanent facilities staffed by Run Leaders who plan out running routes for consumers at home and when they travel. The lounges offer weekly clinics and bring in guest speakers, Nike athletes, and professional experts who provide information and running tips for all levels of runners.[7]

THE RETAILING MARKETING MIX

LO4 Describe the roles and functions of the major components of the retail marketing mix.

IKEA is not a store but rather a cultural phenomenon. While other retailers have to devise marketing strategies to attract shoppers, IKEA has only to plunk itself down in some remote location and its devotees will make pilgrimages to join the throngs of shoppers. The same shoppers complain about IKEA's quality, crowded parking lots, and incomprehensible assembly instructions, yet they have made IKEA one of the most successful retailers on the planet. In 2012 international sales for IKEA were a staggering US$35.5 billion. IKEA operates in 26 countries, and has 298 stores and 139 000 employees.[8]

IKEA's approach to marketing doesn't seem like a winning formula, but buying and assembling its furniture has become a rite of passage for students and young families. There are IKEA fan sites online where enthusiasts—called Tokigs (Swedish for fans)—compare notes, rave about new products, and lobby for IKEA stores in their home communities. "IKEA is dominant in its market and is truly a category killer," says retail analyst Richard Talbot of Talbot Consultants International.[9]

The truth is, IKEA knows its customers and knows how to market. IKEA provides customers with goods of reasonable quality at affordable prices (a good definition of value for many households) and it has revolutionized distribution—one of the most costly components of a retail organization. Its flat-packing technology (everything comes in a flat box ready for assembly) helps save on warehouse, transportation, and retail inventory costs, all of which help lower retail prices.

When devising a marketing strategy, retailers consider numerous elements—all of which have an impact on consumers. The challenge is to select and integrate the right combination of elements, as IKEA has done, that will bring the customers in. The major components of the retailing marketing mix are location, brand identity, atmosphere, merchandise assortment, merchandise control, and marketing communications strategy. Google used pop-up locations in key urban markets, which allowed consumers to experience some of their new technology gadgets. While in the pop-ups consumers could also listen to music, watch videos, and play games. Refer to **Figure 13.11** for an overview.

Location

Many experts suggest that three factors contribute to the success of a retail operation: location, location, and location! Traditional thinking suggests that a good location in a high-traffic area

Figure 13.11
Components of the
Retailing Marketing Mix

Consideration	Concerns
Site Location	Deciding where to locate (e.g., downtown, suburbs, regional shopping mall, power mall)
Brand Identity	Presenting brand banner (logo) in association with other marketing strategies affects consumers' perceptions of store
Atmosphere	Implementing physical characteristics required to create an enjoyable shopping experience (e.g., store layout and design, in-store displays, lighting, open space)
Merchandise Assortment	Determining the breadth and depth of product lines, and the relationship between product lines and stock balance
Merchandise Control	Implementing controls to measure actual performance against planned performance (e.g., analyzing stock turnover)
Marketing Communications	Communicating effectively with consumers to build store image, attract shoppers, and encourage loyalty

gets people into a store. Once they are inside, the quality of the product, the shopping experience, and the service provided will determine whether and how often the customers will return. Consumers today, however, are willing to travel greater distances to obtain better value for their shopping dollars. The popularity of warehouse stores in large cities, outlet malls on major roadways outside of cities, and mega-malls that attract customers from hundreds of kilometres away support the *shopping for value* notion. The ability to buy online from anywhere in the world is another factor that suggests location will be less important in the future. This section outlines the various locations where retailers tend to place themselves.

The **central business district** is normally the hub of retailing activity in the heart of a downtown core (i.e., in the main street and busy cross-streets of a central area). The area usually contains the major financial, cultural, entertainment, and retailing facilities of the city. In Toronto, Bloor Street between Yonge Street and Avenue Road is now considered one of the great shopping locations in the world. It is a street where those with money can find something to spend it on. The Eaton Centre in Toronto, Rideau Centre in Ottawa, and Pacific Centre in Vancouver, all downtown malls, are among the busiest shopping centres in their respective markets. The downtown location is a deterrent for many shoppers, though—the traffic congestion and lack of parking keep them away.

A **suburban mall** is located in a built-up area beyond the core of a city. In Toronto, for example, malls are geographically dispersed. In the east end of the city, there is the Scarborough Town Centre and the west end has Sherway Gardens and the Woodbine Centre. In Ottawa is the Bayshore Shopping Mall in Nepean, a suburb of Ottawa. In Burnaby, British Columbia, there's the Metro Town Centre. These malls draw most of their customers from those who work or live in the immediate area. They are malls for the masses with specialty stores for every interest. Large suburban malls are usually anchored by stores such as The Bay, Target, and Walmart.

A **power centre**, or *power mall*, is a mall that houses a number of superstores in one area. These stores tend to dominate the market they compete in. It is a concept that capitalizes on consumers' expressed interest in shopping in superstores, where value is perceived to be greater. Stores that frequently locate in power malls include Home Depot (household products), Future Shop and Best Buy (consumer electronics), Pet Smart (pet supplies), Moore's (men's wear), Sears Home Furnishings (furniture, appliances, and bedding), Staples Business Depot (business supplies), Chapters (books), and Old Navy (casual clothing). Theatres such as Odeon Cineplex often locate in power malls to help generate (as well as take advantage of) retail traffic.

Outlet malls have become popular in the past decade. An **outlet mall** contains factory outlet stores for well-known manufacturers' brands. One of Canada's newest and largest outlet malls recently opened just west of Toronto. The Toronto Premium Outlet Mall offers consumers the finest international brands in a unique and pleasant outdoor environment. Consumers are drawn to outlet malls for the savings—as much as 25 percent to 65 percent off retail prices. Stores in the Premium Outlet Mall include Adidas, Calvin Klein, Columbia Sportswear, Hugo Boss, J. Crew, Lacoste, Nike, Oakley Vault, and Tommy Hilfiger, among many others. Refer to the image in **Figure 13.12**.

The West Edmonton Mall, one of the world's largest indoor malls, is an example of a **mega-mall**. The mall has an area equivalent to 115 football fields and includes more than 800 stores and services, 110 eating establishments, and 5 amusement areas, including a wave pool and rides for children, a hockey rink, and many other attractions.

Just north of Toronto in the sprawling community of Vaughan is the Vaughan Mills mega-mall. Vaughan Mills combines the regional mall concept with the outlet mall concept. More than half

central business district Normally, the hub of retailing activity in the heart of a downtown core (i.e., the main street and busy cross-streets in a centralized area).

suburban mall Located in built-up areas beyond the core of a city.

power centre (power mall) A mall that houses a number of category-killer superstores in one confined area.

outlet mall Contains factory outlet stores for well-known brands; usually located at a key intersection of a major highway.

mega-mall A destination mall characterized by its incredibly large size and diversity of stores and services; it includes amusements and other attractions to entertain shoppers.

Figure 13.12 Outlet malls offer international brands at much lower prices than traditional retail stores.

Figure 13.13   Lifestyle malls are often described as "outdoor urban villages."

of the stores are outlet versions of the regular retailers mentioned above, while another quarter of the stores are value-priced retailers such as Winners, Designer Depot, Payless, and H&M. The mall also features a bowling-alley-cum-nightclub with a restaurant and art gallery, a go-kart theme park, and other entertainment venues. Almost 8 million people, or 60 percent of Ontario's population, live within 100 kilometres of Vaughan Mills.

Faced with rising costs and waning interest in large, traditional enclosed malls, developers are now experimenting with a lifestyle mall concept. The **lifestyle mall** is a smaller, open-air shopping centre featuring clusters of upscale stores, each with its own entrance onto the main street of the centre along with offices and residential units. The first lifestyle mall in Canada, the Village at Park Royal, opened in Vancouver in 2005. The Village at Park Royal features old-fashioned gas lamps and West Coast-style architecture. Lifestyle malls are about the experience; they offer a back-to-the-community kind of feel.

Other lifestyle malls in Canada include Dartmouth Crossing in Dartmouth, Nova Scotia, Deerfoot Meadows in Calgary, Alberta, and the Shops at Don Mills in Toronto, Ontario, which describes itself as an "outdoor urban village." Refer to the image in **Figure 13.13**. The typical lifestyle-mall shopper is middle-aged (45 to 55 years old) and more affluent (mid- to upper-income level) than the regional-mall shopper. They are well-to-do consumers with money to spend—an attractive target for upscale retailers.

A **strip mall** is usually a small cluster of stores that serve the convenience needs of residents in the immediate area. Such a shopping district is generally composed of a supermarket, a drugstore, a variety store, a dry cleaner, a bank, a hair stylist, and other similar service operations.

A **freestanding store** is an isolated store usually located on a busy street or highway. The nature of the business often influences the location of such a store. Consumers will travel beyond their immediate areas for the products and services these stores provide. As mentioned earlier in this section, shoppers will travel great distances to shop at IKEA, outlets of which may be built far from an urban centre.

Many of the retailers that customarily used freestanding stores have adapted to trends and built new, bigger stores in power malls. Stores such as Rona, Home Depot, and Staples Business Depot have moved in this direction. More recently, these stores and many of their competitors are moving into downtown locations with smaller stores. These stores are designed to meet the different needs of downtown residents, many of whom live in apartments and condominiums. For more insight into this size and location strategy read the Think Marketing box **Big Retailers Are Going Smaller and Downtown**.

With regard to location, research data indicate that people are shopping at traditional-style malls less frequently than they used to. Time-pressed and tired of fighting traffic, consumers are visiting stores that offer convenience, efficient service, and a better overall shopping experience. In that regard, stores located in power malls and destination stores such as Home Depot and IKEA are winning the battle.

lifestyle mall A smaller, open-air shopping centre featuring clusters of 20 to 30 upscale stores, each with its own entrance onto the main street of the centre along with offices and residential units.

strip mall A collection of stores attached together in a neighbourhood plaza.

freestanding store An isolated store usually located on a busy street or highway.

ThinkMarketing

Big Retailers Are Going Smaller and Downtown

A fundamental principle of marketing revolves around how quickly an organization reacts to changes in the market-place. Several changes are causing a return to downtown for many big box retailers. First, consumers are changing their shopping behaviour. They want to buy things closer to home or they want it easy to pick up on the way home. Second, condominium developments in cities like Toronto and Vancouver have brought thousands of people back downtown. Empty nesters who have grown tired of suburban living have returned to the core of big cities. Finally, the ethnic diversity of cities continues to grow.

Most of the condominium developments include substantial retail space on the ground floor. Given the trends, the big-box retailers such as Walmart, Costco, Canadian Tire, Michael's, Winners, and Best Buy, who have maximized the potential of their suburban locations, are opening smaller stores downtown. The first downtown Costco actually opened in 2006. Canadian Tire has a store in the Ryerson University School of Business complex right in the heart of Toronto.

In another Toronto location, Canadian Tire went very small. The company recently opened a 6100 square foot Canadian Tire Express store. An average Canadian Tire store is 35 000 square feet. The Express store carries merchandise suited to the needs of local residents and it also serves as a pickup location for goods ordered online at the Canadian Tire website. Downtown stores are becoming attractive and lucrative. Retailers can sell fewer items more profitably as consumers weigh price against convenience. In contrast, the bigger suburban stores aren't as profitable as they once were. In the big stores, sales revenue per square foot is declining and that is a key measure of a retailer's success.

Walmart is also pursuing opportunities in the downtown core. While it continues to build huge superstores, the company realizes that big cities like Toronto, Vancouver,

Dave Bottoms, Lazy Photographer

Calgary, and Montreal offer significant growth potential. Further, Walmart respects the ethnic diversity of these cities and sees nothing but opportunity for smaller stores designed with local needs in mind.

Walmart recently opened a small-box store in Ceder-brea Mall in Scarborough (a suburb of Toronto). The store is about half the size of a typical Walmart. The immediate area is predominantly high-rise apartments, richly multicultural, hard-working, and blue collar. Residents are heavy users of public transit and have an average household income of $40 000. These people aren't looking for lawn-mowers, patio furniture, and barbecues. Walmart adjusted the product mix accordingly with the grocery section being the area of the store where the individuality of communities is noticed the most.

Question:

Will big retailers continue to open stores in downtown areas of big cities? Are smaller urban stores in conflict with a store's overall marketing strategy?

Adapted from Francine Kopun, "Canadian Tire downsizes on the Danforth," Toronto Star, July 26, 2013, www.thestar.com; and Leanne Delap, "Small-box Walmarts tailored to urban cores," The Globe and Mail, November 13, 2012, p. B15.

Brand Identity

In today's marketplace, a retailer must think more like a brand marketer. Effective branding strategies will influence perceptions that consumers hold of a retailer. To demonstrate, Harry Rosen is not just another men's wear retailer. Successful marketing strategies have separated Harry Rosen from its competitors. The Harry Rosen brand name suggests such attributes as quality, reputation, contemporary fashion, and

Courtesy of Harry Rosen Inc.

Figure 13.14   Harry Rosen's brand image is the retailer's most important asset.

personalized service. The brand identity that Harry Rosen created is the retailer's most valuable asset. Refer to the image in **Figure 13.14**.

The brand name and how it is presented to consumers is the one visual element that, without exception, must be consistently applied to all packaging, advertising, and marketing communications—a strategy employed by Canadian Tire. Canadian Tire is the busiest retailer in Canada. About 85 percent of all Canadians live within a 15-minute drive of a Canadian Tire store; nine out of ten adult Canadians shop there at least twice a year, and 40 percent of Canadians shop at Canadian Tire every week.[10]

Its popularity can be directly linked to its brand identity, an identity created by effective marketing—the familiar red triangle logo appears on all touch points, the red aisle signs appear in creative television ads, the weekly store flyer promoting sale items generates store traffic, and stores are designed attractively to maximize the use of space and make the shopping experience more inspiring.

Atmosphere

atmosphere The physical characteristics of a retail store or group of stores that are used to develop an image and attract customers.

In retailing, **atmosphere** refers to the physical characteristics of a retail store or a group of stores that are used to develop an image and attract customers. Once the consumer is in the store, the shopping experience should be a pleasant one. The image of a store has an impact on the type of customer who shops there, so retailers give their stores an appearance that will attract the sort of patrons they want. Image is created by a combination of elements: exterior appearance, interior appearance, the layout of the store, and interior merchandising and display practices.

Retailers use different strategies to improve the in-store experience for shoppers. Some retailers use a minimalist design concept. *Minimalism* refers to a very simple yet rigidly aesthetic design technique and a devotion to that aesthetic as a lifestyle principle. The minimalist approach cuts away the clutter and lets the merchandise speak for itself. Apple uses the minimalist approach. Its stores are column free and purposely designed to improve product visibility and flow of traffic. Products are displayed so that consumers can test them—a true experience before they decide to buy. The Apple Store isn't so much a shopping experience as it is a total immersive experience.[11]

Electronics retailers have integrated *demonstration centres* into their store designs. With technology becoming more sophisticated, some retailers are showing shoppers how everything works right on the retail floor. Sony, for example, discovered that many of its customers bought expensive equipment but never used all the features the products offered. The company re-engineered its stores to be more "solution-oriented." Consumers can experiment with the equipment to get more comfortable with it.

Lowe's, a competitor in the home improvement store market, tweaked its store formula to compete better with rivals such as Home Depot and Canadian Tire. From consumer insights gained through research, Lowe's decided to focus on some things its competitors weren't doing well. Contractors complained it took too long to find products and female shoppers complained about unreachable product displays. Lowes responded by moving all contractor products into a dedicated section of the store. For female shoppers, items such as faucets, kitchen cabinets and counters, and appliances were moved into a "fashion alley." All products are displayed at eye level. Lowe's also added a power aisle near the store entrance that houses special offers to encourage impulse purchasing.[12]

Separate in-store boutiques (also referred to as a *shop-in-shop*) are another means of improving the shopping experience. A **boutique** is a store-within-a-store, a scaled-down version of a freestanding store within a larger department store. Fashion boutiques for clothing lines such as Ralph Lauren, Tommy Hilfiger, and Nautica are found in The Bay and other department stores. See **Figure 13.15** for an illustration of an in-store boutique.

Samsung has partnered with Best Buy to occupy space in its big-box stores. Facing intense competition from online suppliers of electronics products, Best Buy sees the partnership as a unique way of offering a better in-store shopping experience. The Samsung-operated boutiques will carry mobile devices, cameras and accessories, and televisions. Samsung will train all of the workers employed in the boutique—a strategy that should give it competitive advantage over other brands. Shoppers can pay for products in the boutique, thus avoiding lines at the checkout counter. Best Buy believes

boutique (shop-in-shop) A store-within-a-store concept (e.g., designer-label boutiques in large department stores).

Figure 13.15
In-store boutiques figure prominently in major department stores.

THE CANADIAN PRESS IMAGES/Graham Hughes

this arrangement gives stronger focus to better-selling products and strengthens relationships with its suppliers. Other in-store boutiques will follow.[13]

Merchandise Assortment

merchandise assortment The total variety of products a retailer carries.

Merchandise assortment refers to the product mix; it is the total assortment of products a retailer carries. To ensure that an adequate supply of goods is available to meet customer demand, retailers take into account three merchandising components: breadth and depth of selection, assortment consistency, and stock balance.

breadth of selection The number of goods classifications a store carries.

The **breadth of selection** concerns the number of goods classifications a store carries. For example, a department store carries fashion apparel, furniture, appliances, toys, sporting goods, home furnishings, linens, dry goods, and many more sorts of goods. A drugstore stocks cough and cold remedies, personal-care products, cosmetics, confectionery goods, selected food items, and a mixture of general merchandise.

depth of selection The number of brands and styles carried by a store in each product classification.

The **depth of selection** is the number of brands and styles carried within each classification. For example, a drugstore sells numerous brands of toothpaste in a variety of sizes and flavours. The type of retailer an operation is (e.g., department store, specialty store, convenience store) and the needs of the customers it serves determine the breadth and depth of product assortment.

assortment consistency Product lines that can be used in conjunction with one another or that all relate to the same sorts of activities and needs.

Assortment consistency refers to product lines that can be used in conjunction with one another or that relate to the same sorts of activities and needs. An example of such consistency is a store such as Sport Chek, which carries various lines of sporting goods—baseball, hockey, basketball, and running, for example—as well as clothing and accessories to complement these sports.

scrambled merchandising The addition, in retailing, of unrelated products and product lines to original products.

Some retailers adopt a strategy of assortment inconsistency. Called **scrambled merchandising**, it arises when a retailer begins to carry products and product lines that seem unrelated to the products it already carries. As indicated earlier in the chapter, many large retailers are adding unrelated lines to compete better with Walmart. Loblaws added clothing, for example, and Shoppers Drug Mart added food.

stock balance The practice of maintaining an adequate assortment of goods that will attract customers while keeping inventories of both high-demand and low-demand goods at reasonable levels.

Stock balance is the practice of maintaining an adequate assortment of goods that will attract customers while keeping inventories of both high-demand and low-demand goods at reasonable levels. This is not an easy task, but such factors as profit margin, inventory costs, and stock turnover have a direct impact on cash flow and profitability. In addition, the retailer must know the market and tailor the product mix accordingly. Thus, decisions are made regarding what assortment of name brands and private-label brands to stock, what variety of price ranges to offer, and what mix of traditional (established) products and innovative (new) products to carry.

Video: Abercrombie and Fitch Under Fire "Exclusionary" Tactics

Merchandise Control

There is a direct link between merchandise planning and merchandise control. The best of plans can go awry if proper controls are not implemented to measure the relationship between actual performance and planned performance. The concept of inventory turn or inventory turnover is a key measure of retail control. **Inventory turn** is the number of times during a specific time period that the average inventory is sold. The period for calculating inventory turn is usually one year. Inventory turn is calculated by dividing retail sales at cost (the value of the inventory) by the average inventory. Therefore, if sales at cost were $100 000 and the average inventory was $20 000, the inventory turn would be 5 ($100 000 divided by $20 000). If a retailer determined that this was a poor inventory turn rate, new marketing strategies would be considered to try to improve the situation.

inventory turn The number of times during a specific time period that the average inventory is sold.

Knowing the inventory turn rate allows the retailer to plan inventory (i.e., to match supply with demand) effectively. It also enables the retailer to compare the current turnover with past turnovers, to compare one department to another, and to compare the turnover (performance) of different stores in a chain operation. Inventory turn is a guideline for planning. In large retailing organizations, where advanced information technology is the norm, much of the mystery has been removed from inventory control and the balance of supply and demand. Electronic point-of-sale equipment triggers the entire reordering system.

MARKETING COMMUNICATIONS STRATEGY

LO5 Describe retailing's transition into the digital marketing environment.

Survival today depends on the retailer's ability to build brand loyalty, because consumers are suffering from "time starvation" and are shopping at fewer stores. Further, consumers are thinking of stores the way they do brands, so it follows that stores to which they are extremely loyal will succeed and stores for which they feel little loyalty will fail.

In response to this trend, Canadian Tire's philosophy is to "think like a brand, act like a retailer." Canadian Tire is therefore building bigger and better stores that provide consumers with a pleasant shopping experience, adding new product lines and employing creative advertising campaigns to build its image. Canadian Tire is also one of Canada's largest retail advertisers, with expenditures in television (its presence on *Hockey Night in Canada* is almost institutional), newspaper flyers, and online communications. In spite of the shift to digital communications, Canadian Tire customers openly welcome the weekly sale flyer into their homes. Refer to the image in **Figure 13.16**.

Figure 13.16 Marketing communications is an essential part of Canadian Tire's marketing strategy. The weekly sale flyer plays a key role.

shopper marketing
Understanding how consumers behave as shoppers in all channels (retail, catalogue, and web) and then targeting those channels with appropriate marketing communications to enhance sales.

The customer's shopping experience is increasingly becoming just as important as the products a customer actually buys. Consequently, retailers are becoming more sophisticated in how they look at their entire business. A new practice called *shopper marketing* is taking hold. **Shopper marketing** involves understanding how consumers behave as shoppers in all channels (retail, catalogue, and web) and then targeting those channels with appropriate marketing communications to enhance sales. In the context of retail stores, such communication is vital since some 70 percent of all purchase decisions are made right in the store.

Good shopper marketing programs are the result of partnerships between a supplier and the retailer. The Best Buy/Samsung example cited in the previous section is a good example of how partnerships can benefit both retailer and supplier. These partnerships answer the higher expectations of busy shoppers—essentially the customer experience is a new medium—a medium that offers information, demonstration, and transaction.

A successful shopper marketing campaign relies upon collaboration between the retailer and a supplier. Walmart and Procter & Gamble collaborated on a program of "preparedness" to maximize the sales of the Vicks family of products. Well in advance of the cold season, shoppers were encouraged to stock up on Vicks when they were in Walmart. Product displays and point-of-purchase materials brought attention to the program, and coupons encouraged consumers to buy right away. The campaign ran for several years and Walmart reported sales increases for Vicks products in the +30 percent range.[14]

Media advertising always plays a role in building a retailer's image. It is quite common for large retailers to employ a media mix to encourage customers to visit their stores. Television is effective for positioning the brand and building image, while print media are good for announcing sales (e.g., the weekly flyers so common among grocery stores, hardware stores, and mass merchandise stores). Wise retailers are moving toward direct communications strategies. The rationale for such a move is clear: retaining current customers and securing more purchases from them is much cheaper than trying to attract new customers through the mass media.

As in so many other areas, retailers must examine how they allocate their marketing budgets and how they communicate with their customers. The migration to online communications and web-based buying is happening faster than many retailers think. Refer to the email illustration in **Figure 13.17**.

E-Retailing

When demographic factors such as Canada's cultural diversity and changing family dynamics are considered, there are more reasons for Canadian retailers to be online. Further, Canada has one of the highest Internet penetration rates in the world. That said, Canadians are among the least likely consumers to shop online. A recent study (2013) indicates that 22 percent of Canadians "never buy anything online." Canadian consumers have yet to fully embrace online shopping at the levels of consumers in the United Kingdom, Germany, and the United States. The shopping study confirmed that Canadians still like to look for deals and discounts offline in their weekly flyers.[15] Such data tends to confuse retail decision makers. Should they be aggressive or conservative with their e-commerce activities?

The growing presence of U.S. retailers eyeing expansion into Canada—Target and Nordstrom being the largest among them—could accelerate e-commerce growth in Canada. U.S.-based retailers that operate stores in Canada offer consumers greater product selection, an occurrence that will be extended to their online stores. Canadian retailers must realize that technology cannot be denied. Their future success will depend upon how well they combine offline retailing with online retailing. Despite the conflicting data cited above, smart retailers are moving online. The investment they make now (short-term pain) will pay off in the future (long-term gain).

Retailers that are online have overcome some entry barriers. For example, they have taken advantage of different delivery solutions (e.g., outsourcing delivery to experts

Figure 13.17
Email communications
encourage current
customers to take
advantage of new offers.

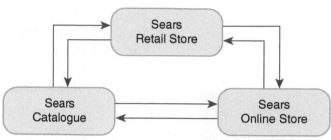

Figure 13.18   Sears operates a hybrid marketing system that requires careful coordination between various marketing channels.

Video: Warby Parker: Vision and Mission

such as UPS and FedEx), adapted their product mix (offering only those products that are suited to online transactions), and simply embraced the new way that customers want to shop. The convenience of online shopping compared to the hassle of finding parking at a busy suburban mall attracts time-pressed consumers to retailers with e-commerce capability.

An online presence offers retailers several advantages. First, it enhances their ability to reach new customers. Second, there is better coordination with their suppliers and partners in the channels of distribution (the concept of supply chain management presented in Chapter 12). Third, the Internet provides an opportunity to solidify relationships with existing customers (the concept of customer relationship management that was presented earlier in the textbook). A good e-commerce website not only will sell goods but also collect valuable information about customers and their buying behaviour—information that can be utilized for improving overall retail marketing strategies.

The transition to electronic retailing has been relatively easy for Sears. Sears was an established catalogue retailer, so an operational infrastructure that included an automated warehouse and distribution system facilitated the transition to online retailing. Sears.ca is consistently one of the top sites in Canada for online traffic. Sears operates a hybrid marketing system that involves several different channels of distribution to target different market segments. Refer to the visual illustration in **Figure 13.18**. The hybrid system offers Sears two key benefits: it allows for better market coverage and it will lower costs, assuming the operations (as in the transfer of information) across all selling channels are coordinated.

Sears' objective with its e-commerce venture is to attract a younger audience—an audience whose members have abandoned department stores but are prime Internet shoppers. Ultimately, the goal is to offer much more product selection than it offers in stores or the catalogue. Thus far, profit margins have been good on e-commerce sales. Rather than Sears carrying the inventory, the suppliers hold onto the goods until they are purchased, at which time they are shipped directly to customers.[16]

Future Shop executives firmly believe a bricks-and-mortar presence helps customers feel more comfortable with online buying. If something goes wrong in cyberspace there is a physical store that people can go to. They also believe that an online presence helps facilitate more in-store purchases. People do their research online and then visit a store to actually buy the product. As discussed elsewhere in this chapter, however, other retailers believe that shoppers visit stores first to examine the product, then go online to buy the product from the cheapest source. No matter how you look at the situation, it seems apparent that retailer must offer a combination of physical stores and online retail to satisfy the needs and behaviour of modern shoppers.

✔ **Experience**Marketing

In order to experience marketing you have to assess situations and make recommendations to change marketing strategies when necessary. What would you do in the following situation?

There was a time when Second Cup was the undisputed leader in the retail specialty coffee market. In 1990 Second Cup operated 160 stores coast to coast. Over the past twenty years things have changed drastically. In Canada, Starbucks is the undisputed leader in the $1 billion a year premium café field. Starbucks now operates 1070 outlets in Canada compared to only 340 for Second Cup.

Second Cup has been languishing in a market that has virtually exploded over the past ten years. Starbucks leads by a wide margin, largely based on its strong brand image and popularity across age groups. Starbucks offers the ambience and convenience that customers are looking for. McDonald's is aggressively pursuing coffee customers with its upgraded coffee offerings. Presently, McDonald's now accounts for 10 percent of coffee sales in fast-food restaurants. That figure is making all competitors squirm a bit! Week-long free coffee promotions played a role in getting people to try their coffee.

Sales at Second Cup are flat. Over a four-year period from 2009 to 2012 sales revenue increased from $191.0 million to $193.5 million, an average annual growth rate of only 0.6 percent. Starbucks' Canadian sales are in the $600 million range and they hold a 60 percent market share.

The Second Cup store design could be more alluring. There was a time when shops were a bit quirky—they were customized to the neighbourhood where they were located. As the company grew the atmosphere of the outlets went more corporate—a consistent look was easier to control.

Right now Second Cup offers 24 varieties of coffee every day. The coffee is good but there aren't enough customers drinking it. Just recently, the company expanded its tea offerings, as many consumers are moving in that direction. A light menu of food items (dessert-oriented) is also available.

Growth is the immediate expectation for Second Cup. New marketing strategies are urgently needed. The company is wrestling with several issues. What product lines should Second Cup concentrate on? Should they be looking at new types of locations? Do they need a new advertising campaign? How can Second Cup differentiate itself from competitors?

Your challenge is to conduct some research on the restaurant coffee market and develop a new marketing strategy that will stimulate growth. What recommendations will you offer?

CHAPTER SUMMARY

L01 Explain the importance of retailing in Canada and identify key trends influencing the industry. *(pp. 271–272)*

Retailing is an important industry in the Canadian economy. It comprises 6.2 percent of the gross domestic product and generates up to $450 billion in annual revenue. The industry accounts for 12 percent of Canada's workforce. The environment of retailing is constantly changing.

There are several key trends that are affecting the industry. Changes in consumer behaviour, such as the shift to online buying, are forcing retailers to combine offline strategies with new online strategies. Price- and value-conscious consumers that have shifted their allegiance to discounters like Walmart and Target are forcing mid-market retailers to re-evaluate their pricing strategies in order to survive. The arrival of more large American retailers is placing added pressure on Canadian retailers.

Advancing technology is another key trend that retailers are responding to. The gradual shift to online buying is directly affecting business in bricks-and-mortar stores. If a retailer is not presently online, they will be in the future. Online buying only accounts for about 5 percent of retail sales presently, but that figure will increase to more significant levels in the next few years.

L02 Define the functions associated with contemporary retailing. *(pp. 272–273)*

This chapter introduces the key elements of retailing activities. Retailing is the activity involved in selling goods and services to final consumers. The primary functions of a retailer are to provide an assortment of goods that consumers need, market goods through effective pricing, engage in marketing communications, use in-store merchandising strategies, provide a means to conduct a transaction, and offer e-commerce capabilities that are in tune with today's consumer expectations.

L03 Describe the various types of retailers based on ownership, products and services offered, and method of operation. *(pp. 273–279)*

Many types of retail operations exist in Canada, and the businesses fall into various classifications. When retailers are classified based on ownership, stores are categorized as retail chain stores, franchised chain stores, and independent stores. When classified according to products and services offered, there are specialty stores, limited-line stores, warehouse outlets, and general merchandise stores. In terms of services provided, there are full-serve stores, limited-serve stores, and self-serve stores. Non-store retailing is an alternative for selling goods. This category of retail operations includes vending machines, direct selling, catalogue marketing, temporary displays and kiosks, pop-up stores, and online retailing.

LO4 Describe the roles and functions of the major components of the retail marketing mix. *(pp. 280–286)*

The key components of the retail marketing mix include selecting a good location, building a brand identity that resonates with targeted consumers, creating an atmosphere conducive to a pleasant shopping experience, carrying an appropriate selection of merchandise, offering appropriate services, and communicating with customers in a meaningful manner. The marketing manager must assess all of these variables and devise marketing strategies that will encourage store traffic, build sales, and ultimately form a strong relationship with customers.

LO5 Describe retailing's transition into the digital marketing environment. *(pp. 287–290)*

The shift to digital retailing in Canada has been slower than expected. Conflicting research regarding how many Canadians

buy online and how frequently they do so has created some confusion among retailers. Consumers' acceptance of online buying in Canada has been much slower than other countries. That said, a good many Canadians buy online and there will be significantly more in the future so retailers must be ready.

The emerging trends described earlier, combined with the growth of large-format warehouse outlets and big-box stores located in power malls, creates challenges and opportunities for retailers. Traditional retailers must adapt to the changes or suffer the consequences. Having e-commerce capabilities is now an essential component of a retailer's operation. Those retailers that have moved online see many benefits. It enhances their ability to reach new customers, it provides for better coordination with suppliers in the channel of distribution, and it provides an opportunity to solidify relationships with existing customers.

The concept of showrooming (people visiting stores to view a product and then searching online for the cheapest source) is reason enough for a retailer to be online. Time-pressed and tech-savvy consumers appreciate the convenience of online buying and the delivery of goods directly to their households. As cited in the chapter, retailers such as Sears, Canadian Tire, and Future Shop have migrated to digital marketing smoothly and are seeing the financial benefits of that investment.

MyMarketingLab   Study, practise, and explore real marketing situations with these helpful resources:
- **Interactive Lesson Presentations:** Work through interactive presentations and assessments to test your knowledge of marketing concepts.
- **Study Plan:** Check your understanding of chapter concepts with self-study quizzes.
- **Dynamic Study Modules:** Work through adaptive study modules on your computer, tablet, or mobile device.
- **Simulations:** Practise decision-making in simulated marketing environments.

REVIEW QUESTIONS

1. What are the key external trends influencing retail marketing strategy today? Briefly explain. (*LO1*)
2. What are the basic functions of a retailer? (*LO2*)
3. By ownership, what are the various classifications of retail stores? Briefly explain each classification. (*LO3*)
4. In the context of retail franchising, what does co-branding refer to? (*LO3*)
5. Based on products and services offered, what are the various types of stores? Briefly describe each type of store. (*LO3*)
6. Identify and briefly explain the various forms of non-store retailing. (*LO3*)
7. What are the location alternatives for a retailer? Briefly describe each alternative. (*LO4*)

8. How important is brand identity in the retail marketing mix? Briefly explain. (*LO4*)
9. How important is atmosphere in the retail marketing mix? Briefly explain. (*LO4*)
10. Briefly explain the concept of a merchandise assortment. (*LO4*)
11. What is scrambled merchandising? (*LO4*)
12. How important is inventory turnover to a retailer? Briefly explain. (*LO4*)
13. What benefits can a retailer gain by shifting some of its business operations into the digital environment? (*LO5*)
14. What is showrooming? Briefly explain. (*LO5*)

DISCUSSION AND APPLICATION QUESTIONS

1. Visit a department store in your local market, then present a brief analysis of your perception of the store's image as conveyed by the atmosphere considerations discussed in this chapter. Do the same analysis for a warehouse outlet.
2. Considering the trends in retailing that were presented in this chapter, what is your assessment of the future direction of retailing? For example, will consumers opt for convenience and flock to the Internet, or will they retreat to neighbourhood

shops and lifestyle malls, where personalized service is more important? What is your opinion?
3. This chapter suggests that location is a crucial aspect of retail marketing planning. Based on your awareness and understanding of recent retailing trends, will location continue to be as important in the future? Evaluate the trends along with changes in consumers' shopping behaviour to formulate a position on this issue.

14

Integrated Marketing Communications and Emerging Media Platforms

Hand-out/LABATT BREWERIES OF CANADA/Newscom

LEARNING OBJECTIVES

LO1 Define integrated marketing communications and describe the components of the integrated marketing communications mix. (pp. 294–295)

LO2 Describe the basic elements that comprise marketing communications planning. (pp. 295–297)

LO3 Explain the nature of creative (message) decisions that are part of an advertising campaign. (pp. 297–301)

LO4 Explain the nature of media decisions that are part of an advertising campaign. (pp. 301–304)

LO5 Assess various media alternatives for delivering messages. (pp. 304–309)

LO6 Describe the role of social media in marketing communications campaigns. (pp. 309–314)

LO7 Describe the role of mobile communications in marketing communications campaigns. (pp. 314–317)

BUDWEISER'S RED LIGHT CAMPAIGN...

created a stir among hockey fans coast to coast in Canada. Budweiser executives were scratching their heads figuring out what to do when the 2013 shortened NHL season began. Fans, players, and advertisers had been on the sidelines for so long, something exciting had to happen to get things going.

Kyle Norrington, marketing director at Labatt, put it this way: "How could we continue to elevate the game and deepen the fans' emotional connection to hockey and to the Budweiser brand?"[1] They determined that a goal was the most exciting thing in hockey, but how could they capitalize on that excitement?

The answer to that question was in every hockey rink. When a goal is scored the red light goes on—Budweiser would use red lights across Canada to signal goals as they happened. Budweiser had to develop the WiFi-enabled die-cast aluminum light. These were lights that people would actually buy at $149 each and they would go off every time that fan's favourite team scored a goal. Once the availability of the lights was announced, they sold out quickly!

The campaign initially launched with a spot on the Super Bowl and was extended to include print and social media content and commercials on CBC's *Hockey Night in Canada*. Budweiser sponsors Don Cherry's Coach's Corner segment and Don wore a suit jacket imprinted with the Budweiser Red Light.

This unique campaign was a success—60 percent advertising awareness was achieved, visits to the Budweiser.ca website increased from 13 000 a month to 451 000, and on Facebook fan interest increased by 15 percent. More to the point, weekly beer consumption increased 17 percent during the months of February and March—Budweiser's rally connected with hockey fans!

Marketing communications strategies are an important component of the marketing mix. That's what this chapter and the next chapter are about.

THE INTEGRATED MARKETING COMMUNICATIONS MIX

LO1 Define integrated marketing communications and describe the components of the integrated marketing communications mix.

integrated marketing communications (IMC) The coordination of various forms of marketing communications into a unified program that maximizes impact on the intended target audience.

Integrated marketing communications (IMC) involves the coordination of appropriate forms of marketing communication into a unified program that maximizes the impact on the intended target audience. It embraces many unique yet complementary forms of communication: media advertising, social media communications, mobile media communications, sales promotion, public relations, experiential marketing, and personal selling. Refer to **Figure 14.1** for a visual illustration of integrated marketing communications. This chapter will focus on media advertising and interactive media communications (social media, mobile communications, and video games).

Different situations require different marketing communications solutions. Rarely are all components used at the same time. Instead, they are selected based on the situation at hand: the manager considers the nature of the problem, the objectives to be achieved, the target market profile, and the size of the budget when making communications decisions.

In the past, media advertising was the driving force behind a marketing communications strategy, particularly when marketers were launching new products. In a rapidly changing external environment where consumers are taking charge of brand messages, marketers now allocate a greater portion of their advertising budgets to social media. The potential buzz that consumers can create for a brand through word-of-mouth communications within their social network makes this investment worthwhile.

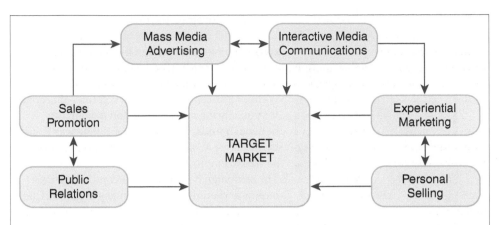

Figure 14.1
Integrated Marketing
Communications Mix

A marketing communications plan may use some or all of the components of the marketing communications mix. The components work in unison to have greater impact on the target market.

Media advertising includes television, radio, newspaper, magazine, out-of-home, direct response, and the Internet.

Interactive media communications embrace social media networks, mobile networks, mobile communications, and video games.

How people consume media is another factor that influences marketing communications decisions. Consumers today are less reliant on traditional media (television, radio, newspaper, and magazines) and more reliant on digital communications (Internet, social media, and mobile communications) for receiving content and commercial messages. As well, people are multi-screening, a behaviour in which two screens are viewed at one time. A study conducted by Google Canada revealed that 51 percent of respondents always have their smartphone or tablet with them when watching television.[2] Consequently, marketers must evaluate different media choices in order to reach their target market effectively.

MARKETING COMMUNICATIONS PLANNING

L02 Describe the basic elements that comprise marketing communications planning.

Marketing communications planning is the process of making systematic decisions regarding which elements of the communications mix to use in marketing communications. Based on the plan's objectives and the target market the message must reach, appropriate components of the marketing communications mix are selected. The key elements of a marketing communications plan are usually included in a brand's marketing plan.

marketing communications planning The process of making systematic decisions regarding which elements of the communications mix to use in marketing communications.

Marketing Communications Objectives

Like other elements of the marketing mix, communications activity must complement the total marketing effort. Thus, each element of the mix is assigned a goal on the basis of what it is capable of contributing to the overall plan. Some typical marketing communications objectives might be the following:

- To create, maintain, or build brand awareness
- To position or reposition the perception of a product in the customer's mind
- To stimulate trial purchase of a product
- To defuse a potentially damaging situation

The list could be longer, but the point is that certain types of marketing communications are better than others at achieving certain objectives. Determining which components to use depends on factors such as the target market, the competitive environment a brand operates in, and the budget available for the challenge.

Ultima Foods

Figure 14.2   A well-planned media campaign crated significant brand awareness for IÖGO in a short period.

Visa Canada

Figure 14.3   Visa Canada's campaign is designed to encourage consumers to use their card more frequently.

To demonstrate the purpose of objectives and their impact on communications decisions, consider a recent campaign by Ultima Foods. The company launched a new yogurt brand called IÖGO. It is a unique brand that is gelatin-free and without artificial flavours and colours—it is good for you! Facing stiff competition from many national brands, the primary objective was to create brand-name awareness. The quickest means to do so was to employ a combination of mass media. The campaign began with 5-second television teasers and outdoor posters in key markets. Their intent was to invoke curiosity among consumers. That was followed by 30-second TV spots, print ads, home takeovers on the Web, bus shelter ads, and subway posters. The word *iögomania* was used in social media to describe the intensity of the blitz campaign. Within three months of launch IÖGO achieved 74 percent awareness and 9.6 percent market share—a clear indication that well-planned advertising works![3] Refer to the image in **Figure 14.2**.

Visa is a well-known credit card brand—it doesn't need to create awareness. Visa launched a campaign recently where the primary objective was to encourage card owners to increase the frequency of use of the card, particularly for smaller purchases. Visa generates its revenue based on the number of transactions made on cards. Therefore, using cards more frequently is the key to growth. An initial wave of media advertising teased consumers by simply asking, "Do you smallenfreuden?"[4] A combination of television, print, and outdoor advertising was used to deliver the message. Refer to the image in **Figure 14.3**.

Marketing Communications Strategy

While objectives state what is to be accomplished, strategy describes how it is to be accomplished. Strategic decisions are made regarding which component of the marketing communications mix to employ. For example, television advertising may be essential for creating awareness, sales promotion essential for encouraging trial purchases, and social media and public relations essential for creating some buzz among the target audience. Then a total budget is determined and funds are allocated across the various activities.

Some forms of marketing communications are effective at reaching consumers who react to the message and pull the product through the channel of distribution. The use of mass media options such as broadcast and print media advertising are frequently used in a **pull strategy**. Some other marketing communications are effective at reaching distributors (e.g., Shoppers Drug Mart or Rexall Drugs) who in turn help market the product on behalf of the manufacturer—in effect, these activities push the product through the channel of distribution. Trade promotion incentives in the form of financial incentives offered to distributors are frequently employed in a **push strategy**. Refer to **Figure 14.4** for a visual image of pull and push strategies.

A marketing communications strategy also involves budget decisions: how much to spend and how to allocate the funds across various activities. Some methods of

Video: OXO: Advertising and Public Relations

pull strategy Creating demand by directing promotional efforts at consumers or final users of a product, who, in turn, put pressure on retailers to carry it.

push strategy Creating demand for a product by directing promotional efforts at middlemen, who, in turn, promote the product among consumers.

determining a budget estimate sales first and then base the budget on sales. Other methods develop the budget first; these methods presuppose that marketing communications are an effective means of achieving sales and marketing objectives. Regardless of the method used, the budget must be carefully calculated and rationalized by the manager responsible for it so that the activities can be implemented as recommended. Refer to **Figure 14.5** for a summary of the various budgeting methods.

When devising a marketing communications budget the manager analyzes several factors, each of which has an impact on the amount of funds required. Those factors include the characteristics and behaviour of the target they are trying to reach, the degree of competition in the market and how much competitors are spending on communications, and the stage of the product in the product life cycle. As you have already learned, budgets are much higher in the introduction and growth stages of the product life cycle.

Pull
- Activity is directed at consumers, who, in turn, request the product from distributors, and pull the product through the channel

| Manufacturer | Wholesaler | Retailer | Consumer |

Push
- Activity is directed at distributors, who resell the product and push the product through the channel

Figure 14.4   The Flow of Push and Pull Marketing Strategies

ADVERTISING AND ITS ROLE

LO3 Explain the nature of creative (message) decisions that are part of an advertising campaign.

Advertising is the placement of persuasive messages in any medium by an identified sponsor. The advertising message promotes the benefits of a product or service. The media could be print (newspaper, magazines, and outdoor), broadcast (radio and television), or interactive (Internet-based messages on computers, tablets, or smartphones). The objective of advertising is to influence the thought patterns of an audience in a favourable manner and ultimately to motivate an action—to purchase a specific good or service.

The task of developing an advertising campaign is usually handled by an advertising agency. **Advertising agencies** are organizations responsible for creating and placing advertising messages for clients (the advertisers). The development of an advertising campaign can be divided into two basic parts: creative (message) and media. Creative decisions focus on what to say to customers and how to say it. Media decisions focus on what media to use and how much on spend on each medium. Let's examine both areas in more detail.

advertising Any paid form of non-personal message communicated through the media by an identified sponsor.

advertising agencies Service organizations responsible for creating, planning, producing, and placing advertising messages for clients.

Figure 14.5
Budgeting Methods

Budget Factor	Influence on Decision
Percentage of Sales	Manager allocates a predetermined percentage of forecasted sales to marketing or marketing communications.
Industry Average	Manager allocates a budget based on the average amount (current or forecasted) spent on marketing or marketing communications by all brands in the market.
Arbitrary Allocation	Manager relies on judgment and experience to assess cost and profit trends and assigns an arbitrary amount to cover marketing or marketing communications expenses.
Task (Objective)	Manager defines the objective to be achieved, determines the activities (strategies required) to achieve the objective, and associates a cost with the activities.

CREATING THE MESSAGE

The key decisions that are made when devising a creative campaign involve what to say (the objectives) in the message and how to say it (the strategy). A marketing manager or brand manager usually identifies the creative objectives and the advertising agency develops the strategy.

creative objectives Statements of what information is to be communicated to a target market.

Creative objectives state what information is to be communicated to a target audience. Typically, an effective ad communicates the key benefit the good or service offers. Body copy and visual illustrations help substantiate the benefit. Consider the advertisement for Excel gum in **Figure 14.6**. The message clearly communicates the brand's fresh breath benefit.

creative strategy Statements outlining how a message is to be communicated to a target market.

The **creative strategy** specifies how a message is to be communicated to the target audience. Ad agencies get paid to come up with the "big ideas" that sell brands! Strategy considerations involve decisions about theme (continuity of message across all media) and the appeal techniques that will be employed in the ads. For example, an ad for a sports car may appeal to a driver's sense of adventure, whereas an ad for a laundry detergent may use a direct comparison technique to show it cleans clothes better than a competitor. This section examines some of the more common appeal techniques used in advertising today.

Humour   In humorous advertisements, the promise and proof are presented in a light-hearted manner. Some form of humour is used in almost half of all television advertising. Humour can make advertising more enjoyable, involving, and memorable. However, advertisers must be careful not to let humour dominate to such a degree that it impedes an ad's effectiveness, specifically in communicating the brand name and the primary message.

Dentyne used humour effectively in a series of television commercials. One commercial for Dentyne Ice shows a young male standing beside a much older female while contemplating what flavour to buy. But the scene and the conversation between the two lead the viewer to think they are in the condom section. The older female says, "This one heats up. This one tingles. And this one is mint flavoured." The male selects a package and she says, "Oh, that's my favourite." The male has an awkward look on his face hearing such details. The tagline for the campaign is "Practise safe breath," a play on words that summarizes the message effectively.

Dentyne extended the campaign by creating the Safe Breath Alliance (SBA), a completely made-up organization committed to educating consumers about the importance of practising safe breath. Actor, comedian, and writer Marlon Wayans is the primary spokesperson for the Safe Breath Alliance. Refer to the image in **Figure 14.7**.

Video: Kmart Goes From 'Shipping Pants' to 'Big Gas Savings'

Excel and all affiliated designs used courtesy of the Wm. Wrigley Jr. Company or its affiliates.

Figure 14.6   A clear and compelling message from Excel.

Comparison   When an advertiser dares to compare, the promise and proof are shown by comparing the attributes of a product with those of competing products—attributes that are important to members of the target market. Comparisons can be direct (e.g., the other brand is mentioned) or indirect (e.g., there is reference to another brand but it is not identified). Comparative campaigns present an element of risk for the initiator, so it must ensure that marketing research data can support any claims of superiority. Any claims that mislead the public could be challenged via legal proceedings.

Emotion   Emotional advertisements concentrate on creating a mood and conveying the message in a manner that arouses the feelings of the audience. The use of emotion-based advertising is increasing due to the shift in how people are consuming media. With more time spent online and less passive attention directed toward television screens, it is more difficult to get a person's attention. The shift to digital media (e.g., watching commercial content on YouTube) allows an advertiser to tell a much longer story that gives the emotional component more time to develop.

The power of a good human story can be compelling. Tim Hortons effectively used emotion to demonstrate how its outlets are part of the Canadian experience. In one commercial, called Welcome to Canada, an apparent African immigrant waits in anticipation at the airport, laden with bags of new winter coats. From the baggage area emerge his wife and two children. After an emotional reunion he hands his wife a cup of fresh coffee. "Welcome to Canada," he says, before gallantly escorting his family into what is presumably their first snowstorm.[5] Emotional appeals help connect Tim's with consumers.

Figure 14.7   Actor and comedian Marlon Wayans effectively spread the word about "safe breath" during red carpet interviews with other celebrities at the 15th Annual Webby Awards.

Lifestyle   Some advertisers attempt to associate their brands with the lifestyles of certain target audiences. The key to success in this type of campaign is in the association. A typical approach is to show the product attached to a lifestyle (e.g., adventurous, fast-paced, urban, and so on) that the target market identifies with. How the customer reacts to the portrayal initiates interest in the product. With reference to **Figure 14.8**, the RAM truck projects an image of strength, power, and toughness, as well as a hint of luxury. It is a truck ideally suited for a hardworking male in any kind of physical occupation or pursuit. The stark colour schemes used in RAM's advertising help develop the tough image for the vehicle.

Celebrity Endorsement   An endorsement involves using a celebrity on whose popularity the advertiser attempts to capitalize. Stars from television, movies, music, and sports form the nucleus of celebrity endorsers. Both Gatorade and Reebok employ Sidney Crosby to endorse their products. Initially, Crosby was a natural fit for Reebok's I Am What I Am advertising campaign, which celebrates authenticity and individuality. The ads show the dedication and determination it takes for athletes to get where they are today. Reebok now markets the Crosby line of SC87 footwear and apparel. The ads feature Crosby diligently training and demonstrate how hard work makes him better.

CCM, a division of Reebok, employs star goaltender Carey Price to endorse its goalie equipment. Having Canada's Olympic gold medal winning goalie (2014 Olympics) as the primary spokesperson for your goalie equipment is a huge benefit for the brand. Refer to the image in **Figure 14.9**.

There is a risk associated with celebrity endorsements. If the image of the endorser goes sour, any brand associated with the celebrity could incur negative publicity and potential damage to its reputation. Brands such as Accenture and Gatorade quickly dumped Tiger Woods once his hidden lifestyle (sexual escapades) became public.

Video: Oxfam America: Strategically Utilizing Music Outreach and Celebrities

Testimonial   In the case of testimonial advertising, a typical user of the product or an apparently objective third party describes the benefits of the item. In the toothpaste market, Colgate Total incorporates the phrase "Colgate Total is the only dentifrice to earn the Canadian Dental

Figure 14.8 The RAM is positioned to fit the lifestyle of hardworking males.

Ram is a registered trademark of Chrysler Group LLC.

Association seal of approval for gingivitis reduction and for the prevention of tooth decay." Such an endorsement by a third party enhances the credibility of the advertiser's message.

THE CANADIAN PRESS/Paul Chiasson

Figure 14.9 Celebrities matched to the right product can be an effective advertising combination.

Sex   The use of sexual appeal in certain product categories is quite common. For example, cosmetics, perfumes, lingerie, and fashion clothing all use sex as an effective motivator. As long as core customers don't find the use of sex offensive, an advertiser may be on to something. Calvin Klein uses sexual imagery effectively to market jeans to twenty-something males and females. Calvin Klein's ads typically show lots of skin and couples enjoying each other's company; the ads are provocative and attention-grabbing. The product is always prominent in the ads. Refer to the image in **Figure 14.10**.

Product Demonstrations   Simply demonstrating how well a product performs can be a convincing way of motivating a person to buy. Several execution options are available. For example, a before-and-after scenario is common for diet-related products and exercise equipment, wherein the message implies usage by

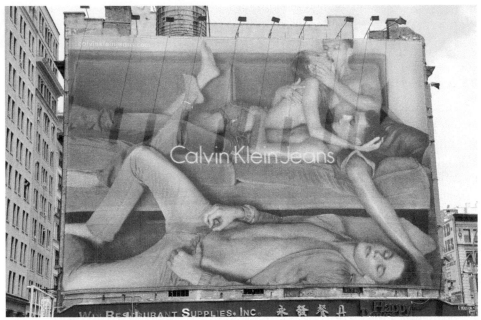

Figure 14.10 Sexual appeals are a popular means of attracting a younger target audience.

Richard Corkery/NY Daily News Archive via Getty Images

the presenter. A second strategy is to simply show the product at work—a technique commonly used in advertising for household products, such as paper towels, cleaners, and floor mops. Sponge Towels, for example, focuses directly on the little pockets in the towel that absorb spills quickly—an important benefit to demonstrate. The brand uses television as its primary medium for its demonstration capability.

As you can see, there are many creative strategy options available to advertisers and some of them work better than others. Some campaigns even include animals and make-believe characters to deliver the message: think of the Geico green gecko, the Aflac duck, the Pillsbury doughboy, and the Maytag repairman, to name just a few.

The media department of an advertising agency is responsible for planning and arranging the placement of advertisements; it schedules and buys advertising time and space for the clients it represents. The media department prepares a document that shows all the details of how a client's budget is spent to achieve advertising objectives. In scheduling, it strives to achieve maximum exposure at the lowest possible cost.

For some insight into how message strategy and media strategy work together to achieve objectives read the Think Marketing box **Koodo Character Makes a Splash.**

PLACING THE MESSAGE: SELECTING THE RIGHT MEDIA

L04 Explain the nature of media decisions that are part of an advertising campaign.

When a manager is involved with **media planning** the key decisions involve what media to use and how much to spend on any particular medium. Typically, several media options are included in a plan and there is much discussion between the agency that develops the plan and the manager who must approve the plan. In a media plan, objectives are stated clearly, strategies for media selection are justified, and budget details are scheduled by activity and timing.

In defining **media objectives**, media planners devise clearly worded guideline statements that guide the planning process. The objective statements focus on who they are trying to reach (the target-market profile is described accurately), what the message is (the message will impact media selection decisions), the best time to reach the target (time of day, season, and so on), and what geographic markets must be reached (national coverage, regional coverage, key cities, and so on).

media planning A precise outline of media objectives, media strategies, and media execution, culminating in a media plan that recommends how funds should be spent to achieve the previously established advertising objectives.

media objectives Media planning statements that consider the target market, the presentation of the message, geographic market priorities, the best time to reach the target, and the budget available to accomplish stated goals.

Think Marketing

Koodo Character Makes a Splash

Good communications plans call for effective collaboration between creative and media planners. Their goal is always to place the right message in the right medium and when they do, good things happen.

Koodo was launched in Canada in 2008 and it led a mobility revolution across Canada with a simple and transparent approach to mobile service. At launch, Koodo was the first to eliminate the System Access Fee and first to introduce Canadians to the revolutionary Koodo Tab. The Tab is an alternative to fixed-term contracts—most competitors offered a discounted price for a phone but customers had to commit to a 3-year plan.

The creative team at Taxi2 (Koodo's creative agency of record) created a new animated character that would ultimately become the spokesperson for the brand in early 2010. The character—El Tabador—a 4-inch animated luchador (an iconic Mexican wrestler) appeared in commercials promoting the benefits of Koodo. His commitment was to fight for Canadians when it came to wireless service.

The media team at the time of the El Tabador launch (Media Experts) recommended an integrated plan embracing TV, outdoor, print, point-of-sale, and digital. Some highlights of the launch: an interactive YouTube game, an online mockumentary with wrestler Bret "The Hitman" Hart, a

Facebook page, and action figurines of the character. El Tabador really got around!

The results have been very positive since launch: Koodo brand awareness reached almost 89 percent (among the target audience). And at the end of 2010, Koodo became the youngest brand ever to be named Brand of the Year by *Strategy* magazine.

Question:

Does a character presenter help or hinder the delivery of a brand message? Consider other characters and brands before forming an opinion.

Adapted from "El Tabador Boosts Koodo," Cassies 2013, Strategy, February 2013, p. 39.

When describing the target market careful consideration is given to their media habits. Consumers now spend much more time online and less time with traditional media. Mobile devices are becoming the centre of an individual's digital universe. Advertisers must follow trends like this and adjust their plans accordingly. Procter & Gamble, the world's largest advertiser, recently announced that it now spends more than a third of its North American marketing budget on digital media. It is an aggressive shift but the company cites the amount of time people are spending online as the motivation for going in that direction.[6]

A **media strategy** describes how the media objectives will be accomplished: how many advertisements or commercials will run, how often, and for what length of time they will appear. A media strategy presents recommendations regarding what media to use and details why certain media are selected and others rejected. The following section presents the key factors that are considered when making media strategy decisions.

media strategy Statements that outline how media objectives will be accomplished; typically, they outline what media will be used and why certain media were selected and others rejected.

Matching the Target with the Medium
The task of an advertising agency's media department is to effectively reach the customers described in the target-market profile. The target-market profile may be broad in scope or it may be narrowly defined based on demographic, psychographic, geographic, or behavioural characteristics. There are three target market media matching strategies: shotgun, profile matching, and rifle. Refer to **Figure 14.11** to see how a target market description influences basic media selection decisions.

reach The total audience potentially exposed, one or more times, to an advertiser's schedule of messages in a given period, usually a week.

Reach, Frequency, and Continuity
The organization must decide on the reach, frequency, and continuity needed to fulfill the media objectives for an advertising message. These factors interact with one another. **Reach** refers to the total audience potentially

Shotgun Strategy	Rifle Strategy	Profile Matching Strategy
The description of the target is very broad. Therefore, mass media with broad reach are appropriate. **EXAMPLE:** To reach adults 18+ years old, newspapers, television and outdoor ads are good options.	The key element of the target description is often an interest or activity. Demographics are less important. **EXAMPLE:** The target is people interested in snowboarding. A special interest magazine titled *Snowboarding* is a good choice.	The target description includes several demographic and psychographic variables that require more selective media choices. **EXAMPLE:** The target is married women, 25–49 years old, who balance household and career responsibilities. A magazine such as *Chatelaine* or *Canadian Living* is a good match.

Figure 14.11 Target Market Media Matching Strategies

exposed to an advertiser's schedule of messages in a given period, usually a week. It could be expressed as a number, for example the circulation or readership of a newspaper or magazine, or as a percentage of the target population in a geographically defined area. Assume a television station is seen by 30 000 households in a geographic area of 150 000 households. The reach would be 20 percent (30 000 divided by 150 000).

Frequency refers to the average number of times an audience is exposed to an advertising message over a period, usually a week. The airing of a television commercial three times on a station during a week would represent its frequency.

Continuity refers to the length of time required to ensure a particular medium affects a target market. For example, an advertiser may schedule television commercials in eight-week flights three times a year, thus covering a total of 24 weeks of the calendar year, or a magazine campaign may run for consecutive months.

The relationship among reach, frequency, and continuity is dynamic. For example, does a media planner recommend more reach at the expense of frequency or vice versa? To overexpose a target to a message can be a waste of money! Altering any one of these variables will affect the others. The budget available for the campaign affects key decisions on reach, frequency, and continuity.

Engagement   **Engagement** refers to a person's degree of involvement with a medium when consuming it. For example, on television there are so many commercials it is easy for the viewer to disengage when a cluster of commercials appear. However, when a person is online he or she is involved in doing something (searching for something) and is more apt to notice an advertising message. When playing a video game a person's involvement may be very intense. Research is showing that gamers do notice advertising messages while playing. The level of engagement varies from one medium to another.

Market Coverage   **Coverage** refers to the number of geographic markets where the advertising is to occur. In deciding the extent of coverage, the advertiser could select national, regional, or particular urban markets, depending on its marketing priorities. Marketers now have the capability of reaching customers wherever they are through mobile communications. The concept of location-based targeting that was discussed earlier in the book takes effect in this situation; a message can be delivered right when the person is ready to buy!

Timing   In determining the best time to reach a target market, marketers may focus on the time of the day, the week, or the year. The best time to advertise a good or service is the time at which it will have the most impact on the consumer's buying decision. For example, the decision to buy a snowmobile is probably made in the fall. Therefore, if advertising is scheduled for the winter, the message will be delivered too late.

The final stage of media planning is **media execution**, where specific media choices are made. In making such decisions the costs of the various media are evaluated for efficiency. Advertisers strive for high reach at reasonable cost—they want to be efficient in

frequency The average number of times an audience is exposed to an advertising message over a given period, usually a week.

continuity The length of time required to create an impact on a target market through a particular medium.

engagement A person's degree of involvement with a medium when consuming it.

coverage The number of geographic markets in which advertising is to occur for the duration of a media plan.

media execution The final stage of media planning; the process of fine-tuning media strategy into specific action plans.

how they spend the budget. Once final decisions are made a media calendar is established that outlines the timing and placement of all media activities, and a budget summary is prepared to show how the budget is allocated across the selected media.

To demonstrate how efficient a medium is at reaching a target market, a manager uses a mathematical formula known as CPM, or cost per thousand, to compare the costs and reach of the media alternatives being considered. **CPM (cost per thousand)** is the cost incurred in delivering a message to 1000 individuals. In magazines, for example, it is calculated by dividing the cost of the ad by the circulation of the magazine in thousands. Therefore, if an ad in a magazine cost $30 000 and the circulation is 750 000, the CPM would be $40 ($30 000 divided by 750). When comparing various magazines, the one with the lowest CPM is the most efficient at reaching the target. CPM calculations can be done when comparing alternatives in other media, as well.

CPM (cost per thousand)
The cost of reaching 1000 people with a message; it is a quantitative measure for comparing the effectiveness of media alternatives.

Simulation: Ethics

ASSESSING MEDIA ALTERNATIVES

L05 Assess various media alternatives for delivering messages.

In an age of rapidly changing technology, all forms of media are converging on the Internet. For example, television is losing viewers because people are watching shows online at a time that is convenient for them. Many viewers are disconnecting their cable cords or satellite services in favour of Netflix. Factor in our insatiable appetite for digital gadgets such as smartphones and tablets, and you quickly see why the Internet and how we access it will become the epicentre of the media universe in years to come.

These behaviour trends are forcing change with traditional media outlets. Television networks are streaming shows and sports events for viewing online. Newspapers and magazines are losing subscribers but have responded by creating their own websites for content distribution. What lies ahead remains uncertain but technology dictates that media consumption will be more digitally based with each passing year.

When selecting which media to use, the most influential factor is the behaviour of the target market. Knowing which media a target refers to more frequently, less frequently, and so on points the media planner in a certain direction. Media are also chosen in keeping with budget constraints. If the budget is small, no need to consider television! Let us briefly examine each of the major media.

Television

Television is a mass reach medium suitable for advertisers wanting to reach diverse target markets. The latest statistics available reveal that 99 percent of Canadian households have televisions and that 90 percent of television households are equipped with satellite or cable TV. The television industry has and will continue to be affected by a few trends. As already mentioned the shift to viewing shows online will continue. The personal video recorder (PVR) allows people to digitally record their favourite shows for later viewing—a phenomenon referred to as *viewing on demand*. Commercials can be skipped in the recording process—a frightening thought to networks and advertisers.

Despite the trends, television remains a dominant medium in terms of advertising impact. A recent consumer research report titled "How Canadians Perceive and Receive Advertising," revealed that television advertising had almost twice the impact of its nearest rival (online media). The driving force behind such dominance is that consumers equate television ads with a form of entertainment.[7]

To compensate for some perceived weaknesses of television advertising, marketers are looking at options such as product placement in shows. **Product placement** refers to the visible placement of a branded product in the television show (the same concept applies in other media as well). Marketers also consider branded content opportunities.

product placement In public relations, the placement of a product in a movie or television show so that the product is exposed to the viewing audience (e.g., the branded product is a prop in the show).

branded content A situation in which the brand name of a product or service is woven into the storyline of a movie or television show.

Branded content is a situation where the brand is written right into the script of the show. For example, the Ford Focus was integrated into a hidden camera stunt on the *Just for Laughs* show on the Comedy Network and its YouTube channel. The stunt featured a 2013 Focus ST pulling up to unsuspecting pedestrians standing by a valet stop. The driver tosses out a bag of money and flees a police pursuit. The unwitting participants become suspects. After they are made aware of the hidden cameras, the scene ends with the line "Find more surprise and delight in every Ford Focus." Ford was looking for a unique way to deliver its brand message, and humour was the way to do it.[8]

Radio

Radio reaches 99 percent of Canadian households and 81 percent of adults on a daily basis—but unlike television, which reaches a mass audience, radio is a local market medium. The amount of time people spend with radio has been affected by technology. People now listen to radio via satellite options and the Internet that are free of advertising. People also download their music (e.g., from iTunes to their iPod or smartphone).

Radio stations attract an audience based on their format. **Format** refers to the nature of the content a station broadcasts. For example, a station may play rock music or another style of music, be an all-news station, or perhaps a sports talk station. The nature (demographic profile) of a station's audience attracts advertisers to the station. The primary advertising benefit of radio is its reach potential in local markets.

format On radio, the nature of the content a station broadcasts.

Newspapers

There are 120+ daily newspapers in Canada that reach 50 percent of adults on a daily basis (weekdays).[9] The circulation of newspapers has been declining for many years—the reader shift to the Internet for news and sports information has had a significant impact on the newspaper industry. **Circulation** refers to the average number of copies per issue of a publication that are sold by subscription or made available through retail distributors. Among the largest newspapers in Canada are the *Toronto Star* (daily circulation of 357 600), *The Globe and Mail* (302 100), and *Le Journal de Montreal* (287 800).[10]

circulation The average number of copies per issue of a publication that are sold by subscription or made available through retail distributors.

Newspapers have been able to maintain their market position on the strength of their brands and their proactive approach to digital formats. The combination of hard copy and digital reaches a mass audience that makes newspapers attractive to advertisers.

Magazines

Just over 1300 consumer magazines are published and distributed in Canada. It seems there is a publication for every conceivable interest. There are also many business magazines in circulation covering a wide variety of industries and business interests. Similar to newspapers, circulation and readership of magazines is declining—they are the victims of people's shift to the Internet for content. Most popular magazines now offer a digital edition, which gives readers access to all or some of the hard copy content.

Among the highest circulation magazines in Canada are *Reader's Digest* (626 000), *Chatelaine* (571 000), *Canadian Living* (519 000), and *Maclean's* (330 000).[11] Advertisers seek magazines that have a readership profile similar to their target-market profile. *Chatelaine*, for example, is an effective magazine for reaching women who balance household responsibilities with a career. The primary advertising benefit of magazines is their ability to reach a target market based on demographic, psychographic, and geographic characteristics.

Out-of-Home Media

Out-of-home media include various forms of outdoor advertising, transit advertising, and in-store advertising. If you drive a car, travel by transit, or stroll through shopping malls, you are constantly exposed to out-of-home advertising messages. Refer to the image in **Figure 14.12**. Some media planners consider that the timing of an advertising exposure is more important than reach and frequency.[12] In that regard, outdoor has an advantage. Outdoor ads reach people when they are ready to buy. As well, new technologies have created new and dynamic interactive formats such as video display boards.

Transit riders represent a captive audience that often has a need for visual stimulation. Bored with travelling on buses and subway cars, riders frequently read advertising messages. Pedestrians, transit riders, and drivers tend to take the same route to and from school or work each day. Therefore, out-of-home media offers an opportunity to reach an audience frequently.

The Canadian Press Images/Libby Yuill

Figure 14.12 Outdoor ads reach a wide cross-section of a market's population frequently.

direct response advertising
Messages that prompt immediate action, such as advertisements containing clip-out coupons, response cards, and order forms; such advertising goes directly to customers and bypasses traditional channels of distribution.

direct mail A form of direct advertising communicated to prospects through the postal service.

direct response television (DRTV) A sales-oriented television commercial message that encourages people to buy right away, usually through 1-800 telephone numbers.

Direct Response Advertising

Direct response advertising is advertising through any medium designed to generate a response by any means that is measurable. The primary forms of direct response communications include direct mail, direct response television (DRTV), direct response print ads, and telemarketing.

Direct response communications play an important role today. In a technological environment, managers have the ability to identify prospective and current customers and the means to communicate with them on an individual basis. Marketing organizations are attracted to direct response advertising because of its targeting capabilities and its ability to account for all dollars spent. The results achieved in a direct response campaign can be directly attributed to the activity!

A shift toward direct response follows on the heels of companies adopting software technology that encourages database management techniques and the implementation of customer relationship programs—concepts discussed earlier in this book. Marketing organizations find that reaching a customer individually and directly is more efficient than reaching a customer through traditional mass media. Shoppers Drug Mart, for example, accumulates considerable data about the buying behaviour of its customers who have a Shoppers Optimum rewards card. From the data, customized mail offers can be sent directly to current customers who have consented to receive such offers. Refer to the image in **Figure 14.13**.

Direct mail is the largest revenue generator among direct response communications alternatives. **Direct mail** is a form of advertising communicated to prospects via the postal service or by a private distribution company. **Direct response television (DRTV)** is becoming more popular with advertisers. Ads that present a product in a very convincing manner get customers to take action immediately—action is the key benefit of this type of advertising. Grab the phone or go online, have the credit card handy, and make the purchase now! Think Vince and the Slap Chop and you'll get the picture!

Shoppers Drug Mart

Figure 14.13 The Shoppers Optimum database provides information that enables offers of interest to be sent to Shoppers Drug Mart customers.

Internet (Online) Advertising

Online advertising is defined as the placement of electronic communications on a website, in an email, or over personal communications devices (e.g., smartphones and tablets) connected to the Internet. The concept of behavioural targeting (discussed earlier in the textbook) applies here. In an online context, **behavioural targeting** involves the delivery of ads based on consumers' previous surfing behaviour. By temporarily placing "cookies" (activity trackers) in a person's Web browser, a user's preferences can be tracked.

Advertising online has grown significantly in recent years. The Internet now ranks second only to television in terms of revenue generated from advertisers. The latest forecast by ZenithOptimedia predicts that online advertising will surpass television to become the largest advertising medium in Canada by 2014. In 2012 (the most recent data available at time of publication), online advertising placements accounted for $2.9 billion in Canada.[13] *Search* and *display* advertising account for the largest portion of this advertising investment, but other options, such as video ads, are growing in popularity.

With **search advertising**, an advertiser's listing is placed within or alongside search results in exchange for a fee that's paid each time someone clicks on the listing in those search results. This is also known as *pay-per-click* advertising. Google, for example, offers a service called AdWords that allows companies, for a small fee, to have a link to their website featured when a user searches for a word that company has specified. If a user types in "investments" and RBC Financial has bought that term, an ad for RBC Financial appears on the screen.

A second option is **display advertising**, which includes banner ads in a variety of sizes. Terms such as *rectangle*, *leaderboard*, and *skyscraper* are used to describe the size of the banner. Historical data show that larger ads (such as a skyscraper) achieve higher scores for brand awareness and message association. They also cost more! Refer to the image in **Figure 14.14**.

Rich media are ads that include animation, sound, video, and interactivity. They are also referred to as *animated banners*. The ads come in a variety of styles to grab the viewer's attention in different ways. Some expand on the screen and some float on the screen—hard to miss if you are exposed to such an ad!

People watch a lot of video content online so video ads seem a natural fit for the medium. Just like television, video ads offer the opportunity to connect with consumers on an emotional level. As more and more television networks stream their shows online, there will be more commercial breaks in the content. Video ads can be placed before, during and after a video is played.

With a **sponsorship** an advertiser commits to an extended relationship with a website. Advertisers are attracted to websites whose content appeals to their target market. Sports junkies, for example, visit sites such as TSN.ca and Sportsnet.ca on a regular basis. TSN runs various contests during the year, all of which are sponsored by national brands. One of the biggest sponsorships is the Kraft Celebration Tour in which TSN goes on the road to 10 towns in 10 days for a news broadcast. The winning communities, as voted by the public, each receive $25 000 to upgrade local sports facilities. The TSN network and website actively promote the contest and its affiliation with Kraft.

Email advertising is similar in concept to direct mail (discussed in the previous section). A big difference, however, is that consumers agree to have the email sent to them—they subscribe to it! Referred to as **permission-based email**, people choose to receive messages from a particular company or brand. Such communication is inexpensive, easy to measure, and targeted at people who have expressed interest in the brand or company—quite a combination of benefits.

Many marketers firmly believe that the key objective of email is to establish and maintain a relationship with customers, which will ultimately generate sales. In many cases, the email message will include special offers or other promotional incentives to spur action. Refer to the illustration in **Figure 14.15**.

Figure 14.14   An Illustration of an Online Display Ad

Figure 14.15 Email is a good medium for building relationships with customers and other interested stakeholders.

online advertising The placement of electronic communications on a website, in an email, or over personal communications devices (e.g., smartphones and tablets) connected to the Internet.

behavioural targeting A database-driven marketing system that tracks a consumer's behaviour to determine his or her interests and then serves ads to that person relevant to that interest.

search advertising An advertiser's listing is placed within or alongside search results and pays a fee each time someone clicks on the listing in those search results (pay-per-click advertising).

display advertising Banner ads in a variety of sizes.

rich media A form of online advertising that incorporates greater use of, and interaction with, animation, audio, and video.

sponsorships The financial support of an event by an organization in return for certain advertising rights and privileges associated with the event.

permission-based email A situation wherein consumers agree to accept online messages from commercial sources.

The Ontario SPCA gives thanks this Thanksgiving for all the wonderful adopters that have given an animal a forever home this past year.

Unfortunately, some animals will find themselves spending this Thanksgiving in a shelter without a loving family to celebrate with. You can help by _____ to give them a meal or a warm place to stay this Thanksgiving.

Many of our animals have been rescued from neglect and abuse. Many have been relinquished to the streets to fend for themselves and have been brought into the Ontario SPCA for protection. Each and every one of these animals give thanks to you for adopting or donating to help other animals in need this Thanksgiving.

To make your Thanksgiving donation now, click _____.

Yours for animals we love,

Marc Ralsky
Director, Community & Donor Development

© 2012 Ontario SPCA

16586 Woodbine Ave, RR3, Newmarket, Ontario , L3Y 4W1
Charitable Business #88969-1044-RR0002

Unsubscribe | Legal Disclaimer | Privacy Statement

Ontario SPCA

Finally, a **website** offers a great means to tell a more complete and compelling story about a brand. All other forms of advertising should encourage consumers to visit the website, Facebook page, or Twitter feed. As discussed elsewhere in this book, people are spending much time online searching for valuable information that will assist them in deciding what products and brands to buy. Consequently, many organizations are investing time and money in content marketing. **Content marketing** involves creating and distributing relevant and valuable content to attract, acquire, and engage an audience, with the objective of driving a profitable customer action.[14]

Content marketing does not have to be confined to website communication. However, websites do present an ideal opportunity to deliver more meaningful information. The difference between content marketing and traditional marketing is that content marketing focuses on owning media rather than renting media (paying for advertising time or space). An organization is in complete control of the content appearing on its website.

The key to successful content marketing lies in its definition. The information posted on a website must be relevant. It must make the person stop, read, think, and behave differently. People visit websites for a reason—they want the content. They also subscribe to emails from organizations assuming the content will be relevant. As you have learned, time spent with a medium is important. Compelling information will extend a consumer's stay at a website.

In conjunction with other strategic factors, the advantages and disadvantages of the various media are considered. An advertiser can rarely use all the media. When assessing media alternatives, a marketer will evaluate the advantages and disadvantages of each. Refer to **Figure 14.16** for details.

content marketing The creation and distribution of relevant and valuable content, to attract, acquire, and engage an audience with the objective of driving profitable customer action.

SOCIAL MEDIA COMMUNICATIONS

L06 Describe the role of social media in marketing communications campaigns.

The future of marketing communications is in interactive marketing communications. People are spending a lot of time online via laptops, tablets, and smartphones, and they are relying more on comments about products from friends in their social network than information from marketing organizations.

A **social media network** connects people with different types of interests at one website. At the website people become friends and form communities—the community could be a potential target market.

The growth of social networks is changing the way in which marketers view their brands, their customers, and the media. Integrating social media into the marketing communications mix should be a priority of marketing organizations today.

Recent data indicates Canadians are married to the social web. Apparently, Canadians spend 25 percent of their total Internet time social networking—approximately 1.2 hours a day.[15] And the number of Canadians on social networks is significant; some 19 million people or 55 percent of the population used social sites in 2013. A recent trend also shows an upswing in mobile access to social media. Of Facebook's Canadian users, 13 million are accessing the site at least once a month by a mobile device, while 9.4 million use a phone or tablet to access Facebook daily.[16]

On a global scale, Facebook is, by far, the largest social network. At the end of 2013, Facebook had 1.2 billion monthly active users.[17] Just 10 years ago Facebook only had one million users. Social media has transformed itself into a mass medium in a very short period. Other popular social network sites include YouTube, Twitter, LinkedIn, Google+, and Pinterest.

Many organizations are moving into the world of social networking without understanding why they are there. They know they want to engage in meaningful communications with consumers, but "the sheer size of the potential audience is overwhelming many marketers, and leaving them feeling unprepared and even inadequate."[18] As well, marketers are uncertain of the benefits that their investment in social media will generate.

Other organizations have entered the social media arena and met with much success. Mondelez Canada, marketer of Oreo cookies, among many other popular brands, is an

social media network A website that connects people with different kinds of interests for the purpose of socializing (e.g., Facebook or Twitter).

Advantages	Disadvantages
Television Impact—sight, sound and motion; demonstration Reach—very high among all age groups	**Television** Cost—high cost for time and commercial production Clutter—too many commercials reduces impact of message
Radio Targeting—reaches a selective audience based on station format Reach and Frequency—reaches same audience frequently	**Radio** Retention—short, single-sense message Fragmentation—many stations in large markets reduces impact
Newspaper Coverage—good reach among adults in local markets Flexibility—message can be inserted quickly	**Newspaper** Lifespan—short; a one day medium Targeting—not appropriate for advertiser with carefully defined targets
Magazine Targeting—specialized magazines reach defined demographic targets Environment—quality of editorial enhances advertising message	**Magazines** Clutter—too many ads in each issue Frequency—low message frequency (monthly)
Out-of-Home Reach and Frequency—message reaches same target frequently (daily travel patterns) Coverage—available on a market-by-market basis	**Out-of-Home** Message—only suitable for short messages Targeting—reaches broad cross-section; can't target specific demographics
Direct Response Targeting—reaches a pre-selected and defined audience Measurement—expenditure directly attributed to advertising effort	**Direct Response** Image—junk image of mail used; hard-sell approach No Editorial Support—message stands alone in medium
Internet Targeting—ads reach individuals based on behaviour (destinations) Timing—ads delivered anytime, anywhere	**Internet** Low Click Rates—only a small audience visits a website for more information Clutter—barrage of banner ads on websites reduces impact

Figure 14.16   Media Advertising Selection Considerations

active participant in social media. Mondelez sees true marketing benefit: "When traditional advertising such as TV is paired with digital and social media, they see a jump: Campaigns are generally two times as effective for the money."[19] For more insight into how Mondelez employs social media in real time, read the Think Marketing Box **Oreo's Olympian Effort**.

The Social Media Environment: Consumers Are in Control

As discussed in Chapter 1, we are in the social media marketing era. In this era consumers have more control over marketing communications. Previously marketers would push their communications onto consumers. In the social media era the communications process is more participative—the goal is to get consumers talking about brands and promoting brands on behalf of the marketing organization. In Chapter 1 this change in control and participative style of communications was referred to as **brand democratization**.

The sooner the marketer adapts to this change and sees the benefit of allowing consumers to participate in the creation of brand content, the easier it will be to integrate social media into a marketing communications strategy. For example, an organization could put out a call for consumer-produced video content to potentially be used in in a promotional campaign. Much of the content on social media networks is

brand democratization A situation in which the customer can interact with a brand, giving the customer some control over the marketing of a brand (as in online user-generated content).

ThinkMarketing

Oreo's Olympian Effort

Smart marketers are making social media work for their brands. For Mondelez Canada, a marketer of food and snack products, the watershed moment came during the 2013 Super Bowl. Mondelez had been working social media communications for three years with mediocre results. Then there was a power blackout that disrupted the big game. The ad agency team immediately went into action.

Mondelez and its agency, Edelman Canada, organize a war room when big events occur. When something happens people spring into action. Within minutes of the blackout Oreo tweeted: "Power out? No problem. You can still dunk in the dark." The tweet included a picture of an Oreo on a dark background. This is what's called *real-time marketing*. Real-time marketing works wonders when a brand has always-on storytelling capability and the event has some relevance to the brand. Oreo's simple tweet generated 280 million impressions (views of the message) and all kinds of buzz in other media.

Real-time marketing doesn't have to be spontaneous—it can be planned in advance. Edelman says about 80 percent of material is planned around events and timed for publication based on audience analytics that determines when the people it wants to reach are online. The remaining 20 percent is spontaneous and is based on conversations happening in the moment.

Mondelez was a sponsor of the Canadian Olympic Committee for the 2014 Winter Olympics in Sochi, Russia. Its sponsorship granted certain advertising privileges. Again, Oreo was at its tweeting best. In one of the preliminary hockey matches, Canada's men's team was in a close game. Oreo sent out a tweet calling the game a "nail-biter" but encouraged people to bite into an Oreo instead. After Canada scored to take the lead Oreo tweeted: "Recipe for gold: 1 part skill, 1 part heart, 1 part awesome comeback." Such comments effectively described Team Canada's performance throughout the tournament.

© Ian Dagnall/Alamy

Oreo and many other brands are investing more money in social media for good reason; they are following consumers' media consumption habits. People are watching the events on television, a tablet or smartphone, or they have two screens going at the same time. The Super Bowl example shows how people use Facebook and Twitter to talk about the game. The key to success, however, is in knowing how to participate in the conversation. That requires an understanding of consumer behaviour along with some communications expertise.

Question:

Social media engages people with a brand. Do these communications have an impact on brand sales? Are social media a good investment for a brand?

Adapted from Susan Krashinsky, "Inside Oreo's Olympic war room," The Globe and Mail, February 21, 2014, p. B5; and Susan Krashinsky, "A Sunday shift: The rise of real-time ads," The Globe and Mail, January 31, 2014, p. B5.

---

created by amateurs. **Consumer-generated content** is content created by consumers for consumers. People will create brand-oriented content without being asked, and in many cases present the brand effectively. People who do this are often called *brand evangelists*, who will do anything to promote their favourite brand. For many people this kind of content carries more weight than marketer-generated content.

When a company invites the public to participate in the marketing of its brands, it is employing a technique referred to as crowdsourcing. **Crowdsourcing** uses public sources to complete marketing tasks that a company would normally assign to a third-party provider (e.g., an advertising agency or production company). Essentially, this approach takes advantage of the creativity and enthusiasm that people have for a brand. The task is

consumer-generated content Online content created by consumers for consumers (often the content is related to a branded good).

crowdsourcing Using public sources to complete marketing tasks normally performed by a third-party provider.

typically completed more quickly and at a much lower cost. Participants gain "personal recognition, a sense of community, or [possibly] a financial incentive."[20]

Perhaps no other brand does crowdsourcing better than Doritos. For the past ten years Doritos has invited the public to submit video content for its Crash the Super Bowl contest. The winning video, as judged by public voting on the finalists, is shown during the Super Bowl game. Surprisingly, Doritos has some of the most effective Super Bowl ads even though they are competing for attention with professionally produced ads for other brands. Apparently Doritos' consumer-generated content resonates with viewers. Some experts feel the Crash ads are effective because they are like mini sitcoms that are authentic and not overly produced like a normal commercial. The grand prize winner gets $1 million—not bad for an amateur production! All ads are posted at a website. The 2013 submissions garnered 3.7 million views.[21]

Marketers now realize that social networks have given real people real power. Whether the expression "any publicity is good publicity" is true or not is debatable, but if consumers create and upload content and it is viewed by millions of people, there must be benefit to the brand. It sounds almost frightening to let consumers take charge, but consumer control is the ultimate form of engagement that marketers are searching for.

TYPES OF SOCIAL NETWORK ADVERTISING AND MARKETING COMMUNICATIONS

Paid social media advertising is still in its infancy. At the end of 2013 it amounted to only $267 million, about 10 percent of what is spent by advertisers on all forms of digital media.[22] Several marketing communications opportunities exist on social networks. Many of the standard Internet advertising options are available along with some interesting company-sponsored opportunities that allow an organization to publish ongoing information about its brands.

Display Advertising

The placement of banner ads is available on social networks. Given the abundance of data that social networks collect about users there are significant targeting opportunities available to advertisers. Facebook, for example, offers a sophisticated demographic filtering process that combines factors such as age, gender, location, education, work history, and interests. Click rates for banner ads are quite low on social sites so advertisers tend to look for more effective options to advertise in this medium.

Sponsored Posts

Sponsored stories allow marketers to amplify the distribution of stories that people have already shared with their friends. For example, should a person check in from a restaurant, their friends will see that in the new feed. The restaurant can purchase sponsored stories to increase the distribution of the story to the person's friends. Facebook has determined that one sponsored post for every 20 posts is an acceptable ratio; apparently the sponsored posts do not interfere with how people engage with the feed.[23]

Brand Page (Fan Page)

Marketers can create their own page or group that users choose to join. Marketers use this to build a subscriber or fan base. Contests and other forms of brand incentives motivate fans to visit the page, resulting in an expanded base that can be utilized for future marketing programs. These pages are proving useful for increasing brand awareness, encouraging participation in contests, and launching new products. Users who "like" a brand become members of the fan page. Among the brand fan leaders on Facebook in Canada are Tim Hortons, Subway, Skittles, Canadian Tire, and Coca-Cola. Refer to the illustration in **Figure 14.17**.

The value of a "like" is questioned by advertisers. Is it a measure of success, they ask? Some recent research studies reveal that only 5 percent of people who like a brand go back to the fan page.[24] Therefore, a brand with one million likes only gets 50 000 people returning to the site. Such limited engagement needs to be evaluated if advertisers want an adequate return on investment. Engagement should be the more important metric for success in this environment.

Referrals from a Friend Network

Referrals from friends play a role in creating interest in a brand. A news feed about someone buying something new, for example, could be received by countless numbers of friends. Word of mouth is often cited as more influential than company-sponsored communication. However, too much word of mouth may not be so good. Many social network users are becoming skeptical of the source of the message. Is the source legitimate? As well, many users now consider such communication an exploitation of personal relationships with friends.

Figure 14.17   Consumers have the opportunity to engage with brands on Facebook.

Company Blogs

A **blog** is a website where journal entries are posted on a regular basis and displayed in reverse chronological order. Company or brand blogs can be effective in delivering relevant information in a positive manner. It gives the brand or company an opportunity to be part of the discussion on matters that are important to customers. The communications occur in a more relaxed manner—readers of blogs are there because they want to read the content—a much different principle than that of traditional advertising. Blogs should provide useful information for the reader to savour.

blog A frequent, chronological publication of personal or corporate thoughts on a webpage that may be updated on a daily basis.

YouTube Channels

Many companies and brands have their own YouTube channel to communicate exciting things in a video format. Axe, a popular male grooming product, is very active in social media. Its dedicated YouTube channel offers highly sexualized content on topics of interest to young males—content that can go beyond anything seen on television! Axe sees YouTube as an essential means of communication. Shelley Brown, CEO of CP+B (Axe's ad agency) says, "Axe is a brand that, as it moves through social space, needs to stay very relevant, very fresh, It needs to be in a state of continual renewal."[25] Placing video content on YouTube makes that happen.

Viral Marketing and Communications

Technology has encouraged marketing organizations to examine the potential of passed-along forms of communication, as when social network members pass on brand information to their friends. **Viral marketing** involves a strategy that encourages individuals to pass on marketing messages to others, creating the potential for exponential growth in the message's exposure and influence. Concepts such as *word of mouth* and *creating buzz* that were introduced earlier are typically part of a viral marketing strategy.

viral marketing A situation whereby the receiver of an online message is encouraged to pass it on to friends.

Marketers can try to plan a viral campaign but it is really up to the receivers of the original message to determine if a campaign goes viral—the receiver of the message is in control. Therefore, the nature of the message must be of high interest to the receiver in order to motivate them to pass it on to others. "Free" is a powerful word in marketing and most successful viral campaigns usually give away something—free email services, free software, free can of soda, etc. In the online environment people are looking for deals! That's the primary reason they become a brand fan.

One of the most talked-about advertising campaigns in recent years, and a campaign that went viral, was Old Spice's The Man Your Man Could Smell Like campaign. In social media it is one of the most popular viral video campaigns of all time. The videos featured the rather handsome actor Isaiah Mustafa. The original videos were viewed 36 million times. The final installment of the campaign, called Old Spice Responses, garnered 6.7 million views

(photo) Dave J Hogan/Getty Images for Old Spice; (graph) Courtesy of Visible Measures Corp

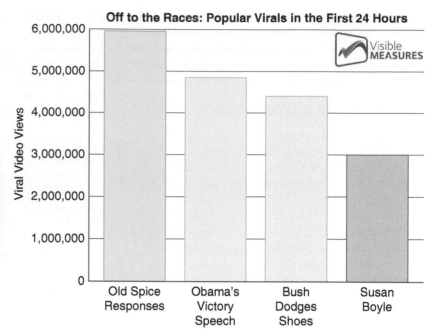

Figure 14.18 The Old Spice social media campaign was a viral success.

within 24 hours, ballooning to 23 million views within 36 hours—that's viral! The response campaign involved the actor responding to comments and questions from people on websites like Facebook, Twitter, Reddit, and Digg in real time. The campaign ran for three days.[26] Viral campaigns take off fast and have a short life cycle. Refer to the illustration in **Figure 14.18**.

Much of the success of the campaign is attributed to the humorous and entertaining nature of the videos. The videos also appeared as commercials on television. The entertainment value helped Old Spice break through the cluster of competitive advertising. In the context of planning a viral campaign, this example clearly demonstrates that "brands don't make viral videos, users make videos go viral."[27]

Benefits of Social Media Communications

There are several good reasons for a marketing organization to engage in social media communications. Historically, one of the most potent forms of influence on brand decisions has been word of mouth, a situation marketers have little control over. On a social network word of mouth is taken to an entirely new level. Simply put, people like to pass on relevant information to their friends.

Social networks now reach all age groups and reaching a target effectively is a priority of a marketing organization. Among 18- to 29-year-olds in North America, 83 percent participate in a stocial network. For the 30- to 49-year age group the figure is 77 percent. Older age groups are on social networks—but not at the same level. Among 50- to 64-year-olds, 52 percent participate on a social site. The 65+ group is much lower at 32 percent.[28]

Marketers have also identified customer engagement as a significant benefit. The participative nature of social media provides marketers the opportunity to converse with customers (a situation that allows them to listen and gain insights into how they feel about the company or brand). Such input could ultimately alter the direction of a brand's marketing strategy.

MOBILE MEDIA COMMUNICATIONS

L07 Describe the role of mobile communications in marketing communications campaigns.

The screen is small, the audience's attention span is short, and the environment is busy—not exactly the best conditions for delivering an advertising message—yet the possibilities of reaching consumers at a critical time (that is, when they are ready to buy) make this medium very attractive to marketers.

There is no doubting the potential impact of mobile technology on marketing strategy. Right now there are 27.3 million wireless subscribers in Canada and, according to recent data from comScore (a research company), smartphone penetration has reached 72 percent. Over the three years from 2011 to 2013, the overall time people spent on the Internet doubled, and traffic from smartphones and tablets accounts for half of that time.[29] Other research indicates that mobile devices have already surpassed desktop computers as the number one channel for Canadians to connect to the Internet.[30]

Mobile is an emerging platform for distributing advertising messages. Right now mobile only generates a small portion of total advertising revenue in Canada (it is less that 5 percent of a typical consumer goods budget), but, since Canadians are emotionally attached to their phones (79 percent of people won't leave home without it), the future looks promising for delivering advertising messages.[31]

Smartphones such as the iPhone, Samsung Galaxy, and BlackBerry typically offer many features: send email messages and access the Web, take photographs and videos, download applications, and play music and video games. Therefore, marketers can communicate with consumers through text messaging, video messaging, applications, and online video games—and they can do so in a highly targeted manner.

Mobile media offer marketers the ability to reach consumers based on where they are located at any point in time—the concept of location-based marketing that was discussed in Chapter 6. Let's refresh your memory. A person's location information (available through GPS chips in smartphones) is factored into a communications effort. For example, if Starbucks knows where you are they could instantly send you an advertising message or promotional offer that would encourage a visit to a nearby location. You might take advantage of such an unexpected incentive. Refer to the image in **Figure 14.19**.

Figure 14.19   Through mobile communications, offers can be sent to consumers in real time.

Through services such as Groupon and Foursquare, consumers can actually check in, announce their whereabouts, and automatically receive offers that may be of interest to them. Let's examine some of the more common means of communicating with consumers through mobile media.

Text Messaging
Text messaging refers to the transmission of text-only messages. While voice calls are the primary function of cell phones, the popularity of smartphones has allowed text messaging to emerge as a popular communications tool. Believe it or not, Canadians send 270 million text messages a day. Texting is popular because of its speed, portability, and low cost.

text messaging The transmission of short, text-only messages on wireless devices.

Marketers interested in reaching younger targets are getting involved with text messaging, running promotions that include *call-to-action* short codes with their marketing material (outdoor posters, transit ads, bottle caps, drink containers, and so on). Mobile phone users can punch in their codes to participate in contests, download free music, and get ring tones and prizes.

There are issues for marketers to consider with mobile phone communications. If the messages are too intrusive they could be perceived as negatively as a telemarketing call. Consumers are concerned about how information about them is used by wireless companies. These companies should have an opt-in from their customers prior to opening their databases to commercial interests. (*Opt-in* means that customers agree to allow messages to be sent to them.)

Video Messaging
Video messaging is going to become more popular in the future. Even though a smartphone screen is small, it shouldn't be surprising that people are watching long-form video content on their mobile phones. In fact, some 40 percent of all video viewing occurs on a smartphone. People view television shows, sports events, and YouTube videos on their phones.[32]

video messaging The transmission of video clips on devices such as smartphones.

Advertisers wanting to reach the next generation of consumers will have to include mobile in the communications mix. Teens and young adults who have grown up with technology and mobile phones will carry their behaviour forward and it will have significant impact on how they learn about and buy products. Smartphones already assist people when they are shopping—anything from finding the nearest store to

Figure 14.20 A quick response code communicates detailed information about a product.

checking prices and availability. Some 39 percent of Canadian smartphone users take a picture or video of a product while shopping and send it to someone for an opinion.[33]

Hugh Dow, a prominent media planner, sees nothing but positives for the small screen. "We're living in a mobile generation now, where consumers are using a variety of methods to stay connected and receive information on the go. It is an important platform for reaching specific target markets."[34]

Mobile Applications

All smartphone suppliers, such as BlackBerry, Apple, and Google (all have different operating systems), offer applications that encourage in-app advertising. Apple introduced a system called iAd that allows for full-screen video and interactive advertising content to be served within an application. The advertisements are wirelessly delivered to the phone. Apple has created a new advertising category called Apple Apps. With some 500 000 and counting applications, Apple has the means to deliver advertising messages.

QR Codes

QR code (quick response code) A two-dimensional barcode that can be scanned and read by smartphones; allows for the sharing of text and data.

A **QR code**, or *quick response code*, is a two-dimensional barcode that can be scanned and read by smartphones. The code allows for the sharing of text and data. The codes are small squares with black-and-white patterns. To read the codes a person needs to download a free QR code reader to their phone, available in various app stores (e.g., Tag Reader for an iPhone and QuickMark for an Android phone).

Marketers have experimented with the codes because they offer opportunities to transfer more detailed information in a cost-efficient manner. If a QR code is included with the ad, the reader can be exposed to much more information by taking a picture of the code. Refer to the image in **Figure 14.20**. That said, the use of QR codes is actually declining among marketing organizations each year. It seems that QR codes have not been popular with consumers. Some experts are predicting the total demise of QR codes in the not-too-distant future.

Video Game Advertising

advergaming The placement of ads in commercially sold games, in games played online, or on mobile phones.

Advertising in video games, or **advergaming**, refers to the placement of ads in commercially sold games, games played online, or on mobile phones. New data suggest that video games, once the domain of young males, are growing in popularity across both genders and all age groups. Games are becoming an accepted form of family entertainment.[35]

An advertiser has the choice of developing their own games or placing ads in commercially sold games. Many brands have developed their own games for visitors at

Figure 14.21 Gamers who are intensely involved with a video game do notice the ads.

their website. These games offer interactivity and entertainment value—things people are looking for when they visit a website. In commercially sold games there is a diverse range of possibilities, including fully integrated opportunities (having a game designed around a brand or brands), interactive product placements, outdoor-style billboards, and 30-second video spots. Refer to the image in **Figure 14.21**.

The presence of advertisements in games are acceptable to gamers. In fact, they expect to see ads and they are receptive to their presence. A study conducted by IGA Worldwide (a game vendor) discovered that 70 percent of respondents thought the ads made them feel better about the brands.[36] Apparently the presence of ads adds some reality to the game! Some traditional blue-chip brands, including Coca-Cola, Pepsi-Cola, Red Bull, Axe, and Burger King, have channelled some of their advertising investment into video games and have been successful with it.

For a summary of the advantages and disadvantages of these emerging media platforms refer to **Figure 14.22**.

Simulation: Online Marketing

Advantages	Disadvantages
Social Media Word-of-Mouth—brand endorsements by friends has positive influence Targeting—can reach precisely defined targets Engagement—consumers interact with brand	**Social Media** Word of Mouth—bad news about a brand travels fast Currency—considerable time required to "refresh" posted information Relevance—too many unsolicited "promotional" ads
Mobile Targeting—effectively reaches younger target Timing—can reach target at point of sale	**Mobile** Cost to Consumers—consumers may balk at data charges for downloads Image—intrusiveness borders on telemarketing image
Video Games Recall—heightened interest while playing game improves brand recall	**Video Games** Message—message can't be changed in commercially sold games

Figure 14.22 Media Selection Considerations—Interactive Media Communications

✔ Experience Marketing

To experience marketing you have to assess situations and make recommendations to change marketing strategies when necessary. What would you do in the following situation?

You are the brand manager for the Audi TT in Canada and have to devise a new advertising campaign to create some excitement for the brand. You have described your target market as progressive-minded males and females who are on the move in their careers, risk-takers who enjoy new challenges, and people who value their work but like to play just as much. This person is 30 to 45 years old, lives in an urban area, has a professional orientation, is willing to move around to get ahead, and lives in a downtown apartment or condominium but longs for open spaces on the weekends.

You know that the luxury sports segment of the market is growing despite the poor economic situation. It seems that people with money will buy cars in any market conditions. Within the target market there is a low level of brand awareness for the Audi TT.

When you look at the car you see confidence: a roofline that extends like a dome sweeping down into a powerful shoulder line, a wide track and aggressive stance—it exudes power! How do you get that image into an advertisement? Your immediate challenge is to develop an effective message and media strategy that will improve awareness and interest in the car among the target market. What will you recommend? Be prepared to justify your message and media decisions.

CHAPTER SUMMARY

L01 Define integrated marketing communications and describe the components of the integrated marketing communications mix. *(pp. 294–295)*

Marketing communications is any means of communication used by marketing organizations to inform, persuade, or remind potential buyers about a product or service. To fulfill these tasks, an organization employs an integrated marketing communications mix comprising media advertising, interactive media communications, sales promotion, public relations, experiential marketing, and personal selling. IMC involves the coordination of all forms of marketing communications in a unified program that maximizes the impact of messages on consumers and other types of customers.

L02 Describe the basic elements comprising marketing communications planning. *(pp. 295–297)*

Marketing communications planning involves setting objectives, making strategic decisions on what components of the communications mix to use, and devising and justifying a budget for all activities that are recommended. Objectives outline what a campaign is to accomplish (e.g., build brand awareness, stimulate trial purchase, etc.). Strategy involves balancing push and pull activities. Push refers to actions that stimulate demand for goods among distributors of products. Pull refers to actions that have an impact the demand for a product among consumers.

L03 Explain the nature of creative (message) decisions that are part of an advertising campaign. *(pp. 297–301)*

The objective of advertising is to motivate a customer to make a purchase. A combination of message and proper media selection are the means to provide such motivation. Creative decisions focus on developing a theme for a campaign and determining what appeal techniques will be used to deliver the message. Creative objectives identify the nature of the message—the key benefits to be communicated. Agency planners then develop a theme and select the appropriate appeal technique to deliver the message. Some of the appeal techniques include humour, comparisons, emotion, lifestyle, celebrity endorsements, testimonials, sex, and product demonstrations.

L04 Explain the nature of media decisions that are part of an advertising campaign. *(pp. 301–304)*

Media decisions focus on what media to select, how much to spend on each medium, and with what frequency and duration. Contemporary marketing organizations have evaluated various media consumption trends and determined that a well-balanced mix of traditional mass media with newer digital media works effectively. Strategically thinking, an advertiser evaluates how broad or how narrow a plan should be in terms of reaching the target market. Factors such as reach, frequency, continuity, market coverage, engagement, and timing are also factored into the media evaluation and selection process. The budget available for the campaign will have an impact on all of these decisions. Advertising agencies prepare media plans for client approval.

L05 Assess the various media alternatiaves for delivering advertising messages. *(pp. 304–309)*

The media options are evaluated for their strengths and weaknesses and are compared for their ability to effectively reach the target market within budget guidelines. Television is the medium with the most impact, but it is also the most costly. Radio is excellent for reaching people in local markets and is relatively inexpensive but it's not possible to show the product on radio. Magazines are a targeted medium that reach people based on demographic, psychographic and geographic characteristics. Newspapers effectively reach readers in local markets. Both newspapers and magazines have to shift their readers to their digital editions to remain relevant. Out-of-home media reach people at a time when they are ready to buy and are effective delivering short messages.

Direct response advertising reaches a predefined target effectively but is associated with the hard-sell approach many consumers dislike. Finally, the Internet is a highly targeted and timely medium but response rates to ads placed online are very low.

LO6 Describe the role of social media in marketing communications campaigns. *(pp. 309–314)*

With such a large segment of the population active on social networks, it has become a logical choice for branded marketing communications. Marketers have discovered that combining traditional media with digital and social media improve the effectiveness of a campaign. Marketers have had to adapt to the lack of control they have on social networks. It is a medium where participants join in the communications process and actually develop content on behalf of brands. Allowing such control is contrary to historical marketing wisdom. Numerous communications options are available including display advertising, sponsored posts, brand pages, referrals from a friend network, blogs, and YouTube channels.

The primary benefits of social media communications are the potential for word of mouth among friends about a brand, the ability to reach all age groups (although there is a skew to the under-35 segment), and the engagement factor. Members of social networks engage with brands because they want to—it is a participative medium. Information garnered from consumers can ultimately have an impact on marketing strategy.

LO7 Describe the role of mobile communications in marketing communications strategies. *(pp. 314–317)*

Mobile media opportunities are in their infancy, but with so many people owning smartphones the opportunities for location-based marketing are significant. The ability to reach a customer in real time right when they could be making a purchase decision is an attractive proposition. Marketing communications opportunities include text messaging, video messaging, advertisements in applications, and video game advertising. An irony of video games is that ads in the games are acceptable—they add an element of reality to the game.

MyMarketingLab

Study, practise, and explore real marketing situations with these helpful resources:
- **Interactive Lesson Presentations:** Work through interactive presentations and assessments to test your knowledge of marketing concepts.
- **Study Plan:** Check your understanding of chapter concepts with self-study quizzes.
- **Dynamic Study Modules:** Work through adaptive study modules on your computer, tablet, or mobile device.
- **Simulations:** Practise decision-making in simulated marketing environments.

REVIEW QUESTIONS

1. What are the components of the integrated marketing communications mix? Briefly describe each component. *(LO1)*
2. What are the key elements of marketing communications planning? *(LO2)*
3. What is the difference between a push strategy and a pull strategy? *(LO2)*
4. Explain the difference between percentage-of-sales budgeting and industry-average budgeting. *(LO2)*
5. In the context of message development, what is the difference between creative objectives and creative strategy? *(LO3)*
6. Briefly explain how the following appeal techniques are used to deliver advertising messages: *(LO3)*
   a. Emotion
   b. Humour
   c. Endorsements
   d. Testimonials
   e. Lifestyle
7. In what situations would the following target-market media strategies be used: shotgun strategy, profile-matching strategy, and rifle strategy? *(LO4)*

8. Explain the following media strategy concepts: reach, frequency, continuity, and engagement. *(LO4)*
9. Briefly explain the concepts of product placement and branded content in television programming. *(LO4)*
10. In the context of advertising, what are the primary strengths and weaknesses of the following media: *(LO5)*
    a. Television
    b. Radio
    c. Magazines
    d. Newspaper
    e. Out-of-home
11. Identify and briefly explain the various forms of Internet advertising. *(LO5)*
12. What are the primary benefits of including social media in the marketing communications mix? Briefly explain. *(LO6)*
13. What is meant by the term *viral marketing*? *(LO6)*
14. What are the primary message delivery options available to advertisers in a mobile communications environment? *(LO7)*

DISCUSSION AND APPLICATION QUESTIONS

1. Assume you are the marketing manager for Gillette Fusion razors (or Gillette Venus razors), and you are considering using a new celebrity in advertising to freshen the image of the brand. What type of celebrity would you select? Would you choose a rising star or an established star? Justify the position you take.
2. Considering the trends in media consumption that are occurring, how quickly should advertisers move into social media

and mobile media advertising? Do budget allocations today reflect the reality of the situation? Some additional research on this topic may be necessary in order to form a sound opinion.
3. How important will mobile communication for advertising purposes be in the future? Will consumers be accepting of advertising messages or will they perceive them to be a nuisance? Describe and defend your opinion on the issue.

15

IMC: Sales Promotion, Public Relations, Experiential Marketing, and Personal Selling

The Canadian Press Images-Mario Beauregard

LEARNING OBJECTIVES

LO1 Identify the roles and functions of various consumer promotion activities. (pp. 321–327)

LO2 Identify the roles and functions of various trade promotion activities. (pp. 327–328)

LO3 Identify the role of public relations in the development of marketing communications strategies. (pp. 329–331)

LO4 Describe the public relations tools and techniques for communications strategies. (pp. 331–334)

LO5 Explain the role of experiential marketing in marketing today. (pp. 335–342)

LO6 Describe the role of personal selling in the marketing communications mix. (pp. 342–343)

LO7 Describe the basic steps in the selling process. (pp. 343–345)

IT SEEMS THAT...

Canadians love their loyalty cards. Nearly nine in ten Canadian adults (86 percent) actively participate in at least one loyalty program. One of the most popular loyalty programs in Canada is operated by Canadian Tire. Its Canadian Tire "money" is as good as cash in any Canadian Tire store.

Canadian Tire money is almost as old as the company itself. The money dates back to 1958 when original owners John W. and Alfred J. Billes wanted to recognize long-standing customers for their loyalty. That formula still works today! Collecting Canadian Tire money is a successful promotion that people have come to know, expect, and love, and it keeps people coming back to shop. Of course, there's an electronic edition of Canadian Tire money today!

Canadian Tire's loyalty program is successful due to its simplicity. It is easy for the customer to understand and easy for them to get their reward. Customers can instantly redeem their money anytime at the cash register. Canadian Tire money remains the backbone of the company's loyalty marketing programs. As you will learn in this chapter, sales promotions such as Canadian Tire money, along with other related strategies, influence customer purchase intentions.

This chapter examines the remaining components of the marketing communications mix: sales promotion, public relations, experiential marketing, and personal selling. All of these activities are given careful consideration when a manager is planning a marketing communications campaign. Each of these activities can serve a specific purpose depending upon the marketing objectives of the company or brand.

SALES PROMOTION

Sales promotion is any activity that provides special incentives to bring about immediate action from consumers, distributors, and an organization's sales force; in other words, it encourages the decision to buy. The expression "advertising appeals to the heart and sales promotion to the wallet" shows the distinction between the two types of activity. Advertising tells us why we should buy a product, whereas sales promotion offers incentives (e.g., cents-off coupon, free sample, chance to win a prize) to encourage consumers to purchase a product. Various discounts and allowances encourage distributors to carry and resell products in the channel of distribution.

sales promotion Activity that provides special incentives to bring about immediate action from consumers, distributors, and an organization's sales force.

Promotions are very important today since we are in an era where consumers are seeking better value for their shopping dollars. In a recent study conducted by Nielsen Canada, 70 percent of respondents said they were only buying products on sale, 52 percent said they used coupons, 37 percent sought out large value packs, and 34 percent shopped at discount retailers.[1] These findings suggest that marketers place a strong focus on promotions.

Sales promotion strategies play a key role in attracting new customers to a brand or retailer. Two principal kinds of sales promotion exist: consumer promotion and trade promotion.

CONSUMER PROMOTION

LO1 Identify the roles and functions of various consumer promotion activities.

Consumer promotion is any activity that promotes extra brand sales by offering the consumer an incentive over and above the product's inherent benefits. These promotions are designed to pull the product through the channel of distribution by motivating consumers to make an immediate purchase. The objectives of consumer promotions are as follows:

consumer promotion Activity promoting extra brand sales by offering the consumer an incentive over and above the product's inherent benefits.

1. *Trial Purchase*—When introducing a new product, marketers want customers to make a first purchase right away so that product acceptance can be secured quickly. Something as simple as a coupon distributed in the media will accomplish this goal.

2. *Repeat Purchases*—Marketers protect loyalty by offering incentives for consumers to buy the item repeatedly. Coupons with a product that can be redeemed on the next purchase is a way of holding loyalty, as are loyalty programs where points or dollars are accumulated for future use.

3. *Multiple Purchases*—Promotions of this nature "load the consumer up." For example, a contest may be run to spur many entries and purchases, or cash refunds may offer savings that increase with each additional purchase of an item. For example, a $1 refund may be available on one purchase and a $3 refund on two purchases.

The major types of consumer promotion are coupons, free samples, contests, cash refunds, premiums, frequent-buyer programs, and delayed-payment incentives.

Coupons

coupon Price-saving incentive offered to consumers by manufacturers and retailers to stimulate purchase of a specified product.

A **coupon** is a price-saving incentive to stimulate quicker purchase of a designated product. The Canadian packaged goods industry is a big distributor of coupons (household, personal care, and food manufacturers). In 2012, this industry distributed 6.8 billion coupons to Canadian households and 86 million of them were redeemed by consumers.[2] Refer to **Figure 15.1** for an illustration.

The objectives of a coupon promotion affect the way that coupons will be delivered. If the objective is trial purchase, media-delivered coupons are appropriate. Media such as newspapers, inserts that are distributed by newspapers, magazines, direct mail, email, and mobile devices are used to deliver the coupons. If the objective is repeat purchase, using the product itself to deliver a coupon is effective—a current customer uses the incentive to buy again. For example, it is quite common for a brand of cereal to include coupons for next purchase inside the package or on the back of the package.

Consumers are now receptive to receiving coupons digitally. According to *eMarketer*, "the number of users who access coupons via computers or smartphones is boosting overall growth of coupons. Smartphones let people access deals on the go and are capable of delivering coupons that are relevant based on location behavior and timeliness."[3]

redemption rate The number of coupons returned to an organization expressed as a percentage of the total number of coupons in distribution for a particular coupon offer.

Savvy shoppers now look to online sources for valuable money-saving coupons. A consumer can select specific goods and services, survey the discounts offered, and obtain the coupon from online sources. Save.ca and Coupons.com offer marketers the opportunity to provide coupons online.

Check-in services such as Groupon and Foursquare are leading the charge in digital coupons. The Groupon model is unique. "Groupon entices a retailer to offer a special deal—say, 50 percent off on an item or service for one day. Groupon then broadcasts the offer to its subscribers. For its matchmaking services, Groupon takes 50 percent of the revenue the offer generates. On average, the retailer makes only about 25 percent of what it would normally

free sample A free product distributed to potential users either in a small trial size or its regular size.

make."[4] This may not sound financially attractive to the retailer but the objective of such a promotion is to get new customers inside the door. Customer satisfaction will determine if there is a return visit.

The effectiveness of a brand-specific coupon campaign is determined by the **redemption rate**, or the number of coupons returned to an organization, expressed as a percentage of the total number of coupons in distribution for a particular coupon offer. A high redemption rate indicates that the coupon offer was attractive (the coupon had a good perceived value) to the target market and had a significant impact on purchases.

Free Samples

A **free sample** is a free product distributed to potential users, either in a small trial size or in its regular size. Sampling is commonly practised when a company is introducing a new product, a line extension of an existing

Figure 15.1   Financial incentives such as coupons encourage trial purchase of a product by new users.

Figure 15.2 In-store sampling encourages trial purchases.

product, or a product improvement, such as a new flavour, blend, or scent. Offering samples is an effective way of getting trial usage because it eliminates the financial risk associated with a new purchase. The downside of free samples is the cost involved; the product, possibility of special packaging, and distribution can be very expensive.

Samples can be distributed in a variety of ways. One of the most common methods is in-store distribution. There are several variations of in-store sampling: product demonstrations and sampling, saleable sample sizes (small replica-pack sizes of the actual product), and cross-sampling (having one product carry a sample size of another product). Packaged-goods companies, such as Kraft and General Mills, frequently employ this type of sampling, as do retailers who are promoting their private-label brands. Refer to the image in **Figure 15.2**.

Contests

Contests are designed to create short-term excitement about a product. A contest usually provides an incentive to buy an item, requiring, for example, the submission of a product label or symbol and an entry form that is included with the product. Consumers are encouraged to enter often and thereby improve their chances of winning a prize. This results in many purchases. While contests tend to attract the current users of a product, they are less effective in inducing trial purchases than are coupons and samples. Consequently, contests are most appropriate in the mature stage of the product life cycle, when the aim is to retain current market share. Sweepstakes and instant wins are two major types of contests.

A **sweepstakes** contest is a chance promotion involving the giveaway of products and services of value to randomly selected participants who have submitted qualified entries. Prizes such as cash, cars, homes, and vacations are given away. Consumers enter sweepstakes by filling in an entry form, usually available at the point of purchase or through print advertising, and submitting it along with a proof of purchase to a central location where a draw is held to determine the winners.

A **game (instant-win contest)** is a promotional vehicle that includes a number of predetermined, pre-seeded winning tickets in the overall, fixed universe of tickets. Packages containing winning certificates are redeemed for prizes. Variations of this type of contest include collect-and-wins and match-and-wins. These types of contests are commonly used by quick-serve restaurants. McDonald's Monopoly contest and Tim Hortons' Roll Up the Rim to Win promotion are good examples. Refer to the image in **Figure 15.3**. The program's simplicity has contributed to the popularity and longevity of Roll Up the Rim. You can win a prize simply by purchasing a morning coffee! This promotion rewards customers for their loyalty.

In the age of database marketing, companies use contests to engage consumers with the brand. To engage consumers, marketers place contest prize codes on packages, food and drink

contest A promotion designed to create short-term excitement about a product.

sweepstakes A type of contest in which large prizes, such as cash, cars, homes, and vacations, are given away to randomly selected participants.

game (instant-win contest) Promotion vehicle that includes a number of predetermined, pre-seeded winning tickets in the overall, fixed universe of tickets. Packages containing winning certificates are redeemed for prizes.

Tim Hortons, the Tim Hortons logo, Tim Card Design, and RRRoll up the Rim to Win are trademarks of Tim Hortons. Used with permission.

Figure 15.3 A popular promotion like Roll up the Rim to Win at Tim Hortons encourages customers to visit the restaurant more often.

containers in fast-food restaurants, and so on. To win a prize, consumers must either send a text message or visit a website to type in their coupon code. Along the way they are exposed to additional brand messages and marketers have an opportunity to collect valuable information about them—information that can be used to fine-tune direct marketing offers at a later date.

Contests are governed by laws and regulations, and any company that runs one must publish certain information: how, where, and when to enter; who is eligible to enter the contest; the prize structure, value, and number of prizes; the odds of winning and the selection procedure; and conditions that must be met before a prize is awarded (e.g., a skill-testing question must be answered). Contest details are made available at point of purchase and on the sponsor's website. Tim Hortons posts all Roll up the Rim to Win rules in each store but it would take a customer all day to read them—rest assured, they do cover all of the legal bases!

Cash Refunds (Rebates)

cash refund (rebate)
Predetermined amount of money returned directly to the consumer by the manufacturer after the purchase has been made.

A **cash refund**, or *rebate* as it is often called, is a predetermined amount of money returned directly to the consumer by the manufacturer after the purchase has been made. For companies in the packaged-goods industry, cash refunds are useful promotion techniques in the mature stage of the product's life cycle because such activity reinforces loyalty. The most common type of refund is the single-purchase refund—consumers receive a portion of their money back on the purchase of a product. However, refunds are designed to achieve different objectives; hence, they can be offered in different formats. For example, they may escalate in value. An offer could be structured as follows: buy one get $1 back; buy two get $2 back; buy three and get $5 back. The reward is greater for buying multiple items. This technique is more suitable to packaged goods brands.

Rebates are very popular in durable-goods markets such as automobiles, appliances, and electronics equipment. Refer to **Figure 15.4**. Automobile companies trying to recover from the recent recession offered "cash back" rebates as high $5000 on cars and $8000 on trucks. The rebates move the cars but place a financial strain on the company. Consumers are adapting to rebates so well, it seems they won't buy a new car unless some kind of incentive is available. Long term, this promotion tactic is not in the best interests of the automobile industry.

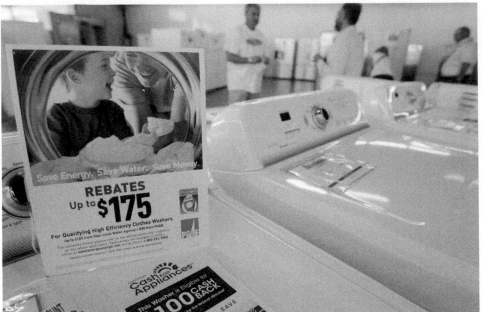

Figure 15.4 Financial incentives in the form of rebates are popular among durable goods manufacturers.

AP Photo/Paul Sakuma/CP Images

Premiums

A **premium** is an item offered free or at a bargain price to consumers who buy another specific item or make a minimum purchase. The goal of a premium offer is to provide added value to new and repeat purchasers.

Premiums are usually offered to consumers in three ways: as a mail-in (send in proofs of purchase and the item will be returned by mail), as an in-pack or on-pack promotion (an item is placed inside a package or attached to a package), or by a coupon offer distributed by in-store shelf advertisements. Distributing premiums with a product is popular because it provides instant gratification. Premiums with high perceived value can encourage brand switching—attractive offers attract new customers, even if only on a temporary basis.

The use of premiums achieves several objectives: it increases the quantity of brand purchases made by consumers, it helps to retain current users, and it provides a merchandising tool to encourage display activity in stores.

In the months preceding the 2014 Sochi Winter Olympics, General Mills launched a unique virtual premium offer across many of its cereal and snack food products. Six million packages were embedded with Blippar technology. By downloading the Blippar application consumers could scan the package to activate an augmented reality experience. Consumers could play games, take a photo beside a virtual image of a Canadian Olympian, and view athlete profiles.[5] Refer to the image in **Figure 15.5**.

Loyalty (Frequent Buyer) Programs

Canadian retailers and a variety of service industries, such as airlines, hotels, and gasoline distributors, have made loyalty or frequent buyer programs popular. In fact, Canadian consumers hold on average 6.4 loyalty cards and 92 percent of consumers belong to at least one loyalty program. Further, 78 percent of consumers shop strategically to accumulate points—people will pass by retailers selling the product they want in order to go to a retailer where they can earn loyalty points.[6]

A **loyalty (frequent buyer) program** offers consumers some kind of bonus or incentive when they make a purchase. The bonus accumulates with each new purchase. For a description of these loyalty programs, refer to **Figure 15.6**.

The goal of such offers is to encourage loyalty. The Intercontinental Group of Hotels, which operates in all price and quality segments of the lodging industry, has a loyalty program called Priority Club Rewards. As a customer's points accumulate they can be

premium An item offered for free or at a bargain price to customers who buy another specific item or make a minimum purchase.

loyalty (frequent buyer) program Offers the consumer a small bonus, such as points or "play money," when they make a purchase; the bonus accumulates with each new purchase.

Figure 15.5 A premium offer will attract new customers and help maintain loyalty with present customers.

Photo by Keith J. Tuckwell

redeemed for merchandise or they can be used for hotel rooms and special travel packages sponsored by the hotel chain and its airline partners. One of the most popular retail loyalty cards in Canada is the Shoppers Optimum program. It is popular since points are easy to accumulate and redeem. The Optimum program has 10 million members.[7] See the illustration in **Figure 15.7**.

Canadian Tire's program is perhaps the best-known and longest-running frequent-buyer program in Canada (it started in 1958). The program rewards regular shoppers who pay for merchandise with cash or a Canadian Tire credit card with Canadian Tire "money." Canadian Tire money captures the essence of a rewards program because customers can obtain something for free—a gratifying experience!

delayed-payment incentive promotion Incentive promotion allowing the consumer a grace period during which no interest or principal is paid for the item purchased.

Delayed-Payment Incentives

In a **delayed-payment incentive promotion**, a consumer is granted a grace period during which no interest or principal is paid for the item purchased. Once the purchase is made from the retailer, a finance company assumes the agreement and charges interest if full payment is not made by the agreed-upon date.

Figure 15.6
Some Different Types of Customer Loyalty Programs

Type	Description of Program
Appreciation	Fast food and coffee chains hand out cards that get stamped or punched with each purchase. After a certain number of purchases, the customer receives a "free" coffee/food item.
Rewards	The consumer collects points, dollars, or miles with rewards related to the company's business (e.g., Canadian Tire money).
Partnerships	Consumers earn points with purchases from partner companies (e.g., Air Miles partners with Shell Canada, Rexall, Safeway, Metro, and Budget car rentals, among others).
Rebates	Shoppers are offered rebates based on the amount they spend. Costco's executive membership offers a 2 percent annual rebate on most purchases.

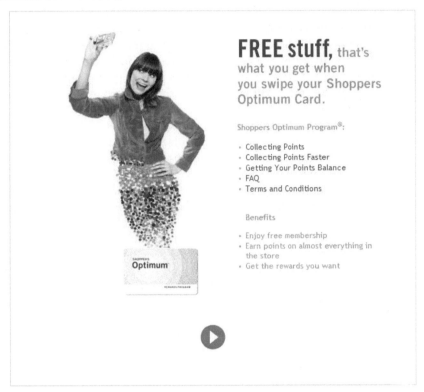

Figure 15.7   An Illustration of a Rewards Loyalty Program from Shoppers Drug Mart

Courtesy of Shoppers Drug Mart

Home Depot offers interest-free loans for up to one year on purchases over a certain value. For example, an installation of new roof shingles may cost $10 000. If installed by Home Depot it can be financed for one year interest free with all payments recorded on the customer's Home Depot credit card statement. If a private contractor did the same job, the consumer would pay as soon as the job was complete. The idea of spreading out payments on an interest-free basis brings customers to Home Depot.

For additional insight into a successful sales promotion program implemented by General Mills Canada, read the Think Marketing box **Going for Gold**.

TRADE PROMOTION

LO2 Identify the roles and functions of various trade promotion activities.

Trade promotion is promotional activity directed at distributors to push a product through the channel of distribution; it is designed to increase the volume purchased and encourage merchandising support for a manufacturer's product. The most commonly used trade promotion activities are co-operative advertising, performance allowances, dealer premiums, and dealer display materials.

Co-operative Advertising

In the case of **co-operative advertising**, a manufacturer allocates funds to pay a portion of a retailer's advertising. For example, a predetermined percentage (say, 3 to 5 percent)

trade promotion Promotional activity directed at distributors that is designed to increase the volume they purchase and encourage merchandising support for a manufacturer's product.

co-operative advertising Funds allocated by a manufacturer to pay for a portion of a retailer's advertising.

of the dollar volume purchased by a distributor accumulates in an account with the company selling the goods. When the selling company wants to run a promotion with the distributor, it draws on the accumulated funds to pay a portion of the retailer's advertising. The advertisements by major supermarket chains showing weekly specials, for example, are partially paid for by the manufacturers participating in the advertisements in any given week.

Trade and Performance Allowances

trade allowance A temporary price reduction designed to encourage larger purchases by distributors (wholesalers and retailers).

performance allowance Discount offered by a manufacturer to a distributor who performs a promotional function on the manufacturer's behalf.

A **trade allowance** is a temporary price reduction designed to encourage larger purchases by distributors (wholesalers and retailers). Such price reductions may be offered in the form of a percentage reduction from list price, a predetermined dollar amount off list price, or as a free goods offer (e.g., buy ten cases, get one free).

A **performance allowance** is a discount offered by manufacturers to encourage retailers to perform specific merchandising functions (e.g., display the product at retail, provide an advertising mention in a flyer, or offer a lower price for a period of time). Before paying the allowance, the manufacturer requires proof of performance from the retailer. Performance allowances are a useful tactic to employ if the marketing objective is to increase sales in the short term.

It is a common strategy to offer co-operative advertising funds, trade allowances, and performance allowances as an integrated offer in order to maximize the impact of a trade promotion. Such plans are attractive to retailers because the financial rewards are much greater and the offer facilitates efficient use of advertising dollars to support the retailer's advertising and merchandising activities.

As discussed in Chapter 12, relatively few large distributors control the grocery and drug store markets. These distributors pressure suppliers for more trade support in the form of financial incentives. To maintain distribution, the suppliers meet these demands. Such control complicates long-term brand planning and curtails investment in other marketing and marketing communications programs.

Dealer Premiums

dealer premium An incentive offered to a distributor by a manufacturer to encourage a special purchase (i.e., a specified volume of merchandise) or to secure additional merchandising support.

dealer-display material (point-of-purchase material) Self-contained, custom-designed merchandising units that either temporarily or permanently display a manufacturer's product.

A **dealer premium** is an incentive offered to a distributor by a manufacturer to encourage a special purchase (e.g., a specified volume of merchandise) or to secure additional merchandising support from a distributor. Premiums are usually offered in the form of merchandise (e.g., a set of golf clubs, or other forms of leisure goods or sporting goods); the value of the premium increases with the amount of product purchased by the retailer.

Its use is often controversial. Some distributors forbid their buyers to accept premiums because they believe only the individual buyer, rather than the organization, benefits. Such a situation, often referred to as *payola*, may lead the buyer to make unnecessary purchases and ignore the objectives of the distributor. These practices are perceived by many to be unethical, and they should not occur. Nonetheless, some dealings do happen under the table, so students should be aware of it.

Dealer-Display Materials

Dealer-display material (point-of-purchase material) consists of self-contained, custom-designed merchandising units, either permanent or temporary, that display a manufacturer's product. It includes shelf extenders (tray-like extensions that project outward from the shelf to extend shelf display), shelf talkers (small posters that hang from shelves), advertising pads or tear pads (tear-off sheets that usually explain details of a consumer promotion offer), and display shippers (shipping cases that convert to display bins or stands when opened). The use of such displays and materials is at the discretion of the retailers whose space they occupy. Refer to the illustration in **Figure 15.8**.

Photo by Keith J. Tuckwell

Figure 15.8   Dealer display materials and product displays attract attention and encourage purchases.

PUBLIC RELATIONS: ITS ROLE IN MARKETING COMMUNICATIONS

LO3 Identify the role of public relations in the development of marketing communications strategies.

Public relations consists of a variety of activities and communications that organizations undertake to monitor, evaluate, and influence the attitudes, opinions, and behaviours of groups or individuals who constitute their publics.

The practice of public relations is used to build rapport with the various publics a company, individual, or organization may have. Those publics may include employees, shareholders, distributors, governments, the financial community, and customers. A good public relations plan involves an open, honest, and constructive relationship with these publics. Public relations communications is useful in four key areas: corporate communications, reputation management, publicity generation, and fundraising. Each of these areas has an impact on how the public perceives a company or brand. Let's examine each area.

public relations A variety of activities and communications that organizations undertake to monitor, evaluate, influence, and adapt to the attitudes, opinions, and behaviours of their publics.

Corporate Communications

Public relations can play a vital role in building an organization's image. Smart companies take a proactive stance and communicate loudly and clearly the good things they are doing. One of the vehicles for announcing good deeds is corporate advertising. **Corporate advertising** is a paid form of advertising designed to convey a favourable image of a company to its various publics. For example, corporate advertising may communicate to the public what a company is doing in terms of social responsibility, or show how it helps resolve customers' problems. **Figure 15.9** shows an example of corporate advertising.

corporate advertising A paid form of advertising designed to create a favourable image for an organization among its publics.

Reputation Management

Public relations plays a vital role when a company faces a crisis. Financial guru Warren Buffett once said, "It takes 20 years to build a reputation and five minutes to ruin it."[8] In today's lightning-speed world of social media it may take only seconds to do the same!

The final outcome of a crisis often depends on how effectively a firm manages its public relations activity. Just recently, the Joe Fresh brand of clothing and its parent company, Loblaw, had to deal with the fallout from the collapse of a Bangladesh garment factory that manufactured their product. With a high death toll, media coverage of Joe Fresh's connection with the event was constant after the disaster. The Joe Fresh image of being a family-friendly brand—good quality at reasonable prices—took a beating once the disaster and connection to exploited workers was exposed. Many Canadians didn't feel good about purchasing or wearing the clothing.

Part of the PR plan to defuse the situation involved sending high-level executives to Bangladesh to explore the situation and figure out a way to prevent similar situations from occurring again. The actions taken by Loblaw were quick and decisive—two trademarks of how to handle a crisis situation effectively. Consumers tend to forgive companies when they know that proper actions are undertaken. In many cases, a brand or company is rewarded with a stronger degree of loyalty because consumers know they can trust the brand for the actions taken now and in the future.

When facing a crisis situation, acting quickly and decisively is the approach recommended by experts. The objective is to reassure the public that everything possible is being done to correct the situation. To do so, a company needs to be ready when crisis situations arise. It must take control of the communications agenda early and ensure that messages are credible from the outset.

Video: Abercrombie and Fitch Sorry After Plus-Size Firestorm

Publicity Generation

Publicity is news about a person, product, service, or idea that appears in the print or broadcast media. In a marketing context, publicity generation can help achieve marketing objectives such as raising awareness, building relationships with customers, engaging target audiences, and attracting new clients. Unlike *paid media*, where the message is

publicity News about a person, product, idea, or service that appears in the print or broadcast media.

Figure 15.9   An illustration of corporate advertising designed to create goodwill for an organization.

predetermined and controlled, the intention of publicity is to generate media coverage or earned media. *Earned media* is essentially free media exposure.

Publicity must be newsworthy. Unfortunately, what seems like news to a company may not be news to the media. Therefore, an organization must be satisfied with whatever media coverage it receives. Red Bull's recent social media event demonstrates how publicity works. Millions of people watched on the Internet as Felix Baumgartner jumped from the edge of space (a 39km jump)—they were literally right there with him.

Baumgartner shattered the sound barrier and safely landed almost nine minutes later. The jump generated 216 000 likes, 10 000 comments and 29 000 shares in 40 minutes. Some 40 television stations in 50 countries carried the live feed and there were eight million simultaneous views on YouTube.[9] You can be the judge of whether this publicity had an impact on Red Bull's sales. Refer to the image in **Figure 15.10**.

Figure 15.10   Red Bull's sponsored jump from the edge of space garnered much publicity for the brand.

Other means of generating publicity for a product could involve a practice called product seeding. With **product seeding** a product is given free to trendsetters who, in turn, influence others to become aware of the product and, the marketer hopes, purchase it. The trendsetters chat about the product whenever the opportunity arises—they act as ambassadors for the brand. In a broader sense, marketers can also take advantage of the influence of ordinary consumers who often recommend goods and services to their friends, a concept referred to as **word-of-mouth marketing**.

The fact that the product is in the hands of a trendsetter helps create publicity for the brand. Typically, a product seeding campaign reaches a well-defined target at much lower cost than a media advertising campaign. Product seeding campaigns are often implemented just prior to the launch of a new product; the objective is to create some buzz for the launch.

Fundraising

In the not-for-profit market sector, public relations plays a key role. A national organization such as the Salvation Army faces a huge challenge each year. Some people perceive the organization to be a big "money hole" and wonder where all the donations go. To change this perception, public relations is used to educate the public about how the funds are used, to solicit commitment, to predispose people to give, and to make people feel good about giving. The goal of the Salvation Army's campaign (or any other similar campaign) is to create a positive image and secure support by sending a message to the public that clearly states what the organization is all about. Refer to the illustration in **Figure 15.11**.

Figure 15.11   A public relations advertisement encouraging the public to support an important social issue.

PUBLIC RELATIONS STRATEGIES

LO4 Describe the public relations tools and techniques for communications strategies.

The tools available to execute public relations programs are diverse. Some are used routinely to communicate newsworthy information and some are used only periodically or on special occasions. The presence of social media is changing the way in which many organizations handle their public relations strategies. This section discusses the vehicles that are routinely used.

Press Release

A **press release** (news release) is a document containing all the essential elements of the story (who, what, when, where, and why). News editors make quick decisions on what to use and what to discard. Copies of the release are mailed or emailed to a list of preferred editors (e.g., established and reliable contacts based on past relationships) and can also be distributed by a national newswire service and posted on the company website. An example of a press release appears in **Figure 15.12**.

Press Conference

A **press conference** is a gathering of news reporters invited to witness the release of important information about a company or product. Because the press conference is time consuming for the media representatives, it is usually reserved for only the most important announcements. Handling a crisis situation, for example, is usually done by means of a press conference. A press kit is usually distributed at a press conference. The **press kit** includes a schedule of conference events, a list of company participants with

product seeding Placing a new product with a group of trendsetters who in turn influence others to purchase the product.

word-of-mouth marketing Recommendations by satisfied consumers to prospective consumers about a good or service.

press release A document prepared by an organization containing public relations information that is sent to the media for publication or broadcast.

press conference A gathering of news reporters invited to a location to witness the release of important information.

press kit The assembly of relevant public relations information into a package (e.g., press releases, photographs, schedules) that is distributed to the media for publication or broadcast.

biographical information, a press release, photographs, copies of speeches, digital material, and any other relevant information.

Websites

Since the purpose of a website is to communicate information about a company and its products it can be an effective public relations tool. Visitors to a website quickly form an impression about a company based on the experience they have at the site. Therefore, the

BCE

News releases

Clara's Big Ride for Bell Let's Talk arrives on Parliament Hill: Clara Hughes completes her epic journey to create a stigma-free nation

- Cycling around Canada for 110 days, Clara shared the goal of a nation free of the stigma around mental illness with Canadians in communities everywhere
- More than 11,000 kilometres, 105 communities, 235 events in every province and territory
- Clara welcomed to Parliament Hill at 1:05 pm by the Honourable Shelly Glover for Canada Day celebrations
- Clara to be welcomed to Rideau Hall later today by Their Excellencies Governor General David Johnston and Mrs. Sharon Johnston
- Drop by Clara's Celebration Plaza in Major's Hill Park to learn more about the incredible journey of Clara Hughes

OTTAWA, July 1, 2014 – Canadian Olympian and mental health champion Clara Hughes rides into Ottawa today to complete her epic 110-day cycling journey around the country, sharing the message that together we can achieve a nation free of the stigma around mental illness.

Over more than 11,000 kilometres, through 105 communities in all 10 provinces and all 3 territories, Clara's Big Ride for Bell Let's Talk engaged Canadians of all kinds in the national conversation about mental health. Clara was welcomed to more than 150 community gatherings and 80 school and youth events from coast to coast to coast – hearing the stories of thousands of Canadians touched by mental illness, and sharing the facts of her own struggle with depression.

"Happy Canada Day and thank you everyone for your incredible support! My journey around this great country has shown me that Canadians everywhere are ready to talk about mental health and eager to make a difference," said Clara. "So many wonderful, open and welcoming people, from Canada's big cities to the small settlements of the North, communities in every province and territory – all sharing the dream of a stigma-free Canada, a place where those who struggle aren't afraid to ask for help."

"1 in 5 will experience mental illness, but the number affected by the disease is 1 in 1. We all know someone impacted, whether in our families, our workplaces or our neighbourhoods. The Big Ride has shown me that talking openly about mental illness, learning that we are all affected in some way, just destroys the stigma. It's the first step in moving mental health forward. Now, let's keep talking Canada and achieve the world's first nation free of the stigma around mental illness!"

Most people who struggle with mental illness will suffer in silence for fear of being judged or rejected because of the continuing stigma around the disease. By talking openly and supportively about mental illness, as so many have done with Clara and their communities during the Big Ride, we can finally break the lingering stigma and truly move Canada's mental health forward.

As Clara circled the country meeting Canadians in communities everywhere, more than 160 elected officials and leaders at all levels of government signed a commitment map carried by Clara throughout the Ride, pledging their communities to building a stigma-free Canada.

Figure 15.12 A Sample Press Release Issued to the Media (*continued*)

Source:http://www.bce.ca/news-and-media/releases/show/claras-big-ride-for-bell-lets-talk-arrives-on-parliament-hill-clara-hughes-completes-her-epic-journey-to-create-a-stigma-free-nation?page=1&month=7&year=2014

"The Bell Let's Talk campaign is helping to shatter the stigma of mental illness one text at a time, one voice at a time and one conversation at a time," said The Honourable Rona Ambrose, Minister of Health. "Clara's journey over the last few months has inspired more people to speak openly about their personal struggles with mental illness. Thank you, Bell Canada, for spearheading this work, and thank you, Clara, for being the brave face of this campaign."

Clara at Rideau Hall
After celebrations on Parliament Hill, Clara will visit the It's An Honour!cross-Canada travelling exhibit at Rideau Hall with Their Excellencies the Right Honourable David Johnston, Governor General of Canada and Mrs. Sharon Johnston. The exhibit introduces visitors to the Canadian Honours System which recognizes extraordinary Canadians who have been honoured for their achievements, including Clara, who is an Officer of the Order of Canada.

Yesterday, after riding into Arnprior with Clara and the Big Ride team, the Governor General presented Clara with the Meritorious Service Cross (Civil Division) in recognition of her work as an advocate for mental health and the success of Clara's Big Ride.

The Clara's Big Ride team
"I'm grateful to the tens of thousands of Canadians – public officials, volunteers, teachers and so many young people – who have committed to making their communities and the entire country stigma free," said Clara. "My thanks go out to all of you, and to everyone who made the Big Ride a reality – our support riders, everyone on the Big Ride support team, our Community Champions, our National Partners. The Big Ride couldn't have happened without all of you!"

"We are all so proud of Clara and how she has engaged Canadians everywhere in creating a stigma-free nation. The Big Ride team offers special thanks to all our Community Champions who organized the more than 200 community and school events that welcomed Clara on her journey, promoting the anti-stigma message at the grassroots level in every corner of the country," said Mary Deacon, Chair of Bell Let's Talk. To learn more about Clara's events and the Big Ride Community Champions who made them happen, please visit Bell.ca/ClarasBigRide.

Clara's Big Ride was powered by our National Partners – Aimia, BMO, Canadian Tire, Cisco, Lundbeck, President's Choice and Samsung – who provided significant support for the Ride. For more information, please visit Bell.ca/ClarasBigRide/Partners.

Clara's Celebration Plaza
Visit Clara's Celebration Plaza in Ottawa today at Major's Hill Park starting at 10 am to celebrate the Big Ride and learn how you can help create a stigma-free Canada. See the extensive collection of gifts, artifacts and mementos from around the country that have been given to Clara during her Big Ride, and enjoy the entertainment on the Bell Stage.

You can also visit Bell.ca/ClarasBigRide or follow the latest Ride news on Twitter at @Bell_LetsTalk or on Facebook at Facebook.com/BellLetsTalk. To learn more about how you can continue the conversation about mental health, please visit Bell.ca/LetsTalk.

Bell Let's Talk
Bell Let's Talk promotes Canadian mental health with national awareness and anti-stigma campaigns, like Clara's Big Ride for Bell Let's Talk and Bell Let's Talk Day, and significant Bell funding of community care and access, research, and workplace initiatives. To learn more, please visit Bell.ca/Lets Talk.

Figure 15.12 (*continued*)

site must load quickly and be easy to navigate. Providing some kind of entertainment or interactive activity also enhances the visit.

The website provides an opportunity to inform the public of an organization's latest happenings. Content can vary from financial information to product information to games and contests. All press releases about the company and its brands are posted at the company website, usually in chronological order starting with the newest releases. A website should also have links to an organization's social media accounts, such as Facebook, Twitter, and Digg.

Social Media

Social media are "the online tools that people use to share content, profiles, opinions, insights, experiences, perspectives, and media itself, thus facilitating conversations and interaction online between groups of people."[10]

As discussed elsewhere in the book, the emergence of social media has transferred control of the message from the organization to the consumer. The consumer can read the message, formulate an opinion on it, perhaps even manipulate it, and send it on to others.

People no longer just want to read about news—they want to interact with it and influence opinions. Organizations that understand this concept now use social sites such as Facebook, YouTube, Twitter, and Instagram to their advantage.

Public relations has long been associated with the word *spin*. Spin implies that the marketer could deliver the message in a tone and manner to their liking. In a social media environment that approach has to change. Many experts recommend "less spin and more humility in their PR communications."[11] Their rationale for this change is based on the fact that millions of Internet users simultaneously scrutinize a brand in the public domain. Therefore, being as transparent as possible while engaging consumers in the conversation is an important consideration when using social media communications. With social media the goal is information sharing in a friend network, a concept referred to as *shared media*. With that in mind, marketers can take advantage of what social media offer.

In social media there are new influencers, such as bloggers who have an audience on sites such as Facebook and Twitter. On Twitter a blogger could have a large following, which provides an opportunity for information to be shared. As introduced in Chapter 14, a *blog* is a frequent, chronological publication of personal thoughts on a website.

A corporate blog enables a company to speak directly to consumers, and as a result traditional media are being pushed out of their central role in public relations. Richard Edelman, president and CEO of Edelman Public Relations Worldwide, believes that "PR practitioners must become more like journalists and rely less on the media to get the message out."[12] Instead of persuading the media to run a story, an organization must speak directly to the public, or try to influence bloggers to post messages on the company's behalf. See **Figure 15.13** for an illustration.

A corporate blog must contain useful information in order to motivate readers to make return visits. The blog should include written commentary, audio content, and video content. It is also prudent to include relevant content provided by everyday people who are intensely engaged with a branded product. As mentioned elsewhere in this textbook, consumer-generated content can have more impact than content produced by professionals.

Figure 15.13
Companies now use corporate blogs to communicate current and relevant information.

Simulation: IMC

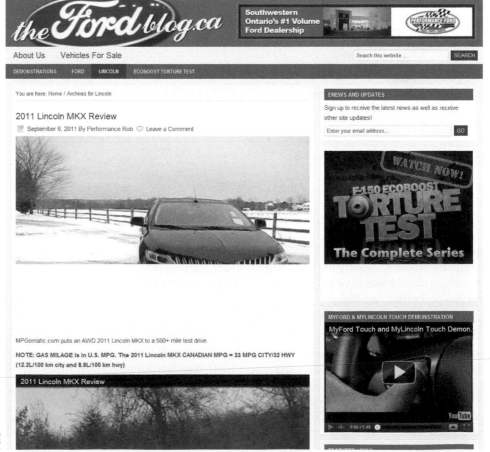

EXPERIENTIAL MARKETING

L05 Explain the role of experiential marketing in marketing today.

Experiential marketing is a form of marketing that creates an emotional connection with the consumer in personally relevant and memorable ways. The objective of this activity is to connect with consumers in such a manner that they "experience" the product. The experience could be something as simple as a free sample distributed at an event, or a planned event at which the brand is the centerpiece as people interact with it.

The term *experiential marketing* is relatively new. It is a contemporary term that embraces several former descriptive terms such as guerilla marketing, impact marketing, engagement marketing, and buzz marketing. Experiential marketing embraces these activities and even more. Brands have always employed product sampling, special product promotions, public relations stunts, product seeding, and street level and other special events in their marketing arsenal but it is just recently that the concept of consumer *engagement* with a brand has taken hold. To engage consumers requires a carefully designed and emotive experience that often integrates various forms of marketing communications.

Traditional forms of marketing and marketing communications have a one-way orientation (marketer to customer) and are usually measured by volume of impressions. In contrast, experiential marketing involves interacting with consumers in such a way that they "feel" the brand—this creates a deeper connection with consumers.[13] Experiential marketing is less about quantity and more about quality. For example, a street level sampling event may only attract a few thousand people and run for a short period, but those people had a hands-on experience with the brand—and they could spread some very good news about it!

Today's consumers expect more from brands. It's not just about transferring information anymore—consumers want to be entertained and enjoy experiences. As discussed earlier in the chapter product sampling is a tried and true sales promotion activity. Loblaws recently took sampling a step further with its Forward to School program, a program based on the premise that mothers have a difficult time selecting healthy foods for their children's lunches. "Mom-approved" products from a selection of brands offered by Loblaws and its suppliers were featured in the campaign. In addition to in-store sampling, product displays, and point-of-sale materials, the program included custom-built food trucks that toured around many cities. Brand ambassadors distributed free samples, coupon booklets, and product information for the featured products.[14]

experiential marketing A type of marketing that creates awareness for a product by having the customer interact directly with the product (e.g., distributing free samples of a product at street level).

Jason DeCrow/Invision for Mountain Dew Kickstart/AP Images

Figure 15.14
Experiential marketing campaigns are designed to engage consumers with brands.

Think Marketing

Reebok's New Way to Experience Fitness

Senior marketing executives want results. They look for tangible benefits gained from their investment in any form of marketing communications. Public relations is no different. In planning a PR program, specific objectives are established; the campaign is implemented and then evaluated. Here is a campaign that effectively combined public relations and experiential marketing techniques.

Reebok set out to change how people think of fitness. The objective of their communications campaign was to change the way people define, view, and experience fitness. Reebok wanted to show people that fitness can be a sport in itself. To launch The Sport of Fitness campaign in Toronto an elaborate stunt was employed in Dundas Square, a very busy downtown public park. Using a crane, Reebok hoisted a 15 000 pound shipping container above the square to raise public curiosity. A week later it was lowered to reveal a mobile CrossFit-branded gym and equipment that the public was encouraged to try. CrossFit is Reebok's strength and conditioning program.

Rich Froning Jr. and Graham Holmberg, both recent winners of the Fittest Men on Earth competition, were there to promote the CrossFit program and encourage consumer participation. Uli Becker, president of Reebok says, "Fitness is tedious and uninspiring to many people but it doesn't have to be. Our event in Toronto shows people that

James Hamilton

CrossFit has all the elements that fuel people's love of sport—community, competition, and challenge."

To create awareness for the CrossFit program, the Canadian launch was supported with television commercials and digital videos showing young people working out strenuously together. Out-of-home advertising helped create an identity for the program.

Question:

What benefits can a marketing organization expect to achieve from experiential activities such as the one described above?

Adapted from Alicia Androich, "Reebok to put focus on fitness in Toronto," Marketing, February 13, 2012, www.marketingmag.ca

Video: Shock Advertising: Does Buzz Lead to Business?

Mountain Dew is positioned as an on-the-edge beverage that appeals to the youth market. Advertising campaigns typically involve thrill-seeking adventures and daredevil types of stunts. Expanding into experiential marketing was a natural fit for the brand. A new series of videos on the brand's YouTube channel shows young people participating in daredevil activities. One video, featuring a featuring a human catapult launching people from a giant slingshot made of bungee cords, garnered 2.4 million views.[15]

Another means of engaging consumers with the brand involved a Super Bowl ticket giveaway. Visitors to Super Bowl boulevard in New York's Times Square were encouraged to text for a chance to win tickets. This activity was part of Mountain Dew KickStart campaign that gets Dew Nation ready for whatever the night will bring. KickStart is an energy drink marketed by Mountain Dew. Refer to the image in Figure 15.14.[16]

For more insight into experiential marketing and public relations strategies read the Think Marketing box **Reebok's New Way to Experience Fitness**.

Event Marketing and Sponsorships

Event marketing and sponsorships are important activities that fall under the umbrella of experiential marketing. A well-planned event will involve consumers with a brand, and once involved they may perceive the brand in a more positive light. Event marketing and sponsorships can be significant investments for a marketing organization.

Event marketing is the process, planned by a sponsoring organization, of integrating a variety of communication elements to support an event theme (e.g., sporting or musical events). For example, Nike plans and executes road races in large urban markets and supports the event with advertising, public relations, and sales promotion activities to achieve runner participation and buzz for the event. To make these events successful, Nike must invest in other forms of communication to generate awareness and encourage participation.

Event sponsorship is the financial support of an event (e.g., an auto race, a theatrical performance, a marathon road race) by a sponsor in return for advertising privileges associated with the event. Perhaps the most elaborate and expensive sponsorship opportunity is an event like the Olympics or FIFA World Cup. Global brands such as Coca-Cola, Visa, and McDonald's commit significant funds to sponsor both events.

Figure 15.15   Participating in the right event allows a brand to effectively reach its target market.

event marketing The process, planned by a sponsoring organization, of integrating a variety of communications elements behind an event theme.

event sponsorship A situation in which a sponsor agrees to support an event financially in return for advertising privileges associated with the event.

Event marketing is big business! The sponsorship market in Canada is estimated to be worth $1.5 billion.[17] Marketers today are reluctant to rely on traditional means of communication; they realize that television viewing and print media readership are declining each year, so they are investing in alternatives such as event marketing and sponsorships. With event marketing and sponsorships there is an opportunity for a brand or company to engage with its target market at a sponsored event.

A survey among North American marketing executives indicates that events deliver a return on investment that exceeds that of media advertising. A brand can form an emotional connection with the fans simply by being at an event, and it can reach certain demographics more effectively than advertising.

Red Bull organizes its own Red Bull Crashed Ice event that takes place in various cities around the world. Its priorities lie with experiential activities. In Canada, the Red Bull Crashed Ice event takes place in Quebec City. Ice cross downhill racers hurtle down a 575m ice track coiling through the city's stunning landscape while navigating huge verticals, jumps, and hairpin turns in a battle to the finish. All Red Bull marketing focuses on adults, starting with college and university students. The audience of such events as Red Bull Crashed Ice is predominantly in their 20s and 30s. Refer to the image in **Figure 15.15**.

In terms of sponsorships, organizations can invest in many different categories. In Canada, the three leading categories are professional and amateur sport (38 percent of investment), followed by fairs, festivals, and annual events (24 percent), and arts and culture (12 percent).[18] Each category reaches a different type of audience.

Sports Sponsorship   Sports sponsorship occurs at amateur and professional levels and can be subdivided into classifications from local events to global events (see **Figure 15.16**). On a global scale, sports accounts for a majority of the money invested in sponsorships—the excitement of sport is a major attraction for sponsors.

Costs associated with sponsorship increase at each level.

| **Local** Minor sports programs, road races for charitable causes | **Regional** Ontario Summer Games, OHL, Western Jr. Hockey League | **National** Canada Summer Games, Canadian Curling Championship | **International** U.S. Open (Golf), Tour de France, British Grand Prix | **Global** Olympic Games |

Figure 15.16   The Various Levels of Sports Event Marketing

Sports sponsorships are a key component of RBC Financial Group's marketing mix. RBC Financial partners with organizations, both professional and amateur, that help create brand exposure nationally while also building regional visibility. RBC Financial has been an active sponsor of the Canadian Olympic Committee (COC) for many Olympic Games. For the 2014 Winter Olympics in Sochi, RBC implemented an emotion-laden advertising campaign with a simple message that would resonate with Canadians. The campaign compared athletes' Olympic dreams to Canadians' dreams, such as buying a home, starting a business, or sending children to college or university. The message the ads delivered was "Your someday is here."[19] RBC effectively used the Olympic dream to tap into what was on peoples' minds. On a national level, RBC Financial sponsors Hockey Canada's premier event: The RBC Cup, a national Junior A championship. What's more Canadian than hockey?

The investment in sports sponsorship increases at each level moving across the chart. Organizations choose between spending locally, to support community events at relatively low cost, to investing in national and international sponsorships at significantly higher cost. Such decisions are based on how sponsorships fit with other marketing communications strategies and the overall marketing strategy of the organization. For example, Visa associates with national and international events, a reflection of the card's status around the world, while Tim Hortons prefers to sponsor local sports programs all across Canada. The local sponsorship program fits nicely with the target audience the company is trying to reach.

venue marketing A form of event marketing in which a company or brand is linked to a physical site, such as a stadium, arena, or theatre.

Venue marketing is another form of event marketing often associated with sports. Here, a company or brand is linked to a physical site, such as a stadium, arena, or theatre. In Canada, there is the Air Canada Centre (home of the Toronto Maple Leafs and Raptors), Rogers Arena (home of the Vancouver Canucks), and the Bell Centre (home of the Montreal Canadiens). See the image in **Figure 15.17**. Pre-eminent title positions like these break through the clutter of other forms of advertising, but it does come at a cost. To have their name on the Bell Centre, Bell pays $3.2 million a year. BMO Field in Toronto (home of Toronto FC) is a $2.3 million annual investment for BMO (Bank of Montreal).[20]

Besides having their name on the building, most naming rights partners receive a luxury box plus a selection of regular seat tickets and rights to use the team's trademark

Vancouver Canucks Limited Partnership

Figure 15.17   Linking a brand name to a venue increases brand exposure and helps build brand image.

in advertising. They may also receive in-arena display areas for their products.[21] It's all a matter of negotiating the right deal.

A recent phenomenon associated with sports event marketing and sponsorship is the illegal practice of ambush marketing. Ambush marketing is a strategy used by non-sponsors to capitalize on the prestige and popularity of an event by giving the false impression that they are sponsors. For insight into how this happens read the Think Marketing box **The Olympic Ambush**.

Think Marketing

The Olympic Ambush

To ambush something almost seems like an unethical tactic; you catch someone off guard and perhaps do harm to them. In contemporary marketing it seems all is fair in love and war. Nike does not sponsor the Olympics but it does employ a creative director whose primary role is to plan and implement strategies that ambush legitimate Olympic sponsors. It's big business with lots of money at stake!

For the 2012 summer Olympics in London, the creative director's focus was on shoes and apparel that would be worn on and off the field by athletes from many different countries. Nike decided all athletes would wear the same colour shoes. Specifically, Nike's trademark execution was the Nike Flyknit Volt shoe in fluorescent green—a colour that really stood out in the crowd! Apparently, it is the most visible colour to the human eye so it wasn't selected by accident. Nike acknowledges that the whole point was to create impact and it did. The shoe garnered all kinds of broadcast, print, and online media exposure during the Games. The result was one of the most iconic images of the 2012 Olympic Games.

Archrival Adidas was an Olympic Games sponsor that paid dearly for the privilege—$155 million! They complained bitterly about the broadcast coverage Nike was receiving but couldn't do much about it. Leslie Smolan, co-founder of Carbone Smolan Agency, says, "Nike's use of the garish shoes was absolutely brilliant. Nike managed to integrate themselves into the games by showing the product, not just talking about it."

The Canadian Olympic Committee (COC) recently threatened legal action against The North Face, claiming that brand associated itself with the 2014 Sochi Winter Olympics. North Face did not pay to be a partner with the COC but it launched a clothing line labelled "village wear" that was decorated with the Canadian flag and a patch with the symbol "RU14," a reference to the Winter Games. The COC claims the clothing line violates its trademarks by suggesting it supports the Canadian Olympic team.

THE CANADIAN PRESS/Sean Kilpatrick

North Face cleverly ambushed legitimate Canadian clothing sponsors but it did not use any protected logos such as the Olympic rings or terms such as Winter Olympics and Sochi 2014 on its clothing or in any promotional materials. It did, however, run a contest in which the grand prize was a trip to Sochi for a major international sports competition.

Question:
Fair or foul? Is this good marketing strategy or not?

Adapted from Susan Krashinsky, "Olympic committee looks to force The North Face out of the village," The Globe and Mail, January 22, 2014, pp. B1, B7; and Shareen Pathak, "How Nike ambushed the Olympics with this neon shoe," Advertising Age, August 20, 2012, pp. 1, 19.

Festivals, Fairs, and Annual Events Sponsorship   Festivals, fairs, and annual events in the realms of film, comedy, and music offer opportunities to reach a cross-section of adult target audiences. At festivals as popular as the Toronto International Film Festival there are waiting lists for top-level sponsorships. It seems that companies are eager to align themselves with the movie stars who attend these types of events. Among the lead sponsors are Bell Canada, RBC Financial, L'Oréal, Visa, and Audi. Refer to the image in **Figure 15.18**. The very popular Montreal International Jazz Festival attracts sponsors such as TD Bank, Loto-Québec, Bell Canada, Heineken, and CBC Radio-Canada.

Film and other types of festivals are becoming popular with marketers because the festivals offer customized packages suitable to a marketer's needs. The Toronto International Film Festival "approaches sponsorships as true partnerships" offering a broad spectrum of associations, from corporate entertaining to brand exposure and product sampling opportunities.[22]

In contrast to sports sponsorships that attract a *mass* audience, sponsorships of festivals and annual events tend to attract a *class* audience—they meet different marketing objectives for an organization. The Toronto International Film Festival reaches a "young, urban, affluent" audience: 30 percent are 18 to 34 years old, 77 percent are

Figure 15.18
Sponsors of the Toronto International Film Festival reach an upscale audience.

Proudly supporting the infinite possibilities of film.

Through our collaboration with the Toronto International Film Festival™, RBC® is committed to helping the film community grow and prosper. We're proud to support filmmakers, new and established, and our city's place on the world arts stage. It continues to be an investment with boundless potential.

RBC® | tiff. toronto international film festival™
OFFICIAL SPONSOR 2014

college or university educated, 60 percent have a household income over $80 000, and all are "culture and experience seekers with high disposable income for entertainment."[23]

Cultural and Arts Sponsorship   Arts and cultural event opportunities embrace dance, film, literature, music, and theatre. Typically, the audience reached is smaller for these sponsorships. Depending on the sponsor, this can be an advantage or a disadvantage. A company such as Molson prefers the mass-audience reach of a sporting event, whereas Mercedes-Benz or BMW may prefer to reach a more selective and upscale audience through an arts event. Perhaps only 2500 people attend a particular cultural event, but those people most likely fit the demographic (age, education and income) and psychographic profile (interests) of the target market. Such an audience profile would be a good match for promoting a new luxury car.

The primary benefit that companies gain from sponsoring the arts is goodwill from the public. Most firms view this type of investment as part of their corporate citizenship objectives (e.g., they are perceived as a good, contributing member of society). BMO Financial Group, for example, is a long-standing sponsor of numerous cultural events and organizations that include the Governor General's Literary Awards, the Stratford Festival, the Toronto Symphony Orchestra, the National Business Book Award, and the National Ballet School.

Cause Marketing Sponsorships   Cause marketing involves a partnership between a company and a non-profit entity for mutual benefit. The relationship between the parties has a significant meaning to consumers. This meaning, when associated with a brand or company, can have a positive effect on the consumer's perception of the brand. Such is one of the benefits that CIBC derives from its ongoing title sponsorship of the Canadian Breast Cancer Foundation CIBC Run for the Cure, in which the overall goal is to raise funds to support the foundation's vision of creating a future without breast cancer.[24] Refer to the image in **Figure 15.19**. Other sponsors of this cause include New Balance, Running Room, and Revlon.

Strategic Considerations for Event Marketing

Advertisers cannot approach event marketing and sponsorships in a haphazard way. Their primary reason for entering into sponsorships is to create a favourable impression with their customers and target groups. To accomplish this, the fit between the event and

Figure 15.19
Associating with a worthy cause helps build brand image and trust with the public.

© Jonny White/Alamy

the sponsor must be a good one. The most effective sponsors adhere to the following principles when considering participation in event marketing.

- *Select events offering exclusivity*—The need for companies to be differentiated within events they sponsor calls for exclusivity, meaning that direct competitors are blocked from sponsorship. Also, a concern among sponsors is the clutter of lower-level sponsors in non-competing categories that reduce the overall impact of the primary sponsor.
- *Use sponsorships to complement other promotional activity*—The role that advertising and promotion will play in the sponsorship must be determined first. Sponsorship of the proper event will enhance a company's other promotional activity. For example, Pepsi-Cola and Doritos (both PepsiCo brands) sponsor the Super Bowl and place several ads during the broadcast. Both brands leverage the Super Bowl sponsorship by implementing a contest where consumers can win game tickets and other prizes. Huge in-store displays are erected to attract attention and encourage purchases. A social media campaign supports the entire effort. The integrated strategy embraces event marketing, advertising, sales promotion (both consumer and trade promotion), and social media communications across key company brands.
- *Choose the target carefully*—Events reach specific targets. For example, while rock concerts attract youth, symphonies tend to reach audiences that are older, urban, and upscale. As suggested earlier, it is the fit, or matching of targets, that is crucial. Do the demographics of the event audience match as closely as possible the demographics of the target market?
- *Select an event with an image that sells*—The sponsor must capitalize on the image of the event and perhaps the prestige or status associated with it. Prominent brands such as McDonald's, RBC Financial, and Coca-Cola bask in the aura of the Olympic Games. The Olympics has the cachet that will make it the cornerstone of a multimedia communications campaign for these brands in the years preceding the games.
- *Establish selection criteria*—In addition to using the criteria cited above, companies evaluating potential events for sponsorship should consider the long-term benefit such sponsorship offers compared to the costs in the short term. The company must establish objectives in terms of awareness and association scores (how consumers link the brand to the event), image improvement, increases in sales, and return on investment so it can properly evaluate its participation in the event.

In summary, organizations now invest more money in experiential marketing. Such an investment is justified based on changing market conditions. In the past, an organization was concerned about making impressions on people (a staple means for measuring the effectiveness of advertising and public relations communications). In a constantly changing media marketplace, markets are shifting their objectives to make quality impressions (fewer but better impressions) while engaging the consumer with the brand. Having the consumer interact with the brand helps establish a stronger reason to buy the product and to build a relationship over an extended period.

PERSONAL SELLING

LO6 Describe the role of personal selling in the marketing communications mix.

personal selling Face-to-face communication involving the presentation of features and benefits of a product or service to a buyer for the purpose of making a sale.

Personal selling is a personalized form of communication that involves a seller presenting the features and benefits of a product or service to a buyer for the purpose of making a sale. It is an integral component of the marketing communications mix, for it is the activity that in many cases clinches a deal, and it does so based on the human touch the sales representative brings. Advertising and sales promotions create awareness and interest for a product. Personal selling creates desire and action. In creating that desire and action, the interaction between the seller and buyer is crucial.

While the purpose of selling is to make the sale, the role of the sales representative goes beyond this task. Essentially, the salesperson is the human component of the marketing communications mix—the face of the marketing organization to customers and the person they call first if a good or service doesn't live up to the expectations promised. For this reason marketing plans and sales plans should be carefully coordinated to ensure that both head in the same direction.

The Role of the Contemporary Salesperson

Gathering Market Intelligence   In a competitive marketplace, salespeople must be attuned to the trends in their industries. They must be alert to what competitors are doing, to their new-product projects, and to their advertising and promotion plans. Salespeople must also listen to feedback from customers regarding their own products' performance. Competitive knowledge is important when the salesperson faces questions involving product comparisons. Data collected by a salesperson can be reported electronically to the company's head office. Managers can retrieve the information and use it appropriately at a later date.

Problem Solving   The only way a salesperson can make a sale is to listen to what a customer wants and ask questions to determine his or her real needs. Asking, listening, and providing information and advice that is in the best interests of the customer is what consultative selling is all about. The seller must demonstrate a sincere concern for the customer's needs and recognize the uniqueness of his or her problem when trying to resolve it.

Locating and Maintaining Customers   Salespeople who locate new customers play a key role in a company's growth. A company cannot be complacent about its current list of customers, because aggressive competitors will attempt to lure them away. To prevent shrinkage and increase sales, salespeople actively pursue new accounts. Their time is divided between finding new accounts and selling and servicing current accounts.

Follow-Up Service   The salesperson is the first point of contact should anything go wrong or more information be required. Maintenance of customers is crucial, and very often it is the quality of follow-up service that determines whether a customer will remain a customer. As the salespeople are the company's direct link to the customer, the importance of their approach to handling customer service cannot be stressed enough. The sale is never over. Once a deal has been closed, numerous tasks arise: arranging for delivery, providing technical assistance, providing customer training, and being readily available to handle any customer problems that emerge during and after delivery. The personalized role of the sales representative is instrumental in building relationships.

THE STEPS IN THE SELLING PROCESS

LO7   Describe the basic steps in the selling process.

Successful salespeople adopt a planned approach to selling. By adhering to a few simple steps they are well on their way to making a sale and establishing a meaningful relationship with a customer. Seven steps are commonly associated with personal selling. Refer to **Figure 15.20** for an illustration.

Prospecting   The first step is **prospecting**, which is a systematic procedure for developing sales leads. If salespeople do not allocate enough time to finding new customers, they risk causing a decline in sales for their company. If their income is geared to the value of the business they produce, they risk the loss of personal compensation, as well.

prospecting A systematic procedure for developing sales leads.

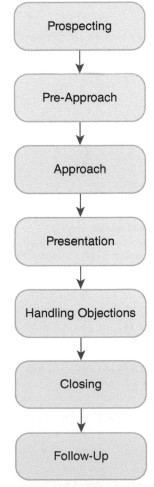

Figure 15.20   Steps in the Selling Process

referral Occurs when a salesperson secures names of potential customers from satisfied customers and makes an initial contact by telephone to arrange a time for a face-to-face meeting.

pre-approach Gathering information about potential customers before actually making sales contact.

approach The initial contact with a prospect, usually a face-to-face selling encounter.

presentation The persuasive delivery and demonstration of a product's benefits.

demonstration An opportunity to show a product in action; it helps substantiate the claims that the salesperson is making.

objection An obstacle that the salesperson must confront and resolve if the sales trans-action is to be completed.

Potential customers, or prospects, are identified by means of published lists and directories, such as Scott's Industrial Directory and Fraser's Canadian Trade Directory. Leads may also arise from a company's own database, which is constantly updated from information gathered at trade shows as well as from telephone calls or online customer inquiries. Sometimes a salesperson gets a referral. A **referral** is a prospect that is recommended by a current customer.

Pre-approach
The **pre-approach** involves gathering information about potential customers before actually making sales contact. During the pre-approach stage, customers are *qualified*, which is the procedure for determining if a prospect needs the product, has the authority to buy it, and has the ability to pay for it. There is little sense in pursuing customers who lack the financial resources to purchase a product or have no need to make the business relationship successful. The seller also gains insights into the customer that can be used in the sales presentation, such as the buyer's likes and dislikes, personal interests and hobbies, buying habits, and special needs and problems.

Approach
The **approach** is the initial contact with the prospect, typically a face-to-face selling situation. Buyers are usually busy, so little time should be wasted in the approach. In the first few minutes of a sales interview, the salesperson must capture the attention and interest of the buyer so that an effective environment is created for the presentation of the product's benefits. At this stage it is important for the salesperson to ask appropriate questions of the buyer and to listen carefully to the answers. Insights learned at this stage can be immediately integrated into the presentation that follows.

Presentation
The actual sales **presentation** consists of a persuasive delivery and demonstration of a product's benefits. An effective sales presentation shows the buyer how the benefits of the product satisfy his or her needs or help resolve a particular problem. In doing so, the seller focuses on the benefits that are most important to the buyer. Critical elements usually focus on lower price, the durability of the product, the dependability of supply, the performance of the product, and the availability of follow-up service.

Similar to the approach stage, during the presentation it is very important for the sales representative to listen attentively. By analyzing what the customer is saying, the sales representative can reconfigure the presentation on the fly to ensure that the buyer's needs are met. Remaining flexible is an important trait for a sales representative to possess. It could be the difference between making the sale and not making the sale.

Demonstrations play a key role in a presentation. A **demonstration** is an opportunity to show a product in action and helps substantiate the claims that the salesperson is making. A good demonstration holds the buyer's attention and creates interest and desire. Laptop computers and tablets now allow for multimedia presentations and precise demonstrations of a product's attributes. While technology helps put the spotlight on the product, it is important not to get carried away with presentation technology—it is the content of the presentation that is important, along with the impression the sales representative makes on the buyer.

Handling Objections
An **objection** is an obstacle that the salesperson must confront and resolve if the sales transaction is to be completed. Prospects almost always express resistance when contemplating the purchase of a product. An objection is a cue that the buyer wants more information before making a decision. The seller must view the objection as useful feedback and should respond to it accordingly. It gives the seller another opportunity to sell the product.

Typical objections involve issues related to price, quality, level of service, and technical assistance. When dealing with objections the salesperson should ask questions of the buyer to confirm his or her understanding of the situation, respond to the objection, and then move on to the next benefit or attempt to close the sale.

Closing   Does the buyer voluntarily say "Yes, I'll buy it"? No! Getting the buyer to say yes is the entire purpose of the sales interview, but this task is accomplished only if the salesperson asks for the order. **Closing** consists of asking for the order, and it is the most difficult step in the process of selling. Salespeople often seem reluctant to ask the big question, even though it is the logical sequel to a good presentation and demonstration. In fact, a good salesperson attempts a close whenever a point of agreement is made with the buyer. If the buyer says no, the close is referred to as a **trial close**, or an attempt to close that failed. The salesperson simply moves on to the next point in the presentation.

Timing a close is a matter of judgment. Good salespeople know when to close—it is often referred to as the *sixth sense* of selling. The salesperson assesses the buyer's verbal and non-verbal responses in an effort to judge when he or she has become receptive, and at the right moment asks the big question.

closing The point in the sales presentation when the seller asks for the order.

trial close An attempt to close that failed.

Follow-Up   There is an old saying: "The sale never ends." There is truth to this statement, for a new sale is nothing more than the start of a new relationship. Keeping current customers satisfied is the key to success. Effective salespeople make a point of providing **follow-up**; that is, they keep in touch with customers to ensure that the delivery and installation of the goods are satisfactory, that promises are kept, and that, generally, the expectations of the buyer are met. When problems do occur, the salesperson is ready to take action to resolve the situation.

follow-up An activity that keeps salespeople in touch with customers after the sale has been made to ensure that the customer is satisfied.

Companies realize that a satisfied customer is a long-term customer. As famous retail clothier Harry Rosen stated, "We don't look at a person in terms of an immediate sale. We look at him in terms of potential lifetime value."[25] Rosen was very quick to understand the importance of customer relationship management programs, a reason his company is well ahead of its competitors.

To be successful in selling requires dedication, determination, and discipline. What separates the successful salesperson from the unsuccessful one usually boils down to how well an individual follows an established set of principles. See **Figure 15.21** for some pointers on what separates professionals from average salespeople.

1. They Are Persistent
Successful salespeople don't let obstacles stand in their way. They are tenacious and are constantly looking for new solutions.

2. They Are Goal Setters
They establish specific goals then visualize their target, determine how they will achieve their goals, and take action daily.

3. They Ask Quality Questions
They ask questions to fully determine the buying situation and needs of the customer. By uncovering concerns they can better present the benefits of their product.

4. They Listen
Great salespeople know that customers will tell them everything they need to know if given the right opportunity. They listen and learn.

5. They Are Passionate
When you love what you do you put more passion into it. Good sales people are passionate about their company and products.

6. They Are Enthusiastic
Good salespeople remain positive even in tough times. When faced with negative situations they focus on the positives.

7. They Take Responsibility for Their Results
They know that their actions alone determine their results. They never look for excuses.

8. They Work Hard
Successful salespeople go after business. They start early, make more calls, and stay later than anyone else. They talk to more people and give more presentations.

9. They Keep in Touch with Their Clients
They send thank-you, birthday, and anniversary cards; make follow-up phone calls; and are always looking for creative ways to help customers.

10. They Show Value
They recognize price is always important but know that buyers look at the value proposition presented by the seller. They know how to create this value with each customer or prospect they encounter.

Source: Adapted from Kelley Robertson, "Characteristics of Successful Salespeople," *SOHO*, Summer 2006, pp. 14, 15.

Figure 15.21   Characteristics of Successful Salespeople

✔ **Experience**Marketing

To experience marketing you have to assess situations and make recommendations to change marketing strategies when necessary. What would you do in the following situation?

You are the brand manager for Maxwell House Coffee at Kraft Canada. You are a leading brand in a very mature market. There is no shortage of competition. Since you are a mature brand you are contemplating various sales promotion and experiential marketing strategies that will help maintain market share. Essentially, you wish to breathe some new life into the brand with something exciting. At this stage of the game, brand loyalty is a priority. What will you recommend? Be prepared to justify your recommendations.

Prior to making any recommendations you should scan the market and a few of your key competitors' activities for additional insights. What your competitors are doing may influence your recommendations.

CHAPTER SUMMARY

L01 **Identify the roles and functions of various consumer promotion activities.**   *(pp. 321–327)*

Sales promotion plays a key role in influencing purchase behaviour and helps boost sales in the short term. Sales promotion activity can be divided into consumer promotions and trade promotions. Consumer promotions involve incentives such as coupons, free samples, and contests that encourage people to buy a certain product immediately or help build brand loyalty. The objectives of a consumer promotion, which include trial purchases, repeat purchases, and multiple purchases, determine which promotion option to use. For example, media-delivered coupons and free samples of a product are ideal for encouraging trial purchase, premium offers and contests are ideal in achieving repeat purchases and multiple purchases, and rewards programs are ideal for maintaining brand loyalty.

L02 **Identify the roles and functions of various trade promotion activities.**   *(pp. 327–328)*

Trade promotions involve financial incentives that help secure distribution and marketing support among channel members who buy and resell the product. The primary trade promotion incentives include trade allowances (discounts off list price for goods purchased), performance allowances (allowances offered to distributors for performing marketing functions on behalf of a manufacturer's product), and co-operative advertising allowances (accumulated discounts based on purchase volumes that goes toward sharing costs of distributor advertising). Collateral materials are made available to distributors to help them resell products.

L03 **Identify the role of public relations in the development of marketing communications strategies.**   *(pp. 329–331)*

Public relations plays a role in developing an organization's image. Corporate advertising is commonly used in image-building campaigns. PR is also an important means of communication in times of crisis. Communicating information in a timely manner about the actions a company is taking to resolve an issue is important. At the product level various activities are undertaken to generate publicity for brands or the company. Free publicity is referred to as earned media. Publicity is generated based on an organization's distribution of newsworthy information.

L04 **Describe the public relations tools and techniques for communications strategies.**   *(pp. 331–334)*

Information is communicated to the media by press releases, press conferences, websites, and social media. Through social media the public can be part of the conversation and help influence behaviour positively by sharing information within a friend network—the concept of shared media. Product seeding (placing free product with trendsetters or social media influencers) is another tactic for generating publicity for a brand.

L05 **Explain the role of experiential marketing in marketing today.**   *(pp. 335–342)*

Experiential marketing creates an emotional connection with consumers in the form of a brand experience. A key benefit of this tactic is consumer engagement at a time and place where consumers are receptive to brand messages. Experiential marketing embraces activities such as product demonstrations and giveaways in public places, activities that consumers can participate in to experience a product, publicity stunts that garner publicity for a brand, and so on. Event marketing and sponsorships can be a key component of a brand marketing strategy. Participating in events or sponsoring events presents an opportunity to reach a defined target directly and offers image-building capabilities in an environment where consumers expect brand participation.

L06 **Describe the role of personal selling in the marketing communications mix.**   *(pp. 342–343)*

Personal selling refers to personal communication between sellers and buyers. The salesperson is responsible for locating customers, gathering marketing intelligence (collecting information on competitive products and on customers needs), problem solving (responding to customers' problems and showing how their product will help them) and maintaining customers (providing the essential follow-up service to ensure customer satisfaction). Salespeople are the human factor in the marketing communications equation. As such, their attitude and disposition with customers play a crucial role in building solid relationships.

LO7 Describe the basic steps in the selling process. *(pp. 343–345)*

There are seven steps in the selling process. *Prospecting* is a procedure for developing sales leads. *Pre-approach* involves gathering information about prospective customers. The *approach* is the initial face-to-face meeting with a customer. During the meeting the salesperson makes a *presentation* where the features and

benefits of a product are presented in the context of how they will resolve a buyer's problem. The presentation may include a product demonstration. During the presentation the salesperson must respond to the buyer's *objections*. If the answer is acceptable the salesperson should ask for the order. Asking for the order is called *closing*. If the close fails, it is referred to as a *trial close*. The salesperson continues with the presentation and may ask for the order (attempt to close) many times. Assuming the customer places an order, the final step is to *follow up* with the customer to ensure goods were delivered properly and to offer service to ensure satisfaction.

MyMarketingLab   Study, practise, and explore real marketing situations with these helpful resources:

- **Interactive Lesson Presentations:** Work through interactive presentations and assessments to test your knowledge of marketing concepts.
- **Study Plan:** Check your understanding of chapter concepts with self-study quizzes.
- **Dynamic Study Modules:** Work through adaptive study modules on your computer, tablet, or mobile device.
- **Simulations:** Practise decision-making in simulated marketing environments.

REVIEW QUESTIONS

1. What are the objectives of consumer promotions? Briefly explain. (*LO1*)
2. What consumer promotions are best suited for the following objectives? Briefly explain. (*LO2*)
   a. Trial purchase
   b. Repeat purchase
3. What are the primary objectives of trade promotions? Briefly explain. (*LO2*)
4. What is the difference between a trade allowance and a performance allowance? Briefly explain. (*LO2*)
5. What are three primary roles public relations can perform in a communications strategy? Briefly explain each role. (*LO3*)

6. What is product seeding and what role does it play in public relations strategy? (*LO4*)
7. What are the purposes of a press release and a press conference? Briefly explain. (*LO4*)
8. What is experiential marketing? Briefly explain and provide a new example of it. (*LO5*)
9. What is the difference between event marketing and event sponsorship? (*LO5*)
10. Briefly explain the key criteria for participating in an event marketing program. (*LO5*)
11. What are the primary roles of a salesperson? (*LO6*)
12. What are the seven steps in the personal selling process? Briefly describe each step. (*LO7*)

DISCUSSION AND APPLICATION QUESTIONS

1. "Social media will change the nature of public relations forever." Is this statement true or false? Evaluate this statement and present an opinion on it.
2. Is cause marketing a worthwhile investment for corporations in Canada? How does the company benefit? Explain.

3. Will experiential marketing play a more significant role in future marketing strategies? Conduct some research on the effectiveness of experiential marketing prior to formulating a position on the matter.

16 Services and Not-for-Profit Marketing

© John Sylvester/Alamy

LEARNING OBJECTIVES

LO1 Outline the characteristics and behaviours that distinguish services marketing from product marketing. (pp. 349–353)

LO2 Describe the elements of the services marketing mix. (pp. 353–356)

LO3 Explain the nature, scope, and characteristics of not-for-profit marketing. (pp. 356–358)

LO4 Describe the types of not-for-profit marketing. (pp. 358–359)

LO5 Discuss the role and importance of marketing strategy in not-for-profit organizations. (pp. 359–360)

ABOUT 20 MILLION PEOPLE ...

visit Canada's national parks each year, but that number has been declining.[1] As a result, Parks Canada is looking for ways to connect with new audiences and encourage more people to come in to natural areas. One strategy has been to establish a youth council to explore ways to get young people interested in nature. Attracting Millenials is important for a variety of reasons, including the fact the average age of park visitors and campers has been increasing. Parks Canada's research shows that young, urban nature enthusiasts remain strongly attached to social media, so the agency is hoping to entice them to a national park by making sure the experience doesn't interrupt their online habits.[2]

"Whether visitors come for a few hours or a few days," says Parks Canada, "they often wish to access the Internet to stay in touch with work, friends or family, stay abreast of the news, share their travel experiences on social media, check weather forecasts, make reservations or monitor security cameras in their homes."[3] In order to make the park experience more accessible, especially for youth and young adults, wireless Internet access is to be installed in as many as 150 locations throughout the park system by 2017. Although this proposal has attracted some negative reaction, Parks Canada maintains that WiFi zones will be restricted to visitor centres and campgrounds—it will not extend to the back country. Parks Canada is hoping that by adapting to changing visitor expectations, more people will enjoy the national park experience, and over time, attendance figures will increase.[4 & 5]

It's clear that service expectations are changing in today's age of digitally empowered consumers and intense competition in the marketplace. Service is demanded 24/7—anytime and anywhere. As you will learn in this chapter, there is more to services marketing than just offering a basic service.

CHARACTERISTICS AND BEHAVIOURS OF SERVICES MARKETING

LO1 Outline the characteristics and behaviours that distinguish services marketing from product marketing.

Services Marketing

The composition of Canada's economy has changed over the years and the country has reached the point at which the service economy dominates. Back in the 1960s the manufacturing sector was pre-eminent, but today the service economy accounts for 70 percent of Canada's gross domestic product.[6] The service industry employs three in four Canadians and accounts for most new jobs each year.[7]

The service industry in Canada is divided into four primary categories: leisure and personal services, food and beverage services, accommodation, and business services. The services industry includes some of Canada's largest employers as it embraces banks and other financial service companies, telecommunications companies, professional firms of accountants and management consultants, real estate companies, advertising agencies, and hotel and food-service businesses.

Characteristics of Services

A **service** is defined as work done by one person (or organization) that benefits another. In a B2B context, a business sells assistance and experience rather than a tangible product. There are four characteristics that distinguish services from products: they are intangible, they are inseparable, they vary in quality, and demand for them is perishable.

Intangibility   **Intangibility** is the quality of not being perceivable by the senses (i.e., a service cannot be seen, heard, tasted, smelled, or touched). For example, a life insurance policy may be worth $1 million, but its true benefit is the security it imparts, and security

services The activities and benefits provided by an organization that satisfy the buyer's needs without conferring ownership of tangible goods; also, intangible offerings required to operate a business efficiently (e.g., repair or maintenance services).

intangibility The quality of not being perceivable by the senses.

Figure 16.1   TD Canada Trust differentiates itself from other banks by combining an exceptional customer service experience with a strong commitment to the environment.

Video: UMPQUA Bank

inseparability The equating of the provider of the service with the service itself.

quality variability The variations in services offered by different individuals, even within the same organization.

Figure 16.2   Westin hotels stresses its value-added services to attract business customers.

cannot be seen or touched. This type of product is quite different from something such as coffee, with a physical aroma and taste.

A marketer deals with the intangibility issue by trying to express the value of the service in tangible terms. In this regard, branding and advertising play a key role. For example, all car rental companies could be perceived by consumers as relative equals—they all provide the same type of service. However, a unique brand name, such as Budget Rent-A-Car or Discount Car and Truck Rentals, suggests price savings. Banks are also perceived as being the same—they all offer the same services, so why choose one bank over another?

TD Canada Trust understands that customers expect their bank to be accessible, helpful, and responsive to their needs. To TD Canada Trust that means supporting customers where they feel most comfortable, whether it's in the branch, on the phone, or via social media channels. The tagline the bank uses in its advertising, "Banking can be this comfortable," aptly summarizes the message. TD Canada Trust's strategy is working, as it continues to rank highest in customer service among the big five retail banks in Canada.[8] Recently TD has gone one step further in differentiating itself from other banks, by combining its legendary customer service experience with a strong commitment to the environment. The bank's new environmentally sustainable branches offer full service seven days a week in a space that facilitates comfortable customer interactions. Refer to the image in **Figure 16.1**.

Inseparability   **Inseparability** equates the provider of the service with the service itself. People feel this way about their doctors, their financial planners, and even their hairstylists. While apparent substitutes are available, the buyer feels more comfortable with his or her preferred and regular source of supply. A close relationship, or inseparability, exists between the service supplier and the customer.

A large service organization must therefore train all employees to perform the service at the desired level. Hotels implement training programs dealing with guest satisfaction—a crucial aspect of achieving repeat business from a customer. Once the desired level of service is in place it must be communicated to the customer. For example, the hotel industry has collectively responded to customers' increasing demand for a good night's sleep. The Sheraton offers the Comfort Bed, Westin offers the Heavenly Bed and the Crowne Plaza promotes its Sleep Advantage program. Refer to **Figure 16.2**.

Variability in Quality   To customers, a quality service is one that meets their expectations, is available when needed, and is administered in a consistent manner. Can a service provider meet this challenge? **Quality variability** refers to the variations in services offered by different individuals, even within the same organization. For example, all life insurance agents employed by Manulife Insurance perform the same service, but they each approach and deal with their customers differently, and some are much more attentive to their clients' needs than others. This presents a challenge for marketers.

Like inseparability, quality variability can be controlled through standardization programs. The growth of franchises and their acceptance by consumers is a result of their ability to offer uniform quality throughout the franchise system. McDonald's promises quality, service, and value, and the intensive training program that all its employees and managers must undergo demonstrates how food can be prepared and delivered in a standardized way.

Perishability of Demand   The demand for services is **perishable**; that is, demand for them varies over a given period. Demand for a service may diminish, but the facilities offering the unwanted service still remain. To understand the concept of uneven demand, consider that hotel rooms sit idle during weekends when business travel is less frequent. However, the building must be large enough, or have sufficient rooms, to accommodate the crowds during peak demand. Hoteliers counter perishability of demand by offering reduced rates for hotel rooms on weekends.

Also consider cafés, like Starbucks, which are typically less busy in the late afternoon and early evening. In order to manage demand and attract customers after morning rush hour, Starbucks plans to turn more of its cafes into destinations for beer and wine in the evenings.[9]

perishable (perishability of demand) Demand for services varies over a given period.

BUYING BEHAVIOUR IN SERVICES

In marketing services, an organization should be aware that there are some differences between consumer behaviour toward services and goods. Differences exist in attitudes, needs and motives, and basic decision-making behaviour.

Attitudes   When deciding whether to purchase a good or a service, customers are obviously influenced by their own attitudes. Because services are intangible, the impression that a customer has of the service and of the supplier is a strong influence on his or her decision to purchase the service. It is also much easier for a customer to express dissatisfaction with a service as a result of the personal nature of a service offering. For example, waiting in line at the front desk of a hotel or an airline ticket area of an airport is a source of frustration, even anger, for many a traveller. It is challenging for customer service representatives to maintain their composure at times.

Customer attitudes are important, and a service organization must take steps to ensure that the quality of services offered remains high so customers are satisfied.

Amazon's mission is to be the world's most customer-centric company, where customers can find and discover anything they might want to buy online. Amazon has teams around the world working on behalf of its customers to provide 24/7 support. According to Amazon, "Although leaders pay attention to competitors, they obsess over customers."[10] Refer to the illustration in **Figure 16.3**.

For insight into a new services marketing strategy in the advertising industry, read the Think Marketing box **A Think-Ferrari, Not a Think-Tank**.

Needs and Motives   Both goods and services satisfy needs and motives, often the same ones. Thus, one could satisfy the need to repair a roof either by

Figure 16.3   Employee attitude plays a key role at Amazon.

ThinkMarketing

A Think-Ferrari, Not a Think-Tank

Normally it can take weeks, if not months, for advertising campaigns to be produced. Now businesses have an option. The World's Fastest Agency (WFA) is a new kind of marketing and communications firm designed to help time-pressured clients keep up with the lightning-fast 24/7 global media and social culture. WFA's service offering is truly unique in that clients are guaranteed a creative solution in 24 hours—for just $999!

So much time is wasted in the process, says WFA founder, Floyd Hayes. "Our clients can say goodbye to 100-page PowerPoint presentations, meetings, weeks of fee negotiation, countless emails, more meetings, lunch meetings, scope of work to-ing and fro-ing, meetings, more emails, Q&A sessions, inaudible conference calls, pitch, feedback, feedback on the feedback, re-briefing, re-pitching, another meeting, more feedback, focus groups, another meeting, more emails. . ." WFA customers follow the simple three-step process shown below, and because all communication is through Twitter, messages are brief.

WFA specializes in providing certain key services, including tag lines, product and service naming, publicity stunts, PR concepts, and experiential and guerrilla marketing ideas. As an example, a client, like the manufacturers of the Cooper Mini—a small car—might send a tweet to WFA saying "We want to gain media and buzz for the Mini—a car that can park anywhere." WFA comes up with an idea and tweets that idea to the client: "Attach replica cars to landmark city buildings."

Question:

Do you think that working this fast might result in inferior creative work? Why or why not?

Adapted from A. Quay, (March 20, 2013). "'World's fastest agency' is Twitter-based, 24-hour response in a tweet." Retrieved from http://designtaxi.com/news/356630/World-s-Fastest-Agency-Is-Twitter-Based-24-Hour-Response-In-A-Tweet/interstitial.html?advertiser=External&return_url=http%3A%2F%2Fdesigntaxi.com%2Fnews%2F356630%2FWorld-s-Fastest-Agency-Is-Twitter-Based-24-Hour-Response-In-A-Tweet%2F; and http://worldsfastestagency.com

STEP 1	STEP 2	STEP 3
Deposit $999* fee via **PayPal** Once received, the project is time stamped and ready to go.	Send a 140 character brief via Twitter Direct Message to: **@FastestAgency** You must be following us to use DM.	Within 24 hours you will receive your 140 character creative pitch from World's Fastest Agency via Twitter Direct Message.

Floyd Hayes, World's Fastest Agency

buying shingles and laying them or by hiring a contractor to provide and lay the shingles. Purchasing the goods and purchasing the service both address the same requirement. The provider of the service offers the customer convenience and expertise in getting the task done. Yet, in addition to satisfying the need for a repaired roof, the service could also cater to another need of the customer—the need for personal attention. People often feel that the personal touch is lacking in their hurried, hectic lives. Customizing the service for individual customers with unique needs gives them the satisfaction of receiving personal attention.

Purchase Behaviour   A customer must decide what to buy, when to buy it, and from whom. The purchase of many services is seasonal. Household improvements are commonly made in the spring and summer, retirement plans sell heavily in the winter, and vacation travel peaks in the summer and winter months. Whatever the time of year, selecting a service takes longer than choosing goods because it is difficult for a buyer to assess the quality and value of a service due to its intangibility.

Marketers must therefore pay a lot of attention to their marketing communications programs and offer ample evidence that their service is the one to buy. Buyers of services pay more attention to advertising, particularly when they are ready to buy. Information placed by the organization in the media and third-party endorsements by others in social media are key influences on what to purchase. Refer to the illustration in **Figure 16.4**.

Buyers of services also value the opinions of other people—friends, neighbours, or relatives—more than do buyers of tangible goods. To illustrate, consider a couple planning a winter ski vacation. Once the information search is complete (e.g., pamphlets, brochures, and Internet search) and potential destinations are identified, the couple will then seek references from acquaintances who have used the facilities. Only then will they make a decision.

THE SERVICES MARKETING MIX

LO2 Describe the elements of the services marketing mix.

The elements of the marketing mix for services are the same elements as those found in the mix for tangible goods. As a product, however, a service differs from other products because the marketing attributes are intangible. Refer to **Figure 16.5** for details.

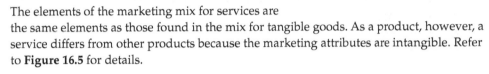

Figure 16.4 Visual images that effectively portray the service will directly influence buying decisions.

Service as a Product With services, the customer is less interested in ownership or physical qualities and more interested in certain conveniences, such as timing, availability, and consistency. Following is a list of some of the intangible qualities that sell a service:

1. *Attitude*—The attitude of those providing the service may be a selling point. Equally important is the degree of personalization between the supplier and the customer. Taking a personal approach and addressing key customers by name, then asking if the quality of the service they received was satisfactory, leads to the formation of a relationship with the customer. Starbucks' baristas ask a customer's name to appear more friendly, and make a point of remembering regular clients' favourite drinks.[11]

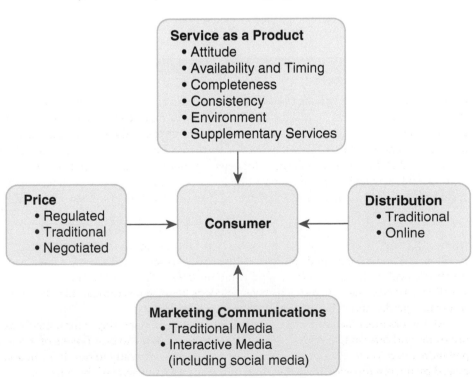

Figure 16.5 The Services Marketing Mix

2. *Availability and Timing*—An airline or bus company that offers frequent and convenient departure times (timing) or ease of entry and accessibility (availability) is adding value to the customer experience. Travelling by bus, for example, can be challenging for people with mobility issues. In response, many city bus systems across the country, including the Winnipeg Transit Commission, have introduced articulated buses that offer more comfortable seating and three doors for improved passenger flow. These buses have a gradual boarding ramp and large aisles, making them fully accessible for wheelchair and mobility device users. Offering a service at the time it is needed is a selling attribute for many customers. For example, the promise of next-day delivery is a crucial service element in the parcel-delivery business.

3. *Completeness*—Some organizations provide a range of conveniences to attract customers. For business travellers, a hotel may offer an express check-in/check-out service or an automated kiosk allowing customers to check in and out themselves, fully stocked rooms with online capabilities, and rooms with the latest telecommunications technology. Business travellers essentially need an office when they are away from the office, and that's the level of service they expect from hotels today.

4. *Consistency*—FedEx, a courier service, uses the slogan "Relax. It's FedEx." The slogan implies reliability and dependability for the services the company provides. For customers with these needs, the decision on what courier to use seems an easy one. FedEx aptly portrays its reliability in a TV commercial where a senior executive counsels a junior executive on what courier service to use. The senior executive is shown excelling at everything he touches (well beyond business) and implies FedEx operates at the same level of excellence.

5. *Environment*—A clean, comfortable environment is an essential component of a service offering. Air travel can be uncomfortable, so many airlines have taken steps to incorporate more comfortable seats that convert to beds. Airports, as well, have taken steps to offer a broader range of services for travellers, including gourmet dining experiences such as the one shown in the illustration in **Figure 16.6**.

6. *Supplementary Services*—A company will often market a primary service and then supplement the basic offering with peripheral services. For example, the primary service supplied by a luxury hotel is clean, comfortable lodging. Yet a hotel can distinguish itself from competitors by offering additional services. W Hotels, an ultra-chic urban hotel (a division of Starwood Hotels), promises customers stylish design, sensual comfort, and sublime services. In fact, it offers a "whatever/whenever" service tailored to the fantasies of its guests, where every desire is satisfied "so long as it's legal and ethical."[12] Such an intriguing services mix distinguishes W Hotels from other upscale competitors.

Figure 16.6
Restaurants at Toronto's Pearson International Airport create a gourmet dining experience by offering a better environment and supplementary services.

Renee Suen

Fairmont Hotels & Resorts offers loyalty club members access to bicycles and luxury automobiles during their stays. BMW (a maker of cars and bicycles) is a partner in this marketing initiative. The addition of peripheral services does increase the amount that a firm must invest in its operations; however, consumers like to choose among services that are clearly differentiated, just as they do with tangible products.

Video: Zappos: Marketing-Creating and Capturing Customer Value

Pricing   The various types of services require various pricing strategies from the supplier. Prices can be determined by regulation, tradition, or negotiation.

1. *Regulated Pricing*—In the case of utilities, telephone service, and cable television, the services provided are regulated by government agencies. The suppliers of the service must present and defend rate increases to the agency prior to changing prices.
2. *Traditional Pricing*—Some services have prices that are established or have become traditional. It could be an established hourly rate for a service provided by an auto mechanic, electrician, or plumber, or a set rate of commission for a real estate agent or financial planning broker.
3. *Negotiated Pricing*—Fees for the services of lawyers and marketing research and management consultants are often negotiated. Typically, these companies will submit bids based on specifications supplied by the client. The client then selects a supplier from among the bids, often after further decreases in price have been negotiated.

A buyer's ability to negotiate can save a company considerable sums of money. For example, corporations will strike deals with hotel suppliers and car rental companies largely based on price negotiation, and they demand the best possible price before committing their business. Traditionally, corporate discounts for hotel rooms are in the 20 to 25 percent range, but sharp negotiation skills can earn a company higher discounts.

Consumers can also negotiate a better room rate if they possess the right negotiation skills. Don't accept the first rate that is quoted to you! It is easy to compare prices associated with travel and other services online. With price comparisons available so quickly, goods and services providers must sharpen their pencils regarding the prices they charge.

Distribution   In the service sector, where the relationship between the supplier and the client is close, the distribution channels tend to be direct. Because services are intangible and cannot be stored, there is often no need for intermediaries. Even if intermediaries are used, and in some businesses they commonly are (e.g., numerous small insurance companies are represented by independent insurance agents), their role is to create demand rather than perform the traditional functions of a distributor.

Technology is also affecting the way consumers access services. For example, the first all-digital public library in North America opened its doors in 2014, and it looks a lot like an Apple Store. Rows of iMacs and iPads invite readers to browse. But this $2.3 million library might be most notable for what it does not have—any actual books.[13] Refer to the image in **Figure 16.7**.

At one time, it was generally thought that personal contact was the key to marketing services, particularly in such industries as insurance, financial investments, and travel planning. Online marketing has changed this way of thinking, and these and other industries have adjusted their marketing strategies accordingly. Now, most people book

Figure 16.7   New BiblioTech, a bookless library, offers only e-books.

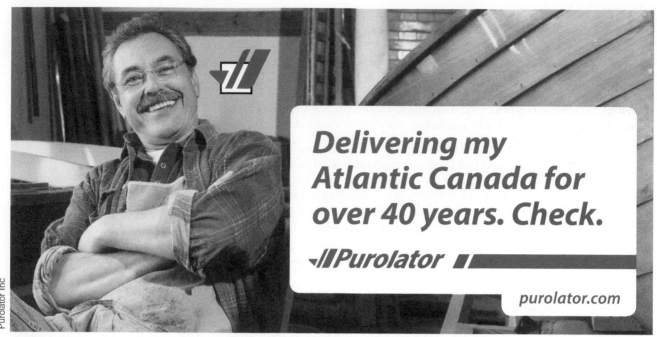

Purolator Inc

Figure 16.8 Advertising plays an essential role in Purolator's marketing strategy.

travel completely online. Traditional (bricks-and-mortar) travel agents have lost considerable business to online travel sites such as Travelocity.ca and Expedia.ca.

Marketing Communications Marketing communications strategies focus on the primary service, detailing what it is and what it does for the customer. In today's competitive market, it is imperative that service companies use all elements of the communications mix. Courier service companies such as UPS and Purolator spend a great deal of money on most forms of advertising to create awareness of and interest in the services they provide. Hotels, airlines, railways, banks, and other financial institutions do the same. Refer to the illustration in **Figure 16.8**.

Information-rich websites reinforce messages from the mass media and provide the details that help convert a prospect into a customer. The Internet and social media channels are widely used for communicating to customers the benefits that services providers offer.

Simulation: Service Marketing

NATURE, SCOPE, AND CHARACTERISTICS OF NOT-FOR-PROFIT MARKETING

LO3 Explain the nature, scope, and characteristics of not-for-profit marketing.

not-for-profit marketing The marketing efforts and activities of not-for-profit organizations.

Not-for-profit marketing refers to the marketing efforts and activities of not-for-profit organizations. These organizations operate in the best interests of the public or champion a particular idea or cause, and they do so without seeking financial profit. The goals and objectives of these groups are quite different from those of profit-based enterprises.

Nature and Scope of Not-for-Profit Marketing

Not-for-profit organizations market goods and services, but they also market people, places, ideas, and organizations. One major goal of not-for-profit marketing is to promote social consciousness. The use of marketing to increase the acceptability of social ideas is referred to as **social marketing**. Examples of social marketing include programs dealing with ecological

social marketing Marketing activity that increases the acceptability of social ideas.

concerns, recycling, the preservation and conservation of natural resources, and spousal abuse, to name a few. Many of these programs are financially supported and promoted by profit-based organizations. For an illustration, refer to **Figure 16.9**.

The Think Marketing box **Missing Children Society's New Social Media Campaign—Milk Carton 2.0** describes an innovative way one not-for-profit is able to get its message out.

Not-for-profit organizations that use marketing strategies effectively include colleges and universities, political parties and politicians, the Canadian Armed Forces, the Humane Society, the Canadian Cancer Society, and the Heart and Stroke Foundation of Canada. This brief listing of organizations indicates that marketing achieves different objectives. It is used to recruit personnel, to raise funds to support causes, and to encourage the public to volunteer time and to make other contributions to worthwhile causes.

Figure 16.9   Profit-based organizations, like tentree Apparel, support social causes by financial means and by helping to raise the profile of the cause through advertising.

Think Marketing

Missing Children Society's New Social Media Campaign—Milk Carton 2.0

Every year, more than 50 000 children go missing in Canada. In the beginning, the police, media, and community band together to help, but over time this effort is reduced. The Missing Children Society of Canada (MCSC) is the only Canadian organization dedicated to the ongoing investigation into, search for, and rescue of missing children.[14] But MCSC has very little money to get word out to the public that a child is missing. Recently, Grey Canada, a full-service advertising agency, offered to assist.

In the past MCSC created awareness by putting a child's photo and name on something people look at every day—milk cartons. Today, however, people spend more time checking in on social media sites like Twitter and Facebook than they do looking at a milk carton. That shift has resulted in Grey's award-winning campaign called Milk Carton 2.0. The campaign invites donors to allow MCSC to use their Facebook or Twitter accounts to help spread the word about a missing child. Donors do not give up control of their accounts—they just give the Missing Children Society the power to send out a message on their behalf. For example, when a child goes missing, an alert goes out to everyone in the donor's social network in those important first few hours when the child is most likely to be found. The campaign has since expanded to include Pinterest and Foursquare. The results? In the first six months following the campaign launch, seven children were found directly due to Milk Carton 2.0. Other positive outcomes have included a 15 percent increase in online donations and a 27 percent rise in corporate sponsorship.

Question:

How could MCSC encourage more people to donate the use of their social media accounts to help spread the word about missing children?

Adapted from: The Missing Children Society of Canada, retrieved from http://mcsc.ca/news/milk-carton-2-0-digital-innovations-transform-the-search-for-missing-children-in-canada/; and M. Weisblott, (February 20, 2014), "Milk Carton 2.0 missing children project wins top Canadian advertising award," retrieved from http://o.canada.com/business/canada-advertising-cassies/

Hand-out/CANADIAN CANCER SOCIETY (BC AND/Newscom

Figure 16.10   Cops for Cancer Tour de Rock is an annual event supporting the Canadian Cancer Society.

CHARACTERISTICS OF NOT-FOR-PROFIT MARKETING

There are many similarities between marketing in a not-for-profit environment and marketing in a profit-oriented environment. In both situations, the customer must choose between competing organizations. A person must decide which charitable groups to support and how much support to give, just as he or she must determine which car to buy and how much to pay for it.

However, there are some differences between not-for-profit and profit-based marketing, especially in the areas of philosophy, exchange (what is exchanged), objectives, benefits derived, and target groups.

Philosophy   Not-for-profit marketing is concerned with the promotion and support of people, causes, ideas, and organizations. It raises funds to support a cause or promote a concept. In the case of profit-based marketing, the goal is to generate a financial return on investment. An illustration of a not-for-profit event is included in **Figure 16.10**.

Exchange   In profit-based marketing, money is exchanged between buyers and sellers for the goods or services provided. While money may change hands in not-for-profit marketing, it does so under different circumstances. What people receive for their money cannot be quantified; they give, for example, for the psychological satisfaction of supporting a cause they believe in.

Objectives   Profit-oriented companies establish objectives in terms of sales, profit, return on investment, and market share. In not-for-profit organizations, the objectives are not always quantifiable and measurable. They establish targets for fundraising, but these are subordinate to other nonfinancial objectives. For example, the objective of the Canadian Cancer Society is to find a cure for the disease. At MADD (Mothers Against Drunk Driving), the objective is to change the public's attitudes or get the public to agree with a certain position. Both of these organizations have extensive websites to educate the public about their cause.

Benefits Derived   In an exchange made for profit, a buyer benefits directly from the good or service supplied by the selling firm. In a not-for-profit environment, only a small portion of "buyers," or supporters, ever receive any material benefits from the supported association or institution. For instance, funds to aid health organizations are solicited from the general population, but only a relatively small portion of the population contracts a particular disease and uses the services of any given health clinic each year. The benefit that is derived by all is the psychological satisfaction of helping a worthwhile cause.

TYPES OF NOT-FOR-PROFIT MARKETING

LO4 Describe the types of not-for-profit marketing.

There are four categories of not-for-profit marketing: organization marketing, people marketing, place marketing, and idea marketing.

Organization Marketing

Organization marketing is marketing that seeks to gain or maintain acceptance of an organization's objectives and services. Colleges, universities, and hospitals engage in such marketing; they turn to fundraising campaigns as a survival tactic in the wake of government restraints on funds for education and health. Educational institutions want the public to both accept their goals and use their services.

People Marketing

People marketing refers to a process of marketing an individual or a group of people to create a favourable impression of that individual or group (e.g., politicians, political parties, sports personalities and their teams) within a target audience.

Figure 16.11 Vivid images attract the attention of prospective travellers.

Politicians, aware that their careers are created or destroyed by their images, call on image-makers to fine-tune their personal and presentation styles. In preparing for political debates on television, all participants are carefully prepared by consultants so that their strengths, and not their weaknesses, will show in the heat of battle. High-profile celebrities, including, for example, NHL stars and their teams, are active in community-minded programs. The Ottawa Senators, for example, offer a number of community-based events that give people the opportunity to see and interact with the team outside of games. The team also offers the Sens@School program, an online educational program for Grades 4 to 6 that focuses on health and physical education, language, and mathematics. The students can be active and test their knowledge through interactive games and activities.

Place Marketing

Place marketing draws attention to and creates a favourable attitude toward a particular place, be it a country, province, region, or city. Places are marketed in much the same way as products. The benefits and advantages of the location are the focal points of advertising and promotion campaigns. Provincial governments, for example, use catchy slogans such as "Spectacular" (Northwest Territories), "More to Discover" (Ontario), "Super, Natural" (British Columbia), and "The Gentle Island" (Prince Edward Island). In place marketing, advertising is the principal strategy, as it creates the image for the destination. Refer to **Figure 16.11** for an illustration. Specific details essential for planning vacations and travel are available on information-rich websites.

Idea Marketing

Idea marketing encourages the public to accept and agree with certain issues and causes. It is often referred to as **cause marketing**. Campaigns aimed at convincing people of the need to wear seat belts, avoid drinking and driving, and exercise regularly are examples of idea marketing. The objective of cause marketing is to induce the majority of the population to accept a given idea, cause, or way of thinking (refer to Figure 16.9 and Figure 16.10).

organization marketing Marketing that seeks to gain or maintain acceptance of an organization's objectives and services.

people marketing The marketing of an individual or group of people to create a favourable impression of that individual or group.

place marketing Drawing attention to and creating a favourable attitude toward a particular place, be it a country, province, region, or city.

idea marketing Marketing activity that enourages the public to accept and agree with certain issues and causes.

cause marketing Marketing activity that increases the acceptability of social ideas.

MARKETING STRATEGY IN A NOT-FOR-PROFIT ORGANIZATION

L05 Discuss the role and importance of marketing strategy in not-for-profit organizations.

A comprehensive marketing strategy is crucial to the success of any not-for-profit group. As suggested earlier, communications plays a prominent role, but all elements of the mix are given due consideration. The charitable marketplace today is just as competitive as any commercial marketplace. Consequently, not-for-profit marketing managers think of their organizations as brands and develop their strategies accordingly. This section briefly examines the contributions of product, price, distribution, and marketing communications to the strategic market planning of not-for-profit organizations.

Product   Product strategy in a not-for-profit organization is virtually the opposite of the strategy employed by a firm driven by the profit motive. Profit-based organizations start by trying to discover what needs the consumer has, and then they formulate a concept—a product or a service—to satisfy those needs. Not-for-profit bodies, on the other hand, believe from the start that they provide what the public needs. Very often, they feel that others only have to be made aware of a certain viewpoint regarding an idea, cause, person, or place for it to become widely accepted. Informational campaigns by such organizations as the Heart and Stroke Foundation of Canada or the Alzheimer Society of Canada exemplify this strategy.

Contemporary not-for-profit organizations are like companies that operate for a profit in that they find it effective to develop a product mix that includes identification (e.g., logos), a package (membership cards to acknowledge contribution), and other product variables.

Price   In a not-for-profit organization, money is not necessarily the only form of exchange. Sometimes no money changes hands; instead, time or expertise is volunteered in return for the psychological satisfaction of helping others or the knowledge that society will be made better. Even if money is involved, the nature of the exchange is different from an exchange made for material profit. While long-term profit is the goal of the profit-based organization, a short-term gain is all a not-for-profit organization seeks. Special events are frequently a means of generating revenue for not-for-profit organizations. For example, Movember, a major fundraising event in which men grow moustaches during the month of November to raise awareness for men's health issues, is supported financially by Canadian corporations and the public. Refer to the image in **Figure 16.12**.

Distribution   Because not-for-profit entities deal in intangibles, channels tend to be direct: the organization tends to work directly with donors. If intermediaries—professional fundraisers, for example—are used, they act on behalf of the organization. They do not assume any responsibility or control.

Video: Save the Children: Social Networking

Marketing Communications   Communication is the most visible aspect of not-for-profit marketing. Advertising and various direct response techniques, including mail and telephone, form the nucleus of an organization's effort, particularly for fundraising programs. Public-service announcements, a low-cost form of advertising, may be used to point out the benefits of contributing to a cause or charitable foundation.

Media advertising plays a big role in people and place marketing. Think of all those ads you see in a federal election campaign that create and maintain an image for a person or party. Very often, a charitable organization will use a known personality as its spokesperson. For example, Canadian actor Michael J. Fox, who has Parkinson's disease, is the primary spokesperson for the Michael J. Fox Foundation for Parkinson's Research.

Personal selling is also common: the Heart and Stroke Foundation and many other worthwhile causes use local residents to solicit funds door to door in their own neighbourhoods. Such campaigns are undertaken annually and supported by advertising to build awareness of the fundraising project.

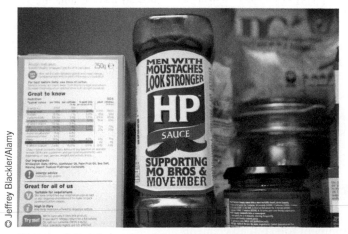

© Jeffrey Blackler/Alamy

Figure 16.12   Annual events, like Movember, are critical components of not-for-profit fundraising.

✔ ExperienceMarketing

To experience marketing you must assess situations and make recommendations to change marketing strategy when necessary. What would you do in the following situation?

You are an enterprising marketing student home for the summer and have decided to start your own business— a window cleaning business. The window cleaning business is usually divided between residential cleaning and institutional/business cleaning. Since you are just starting out you have decided to focus on residential cleaning.

You know what your primary business is but you have several marketing issues to deal with before you can pursue customers. With reference to the "Service as a Product" section of this chapter, how will you describe your service more thoroughly? What will be the name of your business? What are the key benefits you will offer that will differentiate your business from competitors in your market? How will you price your service? What will the nature of your marketing communications be with prospective customers?

As a starting point you may want to review the marketing activities of competitors in your local market. Once you have assessed the market, prepare a summary marketing plan that will get the business going. Include appropriate background information and objectives in your plan.

CHAPTER SUMMARY

LO1 Outline the characteristics and behaviours that distinguish services marketing from product marketing. *(pp. 349–353)*

Services have certain characteristics that distinguish them from products. A service is intangible; it cannot be seen, heard, or touched. It is inseparable from the source of supply, because each supplier is unique despite competitive attempts to imitate a service. The quality of a service also varies, even within a single organization, where different people perform the same service in different ways. Finally, demand for certain services is perishable; in other words, demand is uneven, in some cases seasonal, and this creates a problem for marketers of services. Similar to product marketing situations, when planning a marketing strategy the marketer of a service must consider the attitudes, needs, and motives of potential customers and how an organization goes about buying services.

LO2 Describe the elements of the services marketing mix. *(pp. 353–356)*

Because services are intangible, the marketer must offer things beyond the primary service to make the experience meaningful for the customer. Beyond the primary service, those additional elements include attitude (of employees providing the service), availability and timing (appropriate frequency of offering), completeness (providing a range of conveniences), consistency (reliable and dependable service), environment (pleasing and comfortable to ensure satisfaction), and supplementary services (complementing the primary service with peripheral services). The price of a service is derived more from the value it provides consumers than from direct costs. The channels of distribution are direct, and marketing communications efforts are aimed directly at the final user. Service marketers employ all elements of the marketing mix, but the main planning concern is that the firm understands exactly what it is that the customer is buying. Service organizations market themselves much the way for-profit brands do.

LO3 Explain the nature, scope, and characteristics of not-for-profit marketing. *(pp. 356–358)*

Not-for-profit marketing is used by organizations whose goals do not centre on financial gain. Such organizations operate in the best interests of the public or advocate a particular idea or cause. Some differences between not-for-profit and profit-based marketing are in the areas of philosophy, exchange objectives, benefits derived, and target groups. Rather than aiming for financial targets, not-for-profit bodies attempt to change attitudes. In doing so, they must consider two distinct targets: the clients who use and derive the benefits of the organization, and the donors who provide the organization with resources.

LO4 Describe the types of not-for-profit marketing. *(pp. 358–359)*

There are four categories of not-for-profit marketing: (1) people marketing—fostering certain attitudes toward particular persons; (2) idea marketing—gaining acceptance for ways of thinking; (3) place marketing—encouraging visits to a country, province, or city; and (4) organization marketing—raising funds, cultivating an image, or persuading people to use the facilities.

LO5 Discuss the role and importance of marketing strategy in not-for-profit organizations. *(pp. 359–360)*

Not-for-profit marketing managers must think and act like brand marketers, have a clear brand strategy, and use all elements of the marketing mix to help them reach their goals. In social marketing situations (charities and causes), the marketer assumes that its charity or cause will be of interest to potential supporters and the price is related to any financial donation that is requested. Cause marketers operate in a very competitive environment, however. Distribution strategies tend to be direct and marketing communications utilize personal selling and direct-response advertising techniques. In people and place marketing, mass advertising plays a key role in generating awareness and interest and the marketing is very similar to product marketing. Creating a good brand image is important.

REVIEW QUESTIONS

1. What are the four unique characteristics of services? (*LO1*)
2. What are the tangible and intangible aspects of eating out at a restaurant? (*LO1*)
3. How important a role do customers' attitudes play in their decisions to purchase services? (*LO1*)
4. "A service is an attribute or series of attributes offered to consumers." What does this statement mean? (*LO2*)
5. How is pricing a service different from pricing a tangible product? (*LO2*)
6. Describe the basic differences between marketing for profit-oriented and not-for-profit organizations. (*LO3*)
7. What is one major goal of not-for-profit marketing? (*LO3*)
8. Briefly describe the various types of not-for-profit marketing. (*LO4*)
9. What is cause marketing? Give an example. (*LO4*)
10. What type of distribution channel—direct or indirect—do not-for-profit organizations typically use? Why? (*LO5*)

DISCUSSION AND APPLICATION QUESTIONS

1. If you were in the home-decorating business (painting and wallpapering), how would you convince do-it-yourselfers to use the service?
2. Review the concept of perishability of demand in the service industry. If you were in charge of marketing for the following organizations, what strategies would you recommend to overcome perishability of demand?
   a. Air Canada Centre (or any other major arena)
   b. Your post-secondary institution
3. Assume you are in charge of marketing for the following companies. Describe the quality of service offerings that would be given priority to attract and maintain customers.
   a. Cineplex Odeon Theatres
   b. Starbucks
   c. Mr. Lube

17 Global Marketing

© FogStock/Alamy

LEARNING OBJECTIVES

LO1 Outline the importance of international trade for Canada and Canadian corporations. (pp. 364–365)

LO2 Describe the factors an organization considers when pursuing global markets. (pp. 365–373)

LO3 Outline the various business strategies commonly used when entering foreign markets. (pp. 373–375)

LO4 Describe the nature of marketing strategies used by firms when seeking global market opportunities. (pp. 376–382)

MANY PROMINENT COMPANIES...

operate in industries in Canada where growth potential is flat or only marginal at best. Consequently, these companies look at expansion opportunities in foreign countries as a viable alternative for growth. Such is the case for Yum Brands Inc., parent company of KFC. KFC is the number-one North America-based fast-food chain operating in China. You may automatically think that McDonald's would be the leader, but think a bit longer and you'll realize chicken has been a staple food in China for hundreds of years.

"Our China business continues to fire on all cylinders," says Yum CEO David Novak. "Looking ahead, our international business is strong and new unit development is robust."[1] One of the keys to KFC's success in China is the menu, a menu that has been adapted to fit local tastes. Think rice dishes and hot soy milk alongside fried chicken and hot wings. If size matters, KFC and sister brand Pizza Hut operate 6200 restaurants and plan to open 700 more in 2014. Simply being available gives KFC an advantage as they outnumber their nearest competitor by a two-to-one margin.[2]

In China the economy is growing rapidly and the middle class is adapting to more Western ways. Both situations represent opportunity for North American companies. Many companies are looking at the entire Asia-Pacific region for future growth. China alone could become the biggest market for many companies. Yum Brands thinks so—they see China as the best restaurant opportunity of the twenty-first century where a consuming class is expected to double from 300 million people to 600 million people by 2020. In 2014 they plan on opening 700 new restaurants to serve this new demand.

KFC's success sheds some light on the need for companies to look at global opportunities if growth is their primary business objective.

CANADIAN INTERNATIONAL TRADE AND THE MOVEMENT TO GLOBAL MARKETS

LO1 Outline the importance of international trade for Canada and Canadian corporations.

For Canada, the importance of international trade is significant. In 2013 (the most recent year for which statistics were available for this book), exports to foreign countries amounted to $477.4 billion while imports were $486.5 billion. Historically, Canada has usually had a positive trade balance (meaning that the value of exports exceeds imports). However, the recession of 2009 took its toll on Canada's international trade, and even though our economy has recovered somewhat, there has been a trade deficit of varying amounts each year since.

Canada's largest trading partner by far is the United States, which currently accounts for 74 percent of exports and 64 percent of imports.[3] Other important trading partners include Japan, the United Kingdom, and countries comprising the European Union. Refer to **Figure 17.1** for statistical information on Canada's international trade position.

Canada's leading merchandise exports are energy products, motor vehicles and parts, metal and mineral products, consumer goods, and forestry products. Canada's leading imports are consumer goods, motor vehicles and parts, industrial machinery (including equipment and parts), and energy products.

There are several reasons that companies are moving toward global marketing. First, most opportunities have been exhausted in domestic markets. Coca-Cola, for example, is already a global company, but its primary base is in North America. In North America sales of its core product, Coca-Cola, have been on a slow yet steady decline for the past 10 years. Consumers are showing a preference for healthier beverage alternatives.

Trade Balance Trends ($ billions)

	2011	2012	2013
Exports	456.8	462.5	471.4
Imports	456.0	474.5	475.0
Trade Balance	(0.8)	(12.0)	(3.6)

Brackets = trade deficit

Major Trading Partners (2013)

Country	Exports ($ billions)	% of Exports	Imports ($ billions)	% of Imports
United States	357.5	75.8	247.4	52.1
All Other Countries	113.9	24.2	227.6	47.9

(map) iLoveCoffeeDesign/Shutterstock

Figure 17.1 Canada's Trade Balance Trends and Major Trading Partners

Consequently, greater emphasis is placed on foreign markets. Coca-Cola recently invested $5 billion to expand its operations in India. India, a country of 1.2 billion people, remains one of the last big frontiers for the Atlanta-based beverage giant.[4]

The formation of trading agreements is a second reason for pursuing global markets. European countries have combined forces to form the European Union, a trading community that features a common currency known as the euro. This union presents challenges for North American companies wanting to trade there. The Pacific Rim represents significant opportunity as countries there are now more open to trading with Western countries.

The Asia-Pacific region is very attractive to North American marketing organizations because it represents 60 percent of the world's population, 50 percent of the world's production, and 40 percent of the world's consumption. Some of the world's top restaurant chains have rolled into China, Taiwan, South Korea, and Japan as Asians embrace Western fast food. Both KFC and McDonald's are firmly established in the Asia-Pacific region. Starbucks has aggressive plans there and plans to make China its second largest market by 2014. The company has 600 stores in China but plans to have 1500 by 2017. That's a growth strategy that involves opening almost one store every day for three years. Starbucks enjoys high brand awareness in China and consumers perceive the brand favourably. It is seen as an aspirational brand that offers an international café experience.[5]

ANALYZING GLOBAL MARKETING OPPORTUNITIES

LO2 Describe the factors an organization considers when pursuing global markets.

When a firm is contemplating entry into a foreign market it must assess the benefits and the risks. Similar to analyzing the situation in a domestic market, the firm must assess the foreign country's economic environment, the consumer environment, the political environment, the legal and regulatory environment, the technological environment, and the competitive environment.

Economic Environment

From nation to nation, economies vary considerably. The economic character of any country is shaped by variables that include its natural resources, population, income distribution, employment, system of education, and political system. In a broad sense there are three economy classifications: government-controlled economies, market-controlled economies, and mixed economies. Let's differentiate among the classifications.

government-controlled economy An economic system in which the government makes all the economic decisions on behalf of its people.

A **government-controlled economy** is exactly that. The government makes all the economic decisions on behalf of its people. There is no influence from the free market. Typically there is a strong central government that determines who its trading partners are and which foreign companies operate there, if any. Typically, these countries own the primary industries and companies that operate in these industries. Such countries would include China, Cuba, and North Korea. The times are changing, however, and many government-controlled economies are gradually loosening the reins and giving some control over economic activities to the people. Russia and China are good examples. Both countries are now open to foreign investment by North America-based companies.

market-controlled economy An economic system that operates by voluntary exchange in a free market that is not planned or controlled by a central government.

A **market-controlled economy** operates by voluntary exchange in a free market that is not planned or controlled by a central government. Essentially, it is a capitalistic economy in which a company will succeed or fail based on how well it reads and reacts to changing economic conditions. In this type of economy consumers have an abundance of choices and marketers compete vigorously for their allegiance. The economic laws of supply and demand prevail. Effective marketing strategies are essential. Canada, the United States and Japan are examples of market-controlled economies.

mixed economy An economic system that allows simultaneous operations of publicly and privately owned enterprises.

A **mixed economy** is an economic system that allows simultaneous operations of publicly and privately owned enterprises. Such an economy operates freely but there is some government oversight where necessary. Companies are free to operate as they wish but the government regulates certain areas such as environmental protection, maintenance of employment standards, and maintenance of competition. Thinking internationally, and in the context of competition, a mixed economy could have barriers to entry such as tariffs and quotas—concepts that are discussed later in the chapter. The intent of a trade barrier is to protect the well-being of a domestic industry. Refer to **Figure 17.2** for a summary of these market economies.

Consumer Environment

In assessing the consumer environment, a company will look at how culture, language, and differences in needs and motivation will affect the development of global marketing

Government-Controlled Economy	Market-Controlled Economy	Mixed Economy
• Strong central government makes economic decisions	• Market operates by voluntary exchange	• Simultaneous operations of publicly and privately owned companies
• Consumers usually have much less product choice	• Consumers have much product choice	• Some government control to protect local industries and workers
• Government controls industries and companies	• Laws of supply and demand prevail	• Laws of supply and demand prevail
• Difficult market to enter	• Effective marketing essential for company growth	• Possible barriers to entry for foreign companies

Figure 17.2 The Nature of Global Marketing Economies

strategies. Needless to say, there are significant variations from one part of the world to another. How a company interprets these differences is another matter.

Culture   Segmenting markets on the basis of culture is important in global marketing because the values and beliefs people hold vary from nation to nation. While businesses must think globally, they must act locally. Failing to recognize cultural differences has resulted in marketing blunders by even the savviest marketing organizations.

Nike wanted to make a splash in China and launched a campaign featuring NBA basketball star LeBron James. In a television commercial James played a video-game character who defeats a kung fu master and a pair of dragons. The dragon is an important symbol in traditional Chinese culture. The ad violated regulations that uphold national dignity and respect of the motherland's culture, so the government banned it.[6]

Marketers are learning that North American-style advertising doesn't work elsewhere. In sharp contrast to the Nike example above, Oreo cookies ditched American-style ads in China in favour of a local marketing campaign featuring children—children are the centre of the Chinese family. In recent years Oreo has enjoyed much success in China.[7] It is clear that understanding cultural values is crucial. It is appropriate to place a strong emphasis on group and family values. For certain, marketing communications strategies must be adapted to local customs and preferences if the company is to be successful in a foreign market.

Language   Language is the most obvious barrier to a global marketing program. A product name chosen to appeal to an English-speaking market must be replaced with something that will have greater effect in non–English-speaking countries. Very simple mistakes in judgment, however, or carelessness in checking out local interpretations of names and phrases, have proven costly for many firms. Pepsi-Cola was advertised in Taiwan using the slogan "Come Alive with Pepsi," which translated as "Pepsi brings back your ancestors from the dead." Pepsi devised a new slogan for Taiwan.

Kellogg's had to rename its Bran Buds cereal in Sweden when it discovered that the name roughly translated to "burned farmer." In Mexico, an ad for a Parker pen was to intended to read, "It won't leak in your pocket and embarrass you." In the ad the word "embarazar" was used—the company thought that the word meant "embarrass." Apparently, it meant "impregnate." The ad read "It won't leak in your pocket and make you pregnant"—not exactly the intent of the advertisement.[8]

Symbols are also a factor in communications, and they, too, pose problems for global marketing organizations. In China, the following symbols signify death: shooting stars, upright chopsticks, odd numbers, the number four, white handkerchiefs, and clocks and watches. These symbols should be excluded from any form of marketing communications in that country.[9]

Needs and Motivation   Differences in consumers' needs and motivations for buying products make it difficult to establish marketing strategies that work globally. For example, PepsiCo has found success in China by adapting brands such as Lay's, Tropicana, and Quaker. When it comes to food, taste preferences must be considered. In China, Lay's markets cucumber-flavoured chips, a flavor that wouldn't be popular in North America. In the juice category, PepsiCo recognized that fresh fruit is cheap and readily available in China. It developed a Tropicana juice beverage containing pieces of fruit big enough to bite into.

Countries in East Asia are quickly adopting Western ways, and the changes have been beneficial for fast-food companies such as McDonald's, KFC, and Pizza Hut. Their approach is to give local needs priority over global needs. McDonald's is a master at adapting itself to the idioms and mores of different climes. You can eat McFalafels in Egypt, an egg-topped McHuevos burger in Uruguay, and a McLuks salmon burger in Finland.[10]

Surprisingly, a company can be caught off guard with its desire to accommodate local needs and preferences. IKEA entered China thinking it would market Chinese-inspired designs. Its initial foray into China was not successful. Apparently, Chinese consumers wanted IKEA's modern European look. Ikea reverted to its design roots and has been very successful ever since. Sales in China reached $1 billion in 2013.[11]

Rarely can a product be positioned uniformly around the world, but Philips did just that with its Sense and Simplicity campaign. Philips effectively repositioned the company and its brands under the Sense and Simplicity banner. Philips is a technology company that builds and markets complex products. Its belief, however, is that technology should make life simpler. New and exciting products should be easy to use. Regardless of the market in which the marketing communications occur, the message is easy to understand. Refer to the image in **Figure 17.3**.

Figure 17.3   Philip's products are marketed under the Sense and Simplicity brand promise.

because
only muggers and
pulp novelists
need dark and
lonely streets.

Urban areas can often feel like no-go areas if they're poorly lit. So why not make everyone feel safer by improving visibility? Our LED white light is a simple solution that helps people see faces more clearly and so feel more secure. Find out more at www.philips.com/because

PHILIPS
sense and simplicity

Philips North America

Marketing Strategy

Market Segmentation

Heineken beer is positioned everywhere in the world (except Holland) as a premium-priced, high-quality brew. In its home market, it is a popular-priced brand and is preceived to be "just another beer" by beer drinkers.

Product and Package

In Britain, you can buy cold milk in cans in vending machines. Do you think that canned milk (other than evaporated milk) would sell in Canada?

Psychographics and Demographics

In most countries, psychographic analysis can be more revealing than demographics. Lifestyle-based research provides valuable insights into target-market opportunities. For example, Volvo designed a small, sporty coupe specifically for the European career woman. Is Canada ready for a sporty Volvo? Is this your image of Volvo?

Making Generalizations

Marketers cannot generalize about the Asia-Pacific region. Even within a country, consumers are not alike. In China, there are 60 different ethnic groups and 300 different dialects spoken. The northern Chinese tend to be taller and have long faces. Southern Chinese tend to be shorter and have rounder, fuller faces.

Know Your Customer

Doing business in China revolves around personal relationships. In China, knowing your customer means getting to know them personally. Without a personal relationship, there is no business relationship.

Figure 17.4 Some Facts and Oddities About Global Marketing

For additional details and idiosyncrasies about the cultures, languages, and needs of global consumers, see **Figure 17.4**. Also refer to the Think Marketing box **Oreos Are Different in China** for insight into how Oreo turned failure into success by adapting the brand to local market needs.

Political Environment

The political environment in a foreign country can shape trading policy and have a dramatic impact on a company's profitability. For example, a change in government could alter how a North American company operates in a foreign country. Such was the case for Coca-Cola in India in the late 1970s. A new government ordered Coca-Cola to dilute its investment in its Indian subsidiary and to turn over its secret formula. It was unthinkable that Coke would reveal its formula! Coke pulled up stakes and quit India. One of its Indian bottlers then developed a cola-type product and called it Thums Up. The product caught on immediately and became a top seller in India.

Ironically, when the Indian government liberalized in the late 1990s, foreign investment was encouraged and Coca-Cola returned. Upon its return Coca-Cola acquired an Indian company (Parle Agro Pvt. Ltd.) that marketed four brands: Thums Up, Limca, Gold Spot, and Maaza, giving them an instant 60 percent market share. The acquisition also gave Coca-Cola a nationwide bottling and marketing system it could use to sell its own brands.[12]

Trade Barriers   The purpose of a **trade barrier** is to protect a country from too much foreign competition within its borders. Canada and the United States, for example, believe that the automobile industry needs some form of protection. Consequently, only so many foreign-produced cars are allowed into these countries each year. Such a policy protects employment domestically. **Protectionism** is a belief that foreign trade should be restricted so that domestic industries can be preserved.

trade barrier Intended to protect a country from too much foreign competition within its borders.

protectionism A belief that foreign trade should be restricted so that domestic industry can be preserved.

ThinkMarketing

Oreos Are Different in China

How can the most popular cookie on the planet be a distant follower in China? Everyone likes Oreos, don't they? Well, apparently not, and it all comes down to the fact that Oreos didn't adjust its marketing strategy to suit the needs and expectations of Chinese consumers.

One of the traps that marketers fall into revolves around marketing efficiency. It is so much cheaper to use the same strategy in as many markets as possible. But the savings are false if sales don't materialize. It is more costly to have different strategies in different markets, but in the long term such investment should pay better dividends.

Oreos eventually learned that it had to adapt to what Chinese consumers wanted in a cookie. Working from a base market share in China of 3.5 percent, it was clear that changes were necessary. The result was a new three-pronged marketing strategy that involved extensive new product development, packaging, and marketing communications.

From consumer research the management team determined that American-style Oreos were too sweet for Chinese consumers. Further, they preferred fruit flavours rather than the creamier vanilla and chocolate flavours common in American Oreos. The creamier style of filling was retained but flavours suitable for Chinese consumers were added—for example, a green tea ice cream flavour proved very popular. Double fruit combinations such as orange-mango and blueberry-raspberry were also well received.

Shelf space is scarce in the smaller grocery outlets in China. To solve that problem a smaller package was developed. The smaller size also meant the retail price was more attractive for consumers. Affordability is always an issue in purchase decisions.

Finally, the sub-titled American-style ads were replaced with more meaningful ads that would impact

Imaginechina/AP Images

consumers. They featured children, who are the centre of the Chinese family. Celebrities like Yao Ming, a former NBA basketball star and a Chinese sports legend, were used to promote Oreos. The local marketing strategies have worked. Oreos now has a market share of 15 percent in China!

Question:

What is the moral of this story? Is a local market campaign the only way to be successful in a foreign market?

Adapted from Jeff Beer, "Oreo's Chinese twist," Canadian Business, December 10, 2012, pp. 66, 67.

---

tariff A tax or duty imposed on imported goods.

To restrict trade, governments use tariffs, quotas, embargoes, and local content laws. A **tariff** is a tax or duty imposed on imported goods. In Canada, prices for domestically produced goods and services tend to be high, due to the high costs of labour, raw materials, and parts. In comparison, goods from Asian countries in such markets as toys, clothing, and electronics are produced at much lower cost. To balance the price differences between imported and domestic products in these industries, Canada imposes a tariff on incoming foreign goods. The advantage of a tariff is that it can be specific in nature and protect particular industries when needed.

A **quota** is a specific limit on the amount of goods that may be imported into a country. In Canada, precise quotas are placed on Japanese automobiles each year to restrict their penetration of the domestic market. To circumvent the quota, manufacturers such as Toyota and Honda have significantly increased production capacity in their Canadian facilities. They build cars in Canada for sale in Canada, the United States, and Mexico. The North American Free Trade Agreement (NAFTA), an agreement among Canada, the United States, and Mexico, governs trading practices among these countries.

quota A specific limit imposed on the amount of goods that may be imported into a country.

Tariffs and quotas often work in conjunction with one another. For example, Canada maintains high trade barriers on all dairy products. The barriers protect the domestic dairy industry and are a means of balancing supply with demand. The barriers take the form of tariff rate quotas, which consist of applying high duties and taxes to imports above a certain threshold. Once the import threshold or quota has been met the tariffs charged are significant—a minimum of 200 percent to a maximum of 313 percent.[13] While this system is beneficial to the Canadian dairy industry it may not be in the best interests of consumers. With less competition consumers have less variety to choose from and they face higher prices for the dairy products that are available. For example, Canadians pay significantly more for milk than do American consumers.

A **local content law** is another way of protecting local industry and employment. In this case, a foreign-based manufacturer is required to use a specified amount of locally produced components. As stated above, Honda produces cars in Canada. A local content law calls for a percentage of the car parts Honda uses to be manufactured in Canada. Such a law spurs employment in the domestic auto parts industry.

local content law A way of protecting local industry and employment by requiring a foreign-based manufacturer to use a specified amount of locally produced components.

An **embargo** disallows entry of specified products into a country. Concerns related to health, moral issues, and politics in other countries are often cited as the reasons for imposing embargoes. Fearing the advancement of nuclear weapons in Iran, Canada and many other countries placed a ban on all Iranian imports and exports. Such sanctions helped force the government of Iran to adopt a more moderate stance and open the door to negotiations with the United Nations Security Council. Until the matter is settled diplomatically the embargo will remain in place.[14]

embargo A trade restriction that disallows entry of specified products into a country.

Canada Border Services Agency is responsible for screening various products—pharmaceuticals, chemicals, food, and many others—as they enter the country. Products that do not meet standards are rejected. For example, toys from abroad that do not meet Canadian safety standards are rejected at the border.

Non-governmental organizations and groups can also impose embargoes in the form of a boycott. In a marketing context, a **boycott** calls for consumers to avoid buying a particular product or products based on the actions of a company when the company's actions are contrary to the beliefs of the organization calling for the boycott.

boycott An organized refusal to buy a specific product.

To demonstrate, four organizations—PETA (People for the Ethical Treatment of Animals), Respect for Animals, the Humane Society of the United States, and the International Fund for Animal Welfare—called for a boycott of Canada goods due to the government-subsidized slaughter of nearly one million seals over the last three years. More specifically, these groups called for a boycott of Canadian fish and seafood products. The value of these exports exceed the value of the seal hunt, by far. The Respect for Animals group claim that exports of snow crab to the U.S. have fallen by $200 million a year.[15] Boycotts can have an impact!

Legal and Regulatory Environment

Marketing organizations must know what they can and cannot do with a product in a foreign country. Awareness of local laws and regulations for packaging and advertising is crucial. In the Middle East, for example, advertisements can show only the product; in Austria, children cannot be used in advertisements.

Canada and the United States have their own idiosyncrasies that foreign marketers must deal with or that apply when the two countries are trading with each other. For example, packaging in Canada must be bilingual; a firm manufacturing in the United States must develop separate packaging if it wishes to pursue the Canadian market. Canadian food companies must have separate packaging if they sell their products in the

United States. Such practices are necessary because food labelling laws and nutritional guidelines are not the same in both countries.

Health Canada is responsible for regulations that govern products for consumer goods such as food, toys, beds, jewellery, cosmetics, and medicine. The regulations deal specifically with packaging and labelling, mechanical hazards, flammable hazards, and toxicity hazards. Importers must be aware of these regulations. For example, saccharine is allowed in food products manufactured in the United States, but not in Canada. Any U.S. product containing this ingredient will be automatically destroyed or returned to the country of origin if it reaches Canadian shores.[16]

Technological Environment

When contemplating expansion into a foreign market, the technological environment of that market must be considered. Adapting to changing technologies is one of the biggest challenges an organization faces today. The technological environment includes factors and trends related to innovations that affect the development and production of new products and the marketing of products. Utilizing social media in marketing practices is a good example of how fast technology is changing things. Just a few years ago this option did not exist. Technology presents opportunities for developing new products and how marketing activities are performed.

An organization must ensure that the foreign country has the technology and skill sets required to make and market its products. Alternatively, the organization would provide proper training, which adds to the cost of operations. When the Japanese and South Korean automobile manufacturers built facilities in Canada, they had to deal with this situation to a certain extent. While Canada was knowledgeable in automobile manufacturing and its labour force was skilled, the foreign firms had to educate their Canadian employees in their management style and their way of doing business. Such integration of Canadian and foreign influence allowed the foreign organization to learn about Canadian culture, trade, consumers, and ways of doing business.

Technology is fuelling growth in so many industries that Canadian manufacturers should be concerned. Advancements in Japan, East Asia, and the United States in consumer electronics and telecommunications will have an impact on Canadian companies in these industries. Canada's manufacturing base in Ontario, for example, has suffered significantly as companies move production to foreign countries that offer a combination of technology and lower wage rates.

Perhaps no other company demonstrates the technology principle better than BlackBerry. Once the darling of Canadian technology, it has suffered mightily as competitors such as Apple, Samsung, and Google have shot past it in the mobile communications market. While BlackBerry has undergone considerable management change in recent years, its attempt to resurrect itself has fallen well short of expectations. On the world stage BlackBerry remains a player, particularly in the Asia-Pacific market, but its poor performance in North America could be its ultimate undoing. In marketing terms BlackBerry waited too long to react to changes occurring in the global market-place. The pace at which they operated was much slower than Apple and Samsung. There's an expression in marketing: "Stand still and you're dead." Perhaps that applies here.

Competitive Environment

cartel A group of firms or countries that band together and conduct trade in a manner similar to a monopoly.

A **cartel** is a group of firms or countries that band together to conduct trade in a manner similar to a monopoly. The purpose of a cartel is to improve the bargaining position of its members in the world market. The cartel will typically agree to coordinate pricing and marketing standards with the intention of gaining monopoly status. One of the world's most influential cartels is the Organization of the Petroleum Exporting Countries (OPEC), which comprises 13 oil-producing nations from around the world. OPEC countries can restrict the supply of oil, a resource that is in high demand in other nations, thereby forcing the price up. The higher prices affect the economy of an importing country, because any increase in oil price is added to the cost of manufacturing in that country. This means that consumers ultimately pay more for the products they purchase.

An **orderly market agreement** is an agreement by which nations share a market, eliminating the trade barriers among them. The free trade agreement (NAFTA) among Canada, the United States, and Mexico is an example of an orderly market agreement because it allows the markets to become open to industries across their borders.

Canada has formulated a new free trade agreement with members of the European Union. The agreement will give Canada preferential market access to EU member nations and its more than 500 million consumers. The agreement should be a boon for Canadian exporters who will see the elimination of a 98 percent tariff on a wide range of products.[17] By the same token European goods will have greater access to the Canadian market.

A **common market** is a regional or geographical group of countries that agree to limit trade barriers among members and apply a common tariff to goods from non-member countries. The European Union is an example of a common market. Gradually, the trade barriers that had existed between its members were removed and many EU countries agreed to a common currency—the euro. Unique marketing strategies will be needed for Canadian companies wanting to do business in this region. The Canada–EU free trade agreement should open up doors for new exports of Canadian products to this region.

orderly market agreement An agreement by which nations share a market, eliminating the trade barriers among them.

common market A regional or geographical group of countries that agree to limit trade barriers among their members and apply a common tariff to goods from non-member countries.

GLOBAL BUSINESS STRATEGIES

L03 Outline the various business strategies commonly used when entering foreign markets.

Companies pursuing international opportunities must decide how to enter the various markets. Some of the strategies for doing so include direct investments and acquisitions, joint ventures, and indirect and direct exports. See **Figure 17.5** for an illustration of these strategies.

Direct Investment and Acquisitions

Direct investment refers to a company's financial commitment in a foreign country whereby the investing company owns and operates, in whole or in part, the manufacturing or retailing facility in that foreign country. In many cases a company will acquire an existing business instead of investing in startup operations.

Toys "R" Us is using a direct investment strategy to enter China and plans to open 30 stores within the next few years. This strategy is risky for a North American company but Toys "R" Us sees huge opportunity there. Chinese consumers are becoming

direct investment A company's financial commitment in a foreign country, whereby the investing company owns and operates, in whole or in part, the facility in that country.

Risk Commitment Control

Export	Joint Ventures	Direct Investments
Direct	Licensing	Manufacturing facilities
Indirect	Contract manufacturing	Assembly facilities
	International franchising	Acquire local company

Risk, commitment, and control increase as a marketing organization moves from simply exporting goods to a foreign country to actually manufacturing the goods in a foreign country.

Figure 17.5
Strategies for Entering Global Markets

increasingly affluent and are making sure their children have plenty to play with. The company is emphasizing educational toys in its merchandise mix in an effort to win over strict tiger mothers.[18] "Tiger" is a term referring to the authoritarian and controlling nature of many mothers in China.

Earlier in the chapter it was mentioned that Coca-Cola made a $5 billion direct investment in India. Much of that money is being used to increase capacity at its Indian bottling unit and 13 bottling franchises throughout the country. The investment is intended to expand distribution and help with brand building. Swedish furniture maker IKEA is investing $1.9 billion in India to open 25 stores in the next few years.

Another option is to pursue an acquisition strategy. Rather than build from scratch, a company simply buys a company in a foreign market. Walmart quickly established its presence in Canada by acquiring Woolco. It also acquired Asda stores in the United Kingdom and Seiyu stores in Japan. Walmart's strategy is to procure a piece of the company, then the whole company.

Target entered Canada through the purchase of 220 Zellers stores in a $1.8 billion deal with the U.S. owner of the Hudson's Bay Company. According to retail analyst Wendy Evans, "Canada is now in the midst of a really big wave of American companies moving in . . . there's going to be a lot more competition and that should be worrisome to major Canadian retailers such as Canadian Tire and Loblaws."[19] On the horizon are Nordstrom and Saks. Nordstrom is opening a flagship store in the Toronto Eaton Centre (replacing Sears) in 2016. Saks, which is owned by the Hudson's Bay Company, plans to open seven stores in key urban markets. It seems ironic that an iconic Canadian retailer like The Bay is owned by American interests.

Joint Ventures

joint venture In a global marketing situation, a partnership between a domestic company and a foreign company.

In a global context, a **joint venture** (also called a strategic alliance) is a partnership between a domestic company and a foreign company. Such an arrangement allows a company to produce and market in a foreign country at a lower cost and with less risk to itself than would be the case if it undertook a venture on its own. Even the largest of companies are pursuing joint ventures to reduce the costs of expansion and the costs of developing and marketing new products.

The Kellogg Company and Wilmar International Limited formed a 50:50 joint venture to manufacture, sell, and distribute cereal and snack products in China. Wilmar's subsidiary in China, Yiha Kerry Investments Limited, will be the primary participant with Kellogg's. In the joint venture Wilmar contributes infrastructure, supply chain scale, an extensive sales and distribution network, along with local market expertise. Kellogg's contributes a portfolio of globally recognized brands along with cereal and snack product marketing expertise. From their perspective China represents the largest food and beverage market in the world within the next five years. That fact alone helped foster the formation of the joint venture.[20]

Other options for shared enterprises are licensing, franchising, and contract manufacturing.

licensing One firm legally allowing another firm to use its patent, copyright, brand name, or manufacturing process for a certain period.

Licensing   **Licensing** is the granting of a temporary agreement allowing a company (the licensee) to use a trademark, patent, copyright, or manufacturing process of another company (the licensor). In this type of agreement, the licensee assumes most of the financial risk. In return for the licence, the source company is paid a royalty.

Licensing agreements are also used by manufacturers as a means of staying competitive in a global marketplace. Samsung Electronics and IBM, two very resourceful technology companies, recently announced a patent cross-licensing agreement under which the companies will license their respective patent portfolios to each other. Both companies have built strong patent portfolios in semiconductors, telecommunications, and visual and mobile communications. The cross-licensing agreement enables the two companies to operate freely while using each other's patented inventions to help keep pace with sophisticated technology and business demands.[21] Both companies agree that they will be able to produce better products while maintaining their competitiveness as a result of this licensing.

International Franchising   International franchising is the same as domestic market franchising, except that it is done in other countries. Major fast-food chains, such as McDonald's, Burger King, and Wendy's have franchise networks in many nations (see **Figure 17.6**). In many cases, the products have to be adapted to conform to local tastes if the company is to be successful. In other cases, consumers in foreign countries gradually accept the taste of the original food.

Coffee Time (Chairman's Brands Corp.), a relatively small player in the Canadian doughnut/coffee shop market, has been very successful with its international franchising strategy. Coffee Time is responsible for introducing the Canadian penchant for rings of fried dough to Greece, Egypt, Qatar, Kuwait, Dubai, Saudi Arabia, and Poland. The Canadian business model, based on fresh doughnuts, muffins, and coffee, is working in all these countries.[22]

Figure 17.6   Fast-food outlets such as McDonald's were quick to see the benefits of global market expansion.

Contract Manufacturing   **Contract manufacturing** is a situation where one organization (a marketing organization) forms an agreement with another organization (a manufacturing organization) to produce a product for them. The manufacturing organization produces the product to the specifications of the marketing organization and it is branded with the marketing organization's name.

The motivation for contract manufacturing (often referred to as outsourcing) is the cost saving of such a practice. The manufacturer will claim they can make a quality product for less money than the marketing organization can. The production of the product often takes place offshore where labour and raw material costs are lower.

Gildan Activewear is a successful Canadian company that sells T-shirts, fleece, and sports shirts under the Gildan brand name. At one time Gildan manufactured its products in Canada, but to remain price competitive the company decided to move production to foreign countries such as Honduras, Nicaragua, the Dominican Republic, and the United States. Such a strategy allows the company to capitalize on lower labour rates.

The Microsoft Xbox game console is a very successful product but Microsoft never had any intention of manufacturing the product. Their expertise was in research, design, and product development. The Xbox game console is made by Flextronics Corporation, a company with manufacturing facilities around the world. Flextronics also makes cell phones for Ericsson and printers for HP.

contract manufacturing A situation wherein a manufacturer stops producing a good domestically, preferring to use a foreign plant that can produce the good according to its specifications.

Indirect and Direct Exporting

There are two forms of exporting available to a company: direct and indirect. The difference lies in the distribution strategy. With **indirect exporting** a company employs an intermediary or trading company that specializes in international marketing. This company establishes a distribution system in the foreign country. Generally, the intermediary works for a commission. In terms of control, the foreign company has very little. This is usually an attractive option for firms that are new to the global market scene.

A company engaged in **direct exporting** usually strikes agreements directly with local market companies that would be responsible for distribution in that country. Basically, the company itself performs the role of the intermediary. An export division or export sales force often becomes part of an organization's structure and is responsible for developing the distribution network. The foreign company faces a greater risk than does a company pursuing indirect exporting, but it has greater control over the distribution process.

indirect exporting A form of international distribution in which a company employs a middleman or trading company to establish a distribution network in a foreign country.

direct exporting A form of international distribution whereby the exporting company itself strikes agreements with local market companies that would be responsible for distribution in the importing country.

MARKETING STRATEGIES FOR GLOBAL MARKETS

LO4 Describe the nature of marketing strategies used by firms when seeking global market opportunities.

The first decision the marketing organization must make involves the direction of the overall marketing strategy. Will the organization use a truly global marketing strategy, a country-centred strategy, or a hybrid strategy that combines the best elements of both? That decision will vary from one country to another and will be based on the results of the external analysis (discussed earlier in the chapter) that a manager does on any particular country.

In its purest sense, a **global marketing strategy** involves taking one brand and marketing it in exactly the same way around the world. Adopting a standardized approach keeps costs low and allows for a consistent brand image wherever the product is sold.

Dove is a global brand with a very successful international marketing strategy. Rather than perpetuate the myth of beauty with stifling stereotypes like so many of its competitors, Dove markets a healthier view of beauty. Dove's campaign includes advertising that inspires women and society to think differently about what is defined as beautiful, fundraising initiatives (sponsored by the Dove Self-Esteem Fund) to help young girls with body-related low self-esteem, and the creation of a forum for women to participate in a dialogue and debate about the definition and standards of beauty in society.[23] Refer to **Figure 17.7** for an illustration.

Doritos launched its first global campaign in 2013. Doritos is the world's largest tortilla/corn chip brand with a 39 percent market share. Prior to the global campaign the brand was marketed in 25 different package variations around the world. Logo design, marketing, and packaging are key elements of the new campaign. Recognizing that the world was becoming smaller with the rise of social media, PepsiCo saw a need for consistency in package design and message. Refer to the image in **Figure 17.8**. The marketing communications component of the campaign focuses on the phrase "For the Bold," a clear reference to the nature of the product and the target market the brand pursues.[24]

If a firm uses a **country-centred strategy**, it develops a unique marketing strategy for each foreign market it enters. It does so because of the unique needs, values, and beliefs of consumers in that market. Such an approach does add to the marketing costs of an organization.

Cadbury is a leading brand of chocolate products around the world. It uses all the usual marketing tools to promote its confectionery brands while acknowledging local tastes. According to Dora McCabe, head of group PR at Cadbury Schweppes, "We run our business on a regional, not global, basis and tailor our products and marketing strategies to the local markets." Cadbury has been particularly successful in markets such as Russia and China, where chocolate preference is less established.[25]

global marketing strategy
A plan whereby a product is marketed in essentially the same way in all countries, though some modification to particular elements of the marketing mix is often necessary.

country-centred strategy
The development of a unique marketing approach for each country a product is marketed in.

Figure 17.7 Dove's global campaign helps redefine beauty.

Ruby Washington/The New York Tim/Redux

When determining which strategy to use, answers are required to three basic questions:

1. How does market development differ from one country to another?
2. Do the needs of consumers vary from country to country?
3. Are the characteristics of the target-market profile different?

Starbucks has been a huge success on a global scale and it utilizes a **hybrid marketing strategy**. The nature of the products served will vary from country to country but the experience of being in a Starbucks remains the same everywhere. The Starbucks experience is about passion for a quality product, excellent customer service, and people. It's a place where people can meet friends and family or simply enjoy a quiet moment alone with a book.

Starbucks operates 16 500 stores in 50 countries around the world. Such growth clearly indicates that its passion transcends language and culture. According to CEO Howard Shultz, the company firmly believes in local relevance.

Old   New

Figure 17.8   Old and new packaging for Doritos. A redesigned package is a key component of the Doritos global marketing strategy.

"We remain highly respectful of the culture and traditions of the countries in which we do business," he says. "We must continue to earn the trust and respect of customers each day."[26] This is a good lesson for any company with international aspirations.

The Starbucks brand carries a cachet of wealth, success, and status that is attractive to an emerging Asian middle class willing to pay a premium price for a cup of coffee. Consequently, Starbucks has plans to make China its biggest market outside the United States. Refer to the image in **Figure 17.9**. In terms of marketing strategy it's all about the coffee and the experience. Starbucks gives the customers in foreign countries what they want (unique food and coffee beverages) in Starbucks' North American retail environment.

Product

When it comes to global product strategy, a company has three options: to market a standardized product in all markets, to adapt the product to suit local markets, or to develop a new product.

Using standardized products in all markets can be a successful strategy. Products such as cell phones, digital cameras, and even automobiles can be essentially the same regardless of the country they are marketed in. Even fast-food marketers such as McDonald's and KFC find that many foreign markets are accepting of American fare. They do, however, add local dishes to their menus to round out their offerings.

Adapting a product to local tastes and preferences is common in the fast-food industry. Different ingredients may be used to make a fairly uniform product more attractive to local customers. Coca-Cola's formula is a secret, but there are about a dozen versions of it around the world. In fact, the Canadian formula is a little sweeter than the U.S. version. In China, KFC has given its menu a Chinese twist, adding dishes similar to the fast food that tens of millions of Chinese grab from street stalls or hole-in-the-wall restaurants.

The final alternative, developing a new product, is the most costly. A company employs such a strategy

Figure 17.9   Starbucks has successfully penetrated the market in China.

only when its market analysis indicates the existence of a sizeable market opportunity. This strategy presents a high degree of risk, because the company may not fully understand the needs and customs of the local market in different countries. The assistance of local marketing consultants is essential to ensure that development heads in the right direction.

L'Oréal saw great opportunity in China and developed many new products at great expense using traditional Chinese medicine remedies, including ginseng and white fungus. In high-end cosmetics its Lancôme brand is a market leader. There is a drawback to such investment. Very often local companies churn out copycat products and place them in stores at much lower prices. The nature of competition is a factor in a company's decision to use a global strategy or a local market strategy.

As indicated by the Doritos and Starbucks examples mentioned earlier in the chapter, the value of an existing brand name is important. If a brand can be extended to foreign markets, the development and marketing costs are spread over a larger market. Strong brands should be used in as many markets as possible and weak brands should be replaced if a stronger name is available. In Canada, for example, Kraft Dinner is a popular brand name and the product is the dominant leader in its category. In the United States, the same product is called Kraft Macaroni and Cheese (a rather generic name). The management structure of Kraft's marketing in North America is now controlled by managers based in the United States. It will be interesting to see which brand name survives as Kraft searches for efficiencies in marketing costs. For insight into what constitutes a truly global brand name, refer to **Figure 17.10**.

Figure 17.10
Characteristics of Truly Global Brands

Source: Statistical rankings from BRANDZ Top 100 Most Valuable Brands 2013, Millward Brown, www.millwardbrown.com.

Rank	Brand	Value ($US billions)	Market	Origin
1	Apple	185.1	Technology	U.S.
2	Google	113.6	Technology	U.S.
3	IBM	112.6	Technology	U.S.
4	McDonald's	90.3	Restaurants	U.S.
5	Coca-Cola	78.4	Beverages	U.S.
6	AT & T	76.5	Telecommunications	U.S.
7	Microsoft	69.6	Technology	U.S.
8	Marlboro	69.3	Tobacco	U.S.
9	Visa	58.1	Finance	U.S.
10	China Mobile	56.3	Telecommunications	China

The characteristics of a strong brand are many; here are a few:

- Has leadership at home
- Is associated with its country of origin
- Has a compelling platform that propels it beyond domestic borders
- Is ever–renewing and is tailored to local markets
- Is obsessed with innovation
- Makes money

Aldo Group Inc., a Canadian-based shoe company, is one of the most successful shoe companies in the world. Having the right product at the right time is one of its keys to success. For insight into how Aldo does things, read the Think Marketing box **Aldo Group: Masters of Change**.

Price

Among the factors affecting price are local competition, the value of currency, dumping, and tariffs. McCain Foods Limited of Florenceville, New Brunswick, the world's biggest producer of frozen french fries, had a difficult time penetrating the U.S. market. The sheer size and reputation of McCain meant nothing to food-service customers. Alternate sources of supply were cheaper so McCain's had no alternative but to lower its prices.

The value of the Canadian dollar in relation to foreign currencies also has an impact on the level of demand for Canadian goods. When the value of the Canadian

Think Marketing

Aldo Group: Masters of Change

If someone asked you "Who is the most successful shoe retailer in the world?" would your answer be Aldo? Probably not! The reality, however, is that Aldo Group Inc. is one of the most successful shoe companies in the world. Not bad for a Canadian-based company with humble beginnings.

So how did Aldo do it? The company is led by an extremely smart businessman, Aldo Bensadoun. Under his guidance Aldo has expanded to 1500 stores in 55 countries, generating $1.5 billion in revenue. Other retail shoe banners in the Aldo Group include FeetFirst, Stone Ridge, and Spring.

Bensadoun cites keeping pace with change and being adaptable, quickly, as a key to the company's success. "Aldo brings products to market lightning fast and is constantly tempting customers with new trends. There is constant reinvention of the company. Nobody is quicker at adjusting to shoe styles, retail concepts, and factory sourcing to suit the demands of fickle, fashion-obsessed customers."

Once Aldo spots an idea it takes only 12 weeks to get the shoes produced and into retail stores; the industry average is 17 weeks—advantage Aldo! Aldo manages to produce $1000-plus sales per square foot in Canada, more than twice that of other shoe stores—advantage Aldo! Tim McGuire, partner at McKinsey & Co, a consultancy that advises Aldo, says, "They're the best at what they do, and they're doing it everywhere in the world."

Bensadoun's marketing sense is second to none. "Everybody has shoes—there's no shortage of competitors," says retail analyst George Hartman. "But he has a sense of control of where's he's buying and whom he's targeting as his customers—better than anyone else."

Mario Beauregard/CPI/The Canadian Press

Bensadoun segments his business and targets his stores to serve those different segments. FeetFirst was launched in the 1990s to serve boomers wanting comfortable shoes. Today, boomers want fashion first rather than "granny shoe" comfort. The solution: a fashionable shoe that is "secretly" comfortable—advantage, Aldo! Aldo is currently converting its FeetFirst stores to a higher-end chain called Locale. It will be Aldo's next global brand. Another example of adapting to change—advantage Aldo!

What lies ahead globally? New markets such as China, Japan, Brazil, and Germany are on the horizon. As David Bensadoun puts it, "It's a changing world, and Aldo is determined to fit into it."

Question:

Which components of the marketing mix have had the most impact on Aldo's success? Briefly discuss your point of view and identify any other factors that have contributed the company's success.

Adapted from Christine Muschi, "Aldo's global footprint," The Globe and Mail, September 4, 2010, pp. B1, B4.

dollar is low in relation to the U.S. dollar, the prices for our goods are more attractive to American buyers; therefore, demand for Canadian goods increases and exports to the United States increase. Conversely, if the Canadian dollar rises in relation to the U.S. dollar, the prices of our goods are less attractive to U.S. buyers and demand for Canadian goods decreases. In recent years our dollar has been relatively even with the U.S dollar. A strong dollar in a recovering economy produced a negative international trade balance in Canada between 2009 and 2013.

Earlier in the chapter it was mentioned that several fast-food chains have been successful in entering Asian markets. An initial concern was price, considering the generally lower personal incomes of a large portion of the Asian population. But with the middle class growing in numbers, the more affluent among them were willing to spend a little more for extra treats beyond traditional local fare. However, the competitive nature of most markets dictates that the pricing strategy of all participants remain competitive.

dumping The practice of selling goods in a foreign market at a lower price than they are sold in the domestic market.

Dumping is the practice of selling goods in a foreign market at a price lower than they are sold for in the domestic market. Used as a means of penetrating foreign markets, it is judged by most countries to be unfair, since it can undermine domestic companies and the workforce they employ. To protect themselves against such undermining and to maintain a reasonable level of competition between foreign and domestic marketers, countries impose tariffs (see discussion earlier in this chapter).

Marketing Communications

While a product may be suited for worldwide distribution, it is very difficult to promote it in the same way everywhere. In similar markets, such as the Canadian and U.S. markets, a uniform marketing communications program can be successfully implemented, but regional differences will often dictate that alternative strategies be used. Organizations like to protect their brand image, so it is common for standard communications to be made available for foreign markets. Regional or local managers often decide if and how such communications are employed.

On a global scale, marketing communications is more complex. Because of the differences in language and culture around the world, companies often adapt a communications strategy to meet local tastes. Standardized advertising is effective only if consumers think, act, and buy in the same manner. As discussed earlier in the chapter, language poses the main challenge to global advertising. When KFC entered China it wanted to use the famous slogan "Finger-lickin' good"—which, when translated to Chinese, read as "So good you will eat your fingers off." Ouch!

Levi's, the world's top-selling brand of jeans, launched a global advertising campaign recently using the Go Forth theme. The intent of the campaign was to appeal to consumers of all ages with an inspiring message. Attracting the youth market has been a challenge for Levi's, so the campaign used a youth-stirring tagline, "Now is our time." Launched in 19 languages, the campaign embraced traditional media and social media. The message celebrates America's pioneering spirit (how that will play internationally is open for debate) that is in keeping with the brand's utilitarian footprint. The ads feature naturally, good-looking, rebellious youth. On Facebook there was a social responsibility component that encouraged fans of the brand to support Water.org, an organization dedicated to providing sustainable water and sanitation services to people living in poverty.[27] Refer to the image in **Figure 17.11**.

Figure 17.11 Levi's delivers an inspiring and empowering message in its Go Forth global campaign.

Today, there is a movement toward globalization in the advertising industry, because most large advertising firms now have offices or subsidiaries around the world to help multinational clients adapt their advertising to local ways. Appropriateness is the key element of the global advertising equation.

The Philips ads that appear in Figure 17.3 and **Figure 17.12** are executions of a global advertising strategy. Philip's global advertising strategy involves a consistent message and experience via the ads' copy, photography, content, and interaction, and shows that solutions and propositions offered by Philips are designed around people, are advanced and easy to experience, and improve the quality of people's lives.

The general perception the public holds about Philips is that it is a consumer electronics company; its brand name is well known. The primary objective of the Philips

Figure 17.12
An execution of Philips' global advertising strategy.

because there's no place like home, especially when you're sick.

Hospitals are excellent establishments. It's just that no-one likes going into them unless they have to. So why not have the hospital come to the patient instead? Getting healthcare at home is a simple solution that makes patients less anxious and hospitals less crowded. Find out more at www.philips.com/because

PHILIPS
sense and simplicity

Philips North America

advertising campaign is to alter perceptions and make the public aware that it is more than an electronics company. The campaign employs a theme line, "Sense and simplicity," which replaces the longstanding "Let's make things better."

Distribution

Firms generally secure distribution in international markets in two ways. They either use existing channels employing intermediaries, or they introduce new channels; their choice depends on the needs of the marketing organization. If they choose existing channels, firms may employ trading companies in their home countries, making them responsible for distributing goods to other distributors and final users in the foreign country. Walmart's expansion into Hong Kong, China, and Japan would not have happened had it not formed a partnership agreement with a trading company in Hong Kong and existing department stores in China and Japan.

A company may also decide to use a specialized sales force of its own that sells directly to existing foreign-market agents, distributors, or final users. See **Figure 17.13** for an illustration of global distribution channels. On the other hand, new channels of distribution can be developed. To illustrate, two North American fast-food outlets, McDonald's and KFC, have successfully extended their distribution strategies into the European and Asian markets. The acceptance of superstores (stores selling groceries and general merchandise under one roof) in the United States and Canada is an example of European distribution systems working in North America.

Shipping overseas involves water transportation, so the port facilities of foreign-market destinations are an important consideration in distribution planning. For example, some ports are unequipped to load and unload containerized ships, a circumstance that makes water transportation impractical for some countries. Distribution capabilities must be evaluated when a company is considering marketing products in other countries.

In summary, many prominent Canadian companies are global marketing organizations. Among them are Thomson Reuters (information, health care, financial, and scientific interests), Magna (automotive parts and assembly), Four Seasons (hotels and resorts), and Bombardier (aerospace, transportation, and recreational vehicles). Companies such as Magna and Bombardier rely less on brand names and brand image to be successful. Their keys to success are strong customer and supplier relationships and a reputation for quality or unique technology.

Video: Marketing a Movie Globally: The Global Marketplace

Simulation: Managing in a Global Environment

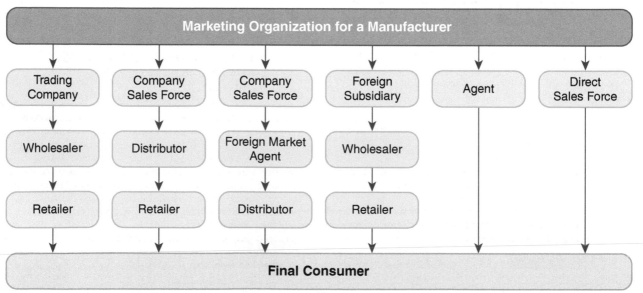

Figure 17.13   Global Distribution Channels

✔ ExperienceMarketing

To experience marketing you have to assess situations, develop strategies, and make decisions that fit a particular situation. What would you recommend in the following situation?

Kevin Van Paassen/The Globe and Mail/CP Images

You are the marketing manager for Roots Canada. You have been asked to explore opportunities to expand Roots into Europe. Currently, Roots operates 120 retail locations in Canada and the United States, and 40 outlets in Asia. Roots is a famous Canadian brand synonymous with a casual, athletic, hip, and outdoor lifestyle. Will that lifestyle resonate with consumers in a European country?

Your challenge is to conduct the necessary secondary research (Web-based) to determine if Roots should expand to one of the following countries: United Kingdom, France, Germany, or Austria. What business strategy would you use to enter the market? What marketing strategy (marketing mix utilization) would you recommend? Will the marketing strategy be significantly different than what Roots uses in Canada?

CHAPTER SUMMARY

LO1 Outline the importance of international trade for Canada and Canadian corporations. (pp. 364–365)

International trade is extremely important to Canada's economy. Having a healthy balance between imports and exports helps keep Canadian industries running and people employed. Historically, Canada has had a positive trade balance, meaning the value of exports exceeds the value of imports. Since 2009 Canada's imports have exceeded exports, resulting in a trade deficit. Our largest trading partner is the United States, which accounts for 74 percent of exports and 64 percent of imports. Such high numbers indicates how much Canada depends on the United States. Canada's priority now is to expand trade with other nations. Europe and the Asia-Pacific region are areas where Canadian industry will be exploiting growth.

LO2 Describe the factors an organization considers when pursuing global markets. (pp. 365–373)

To analyze global market opportunities, a marketing organization considers a host of factors, including the economy, culture, language barriers, varying consumer needs, politics, laws and regulations, technology, and competition in countries where potential markets exist. Before entering a foreign market, a firm must understand that market if it is to develop appropriate marketing strategies for penetrating it.

LO3 Outline the various business strategies commonly used when entering foreign markets. (pp. 373–375)

Several options are available to a firm going into an international market. Among the more common strategies are direct investment and acquisition, and such joint ventures as partnerships, licensing agreements, franchising, and contract manufacturing. Exporting goods indirectly through intermediaries or directly by the company are other options. Decisions about which option to use depend on the financial resources of the organization and the degree of marketing expertise they possess.

LO4 Describe the nature of marketing strategies used by firms when seeking global market opportunities. (pp. 376–382)

The company can use either a global strategy, in which a standardized product is marketed in a uniform manner in all markets where it is available; a country-centred strategy, in which the marketing mix is tailored to the specific needs of individual countries; or a hybrid marketing strategy that combines the best elements of global strategy with a country-centred strategy. Where possible, the global approach should be used because it saves money, but necessary changes should be made as dictated by local market circumstances. As in domestic marketing, a company developing a marketing strategy for a foreign market considers the elements of the marketing mix: product, price, marketing communications, and distribution.

MyMarketingLab   Study, practise, and explore real marketing situations with these helpful resources:
- **Interactive Lesson Presentations:** Work through interactive presentations and assessments to test your knowledge of marketing concepts.
- **Study Plan:** Check your understanding of chapter concepts with self-study quizzes.
- **Dynamic Study Modules:** Work through adaptive study modules on your computer, tablet, or mobile device.
- **Simulations:** Practise decision-making in simulated marketing environments.

REVIEW QUESTIONS

1. How important is international trade to Canada and who are our largest trading partners? (*LO1*)
2. What are the key external environments a company analyzes when considering entry to a foreign market? (*LO2*)
3. What is the difference between a government-controlled economy and a market-controlled economy? Briefly explain. (*LO2*)
4. When an economy is described as a "mixed economy," what does that mean? Briefly explain. (*LO2*)
5. Why do countries impose trade barriers? (*LO2*)
6. What are the differences among the following trade barriers? (*LO2*)
   a. Tariff
   b. Quota
   c. Local content law
   d. Embargo
7. What is a joint venture, and what benefits does it provide participants? (*LO3*)
8. Distinguish between licensing and contract manufacturing as strategies for pursuing global market opportunities. (*LO3*)
9. What is the difference between a global marketing strategy, a country-centred marketing strategy, and a hybrid marketing strategy? (*LO4*)

DISCUSSION AND APPLICATION QUESTIONS

1. "Because of the cultural differences that exist from nation to nation, marketing communications strategies must be tailored to each country." Discuss the validity of this statement.
2. Are Canadian corporations a likely target for takeover by foreign-based companies? Conduct some secondary research about acquisition strategies by foreign companies prior to reaching any conclusions. Present your views on this statement.
3. If you were marketing a soft drink such as Pepsi-Cola or 7-Up in Latin America, what factors would you consider when developing a marketing strategy?

Glossary

accessory equipment Items, such as computers and power tools, that facilitate an organization's operations.

acquisition strategy A corporate strategy in which a company decides to acquire other companies that represent attractive financial opportunities.

administered VMS A cooperative system in which the organization with the greatest economic influence has control of planning the marketing program and identifies and coordinates the responsibilities of each member.

adoption A series of stages a consumer passes through on the way to purchasing a product on a regular basis.

advergaming The placement of ads in commercially sold games, in games played online, or on mobile phones.

advertising Any paid form of non-personal message communicated through the media by an identified sponsor.

advertising agencies Service organizations responsible for creating, planning, producing, and placing advertising messages for clients.

approach The initial contact with the prospect, usually a face-to-face selling encounter.

assortment consistency Product lines that can be used in conjunction with one another or that all relate to the same sorts of activities and needs.

atmosphere The physical characteristics of a retail store or group of stores that are used to develop an image and attract customers.

attitudes An individual's feelings, favourable or unfavourable, toward an idea or object.

backward pricing An organization determines the optimum retail selling price that consumers will accept and then subtracts the desired profit margin and marketing expenses to arrive at the cost at which the product should be produced.

behaviour response segmentation The division of buyers into groups according to their occasion for using a product, the benefits they require in a product, the frequency with which they use the product, and their degree of brand loyalty.

bait and switch A situation in which a company advertises a bargain price for a product that is not available in reasonable quantity; when customers arrive at the store they are directed to another product, often priced higher than the product advertised.

behavioural targeting A database-driven marketing system that tracks a consumer's behaviour to determine his or her interests and then serves ads to that person relevant to those interests.

bid A written tender submitted by a specific deadline.

bill-back A discount in which the manufacturer records sales volume purchased by a customer and then pays the customer the total accumulated discount at the end of a deal period.

blended family A family structure created by separation or divorce; two separate families merge into a single household as spouses remarry.

blog A frequent, chronological publication of personal or corporate thoughts on a webpage that may be updated on a daily basis.

bonus pack Offers customers more volume or weight for the same price as the original size.

boutique (shop-in-shop) A store-within-a-store concept (e.g., designer-label boutiques in large department stores).

boycott An organized refusal to buy a specific product.

brand A name, term, symbol, or design, or some combination of these, that identifies a good or service.

brand democratization A situation in which the customer can interact with a brand, giving the customer some control over the marketing of a brand (as in online user-generated content).

brand design Designing the brand experience into the product or service.

brand equity The value a consumer derives from a product over and above the value derived from its physical attributes.

brand insistence At this stage, a consumer will search the market extensively for the brand he or she wants.

brand loyalty The degree of consumer attachment to a particular brand, product, or service.

brand manager An individual assigned responsibility for the development and implementation of effective and efficient marketing programs for a specific product or group of products.

brand name That part of a brand that can be vocalized.

brand preference The stage of a product's life at which it is an acceptable alternative and will be purchased if it is available when needed.

brand recognition Customer awareness of the brand name and package.

branded content A situation in which the brand name of a product or service is woven into the storyline of a movie or television show.

breadth of selection The number of goods classifications a store carries.

break-even analysis Determining the sales in units or dollars that are necessary for total revenue to equal total costs at a certain price.

business analysis A formal review of some of the ideas accepted in the screening stage, the purpose of which is again to rank potential ideas and eliminate those judged to have low financial promise.

business ethics The study and examination of moral and social responsibility in relation to business practices and decision making in business.

business-to-business (B2B) Markets comprising individuals and organizations that acquire goods and services that are then used in the production of other goods or services that are sold or supplied to others.

buying centre An informal purchasing group in which individuals with a variety of roles influence the purchase decision but may not have direct responsibility for the decision to purchase.

buying committee A formal purchasing group involving members from across a business organization who share responsibility for making a purchase decision.

capital items Expensive goods with a long life-span that are used directly in the production of another good or service.

cartel A group of firms or countries that band together and conduct trade in a manner similar to a monopoly.

cash discounts Discounts granted for prompt payment within a stated period.

cash refund (rebate) Predetermined amount of money returned directly to the consumer by the manufacturer after the purchase has been made.

category manager An individual assigned responsibility for developing and implementing marketing activity for a group of related products or product lines.

cause marketing (1) An organization's support of causes that benefit society. (2) Marketing activity that increases the acceptability of social ideas.

census metropolitan area (CMA) An area that encompasses all rural and urban areas that are linked to a city's urban core, either socially or economically.

central business district Normally, the hub of retailing activity in the heart of a downtown core (i.e., the main street and busy cross-streets in a centralized area).

chain store An organization operating four or more retail stores in the same kind of business under the same legal ownership.

channel captain A leader that integrates and coordinates the objectives and policies of all other members.

channel length Refers to the number of intermediaries or levels in the channel of distribution.

channel width Refers to the number of intermediaries at any one level of the channel of distribution.

circulation The average number of copies per issue of a publication that are sold by subscription or made available through retail distributors.

closed bid A written, sealed bid submitted by a supplier for review and evaluation by the purchaser on a particular date.

closing The point in the sales presentation when the seller asks for the order.

co-branding Occurs when a company uses the equity in another brand name to help market its own brand-name product or service; also applies to two organizations sharing common facilities for marketing purposes.

cognitive dissonance An individual's unsettled state of mind after an action he or she has taken.

commercialization The full-scale production and marketing plan for launching a product on a regional or national basis.

common market A regional or geographical group of countries that agrees to limit trade barriers among their members and apply a common tariff to goods from non-member countries.

Competition Act Brings together a number of related laws to help consumers and businesses function in Canada.

competitive bidding A situation in which two or more firms submit written price quotations to a purchaser on the basis of specifications established by the purchaser.

competitive pricing Placing prices above, equal to, or below those of competitors.

component parts Goods used in the production of another product but that do not change form as a result of the manufacturing process.

consumer analysis The monitoring of consumer behaviour changes (tastes, preferences, lifestyles) so that marketing strategies can be adjusted accordingly.

consumer behaviour The acts of individuals in obtaining goods and services, including the decision processes that precede and determine these acts.

consumer goods Products and services ultimately purchased for personal use.

consumer promotion Activity promoting extra brand sales by offering the consumer an incentive over and above the product's inherent benefits.

consumer-generated content Online content created by consumers for consumers (often the content is related to a branded good).

containerization The grouping of individual items into an economical shipping quantity that is sealed in a protective container for intermodal transportation to a final customer.

content marketing A marketing format that involves the creation and sharing of relevant brand-oriented content in order to acquire customers.

contest A promotion designed to create short-term excitement about a product.

contingency plan Alternative courses of action that can be used to modify an original plan if and when new circumstances arise.

continuity The length of time required to create an impact on a target market through a particular medium.

contract manufacturing A situation wherein a manufacturer stops producing a good domestically, preferring to find a foreign country that can produce the good according to its specifications.

contractual VMS A legal agreement that binds the members in the marketing channel.

convenience goods Those goods that consumers purchase frequently, with a minimum of effort and evaluation.

co-operative advertising Funds allocated by a manufacturer to pay for a portion of a retailer's advertising.

corporate advertising A paid form of advertising designed to create a favourable image for an organization among its publics.

corporate objectives Statements of a company's overall goals.

corporate plan Identifies the corporate objectives to be achieved over a specific period.

corporate strategies Plans outlining how the objectives are to be achieved.

corporate VMS A tightly controlled arrangement in which a single corporation owns and operates in each level of the channel.

cost-based pricing A type of pricing whereby a company calculates its total costs and then adds a desired profit margin to arrive at a list price for a product.

cost reductions Reduction of the costs involved in the production process.

country-centred strategy The development of a unique marketing strategy for each country a product is marketed in.

coupon Price-saving incentive offered to consumers by manufacturers and retailers to stimulate purchase of a specified product.

coverage The number of geographic markets in which advertising is to occur for the duration of a media plan.

CPM (cost per thousand) The cost of reaching 1000 people with a message; it is a quantitative measure for comparing the effectiveness of media alternatives.

creative objectives Statements of what information is to be communicated to a target market.

creative strategy Statements outlining how a message is to be communicated to a target market.

cross-selling Customer campaign that includes selling related products and services.

cross-tabulation Comparison and contrast of the answers of various subgroups or of particular subgroups and the total response group.

crowdsourcing Using the collective talents of the public to complete marketing tasks normally undertaken by a third-party provider.

cult brand A brand that captures the imagination of a small group of devotees who then spread the word, make converts, and help turn a fringe product into a mainstream name.

culture Behaviour learned from external sources that influences the formation of value systems that hold strong sway over every individual.

customary pricing The strategy of matching prices to a buyer's expectations: the price reflects tradition or is a price that people are accustomed to paying.

customer relationship management (CRM) Strategies designed to optimize profitability, revenue, customer retention, and customer satisfaction.

customer relationship management program Analyzes data about customers' buying behaviour, their preferences when buying, and their likes and dislikes to create individualized marketing programs to meet unique customer needs.

data analysis The evaluation, in market research, of responses on a question-by-question basis, a process that gives meaning to the data.

data interpretation Relating accumulated data to the problem under review and to the objectives and hypotheses of the research study.

data mining The analysis of information so that relationships are established between pieces of information and more effective marketing strategies can be identified and implemented.

data transfer A process whereby data from a marketing research questionnaire is transferred to a computer.

dealer premium An incentive offered to a distributor by a manufacturer to encourage a special purchase (i.e., a specified volume of merchandise) or to secure additional merchandising support.

dealer-display material (point-of-purchase material) Self-contained, custom-designed merchandising units that either temporarily or permanently display a manufacturer's product.

decision support system (DSS) An interactive information system that marketers can use to obtain and manipulate information that will assist them in the decision-making process.

decline stage Stage in the product's life cycle when sales begin to drop rapidly and profits are eroded.

delayed-payment incentive promotion Incentive promotion allowing the consumer a grace period during which no interest or principal is paid for the item purchased.

demographic segmentation The division of a large market into smaller segments based on combinations of age, gender, income, occupation, education, marital status, household formation, and ethnic background.

demographics The study of the characteristics of a population.

demonstration An opportunity to show a product in action; it helps substantiate the claims that the salesperson is making.

depth of selection The number of brands and styles carried by a store in each product classification.

derived demand Demand for products sold in the business-to-business market that is actually driven by consumer demand.

diffusion of innovation The gradual acceptance of a product from its introduction to market saturation.

direct channel A short channel of distribution.

direct competition Competition from alternative products and services.

direct exporting A form of international distribution whereby the exporting company itself strikes agreements with local market companies that would be responsible for distribution in the importing country.

direct investment A company's financial commitment in a foreign country, whereby the investing company owns and operates, in whole or in part, the facility in that country.

direct mail A form of direct advertising communicated to prospects through the postal service.

direct response advertising Messages that prompt immediate action, such as advertisements containing clip-out coupons, response cards, and order forms; such advertising goes directly to customers and bypasses traditional channels of distribution.

direct response television (DRTV) A sales-oriented television commercial message that encourages people to buy right away, usually through 1-800 telephone numbers.

direct segmentation (or *one-to-one marketing* or *individual marketing*) A situation in which unique marketing programs are designed specifically to meet the needs and preferences of individual customers.

directory databases A commercial database that provides quick information about a company (e.g., size, sales, location, and number of employees).

display advertising Banner ads in a variety of sizes.

disposable income Actual income after taxes and other expenses; it is income available for basic necessities and optional purchases.

distribution Includes all activities related to the transfer of goods and services from one business to another or from a business to a consumer.

distribution planning A systematic decision-making process regarding the physical movement and transfer of ownership of goods and services from producers to consumers.

distribution strategy The selection and management of marketing channels and the physical distribution of products.

distribution warehouse (distribution centre) A warehouse that assembles and redistributes merchandise, usually in smaller quantities or shorter periods of time.

diversification A situation in which a company invests its resources in a totally new direction (e.g., a new industry or market).

divesting Removing an entire division of a company through sale or liquidation.

double targeting Devising a single marketing strategy for both sexes.

double ticketing A situation in which more than one price tag appears on an item.

dumping The practice of selling goods in a foreign market at a lower price than they are sold in the domestic market.

durable good A tangible good that survives many uses.

editing In marketing research, a stage when completed questionnaires are reviewed for consistency and completeness.

elastic demand A situation in which a small change in price results in a large change in volume.

electronic data interchange (EDI) The computerized transfer of information among business partners to facilitate efficient transfer of goods.

embargo A trade restriction that disallows entry of specified products into a country.

engagement A person's degree of involvement with a medium when consuming it.

e-procurement An Internet-based business-to-business marketplace through which participants are able to purchase goods from one another.

ethnographic research The study of human behaviour in a natural setting.

event marketing The process, planned by a sponsoring organization, of integrating a variety of communications elements behind an event theme.

event sponsorship A situation in which a sponsor agrees to support an event financially in return for advertising privileges associated with the event.

evoked set A group of brands that a person would consider acceptable among competing brands in a class of product.

execution (*tactics*) Action plan that outlines in specific detail how strategies are to be implemented.

experiential marketing A type of marketing that creates awareness for a product by having the customer directly interact with the product (e.g., distributing free samples of a product at street level).

experimental research Research in which one or more factors are manipulated under controlled conditions, while other elements remain constant, so that respondents' reactions can be evaluated.

exploratory research A preliminary form of research that clarifies the nature of a problem.

F.O.B. destination pricing A geographic pricing strategy whereby the seller agrees to pay freight charges between point of origin and point of destination (title does not transfer to the buyer until the goods arrive at their destination).

F.O.B. origin pricing A geographic pricing strategy whereby the price quoted by the seller does not include freight charges (the buyer assumes title when the goods are loaded onto a common carrier).

fad A product that has a reasonably short selling season, perhaps one or a few financially successful seasons.

family brand The use of the same brand name for a group of related products.

fashion A cycle for a product that recurs through many selling seasons.

fixed costs Costs that do not vary with different quantities of output.

fixed-response questioning Questionnaire used for a large sample that contains predetermined questions and a choice of answers that are easily filled in by the respondent or interviewer.

flexible pricing Charging different customers different prices.

focus group A small group of 8 to 10 people with common characteristics brought together to discuss issues related to the marketing of a product or service.

follow-up An activity that keeps salespeople in touch with customers after the sale has been made to ensure that the customer is satisfied.

format On radio, the nature of the content a station broadcasts.

forward buying The practice of buying deal merchandise in quantities sufficient to carry a retailer through to the next deal period offered by the manufacturer.

forward pricing A pricing strategy where all costs and profit expectations are established at the point of manufacture, with appropriate profit margins added for various distributors, thus arriving at a retail selling price that the marketing company hopes is in line with consumer expectations.

franchise agreement A franchisee (retailer) conducts business using the franchiser's name and operating methods in exchange for a fee.

free sample A free product distributed to potential users either in a small trial size or its regular size.

freestanding store An isolated store usually located on a busy street or highway.

frequency distribution In a survey, the number of times each answer was chosen for a question.

frequency The average number of times an audience is exposed to an advertising message over a given period, usually a week.

full-cost pricing A desired profit margin is added to the full cost of producing a product.

full-payout lease A type of lease where the lessor recovers the full value of the goods leased to a customer.

full-serve store A retailer that carries a variety of shopping goods that require sales assistance and a variety of services to facilitate the sale of the goods (such services may include fitting rooms, delivery, and installations).

funnelling Dividing a subject into manageable variables so that specifically directed research can be conducted.

game (instant-win contest) Promotion vehicle that includes a number of predetermined, pre-seeded winning tickets in the overall, fixed universe of tickets. Packages containing winning certificates are redeemed for prizes.

general-merchandise store A store offering a wide variety of product lines and a selection of brand names within those product lines (e.g., a department store).

generic brand A product without a brand name or identifying features.

geodemographic segmentation The isolation of dwelling areas through a combination of geographic and demographic information, based on the assumption that people seek out residential neighbourhoods in which to cluster with their lifestyle peers.

geographic pricing Pricing strategy based on the question, "Who is paying the freight?"

geographic segmentation The division of a large geographic market into smaller geographic or regional units.

geo-targeting The practice of customizing an advertisement for a product or service to a specific market based on the geographic location of potential buyers.

global marketing strategy A marketing strategy whereby a product is marketed in essentially the same way in all countries, though some modification to particular elements of the marketing mix is often necessary.

government-controlled economy An economic system in which the government makes all the economic decisions on behalf of its people.

gross domestic product (GDP) The total value of goods and services produced in a country on an annual basis.

growth stage The period of rapid consumer acceptance.

head-on positioning A marketing strategy in which one brand is presented as an equal or better alternative to a competing brand.

hierarchy of needs The classification of consumers' needs in an ascending order from lower-level needs to higher-level needs.

horizontal conflict Conflict between similar organizations at the same level in the channel of distribution.

horizontal integration strategy A corporate strategy in which one organization owns and operates several companies at the same level in the channel of distribution.

horizontal marketing system A situation in which many channel members at one level in the channel have the same owner.

hypotheses Statements of predicted outcomes.

idea marketing Marketing activity that encourages the public to accept and agree with certain issues and causes.

independent retailer A retailer operating one to three stores, even if the stores are affiliated with a large retail organization.

indirect channel A long channel of distribution.

indirect competition Competition from substitute products that offer customers the same benefit.

indirect exporting A form of international distribution in which a company employs a middleman or trading company to establish a distribution network in a foreign country.

individual brand strategy The identification of each product in a company's product mix with its own name.

industrial (business) goods Products and services purchased to be used directly or indirectly in the production of other goods for resale.

Industry Canada Regulates the legal environment for marketing and other business practices in Canada.

inelastic demand A situation in which a change in price does not have a significant impact on the quantity purchased.

inflation The rising price level for goods and services that results in reduced purchasing power.

information search Conducted by an individual once a problem or need has been defined.

inseparability The equating of the provider of the service with the service itself.

installations Major capital items used directly in the production of another product.

instant bust A product that a firm had high expectations of and launched with marketing fanfare but that consumers rejected very quickly.

intangibility The quality of not being perceivable by the senses.

integrated marketing communications (IMC) The coordination of various forms of marketing communications into a unified program that maximizes impact on consumers and other types of customers.

intensive distribution The availability of a product in the widest possible channel of distribution.

intermediary Offers producers of goods and services the advantage of being able to make goods and services readily available to target markets.

intermodal transportation Moving goods using two or more modes of transportation, with goods being transferred from one mode to another.

introduction stage The period after the product is introduced into the marketplace and before significant growth begins.

inventory management A system that ensures continuous flow of needed goods by matching the quantity of goods in inventory to sales demand so that neither too little nor too much stock is carried.

inventory turn The number of times during a specific time period that the average inventory is sold.

joint or shared demand A situation in which industrial products can be used only in conjunction with others, when the production and marketing of one product is dependent on another.

joint venture In a global marketing situation, a partnership between a domestic company and a foreign company.

just-in-time (JIT) inventory system A system that reduces inventory on hand by ordering small quantities frequently.

knock-off A look-alike product that often is a copy of a patented product.

labels Printed sheets of information affixed to a package container.

law of supply and demand The law declaring that an abundant supply and low demand lead to a low price, while a high demand and limited supply lead to a high price.

lease A contractual agreement whereby a lessor, for a fee, agrees to rent an item to a lessee over a specified period.

licensed brand Occurs when a brand name or trademark is used by a licensee.

licensing One firm legally allowing another firm to use its patent, copyright, brand name, or manufacturing process for a certain period.

lifestyle A person's pattern of living as expressed in his or her activities, interests, opinions, and values.

lifestyle mall A smaller, open-air shopping centre featuring clusters of 20 to 30 upscale stores, each with its own entrance onto a main street of the centre along with offices and residential units.

limited-line store A store that carries a large assortment of one product line or a few related product lines.

limited-service stores A type of retailer that offers only a small range of services in order to keep operating costs to a minimum.

line extensions Products added to rejuvenate a mature brand by stretching the line into new areas.

list price The rate normally quoted to potential buyers.

local content law A way of protecting local industry and employment by requiring a foreign-based manufacturer to use a specified amount of locally produced components.

location-based targeting An effort to integrate consumers' location information into a marketing strategy.

logistics marketing The range of activities involved in the flow of materials, finished goods, and related information from points of origin to points of consumption to meet customer requirements at a profit.

loss leaders Products offered for sale at or slightly below cost.

loyalty (frequent buyer) program Offers the consumer a small bonus, such as points or "play money," when they make a purchase; the bonus accumulates with each new purchase.

mail interviews A silent process of collecting information; reaches a highly dispersed sample in a cost-efficient manner.

manufacturer's agent Carries and sells similar products for non-competing manufacturers in an exclusive territory.

manufacturer's suggested list price (MSLP) The price manufacturers suggest retailers should charge for a product.

market A group of people who have a similar need for a product or service, the resources to purchase it, and the willingness and ability to buy it.

market analysis The collection of appropriate information (i.e., information regarding demand, sales volume potential, production capabilities, and resources necessary to produce and market a given product) to determine if a market is worth pursuing.

market challenger Firm or firms attempting to gain market leadership through aggressive marketing efforts.

market development A strategy whereby a company attempts to market existing products to new target markets.

market follower A company that is generally satisfied with its market-share position.

market leader The largest firm in the industry and the leader in strategic action.

market nicher A firm that concentrates resources on one or more distinguishable market segments.

market penetration A strategy whereby a company attempts to improve the market position of existing products in existing markets.

market segmentation The division of a large market (mass market) into smaller homogeneous markets (targets) on the basis of common needs and/or similar lifestyles.

market share The sales volume of one competing product or company expressed as a percentage of total market sales volume.

market-controlled economy An economic system that operates by voluntary exchange in a free market that is not planned or controlled by a central government.

marketing The process of planning the conception, pricing, promotion, and distribution of ideas, goods, and services to create exchanges that satisfy individual and organization objectives.

marketing channel A series of firms or individuals that participate in the flow of goods and services from producer to final users or customers.

marketing communications planning The process of making systematic decisions regarding which elements of the communications mix to use in marketing communications.

marketing communications strategy The blending of advertising, sales promotion, event marketing and sponsorship, personal selling, and public relations to present a consistent and persuasive message about a product or service.

marketing concept The process of determining the needs and wants of a target market and delivering a set of desired satisfactions to that target market more effectively than the competition does.

marketing control The process of measuring and evaluating the results of marketing strategies and plans, and taking corrective action to ensure that marketing objectives are attained.

marketing execution (or *marketing tactics*) Planning that focuses on specific program details that stem directly from the strategy section of the plan.

marketing mix The four strategic elements of product, price, distribution, and marketing communications.

marketing objectives Statement outlining what a product or service will accomplish in one year, usually expressed in terms of sales volume, market share, or profit.

marketing plan A plan that is short-term and specific, and combines both strategy and tactics.

marketing planning The analysis, planning, implementation, evaluation, and control of marketing initiatives in order to satisfy target-market needs and organizational objectives.

marketing research A function that links the consumer, customer, and public to the marketer through information—information used to define marketing opportunities and problems; generate, refine, and evaluate marketing actions; monitor marketing performance; and improve understanding of marketing as a process.

marketing strategies Strategies that identify target markets and satisfy the needs of those targets with a combination of marketing mix elements within budget constraints.

mass customization The creation of systems that can produce products and personalize messages to a target audience of one.

mass marketing The use of one basic marketing strategy to appeal to a broad range of consumers without addressing any distinct characteristics among them.

mature stage The stage of a product's life cycle when it has been widely adopted by consumers; sales growth slows and eventually declines slightly.

media execution The final stage of media planning; the process of fine-tuning media strategy into specific action plans.

media objectives Media planning statements that consider the target market, the presentation of the message, geographic market priorities, the best time to reach the target, and the budget available to accomplish stated goals.

media planning A precise outline of media objectives, media strategies, and media execution, culminating in a media plan that recommends how funds should be spent to achieve the previously established advertising objectives.

media strategy Statements that outline how media objectives will be accomplished; typically, they outline what media will be used and why certain media were selected and others rejected.

mega-mall A destination mall characterized by its incredibly large size and diversity of stores and services; it includes amusements and other attractions to entertain shoppers.

merchandise assortment The total variety of products a retailer carries.

micro-marketing The development of marketing strategies on a regional basis, giving consideration to the unique needs and geodemographics of different regions.

mission statement A statement of purpose for an organization reflecting the operating philosophy and direction the organization is to take.

mixed economy An economic system that allows simultaneous operations of publicly and privately owned enterprises.

monopolistic competition A market in which there are many competitors, each offering a unique marketing mix based on price and other variables.

monopoly A market in which there is a single seller of a particular good or service for which there are no close substitutes.

motives The conditions that prompt the action necessary to satisfy a need.

mugging Fraudulent marketing under the guise of interviewing, in which sellers pretend to be conducting a marketing research interview.

multibrand strategy The use of a different brand name for each item a company offers in the same product category.

multi-channelling A type of distribution for which different kinds of intermediaries are used at the same level in the channel of distribution.

multiple-unit pricing Offering items for sale in multiples, usually at a price below the combined regular price of each item.

need A state of deprivation or the absence of something useful.

need description In business-to-business marketing, a stage where a buying organization identifies the general characteristics of the items and services it requires.

needs assessment The initial stage of marketing planning in which a company collects appropriate information to determine if a market is worth pursuing.

new product A product that is truly unique and meets needs that have previously been unsatisfied.

new-products strategy A corporate strategy that calls for significant investment in research and development to develop innovative products.

niche marketing Targeting a product line to one particular segment and committing all marketing resources to the satisfaction of that segment.

nondurable good A tangible good normally consumed after one or a few uses.

non-probability sample The respondents have an unknown chance of selection, and their being chosen is based on such factors as convenience for the researcher or the judgment of the researcher.

not-for-profit marketing The marketing efforts and activities of not-for-profit organizations.

objection An obstacle that the salesperson must confront and resolve if the sales transaction is to be completed.

objectives Statements that outline what is to be accomplished in a corporate plan or marketing plan.

observation research A form of research in which the behaviour of the respondent is observed and recorded.

odd–even pricing A psychological pricing strategy that capitalizes on setting prices below even-dollar amounts.

off-invoice allowance A temporary allowance that is deducted from the invoice at the time of customer billing.

oligopolistic market A market situation in which a few large firms control the market.

oligopoly A market situation in which a few large firms control the market.

online advertising The placement of electronic communications on a website, in email, or over personal communications devices (e.g., smartphones and tablets) connected to the Internet.

online databases A public information database accessible to anyone with proper communications facilities.

online surveys Surveys conducted via the Internet.

open bid An informal submission of a price quotation in written or verbal form by a potential supplier.

operating lease A short-term lease involving monthly payments for use of equipment, which is returned to the lessor.

order and reorder routine In business-to-business marketing, the placing of an order and the establishment of a repeat order process with a supplier.

order processing A distribution activity that involves checking credit ratings of customers, recording a sale, making the necessary accounting entries, and then locating the item for shipment.

orderly market agreement An agreement by which nations share a market, eliminating the trade barriers among them.

organization marketing Marketing that seeks to gain or maintain acceptance of an organization's objectives and services.

organizational buying The decision-making process that firms follow to establish what products they need to purchase, and then identify, evaluate, and select a brand and a supplier for those products.

outlet mall Contains factory outlet stores for well-known brands; usually located at a key intersection of a major highway.

outsourcing The contracting out of services or functions previously done in-house (e.g., a firm contracts out its computer services function).

packaging Those activities related to the design and production of the container or wrapper of a product.

partnership marketing A process that involves cooperation and collaboration among members of a channel of distribution that do business with one another.

parts and materials Less expensive goods that directly enter another manufacturer's production process.

patent A provision that gives a manufacturer the sole right to develop and market a new product, process, or material.

penetration strategy A corporate strategy that calls for aggressive and progressive action on the part of an organization—growth is achieved by investing in existing businesses.

pop-up stores (flash retailing) A retail trend where stores open for sales in a temporary space and then disappear anywhere from one day to a few weeks later.

people marketing The marketing of an individual or group of people to create a favourable impression of that individual or group.

perception How individuals receive and interpret messages.

performance allowance Discount offered by a manufacturer to a distributor who performs a promotional function on the manufacturer's behalf.

performance reviews The final step in the buying process, where the buying organization establishes a system of obtaining and evaluating feedback on the performance of the supplier's products.

perishable (perishability of demand) Demand for services varies over a given period.

permission-based email A situation wherein consumers agree to accept online messages from commercial sources.

personal interviews Face-to-face communication with groups or individuals, usually done through quantitative questionnaires.

personal selling Face-to-face communication involving the presentation of features and benefits of a product or service to a buyer for the purpose of making a sale.

personality Distinguishing psychological characteristics of a person that produce relatively consistent and enduring responses to the environment in which that person lives.

phantom freight The amount by which average transportation charges exceed the actual cost of shipping for customers near the source of supply.

piggybacking A system in which the entire load of a truck trailer is placed in a rail flatcar for movement from one place to another. In retailing, piggybacking also means the sharing of facilities for marketing purposes.

place marketing Drawing attention to and creating a favourable attitude toward a particular place, be it a country, province, region, or city.

planned obsolescence Deliberately outdating a product before the end of its useful life by stopping its supply or introducing a newer version.

population A group of people with certain specific age, gender, or other demographic characteristics.

positioning Designing and marketing a product to meet the needs of a target market, and creating the appropriate appeals to make the product stand out from the competition in the minds of customers.

positioning strategy statement Statement that acts as a focal point for the development of marketing strategies and the utilization of the marketing mix.

power centre (power mall) A mall that houses a number of category-killer superstores in one confined area.

pre-approach Gathering information about potential customers before actually making sales contact.

predatory pricing A situation in which a large firm sets an extremely low price in an attempt to undercut all other competitors, thus placing them in a difficult financial position.

premium An item offered for free or at a bargain price to customers who buy another specific item or make a minimum purchase.

presentation The persuasive delivery and demonstration of a product's benefits.

press conference A gathering of news reporters invited to a location to witness the release of important information.

press kit The assembly of relevant public relations information into a package (e.g., press releases, photographs, schedules) that is distributed to the media for publication or broadcast.

press release A document prepared by an organization containing public relations information that is sent to the media for publication or broadcast.

prestige pricing A high price charged for luxury goods that enhances the image of a product and to the status of the buyer.

price The exchange value of a good or service in the marketplace.

price elasticity of demand Measures the effect a price change has on the volume purchased.

price fixing Competitors banding together to raise, lower, or stabilize prices.

price lining The adoption of price points for the various lines of merchandise a retailer carries.

price penetration Establishing a low entry price to gain wide market acceptance quickly.

price skimming Establishing a high entry price so that a firm can maximize its revenue early.

price strategy The development of a pricing structure that is fair and equitable for consumers and still profitable for the organization.

primary package The package containing the actual product (e.g., the jar that contains the jam).

primary research Data collected and recorded for the first time to resolve a specific problem.

private-label brand A brand produced to the specifications of the distributor, usually by national brand manufacturers that make similar products under their own brand names.

probability sample A sample in which the respondents have a known or equal chance of selection and are randomly selected from across the country.

problem recognition In the consumer buying process, a stage in which a consumer discovers a need or an unfulfilled desire.

processed materials Materials that are used in the production of another product but that are not readily identifiable with the product.

product A bundle of tangible and intangible benefits that a buyer receives in exchange for money and other considerations.

product descriptions (specifications) In a B2B context, a description of the characteristics of a product an organization requires. The description is used by potential suppliers when preparing bids to supply the product.

product development A strategy whereby a company markets new products or modifies existing products to current customers.

product differentiation A strategy that focuses on the unique attributes or benefits of a product that distinguish it from another product.

product item A unique product offered for sale by an organization.

product life cycle The stages a product goes through from its introduction to the market to its eventual withdrawal.

product line A grouping of product items that have major attributes in common but that may differ in size, function, or style.

product line depth Number of items in the line.

product line width Number of lines in the mix.

product mix The total range of products offered for sale by a company.

product placement In public relations, the placement of a product in a movie or television show so that the product is exposed to the viewing audience (e.g., the branded product is a prop in the show).

product research Produces information about how people perceive product attributes.

product seeding Placing a new product with a group of trendsetters who in turn influence others to purchase the product.

product strategy Making decisions about such variables as product quality, product features, brand names, packaging, customer service, guarantees, and warranties.

product stretching The sequential addition of products to a product line to increase its depth or width.

production orientation Occurs when organizations pay little attention to what customers need, concentrating instead on what they are capable of producing.

profit maximization To achieve this, an organization sets some type of measurable and attainable profit objective on the basis of its situation in the market.

project teams Groups of sales representatives formed to deal with customers' needs more effectively.

promotional pricing The temporary lowering of prices to attract customers.

proposal solicitation A situation whereby a buying organization seeks and evaluates written proposals from acceptable suppliers.

prospecting A systematic procedure for developing sales leads.

protectionism A belief that foreign trade should be restricted so that domestic industry can be preserved.

prototype A physical version of a potential product—that is, of a product designed and developed to meet the needs of potential customers; it is developmental in nature and refined according to feedback from consumer research.

psychographic segmentation Market segmentation based on the activities, interests, and opinions of consumers.

psychological pricing Pricing strategies that appeal to tendencies in consumer behaviour other than rational ones.

public image The reputation that a product, service, or company has among its various publics.

public relations A variety of activities and communications that organizations undertake to monitor, evaluate, influence, and adapt to the attitudes, opinions, and behaviours of their publics.

publicity News about a person, product, idea, or service that appears in the print or broadcast media.

pull strategy Creating demand by directing promotional efforts at consumers or final users of a product, who, in turn, put pressure on the retailers to carry it.

pure competition A market in which many small firms market similar products.

push strategy Creating demand for a product by directing promotional efforts at middlemen, who, in turn, promote the product among consumers.

QR code (quick response code) A two-dimensional barcode that can be scanned and read by smartphones; allows for the sharing of text and data.

qualitative data Collected from small samples in a controlled environment, the data result from questions concerned with *why* and from in-depth probing of the participants.

quality variability The variations in services offered by different individuals, even within the same organization.

quantitative data Collected using a structured procedure and a large sample, the data provide answers to questions concerned with *what, when, who, how many,* and *how often.*

quantity discounts Offered on the basis of volume purchased in units or dollars.

quota A specific limit imposed on the amount of goods that may be imported into a country.

quotation A written document, usually from a sales representative, that states the terms of the price quoted.

radio frequency identification (RFID) The next wave of intelligent technology to impact inventory planning: RFID tags will be placed on goods so they can be instantly tracked anywhere in the world.

rain cheque A guarantee by a retailer to provide an original product or one of comparable quality to a consumer within a reasonable time.

raw materials Farm goods and other materials derived directly from natural resources.

reach The total audience potentially exposed, one or more times, to an advertiser's schedule of messages in a given period, usually a week.

rebates Temporary price discounts in the form of cash returns made directly to consumers, usually by manufacturers.

redemption rate The number of coupons returned to an organization expressed as a percentage of the total number of coupons in distribution for a particular coupon offer.

reference group A group of people with a common interest that influences the members' attitudes and behaviour.

referral Occurs when a salesperson secures names of potential customers from satisfied customers and makes an initial contact by telephone to arrange a time for a face-to-face meeting.

regional marketing management system The management of marketing activity based on the needs of customers in different geographical locations (e.g., Ontario, Western Canada, Quebec).

reliability Refers to similar results being achieved if another research study were undertaken under similar circumstances.

repositioning Changing the place a product occupies in the consumer's mind, relative to competitive products.

research objectives Statements that outline what the research is to accomplish.

retail cooperatives Retailers that join together to establish a distribution centre that performs the role of the wholesaler in the marketing channel.

retail franchise A contractual agreement between a franchiser and a franchisee.

retailing Activities involved in the sale of goods and services to final consumers for personal, family, or household use.

retailing marketing mix The plan a retailer uses to attract customers.

reverse marketing An effort by organizational buyers to build relationships that allow them to influence the specifications of suppliers' goods and services to fit the buyer's (and, by extension, the customers') needs.

rich media A form of online advertising that incorporates greater use of, and interaction with, animation, audio, and video.

sales promotion Activity that provides special incentives to bring about immediate action from consumers, distributors, and an organization's sales force.

sales volume maximization A firm strives for growth in sales that exceeds the growth in the size of the total market so that its market share increases.

sample A representative portion of an entire population used to obtain information about that population.

sampling frame A listing that can be used for reaching a population.

sandwich generation A generation of parents who are simultaneously caring for children and aging relatives.

scrambled merchandising The addition, in retailing, of unrelated products and product lines to original products.

screening An early stage in the new-product development process in which new ideas are quickly eliminated.

search advertising An advertiser's listing is placed within or alongside search results in exchange for paying a fee each time someone clicks on the listing in those search results (pay-per-click advertising).

seasonal discounts Discounts that apply to off-season or pre-season purchases.

secondary data Data that have been compiled and published for purposes other than that of solving the specific problem under investigation.

secondary package An outer wrapper that protects the product, often discarded once the product is used the first time.

selective distribution The availability of a product in only a few outlets in a particular market.

self-concept theory States that the self has four components: real self, self-image, looking-glass self, and ideal self.

self-regulation A form of regulation whereby an industry sets standards and guidelines for its members to follow.

self-serve store A retailer characterized by the limited number of services offered. Such a store tends to rely on in-store displays and merchandising to sell products.

selling orientation Occurs when companies believe that the more they sell the more profit they will make.

shipping carton Packaging that can be marked with product codes to facilitate storage and transportation of merchandise.

shopper marketing Understanding how consumers behave as shoppers in all channels (retail, catalogue, and Web) and then targeting those channels with appropriate marketing communications to enhance sales.

shopping goods Goods that the consumer compares on such bases as suitability, quality, price, and style before making a selection.

showrooming A situation in which consumers physically review a product in a retail store and then search the Internet for a supplier offering the same product at a lower price.

situation analysis (also *environmental analysis/scan*) Collecting information from knowledgeable people inside and outside the organization and from secondary sources.

slotting allowance Discount offered by a supplier to a retail distributor for the purpose of securing shelf space in retail outlets; such allowances are commonly associated with product introductions.

social class The division of people into ordered groups on the basis of similar values, lifestyles, and social history.

social marketing Marketing activity that increases the acceptability of social ideas.

social media network A website that connects people with different kinds of interests for the purpose of socializing (e.g., Facebook or Twitter).

social network A website that connects people with different kinds of interests for the purpose of socializing (e.g., Facebook or Twitter).

socially responsible marketing The notion that business should conduct itself in the best interests of consumers and society.

specialty goods Goods that consumers will make an effort to find and purchase because the goods possess some unique or important characteristic.

specialty store A store selling a single line or limited line of merchandise.

sponsorships The financial support of an event by an organization in return for certain advertising rights and privileges associated with the event.

stock balance The practice of maintaining an adequate assortment of goods that will attract customers while keeping inventories of both high-demand and low-demand goods at reasonable levels.

stockout Items that are not available when a customer's order is received.

storage warehouse A warehouse that holds products for long periods of time in an attempt to balance supply and demand for producers and purchasers.

strategic alliance A partnering process whereby two firms combine resources in a marketing venture for the purpose of satisfying the customers they share; the firms have strengths in different areas.

strategic planning The process of determining objectives and identifying strategies and tactics within the framework of the business environment that will contribute to the achievement of objectives.

strategies Statements that outline how objectives will be achieved.

strip mall A collection of stores attached together in a neighbourhood plaza.

structured survey Follows a planned format: screening questions at the beginning, central-issue questions in the middle, and classification questions at the end.

subculture A subgroup of a culture that has a distinctive mode of behaviour.

suburban mall Located in built-up areas beyond the core of a city.

supplier search A stage in the business-to-business buying process in which a buyer looks for potential suppliers.

supplier selection The stage in the business-to-business buying process in which the buying organization evaluates the proposals from various suppliers and selects the one that matches its needs.

supplies Standardized products that are routinely purchased with a minimum of effort.

supply chain A sequence of companies that perform activities related to the creation and delivery of a good or service to consumers or business customers.

supply chain management The integration of information among members of a supply chain to facilitate efficient production and distribution of goods to customers.

survey research Data collected systematically through some form of communication with a representative sample by means of a questionnaire.

sweepstakes A type of contest in which large prizes, such as cash, cars, homes, and vacations, are given away to randomly selected participants.

SWOT analysis The examination of critical factors that have an impact on the nature and direction of a marketing strategy (strengths, weaknesses, opportunities, and threats).

tabulation Counting the various responses for each question and arriving at a frequency distribution.

target market A group of customers who have certain characteristics in common.

target-market management system The management of marketing activity based on the requirements of different customer groups (e.g., industry, government, consumers).

target-market profile Describes the ideal customer around which the marketing strategy will be devised and delivered.

target pricing A pricing strategy designed to generate a desirable rate of return on investment and based on the full costs of producing a product.

tariff A tax or duty imposed on imported goods.

telephone interviews Communication with individuals via the telephone, usually conducted from central locations.

test marketing Placing a product for sale in one or more representative markets to observe performance under a proposed marketing plan.

text messaging The transmission of short, text-only messages on wireless devices.

total product concept The package of benefits a buyer receives when he or she purchases a product.

trade allowance A temporary price reduction designed to encourage larger purchases by distributors (wholesalers and retailers).

trade barrier Intended to protect a country from too much foreign competition within its borders.

trade promotion Promotional activity directed at distributors that is designed to increase the volume they purchase and encourage merchandising support for a manufacturer's product.

trade-in allowance Price reduction granted for a new product when a similar used product is turned in.

trademarks That part of a brand granted legal protection so that only the owner can use it.

trial close An attempt to close that failed.

uniform delivered pricing A geographic pricing strategy that includes an average freight charge for all customers regardless of their location.

unique selling point (USP) The primary benefit of a product or service, the one feature that distinguishes a product from competing products.

unit pricing The expression of price in terms of a unit of measurement (e.g., cost per gram or cost per millilitre).

unstructured survey Gives researcher some leeway in determining how the questions are asked; questions may be of an open-ended nature.

up-selling Customer campaign that includes selling more expensive products and services.

validity Refers to a research procedure's ability to actually measure what it is intended to measure.

values statement A statement (or set of statements) that reflects an organization's culture and priorities.

variable costs Costs that change according to the level of output.

vendor analysis An evaluation of potential suppliers based on an assessment of their technological ability, consistency in meeting product specifications, quantity, delivery, ability to provide needed quantity, and price.

venue marketing A form of event marketing in which a company or brand is linked to a physical site, such as a stadium, arena, or theatre.

vertical conflict Conflict that occurs when a channel member feels that another member at a different level is engaging in inappropriate conduct.

vertical integration strategy A corporate strategy in which a company owns and operates businesses at different levels of the channel of distribution.

vertical marketing system (VMS) The linking of channel members at different levels in the marketing process to form a centrally controlled marketing system in which one member dominates the channel.

video messaging The transmission of video clips on devices such as smartphones.

viral marketing A situation whereby the receiver of an online message is encouraged to pass it on to friends.

vision statement A statement that defines plans for the future, what the company is and does, and where it is headed.

voluntary chain A wholesaler-initiated organization consisting of a group of independent retailers who agree to buy from a designated wholesaler.

warehouse A distribution centre that receives, sorts, and redistributes merchandise to customers.

warehouse outlets (big-box stores) No-frills, cash-and-carry outlets that offer customers name-brand merchandise at discount prices.

wholesaling Buying or handling merchandise and subsequently reselling it to organizational users, other wholesalers, and retailers.

word-of-mouth marketing Recommendations by satisfied consumers to prospective consumers about a good or service.

zone pricing The division of a market into geographic zones and the establishment of a uniform delivered price for each zone.

Endnotes

Chapter 1

1. American Marketing Association, http://marketingpower.com/AboutAMA/Pages/DefinitionofMarketing
2. Jeffrey Merrihue, "Marketing must rule again," *Advertising Age*, March 1, 2004, p. 16.
3. Alicia Androich and Kristin Laird, "Best Reputations in 2013, *Marketing*, May 20, 2013, p. 41.
4. Frank Plamer, "Where are all the bold clients?" *Marketing*, February 26, 2007, p. 3.
5. http://corp.canadiantire.ca/EN/AboutUs/Pages/Loyalty.aspx
6. Ellen Rosema, "Most want socially responsible companies," *Toronto Star*, February 1, 2002, p. E2.
7. "Bell Takes Mental Health Out of the Shadows," *Strategy*, May 2013, p. 23.
8. "Products reformulated to respond to healthy, active living," supplement to *The Globe and Mail*, March 26, 2008, p. EW1.
9. "Naya Waters to Introduce 100% Recycled Plastic Bottle," Green at Work, February 2, 2010, http://greenatwork.com
10. David Brown, "Unilever CMO says company will double digital spending this year," *Marketing*, June 28, 2010, www.marketingmag.ca
11. "What are the benefits of social marketing?" www.mashable.com/2008/12/29/benefits-of-social-media-marketing.html
12. "The Rise of Branded Content," *Strategy*, December/January 2014, p. 55.
13. Alicia Androich and Kristin Laird, "Best Reputations in 2013," *Marketing*, May 20, 2013, p. 40.
14. Ibid., p. 45.
15. "Coke Zero Delivers Explosive Growth," http://cokesolutions.com/OurProducts/Pages/SitePages/Details
16. Jack Neff, "Tide Pods winning $7 billion detergent wars by redefining value," *Advertising Age*, December 12, 2012, p. 10.
17. "Digital natives adopt and adapt," *eMarketer*, September 7, 2010, www.emarketer.com
18. "Canadian online shopping rises 24% in two years," *Marketing*, October 28, 2013, www.marketingmag.ca
19. "Lululemon founder and chairman Chip Wilson resigns," *Marketing*, December 10, 2013, www.marketingmag.ca
20. AMA Dictionary of Marketing Terms, www.marketingpower.com
21. "Shoppers targets customers with individualized offers, says CEO," *Marketing*, November 15, 2013, www.marketingmag.ca
22. George S. Day, "No two consumers alike," *Financial Post*, June 16, 2003, p. FE5.
23. http://dictionary.reference.com/browse/business+ethics
24. http://marketingpower.com/AboutAMA/Pages/Statementofethics
25. www.the-cma.org/regulatory/code-of-ethics
26. http://sustainability.com/sustainability
27. "Responsible Consumerism: Greening the Way," supplement to *Macleans*, March 28, 2011.
28. Hollie Shaw, "Voicing doubts over green claims," *Financial Post*, August 1, 2008, p. FP11.
29. Rebecca Harris, "Cleaning up by saving the world," *Marketing*, April 12, 2013, pp. 37–40.
30. Ellen Moorhouse, "When compostable is anything but green," *Toronto Star*, June 23, 2012, p. H10.

Chapter 2

1. www.cbc.ca/thecurrent/episode/2014/01/17/monday-internet-of-things/; www.howstuffworks.com/internet/basics/google4; and http://techcrunch.com/2014/01/13/google-just-bought-connected-device-company-nest-for-3-2b-in-cash/; and www.theglobeandmail.com/life/home-and-garden/the-smart-home-is-coming-soon-and-heres-what-it-will-mean/article17113916/
2. Statistics Canada, CANSIM, table 228-0058, www5.statcan.gc.ca/cansim/home-accueil?lang=eng&p2=50&HPA
3. The Conference Board of Canada. "Canadian Outlook Economic Forecast: Autumn 2013." www.conferenceboard.ca/e-library/abstract.aspx?did=5788
4. Ibid.
5. Statistics Canada, CANSIM, table 228-0058. www5.statcan.gc.ca/cansim/home-accueil?lang=eng&p2=50&HPA
6. M. Babad, "Canadian dollar plunges: How to target an exchange rate without saying so." *The Globe and Mail*, January 22, 2014, www.theglobeandmail.com
7. "Canada-EU trade deal—How the historic agreement will affect Canadian industries," (October 18, 2013), www.cbc.ca/news/politics/ceta-canada-eu-free-trade-deal-lauded-by-harper-barroso-1.2125122
8. "Exchange rates." Bank of Canada. (January, 2014). www.bankofcanada.ca/rates/exchange/
9. D. Hood, "It's finally the year we've all been waiting for." *Canadian Business*, February, 2014, p. 4.

10. Bank of Canada, "Monthly average exchange rates," www.bankofcanada.ca/rates/exchange/exchange-rates-in-pdf/

11. Statistics Canada, CANSIM, table 282-0087, www5.statcan.gc.ca/cansim/home-accueil?lang=eng&p2=50&HPA

12. The Conference Board of Canada. (2013), www.conferenceboard.ca/topics/economics/default.aspx

13. Statistics Canada. (2013). Labour Market Survey, www5.statcan.gc.ca/subject-sujet/sub-theme-soustheme.action?pid=2621&id=1803&lang=eng&more=0

14. Statistics Canada, CANSIM, table 080-0023, www5.statcan.gc.ca/cansim/home-accueil?lang=eng&p2=50&HPA

15. Bank of Canada, www.bankofcanada.ca/rates/interest-rates/canadian-interest-rates/

16. H. Shaw, "Dollarama sales feel chill of winter storms: 80 stores hit." *National Post*, January 18, 2014, http://business.financialpost.com/2014/01/17/dollarama-sales-feel-chill-of-winter-storms-power-outages/

17. Marina Strauss, "Lululemon's plan for lean times," *The Globe and Mail*, March 28, 2009, p. B3.

18. Statistics Canada, CANSIM, table 080-0022, www5.statcan.gc.ca/cansim/home-accueil?lang=eng&p2=50&HPA

19. Phillip Kotler and Gary Armstrong, Principles of Marketing, 10th edition (Upper Saddle River, NJ: Prentice-Hall, 2004), p. 56.

20. "Subway: Explore Our World," www.subway.com/subwayroot/ExploreOurWorld.aspx

21. S. Krashinsky, "Subway's Fred DeLuca: The accidental sandwich tycoon," *The Globe and Mail*, August, 30, 2013, www.theglobeandmail.com/report-on-business/careers/careers-leadership/subways-fred-deluca-the-accidental-sandwich-tycoon/article14052931/

22. D. Deveau, "Franchises putting millennials on the marketing menu are grabbing market share," *Financial Post*, http://business.financialpost.com/2013/11/25/franchises-putting-millennials-on-the-marketing-menu-are-grabbing-market-share/

23. N. Heath, "Android's dominance cements Samsung's place ahead of Apple as world's biggest chip buyer," *ZDNet*, January 23, 2014.

24. "Porter Airlines takes flight," press release, October 23, 2006, CNW Group, www.newswire.ca

25. J. Castaldo & M. Luxen, "Canada's three new discount airlines get ready to rumble." *Canadian Business*, July 19, 2013, www.canadianbusiness.com/companies-and-industries/air-wars/

26. www.reuters.com/article/2014/01/09/us-calories-idUSBREA081DP20140109

27. www.unilever.ca/brands/nutrition/diethealthandthefightagainstobesity/

28. Lesley Young, "In the fat seat," *Marketing*, August 11, 2003, pp. 8–11.

29. http://drinkrumble.com

30. www.panasonic.com/business-solutions/green-solutions.asp

31. Statistics Canada, *The Daily*, September 26, 2013, www.statcan.gc.ca/daily-quotidien/130926/dq130926b-eng.htm

32. Statistics Canada, *The Daily*, September 26, 2013, www.statcan.gc.ca/daily-quotidien/130926/dq130926b-eng.htm

33. www.socialmarketing.org/newsletter/features/generation3.htm

34. www.forbes.com/sites/theyec/2013/12/16/five-tips-for-marketing-to-generation-z/

35. www.marketingmagazine.co.uk/article/1214118/generation-z-holy-grail-brands

36. M. Thrasher, "11 ways big brands are chasing millennials," *Business Insider*, August 2, 2013, www.businessinsider.com/top-brands-are-marketing-to-millennials-2013-8

37. Statistics Canada, CANSIM, Matrix 6900.

38. Caroline Alphonso and Tenille Bonoguore, "Aging population set to alter landscape," *The Globe and Mail*, July 18, 2007, p. A10.

39. Statistics Canada. (2011), Population, urban and rural by province and territory. www.statcan.gc.ca/tables-tableaux/sum-som/l01/cst01/demo62a-eng.htm

40. Statistics Canada, "Portrait of the Canadian population in 2006: Subprovincial population dynamics," www.statcan.ca.

41. Statistics Canada. (2011), Portraits of families and living arrangements in Canada. www.statcan.gc.ca/daily-quotidien/120912/dq120912c-eng.htm

42. Siri Agrell, "Then your in-laws move in," *The Globe and Mail*, September 13, 2007, p. L1.

43. O'Reilly, T. (2012, June 2). Under the influence. Retrieved from http://www.cbc.ca/undertheinfluence

44. Andrea Zoe Aster, "Defining pink consumers," *Marketing*, April 19, 2004, p. 4.

45. Statistics Canada, "2006 Census: Families, marital status, households and dwelling characteristics," *The Daily*, September 12, 2007, www.statcan.ca

46. Statistics Canada, "Income of Canadians," *The Daily*, May 3, 2007, www.statcan.ca

47. OECD Indicators. (2012), Education at a glance, www.oecd.org/edu/eag2012

48. Statistics Canada. (2011), Census, www12.statcan.gc.ca/census-recensement/index-eng.cfm

49. Canadian Press, "Young, suburban and mostly Asian: Canada's immigrant population surges," *National Post*, May 8, 2013. Retrieved from

http://news.nationalpost.com/2013/05/08/young-suburban-and-mostly-asian-canadas-immigrant-population-surges/

50. "Study: Canada's visible minority population in 2017," Statistics Canada, www.statcan.gc.ca/daily-quotidien/050322/dq050322b-eng.html

51. M. Oliveira, "25% of grade 4 students have cellphone: Canadian survey," *The Star*, January 22, 2014, www.thestar.com/news/canada/2014/01/22/25_of_grade_4_students_have_cellphone_canadian_survey.html

52. Gariné Tcholakian, "Internet top media grabber among Canadian youth, says new IAB study," *Media in Canada*, February 2, 2009, www.mediaincanada.ca

53. CBC News, "Canadians spent $18.9B online in 2012, StatsCan says," www.cbc.ca/news/business/canadians-spent-18-9b-online-in-2012-statscan-says-1.2254150

54. www.elementbars.com

55. Canadian Press, September 17, 2013. Sweet news for chocolate lovers: $23M price fixing settlement offers consumers potential cash compensation. http://business.financialpost.com/2013/09/17/chocolate-settlement-price-fixing/

56. "Privacy legislation in Canada," fact sheet published by the Office of the Privacy Commissioner, www.privcom.gc.ca

57. Iain Marlow, "Bell fined $1.3 million for violating no-call rules," *The Globe and Mail*, December 2, 2010, p. A9.

58. "About the Office of Consumer Affairs," Industry Canada, www.consumer.ic.gc.ca

Chapter 3

1. "Shoppers targets customers with individualized offers, says CEO," *Marketing*, November 14, 2013, www.marketingmag.ca

2. American Marketing Association, *Dictionary of Marketing Terms*, www.marketingpower.com

3. Kelly Gadzala, "Explorer Group launches high-tech shopper insight facility," *Strategy*, September 20, 2011, vwww.strategyonline.ca

4. "E.D. Smith looks to sweeten the market spread," *Financial Post*, May 31, 2005, p. FP9.

5. Nielsen Consumer Research, Nielsen Canada, www.nielsen.com

6. PRIZM C2 Consumer Segmentation System for Canada, Environics Analytics, www.environics-analytics.ca

7. Paul Smailes, "Dos Equis," in America's Hottest Brands feature supplement, *Advertising Age*, November 15, 2010, p. 20.

8. Annette Boudreau, "No more pencils, no more (note) books," *Strategy*, February 2006, p. 34.

9. Lisa D'Innocenzo, "Cozying up to shoppers," *Marketing*, November 22, 2004, p. 31.

10. Shawna Richer, "Dairy Queen tests tasty new brands in Maritimes," *The Globe and Mail*, July 23, 2003, p. B21.

11. Jody Temkin, "How focus groups work," http://money.howstuffworks.com/business-communications/how-focus-groups-work

12. "Mugging and sugging," *Marketing*, September 26, 2005, p. 29.

13. Andrea Zoe Aster, Consumer research goes online," *Marketing*, June 7, 2004, p. 13.

14. Jack Neff, "Chain the cheaters who undermine online research," *Advertising Age*, March 31, 2008, p. 12.

15. Sarah Dobson, "Coffee Crisp targets caffeine crowd," *Marketing*, February 10, 2003, p. 3.

16. Ron Waring, "The promise and reality of data mining," *Strategy*, June 7, 1999, p. D9.

17. Chris Daniels, "It's in the cards," Loyalty + Incentive Report, *Marketing*, August 30, 2010, p. L12.

18. Michelle Warren, "Too much information," *Marketing*, November 28, 2011, p. 46.

Chapter 4

1. S. Krashinsky, "Target take note: Quebec market tricky for outsiders." *The Globe and Mail*, March 4, 2013, www.theglobeandmail.com/report-on-business/industry-news/marketing/target-take-note-quebec-market-tricky-for-outsiders/article9259193/#dashboard/follows/

2. Target website, http://pressroom.target.ca/news/target-to-continue-canadian-expansion-in-2014

3. James F. Engel, David T. Kollatt, and Roger D. Blackwell, *Consumer Behaviour*, 2nd edition (New York: Holt Rinehart and Winston, 1973), p. 5.

4. S. Begley, "Food, beverage companies slash calories in obesity fight," www.reuters.com/article/2014/01/09/us-calories-idUSBREA0805F20140109

5. Bradley Johnson, "Consumers cite past experience as the No. 1 influence when buying," *Advertising Age*, November 20, 2006, p. 21.

6. Statistics Canada. "Individual internet use and e-commerce," *The Daily*, www.statcan.gc.ca/daily-quotidien/131028/dq131028a-eng.htm

7. P. Redsicker, "7 social media trends for consumers: New research," *Social Media Examiner*, www.socialmediaexaminer.com/7-social-media-trends-for-consumers-new-research/

8. P. Redsicker, "9 consumer social media trends that could impact marketers," *Social Media Examiner*, www.socialmediaexaminer.com/9-consumer-social-media-trends-that-could-impact-marketers/

9. John Douglas, George Field, and Lawrence Tarpay, *Human Behaviour in Marketing* (Columbus, OH: Charles E. Merrill Publishing, 1987), p. 5.

10. H. Wee, "No more ironing boards: Engineer aims to reinvent toys for girls." NBC News, July 14, 2013, www.nbcnews.com/business/consumer/no-more-ironing-boards-engineer-aims-reinvent-toys-girls-f6C10629732

11. Y. Kageyama, "Toyota crowned king of global auto sales," *Times Colonist*, January 24, 2014, www.timescolonist.ca/

12. Philip Kotler, Gordon McDougall, and Gary Armstrong, *Marketing*, Canadian Edition (Scarborough, ON: Prentice-Hall Inc., 1988), p. 42.

13. K. Naughton, "Honda appeals to female buyers with costly Acura ad campaign," *Bloomberg Business Week*, www.businessweek.com/news/2013-06-24/honda-appeals-to-female-buyers-with-costliest-acura-ad-campaign

14. Jack Neff, "Time to rethink your message: Now the cart belongs to daddy," *Advertising Age*, January 17, 2011, pp. 1, 20.

15. A. Mancuso, "5 old brands that won over millennials," *imedia Connection*, September 12, 2013, www.imediaconnection.com/printpage/printpage.aspx?id=34928

16. Huffington Post Canada, "World's heaviest internet users: Canada tops list despite uncompetitive prices and speeds," January 22, 2013, www.huffingtonpost.ca/2013/01/22/canada-worlds-heaviest-internet-users_n_2527319.html

17. Statistics Canada, "Canadian internet use survey," *The Daily*. Retrieved from www.statcan.gc.ca/daily-quotidien/131126/dq131126d-eng.htm; and Statistics Canada, CANSIM, table 358-0153, www.statcan.gc.ca/

18. M. Oliveira, "Canadian kids can navigate a tablet before they can tie their laces," *The Globe and Mail*, February 9, 2014. Retrieved from www.theglobeandmail.com/technology/canadian-kids-can-navigate-a-tablet-before-they-can-tie-their-laces-report/article16765300/

19. Huffington Post, "Tesco's facial recognition scanners raise privacy concerns," November 8, 2013, www.huffingtonpost.ca/2013/11/08/tesco-facial-recognition-scanners_n_4241801.html; and S. Krashinsky, "Tesco to use face scanners for targeted advertising," *The Globe and Mail*, November 7, 2013, www.theglobeandmail.com/report-on-business/industry-news/marketing/tesco-rolls-out-face-scanners-to-deliver-targeted-ads/article15243513/

20. CBC News, "Smartphone use way up in Canada," July 29, 2013, www.cbc.ca/news/business/smartphone-use-way-up-in-canada-google-finds-1.1384916

21. G. Kennedy, "Six trends for 2014 in mobile marketing and advertising," *Marketing Profs*, December 2, 2013, www.marketingprofs.com/articles/2013/12167/six-trends-for-2014-in-mobile-marketing-and-advertising

22. MC Marketing Charts, "Millennials 'most-loved' brand is…" October 2, 2013, www.marketingcharts.com/wp/traditional/millennials-most-loved-brand-is-37076/

23. Karen Mazurkewich, "The pink purse strings," *Financial Post*, September 15, 2007, www.canada.com

24. L. Lowe, "Report: Men spending more time at the grocery store," October 22, 2013, http://parade.condenast.com/218427/linzlowe/report-men-spending-more-time-at-the-grocery-store/

25. M. White, M. "American families increasingly let kids make buying decisions," *Time*, April 11, 2013, http://business.time.com/2013/04/11/american-families-increasingly-let-kids-make-buying-decisions/

26. "The state of affairs in the nation today," *Consumer TrendZ 2003* (Toronto: Millward Brown Goldfarb, 2003).

27. Ibid.

28. X. de Lecaros Aquise, "The rise of collaborative consumption and the experience economy," *The Guardian*, January 3, 2014, www.theguardian.com/technology/2014/jan/03/collaborative-consumption-experience-economy-startups

29. Alain Belanger and Eric Caron Malenfant, "Ethnocultural diversity in Canada: Prospects for 2017," *Canadian Social Trends*, Winter 2005, pp. 18–21.

30. "What Quebec Wants," *Sales and Marketing Management in Canada*, July 1991, p. 16.

31. Matt Semansky, "Plus ça change . . ." *Marketing*, October 27, 2008, p. 27.

32. Matt Semansky, "Adopt, adapt, or create," *Marketing*, October 27, 2008, p. 25.

33. "Getting to know Western Canada," *Strategy*, October 8, 2001, p. 21.

34. www.avcommunications.ca/case_study_3.html

35. *Macleans*, "Ontario colleges targeting aboriginal students," April 18, 2011, http://oncampus.macleans.ca/education/2011/04/18/ontario-colleges-targeting-aboriginal-students/

36. Colleges Ontario, "New ad campaign encourages Aboriginal peoples to explore higher education," www.newswire.ca/en/story/792985/new-ad-campaign-encourages-aboriginal-peoples-to-explore-higher-education

Chapter 5

1. Level Ground Trading Ltd., www.levelground.com/

2. Ibid.

3. Statistics Canada. (2013). CANSIM table 379-0031, www76.statcan.gc.ca/stcsr/query.html?style=emp&qt=CANSIM+table+379-0031&GO%21=Search&la=en&qm=1&st=1&oq=&rq=0&rf=0
4. Ibid.
5. The Talent Project, "6 key trends in outsourcing," Kelly OCG, www.kellyocg.com/Knowledge/Ebooks/6_Key_Trends_in_Outsourcing/
6. M. Strauss, "Canadian grocery suppliers strike back against heavy discounting," *The Globe and Mail*, March 6, 2014, www.theglobeandmail.com/report-on-business/canadian-grocery-suppliers-strike-back-against-heavy-discounting/article17360748/#dashboard/follows/
7. M. Strauss, "Grocers call for a code of conduct between retailers, suppliers," *The Globe and Mail*, www.theglobeandmail.com/report-on-business/grocers-call-for-code-of-conduct-between-retailers-suppliers/article17381094/#dashboard/follows/
8. Statistics Canada, CANSIM, table 304-0014, www.statcan.gc.ca/tables-tableaux/sum-som/l01/cst01/manuf32a-eng.htm
9. Statistics Canada, CANSIM table 281-0024, www76.statcan.gc.ca/stcsr/query.html?style=emp&qt=CANSIM+table+281-0024&GO%21=Search&la=en&qm=1&st=1&oq=&rq=0&rf=0
10. Monk Office Corporate Social Responsibility 2014 Report, www.monk.ca/
11. Canadian News Wire (April 23, 3014). Office-Max Grand & Toy to close retail stores as business customers shift to growing e-commerce and direct sales channels. Retrieved from www.newswire.ca/en/story/1343293/officemax-grand-toy-to-close-retail-stores-as-business-customers-shift-to-growing-e-commerce-and-direct-sales-channels
12. "GM outlines efforts to transform transportation." Retrieved May 19, 2014, from http://media.gm.ca/media/ca/en/gm/news.detail.html/content/Pages/news/ca/en/2014/May/0520_Sustainability.html
13. Nirihiko Shirouzu, "Ford, GM push suppliers for aggressive price cuts," *The Globe and Mail*, November 18, 2003, p. B16.

Chapter 6

1. "2012 Rankings of Canada's 350 biggest private companies," *The Globe and Mail*, June 29, 2012, www.globeandmail.ca
2. www.additionelle.com
3. "Ashley Graham second signature lingerie collection," press release, February 6, 2014, www.additionelle.com
4. Marsha Lindsay, "Today's niche marketing is about narrow, not small," *Advertising Age*, June 4, 2007, p. 30.

5. "The State of Canadian Connectedness: Internet Usage, Mobile, Search, and Social Media," 6S Marketing, http://6smarketing.com/blog/infographic-canadian-internet-usage
6. Stefania Moretti, "Coupon war heats up," *Kingston Whig-Standard*, December 1, 2010, p. 14.
7. Tessa Wegert, "Online marketing consumers give consumers a say," *The Globe and Mail*, October 13, 2005, p. B11.
8. Shayne Rice, ""Days of wild user growth appear over at Facebook," *The Wall Street Journal*, June 11, 2012, http://online.wsj.com/news/articles/SB10001424052702303296604577454970244896342
9. Robert Klara, "Tweeters of the pack: Harley-Davidson turns to its riders and Twitter in new social media effort," *Adweek*, March 6, 2012, www.adweek.com/news/harley-davidson/tweeters-pack-138690
10. Staci Sturrock, "Power of the purse," *National Post*, June 3, 2006, p. FW3.
11. Kristin Laird, "Hitting the mark," *Marketing*, April 19, 2010, p. 18+.
12. Guy Dixon, "What women want, and don't want in ads," *The Globe and Mail*, April 18, 2003, p. 38.
13. "Retailers move to cash in on new, loyal ethnic customers," *The Globe and Mail*, September 24, 2010, p. B7.
14. Caroline Fortin, "Dr. Pepper seeks prescription for growth in Quebec, *Marketing*, May 8, 2013, www.marketingmag.ca/brands/dr-pepper-seeks-prescription-for-growth-in-quebec-78112
15. J. Rice, "Succinct positioning," *Brand Mantra*, April 22, 2007, www.brand.blogs.com.

Chapter 7

1. Information from High Liner Foods website, www.highlinerfoods.com.
2. "Sobeys to acquire Safeway, but uncertain about rebranding," *Marketing*, June 13, 2013, www.marketingmag.ca
3. "Furniture retailer Leon's buys The Brick for $700 million," *Marketing*, November 12, 2012, www.marketingmag.ca
4. E.J. Shultz and Natalie Zmuda, "No solo Mio: Kraft's smash product attracts rival in Coke's Dasani," *Advertising Age*, November 5, 2012, p. 10., www.adage.com
5. Kristin Laird, "Kraft launches TV spots for expanding peanut butter lineup," *Marketing*, September 24, 2013, www.marketingmag.ca
6. Jack Neff, "P&G plots growth path through services," *Advertising Age*, March 22, 2010, pp. 2, 22.
7. Roman Loyola, "Financial history of the Apple retail store," *Macworld*, May 19, 2011, www.macworld.com

8. "Cara Operations announces plan to acquire Fairfax's restaurant holdings," *The Toronto Star*, October 31, 2013, www.thestar.com.

9. Alicia Androich, "Target Canada gets its roast on with Starbucks Coffee Canada," *Marketing*, February 15, 2012, www.marketingmag.ca/news/marketer-news/target-canada-gets-its-roast-on-with-starbucks-coffee-canada-46363

10. "Nestlé, General Mills open Cereal Innovation Centre," *Media Post Marketing Daily*, February 2, 2011, www.mediapost.com

11. Thom Forbers, "P&G kicks the Pringle can to Kellogg," *Marketing Daily*, February 16, 2012, www.mediapost.com

12. Iain Marlow, Sean Silcoff and Susan Krashinsky, "Flying south: Bain buys into Canada Goose," *The Globe and Mail*, December 11, 2013, pp. B1, B10.

13. Sophie Cousineau, "Retailer Simons crashes Canada, one door at a time," *The Globe and Mail*, September 5, 2013, www.theglobeandmail.com

14. Meghan Haynes, "Transforming Maple Leaf," *Strategy*, April 2013, pp. 17–19.

15. Leander Kahney, "Courting consumers, Dell takes page from Apple's playbook," *Wired*, May 2007, www.wired.com

16. "Apple iTunes accounts for 75% of global digital music market, worth $6.9 billion a year," *Apple Insider*, June 20, 2013, www.appleinsider.com

17. "Apple's share of tablet market drops on increased Android sales," *Business Insider*, October 31, 2013, www.businessinsider.com

Chapter 8

1. D. Friend, (2013, November 4). Canadian business owners see big growth in tea drinkers *The Globe and Mail*. Retrieved from www.theglobeandmail.com/report-on-business/small-business/sb-growth/day-to-day/canadian-business-owners-see-big-growth-in-tea-drinkers/article15240864/#dashboard/follows/

2. K. Moore, (2011, August 10). A less intimidating tea shop. *The Globe and Mail*. Retrieved from www.theglobeandmail.com/report-on-business/transcript-a-less-intimidating-tea-shop/article601057/#dashboard/follows/

3. Lawrence Renet, et al. *Decisions in Marketing* (Plano, TX: Business Publications Inc., 1984), p. 20.

4. Raising David: A Lululemon history. (nd). Retrieved from: http://lululemonmis.blogspot.ca/p/strategy-and-challenges-life-is-full-of.html

5. www.lululemon.com

6. M. Strauss, (2014, April 17). Lululemon stretching out to become a big player in men's wear. *The Globe & Mail*. Retrieved from www.theglobeandmail.com/globe-investor/lululemon-stretching-out-to-become-a-big-player-in-mens-wear/article18062785/

7. L. Rupp, (2013, June 13). Lululemon Atheletica Inc. to open standalone men's stores by 2016. *Financial Post*. Retrieved from http://business.financialpost.com/2013/06/13/lululemon-mens-stores/

8. D. Bronnikov (2013, November 4). Google Android and Nestle KitKat: The ultimate co-branding marketing takeaways. *Modern Marketing*. Retrieved from http://blog.marketo.com/2013/11/google-android-and-nestle-kitkat-the-ultimate-co-branding-marketing-takeaways.html

9. www.android.com/versions/kit-kat-4-4/

10. Marina Strauss, "(Re)making a name in NO name," *The Globe and Mail*, March 21, 2009, p. B3.

11. Diane Brady, "Cult brands," *BusinessWeek*, August 2, 2004.

12. D. Schlanger and K. Bhasin (2012, June 25). 16 brands that have fanatical cult followings. *Business Insider*. Retrieved from www.businessinsider.com/cult-brands-2012-6?op=1

13. Andrea Zoe Aster, "Good drinks come in smart packages," *Marketing*. October 4–11, 2004, pp. 13, 15.

14. Creative Bloq, (2014, February 24). "Packaging: 58 awesome packaging designs." Retrieved from www.creativebloq.com/packaging/inspirational-packaging-912837

15. B. Bruce (2013, August 23). "Water in a Box from Vivid Waters." FoodBev.com. Retrieved from www.foodbev.com/news/water-in-a-box-from-vivid-waters#.U1Gj7cKPJdg

16. Jo Marney, "More than a pretty face," *Marketing*, April 10, 1995, p. 25.

17. Mya Frazier, "How can your package stand out? Eye tracking looks hard for answers," *Advertising Age*, October 16, 2006, p. 14.

18. A. Petru (2011, July 5). "Puma bag dissolves in 3 minutes." Earth 911. Retrieved from www.earth911.com/news/2011/07/05/video-puma-shopping-bag-dissolves-in-3-minutes/

19. Herrera, G. (2011, June 24). The Dieline Awards 2011: Best of Show—Puma Clever Little Bag. Retrieved from www.thedieline.com/blog/2011/6/24/the-dieline-awards-2011-best-of-show-puma-clever-little-bag.html

20. Think Outside the Bin (2011, June 2). A sea of plastic: More plastic than plankton in our ocean. Retrieved from http://thinkoutsidethebin.com/2011/06/02/a-sea-of-plastic-more-plastic-than-plankton-in-our-ocean/

21. Method, http://methodhome.com/ocean-plastic/

22. Food Allergies & Allergen Labelling—Information for Consumers. Canadian Food Inspection Agency. Retrieved from www.inspection.gc.ca/food/information-for-consumers/fact-sheets/food-allergies/eng/1332442914456/1332442980290

23. *Marketing Magazine*, (2013, April 29). *Canadian Business* releases Canada's top brands 2013. Retrieved from www.marketingmag.ca/news/marketer-news/canadian-business-releases-canadas-top-brands-2013-77495

24. The Canadian Press. (2014, April 18). "Apple tightens grip on tablet market." *Times Colonist*, page C12.

25. "Design's new blueprint," *Strategy*, October, 2007, pp. 38–42.

26. M. Strauss (2014, February 20). "Loblaw's Joe Fresh embarks on major international expansion." *The Globe and Mail*. Retrieved from www.theglobeandmail.com/report-on-business/loblaw-profit-sales-beat-forecasts/article16992654/#dashboard/follows/

27. H. Shaw (2014, February 20). "Loblaw opening 140 Joe Fresh stores in Africa, Asia, Middle East and Europe." *Financial Post*. Retrieved from http://business.financialpost.com/2014/02/20/loblaw-opening-up-to-140-joe-fresh-stores-in-south-korea-eastern-europe-middle-east/

28. Larry Light, "Brand design takes more than style." *Advertising Age,* November 6, 2006, p. 74.

29. Dale Beckman et al., *Foundations of Marketing* (Toronto: Holt, Rinehart, and Winston, 1988), pp. 316–317.

30. *Canadian Business*. "Brands we love: Canada's top brands 2013," www.canadianbusiness.com/lists-and-rankings/canadas-top-brands-2013/

31. *A Dictionary of Marketing Terms*, www.landor.com

32. Brand Directory 2013. Retrieved from http://brandirectory.com/league_tables/table/canada-50-2013

33. Interbrand. Best Global Brands 2013. Retrieved from www.interbrand.com/en/best-global-brands/2013/Best-Global-Brands-2013-Brand-View.aspx

34. L. Cooper (2010, June 10). "Brand loyalty starts from a very early age." *Marketing Week*. Retrieved from www.marketingweek.co.uk/brand-loyalty-starts-from-a-very-early-age/3014359.article

35. M. Harris (2009, October 25). "Brand loyalty starts in babyhood." *Times Colonist*. Retrieved from www.timescolonist.com/life/Brand+loyalty+starts+babyhood+study/2143307/story.html

36. The Huffington Post Canada. (2014, February 5). Ivivva Athletica—Lululemon's brand for kids is retailer's new hope. Retrieved from www.huffingtonpost.ca/2014/02/05/ivivva-lululemon-kids_n_4732901.html

37. www.ivivva.com/

Chapter 9

1. L. Nguyen, (2013, June 18). "Mountain Equipment Co-op rebrands to woo urban customers." *The Globe and Mail*. Retrieved from www.theglobeandmail.com/report-on-business/mountain-equipment-co-op-rebrands-to-woo-urban-customers/article12631320/#dashboard/follows/

2. www.bell.ca/Residential_services

3. (2014, March 24). Personal interview with Bell Canada Residential Services supervisor – Ron. 1-800-668-6878.

4. (2013, December 30). Bell Canada Enterprises Annual Report. Retrieved from www.bce.ca/assets/investors/AR-2012/BCE_AIF_2012Eng_Mar12_FINAL.pdf

5. Lara Mills, "Molson overhauls marketing team," *Marketing*, September 20, 1999, p. 3.

6. Grant Robertson, "Kraft unites North American divisions," *The Globe and Mail*, March 12, 2007, www.theglobeandmail.com

7. H. Fleishman, (2012, November 30). "10 businesses we admire for brilliant global marketing. "Hubspot. Retrieved from http://blog.hubspot.com/blog/tabid/6307/bid/33857/10-Businesses-We-Admire-for-Brilliant-Global-Marketing.aspx

8. www.airbnb.ca/about/about-us

9. L. Mills, (2013, March 19). "Starbucks celebrates five year anniversary of My Starbucks Idea." *Business Wire*. Retrieved from www.businesswire.com/news/home/20130328006372/en/Starbucks-Celebrates-Five-Year-Anniversary-Starbucks-Idea#.Uy9dPMKPJdg

10. www.starbucks.com

11. C. Han, (2010, April 19). "Tips for generating and screening ideas from Facebook, IDEO, Google, and others." Retrieved from www.han.co/blog/?p=98

12. (2013, November 21). "Automakers target younger consumers at Tokyo Motor Show." *The Asahi Shimbun*. Retrieved from http://ajw.asahi.com/article/economy/business/AJ201311210076

13. S. Murphy, (2013, November 22). "Why Canada is a testing ground for apps." *Mashable*. Retrieved from http://mashable.com/2013/11/22/apps-canada-testing-ground/

14. J. Schneider and J. Hall. (2011, April). Why most product launches fail. *Harvard Business Review*. Retrieved from: http://hbr.org/2011/04/why-most-product-launches-fail/ar/1

15. Global News. (2013, December 3). Young entrepreneur promotes the East Coast lifestyle. Retrieved from: http://globalnews.ca/video/1005323/young-entrepreneur-promotes-the-east-coast-lifestyle

16. A. MacLean, (2014, February 19). Atlantic Canadians can't get enough of this brand! Retrieved from: http://eastcoastlifestyle.ca/blogs/news/12387369-macleans-magazine-article

17. www.unilever.com/brnads/hpc/dove.asp

18. D. Smith, (2011, October 4). "Microsoft Zune discontinued (2006–2011)." www.ibtimes.com/Microsoft-zune-discontinued-2006-2011-321118

19. iPhonenomics. (2014, March 8–14). "One phone, many countries." *The Economist*, p. 39.

20. C. Hutton, (2013, November 4). "Ikea in China: Store or theme park?" BBC News, Beijing. Retrieved from www.bbc.com/news/world-asia-china-24769669

21. J. Stewart, (2014, February 28). "For Coke, challenge is staying relevant." *New York Times*. Retrieved from: www.nytimes.com/2014/03/01/business/challenges-for-coke-to-stay-on-top.html?_r=0

22. Marina Strauss, "Micro-size this: Snack business seeks profits in smaller portions," *The Globe and Mail,* October 20, 2005, pp. B1, B5.

23. Media Advisory. (2013, October 1). Danone. Retrieved from www.danone.ca/sites/default/files/press-pdfs/Danino_Press%20release.pdf

24. J. Cosgrove, (2012, April 9). "The market for nutraceutical gums. Though mature, the gum market continues to transition into the role of a value-added product." *Nutraceuticals World*. Retrieved from www.nutraceuticalsworld.com/contents/view_online-exclusives/2012-04-09/the-market-for-nutraceutical-gums/ [Related articles include: M. Bellis, "The history of bubble and chewing gum." About.com Inventors. Retrieved from http://inventors.about.com/od/gstartinventions/a/gum.htm; and "Global gums market to reach US $23.1 billion by 2017 according to new report by Global Industry Analysts, Inc." Retrieved from www.prweb.com/releases/gums_chewing_gum/sugarless_bubble_gum/prweb9246521.htm]

25. G. Burns, (2014, March 7). "Yogurt: The most versatile grocery aisle product." *Marketing*. Retrieved from www.marketingmag.ca/news/marketer-news/yogurt-the-most-versatile-grocery-aisle-product-103040

26. Sturgeon, J. (2013, August 9). "Target, Starbucks partnership brews up perfect blend." Global News. Retrieved from http://globalnews.ca/news/771537/target-starbucks-partnership-brews-up-perfect-blend/

27. Everett M. Rogers, *Diffusion of Innovations*, 3rd edition (New York: Free Press, 1982), p. 246.

28. Jermyn, D. (2014, March 19). Cyclist wants you to try the drink that made him healthy again. Globe and Mail. Retrieved from http://www.theglobeandmail.com/report-on-business/small-business/sb-growth/the-challenge/cyclist-markets-drink-that-he-says-brought-him-back-to-health/article17540393/#dashboard/follows/ http://www.drinkrumble.com

29. Ibid.

Chapter 10

1. Kristin Laird, "Holts bets on affordable luxury," *Marketing*, April 22, 2013, p. 10.

2. "Facts & Figures: Wireless Phone Subscribers in Canada," CWTA, 2013, www.cwta.ca/facts-figures/

3. Marina Strauss, "Suppliers brace for more price cuts as grocery fight heats up," *The Globe and Mail*, January 10, 2014, p. B1, B7.

4. Anjali Cordeiro, "Kellogg dishes out smaller box sizes," *The Globe and Mail*, June 16, 2008, p. B7.

5. Advertising notice that appeared in the *Financial Post*, August 5, 2006, p. A7.

6. "Many Canadians cutting the cord on traditional cable," *CTV News*, July 4, 2013, http://bc.ctvnews.ca/many-canadians-cutting-the-cord-on-traditional-cable-1.1352405

7. Practices Branch, Consumer and Corporate Affairs Canada, Misleading Advertising Bulletin, 1984, p. 34.

8. Ibid.

9. Dana Flavelle, "Hershey Canada fined $4 million for conspiracy to fix price of chocolate," *Toronto Star*, June 21, 2013, www.thestar.com/business

Chapter 11

1. Gabrielle A. Brenner and Rauven Brenner, "Memory and markets, or why you pay $2.99 for a widget," *Journal of Business*, Vol. 55, no.1, 1982, pp. 147–158.

2. Ibid.

3. Canadian Finance and Leasing Association, 2013, www.cfla.acfl.ca

4. Jeremy Cato, "Trending topics in the auto industry, *The Globe and Mail*, August 22, 2012, www.theglobeandmail.com

Chapter 12

1. www.walmartstores.com.

2. Joel Evans and Barry Berman, *Marketing*, 3rd edition (New York: MacMillan Publishing Company, 1987), p. 234.

3. Robert Gray, "Apple's retail stores key to tech giant's success," *Fox Business*, January 27, 2014, www.foxbusiness.com

4. Canadian Industry Statistics, Industry Canada, www.ic.gc.app/scr/sbms/sbb/cis/wholesaler-evenues.html
5. "Canadian e-commerce hits $18.9 billion in 2012; Seniors up internet use," *Betakit,* www.betakit.com/canadian-ecommerce-hits-18-9-billion-in-2012-seniors-up-internet-use/
6. Jack Neff, "Walmart weans suppliers," *Advertising Age,* December 1, 2003, pp. 1, 33.
7. Megan Haynes, "Febreze explores new distribution channels for car freshener," *Strategy,* May 15, 2012, www.strategyonline.ca
8. "Costco nixes Coke over pricing dispute," *Kingston Whig-Standard,* November 18, 2009, p. 14.
9. Jack Neff, "Walmart vendor cuts likely to hit small players," *Advertising Age,* August 10, 2009, p. 8.
10. www.calgarycoop.com/about_us
11. www.couche-tard.com
12. "Supply chain management," http://en.wikipedia.org/wiki/http://en.wikipedia.org/wiki/Supply_chain_management
13. "What is EDI?" *1EDISource,* www.1edisource.com
14. Chris Atchison, "Virtual buying pushes warehouses to new heights," *The Globe and Mail,* February 21, 2012, p. B7.
15. "Canada moves by truck," www.cantruck.ca

Chapter 13

1. "We love Shoppers," *Strategy,* November 2006, pp. 38, 39.
2. Adapted from data at http://statcan.gc.ca/tables-tableaux/sum-som/101/cst01/trad42a-eng.htm
3. "Retail Revenues and Expenses," Industry Canada, www.ic.gc.ca/app/scr/sbms/sbb/cis/revenues.html?code=44-45
4. "Best fast food franchises to own in Canada," *MSN Money,* http://money.ca.msn.com/small-business/gallery/best-fast-food-franchises-to-own-in-canada
5. Chris Powell, "Canadian Tire launches automotive magalogue," *Marketing,* May 3, 2011, www.marketingmag.ca
6. "Retail non-store industries, operating statistics," Statistics Canada, www.statcan.gc.ca/tables-tableaux/sum-som/l01/cst01/trad40a-eng.htm
7. www.inside.nike.com/nikerunning_/nike-runner-s-lounge-101
8. "Welcome Inside," IKEA Group Yearly Summary, 2012, www.ikea.com
9. Lianne George, "It's Swedish for invincible," *Maclean's,* August 14, 2006, pp. 33–35.
10. Canadian Tire Corporation, Limited, Reference for Business, Encyclopedia for Business, www.referenceforbusiness.com/history/Ca-Ch/Canadian-Tire-Corporation-Limited.html

11. Chris Atchison, "Retail stores download lessons from the Net," *The Globe and Mail,* February 15, 2011, p. B11.
12. Marina Strauss, "Lowe's tweaks store formula," *The Globe and Mail,* January 30, 2014, p. B5.
13. Ann Zimmerman, "Best Buy pairs with Samsung in bid to lure shoppers," *The Wall Street Journal,* reprinted in *The Globe and Mail,* April 4, 2013, p. B9.
14. "What is shopper marketing? Examples of it in action," *Visualise News,* January 20, 2012, www.visualise.ie/what-is-shopper-marketing-examples-of-it-in-action
15. Russ Martin, "More data on Canada's online shopping lag," *Marketing,* August 21, 2013, www.marketingmag.ca
16. Marina Strauss, "Turning to the Web for an 'endless aisle,'" *The Globe and Mail,* February 19, 2010, p. B3.

Chapter 14

1. "Behind the scenes of Canada's best advertising campaigns of 2013," 2014 Cassies Awards, *The Globe and Mail,* February 21, 2014, p. B9.
2. Jeff Fraser, "Google's Canadian multiscreen study vindicates second screen skeptics, *Marketing,* December 5, 2013, www.marketingmag.ca
3. "Behind the scenes of Canada's best advertising campaigns of 2013," 2014 Cassies Awards, *The Globe and Mail,* February 24, 2104, p. B8.
4. Susan Krashinsky, "A made-up word with a serious purpose," *The Globe and Mail,* May 10, 2013, p. B4.
5. Matthew McClearn, "Brands we trust: On a first-name basis," *Canadian Business,* May 10, 2010, p. 31.
6. Serena Ng and Suzanne Vranica, "P&G shifts marketing dollars to online, mobile," *Wall Street Journal,* August 1, 2013, www.wsj.com
7. Russ Martin, "Doom, gloom and the downwardly mobile," *Marketing,* April 22, 2013, p. 11, www.marketingmag.ca
8. Michelle DiPardo, "Ford teams up with Just for Laughs Gags for Focus stunt," *Marketing,* November 14, 2014, www.marketingmag.ca
9. Data from Canadian Media Directors' Council *Media Digest,* 2013–2014, p. 62,
10. Data from Canadian Media Directors' Council *Media Digest,* 2013–2014, p. 53.
11. Data from Canadian Media Directors' Council *Media Digest,* 2013–2014, p. 77.
12. Joe Mendese, "New outdoor media options challenge conventional media planning wisdom," *Media Post,* August 13, 2003, www.mediapost.com.
13. Data from Canadian Media Directors' Council *Media Digest,* 2013–2014, pp. 11, 12.
14. "What is content marketing?" Content Marketing Institute, http://contentmarketinginstitute.com

15. "Social networking dominates time spent online in Canada," *eMarketer*, July 3, 2013, www.emarketer.com/articles/print.aspx?r=1010023

16. "Facebook releases stats about Canadian usage; 14 million daily users," Maclean's, August 13, 2013, www.macleans.ca/news/facebook-releases-stats-about-canadian-usage-14-million-daily-users/

17. Data from Facebook Newsroom, http://newsroom.fb.com/Key-Facts

18. Gavin O'Malley, "Lessons from top brands on Facebook," *Media Post News*, August 16, 2010, www.mediapost.com

19. Susan Krashinsky, Inside Oreo's Olympic war room," *The Globe and Mail*, February 21, 2014, p. B5.

20. Jennifer Alsever, "What is crowdsourcing?" *BNET*, March 7, 2007, www.bnet.com

21. E.J. Shultz, "Why 'Crash the Super Bowl' burned out for Doritos," *Advertising Age*, January 24, 2013, www.adage.com

22. "Social media ad spend rises to $267 million," *Marketing*, October 7, 2013, www.marketingmag.ca

23. Michael Oliveira, "Facebook's mobile revolution," *Toronto Star*, February 20, 2104, p. B3.

24. Mark Walsh, "Engagement: Brands should drive traffic to Facebook page," *Online Media Daily*, June 14, 2012, www.mediapost.com/publications/article/176841/engagement-brands-should-drive-traffic-to-facebook.html

25. Chris Powell, "Axe launches its own web channel," *Marketing*, August 25, 2011, www.marketingmag.ca

26. "Behind the curtain of Old Spice's viral video mega hit," http://socialfresh.com/old-spice-viral-videos

27. "The Old Spice social media campaign by the numbers," *Mashable*, July 15, 2010, http://mashable.com/2010/01/15/pld-spics-stats/

28. Leo Widrich, "Social media 2013: User demographics for Twitter, Facebook, Pinterest and Instagram," May 2, 2013, http://blog.bufferapp.com/social-media-in-2013-user-demographics

29. Susan Krashinksy, "ComScore bringing mobile measurement system to Canada," *The Globe and Mail*, November 5, 2013, www.theglobeandmail.com

30. Jeff Fraser, "Online use has caught up to TV viewing," *Marketing*, December 5, 2013, www.marketingmag.ca

31. "The state of Canadian Internet usage statistics on mobile, search and social," 6S Marketing, http://6smarketing.com/blog/infographic-canadian-internet-usage

32. Daisy Whitney, "Prime time is mobile time; Study shows online mobile video use skyrocketing," *VidBlog*, May 31, 2012, www.mediapost.com

33. Chris Powell, "Mobile devices becoming a bigger part of retail: Study," *Marketing*, May 31, 2012, www.marketingmag.ca/news/media-news/mobile-devices-becoming-a-bigger-part-of-retail-study-53799

34. "New in Mobile," *Mobile in Motion*, 2006, p. 15.

35. Aaron Barr, "Video games becoming mainstream choice," *MediaPost*, January 19, 2009, www.mediapost.com

36. Mike Shields, "IGA: Most gamers cool with in-game ads," *MediaWeek.com*, June 17, 2008, www.mediaweek.com

Chapter 15

1. Matt Semansky, "Nielsen tells marketers to focus on promotions," *Marketing*, May 13, 2011, www.marketingmag.ca

2. "Coupon redemption in Canada; some interesting data," Canadian Deals and Coupon Association, www.canadiandealsassociation.com

3. "Mobile spurs digital coupon user growth," *eMarketer*, January 31, 2013, www.emarketer.com

4. Daniel Lyons, "Click and save," *Newsweek*, November 29, 2010, p. 25.

5. Jennifer Horn, "General Mills, Mondelez and P&G cheer for Canada," *Strategy*, www.strategyonline.ca

6. Hollie Shaw, "Canadians are downright loyal," *Financial Post*, March 2, 2012, http://business.financialpost.com/2012/03/02/Canadians-are-down-right-loyal

7. Omar El Akkad and Josh Kerr, "Beyond loyalty: Why retailers track your every purchase," *The Globe and Mail*, July 20, 2013, p. B1, B8.

8. Angela Scardillo, "Old Spice Guy's lessons in crisis management," *Marketing*, August 30, 2010, p. 27.

9. Chris Pow, "Branded content offers high growth opportunity for Canadian producers: Study," *Marketing*, September 13, 2013, www.marketingmag.ca

10. Brian Solis, "The definition of social media," *WebProNews*, June 29, 2007, www.webpronews.com/blogtalk

11. Kenneth Evans, Stop the spin," *Marketing*, Public Relations Report, June 1, 2009, p. 11.

12. Keith McArthur, "Online media leaves media out of the loop: PR expert," *The Globe and Mail*, March 21, 2005, p. B5.

13. Edmund Lawlor, "The rise of experiential marketing, *Advertising Age*, November 18, 2013, p. C1.

14. "Launch! takes brand interaction on the road," sponsored supplement, *Strategy*, April 2014, p. S54.

15. Edmund Lawlor, "The rise of experiential marketing," *Advertising Age*, November 18, 2013, p.C2.

16. www.pepsico.com/Story/Mtn-Dew-Kickstart-starts-fans-nights-right-with-new-flavors011320141295.html

17. Data obtained from "Sponsorship Today," presentation by Partnership Group, Change the Conversation Conference, Ottawa, June 11, 2013.

18. "Canadian Sponsorship Landscape Study 2012," www.partnershipgroup.ca

19. Susan Krashinsky, "Making a Connection," *The Globe and Mail*, February 7, 2014, p. B7.

20. Data obtained from "Sponsorship Today," presentation by Partnership Group, Change the Conversation Conference, Ottawa, June 11, 2013.

21. Rick Westhead, "What's in a name? $$$," *Toronto Star*, August 19, 2003, p. E3.

22. Toronto International Film Festival, http://tiff.net/abouttiff/acknowledgements/sponsorship

23. "Sponsorship versus Marketing: What Does the Future Look Like?" Partnership Group, June 2012, www.partnershipgroup.ca

24. Kate McNamara, "Too much pink you think," *National Post*, December 16, 2006, p. FW3.

25. "Relationship Marketing," *Venture* (Canadian Broadcasting Corporation), broadcast on April 7, 1998.

Chapter 16

1. Parks Canada Attendance Reports 2013. Retrieved from www.pc.gc.ca/eng/docs/pc/attend/table3.aspx and www.pc.gc.ca/eng/docs/pc/attend/table2.aspx

2. T. Alvarez, (n.d.). "Canadian national parks get WiFi," *Backpacker*. Retrieved from www.backpacker.com/laugh/destinations/18575

3. Canadian Press. (2014, April 28). Parks Canada accepting bids to bring wireless to the wilderness. Retrieved from www.ctvnews.ca/canada/parks-canada-accepting-bids-to-bring-wireless-to-the-wilderness-1.1795897

4. D. Butler, (2014, April 28, 2014). Call of the Wi-Fi? Parks Canada rolling out wireless Internet access in national parks. Retrieved from www.calgaryherald.com/news/alberta/Call+Parks+Canada+rolling+wireless+Internet+access+national+parks/9785080/story.html

5. A. M. Tremonti, "WiFi in some of Canada's national parks gets a fuzzy reception from campers," *The Current*. Retrieved May 1, 2014, from www.cbc.ca/thecurrent/episode/2014/05/01/wifi-in-some-of-canadas-national-parks-gets-a-fuzzy-reception-from-campers/

6. Statistics Canada. Gross domestic product at basic prices by industry. Table 379-0031. Retrieved April 30, 2014, from www.statcan.gc.ca/tables-tableaux/sum-som/l01/cst01/gdps04a-eng.htm

7. Statistics Canada. Employment by industry. Table 282-0008. Retrieved January 10, 2014, from www.statcan.gc.ca/tables-tableaux/sum-som/l01/cst01/econ40-eng.htm

8. TD Bank Group. (November 9, 2013). "New TD branch in Mississauga combines legendary customer service with a commitment to environment." Retrieved from www.newswire.ca/en/story/1258381/new-td-branch-in-mississauga-combines-legendary-customer-service-with-commitment-to-environment

9. The Associated Press. (March 20, 2014). "Starbucks to expand evening beer and wine service," *The Guardian*. Retrieved from www.theguardian.com/business/2014/mar/20/starbucks-expand-beer-and-wine-service

10. A. von der Heydt, A. (January 6, 2014). "How Apple, Disney & Co. delight customers," LinkedIn. Retrieved from www.linkedin.com/today/post/article/20140106100700-175081329-how-apple-disney-co-delight-customers

11. V. Barford, (2012, March 14). "Will you tell Starbucks your name?" *BBC News Magazine*. Retrieved from www.bbc.com/news/magazine-17356957

12. Misty Harris, "Hotels add fantasies to room service," *National Post*, November 5, 2004, p. A2.

13. P. Weber, (January 4, 2014). "Texas library offers glimpse of bookless future," *USA Today*. Retrieved from www.usatoday.com/story/money/business/2014/01/04/san-antonio-bookless-public-library/4310655/

14. S. Krashinsky, S. (July 10, 2013). "23 award-winning Canadian ads and marketing campaigns," *The Globe and Mail*. Retrieved from www.theglobeandmail.com/report-on-business/industry-news/marketing/canadian-winners-at-the-cannes-lions-ad-festival/article13124965/#dashboard/follows/

Chapter 17

1. Carolynne Wheeler, "Yum Brands' recipe for fast-food success in china? Adapt to local tastes," *The Globe and Mail*, https://secure.globeadvisor.com/servlet/ArticleNews/story/gam/20110511/RBCHINAFASTFOODATL

2. www.yum.com/brands/china.asp

3. 'Imports, exports, and trade balance of goods on a balance of payments basis, by country, or country grouping," Statistics Canada, http://www.statcan.gc.ca/tables-tableaux/sum-som/l01/cst01/gblec02a-eng.htm

4. Nikhil Gulati and Rumman Ahmed (*Wall Street Journal*), "Coca-Cola makes a $5-billion bet on

India," reprinted in *The Globe and Mail*, June 27, 2012, p. B11.

5. Anita Chang Beattie, "Can Starbucks make China love joe?" *Advertising Age*, November 5, 2012, p. 20.

6. Geoffrey Fowler, "Nike's kung fu ad trips up in China," *The Globe and Mail*, December 7, 2004, p. B10.

7. Jeff Beer, "Oreo's Chinese Twist," *Canadian Business*, December 10, 2012, pp. 66–67.

8. Mike Fromowitz, "Cultural blunders: Brands gone wrong," *Campaign Asia*, October 7, 2013, www.campaignasia.com/BlogEntry/359532,Cultural+blunders

9. Ronnie Lipton, "Symbols to avoid like death," *Strategy*, September 23, 2002, p. 24.

10. Jeet Heer and Steve Penfold, "Fast food celebrate regional differences," *National Post*, February 12, 2003, pp. B1, B4.

11. "Why Ikea encourages Chinese to literally make its stores their own," *Advertising Age*, December 9, 2013, p. 19.

12. Nikhil Gulati and Rumman Ahmed, "Coca-Cola makes a $5-billion bet on India, *The Globe and Mail*, June 27, 2012, p. B11, reprinted from the *Wall Street Journal*.

13. "Dairy Trade between the US and Canada," *The Dairy Site*, www.thedairysite.com

14. "Statement on Iran's Nuclear Program," Foreign Affairs, Trade and Development Centre, Government of Canada, November 24, 2013, www.international.gc.ca/media/aff/news-communiques/2013/11/24

15. "Ethical Consumer List of Consumer Boycotts," www.ethicalconsumer.org/boycotts/boycottslist.aspx

16. "Import regulations for small business," *Small Business BC*, October 14, 2011, www.smallbusinessbc.ca

17. "Summary of Canada-EU free trade deal tabled," *CBC News*, October 29, 2013, www.cbcnews.ca

18. Laurie Burkitt and Ann Zimmerman, "Toys "R" Us maps China growth," *The Globe and Mail* (reprinted from the *Wall Street Journal*), November 20, 2012, p. B11.

19. Emily Senger, "Who will target Canada next?" *Canadian Business*, February 28, 2011, p. 26.

20. "Kellogg Company and Wilmar International Limited Announce China Joint Venture," news release, Kellogg Company, September 24, 2012, http://newsroom.kelloggcompany.com.

21. "Samsung Electronics and IBM announce patent cross-license agreement," press release, IBM, February 22, 2011, www-03.ibm.com/press/us/en/pressrelease/33588.wss

22. Global entrepreneur, *National Post*, April 16, 2007, p. EN7.

23. www.campaignforrealbeauty.ca/flat2.asp?id=6960

24. E. J. Shulz, "Doritos launches first global campaign," *Advertising Age*, March 6, 2013, www.adage.com

25. Stephanie Margolin, "The chocolate market unwrapped," *Brand Channel*, May 5, 2003, www.brandchannel.com,

26. www.starbucks.com/aboutus/international.asp

27. Mark. J. Miller, "Levi's takes Go Forth campaign global," *Brand Channel*, August 9, 2011, www.brandchannel.com

Index

data transfer and processing, 70
ethnographic research, 66
experimental research, 66
exploratory research, 57–58, 58*f*
hypotheses, 63
information collection. *See* information collection
key marketing decisions, 62
observation research, 65–66
primary research, 62–71, 63*f*
process, 56–58, 57*f*
qualitative data, 66–68, 68*f*
quantitative data, 68, 68*f*, 70*f*
recommendations and implementation, 71
research objectives, 63
role and scope, 55–56
sample design, 63–64
secondary data collection, 59–61, 61*f*
survey methodology, 68–69, 70*f*
survey research, 64–65
Marketing Research and Intelligence Association (MIRA), 68
marketing research process, 56–58, 57*f*
marketing strategies, 154–155, 158*f*
    creative strategy, 298
    diversification, 160–161
    global marketing, 376–382
    market development, 158–159
    market penetration, 158
    marketing communications, 296–297
    media strategy, 302
    for not-for-profit organization, 359–360
    price strategy, 17, 201
    product development, 159–160
    product strategy. *See* product strategy
    profile matching strategy, 303*f*
    public relations strategies, 331–334
    pull strategy, 296, 297*f*
    push strategy, 296, 297*f*
    rifle strategy, 303*f*
    shotgun strategy, 303*f*
marketing tactics, 157
Mark's, 91, 91*f*
Mars, 203, 228
Maslow, Abraham, 83
mass customization, 49, 123
mass marketing, 118–119
mass merchandise, 275
master plans, 154
mature stage, 201–202
maximization of customer value, 22–23
Maxwell House, 119, 179
Maytag, 171
Mazda, 18, 34, 134, 155, 183
McCabe, Dora, 376
McCain Foods Limited, 185, 379
McDonald's, 2, 3, 12, 22, 34, 38, 41, 62, 123, 158, 291, 323, 337, 342, 351, 365, 367, 375, 377, 382

McGuire, Tim, 379
McKenzie, James, 110
McKinsey & Co., 379
media, 153
media alternatives, assessment of, 304–309
media execution, 303–304
media objectives, 301
media planning, 301–304
media strategy, 302
Media Technology Monitor, 183
megamall, 281
Menu Foods, 107
Mercedes-Benz, 34, 44*f*, 125, 133*f*
merchandise assortment, 286
merchandise control, 286
MERX Canadian Public Tenders, 102
Method, 181, 182
Metro, 35, 55, 102, 104, 217, 235, 243, 257
Mexico, 105, 373
Michael J. Fox Foundation for Parkinson's Research, 360
Michael Kors, 171, 174
Michael's, 283
micro-marketing, 131
Microsoft, 34, 89, 185, 199–200, 278, 279, 375
middlemen, 248
Milk Carton 2.0 campaign, 357
Millennials, 14, 156
    see also Generation Y
Mimran, Joseph, 183
Ministry of Industry, 50
Missing Children Society of Canada (MCSC), 357
mission statement, 146, 146*f*
mixed economy, 366, 366*f*
mobile media communications, 314–317
    QR code (quick response code), 316
    text messaging, 315
    video game advertising, 316–317
    video messaging, 315–316
Molson Coors Brewing Company, 121, 192
Mondelez, 203
Mondelez Canada, 309–310, 311
Monk Office, 110
monopolistic competition, 34, 214*f*, **215,** 216
monopoly, 33, 214*f*, **215**–216
Monster, 168, 202
Montreal International Jazz Festival, 340
motives, 83–84, 351–352, 367–369
Mountain Dew, 135, 335
Mountain Equipment Co-op, 190, 198
The Movie Out Here, 10–11, 11*f*
Mr. Sub, 37, 158
MSN, 118
mugging, 69
multibrand strategy, 174–175
multi-channeling, 253–254
multicultural marketing, 94